D0604521

FUNK & WAGNALLS HAMMOND WORLD ATLAS

INCLUDING

WORLD HISTORY

SECTION

FUNK & WAGNALLS, INC., NEW YORK

CONTENTS

COLOR MAP SECTION

PRINTED IN THE UNITED STATES OF AMERICA

CONTENTS

WORLD HISTORY SECTION

GAZETTEER OF THE WORLD

This alphabetical list of grand divisions, countries, states, colonial possessions, etc., gives area, population, capital or chief town, and index references and page numbers on which they are shown on the largest scale. The index reference shows the square on the respective map in which the name of the entry may be located.

Country	Area (Sq. Miles)	Population	Capital or Chief Town	Index Ref.	Plate No.
Afars & Issas, Terr. of the ..	8,880	101,000	Djibouti	P 9	38
*Afghanistan	250,775	18,700,000	Kabul	A 2	34
Africa	11,707,000	374,000,000	....		38-39
Alabama, U.S.A.	51,609	3,577,000	Montgomery		65
Alaska, U.S.A.	586,412	337,000	Juneau		66
*Albania	11,100	2,400,000	Tiranë	B 3	29
Alberta, Canada	255,285	1,759,000	Edmonton		58
*Algeria	919,591	16,275,000	Algiers	F 6	38
American Samoa	76	32,000	Pago Pago	J 7	41
Andorra	188	23,000	Andorra la Vella	G 1	27
Angola	481,351	6,100,000	Luanda	K14	39
Antarctica	5,500,000	....	....		20
Antigua	171	75,000	St. Johns	G 3	45
*Argentina	1,068,296	24,500,000	Buenos Aires		43
Arizona, U.S.A.	113,909	2,153,000	Phoenix		67
Arkansas, U.S.A.	53,104	2,062,000	Little Rock		68
Ascension, St. Helena	34	1,200	Georgetown	E15	39
Asia	17,128,500	2,267,000,000	....		32
*Australia	2,967,909	13,417,000	Canberra		40
*Austria	32,375	7,550,000	Vienna		29
*Bahamas	5,382	197,000	Nassau	C 1	45
*Bahrain	240	227,000	Manama	F 4	33
*Bangladesh	55,126	71,614,000	Dacca	F 4	34
*Barbados	166	243,000	Bridgetown	G 4	45
*Belgium	11,781	9,800,000	Brussels		24
Belize	8,867	132,000	Belmopan	B 1	46
*Benin	43,483	3,029,000	Porto-Novo	G10	38
Bermuda	21	55,000	Hamilton	H 3	45
*Bhutan	18,147	1,100,000	Thimphu	G 3	34
*Bolivia	424,162	5,470,000	La Paz, Sucre	H 7	42
*Botswana	224,764	709,000	Gaborone	L16	39
*Brazil	3,265,058	104,642,000	Brasília		42-43
British Columbia, Canada	366,255	2,452,000	Victoria		59
British Indian Ocean Terr.	87	550	Victoria (Seychelles)	L10	32
Brunei	2,226	145,000	Bandar Seri Begawan	E 5	36
*Bulgaria	42,823	8,706,000	Sofia	C 3	29
*Burma	261,789	30,200,000	Rangoon	B 2	35
*Burundi	10,747	3,600,000	Bujumbura	M12	39
California, U.S.A.	158,693	20,907,000	Sacramento		69
*Cambodia	69,898	8,000,000	Phnom Penh	D 4	35
*Cameroon	179,557	6,300,000	Yaoundé	J11	38
*Canada	3,851,809	22,737,000	Ottawa		47
Canal Zone	553	46,000	Balboa Heights	E 3	46
*Cape Verde	1,557	300,000	Praia	H 5	19
Cayman Islands	100	12,000	Georgetown	B 3	45
*Central African Republic	236,293	2,370,000	Bangui	K10	38
Central America	197,559	18,800,000	....		46
*Ceylon (Sri Lanka)	25,332	13,600,000	Colombo	E 7	34
*Chad	495,752	4,000,000	N'Djamena	K 8	38
Channel Islands	74	126,000	St. Helier, St. Peter Port	E 6	23
*Chile	292,256	10,494,000	Santiago	G10	43
*China (People's Rep.)	3,691,000	887,000,000	Peking		37
China (Taiwan)	13,971	15,700,000	Taipei	K 7	37
*Colombia	439,735	23,952,000	Bogotá	F 3	42
Colorado, U.S.A.	104,247	2,496,000	Denver		70
*Comoro Islands	863	300,000	Moroni	P14	39
*Congo	132,046	1,300,000	Brazzaville	J12	39
Connecticut, U.S.A.	5,009	3,088,000	Hartford		71
Cook Islands	91	19,000	Avarua	K 7	41
*Costa Rica	19,652	1,921,000	San José	C 3	46
*Cuba	42,827	9,100,000	Havana	B 2	45
*Cyprus	3,473	659,000	Nicosia	B 3	33
*Czechoslovakia	49,370	14,700,000	Prague		29
Delaware, U.S.A.	2,057	573,000	Dover		83
*Denmark	16,629	5,100,000	Copenhagen	B 3	24
District of Columbia, U.S.A.	67	723,000	Washington	B 5	83
Dominica	290	73,000	Roseau	G 4	45
*Dominican Republic	18,704	4,600,000	Santo Domingo	D 3	45
*Ecuador	105,685	6,600,000	Quito	E 4	42
*Egypt	386,659	36,417,000	Cairo	M 6	38
*El Salvador	8,260	3,980,000	San Salvador	B 2	46
England, U.K.	50,516	46,436,000	London	F 4	23
*Equatorial Guinea	10,831	300,000	Malabo	H11	39
*Ethiopia	471,776	27,900,000	Addis Ababa	O 9	38
Europe	4,057,000	657,000,000	....		21
Faerøe Is., Denmark	540	42,000	Tórshavn	D 2	21
Falkland Is.	4,618	2,000	Stanley	H14	43
*Fiji	7,055	560,000	Suva	H 8	41
*Finland	130,128	4,692,000	Helsinki	E 2	24
Florida, U.S.A.	58,560	8,090,000	Tallahassee		72
France	212,821	52,507,000	Paris		26
French Guiana	35,135	52,000	Cayenne	K 3	42
French Polynesia	1,544	120,000	Papeete	M 8	41
*Gabon	103,346	515,000	Libreville	J12	39
*Gambia	4,361	510,000	Banjul	C 9	38
Georgia, U.S.A.	58,876	4,882,000	Atlanta		73
*Germany, East (German Democratic Republic)	41,768	16,980,000	Berlin		25
*Germany, West (Federal Republic)	95,979	62,101,000	Bonn		25
*Ghana	92,099	9,607,000	Accra	F10	38
Gibraltar	2	30,000	Gibraltar	D 4	27
Gilbert & Ellice Islands	412	58,000	Bairiki	J 6	41
*Great Britain & Northern Ireland (United Kingdom)	94,399	56,094,000	London		23
*Greece	50,944	9,000,000	Athens	C 4	29
Greenland, Denmark	840,000	51,000	Godthåb	B12	20
*Grenada	133	96,000	St. George's	G 4	45
Guadeloupe & Dependencies..	687	342,000	Basse-Terre	F 3	45
Guam	212	107,000	Agaña	E 4	41
*Guatemala	42,042	5,548,000	Guatemala	B 2	46
*Guinea	94,925	5,143,000	Conakry	D 9	38
*Guinea-Bissau	13,948	509,000	Bissau	C 9	38
*Guyana	83,000	784,000	Georgetown	J 2	42
*Haiti	10,683	5,300,000	Port-au-Prince	D 3	45
Hawaii, U.S.A.	6,450	847,000	Honolulu		74
*Holland (Netherlands)	15,892	13,573,000	Amsterdam, The Hague		24
*Honduras	43,277	2,781,000	Tegucigalpa	C 2	46
Hong Kong	403	4,249,000	Victoria	H 7	37
*Hungary	35,919	10,510,000	Budapest		29
*Iceland	39,768	215,000	Reykjavík	C 2	21
Idaho, U.S.A.	83,557	799,000	Boise		75
Illinois, U.S.A.	56,400	11,131,000	Springfield		76
*India	1,269,339	586,056,000	New Delhi		34
Indiana, U.S.A.	36,291	5,330,000	Indianapolis		77
*Indonesia	782,658	129,000,000	Djakarta		36
Iowa, U.S.A.	56,290	2,855,000	Des Moines		78
*Iran	636,293	31,925,000	Tehran	F 3	33
*Iraq	172,476	10,765,000	Baghdad	D 3	33
*Ireland	27,136	3,086,000	Dublin		23
Isle of Man	227	60,000	Douglas	D 3	23
*Israel	7,847	3,450,000	Jerusalem		31
*Italy	116,303	55,586,000	Rome		28
*Ivory Coast	124,198	5,400,000	Abidjan	E10	38
*Jamaica	4,232	2,000,000	Kingston	C 3	45
*Japan	143,733	110,000,000	Tokyo		36
*Jordan	37,737	2,646,000	Amman		31
Kansas, U.S.A.	82,264	2,270,000	Topeka		79
Kentucky, U.S.A.	40,395	3,357,000	Frankfort		80
*Kenya	224,960	12,912,000	Nairobi	O11	39
Korea, North	46,540	15,500,000	P'yŏngyang	C 2	36
Korea, South	38,004	33,959,000	Seoul	C 3	36
*Kuwait	6,880	929,000	Al Kuwait	E 4	33
*Laos	91,428	3,257,000	Vientiane	E 3	35
*Lebanon	3,950	3,100,000	Beirut	C 3	33
*Lesotho	11,720	1,143,000	Maseru	M17	39
*Liberia	43,000	1,700,000	Monrovia	E10	38
*Libya	679,358	2,257,000	Tripoli	K 6	38
Liechtenstein	61	23,000	Vaduz	E 1	27
Louisiana, U.S.A.	48,523	3,764,000	Baton Rouge		81
*Luxembourg	999	353,000	Luxembourg	H 8	24

*Members of the United Nations

GAZETTEER OF THE WORLD

Country	Area (Sq. Miles)	Population	Capital or Chief Town	Index Ref.	Plate No.
Macao	6.2	262,000	Macao	H 7	37
Maine, U.S.A.	33,215	1,047,000	Augusta		82
*Malagasy Republic	226,657	7,655,000	Tananarive	R16	39
*Malawi	45,747	4,900,000	Lilongwe	N14	39
Malaya, Malaysia	50,670	8,978,000	Kuala Lumpur	D 6	35
*Malaysia	128,308	12,200,000	Kuala Lumpur	D 5	36
*Maldives	115	123,000	Male	C 8	34
*Mali	464,873	5,376,000	Bamako	E 9	38
*Malta	122	331,000	Valletta	E 7	28
Manitoba, Canada	251,000	1,016,000	Winnipeg		56
Martinique	425	343,000	Fort-de-France	G 4	45
Maryland, U.S.A.	10,577	4,094,000	Annapolis		83
Massachusetts, U.S.A.	8,257	5,800,000	Boston		84
*Mauritania	418,810	1,290,000	Nouakchott	D 8	38
*Mauritius	790	868,000	Port Louis	S19	39
*Mexico	759,530	58,118,000	Mexico City		46
Michigan, U.S.A.	58,216	9,098,000	Lansing		85
Midway Islands	2	2,000	....	B 5	74
Minnesota, U.S.A.	84,068	3,917,000	St. Paul		86
Mississippi, U.S.A.	47,716	2,324,000	Jackson		87
Missouri, U.S.A.	69,686	4,777,000	Jefferson City		88
Monaco	374 acres	25,000	Monaco	G 6	26
*Mongolia	604,247	1,400,000	Ulan Bator	F 2	37
Montana, U.S.A.	147,138	735,000	Helena		89
Montserrat	40	13,000	Plymouth	G 3	45
*Morocco	172,413	16,880,000	Rabat	E 5	38
*Mozambique	308,641	9,000,000	Maputo	N16	39
Nauru	8	7,000	Yaren dist.	G 6	41
Nebraska, U.S.A.	77,227	1,543,000	Lincoln		90
*Nepal	54,663	12,400,000	Kathmandu	E 3	34
*Netherlands	15,892	13,592,000	Amsterdam, The Hague		24
Netherlands Antilles	390	234,000	Willemstad	E 4	45
Nevada, U.S.A.	110,540	573,000	Carson City		91
New Brunswick, Canada	28,354	673,000	Fredericton		52
New Caledonia & Dependencies	7,335	126,000	Nouméa	G 8	41
Newfoundland, Canada	156,185	548,000	St. John's		50
New Hampshire, U.S.A.	9,304	808,000	Concord		92
New Hebrides	5,700	93,000	Vila	G 7	41
New Jersey, U.S.A.	7,836	7,330,000	Trenton		93
New Mexico, U.S.A.	121,666	1,122,000	Santa Fe		94
New York, U.S.A.	49,576	18,111,000	Albany		95
*New Zealand	103,736	3,045,000	Wellington	L 7	40
*Nicaragua	45,698	2,084,000	Managua	C 2	46
*Niger	489,189	4,476,000	Niamey	H 8	38
*Nigeria	379,628	79,800,000	Lagos	H10	38
Niue	100	5,000	Alofi	K 7	41
North America	9,363,000	339,000,000	....		44
North Carolina, U.S.A.	52,586	5,363,000	Raleigh		96
North Dakota, U.S.A.	70,665	637,000	Bismarck		97
Northern Ireland, U.K.	5,462	1,550,000	Belfast	C 3	23
Northwest Territories, Canada	1,304,903	37,000	Yellowknife		60
*Norway	125,181	4,002,000	Oslo	B 2	24
Nova Scotia, Canada	21,425	821,000	Halifax		51
Ohio, U.S.A.	41,222	10,737,000	Columbus		98
Oklahoma, U.S.A.	69,919	2,709,000	Oklahoma City		99
*Oman	82,030	722,000	Muscat	G 5	33
Ontario, Canada	412,582	8,200,000	Toronto		54-55
Oregon, U.S.A.	96,981	2,266,000	Salem		100
Pacific Islands, Terr. of the (U.S. Trust.)	717	115,000	Garapan (Saipan)	F 5	41
*Pakistan	310,403	68,214,000	Islamabad	B 3	34
*Panama	29,208	1,631,000	Panamá	D 3	46
Papua New Guinea	183,540	2,700,000	Port Moresby	B 7	36
*Paraguay	157,047	2,674,000	Asunción	J 8	43
Pennsylvania, U.S.A.	45,333	11,835,000	Harrisburg		101
*Persia (Iran)	636,293	31,925,000	Tehran	F 3	33
*Peru	496,222	15,383,000	Lima	E 5	42
Philippines	115,830	42,108,000	Quezon City	H 4	36
Pitcairn Islands	18	61	Adamstown	O 8	41
*Poland	120,725	33,869,000	Warsaw		31
*Portugal	35,549	8,564,000	Lisbon		27
Portuguese Timor	5,763	639,000	Dili	H 7	36
Prince Edward I., Canada	2,186	119,000	Charlottetown	E 2	51
Puerto Rico	3,435	2,987,000	San Juan	G 1	45
Qatar	4,247	140,000	Doha	F 4	33
Québec, Canada	594,860	6,176,000	Québec		53-54
Réunion	969	479,000	St-Denis	R20	39
Rhode Island, U.S.A.	1,214	937,000	Providence		84
Rhodesia	150,803	6,100,000	Salisbury	M15	39
Rumania	91,699	20,900,000	Bucharest	D 2	29
Rwanda	10,169	4,123,000	Kigali	N12	39

Country	Area (Sq. Miles)	Population	Capital or Chief Town	Index Ref.	Plate No.
Sabah, Malaysia	28,460	695,000	Kota Kinabalu	F 4	36
St. Christopher-Nevis-Anguilla	136	66,000	Basseterre	F 3	45
St. Helena & Dependencies	162	6,600	Jamestown	E15	39
St. Lucia	238	107,000	Castries	G 4	45
St-Pierre & Miquelon	93.5	6,000	St-Pierre	C 4	50
St. Vincent	150	94,000	Kingstown	G 4	45
San Marino	23.4	19,000	San Marino	D 3	28
*São Tomé e Príncipe	372	78,000	São Tomé	H11	39
Sarawak, Malaysia	48,050	999,000	Kuching	E 5	36
Saskatchewan, Canada	251,700	915,000	Regina		57
*Saudi Arabia	829,995	8,600,000	Riyadh, Mecca	D 4	33
Scotland, U.K.	30,414	5,215,000	Edinburgh	D 2	23
*Senegal	75,954	4,227,000	Dakar	D 9	38
Seychelles & Dependencies	145	56,000	Victoria	J10	32
*Siam (Thailand)	198,455	41,023,000	Bangkok	D 3	35
*Sierra Leone	27,925	2,861,000	Freetown	D10	38
*Singapore	226	2,230,000	Singapore	F 6	35
Solomon Islands	11,157	185,000	Honiara	G 6	41
*Somalia	246,199	3,100,000	Mogadishu	R10	38
*South Africa	472,359	24,920,000	Cape Town, Pretoria	L18	39
South America	6,885,700	206,000,000	....		42-43
South Carolina, U.S.A.	31,055	2,784,000	Columbia		102
South Dakota, U.S.A.	77,047	682,000	Pierre		103
South-West Africa	317,827	673,000	Windhoek	K16	39
*Spain	194,881	35,225,000	Madrid		27
Spanish Sahara	102,703	108,000	El Aaiún	D 7	38
*Sri Lanka	25,332	13,600,000	Colombo	E 7	34
*Sudan	967,494	17,324,000	Khartoum	M 9	38
*Surinam	60,239	432,000	Paramaribo	J 3	42
*Swaziland	6,705	494,000	Mbabane	N17	39
*Sweden	170,210	8,177,000	Stockholm	C 2	24
Switzerland	15,941	6,431,000	Bern		27
*Syria	71,227	7,121,000	Damascus	C 2	33
*Tanzania	363,708	14,763,000	Dar es Salaam	N13	39
Tennessee, U.S.A.	42,244	4,129,000	Nashville		104
Texas, U.S.A.	267,338	12,050,000	Austin		105
*Thailand	198,455	41,023,000	Bangkok	D 3	35
*Togo	21,622	2,171,000	Lomé	G10	38
Tokelau Islands	3.9	1,600	Fenuafala	J 6	41
Tonga	270	96,000	Nuku'alofa	J 8	41
*Trinidad & Tobago	1,980	1,064,000	Port of Spain	G 5	45
Tristan da Cunha	38	275	Edinburgh	J 7	19
*Tunisia	63,170	5,641,000	Tunis	H 5	38
*Turkey	300,946	38,270,000	Ankara	B 2	33
Turks & Caicos Islands	166	6,000	Cockburn Town	D 2	45
*Uganda	91,076	11,172,000	Kampala	N11	39
*Ukrainian S.S.R., U.S.S.R.	233,089	48,521,000	Kiev	C 5	30
*Union of Soviet Socialist Republics	8,649,489	252,064,000	Moscow		30
*United Arab Emirates	32,278	250,000	Abu Dhabi	F 5	33
*United Kingdom	94,399	56,094,000	London		23
*United States of America, land land & water	3,536,855 3,615,122	212,812,000	Washington		61
*Upper Volta	105,869	5,737,000	Ouagadougou	F 9	38
*Uruguay	68,536	3,028,000	Montevideo	J10	43
Utah, U.S.A.	84,916	1,173,000	Salt Lake City		106
Vatican City	109 acres	700	....	B 6	28
*Venezuela	352,143	11,632,000	Caracas	G 2	42
Vermont, U.S.A.	9,609	470,000	Montpelier		107
Vietnam, North	61,293	23,787,000	Hanoi	E 3	35
Vietnam, South	67,112	20,100,000	Saigon	F 4	35
Virginia, U.S.A.	40,817	4,908,000	Richmond		108
Virgin Islands, British	59	12,000	Road Town	H 1	45
Virgin Islands (U.S.A.)	133	73,000	Charlotte Amalie	G 1	45
Wake Island	2.5	437	....	G 4	41
Wales, U.K.	8,017	2,759,000	Cardiff	E 4	23
Wallis & Futuna	106	9,000	Matautu	J 7	41
Washington, U.S.A.	68,192	3,476,000	Olympia		109
Western Samoa	1,133	155,000	Apia	J 7	41
West Virginia, U.S.A.	24,181	1,791,000	Charleston		110
*White Russian (Byelorussian) S.S.R., U.S.S.R.	80,154	9,268,000	Minsk	C 4	30
Wisconsin, U.S.A.	56,154	4,566,000	Madison		111
World	52,470,000	3,866,000,000	....		17,19
Wyoming, U.S.A.	97,914	359,000	Cheyenne		112
*Yemen Arab Republic	77,220	6,700,000	San'a	D 6	33
*Yemen, Peoples Democratic Republic of	111,101	1,633,000	Aden	E 7	33
*Yugoslavia	98,766	21,262,000	Belgrade	B 2	29
Yukon Territory, Canada	207,076	21,000	Whitehorse		60
*Zaire	918,962	24,222,000	Kinshasa	L12	39
*Zambia	290,586	4,751,000	Lusaka	M14	39

GAZETTEER OF THE UNITED STATES

This section lists the major cities and all state capitals and territorial capitals of the United States. Listings for the states and territories can be found on pages 4 and 5. Population figures are derived from the 1970 U.S. Final Census, as revised.

Name	Index Ref.	Plate No.
Abilene, Tex., 89,653	E 5	105
Abington, Pa., 62,786	M 5	101
Agaña (cap.), Guam, 2,119	E 4	41
Akron, Ohio, 275,425	G 3	98
Alameda, Calif., 70,968	J 2	69
Albany, Ga., 72,623	D 7	73
Albany (cap.), N.Y., 115,781	N 5	95
Albuquerque, N. Mex., 243,751	C 3	94
Alexandria, La., 41,557	E 4	81
Alexandria, Va., 110,927	L 3	108
Alhambra, Calif., 62,125	C10	69
Allen Park, Mich., 40,747	B 7	85
Allentown, Pa., 109,871	L 4	101
Alton, Ill., 39,700	A 6	76
Altoona, Pa., 63,115	F 4	101
Amarillo, Tex.,127,010	C 2	105
Ames, Iowa, 39,505	F 4	78
Anaheim, Calif., 166,408	D11	69
Anchorage, Alaska, 49,126	B 1	66
Anderson, Ind., 70,787	F 4	77
Annapolis (cap.), Md.,30,095	H 5	83
Ann Arbor, Mich., 99,797	F 6	85
Appleton, Wis., 56,377	J 7	111
Arcadia, Calif., 45,138	C10	69
Arden-Arcade, Calif., 82,492	B 8	69
Arlington, Mass., 53,534	C 6	84
Arlington, Tex., 90,032	F 2	105
Arlington, Va., 174,284	K 3	108
Arlington Hts., Ill., 64,884	A 1	76
Arvada, Colo., 49,083	J 3	70
Asheville, N.C., 57,681	E 8	96
Athens, Ga., 44,342	F 3	73
Atlanta (cap.), Ga., 497,421	D 3	73
Atlantic City, N.J., 47,859	E 5	93
Augusta, Ga., 59,864	J 4	73
Augusta (cap.), Maine, 21,945	D 7	82
Aurora, Colo., 74,974	K 3	70
Aurora, Ill., 74,182	E 2	76
Austin (cap.), Tex., 251,808	G 7	105
Bakersfield, Calif., 69,515	G 8	69
Baldwin Park, Calif., 47,285	D10	69
Baltimore, Md., 905,787	H 3	83
Baton Rouge (cap.), La., 165,921	K 2	81
Battle Creek, Mich., 38,931	D 6	85
Bayamón, P.R., 147,552	G 1	45
Bay City, Mich., 49,449	F 5	85
Bayonne, N.J., 72,743	B 2	93
Baytown, Tex., 43,980	L 2	105
Beaumont, Tex., 117,548	K 7	105
Belleville, Ill., 41,699	B 6	76
Bellevue, Wash., 61,196	B 2	109
Bellflower, Calif., 51,454	C11	69
Bellingham, Wash., 39,375	C 2	109
Berkeley, Calif., 116,716	J 2	69
Berwyn, Ill., 52,502	B 2	76
Bethesda, Md., 71,621	A 4	83
Bethlehem, Pa., 72,686	M 4	101
Beverly, Mass., 38,348	E 5	84
Billings, Mont., 61,581	H 5	89
Biloxi, Miss., 48,486	G10	87
Binghamton, N.Y., 64,123	J 6	95
Birmingham, Ala., 300,910	D 3	65
Bismarck (cap.), N. Dak., 34,703	J 6	97
Bloomfield, N.J., 52,029	B 2	93
Bloomington, Ill., 39,992	D 3	76
Bloomington, Ind., 43,262	D 6	77
Bloomington, Minn., 81,970	G 6	86
Boise (cap.), Idaho, 74,990	B 6	75
Bossier City, La., 41,595	C 1	81
Boston (cap.), Mass., 641,071	D 7	84
Boulder, Colo., 66,870	J 2	70
Bridgeport, Conn., 156,542	C 4	71
Bristol, Conn., 55,487	D 2	71
Bristol, Pa., 67,498	N 5	101
Brockton, Mass., 89,040	K 4	84
Brookline, Mass., 58,689	C 7	84
Brownsville, Tex., 52,522	G12	105
Buena Park, Calif., 63,646	D11	69
Buffalo, N.Y., 462,768	B 5	95
Burbank, Calif., 88,871	C10	69
Burlington, Vt., 38,633	A 2	107
Caguas, P.R., 63,215	G 1	45
Cambridge, Mass.,100,361	C 6	84
Camden, N.J., 102,551	B 3	93
Canton, Ohio, 110,053	H 4	98
Carson, Calif., 71,150	C11	69
Carson City (cap.), Nev., 15,468	B 3	91
Casper, Wyo., 39,361	F 3	112
Catonsville, Md., 54,812	H 3	83
Cedar Rapids, Iowa, 110,642	K 5	78
Champaign, Ill., 56,837	E 3	76
Charleston, S.C., 66,945	G 6	102
Charleston (cap.), W.Va., 71,505	C 4	110
Charlotte, N.C., 241,178	D 4	96
Charlotte Amalie (cap.), Virgin Is., 12,220	H 1	45
Charlottesville, Va., 38,880	G 4	108
Chattanooga, Tenn., 119,923	K 4	104
Cheektowaga, N.Y., 113,844	C 5	95
Cheltenham, Pa., 40,238	M 5	101
Cherry Hill, N.J., 64,395	B 3	93
Chesapeake, Va., 89,580	M 7	108
Chester, Pa., 56,331	L 7	101
Cheyenne (cap.), Wyo., 40,914	H 4	112
Chicopee, Mass., 66,676	D 4	84
Chicago, Ill., 3,369,357	B 2	76
Chicago Hts., Ill., 40,900	B 3	76
Chula Vista, Calif., 67,901	J11	69
Cicero, Ill., 67,058	B 2	76
Cincinnati, Ohio, 451,455	B 9	98
Clearwater, Fla., 52,074	B 2	72
Clifton, N.J., 82,437	B 2	93
Cleveland, Ohio, 750,879	H 9	98
Cleveland Hts., Ohio, 60,767	H 9	98
Colorado Springs, Colo., 135,060	K 5	70
Columbia, Mo., 58,812	H 5	88
Columbia (cap.), S.C., 113,542	F 4	102
Columbus, Ga., 167,377	C 6	73
Columbus (cap.), Ohio, 540,025	E 6	98
Compton, Calif., 78,547	C11	69
Concord, Calif., 85,164	K 1	69
Concord (cap.), N.H., 30,022	C 5	92
Coral Gables, Fla., 42,494	B 5	72
Corpus Christi, Tex., 204,525	G10	105
Costa Mesa, Calif., 72,660	D11	69
Council Bluffs, Iowa, 60,348	B 6	78
Covington, Ky., 52,535	K 1	80
Cranston, R.I., 74,287	J 5	84
Cuyahoga Falls, Ohio, 49,678	G 3	98
Dallas, Tex., 844,401	H 2	105
Daly City, Calif., 66,922	H 2	69
Danbury, Conn., 50,781	B 3	71
Danville, Ill., 42,570	F 3	76
Danville, Va., 46,391	E 7	108
Davenport, Iowa, 98,469	M 5	78
Dayton, Ohio, 242,917	B 6	98
Daytona Bch., Fla., 45,327	F 2	72
Dearborn, Mich., 104,199	B 7	85
Dearborn Heights, Mich., 80,069	B 7	85
Decatur, Ala., 38,044	D 1	65
Decatur, Ill., 90,397	E 4	76
Denton, Tex., 39,874	G 4	105
Denver (cap.), Colo., 514,678	K 3	70
Des Moines (cap.), Iowa, 201,404	G 5	78
Des Plaines, Ill., 57,239	A 1	76
Detroit, Mich., 1,513,601	B 7	85
Dover (cap.), Del., 17,488	M 4	83
Downey, Calif., 88,442	C11	69
Dubuque, Iowa, 62,309	M 3	78
Duluth, Minn., 100,578	F 4	86
Dundalk, Md., 85,377	J 3	83
Durham, N.C., 95,438	H 2	96
East Chicago, Ind., 46,982	C 1	77
E. Cleveland, Ohio, 39,600	H 9	98
E. Detroit, Mich., 45,920	B 6	85
E. Hartford, Conn., 57,583	E 1	71
E. Lansing, Mich., 47,540	E 6	85
E. Los Angeles, Calif., 105,033	C10	69
E. Orange, N.J., 75,471	B 2	93
E. Point, Ga., 39,315	C 3	73
E. Providence, R.I., 48,207	J 5	84
E. St. Louis, Ill., 69,996	B 6	76
Eau Claire, Wis., 44,619	D 6	111
Edina, Minn., 44,046	G 5	86
Edison, N.J., 67,120	E 2	93
El Cajon, Calif., 52,273	J11	69
Elgin, Ill., 55,691	E 1	76
Elizabeth, N.J., 112,654	B 2	93
Elkhart, Ind., 43,152	F 1	77
Elmhurst, Ill., 48,887	A 2	76
Elmira, N.Y., 39,945	G 6	95
El Monte, Calif., 69,892	D10	69
El Paso, Tex., 322,261	A10	105
Elyria, Ohio, 53,427	F 3	98
Enfield, Conn., 46,189	E 1	71
Enid, Okla., 44,986	G 2	99
Erie, Pa., 129,231	B 1	101
Euclid, Ohio, 71,552	J 9	98
Eugene, Oreg., 79,028	D 3	100
Evanston, Ill., 80,113	B 1	76
Evansville, Ind., 138,764	C 9	77
Everett, Mass., 42,485	D 6	84
Everett, Wash., 53,622	C 3	109
Fairfield, Calif., 44,146	K 1	69
Fairfield, Conn., 56,487	B 4	71
Fall River, Mass., 96,898	K 6	84
Fargo, N.D., 53,365	S 6	97
Fayetteville, N.C., 53,510	H 4	96
Fitchburg, Mass., 43,343	G 2	84
Flint, Mich., 193,717	F 6	85
Florissant, Mo., 65,903	P 2	88
Fort Collins, Colo., 43,337	J 1	70
Ft. Lauderdale, Fla., 139,590	C 4	72
Ft. Smith, Ark., 62,802	B 3	68
Ft. Wayne, Ind., 178,021	G 2	77
Ft. Worth, Tex., 393,476	E 2	105
Framingham, Mass., 64,048	A 7	84
Frankfort (cap.), Ky., 21,902	H 4	80
Freeport, N.Y., 40,374	B 3	95
Fremont, Calif., 100,869	K 3	69
Fresno, Calif., 165,972	F 7	69
Fullerton, Calif., 85,987	D11	69
Gadsden, Ala., 53,928	G 2	65
Gainesville, Fla., 64,510	D 2	72
Galveston, Tex., 61,809	L 3	105
Gardena, Calif., 41,021	C11	69
Garden Grove, Calif., 121,357	D11	69
Garfield Hts., Ohio, 41,417	J 9	98
Garland, Tex., 81,437	H 1	105
Gary, Ind., 175,415	C 1	77
Gastonia, N.C., 47,142	C 4	96
Glendale, Calif., 132,664	C10	69
Grand Forks, N. Dak., 39,008	R 4	97
Grand Prairie, Tex., 50,904	G 2	105
Grand Rapids, Mich., 197,649	D 5	85
Granite City, Ill., 40,685	B 6	76
Great Falls, Mont., 60,091	E 3	89
Greece, N.Y., 75,136	E 4	95
Greeley, Colo., 38,902	K 2	70
Green Bay, Wis., 87,809	K 6	111
Greensboro, N.C., 144,076	F 2	96
Greenville, Miss., 39,648	B 4	87
Greenville, S.C., 61,436	C 2	102
Greenwich, Conn., 59,755	A 4	71
Groton, Conn., 38,244	G 3	71
Gulfport, Miss., 40,791	F10	87
Hamden, Conn., 49,357	D 3	71
Hamilton, Ohio, 67,865	A 7	98
Hammond, Ind., 107,885	B 1	77
Hampton, Va., 120,779	M 6	108
Harrisburg (cap.), Pa., 68,061	H 5	101
Hartford (cap.), Conn., 158,017	E 1	71
Hattiesburg, Miss., 38,277	F 8	87
Haverford, Pa., 55,132	M 6	101
Haverhill, Mass., 46,120	K 1	84
Hawthorne, Calif., 53,304	C11	69
Hayward, Calif., 93,058	K 2	69
Helena (cap.), Mont., 22,730	E 4	89
Hempstead, N.Y., 39,411	A 2	95
Hialeah, Fla., 102,452	B 4	72
High Point, N.C., 63,259	E 3	96
Hoboken, N.J., 45,380	C 2	93
Hollywood, Fla., 106,873	B 4	72
Holyoke, Mass., 50,112	D 4	84
Honolulu (cap.), Hawaii, 324,871	C 4	74
Houston, Tex., 1,232,802	J 2	105
Huntington, W.Va., 74,315	A 4	110
Huntington Beach, Calif., 115,960	C11	69
Huntsville, Ala., 139,282	E 1	65
Independence, Mo., 111,630	R 5	88
Indianapolis (cap.), Ind., 746,302	E 5	77
Inglewood, Calif., 89,985	B11	69
Inkster, Mich., 38,595	B 7	85
Iowa City, Iowa, 46,850	L 5	78
Irondequoit, N.Y., 63,675	E 4	95
Irving, Tex., 97,260	G 2	105
Irvington, N.J., 59,473	B 2	93
Jackson, Mich., 45,484	E 6	85
Jackson (cap.), Miss., 153,968	D 6	87
Jackson, Tenn., 39,996	D 3	104
Jacksonville, Fla., 528,865	E 1	72
Jamestown, N.Y., 39,795	B 6	95
Janesville, Wis., 46,426	H10	111
Jefferson City (cap.), Mo., 32,407	H 5	88
Jersey City, N.J., 260,350	B 2	93
Johnstown, Pa., 42,476	D 5	101
Joliet, Ill., 78,887	E 2	76
Joplin, Mo., 39,256	C 8	88
Juneau (cap.), Alaska, 13,556	N 1	66
Kalamazoo, Mich., 85,555	D 6	85
Kansas City, Kans., 168,213	H 2	79
Kansas City, Mo., 507,330	P 5	88
Kenosha, Wis., 78,805	M 3	111
Kettering, Ohio, 71,864	B 6	98
Knoxville, Tenn., 174,587	O 3	104
Kokomo, Ind., 44,042	E 4	77
La Crosse, Wis., 51,153	D 8	111

GAZETTEER OF THE UNITED STATES

Name	Index Ref.	Plate No.
Lafayette, Ind., 44,955	D 4	77
Lafayette, La., 68,908	F 6	81
La Habra, Calif., 41,350	D11	69
Lake Charles, La., 77,998	D 6	81
Lakeland, Fla., 41,550	D 3	72
Lakewood, Calif., 83,025	C11	69
Lakewood, Colo., 92,743	J 3	70
Lakewood, Ohio, 70,173	G 9	98
La Mesa, Calif., 39,178	H11	69
Lancaster, Pa., 57,690	K 5	101
Lansing (cap.), Mich., 131,403	E 6	85
Laredo, Tex., 69,024	E10	105
Las Vegas, Nev., 125,787	F 6	91
Lawrence, Kans., 45,698	G 3	79
Lawrence, Mass., 66,915	K 2	84
Lawton, Okla., 74,470	F 5	99
Levittown, N.Y., 65,440	B 2	95
Lewiston, Maine, 41,779	C 7	82
Lexington, Ky., 108,137	H 4	80
Lima, Ohio, 53,734	B 4	98
Lincoln (cap.), Nebr., 149,518	H 4	90
Lincoln Park, Mich., 52,984	B 7	85
Linden, N.J., 41,409	A 3	93
Little Rock (cap.), Ark., 132,483	F 4	68
Livonia, Mich., 110,109	F 6	85
Long Beach, Calif., 358,879	C11	69
Longview, Tex., 45,547	K 5	105
Lorain, Ohio, 78,185	F 3	98
Los Angeles, Calif., 2,809,813	C10	69
Louisville, Ky., 361,706	F 4	80
Lowell, Mass., 94,239	J 2	84
Lubbock, Tex., 149,101	C 4	105
Lynchburg, Va., 54,083	F 6	108
Lynn, Mass., 90,294	D 6	84
Lynwood, Calif., 43,354	C11	69
Macon, Ga., 122,423	E 5	73
Madison (cap.), Wis., 171,769	H 9	111
Madison Hts., Mich., 38,599	F 6	85
Malden, Mass., 56,127	D 6	84
Manchester, Conn., 47,994	E 1	71
Manchester, N.H., 87,754	C 6	92
Mansfield, Ohio, 55,047	F 4	98
Marion, Ind., 39,607	F 3	77
Marion, Ohio, 38,646	D 4	98
Mayagüez, P.R., 68,872	F 1	45
Medford, Mass., 64,397	C 6	84
Melbourne, Fla., 40,236	F 3	72
Memphis, Tenn., 623,530	B 4	104
Meriden, Conn., 55,959	D 2	71
Meridian, Miss., 45,083	G 6	87
Mesa, Ariz., 62,853	D 5	67
Mesquite, Tex., 55,131	H 2	105
Metairie, La., 136,477	O 4	81
Miami, Fla., 334,859	B 5	72
Miami Bch., Fla., 87,072	C 5	72
Michigan City, Ind., 39,369	C 1	77
Middletown, N.J., 54,623	E 3	93
Middletown, Ohio, 48,767	A 6	98
Midland, Tex., 59,463	C 6	105
Midwest City, Okla., 48,212	H 4	99
Milford, Conn., 50,858	C 4	71
Milwaukee, Wis., 717,372	M 1	111
Minneapolis, Minn., 434,400	G 5	86
Mobile, Ala., 190,026	B 9	65
Modesto, Calif., 61,712	D 6	69
Moline, Ill., 46,237	C 2	76
Monroe, La., 56,374	F 1	81
Montclair, N.J., 44,043	B 2	93
Montebello, Calif., 42,807	C10	69
Montgomery (cap.), Ala., 133,386	F 6	65
Monterey Park, Calif., 49,166	C10	69
Montpelier (cap.), Vt., 8,609	B 2	107
Mountain View, Calif., 54,304	K 3	69
Mount Lebanon, Pa., 39,596	B 7	101
Mt. Prospect, Ill., 45,228	A 1	76
Mt. Vernon, N.Y., 72,778	H 1	95
Muncie, Ind., 69,082	G 4	77
Muskegon, Mich., 44,631	C 5	85
Nashua, N.H., 55,820	C 6	92
Nashville (cap.), Tenn., 447,877	H 2	104
National City, Calif., 43,184	J11	69

Name	Index Ref.	Plate No.
New Albany, Ind., 38,402	F 8	77
Newark, N.J., 381,930	B 2	93
Newark, Ohio, 41,836	F 5	98
New Bedford, Mass., 101,777	K 6	84
New Britain, Conn., 83,441	E 2	71
New Brunswick, N.J., 41,885	E 3	93
New Castle, Pa., 38,559	B 3	101
New Haven, Conn., 137,707	D 3	71
New Orleans, La., 593,471	O 4	81
Newport Bch., Calif., 49,422	D11	69
Newport News, Va., 138,177	L 6	108
New Rochelle, N.Y., 75,385	J 1	95
Newton, Mass., 91,263	C 7	84
New York, N.Y., 7,895,563	C 2	95
Niagara Falls, N.Y., 85,615	C 4	95
Norfolk, Va., 307,951	M 7	108
Norman, Okla., 52,117	H 4	99
Norristown, Pa., 38,169	M 5	101
North Bergen, N.J., 47,751	B 2	93
N. Charleston, S.C., 53,617	G 6	102
N. Chicago, Ill., 47,275	F 1	76
N. Little Rock, Ark., 60,040	F 4	68
Norwalk, Calif., 91,827	C11	69
Norwalk, Conn., 79,288	B 4	71
Norwich, Conn., 41,739	G 2	71
Oakland, Calif., 361,561	J 2	69
Oak Lawn, Ill., 60,305	B 2	76
Oak Park, Ill., 62,511	B 2	76
Oceanside, Calif., 40,494	H10	69
Odessa, Tex., 78,380	B 6	105
Ogden, Utah, 69,478	C 2	106
Oklahoma City (cap.), Okla., 368,377	G 4	99
Old Bridge, N.J., 48,715	E 3	93
Olympia (cap.), Wash., 23,296	C 3	109
Omaha, Nebr., 346,929	J 3	90
Ontario, Calif., 64,118	D10	69
Orange, Calif., 77,365	D11	69
Orlando, Fla., 99,006	E 3	72
Oshkosh, Wis., 53,082	J 8	111
Overland Park, Kans., 79,034	H 3	79
Owensboro, Ky., 50,329	C 5	80
Oxnard, Calif., 71,225	F 9	69
Pago Pago (cap.), American Samoa, 2,451	J 7	41
Palo Alto, Calif., 55,835	K 3	69
Parkersburg, W.Va., 44,208	D 2	110
Park Ridge, Ill., 42,614	A 1	76
Parma, Ohio, 100,216	H 9	98
Parsippany-Troy Hills, N.J., 55,112	E 2	93
Pasadena, Calif., 112,951	C10	69
Pasadena, Tex., 89,277	J 2	105
Passaic, N.J., 55,124	B 2	93
Paterson, N.J., 144,824	B 2	93
Pawtucket, R.I., 76,984	J 5	84
Peabody, Mass., 48,080	E 5	84
Pensacola, Fla., 59,507	B 6	72
Peoria, Ill., 126,963	D 3	76
Perth Amboy, N.J., 38,798	E 2	93
Petersburg, Va., 44,124	J 6	108
Philadelphia, Pa., 1,949,996	M 6	101
Phoenix (cap.), Ariz., 582,500	C 5	67
Pico Rivera, Calif., 54,170	C10	69
Pierre (cap.), S. Dak., 9,699	J 5	103
Pine Bluff, Ark., 57,389	F 5	68
Pittsburgh, Pa., 520,117	B 7	101
Pittsfield, Mass., 57,020	A 3	84
Plainfield, N.J., 46,862	E 2	93
Pocatello, Idaho, 40,036	F 7	75
Pomona, Calif., 87,384	D10	69
Pompano Bch., Fla., 38,587	F 5	72
Ponce, P.R., 128,233	G 1	45
Pontiac, Mich., 85,279	F 6	85
Port Arthur, Tex., 57,371	K 8	105
Portland, Maine, 65,116	C 8	82
Portland, Oreg., 379,967	B 2	100
Portsmouth, Va., 110,963	L 7	108
Prichard, Ala., 41,578	B 9	65
Providence (cap.), R.I., 179,116	J 5	84
Provo, Utah, 53,131	C 3	106
Pueblo, Colo., 97,453	K 6	70
Quincy, Ill., 45,288	B 4	76
Quincy, Mass., 87,966	D 7	84

Name	Index Ref.	Plate No.
Racine, Wis., 95,162	M 3	111
Raleigh (cap.), N.C., 123,793	H 3	96
Rapid City, S. Dak., 43,836	C 5	103
Reading, Pa., 87,643	L 5	101
Redondo Bch., Calif., 57,451	B11	69
Redwood City, Calif., 55,686	J 3	69
Reno, Nev., 72,863	B 3	91
Revere, Mass., 43,159	D 6	84
Richardson, Tex., 48,582	G 1	105
Richfield, Minn., 47,231	G 6	86
Richmond, Calif., 79,043	J 1	69
Richmond, Ind., 43,999	H 5	77
Richmond(cap.), Va., 249,431	K 5	108
Riverside, Calif., 140,089	E10	69
Roanoke, Va., 92,115	D 6	108
Rochester, Minn., 53,766	F 6	86
Rochester, N.Y., 296,233	E 4	95
Rockford, Ill., 147,370	D 1	76
Rock Island, Ill., 50,166	C 2	76
Rockville, Md., 41,821	F 4	83
Rome, N.Y., 50,148	J 4	95
Rosemead, Calif., 40,972	D10	69
Roseville, Mich., 60,529	G 6	85
Royal Oak, Mich., 86,238	B 6	85
Sacramento (cap.), Calif., 257,105	B 8	69
Saginaw, Mich., 91,849	F 5	85
Saint Clair Shores, Mich., 88,093	G 6	85
St. Cloud, Minn., 39,691	D 5	86
St. Joseph, Mo., 72,691	C 3	88
St. Louis, Mo., 622,236	P 3	88
St. Louis Park, Minn., 48,922	G 5	86
St. Paul (cap.), Minn., 309,714	G 5	86
St. Petersburg, Fla., 216,159	B 3	72
Salem, Mass., 40,556	E 5	84
Salem (cap.), Oreg., 68,480	A 3	100
Salinas, Calif., 58,896	D 7	69
Salt Lake City (cap.), Utah, 175,885	C 3	106
San Angelo, Tex., 63,884	D 6	105
San Antonio, Tex., 654,153	F 8	105
San Bernardino, Calif., 106,869	E10	69
San Diego, Calif., 697,027	H11	69
San Francisco, Calif., 715,674	H 2	69
San Jose, Calif., 445,779	L 3	69
San Juan (cap.), P.R., 452,749	G 1	45
San Leandro, Calif., 68,698	J 2	69
San Mateo, Calif., 78,991	J 3	69
San Rafael, Calif., 38,977	J 1	69
Santa Ana, Calif., 155,762	D11	69
Sta. Barbara, Calif., 70,215	F 9	69
Sta. Clara, Calif., 87,717	K 3	69
Sta. Fe (cap.), N. Mex., 41,167	C 3	94
Sta. Monica, Calif., 88,289	B10	69
Sta. Rosa, Calif., 50,006	C 5	69
Sarasota, Fla., 40,237	D 4	72
Savannah, Ga., 118,349	L 6	73
Schenectady, N.Y., 77,958	M 5	95
Scottsdale, Ariz., 67,823	D 5	67
Scranton, Pa., 103,564	L 3	101
Seattle, Wash., 530,831	A 2	109
Sheboygan, Wis., 48,484	L 8	111
Shreveport, La., 182,064	C 1	81
Silver Spring, Md., 77,411	B 4	83
Simi Valley, Calif., 59,832	G 9	69
Sioux City, Iowa, 85,925	A 3	78
Siouy Falls, S. Dak., 72,488	R 6	103
Skokie, Ill., 68,322	B 1	76
Somerville, Mass., 88,779	C 6	84
South Bend, Ind., 125,580	E 1	77
Southfield, Mich., 69,285	F 6	85
South Gate, Calif., 56,909	C11	69
South San Francisco, Calif., 46,646	J 2	69
Spartanburg, S.C., 44,546	C 1	102
Spokane, Wash., 170,516	H 3	109
Springfield (cap.), Ill., 91,753	D 4	76
Springfield, Mass., 163,905	D 4	84
Springfield, Mo., 120,096	F 8	88
Springfield, Ohio, 81,941	C 6	98
Stamford, Conn., 108,798	A 4	71
Sterling Heights, Mich., 61,365	B 6	85

Name	Index Ref.	Plate No.
Stockton, Calif., 109,963	D 6	69
Stratford, Conn., 49,775	C 4	71
Suffolk, Va., 45,024	L 7	108
Sunnyvale, Calif., 95,408	K 3	69
Syracuse, N.Y., 197,297	H 4	95
Tacoma, Wash., 154,407	C 3	109
Tallahassee (cap.), Fla., 72,624	B 1	72
Tampa, Fla., 277,753	C 2	72
Taunton, Mass., 43,756	K 5	84
Taylor, Mich., 70,020	B 7	85
Teaneck, N.J., 42,355	B 2	93
Tempe, Ariz., 63,550	D 5	67
Terre Haute, Ind., 70,335	C 6	77
Texas City, Tex., 38,908	K 3	105
Toledo, Ohio, 383,105	D 2	98
Topeka (cap.), Kans., 125,011	G 2	79
Torrance, Calif., 134,968	C11	69
Towson, Md., 77,768	H 3	83
Trenton (cap.), N.J., 104,786	D 3	93
Troy, Mich., 39,419	B 6	85
Troy, N.Y., 62,918	N 5	95
Tucson, Ariz., 262,933	D 6	67
Tulsa, Okla., 330,350	K 2	99
Tuscaloosa, Ala., 65,773	C 4	65
Tyler, Tex., 57,770	J 5	105
Union, N.J., 53,077	A 2	93
Union City, N.J., 57,305	B 2	93
University City, Mo., 47,527	P 3	88
Upper Arlington, Ohio, 38,727	D 6	98
Upper Darby, Pa., 95,910	M 6	101
Utica, N.Y., 91,340	K 4	95
Vallejo, Calif., 71,710	J 1	69
Valley Stream, N.Y., 40,413	A 2	95
Vancouver, Wash., 41,859	C 5	109
Ventura, Calif., 57,964	F 9	69
Victoria, Tex., 41,349	H 9	105
Vineland, N.J., 47,399	C 5	93
Virginia Bch., Va., 172,106	M 7	108
Waco, Tex., 95,326	G 6	105
Walnut Creek, Calif., 39,844	K 2	69
Waltham, Mass., 61,582	B 6	84
Warren, Mich., 179,260	B 6	85
Warren, Ohio, 63,494	J 3	98
Warwick, R.I., 83,694	J 6	84
Washington, D.C. (cap.), U.S., 756,510	B 5	83
Waterbury, Conn., 108,033	C 2	71
Waterloo, Iowa, 75,533	J 4	78
Watertown, Mass., 39,307	C 6	84
Waukegan, Ill., 65,134	F 1	76
Waukesha, Wis., 39,695	K 1	111
Wauwatosa, Wis., 58,676	L 1	111
Wayne, N.J., 49,141	A 1	93
West Allis, Wis., 71,649	L 1	111
W. Covina, Calif., 68,034	D10	69
W. Hartford, Conn., 68,031	D 1	71
W. Haven, Conn., 52,851	D 3	71
Westland, Mich., 86,749	F 6	85
Westminster, Calif., 59,874	D11	69
West New York, N.J., 40,627	C 2	93
W. Orange, N.J., 43,715	A 2	93
W. Palm Bch., Fla., 57,375	F 5	75
W. Seneca, N.Y., 48,404	C 5	95
Weymouth, Mass., 54,610	D 8	84
Wheaton, Md., 66,280	A 3	83
Wheeling, W. Va., 48,188	K 5	110
White Plains, N.Y., 50,346	J 1	95
Whittier, Calif., 72,863	D11	69
Wichita, Kans., 276,554	E 4	79
Wichita Falls, Tex., 96,265	F 4	105
Wilkes-Barre, Pa., 58,856	L 3	101
Willingboro, N.J., 43,386	D 3	93
Wilmington, Del., 80,386	M 2	83
Wilmington, N.C., 46,169	J 6	96
Winston-Salem, N.C., 133,683	E 2	96
Woodbridge, N.J., 98,944	E 2	93
Woonsocket, R.I., 46,820	J 4	84
Worcester, Mass., 176,572	H 3	84
Wyandotte, Mich., 41,061	B 7	85
Wyoming, Mich., 56,560	D 6	85
Yakima, Wash., 45,588	E 4	109
Yonkers, N.Y., 204,297	H 1	95
York, Pa., 50,335	J 6	101
Youngstown, Ohio, 140,909	J 3	98

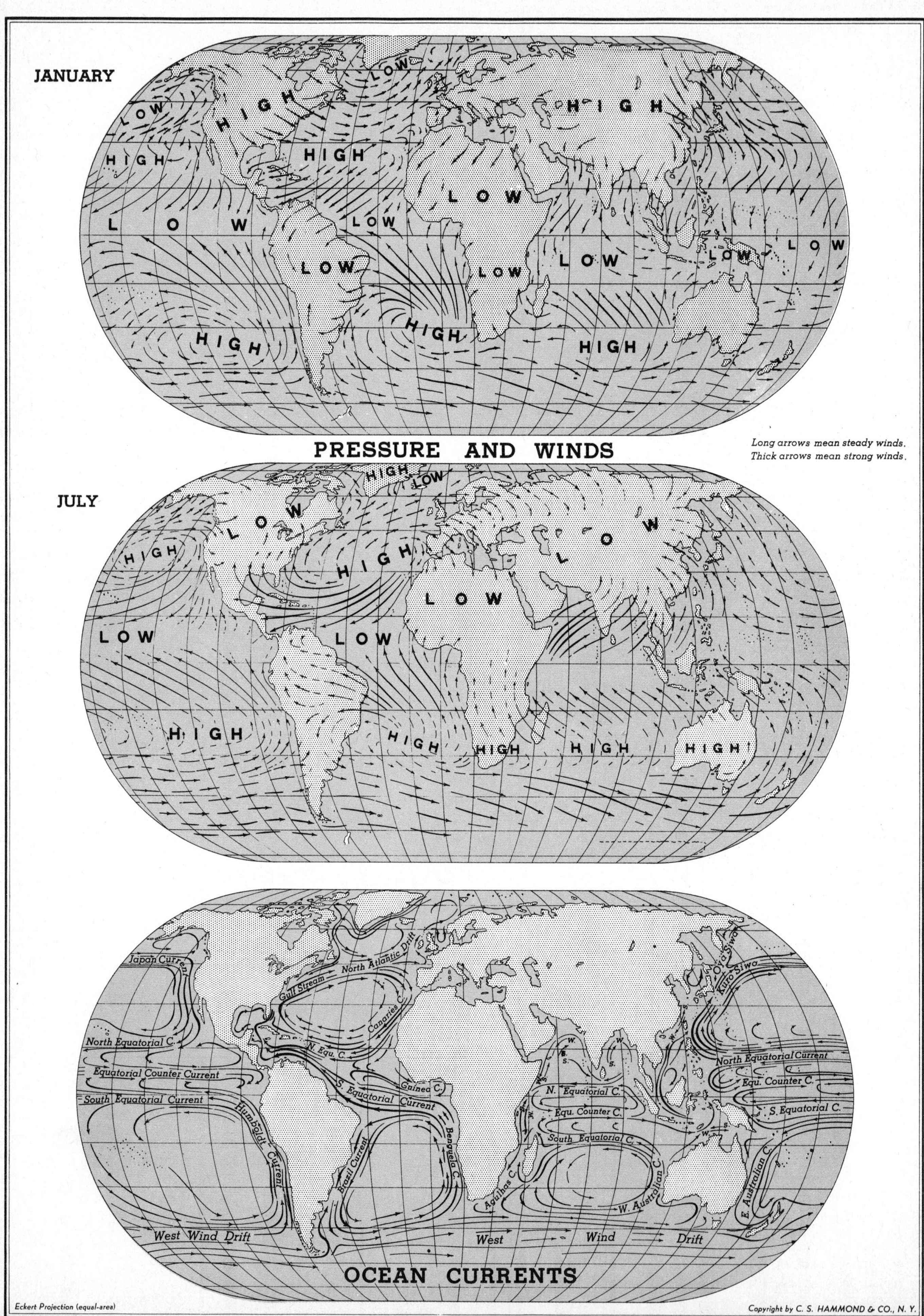
JANUARY
LOW
HIGH
HIGH
HIGH
LOW
HIGH
LOW
LOW
LOW
LOW
LOW
LOW
LOW
LOW
HIGH
HIGH
HIGH
PRESSURE AND WINDS
Long arrows mean steady winds.
Thick arrows mean strong winds.
JULY
HIGH
LOW
LOW
HIGH
HIGH
LOW
LOW
LOW
LOW
HIGH
HIGH
HIGH
HIGH
HIGH
Japan Current
North Atlantic Drift
Gulf Stream
Oya Siwo
Kuro Siwo
Canaries C.
North Equatorial C.
N. Equ. C.
North Equatorial Current
Equatorial Counter Current
Guinea C.
Equ. Counter C.
South Equatorial Current
S. Equatorial Current
N. Equatorial C.
Equ. Counter C.
S. Equatorial C.
Humboldt Current
Benguela C.
Brazil Current
South Equatorial C.
Agulhas C.
W. Australian C.
E. Australian C.
West Wind Drift
West Wind Drift
OCEAN CURRENTS
Eckert Projection (equal-area)

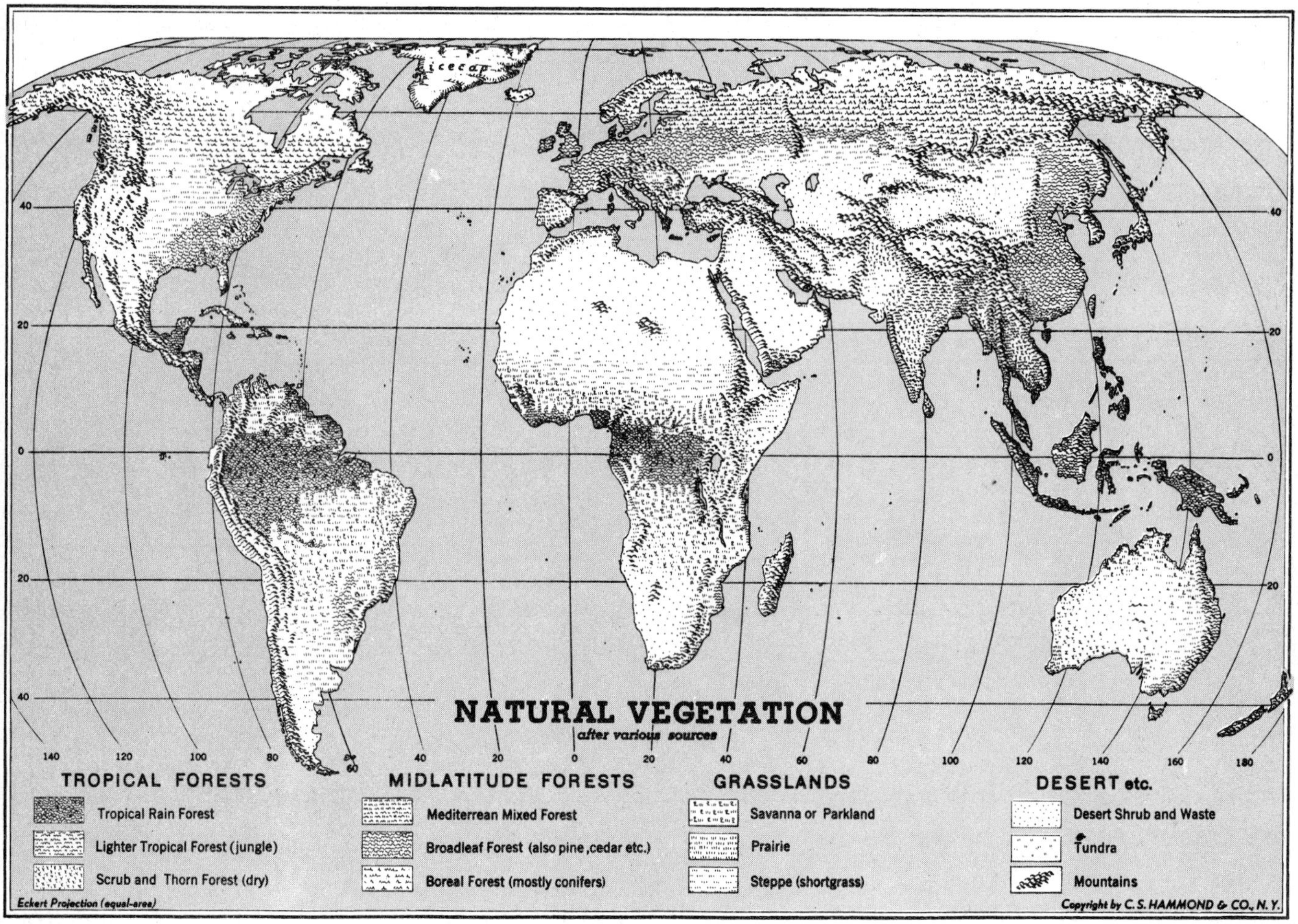
icecap
NATURAL VEGETATION
after various sources
TROPICAL FORESTS
Tropical Rain Forest
Lighter Tropical Forest (jungle)
Scrub and Thorn Forest (dry)
MIDLATITUDE FORESTS
Mediterrean Mixed Forest
Broadleaf Forest (also pine, cedar etc.)
Boreal Forest (mostly conifers)
GRASSLANDS
Savanna or Parkland
Prairie
Steppe (shortgrass)
DESERT etc.
Desert Shrub and Waste
Tundra
Mountains
Eckert Projection (equal-area)
Copyright by C. S. HAMMOND & CO., N. Y.

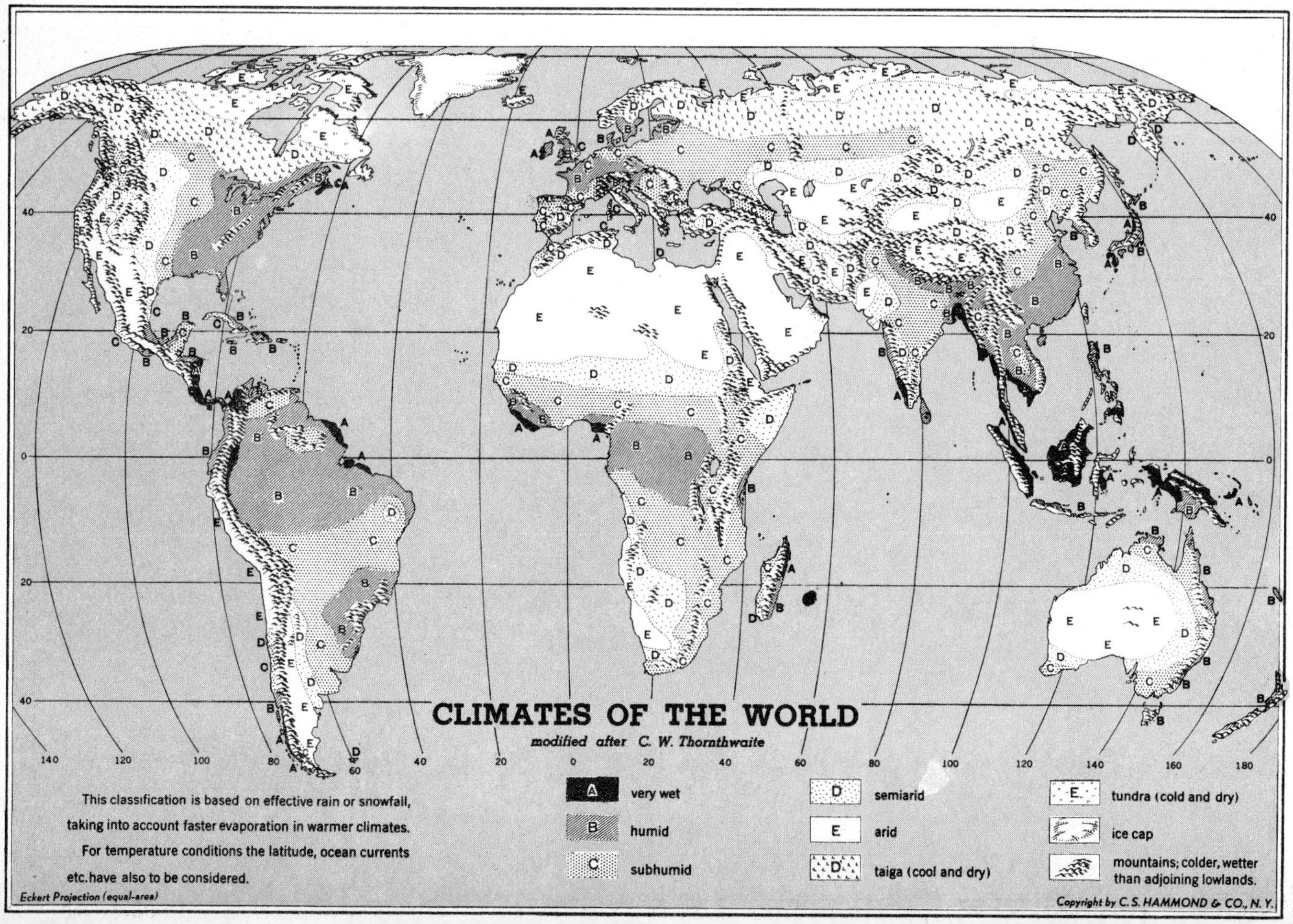
CLIMATES OF THE WORLD
modified after C. W. Thornthwaite
This classification is based on effective rain or snowfall, taking into account faster evaporation in warmer climates. For temperature conditions the latitude, ocean currents etc. have also to be considered.
A very wet
B humid
C subhumid
D semiarid
E arid
D taiga (cool and dry)
E tundra (cold and dry)
ice cap
mountains; colder, wetter than adjoining lowlands.
Eckert Projection (equal-area)
Copyright by C. S. HAMMOND & CO., N. Y.

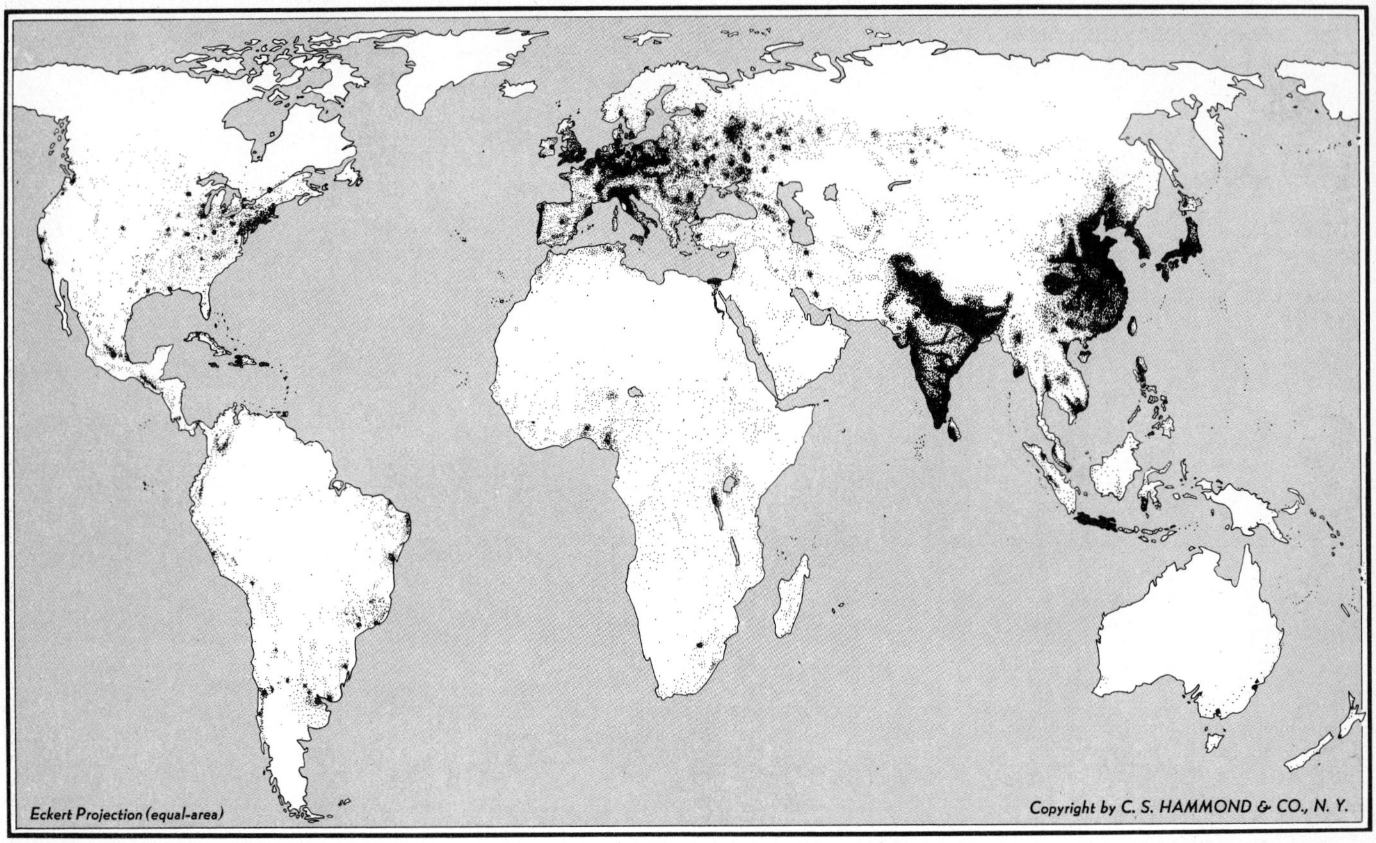
Eckert Projection (equal-area)
Copyright by C. S. HAMMOND & CO., N. Y.

DENSITY OF POPULATION. *One of the most outstanding facts of human geography is the extremely uneven distribution of people over the Earth. One-half of the Earth's surface has less than 3 people per square mile, while in the lowlands of India, China, Java and Japan rural density reaches the incredible congestion of 2000-3000 per square mile. Three-fourths of the Earth's population live in four relatively small areas; Northeastern United States, North-Central Europe, India and the Far East.*

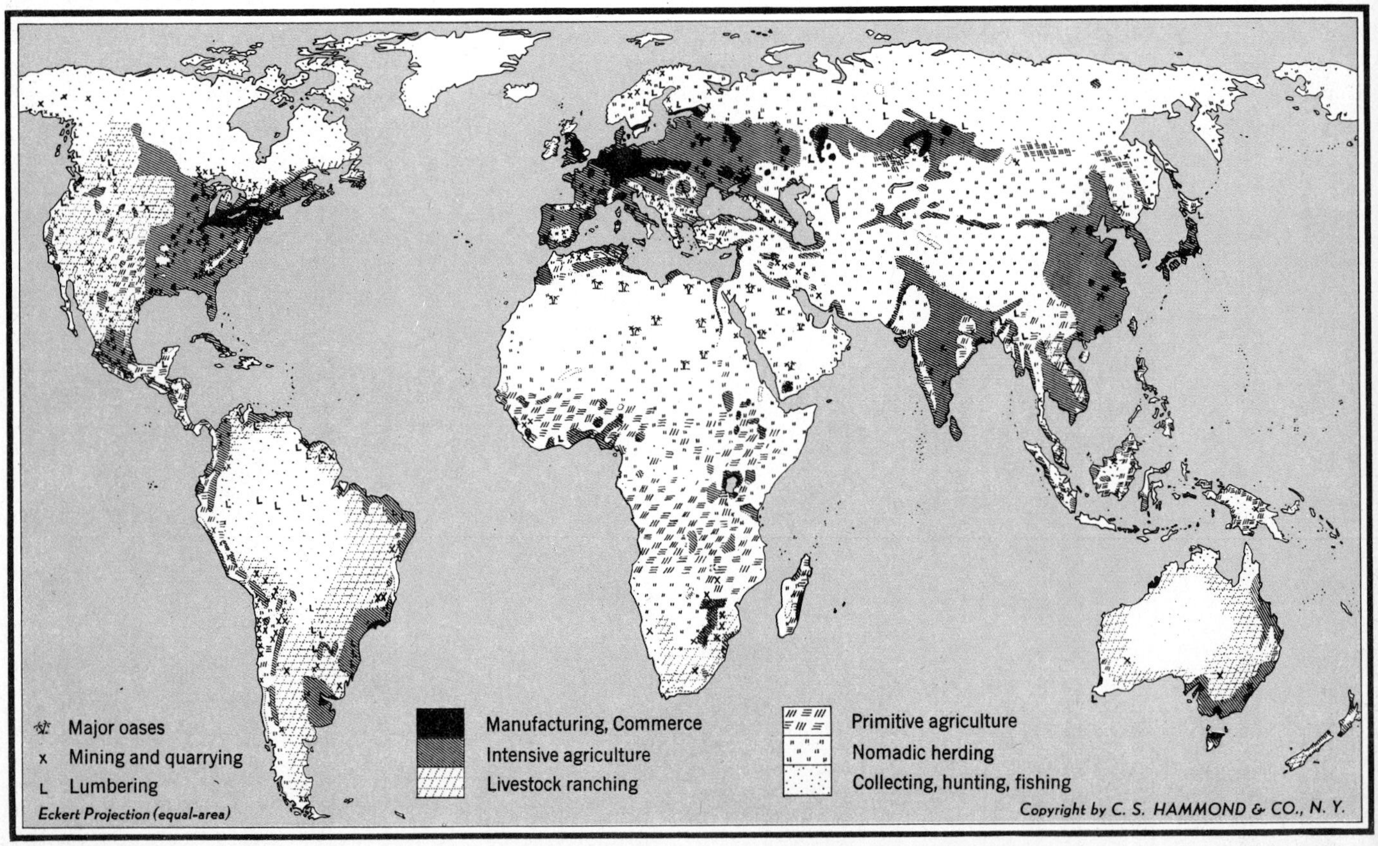
Major oases
Mining and quarrying
Lumbering
Manufacturing, Commerce
Intensive agriculture
Livestock ranching
Primitive agriculture
Nomadic herding
Collecting, hunting, fishing
Eckert Projection (equal-area)
Copyright by C. S. HAMMOND & CO., N. Y.

OCCUPATIONS. *Correlation with the density of population shows that the most densely populated areas fall into the regions of manufacturing and intensive farming. All other economies require considerable space. The most sparsely inhabited areas are those of collecting, hunting and fishing. Areas with practically no habitation are left blank.*

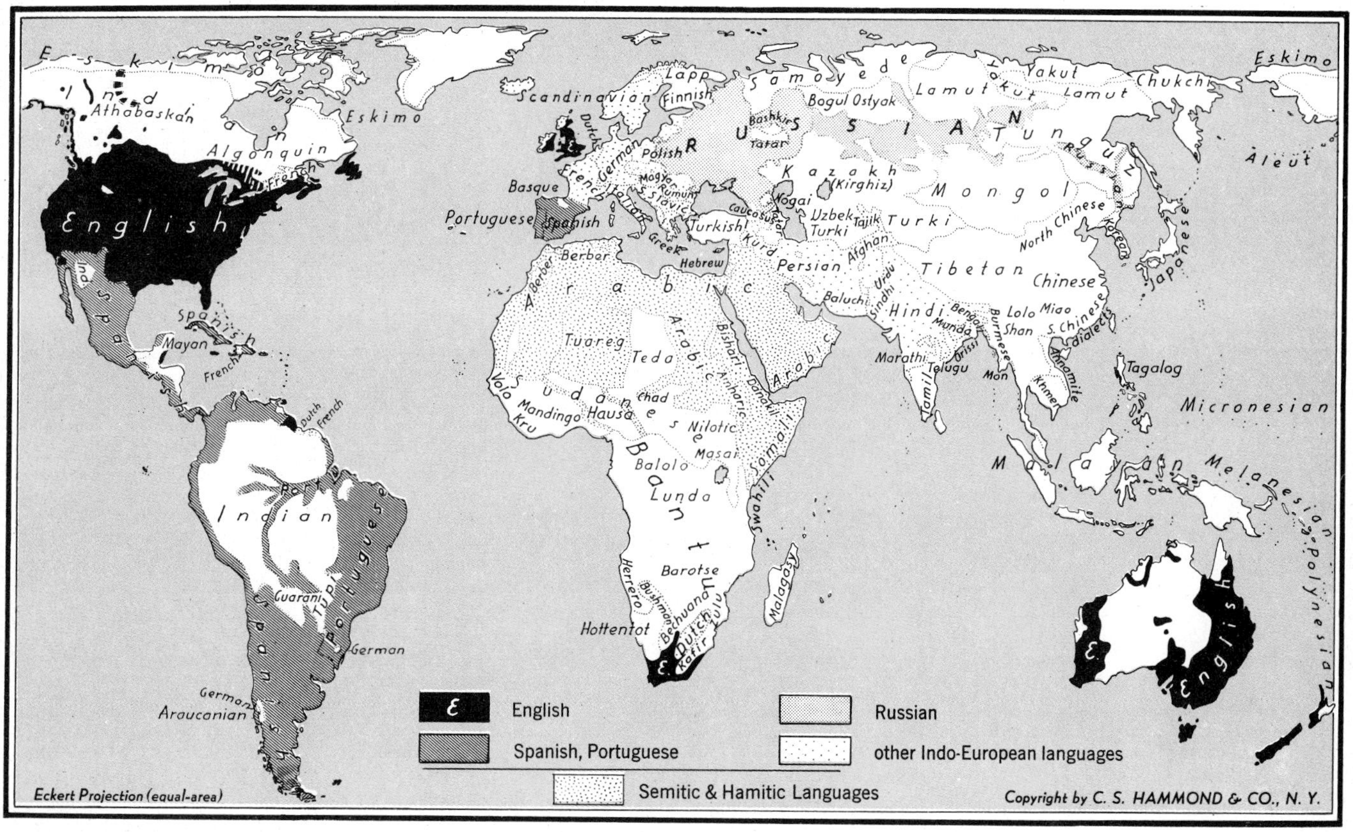

English
Spanish, Portuguese
Russian
other Indo-European languages
Semitic & Hamitic Languages

Eckert Projection (equal-area)

LANGUAGES. *Several hundred different languages are spoken in the World, and in many places two or more languages are spoken, sometimes by the same people. The map above shows the dominant languages in each locality. English, French, Spanish, Russian, Arabic and Swahili are spoken by many people as a second language for commerce or travel.*

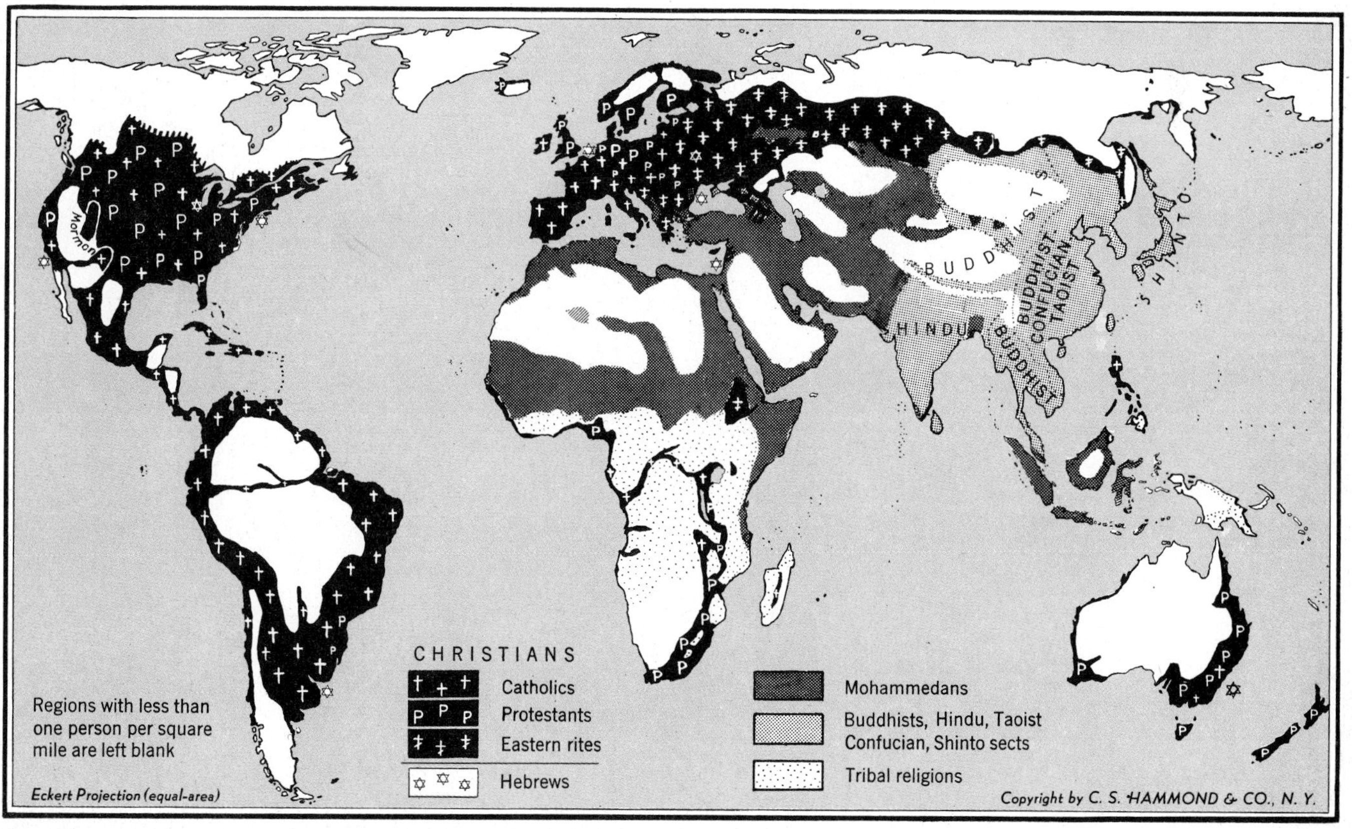

Regions with less than one person per square mile are left blank

CHRISTIANS
Catholics
Protestants
Eastern rites
Hebrews
Mohammedans
Buddhists, Hindu, Taoist Confucian, Shinto sects
Tribal religions

Eckert Projection (equal-area)

RELIGIONS. *Most people of the Earth belong to four major religions: Christians, Mohammedans, Brahmans, Buddhists and derivatives. The Eastern rites of the Christians include the Greek Orthodox, Greek Catholic, Armenian, Syrian, Coptic and more minor churches. The lamaism of Tibet and Mongolia differs a great deal from Buddhism in Burma and Thailand. In the religion of China the teachings of Buddha, Confucius and Tao are mixed, while in Shinto a great deal of ancestor and emperor worship is added. About 11 million Hebrews live scattered over the globe, chiefly in cities and in the state of Israel.*

WORLD STATISTICS

EARTH AND SOLAR SYSTEM

Elements of the Solar System

	Mean Distance From Sun in Miles	Period of Revolution Around Sun	Period of Rotation on Axis	Equatorial Diameter in Miles	Surface Gravity (Earth=1)	Mean Density (Water=1)	Number of Satellites
SUN	....	....	25.4 days	864,000	27.95	1.4	....
MERCURY	36,001,000	87.97 days	59 days	3,010	0.38	5.3	0
VENUS	67,235,000	224.70 days	247 days	7,600	0.88	4.9	0
EARTH	93,003,000	365.26 days	23h 56m	7,927	1.00	5.5	1
MARS	141,708,000	687 days	24h 37m	4,200	0.39	4.0	2
JUPITER	483,880,000	11.86 years	9h 50m	88,698	2.65	1.3	12
SATURN	887,141,000	29.46 years	10h 14m	75,060	1.17	0.7	10
URANUS	1,783,000,000	84.02 years	10h 45m	29,200	1.05	1.3	5
NEPTUNE	2,795,000,000	164.79 years	15h 48m	27,700	1.23	1.6	2
PLUTO	3,664,000,000	248.5 years	6.4 days	3,725	0.7	?	0

Dimensions of the Earth

Superficial area	192,251,000	sq. miles
Land surface	52,470,000	" "
North America	9,363,000	" "
South America	6,885,700	" "
Europe	4,057,000	" "
Asia	17,128,500	" "
Africa	11,707,000	" "
Australia	2,941,500	" "
Water surface	139,781,000	" "
Atlantic Ocean	31,862,000	" "
Pacific Ocean	64,186,000	" "
Indian Ocean	28,350,000	" "
Arctic Ocean	5,427,000	" "
Equatorial circumference	24,894	miles
Meridional circumference	24,811	"
Equatorial diameter	7,926.677	"
Polar diameter	7,899.988	"
Equatorial radius	3,963.34	"
Polar radius	3,949.99	"
Volume of the Earth	260,000,000,000	cubic miles
Mass, or weight	5,890,000,000,000,000,000,000	tons
Mean distance from the Sun	93,003,000	miles

The Moon is the Earth's natural satellite. The mean distance which separates the Earth from the Moon is 237,087 miles. The Moon's true period of revolution (sidereal month) is 27⅓ days. The Moon rotates on its own axis once during this time. The phase period or time between new moons (synodic month) is 29½ days. The Moon's diameter is 2,160 miles, its density is 3.3 and its surface gravity is 0.2.

PRINCIPAL LAKES AND INLAND SEAS

	AREA IN SQ. MILES
Caspian Sea	143,243
Lake Superior	32,483
Lake Victoria	26,724
Aral Sea	25,676
Lake Huron	23,860
Lake Michigan	22,400
Lake Tanganyika	12,650
Lake Baykal	12,162
Great Bear Lake	12,096
Lake Nyasa	11,555
Great Slave Lake	11,269
Lake Erie	9,889
Lake Winnipeg	9,417
Lake Ontario	7,313
Lake Ladoga	7,104
Lake Balkhash	7,027
Lake Chad	5,300
Lake Onega	3,710
Lake Titicaca	3,200
Lake Nicaragua	3,100
Lake Athabasca	3,064
Reindeer Lake	2,568
Lake Rudolf	2,463
Issyk-Kul'	2,425
Vänern	2,156
Lake Winnipegosis	2,075
Lake Albert	2,075
Kariba Lake	2,050
Lake Urmia	1,815
Lake of the Woods	1,695
Lake Peipus	1,400
Lake Tana	1,219
Great Salt Lake	1,100
Lake Iliamna	1,000
Vättern	733
Dead Sea	400
Lake Balaton	228
Lake Geneva	224
Lake of Constance	208
Lake Tahoe	192
Lake Garda	143
Lake Como	56
Lake of Lucerne	44
Lake of Zürich	34

OCEANS AND SEAS OF THE WORLD

	AREA IN SQ. MILES	GREATEST DEPTH IN FEET	VOLUME IN CUBIC MILES
Pacific Ocean	64,186,000	36,198	167,025,000
Atlantic Ocean	31,862,000	28,374	77,580,000
Indian Ocean	28,350,000	25,344	68,213,000
Arctic Ocean	5,427,000	17,880	3,026,000
Caribbean Sea	970,000	24,720	2,298,400
Mediterranean Sea	969,000	16,896	1,019,400
South China Sea	895,000	15,000	....
Bering Sea	875,000	15,800	788,500
Gulf of Mexico	600,000	12,300	....
Sea of Okhotsk	590,000	11,070	454,700
East China Sea	482,000	9,500	52,700
Japan Sea	389,000	12,280	383,200
Hudson Bay	317,500	846	37,590
North Sea	222,000	2,200	12,890
Black Sea	185,000	7,365	....
Red Sea	169,000	7,200	53,700
Baltic Sea	163,000	1,506	5,360

GREAT SHIP CANALS

	LENGTH IN MILES	DEPTH IN FEET
Karakum, U.S.S.R.	332	....
Volga-Baltic, U.S.S.R.	225	....
Baltic-White Sea, U.S.S.R.	138	....
Suez, Egypt	100.76	34
Albert, Belgium	81	16.5
Moscow-Volga, U.S.S.R.	78	18
Kiel, West Germany	61	37
Göta, Sweden	54	10
Panama, Canal Zone	50.72	41
Houston Ship, U.S.A.	50	36
Amsterdam-Rhine, Netherlands	45	41
Beaumont-Port Arthur, U.S.A.	40	32
Manchester Ship, England	35.5	28
Chicago Sanitary and Ship, U.S.A.	30	22
Welland, Canada	27.6	30
Juliana, Netherlands	21	11.8
Chesapeake and Delaware, U.S.A.	19	27
Cape Cod, U.S.A.	13	25
Lake Washington, U.S.A.	8	30
Corinth, Greece	4	26.25
Sault Ste. Marie, U.S.A.	1.6	24.5
Sault Ste. Marie, Canada	1.4	18.25

WORLD STATISTICS

PRINCIPAL ISLANDS OF THE WORLD

Island	AREA IN SQ. MILES
Greenland	840,000
New Guinea	305,000
Borneo	290,000
Madagascar	226,400
Baffin	195,928
Sumatra	164,000
Philippines	115,830
New Zealand	103,736
Great Britain	88,764
Honshu	88,000
Victoria	83,896
Ellesmere	75,767
Celebes	72,986
Java	48,842
Newfoundland	42,031
Cuba	40,543
Luzon	40,420
Iceland	39,768
Mindanao	36,537
Molucca Islands	32,307
Novaya Zemlya	31,900
Ireland	31,743
Sakhalin	29,500
Hispaniola	29,399
Hokkaido	28,983
Banks	27,038
Tasmania	26,383
Ceylon	25,332
Svalbard	23,958
Devon	21,331
Bismarck Arch.	18,976
Tierra del Fuego	17,900
Melville	16,274
Southampton	15,913
Solomon Islands	15,600
New Britain	14,100
Taiwan (Formosa)	13,836
Kyushu	13,770
Hainan	13,000
Prince of Wales	12,872
Vancouver	12,079
Timor	11,527
Sicily	9,926
Somerset	9,570
Sardinia	9,301
Fiji Islands	7,055
Shikoku	6,860
New Caledonia	6,530
Kuril Islands	6,025
New Hebrides	5,700
Bahama Islands	5,382
Falkland Islands	4,618
Jamaica	4,232
Hawaii	4,038
Cape Breton	3,981
Cyprus	3,572
Puerto Rico	3,435
Corsica	3,367
New Ireland	3,340
Crete	3,218
Galápagos Islands	3,075
Wrangel	2,819
Hebrides	2,812
Canary Islands	2,808
Kerguélen	2,700
Prince Edward	2,170
Trinidad and Tobago	1,980
Balearic Islands	1,936
Ryukyu Islands	1,767
Madura	1,752
Cape Verde Islands	1,557
South Georgia	1,450
Long I., New York	1,401
Socotra	1,400
Samoa	1,209
Gotland	1,153
Réunion	969
Azores	902
Isle of Pines	849
Macías Nguema Biyogo	779
Tenerife	745
Maui	729
Mauritius	720
Zanzibar	641
Oahu	608
Guadeloupe	584
Åland Is.	581
Kauai	553
Shetland Islands	552
Rhodes	542
Caroline Islands	463
Martinique	425
Tahiti	402
Pemba	380
Orkney Islands	372
Madeira Islands	307
Dominica	290
Tonga	270
Molokai	261
St. Lucia	238
Corfu	229
Bornholm	227
Isle of Man	227
Singapore	226
Guam	212
Isle Royale	196
Virgin Islands	192
Curaçao	182
Barbados	166
Isle of Wight	145
Lanai	140
St. Vincent	131
Maltese Islands	122
Grenada	120
Tobago	116
Martha's Vineyard	93
Seychelles	85
Channel Islands	74
St. Helena	47
Nantucket	46
Ascension	34
Hong Kong	30
Manhattan, New York	22
Bermuda Islands	21

PRINCIPAL MOUNTAINS OF THE WORLD

Mountain	FEET
Everest, Nepal-China	29,028
Godwin Austen (K2), India	28,250
Kanchenjunga, Nepal-India	28,208
Lhotse, Nepal-China	27,923
Makalu, Nepal-China	27,824
Dhaulagiri, Nepal	26,810
Nanga Parbat, India	26,660
Annapurna, Nepal	26,504
Nanda Devi, India	25,645
Kamet, India	25,447
Tirich Mir, Pakistan	25,230
Minya Konka, China	24,902
Muztagh Ata, China	24,757
Communism Peak, U.S.S.R.	24,599
Pobeda Peak, U.S.S.R.	24,406
Chomo Lhari, Bhutan-China	23,997
Muztagh, China	23,891
Aconcagua, Argentina	22,831
Ojos del Salado, Chile-Arg.	22,572
Tupungato, Chile-Argentina	22,310
Mercedario, Argentina	22,211
Huascarán, Peru	22,205
Llullaillaco Volcano, Chile-Arg.	22,057
Ancohuma, Bolivia	21,489
Illampu, Bolivia	21,276
Chimborazo, Ecuador	20,561
McKinley, Alaska	20,320
Logan, Yukon	19,850
Cotopaxi, Ecuador	19,347
Kilimanjaro, Tanzania	19,340
El Misti, Peru	19,101
Huila, Colombia	18,865
Citlaltépetl (Orizaba), Mexico	18,855
El'brus, U.S.S.R.	18,510
Demavend, Iran	18,376
St. Elias, Alaska-Yukon	18,008
Popocatépetl, Mexico	17,887
Kenya, Kenya	17,058
Dykh-Tau, U.S.S.R.	17,070
Ararat, Turkey	16,946
Vinson Massif, Antarctica	16,864
Margherita (Ruwenzori), Africa	16,795
Kazbek, U.S.S.R.	16,512
Djaja, Indonesia	16,503
Blanc, France	15,771
Klyuchevskaya Sopka, U.S.S.R.	15,584
Rosa (Dufourspitze), Italy-Switzerland	15,203
Ras Dashan, Ethiopia	15,157
Matterhorn, Switzerland	14,688
Whitney, California	14,494
Elbert, Colorado	14,433
Rainier, Washington	14,410
Blanca Peak, Colorado	14,317
Markham, Antarctica	14,272
Shasta, California	14,162
Pikes Peak, Colorado	14,110
Finsteraarhorn, Switzerland	14,022
Tajumulco, Guatemala	13,845
Mauna Kea, Hawaii	13,796
Mauna Loa, Hawaii	13,680
Toubkal, Morocco	13,665
Jungfrau, Switzerland	13,642
Cameroon, Cameroon	13,350
Gran Paradiso, Italy	13,323
Robson, British Columbia	12,972
Grossglockner, Austria	12,461
Fuji, Japan	12,389
Cook, New Zealand	12,349
Pico de Teide, Canary Is.	12,172
Semeru, Java, Indonesia	12,060
Mulhacén, Spain	11,411
Etna, Italy	11,053
Lassen Peak, California	10,457
Kosciusko, Australia	7,316
Mitchell, North Carolina	6,684

LONGEST RIVERS OF THE WORLD

River	LENGTH IN MILES
Nile, Africa	4,145
Amazon, S.A.	3,915
Mississippi-Missouri, U.S.A.	3,710
Yangtze, China	3,434
Ob-Irtysh, U.S.S.R.	3,362
Yenisey-Angara, U.S.S.R.	3,100
Hwang (Yellow), China	2,903
Amur, Asia	2,744
Lena, U.S.S.R.	2,734
Congo, Africa	2,718
Mackenzie, Canada	2,635
Mekong, Asia	2,600
Niger, Africa	2,585
Paraná, S.A.	2,450
Murray-Darling, Australia	2,310
Volga, U.S.S.R.	2,194
Madeira, S.A.	2,013
Purus, S.A.	1,995
Yukon, Alaska-Canada	1,979
St. Lawrence, Canada-U.S.A.	1,900
Rio Grande, U.S.A.-Mexico	1,885
Syr-Dar'ya, U.S.S.R.	1,859
São Francisco, Brazil	1,811
Indus, Asia	1,800
Danube, Europe	1,775
Salween, Asia	1,770
Brahmaputra, Asia	1,700
Euphrates, Asia	1,700
Zambezi, Africa	1,600
Tocantins, Brazil	1,677
Si, China	1,650
Amu-Dar'ya, Asia	1,616
Nelson, Canada	1,600
Orinoco, S.A.	1,600
Paraguay, S.A.	1,584
Kolyma, U.S.S.R.	1,562
Ganges, Asia	1,550
Ural, U.S.S.R.	1,509
Japurá, S.A.	1,500
Arkansas, U.S.A.	1,450
Colorado, U.S.A.-Mexico	1,450
Negro, S.A.	1,400
Dnieper, U.S.S.R.	1,368
Irrawaddy, Burma	1,325
Orange, Africa	1,350
Ohio-Allegheny, U.S.A.	1,306
Red, U.S.A.	1,270
Kama, U.S.S.R.	1,262
Columbia, U.S.A.-Canada	1,243
Don, U.S.S.R.	1,222
Brazos, U.S.A.	1,210
Saskatchewan, Canada	1,205
Peace-Finlay, Canada	1,195
Tigris, Asia	1,181
Darling, Australia	1,160
Angara, U.S.S.R.	1,151
Sungari, Asia	1,130
Pechora, U.S.S.R.	1,124
Snake, U.S.A.	1,038
Churchill, Canada	1,000
Pilcomayo, S.A.	1,000
Uruguay, S.A.	1,000
Magdalena, Colombia	1,000
Platte-N. Platte, U.S.A.	990
Oka, U.S.S.R.	918
Canadian, U.S.A.	906
Tennessee, U.S.A.	900
Colorado, Texas, U.S.A.	894
Dniester, U.S.S.R.	876
South Saskatchewan, Canada	865
Fraser, Canada	850
Rhine, Europe	820
Northern Dvina, U.S.S.R.	809
Tisza, Europe	800
North Canadian, U.S.A.	784
Athabasca, Canada	765

Between Principal Cities in the United States

FROM/TO	Albuquerque, N. Mex.	Atlanta, Ga.	Baltimore, Md.	Boise, Idaho	Boston, Mass.	Brownsville, Tex.	Buffalo, N. Y.	Chicago, Ill.	Cincinnati, Ohio	Cleveland, Ohio	Denver, Colo.	Des Moines, Iowa	Detroit, Mich.	El Paso, Tex.	Fargo, N. Dak.	Fort Worth, Tex.	Galveston, Tex.	Hastings, Nebr.	Hot Springs, Ark.	Houghton, Mich.	Jacksonville, Fla.	Kansas City, Mo.	Los Angeles, Calif.	Louisville, Ky.	Memphis, Tenn.	Miami, Fla.	Minneapolis, Minn.	Missoula, Mont.	Nashville, Tenn.	New Orleans, La.	New York, N. Y.	Norfolk, Va.	Oklahoma, Okla.	Omaha, Nebr.	Philadelphia, Pa.	Phoenix, Ariz.	Pittsburgh, Pa.
Albuquerque, N. Mex.	....	1273	1670	774	1967	838	1577	1126	1248	1417	332	833	1360	228	968	561	803	588	773	1252	1492	717	663	1174	938	1710	980	895	1117	1030	1810	1696	518	718	1748	330	1498
Atlanta, Ga.	1273	....	575	1830	933	960	695	583	368	550	1208	738	595	1293	1112	750	688	901	498	947	286	675	1935	317	335	610	905	1790	218	427	747	507	753	815	663	1592	520
Baltimore, Md.	1670	575	....	2055	358	1525	273	603	423	305	1505	913	398	1750	1143	1239	1245	1154	964	808	682	962	2313	498	792	958	948	1947	597	1001	170	167	1173	1026	90	2002	194
Boise, Idaho	774	1830	2055	....	2266	1610	1872	1453	1663	1754	637	1155	1671	969	975	1263	1538	934	1384	1367	2098	1158	663	1623	1506	2368	1140	252	1631	1713	2153	2137	1138	1044	2113	733	1863
Boston, Mass.	1967	933	358	2266	....	1881	398	849	737	550	1766	1159	613	2067	1304	1574	1598	1415	1302	922	1015	1250	2590	823	1133	1258	1125	2124	941	1359	188	467	1490	1280	268	2295	478
Brownsville, Tex.	838	960	1525	1610	1881	....	1575	1234	1184	1402	1047	1102	1398	682	1445	471	287	1013	650	1543	1025	923	1370	1093	777	1100	1335	1706	952	536	1695	1465	659	1061	1614	1023	1424
Buffalo, N. Y.	1577	695	273	1872	398	1575	....	454	392	175	1368	762	218	1690	923	1221	1289	1019	956	560	880	862	2195	483	802	1184	733	1740	626	1087	291	435	1117	883	278	1904	178
Chicago, Ill.	1126	583	603	1453	849	1234	454	....	249	307	918	310	236	1249	571	820	954	566	585	367	861	413	1741	268	481	1190	356	1348	394	831	711	696	689	432	664	1451	411
Cincinnati, Ohio	1248	368	423	1663	737	1184	392	249	....	218	1090	509	234	1333	818	839	897	742	569	589	628	541	1892	92	410	957	603	1578	239	708	568	474	755	620	501	1578	258
Cleveland, Ohio	1417	550	305	1754	550	1402	175	307	218	....	1223	617	94	1521	838	1046	1116	871	787	518	768	700	2044	309	627	1088	632	1640	456	922	404	429	946	738	343	1745	115
Denver, Colo.	332	1208	1505	637	1766	1047	1368	918	1090	1223	....	607	1153	554	642	643	925	353	749	970	1468	555	828	1035	878	1732	699	670	1018	1079	1628	1562	503	485	1575	585	1320
Des Moines, Iowa	833	738	913	1155	1159	1102	762	310	509	617	607	....	545	980	397	640	851	256	488	458	1024	180	1433	477	485	1338	235	1074	523	825	1023	983	469	122	972	1154	718
Detroit, Mich.	1360	595	398	1671	613	1398	218	236	234	94	1153	545	....	1475	745	1018	1111	800	761	427	832	643	1976	315	621	1156	542	1552	468	938	483	522	905	666	444	1685	208
El Paso, Tex.	228	1293	1750	969	2067	682	1690	1249	1333	1521	554	980	1475	....	1161	543	723	757	802	1422	1481	836	702	1253	978	1662	1156	1115	1169	986	1902	1755	578	875	1834	347	1592
Fargo, N. Dak.	968	1112	1143	975	1304	1445	923	571	818	838	642	397	745	1161	....	973	1218	440	875	393	1400	548	1426	818	882	1721	219	819	900	1221	1213	1258	786	390	1186	1225	952
Fort Worth, Tex.	561	750	1239	1263	1574	471	1221	820	839	1046	643	640	1018	543	973	....	283	544	273	1093	943	460	1212	751	448	1150	870	1312	643	470	1398	1226	188	590	1324	858	1097
Galveston, Tex.	803	688	1245	1538	1598	287	1289	954	897	1116	925	851	1111	723	1218	283	....	808	375	1277	799	677	1423	807	492	941	1087	1595	666	288	1415	1195	456	828	1336	1065	1140
Hastings, Nebr.	588	901	1154	934	1415	1013	1019	566	742	871	353	256	800	757	440	544	808	....	513	666	1178	226	1177	693	591	1468	399	891	697	870	1275	1216	357	135	1222	901	967
Hot Springs, Ark.	773	498	964	1384	1302	650	956	585	569	787	749	488	761	802	875	273	375	513	....	901	728	326	1437	480	176	983	722	1385	370	358	1125	955	260	490	1051	1094	825
Houghton, Mich.	1252	947	808	1367	922	1543	560	367	589	518	970	458	427	1422	393	1093	1277	666	901	....	1216	633	1787	636	830	1545	272	1208	760	1187	849	946	926	547	827	1550	630
Jacksonville, Fla.	1492	286	682	2098	1015	1025	880	861	628	768	1468	1024	832	1481	1400	943	799	1178	728	1216	....	952	2153	595	591	328	1192	2070	502	511	838	548	988	1098	758	1800	703
Kansas City, Mo.	717	675	962	1158	1250	923	862	413	541	700	555	180	643	836	548	460	677	226	326	633	952	....	1352	480	370	1247	413	1117	472	678	1097	1009	293	165	1037	1045	784
Los Angeles, Calif.	663	1935	2313	663	2590	1370	2195	1741	1892	2044	828	1433	1976	702	1426	1212	1423	1177	1437	1787	2153	1352	....	1825	1602	2355	1522	910	1777	1675	2446	2352	1182	1312	2388	357	2135
Louisville, Ky.	1174	317	498	1623	823	1093	483	268	92	309	1035	477	315	1253	818	751	807	693	480	636	595	480	1825	....	319	923	605	1550	153	623	650	528	675	579	580	1512	345
Memphis, Tenn.	938	335	792	1506	1133	777	802	481	410	627	878	485	621	978	882	448	492	591	176	830	591	370	1602	319	....	878	700	1483	195	358	953	778	422	529	878	1264	660
Miami, Fla.	1710	610	958	2368	1258	1100	1184	1190	957	1088	1732	1338	1156	1662	1721	1150	941	1468	983	1545	328	1247	2355	923	878	....	1516	2359	821	681	1095	802	1233	1402	1023	1998	1014
Minneapolis, Minn.	980	905	948	1140	1125	1335	733	356	603	632	609	235	542	1156	219	870	1087	399	722	272	1192	413	1522	605	700	1516	....	1010	695	1050	1019	1047	692	291	985	1279	745
Missoula, Mont.	895	1790	1947	252	2124	1706	1740	1348	1578	1640	670	1074	1552	1115	819	1312	1595	801	1385	1208	2070	1117	910	1550	1483	2359	1010	....	1582	1733	2030	2045	1162	978	1997	932	1754
Nashville, Tenn.	1117	218	597	1631	941	952	626	394	239	456	1018	523	468	1169	900	643	666	697	370	760	502	472	1777	153	195	821	605	1582	....	470	758	586	602	604	683	1445	472
New Orleans, La.	1030	427	1001	1713	1359	536	1087	831	708	922	1079	825	938	986	1221	470	288	870	358	1187	511	678	1675	623	358	681	1050	1733	470	....	1173	932	575	845	1090	1318	923
New York, N. Y.	1810	747	170	2153	188	1695	291	711	568	404	1628	1023	483	1902	1213	1398	1415	1275	1125	849	838	1097	2446	650	953	1095	1019	2030	758	1173	....	293	1324	1144	83	2142	313
Norfolk, Va.	1696	507	167	2137	467	1465	435	696	474	429	1562	983	522	1755	1258	1226	1195	1216	955	946	548	1009	2352	528	778	802	1047	2045	586	932	293	....	1186	1095	220	2027	316
Oklahoma, Okla.	518	753	1173	1138	1490	659	1117	689	755	946	503	469	905	578	786	188	456	357	260	926	988	293	1182	675	422	1233	692	1162	602	575	1324	1186	....	405	1256	843	1013
Omaha, Nebr.	718	815	1026	1044	1280	1061	883	432	620	738	485	122	666	875	390	590	828	135	490	547	1098	165	1312	579	529	1402	291	978	604	845	1144	1095	405	....	1094	1032	837
Philadelphia, Pa.	1748	663	90	2113	268	1614	278	664	501	343	575	972	444	1834	1186	1324	1335	1222	1051	827	758	1037	2388	580	878	1023	985	1997	683	1090	83	220	1256	1094	....	2079	254
Phoenix, Ariz.	330	1592	2002	733	2295	1023	1904	1451	1578	1745	585	1154	1685	347	1225	858	1065	901	1094	1550	1800	1045	357	1512	1264	1998	1279	932	1445	1318	2142	2027	843	1032	2079	....	1829
Pittsburgh, Pa.	1498	520	194	1863	478	1424	178	411	258	115	1320	718	208	1592	952	1097	1140	967	825	530	703	784	2135	345	660	1014	745	1754	472	923	313	316	1013	837	254	1829	....
Portland, Me.	2015	1022	446	2282	100	1961	438	892	802	603	1803	1197	657	2126	1313	1642	1678	1454	1371	924	1113	1300	2631	892	1205	1357	1145	2133	1015	1445	277	565	1550	1318	360	2345	545
Portland, Oreg.	1107	2172	2367	349	2553	1944	2167	1765	1987	2063	985	1479	1975	1286	1248	1612	1885	1271	1733	1638	2442	1397	825	1953	1852	2716	1435	430	1970	2063	2455	2458	1488	1373	2419	1007	2174
Richmond, Va.	1628	470	128	2060	471	1428	375	618	399	353	1488	905	445	1695	1180	1170	1154	1142	897	870	953	937	2283	457	722	831	968	1967	526	899	287	79	1122	1020	205	1960	242
St. Louis, Mo.	938	467	731	1389	1036	975	662	259	308	490	793	270	452	1033	658	568	697	455	325	591	755	238	1585	242	242	1067	464	1331	253	599	873	771	456	352	808	1270	561
Salt Lake City, Utah	483	1580	1858	292	2099	1317	1701	1260	1450	1567	372	952	1490	689	865	977	1249	708	1116	1242	1840	922	577	1400	1250	2098	988	435	1390	1433	1972	1925	862	833	1923	504	1670
San Francisco, Calif.	893	2133	2451	516	2696	1675	2298	1855	2037	2163	946	1547	2087	993	1447	1454	1693	1297	1648	1833	2375	1500	345	1983	1800	2603	1585	762	1958	1923	2568	2510	1386	1425	2518	652	2264
Schenectady, N. Y.	1823	840	278	2120	150	1770	249	702	605	408	1618	1012	467	1930	1157	1445	1487	1267	1175	776	960	1107	2445	695	1010	1229	975	1978	820	1259	142	426	1354	1133	205	2152	350
Seattle, Wash.	1178	2180	2341	405	2508	2015	2130	1743	1974	2035	1020	1470	1945	1373	1206	1658	1938	1288	1759	1588	2450	1505	956	1945	1867	2740	1403	395	1973	2098	2419	2440	1523	1372	2388	1112	2145
Shreveport, La.	764	548	1064	1433	1410	510	1080	725	688	904	799	624	891	752	1002	209	233	615	142	1043	733	326	1420	598	279	950	859	1457	470	280	1230	1037	297	617	1153	1067	939
Spokane, Wash.	1028	1960	2110	290	2279	1852	1900	1514	1746	1804	827	1243	1715	1238	976	1470	1753	1061	1552	1360	2239	1286	939	1720	1652	2528	1173	170	1752	1898	2190	2211	1324	1149	2159	1020	1918
Springfield, Mass.	1889	863	282	2196	79	1805	325	774	659	473	1692	1085	540	1990	1240	1495	1524	1340	1224	860	957	1173	2515	745	1055	1210	1056	2060	863	1287	120	411	1412	1205	201	2220	400
Vermillion, S. Dak.	742	917	1083	973	1314	1161	916	479	694	785	468	187	705	920	284	689	938	167	605	510	1203	280	1291	663	642	1510	238	887	704	960	1189	1166	502	115	1143	1043	891
Washington, D. C.	1648	542	33	2045	392	1493	290	594	403	303	1490	895	397	1726	1141	1210	1214	1139	936	813	647	943	2295	473	763	927	936	1940	567	968	204	145	1150	1012	122	1980	188

Between Principal Cities of Europe

FROM/TO	Amsterdam	Athens	Baku	Barcelona	Belgrade	Berlin	Brussels	Bucharest	Budapest	Cologne	Copenhagen	Istanbul	Dresden	Dublin	Frankfort	Hamburg	Leningrad	Lisbon	London	Lyon	Madrid	Marseilles	Milan	Moscow	Munich	Oslo	Paris	Riga	Rome	Sofia	Stockholm	Toulouse	Warsaw	Vienna	Zurich
Amsterdam	....	1340	2218	770	875	365	105	1100	710	128	381	1360	385	468	228	232	1090	1140	220	458	912	627	517	1325	415	568	257	820	808	1073	695	625	673	580	375
Athens	1340	....	1395	1160	500	1112	1292	460	698	1200	1320	350	1022	1765	1113	1250	1535	1770	1476	1100	1463	1025	900	1388	925	1610	1300	1310	650	335	1495	1215	990	795	1000
Baku	2218	1395	....	2427	1487	1867	2240	1220	1562	2127	1980	1070	1837	2490	2055	2020	1570	3050	2435	2238	2742	2238	2028	1175	1912	2118	2335	1590	1900	1360	1862	2425	1555	1700	2050
Barcelona	770	1160	2427	....	998	925	658	1210	924	692	1085	1380	860	919	665	910	1740	610	707	327	316	211	450	1852	648	1330	518	1440	530	1072	1410	156	1150	830	513
Belgrade	875	500	1487	998	....	618	850	295	205	750	840	502	530	1327	652	760	1165	1555	1040	752	1235	750	540	1160	475	1112	890	855	440	231	1005	930	510	300	590
Berlin	365	1112	1867	925	618	....	401	798	425	300	225	1068	95	815	268	165	815	1410	575	601	1149	730	570	995	310	520	540	520	730	810	503	815	320	322	410
Brussels	105	1292	2240	658	850	401	....	1110	700	110	475	1345	407	480	198	301	1175	998	202	352	807	521	435	1392	372	672	170	900	730	945	793	515	720	568	312
Bucharest	1100	460	1220	1210	295	798	1110	....	295	982	970	272	725	1560	890	950	1080	1842	1285	1025	1518	1020	819	920	725	1245	1152	870	700	194	1080	1210	580	520	855
Budapest	710	698	1562	924	205	425	700	295	....	590	629	650	345	1176	504	572	965	1515	900	680	1214	718	476	965	350	920	770	685	500	395	820	883	342	128	498
Cologne	128	1200	2127	692	750	300	110	982	590	....	400	1240	292	585	93	228	1090	1126	308	370	875	528	390	1285	282	635	250	805	675	945	722	875	602	460	259
Copenhagen	381	1320	1960	1085	840	225	475	970	629	400	....	1240	315	768	412	180	708	1520	590	760	1272	906	720	970	520	303	634	453	948	1010	330	962	415	538	595
Istanbul	1360	350	1070	1380	502	1068	1345	272	650	1240	1240	....	995	1830	1150	1222	1292	2005	1540	1238	1690	1205	1030	1180	975	1505	1390	1115	840	315	1340	1400	852	790	1090
Dresden	385	1022	1837	860	530	95	407	725	345	292	315	995	....	852	236	238	885	1380	592	540	1100	655	435	1200	227	620	523	585	630	730	598	762	325	235	342
Dublin	468	1765	2490	919	1327	815	480	1560	1176	585	768	1830	852	....	671	668	1440	1015	300	720	902	875	880	1728	855	786	480	1210	1175	1525	1010	761	1130	1040	768
Frankfort	228	1113	2055	665	652	268	198	890	504	93	412	1150	236	671	....	250	1075	1160	392	350	888	492	323	1240	193	675	295	780	698	860	730	560	550	370	193
Hamburg	232	1250	2020	910	760	165	301	950	572	228	180	1222	238	668	250	....	880	1301	448	580	1098	730	570	1100	378	445	459	600	810	954	502	780	462	460	432
Leningrad	1090	1535	1570	1740	1165	815	1175	1080	965	1090	708	1292	885	1440	1075	880	....	2235	1300	1420	1980	1540	1315	391	1100	670	1335	300	1440	1218	435	1635	640	975	1225
Lisbon	1140	1770	3050	610	1555	1410	998	1842	1515	1126	1520	2005	1380	1015	1160	1301	2235	....	975	850	313	810	1350	430	1208	1690	890	1940	1150	1685	1848	640	1700	1415	1058
London	220	1476	2435	707	1040	575	202	1285	900	308	590	1540	592	300	392	448	1300	975	....	455	777	620	595	1540	526	720	210	1035	890	1235	885	550	890	762	480
Lyon	458	1100	2238	327	752	601	352	1025	680	370	760	1238	540	720	350	580	1420	850	455	....	577	170	210	1560	352	1005	248	1122	462	928	1080	228	850	562	206
Madrid	912	1463	2742	316	1235	1149	807	1518	1214	875	1272	1690	1100	902	888	1098	1980	313	777	557	....	394	728	2120	910	1474	645	1670	840	1385	1598	344	1410	1110	765
Marseilles	627	1025	2238	211	750	730	521	1020	718	528	906	1205	655	875	492	730	1540	810	620	170	394	....	238	1642	445	1165	410	1238	372	895	1225	196	950	620	318
Milan	517	900	2028	450	540	570	435	819	476	390	720	1030	435	880	323	570	1315	1350	595	210	728	238	....	1408	215	1000	400	1010	295	715	1020	400	705	385	137
Moscow	1325	1388	1175	1852	1160	995	1392	920	965	1285	970	1180	1200	1728	1240	1100	391	430	1540	1560	2120	1642	1408	....	1220	1030	1538	520	1462	1100	770	1770	710	1028	1350
Munich	415	925	1912	648	475	310	372	725	350	282	520	975	227	855	193	378	1100	1208	526	352	910	445	215	1220	....	810	425	800	430	672	811	570	500	222	158
Oslo	568	1610	2118	1330	1112	520	672	1245	920	635	303	1505	620	786	675	445	670	1690	720	1005	1474	1165	1000	1030	810	....	830	531	1242	1295	267	1140	653	835	869
Paris	257	1300	2335	518	890	540	170	1152	770	250	634	1390	523	480	295	459	1335	890	210	248	645	410	400	1538	425	830	....	1050	690	1080	950	431	845	770	295
Riga	820	1310	1590	1440	855	520	900	870	685	805	453	1115	585	1210	780	600	300	1940	1035	1122	1670	1238	1010	520	800	531	1050	....	1155	985	276	1335	350	685	930
Rome	808	650	1900	530	440	730	730	700	500	675	948	840	630	1175	698	810	1440	1150	890	462	840	372	295	1462	430	1242	690	1155	....	545	1220	569	810	470	421
Sofia	1073	335	1360	1072	231	810	945	194	395	945	1010	315	730	1525	860	954	1218	1685	1235	928	1385	895	715	1100	672	1295	1080	985	545	....	1170	1080	662	500	780
Stockholm	695	1495	1862	1410	1005	503	793	1080	820	722	330	1340	598	1010	730	502	435	1848	885	1080	1598	1225	1020	770	811	267	950	276	1220	1170	....	1281	500	770	908
Toulouse	625	1215	2425	156	930	815	515	1210	883	875	962	1400	762	761	560	780	1635	640	550	228	344	196	400	1770	570	1140	431	1335	569	1080	1281	....	1062	725	425
Warsaw	673	990	1555	1150	510	320	720	580	342	602	415	852	325	1130	550	462	640	1700	890	850	1410	950	705	710	500	653	845	350	810	662	500	1062	....	345	640
Vienna	580	795	1700	830	300	322	568	520	128	460	538	790	235	1040	370	460	975	1415	762	562	1110	620	385	1028	222	835	770	685	470	500	770	725	345	....	365
Zurich	375	1000	2050	513	590	410	312	855	498	259	595	1090	342	768	193	432	1225	1058	480	206	765	318	137	1350	158	869	295	930	421	780	908	425	640	365	....

AIRLINE DISTANCES

All Distances in Statute Miles

Richmond, Va.	St. Louis, Mo.	Salt Lake City, Utah	San Francisco, Calif.	Schenectady, N. Y.	Seattle, Wash.	Shreveport, La.	Spokane, Wash.	Springfield, Mass.	Vermillion, S. Dak.	Washington, D.
628	938	483	893	1823	1178	764	1028	1889	742	1648
470	467	1580	2133	840	2180	548	1960	863	917	542
128	731	1858	2451	278	2341	1064	2110	282	1083	33
060	1389	292	516	2120	405	1433	290	2196	973	2045
471	1036	2099	2696	150	2508	1410	2279	79	1314	392
428	975	1317	1675	1770	2015	510	1852	1805	1161	1493
375	662	1701	2298	249	2130	1080	1900	325	916	290
618	259	1260	1855	702	1743	725	1514	774	479	594
399	308	1450	2037	605	1974	688	1746	659	694	403
353	490	1567	2163	408	2035	904	1804	478	785	303
488	793	372	946	1618	1020	799	827	1692	468	1490
05	270	952	1547	1012	1470	624	1243	1085	187	895
445	452	1490	2087	467	1945	891	1715	540	705	397
95	1033	689	993	1930	1373	752	1238	1990	920	1726
180	658	865	1447	1157	1206	1002	976	1240	284	1141
170	568	977	1454	1445	1658	209	1470	1495	689	1210
154	697	1249	1693	1487	1938	233	1753	1524	938	1214
142	455	708	1297	1267	1288	615	1061	1340	167	1139
397	325	1116	1648	1175	1759	142	1552	1224	605	936
370	591	1242	1833	776	1588	1043	1360	860	510	813
953	755	1840	2375	960	2450	733	2239	957	1203	647
037	238	922	1500	1107	1505	326	1286	1173	280	943
283	1585	577	345	2445	956	1420	939	2515	1291	2295
457	242	1400	1983	695	1945	598	1720	745	663	473
722	242	1250	1800	1010	1867	279	1652	1055	642	763
331	1067	2098	2603	1229	2740	950	2528	1210	1510	927
968	464	988	1585	975	1403	859	1173	1056	238	936
967	1331	435	762	1978	395	1457	170	2060	887	1940
526	253	1390	1958	820	1973	470	1752	863	704	567
399	599	1433	1923	1259	2098	280	1898	1287	960	968
287	873	1972	2568	142	2419	1230	2190	120	1189	204
79	771	1925	2510	426	2440	1037	2211	411	1166	145
22	456	862	1386	1354	1523	297	1324	1412	502	1150
020	352	833	1425	1133	1372	617	1149	1205	115	1012
205	808	1923	2518	205	2388	1153	2159	201	1143	122
960	1270	504	652	2152	1112	1067	1020	2220	1043	1980
242	561	1670	2264	350	2145	939	1918	400	891	188
565	1094	2127	2725	197	2513	1484	2285	159	1345	480
381	1723	636	536	2405	143	1783	295	2488	1293	2360
..	699	1850	2436	406	2362	985	2133	407	1089	96
99	....	1158	1738	898	1722	466	1500	958	450	710
350	1158	....	592	1950	697	1155	548	2027	785	1845
436	1738	592	....	2548	680	1655	730	2625	1383	2437
406	898	1950	2548	....	2363	1290	2139	86	1165	313
362	1722	697	680	2363	....	1820	229	2445	1282	2335
985	466	1155	1655	1290	1820	....	1621	1333	726	1035
133	1500	548	730	2139	229	1621	....	2216	1055	2105
407	958	2027	2625	86	2445	1333	2216	....	1242	321
089	450	785	1383	1165	1282	726	1055	1242	....	1073
96	710	1845	2437	313	2335	1035	2105	321	1073	....

Between Representative Cities of the United States and Latin America

New York to	Miles	San Francisco to	Miles	Seattle to	Miles	Washington to	Miles
Buenos Aires	5,295	Buenos Aires	6,487	Buenos Aires	6,956	Buenos Aires	5,205
Bogota	2,474	Bogota	3,863	Bogota	4,166	Bogota	2,344
Caracas	2,100	Caracas	3,900	Caracas	4,100	Caracas	2,040
Guatemala City	2,060	Guatemala City	2,525	Guatemala City	2,930	Guatemala City	1,835
Havana	1,302	Havana	2,600	Havana	2,805	Havana	1,110
La Paz	3,905	La Paz	5,080	La Paz	5,110	La Paz	3,780
Panama	2,211	Panama	3,349	Panama	3,680	Panama	2,020
Para	3,281	Para	5,430	Para	5,550	Para	3,270
Managua	2,100	Managua	2,860	Managua	3,240	Managua	1,920
Rio de Janeiro	4,810	Rio de Janeiro	6,655	Rio de Janeiro	6,945	Rio de Janeiro	4,710
San Jose	2,200	San Jose	3,070	San Jose	3,430	San Jose	2,030
Santiago	5,134	Santiago	5,960	Santiago	6,466	Santiago	4,965
Tampico	1,880	Tampico	1,790	Tampico	2,200	Tampico	1,665

Chicago to	Miles	Denver to	Miles	Los Angeles to	Miles	New Orleans to	Miles
Buenos Aires	5,598	Buenos Aires	5,935	Buenos Aires	6,148	Buenos Aires	4,902
Bogota	2,691	Bogota	3,100	Bogota	3,515	Bogota	1,996
Caracas	2,480	Caracas	3,105	Caracas	3,610	Caracas	1,990
Guatemala City	1,870	Guatemala City	1,935	Guatemala City	2,190	Guatemala City	1,050
Havana	1,315	Havana	1,760	Havana	2,320	Havana	672
La Paz	4,130	La Paz	4,445	La Paz	4,805	La Paz	3,480
Panama	2,320	Panama	2,620	Panama	3,025	Panama	1,600
Para	3,820	Para	4,580	Para	5,110	Para	3,470
Managua	2,060	Managua	2,230	Managua	2,540	Managua	1,250
Rio de Janeiro	5,320	Rio de Janeiro	5,900	Rio de Janeiro	6,330	Rio de Janeiro	4,798
San Jose	2,100	San Jose	2,420	San Jose	2,725	San Jose	1,425
Santiago	5,320	Santiago	5,495	Santiago	5,595	Santiago	4,553
Tampico	1,460	Tampico	1,240	Tampico	1,470	Tampico	720

Between Principal Cities of the World

FROM/TO	Azores	Bagdad	Berlin	Bombay	Buenos Aires	Callao	Cairo	Cape Town	Chicago	Istanbul	Guam	Honolulu	Juneau	London	Los Angeles
Azores	....	3906	2148	5930	5385	4825	3325	5670	3305	2880	8985	7421	4715	1562	5034
Bagdad	3906	....	2040	2022	8215	8618	785	4923	6490	1085	6380	8445	6180	2568	7695
Berlin	2148	2040	....	3947	7411	6937	1823	5949	4458	1068	7158	7384	4638	575	5849
Bombay	5930	2022	3947	....	9380	10530	2698	5133	8144	3043	4831	8172	6992	4526	8810
Buenos Aires	5385	8215	7411	9380	....	1982	7428	4332	5598	7638	10516	7653	7964	6919	6148
Callao	4825	8618	6937	10530	1982	....	7870	6195	3765	7666	9760	5993	5806	6376	4155
Cairo	3325	785	1823	2698	7428	7870	....	4476	6231	780	7175	8925	6352	2218	7675
Cape Town	5670	4923	5949	5133	4332	6195	4476	....	8551	5210	8918	11655	10382	5975	10165
Chicago	3305	6490	4458	8144	5598	3765	6231	8551	....	5530	7510	4315	2310	4015	1741
Istanbul	2880	1085	1068	3043	7638	7666	780	5210	5530	....	7015	8200	5665	1540	6895
Guam	8985	6380	7158	4831	10516	9760	7175	8918	7510	7015	....	3896	5225	7605	6255
Honolulu	7421	8445	7384	8172	7653	5993	8925	11655	4315	8200	3896	....	2825	7320	2620
Juneau	4715	6180	4638	6992	7964	5806	6352	10382	2310	5665	5225	2825	....	4496	1835
London	1562	2568	575	4526	6919	6376	2218	5975	4015	1540	7605	7320	4496	....	5496
Los Angeles	5034	7695	5849	8810	6148	4155	7675	10165	1741	6895	6255	2620	1835	5496	....
Melbourne	12190	8150	9992	6140	7336	8196	8720	6510	9837	9189	3497	5581	8162	10590	8098
Mexico City	4584	8155	6119	9818	4609	2619	7807	8620	1690	7160	7690	3846	3210	5605	1445
Montreal	2548	5814	3776	7582	5619	3954	5502	7975	750	4825	7840	4992	2647	3370	2468
New Orleans	3718	7212	5182	8952	4902	2990	6862	8390	827	6220	7895	4305	2860	4656	1695
New York	2604	6066	4025	7875	5295	3633	5701	7845	727	5060	8115	5051	2874	3500	2466
Panama	3918	7807	5902	9832	3319	1450	7230	7090	2320	6797	9220	5347	4456	5310	3025
Paris	1617	2385	540	4391	6891	6455	2020	5762	4219	1390	7675	7525	4700	210	5711
Rio de Janeiro	4312	7012	6246	8438	1230	2400	6242	3850	5320	6420	11710	8400	7611	5747	6330
San Francisco	5114	7521	5744	8523	6487	4500	7554	10340	1875	6770	5952	2407	1530	5440	345
Santiago	5718	8876	7842	10127	731	1548	8100	5080	5325	8230	9946	6935	7320	7275	5595
Seattle	4720	6848	5121	7830	6956	4964	6915	10305	1753	6124	5785	2707	870	4850	961
Shanghai	7324	4468	5323	3219	12295	10760	5290	8179	7155	5084	1945	5009	4968	5841	6598
Singapore	8338	4443	6226	2425	9940	11700	5152	6025	9475	5440	2990	6874	7375	6818	8955
Tokyo	7370	5242	5623	4247	11601	9740	6005	9234	6410	5649	1596	3940	4117	6050	5600
Wellington	11475	9782	11384	7752	6341	6696	10360	7149	8465	10790	4206	4676	7501	11790	6806

FROM/TO	Melbourne	Mexico City	Montreal	New Orleans	New York	Panama	Paris	Rio de Janeiro	San Francisco	Santiago	Seattle	Shanghai	Singapore	Tokyo	Wellington
Azores	12190	4584	2548	3718	2604	3918	1617	4312	5114	5718	4720	7324	8338	7370	11475
Bagdad	8150	8155	5814	7212	6066	7807	2385	7012	7521	8876	6848	4468	4443	5242	9782
Berlin	9992	6119	3776	5182	4026	5902	540	6246	5744	7842	5121	5323	6226	5623	11384
Bombay	6140	9818	7582	8952	7875	9832	4391	8438	8523	10127	7830	3219	2425	4247	7752
Buenos Aires	7336	4609	5619	4902	5295	3319	6891	1230	6487	731	6956	12295	9940	11601	6341
Callao	8196	2619	3954	2990	3633	1450	6455	2400	4500	1548	4964	10760	11700	9740	6696
Cairo	8720	7807	5502	6862	5701	7230	2020	6242	7554	8100	6915	5290	5152	6005	10360
Cape Town	6510	8620	7975	8390	7845	7090	5732	3850	10340	5080	10305	8179	6025	9234	7149
Chicago	9837	1690	750	827	727	2320	4219	5320	1875	5325	1753	7155	9475	6410	8465
Istanbul	9189	7160	4825	6220	5060	6797	1390	6420	6770	8230	6124	5084	5440	5649	10790
Guam	3497	7690	7840	7895	8115	9220	7675	11710	5952	9946	5785	1945	2990	1596	4206
Honolulu	5581	3846	4992	4305	5051	5347	7525	8400	2407	6935	2707	5009	6874	3940	4676
Juneau	8162	3210	2647	2860	2874	4456	4700	7611	1530	7320	870	4968	7375	4117	7501
London	10590	5605	3370	4656	3500	5310	210	5747	5440	7275	4850	5841	6818	6050	11790
Los Angeles	8098	1445	2468	1695	2466	3025	5711	6330	345	5595	961	6598	8955	5600	6806
Melbourne	....	8599	10553	9455	10541	9211	10500	8340	7970	7130	8330	4967	3768	5172	1655
Mexico City	8599	....	2247	940	2110	1532	5800	4810	1870	4122	2339	8120	10495	7190	7003
Montreal	10553	2247	....	1390	340	2545	3490	5110	2557	5461	2309	7141	9280	6546	9206
New Orleans	9455	940	1390	....	1161	1600	4846	4798	1960	4553	2137	7830	10255	6993	7950
New York	10541	2110	340	1161	....	2211	3600	4810	2606	5134	2440	7460	9617	6846	9067
Panama	9211	1532	2545	1600	2211	....	5440	3311	3349	3000	3680	9430	11800	8560	7580
Paris	10500	5800	3490	4846	3600	5440	....	5710	5680	7300	5080	5855	6730	6132	11865
Rio de Janeiro	8340	4810	5110	4798	4810	3311	5710	....	6655	1852	6945	11510	9875	11600	7510
San Francisco	7970	1870	2557	1960	2606	3349	5680	6655	....	5960	692	6245	8440	5250	6800
Santiago	7130	4122	5461	4553	5134	3000	7300	1852	5960	....	6466	11850	10270	10850	5925
Seattle	8330	2339	2309	2137	2440	3680	5080	6945	692	6466	....	5780	8200	4863	7310
Shanghai	4967	8120	7141	7830	7460	9430	5855	11510	6245	11850	5780	....	2395	1095	6080
Singapore	3768	10495	9280	10255	9617	11800	6730	9875	8440	10270	8200	2395	....	3350	5360
Tokyo	5172	7190	6546	6993	6846	8560	6132	11600	5250	10850	4863	1095	3350	....	5730
Wellington	1655	7003	9206	7950	9067	7580	11865	7510	6800	5925	7310	6080	5360	5730	.....

COLOR MAP SECTION

FOREIGN GEOGRAPHICAL TERMS

A. = Arabic Camb. = Cambodian Ch. = Chinese Czech. = Czechoslovakian Dan. = Danish Du. = Dutch Finn. = Finnish Fr. = French Ger. = German Ice. = Icelandic It. = Italian Jap. = Japanese Mong. = Mongol Nor. = Norwegian Per. = Persian Port. = Portuguese Russ. = Russian Sp. = Spanish Sw. = Swedish Turk. = Turkish

A	Nor., Sw.	Stream
Aas	Dan., Nor.	Hills
Abajo	Sp.	Lower
Ada, Adasi	Turk.	Island
Altipiano	It.	Plateau
Altiplano	Sp.	Plateau
Alv, Alf, Elf	Sw.	River
Arrecife	Sp.	Reef
Asa	Nor., Sw.	Hill
Asaga	Turk.	Lower
Austral	Sp.	Southern
Baai	Du.	Bay
Bab	Arabic	Gate or Strait
Bahia	Sp.	Bay
Bahr	Arabic	Marsh, Lake, Sea, River
Baia	Port.	Bay
Baie	Fr.	Bay, Gulf
Baizo	Port.	Low
Bakke	Dan.	Hill
Bana	Jap.	Cape
Bañados	Sp.	Marshes
Band	Per.	Mt. Range
Barra	Sp.	Reef
Bel	Turk.	Pass
Belt	Ger.	Strait
Ben	Gaelic	Mountain
Bera	Du.	Mountain
Berg	Ger., Du.	Mountain
Bir	Arabic	Well
Birket	Arabic	Pond
Boca	Sp.	Gulf, Inlet
Boğhaz	Turk.	Strait
Bolshoi, Bolshaya	Russ.	Big
Bolson	Sp.	Depression
Bong	Korean	Mountain
Boreal	Sp.	Northern
Breen	Nor.	Glacier
Bro	Dan., Nor., Sw.	Bridge
Bucht	Ger.	Bay
Bugt	Dan.	Bay
Bukhta	Russ.	Bay
Bukit	Malay	Hill, Mountain
Bukt	Nor., Sw.	Bay, Gulf
Burnu, Burun	Turk.	Cape, Point
By	Dan., Nor., Sw.	Town
Cabo	Port., Sp.	Cape
Campos	Port.	Plains
Canal	Port., Sp.	Channel
Cap, Capo	Fr., It.	Cape
Cataratas	Sp.	Falls
Catena	It.	Mt. Range
Catingas	Port.	Open Woodlands
Central, Centrale	Fr., It.	Middle
Cerrito, Cerro	Sp.	Hill
Cerros	Sp.	Hills, Mountains
Chai	Turk.	River
Chow	Ch.	Town of the second rank
Ciénaga	Sp.	Swamp
Ciudad	Sp.	City
Col	Fr.	Pass
Cordillera	Sp.	Mt. Range, Mts.
Côte	Fr.	Coast
Csatoria	Magyar	Canal
Cuchilla	Sp.	Mt. Range
Curiche	Sp.	Swamp
Dag, Dagh	Turk.	Mountain
Dağlari	Turk.	Mt. Range
Dal	Nor., Sw.	Valley
Dar	Arabic	Land
Darya	Per.	Salt Lake
Dasht	Per.	Desert, Plain
Deniz, Denizi	Turk.	Sea, Lake
Desierto	Sp.	Desert
Détroit	Fr.	Strait
Djeziret	Arabic, Turk.	Island
Do	Korean	Island
Doi	Thai	Mountain
Eiland	Du.	Island
Elv	Dan., Nor.	River
Embalse	Sp.	Reservoir
Emi	Berber	Mountain
Erg	Arabic	Dune, Desert
Eski	Turk.	Old
Est, Este	Fr., Port., Sp.	East
Estero	Sp.	Estuary, Creek
Estrecho, Estreito	Sp., Port.	Strait
Etang	Fr.	Pond, Lagoon, Lake
Fedja, Feij	Arabic	Pass
Fiume	It.	River
Fjäll	Sw.	Mountain
Fjeld, Fjell	Nor.	Hills, Mountain
Fjord	Dan., Nor., Sw.	Fiord
Fleuve	Fr.	River
Fljót	Icelandic	Stream
Fluss	Ger.	River
Fokani, Fukani	Arabic	Upper
Fors	Sw.	Waterfall
Fos, Foss	Dan., Nor.	Waterfall
Fu	Ch.	Town of importance
Gamla	Nor.	Old
Gamle	Dan.	Old
Gata	Jap.	Lake
Gawa	Jap.	River
Gebel	Arabic	Mountain
Gebergte	Du.	Mt. Range
Gebirge	Ger.	Mt. Range
Ghubbet	Arabic	Bay
Gobi	Mongol	Desert
Goe	Jap.	Pass
Gol	Mongol, Turk.	Lake, Stream
Golf	Ger., Du.	Gulf
Golfe	Fr.	Gulf
Golfo	Sp., It., Port.	Gulf
Gölü	Turk.	Lake
Gora	Russ.	Mountain
Grand, Grande	Fr., Sp.	Big
Groot	Du.	Big
Gross	Ger.	Big
Grosso	It., Port.	Big
Guba	Russ.	Bay, Gulf
Gunto	Jap.	Archipelago
Gunung	Malay	Mountain
Hai	Ch.	Sea
Halbinsel	Ger.	Peninsula
Hamáda, Hammada	Arabic	Rocky Plateau
Hamn	Sw.	Harbor
Hamún	Per.	Marsh
Hanto	Jap.	Peninsula
Has, Hassi	Arabic	Well
Hav	Dan., Nor., Sw.	Sea, Ocean
Havet	Nor.	Bay
Havn	Dan., Nor.	Harbor
Havre	Fr.	Harbor
Higashi, Higasi	Jap.	East
Ho	Ch.	River
Hochebene	Ger.	Plateau
Hoek	Du.	Cape
Hoku	Jap.	North
Holm	Dan., Nor., Sw.	Island
Hory	Czech.	Mountains
Hoved	Dan., Nor.	Cape, Promontory
Hsien	Ch.	Town of the third class
Hu	Ch.	Lake
Huk	Dan., Nor., Sw.	Point
Hus, Huus	Dan., Nor., Sw.	House
Hwang	Ch.	Yellow
Ile	Fr.	Island
Ilet	Fr.	Islet
Ilot	Fr.	Islet
Indre	Dan., Nor.	Inner
Inferieur, Inferiore	Fr., It.	Lower
Inner, Inre	Sw.	Inner
Insel	Ger.	Island
Irmak	Turk.	River
Isla	Sp.	Island
Isola	It.	Island
Jabal, Jebel	Arabic	Mountains
Järvi	Finn.	Lake
Jaure	Sw.	Lake
Jezira	Arabic	Island
Jima	Jap.	Island
Joki	Finn.	River
Kaap	Du.	Cape
Kabir, Kebir	Arabic	Big
Kai	Jap.	Sea
Kaikyo	Jap.	Strait
Kami	Turk.	Upper
Kanaal	Du.	Canal
Kanal	Russ., Ger.	Canal, Channel
Kao	Thai	Mountain
Kap, Kapp	Nor., Sw., Ice.	Cape
Kaupunki	Finn.	Town
Kawa	Jap.	River
Khao	Thai	Mountain
Khrebet	Russ.	Mt. Range
Kiang	Ch.	River
Kiao	Ch.	Point
Kita	Jap.	North
Klein	Du., Ger.	Small
Klint	Dan.	Promontory
Kô	Jap.	Lake
Ko	Thai	Island
Koh	Camb., Khmer	Island
Kong	Ch.	River
Kop	Du.	Peak, Head
Köping	Sw.	Market, Borough
Körfez, Körfezi	Turk.	Gulf
Kosa	Russ.	Spit
Kosui	Jap.	Lake
Kraal	Du.	Native Village
Kuchuk	Turk.	Small
Kuh	Per.	Mountain
Kul	Sinkiang Turki	Lake
Kum	Turk.	Desert
Kuro	Jap.	Black
Laag	Du.	Low
Lac	Fr.	Lake
Lago	Port., Sp., It.	Lake
Lagoa	Port.	Lagoon
Laguna	Sp.	Lagoon
Lagune	Fr.	Lagoon
Lahti	Finn.	Bay, Bight
Län	Sw.	County
Lilla	Sw.	Small
Lille	Dan., Nor.	Small
Llanos	Sp.	Plains
Loch	Scottish	Lake
Mae Nam	Thai	River
Mali, Malaya	Russ.	Small
Man	Korean	Bay
Mar	Sp., Port.	Sea
Mare	It.	Sea
Medio	Sp.	Middle
Meer	Du.	Lake
Meer	Ger.	Sea
Mer	Fr.	Sea
Meridionale	It.	Southern
Meseta	Sp.	Plateau
Middelst, Midden	Du.	Middle
Minami	Jap.	Southern
Mir	Per.	Mountain
Mis	Russ.	Cape
Misaki	Jap.	Cape
Mittel	Ger.	Middle
Mont	Fr.	Mountain
Montagne	Fr.	Mountain
Montaña	Sp.	Mountains
Monte	Sp., It., Port.	Mountain
More	Russ.	Sea
Morro	Port., Sp.	Mountain, Promontory
Morue	Fr.	Hill
Moyen	Fr.	Middle
Muong	Siamese	Town
Mys	Russ.	Cape
Nada	Jap.	Sea
Naka	Jap.	Middle
Nam	Burm., Lao	River
Nan	Ch., Jap.	South
Nes	Nor.	Cape, Point
Nevado	Sp.	Snow covered peak
Nieder	Ger.	Lower
Nishi, Nisi	Jap.	West
Nizhni, Nizhnyaya	Russ.	Lower
Njarga	Finn.	Peninsula, Promontory
Nong	Thai	Lake
Noord	Du.	North
Nor	Mong.	Lake
Nord	Fr., Ger.	North
Norte	Sp., It., Port.	North
Nos	Russ.	Cape
Novi, Novaya	Russ.	New
Nusa	Malay	Island
Ny, Nya	Nor., Sw.	New
O	Jap.	Big
Ö	Nor., Sw.	Island
Ober	Ger.	Upper
Occidental, Occidentale	Sp., It.	Western
Odde	Dan.	Point
Oeste	Port.	West
Ola	Mong.	Mountains
Ooster	Du.	Eastern
Opper, Over	Du.	Upper
Oriental	Sp., Fr.	Eastern
Orientale	It.	Eastern
Orta	Turk.	Middle
Ost	Ger.	East
Ostrov	Russ.	Island
Ouest	Fr.	West
öy	Nor.	Island
Ozero	Russ.	Lake
Pampa	Sp.	Plain
Pas	Fr.	Channel, Strait
Paso	Sp.	Pass
Passo	It., Port.	Pass
Peh, Pei	Ch.	North
Peña	Sp.	Rock, Mountain
Penisola	It.	Peninsula
Pequeño	Sp.	Small
Pereval	Russ.	Pass
Peski	Russ.	Desert
Petit	Fr.	Small
Phu	Lao, Annamese	Mtn.
Pic	Fr.	Mountain
Piccolo	It.	Small
Pico	Port., Sp.	Mountain, Peak
Pik	Russ.	Mountain, Peak
Piton	Fr.	Mountain, Peak
Planalto	Port.	Plateau
Plato	Russ.	Plateau
Pointe	Fr.	Point
Poluostrov	Russ.	Peninsula
Ponta	Port.	Point
Presa	Sp.	Reservoir
Presqu'île	Fr.	Peninsula
Proliv	Russ.	Strait
Pulou, Pulo	Malay	Island
Punt	Du.	Point
Punta	Sp., It., Port.	Point
Qum	Turk.	Desert
Rada	Sp.	Inlet
Rade	Fr.	Bay, Inlet
Ras	Arabic	Cape
Reka	Russ.	River
Retto	Jap.	Archipelago
Ria	Sp.	Estuary
Río	Sp.	River
Rivier, Rivière	Du., Fr.	River
Rud	Per.	River
Saghir	Arabic	Small
Sai	Jap.	West
Saki	Jap.	Cape
Salar, Salina	Sp.	Salt Deposit
Salto	Sp., Port.	Falls
San	Ch., Jap., Korean	Hill
Sanmaek	Korean	Mt. Range
Schiereiland	Du.	Peninsula
Se	Camb., Khmer	River
See	Ger.	Sea, Lake
Selvas	Sp., Port.	Woods, Forest
Seno	Sp.	Bay, Gulf
Serra	Port.	Mts.
Serranía	Sp.	Mts.
Seto	Jap.	Strait
Settentrionale	It.	Northern
Severni, Severnaya	Russ.	North
Shan	Ch., Jap.	Hill, Mts.
Shang	Ch.	Upper
Shatt	Arabic	River
Shima	Jap.	Island
Shimo	Jap.	Lower
Shin	Jap.	Land
Shiro	Jap.	White
Shoto	Jap.	Islands
Si	Ch.	West
Siao	Ch.	Small
Sierra	Sp.	Mt. Range, Mts.
Sjö	Nor., Sw.	Lake, Sea
Sok, Suk, Souk	Arabic, Ar. Fr.	Market
Song	Annamese	River
Sopka	Russ.	Volcano
Spitze	Ger.	Mt. Peak
Sredni, Srednyaya	Russ.	Middle
Stad	Dan., Nor., Sw.	City
Stari, Staraya	Russ.	Old
Step	Russ.	Treeless Plain
Straat	Du.	Strait
Strasse	Ger.	Strait
Stretto	It.	Strait
Ström	Dan., Nor., Sw.	Sound
Stung	Camb., Khmer	River
Su	Turk.	River
Sud, Süd	Sp., Fr., Ger.	South
Suido	Jap.	Strait, Channel
Sul	Port.	South
Sund	Dan., Nor., Sw.	Sound
Sungei	Malay	River
Supérieur	Fr.	Upper
Superior, Superiore	Sp., It.	Upper
Sur	Sp.	South
Suyu	Turk.	River
Ta	Ch.	Big
Tafelland	Du.	Plateau
Tagh	Turk.	Mt. Range
Take	Jap.	Peak, Ridge
Takht	Arabic	Lower
Tal	Ger.	Valley
Tandjong, Tanjung	Malay	Cape, Point
Tao	Ch.	Island
Tell	Arabic	Hill
Thale	Thai	Sea, Lake
Tind	Nor.	Peak
Tö	Jap.	East
To	Jap.	Island
Toge	Jap.	Pass
Trask	Finn.	Lake
Tso	Tibetan	Lake
Tugh	Somali	Dry River
Tung	Ch.	Eastern
Udjung	Malay	Point
Umi	Jap.	Bay
Unter	Ger.	Lower
Ura	Jap.	Inlet
Val	Fr.	Valley
Vatn	Nor.	Lake
Vecchio	It.	Old
Veld	Du.	Plain, Field
Velho	Port.	Old
Verkhni	Russ.	Upper
Vesi	Finn.	Lake
Vieho	Sp.	Old
Vik	Nor., Sw.	Bay
Vishni, Vishnyaya	Russ.	High
Vodokhranilishche	Russ.	Reservoir
Volcán	Sp.	Volcano
Vostochni, Vostochnaya	Russ.	East, Eastern
Wadi	Arabic	Dry River
Wald	Ger.	Forest
Wan	Jap.	Bay
Westersch	Du.	Western
Wüste	Ger.	Desert
Yama	Jap.	Mountain
Yarim Ada	Turk.	Peninsula
Yokara	Turk.	Upper
Yug, Yuzhni, Yuzhnaya	Russ.	South, Southern
Zaki	Jap.	Cape
Zaliv	Russ.	Bay, Gulf
Zapadni, Zapadnaya	Russ.	Western
Zee	Du.	Sea
Zemlya	Russ.	Land
Zuid	Du.	South

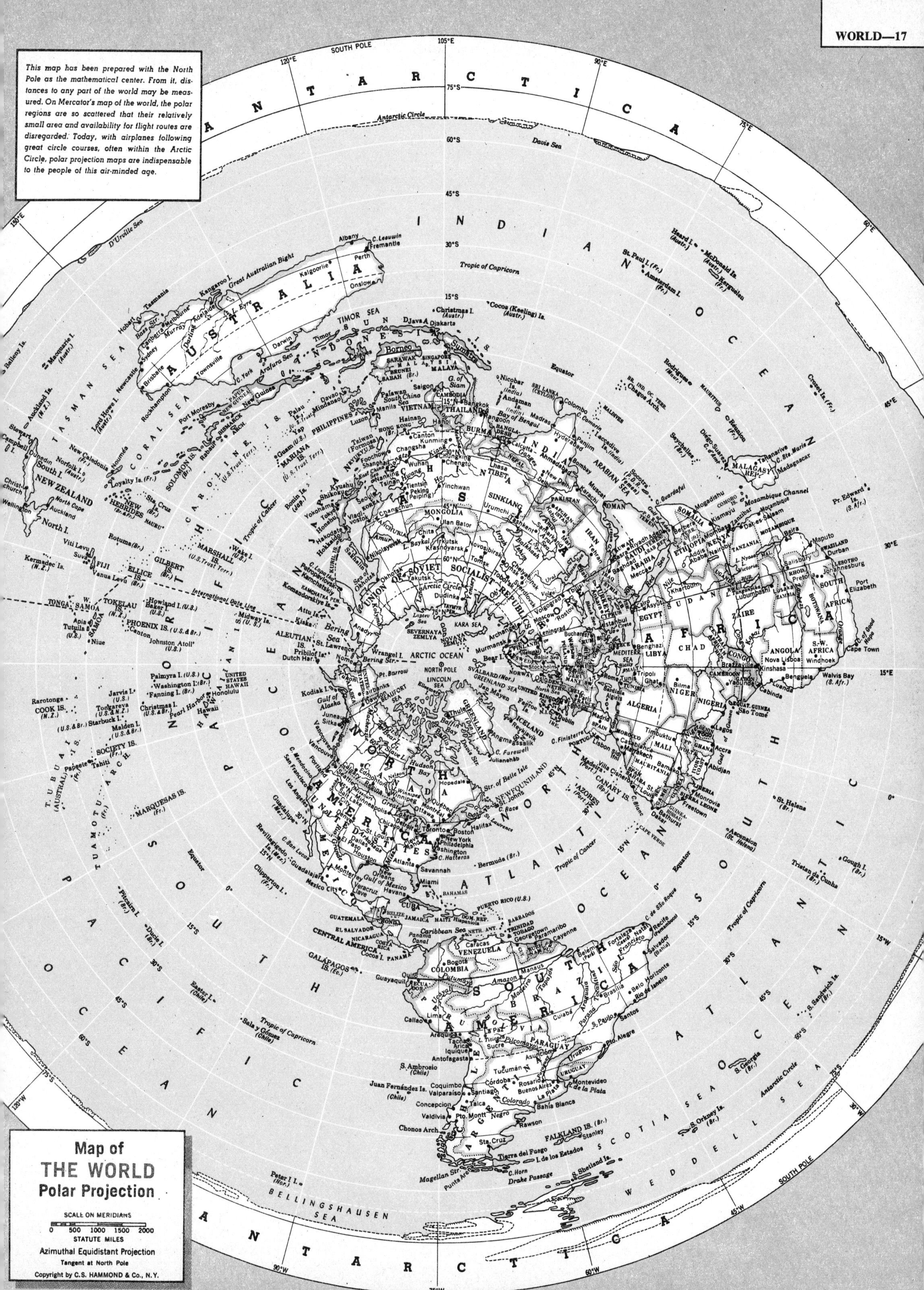
This map has been prepared with the North Pole as the mathematical center. From it, distances to any part of the world may be measured. On Mercator's map of the world, the polar regions are so scattered that their relatively small area and availability for flight routes are disregarded. Today, with airplanes following great circle courses, often within the Arctic Circle, polar projection maps are indispensable to the people of this air-minded age.
Map of
THE WORLD
Polar Projection
SCALE ON MERIDIANS
0 500 1000 1500 2000
STATUTE MILES
Azimuthal Equidistant Projection
Tangent at North Pole
Copyright by C.S. HAMMOND & Co., N.Y.
SOUTH POLE
ANTARCTICA
INDIAN OCEAN
AUSTRALIA
ASIA
UNION OF SOVIET SOCIALIST REPUBLICS
EUROPE
AFRICA
NORTH AMERICA
SOUTH AMERICA
NORTH PACIFIC OCEAN
SOUTH PACIFIC OCEAN
NORTH ATLANTIC OCEAN
SOUTH ATLANTIC OCEAN
ARCTIC OCEAN
NORTH POLE
Tropic of Cancer
Tropic of Capricorn
Equator
Arctic Circle
Antarctic Circle
International Date Line
BELLINGSHAUSEN SEA
WEDDELL SEA
SCOTIA SEA
Davis Sea
D'Urville Sea

THE WORLD'S CONTINENTS BY SIZE

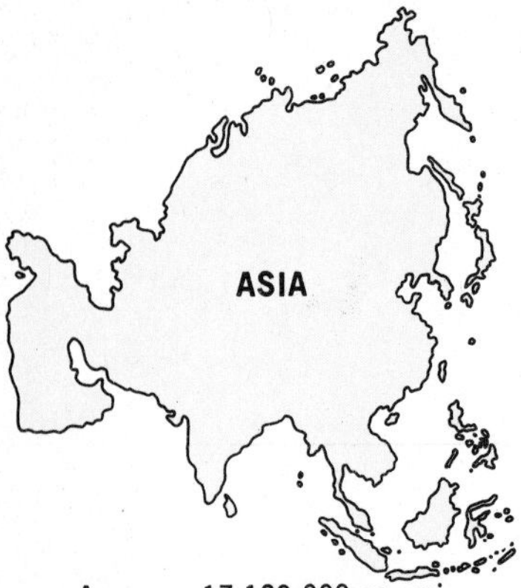

Continent	Area	Population
Asia	17,129,000 sq. mi. 44 363 000 sq. km.	2,265,000,000
Africa	11,707,000 sq. mi. 30 320 000 sq. km.	374,000,000
North America	9,363,000 sq. mi. 24 249 000 sq. km.	335,000,000
South America	6,886,000 sq. mi. 17 834 000 sq. km.	206,000,000
Antarctica	5,500,000 sq. mi. 14 245 000 sq. km.	No permanent population
Europe	4,056,000 sq. mi. 10 505 000 sq. km.	657,000,000
Australia	2,968,000 sq. mi. 7 687 000 sq. km.	13,132,000

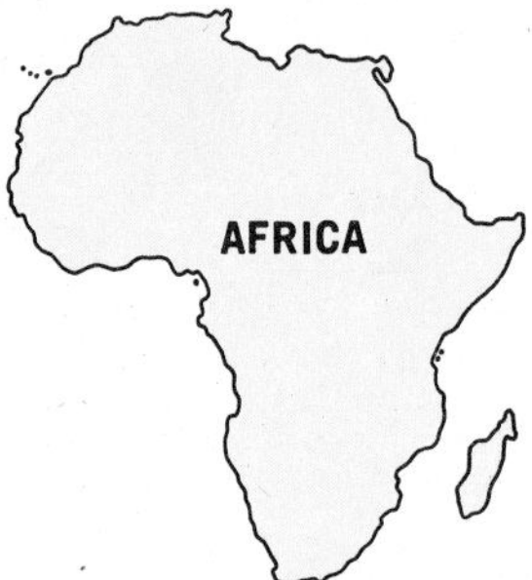

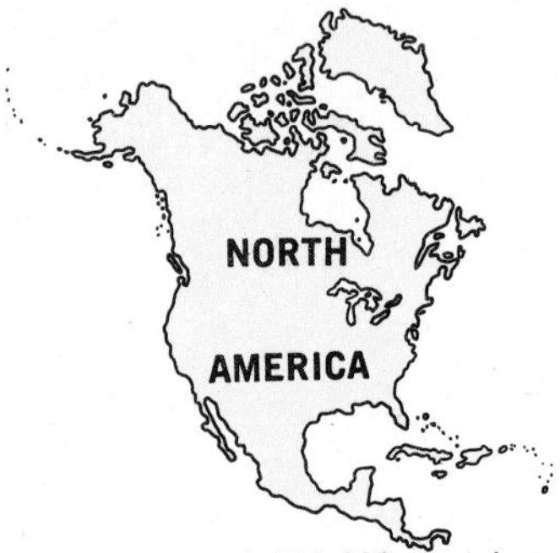

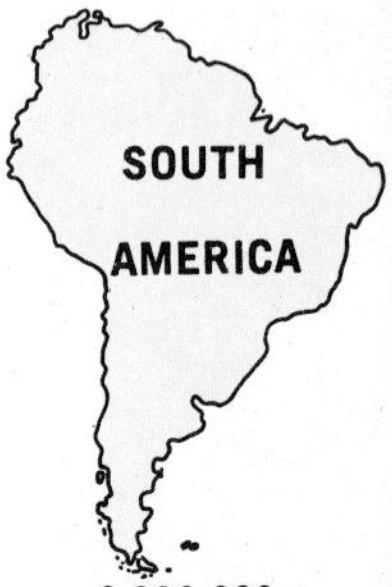

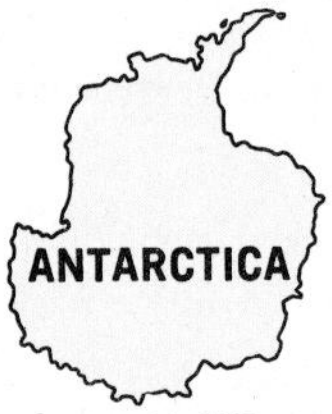

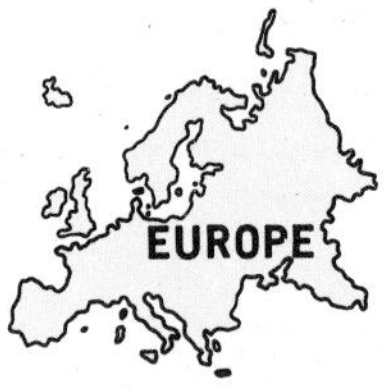

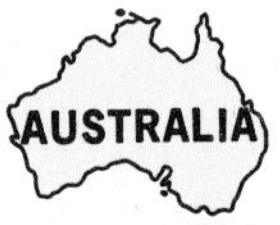

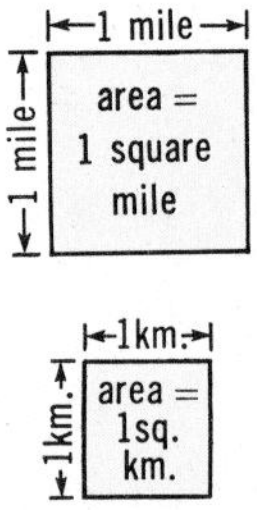

km. = kilometer
sq. km. = square kilometer

WORLD TIME ZONES

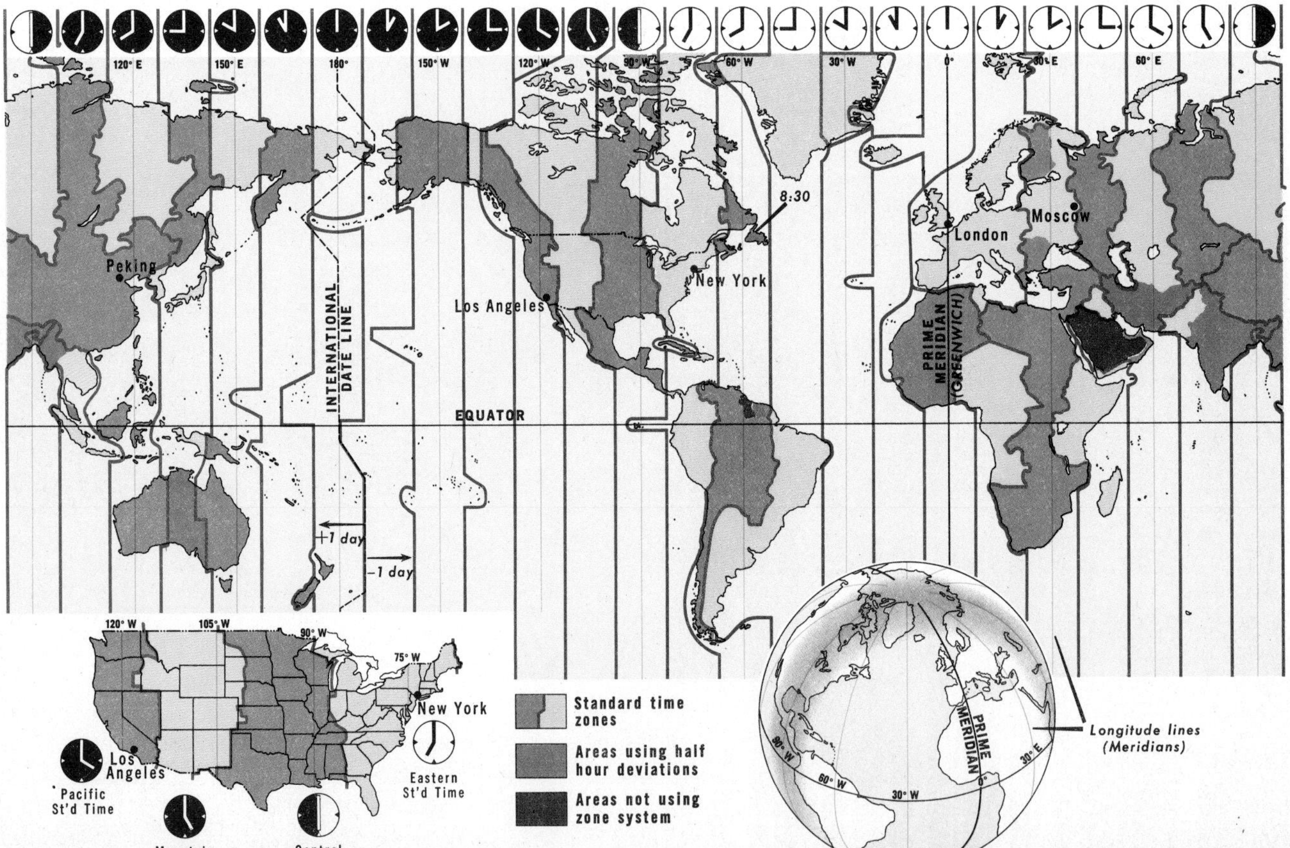

THE WORLD
MILLER CYLINDRICAL PROJECTION
(MODIFIED MERCATOR)
SCALE ALONG EQUATOR
MILES
0 500 1000 1500 2000 2500
KILOMETRES
0 500 1000 1500 2000 2500
Capitals of Countries
© Copyright HAMMOND INCORPORATED, Maplewood, N. J.
ANTARCTICA
SCALE ON MERIDIANS
MILES
0 200 400 600 800 1000
KILOMETRES
0 200 400 600 800 1000
Longitude West of Greenwich
Longitude East of Greenwich
International Date Line
ARCTIC OCEAN
NORTH PACIFIC OCEAN
SOUTH PACIFIC OCEAN
NORTH ATLANTIC OCEAN
SOUTH ATLANTIC OCEAN
INDIAN OCEAN
NORTH AMERICA
SOUTH AMERICA
EUROPE
ASIA
AFRICA
AUSTRALIA
ANTARCTICA
UNION OF SOVIET SOCIALIST REPUBLICS
GREENLAND (Den.)
WEDDELL SEA
Tropic of Cancer
Equator
Tropic of Capricorn
Arctic Circle
Antarctic Circle

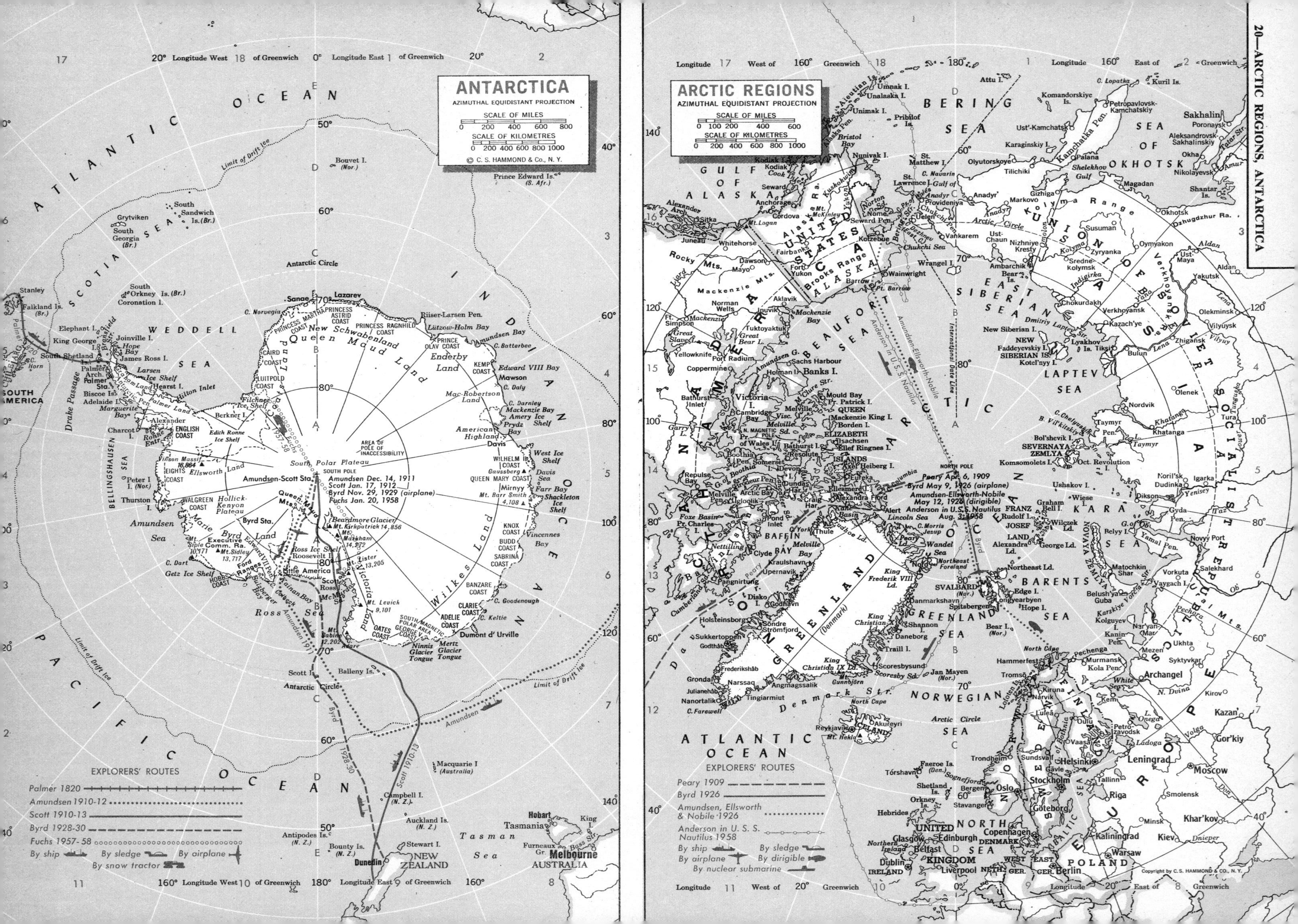
ANTARCTICA
AZIMUTHAL EQUIDISTANT PROJECTION
SCALE OF MILES
0 200 400 600 800
SCALE OF KILOMETRES
0 200 400 600 800 1000
© C. S. HAMMOND & Co., N. Y.
ATLANTIC OCEAN
INDIAN OCEAN
PACIFIC OCEAN
WEDDELL SEA
SCOTIA SEA
BELLINGSHAUSEN SEA
Amundsen Sea
Ross Sea
Antarctic Circle
Limit of Drift Ice
Queen Maud Land
Wilkes Land
Victoria Land
Byrd Land
SOUTH POLE
Amundsen Dec. 14, 1911
Scott Jan. 17, 1912
Byrd Nov. 29, 1929 (airplane)
Fuchs Jan. 20, 1958
Amundsen-Scott Sta.
South Polar Plateau
AREA OF POLE OF INACCESSIBILITY
EXPLORERS' ROUTES
Palmer 1820
Amundsen 1910-12
Scott 1910-13
Byrd 1928-30
Fuchs 1957-58
By ship
By sledge
By airplane
By snow tractor
160° Longitude West 10 of Greenwich 180° Longitude East 9 of Greenwich 160°
20° Longitude West 18 of Greenwich 0° Longitude East 1 of Greenwich 20°
ARCTIC REGIONS
AZIMUTHAL EQUIDISTANT PROJECTION
SCALE OF MILES
0 100 200 400 600
SCALE OF KILOMETRES
0 200 400 600 800 1000
ARCTIC OCEAN
ATLANTIC OCEAN
BERING SEA
SEA OF OKHOTSK
GULF OF ALASKA
BEAUFORT SEA
EAST SIBERIAN SEA
LAPTEV SEA
KARA SEA
BARENTS SEA
GREENLAND SEA
NORWEGIAN SEA
NORTH SEA
UNION OF SOVIET SOCIALIST REPUBLICS
UNITED STATES
ALASKA
CANADA
GREENLAND (Denmark)
EUROPE
NORTH POLE
Peary Apr. 6, 1909
Byrd May 9, 1926 (airplane)
Amundsen-Ellsworth-Nobile May 12, 1926 (dirigible)
Anderson in U.S.S. Nautilus Aug. 3, 1958
International Date Line
Arctic Circle
EXPLORERS' ROUTES
Peary 1909
Byrd 1926
Amundsen, Ellsworth & Nobile 1926
Anderson in U. S. S. Nautilus 1958
By ship
By sledge
By airplane
By dirigible
By nuclear submarine
Longitude 17 West of 160° Greenwich 18 180° 1 Longitude 160° East of 2 Greenwich
Longitude 11 West of 20° Greenwich 10 0° 9 Longitude 20° East of 8 Greenwich
Copyright by C. S. HAMMOND & CO., N. Y.

EUROPE
LAMBERT AZIMUTHAL EQUAL AREA PROJECTION
SCALE OF MILES
0 100 200 300 400 500
SCALE OF KILOMETERS
0 100 200 300 400 500
Capitals of Countries
International Boundaries
Canals
Copyright by C.S. HAMMOND & CO., N.Y.
The government of the United States has not recognized the incorporation of Estonia, Latvia and Lithuania into the Soviet Union, nor does it recognize as final the de facto western limit of Polish administration in Germany (the Oder-Neisse line).
Longitude West of Greenwich
Longitude East of Greenwich
Arctic Circle
ATLANTIC OCEAN
NORWEGIAN SEA
BARENTS SEA
NORTH SEA
BALTIC SEA
MEDITERRANEAN SEA
TYRRHENIAN SEA
IONIAN SEA
BLACK SEA
CASPIAN SEA
Bay of Biscay
English Channel
White Sea
ICELAND
Reykjavik
BRITISH ISLES
UNITED KINGDOM
IRELAND
NO. IRELAND
LONDON
Dublin
NORWAY
Oslo
SWEDEN
Stockholm
FINLAND
Helsinki
DENMARK
Copenhagen
NETHERLANDS
Amsterdam
BELGIUM
Brussels
LUX.
GERMANY
EAST BERLIN
Bonn
FRANCE
PARIS
SWITZERLAND
Bern
AUSTRIA
VIENNA
CZECHOSLOVAKIA
Prague
POLAND
WARSAW
HUNGARY
Budapest
RUMANIA
Bucharest
YUGOSLAVIA
Belgrade
BULGARIA
Sofia
ALBANIA
Tiranë
GREECE
Athens
ITALY
ROME
VATICAN CITY
SAN MARINO
MONACO
ANDORRA
SPAIN
MADRID
PORTUGAL
Lisbon
GIBRALTAR
MALTA
Valletta
CYPRUS
Nicosia
TURKEY
Ankara
ISTANBUL
SYRIA
IRAN
MOROCCO
Rabat
ALGERIA
Algiers
TUNISIA
Tunis
UNION OF SOVIET SOCIALIST REPUBLICS
MOSCOW
LENINGRAD
ESTONIAN S.S.R.
Tallinn
LATVIAN S.S.R.
Riga
LITHUANIAN S.S.R.
Vilna
WHITE RUSSIAN S.S.R.
Minsk
UKRAINIAN S.S.R.
Kiev
MOLDAVIAN S.S.R.
Kishinev
GEORGIAN S.S.R.
Tbilisi
ARMENIAN S.S.R.
Yerevan
AZERBAIDZHAN S.S.R.
Baku

WESTERN and
CENTRAL EUROPE
CONIC PROJECTION
SCALE OF MILES
0 50 100 200 300
SCALE OF KILOMETERS
0 50 100 200 300
National Capitals
Administrative Centers
International Boundaries
Internal Boundaries
Canals
Longitude West of Greenwich
Longitude East of Greenwich
The government of the United States has not recognized the incorporation of Estonia, Latvia and Lithuania into the Soviet Union, nor does it recognize as final the de facto western limit of Polish administration in Germany (the Oder-Neisse line).
Arctic Circle
NORWEGIAN SEA
NORTH SEA
ATLANTIC OCEAN
Bay of Biscay
MEDITERRANEAN SEA
TYRRHENIAN SEA
IONIAN SEA
ADRIATIC SEA
BALTIC SEA
Gulf of Bothnia
Gulf of Finland
Gulf of Riga
Gulf of Lions
LIGURIAN SEA
English Channel
Skagerrak
Kattegat
FAERØE IS. (Den.)
SHETLAND ISLANDS
ORKNEY IS.
HEBRIDES
CHANNEL IS. (Br.)
SCILLY IS.
BALEARIC IS.
UNITED KINGDOM
GREAT BRITAIN
SCOTLAND
IRELAND
NORTHERN IRELAND
NORWAY
SWEDEN
DENMARK
FINLAND
ESTONIAN S.S.R.
LATVIAN S.S.R.
LITHUANIAN S.S.R.
R.S.F.S.R.
NETHERLANDS
BELGIUM
LUX.
WEST GERMANY
EAST GERMANY
POLAND
CZECHOSLOVAKIA
AUSTRIA
HUNGARY
SWITZERLAND
LIECH.
FRANCE
SPAIN
PORTUGAL
ANDORRA
MONACO
SAN MARINO
VATICAN CITY
ITALY
YUGOSLAVIA
ALBANIA
ALGERIA
TUNISIA
MOROCCO
Corsica (Corse)
Sardinia (Sardegna)
Sicily (Sicilia)
MALTA
GIBRALTAR (Br.)
LONDON
PARIS
Amsterdam
Brussels
BERLIN
Oslo
Stockholm
Copenhagen
Helsinki
Bern
Vienna
Prague
Budapest
Warsaw
Madrid
Lisbon
ROME
Dublin
Luxembourg
Algiers
Tunis
Valletta
Copyright by C. S. HAMMOND & Co., N. Y.

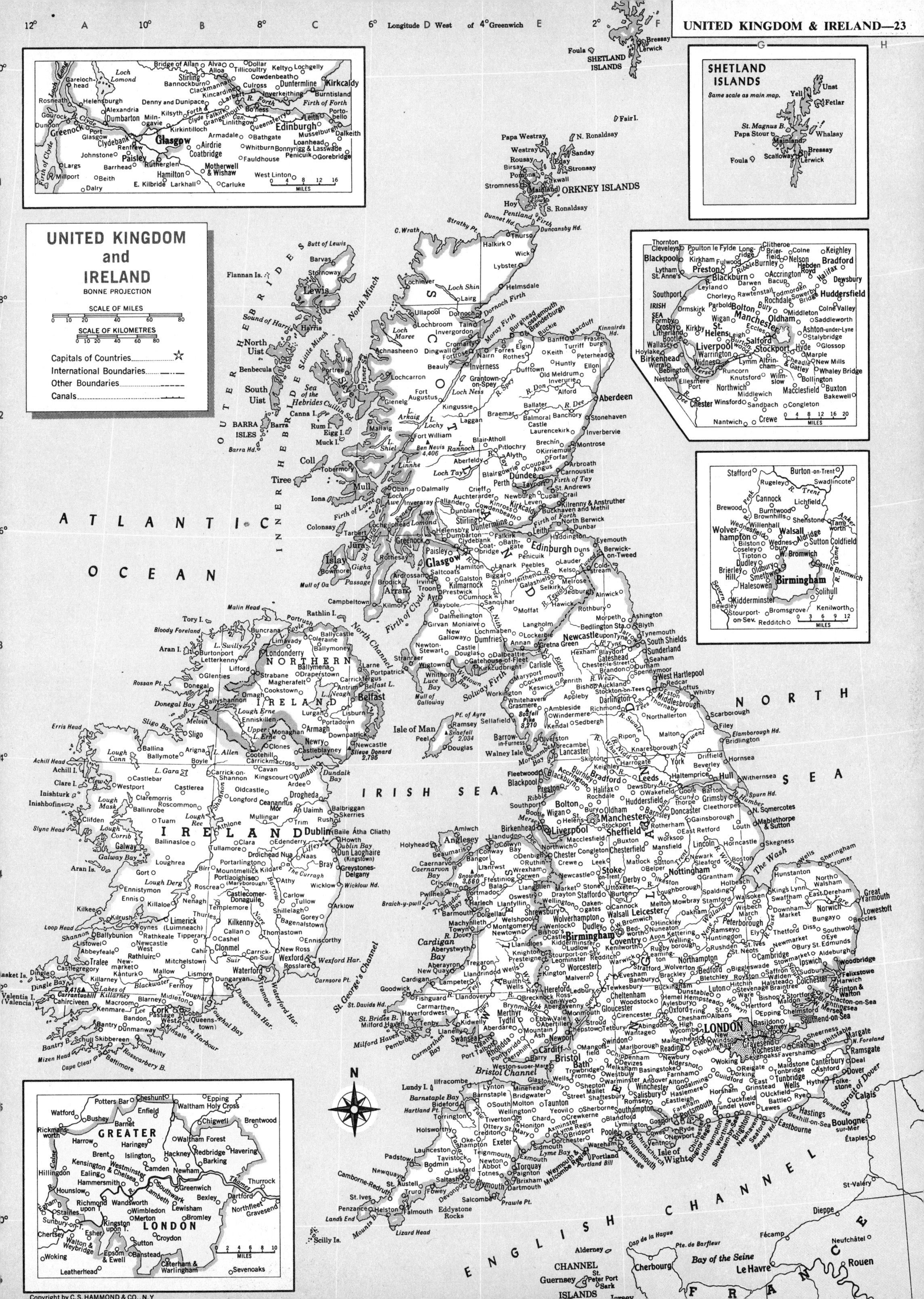
UNITED KINGDOM and IRELAND
BONNE PROJECTION
SCALE OF MILES
0 10 20 40 60 80
SCALE OF KILOMETRES
0 10 20 40 60 80
Capitals of Countries
International Boundaries
Other Boundaries
Canals
SHETLAND ISLANDS
Same scale as main map.
ORKNEY ISLANDS
ATLANTIC OCEAN
NORTH SEA
IRISH SEA
ENGLISH CHANNEL
CHANNEL ISLANDS
SCOTLAND
ENGLAND
WALES
NORTHERN IRELAND
IRELAND
FRANCE
OUTER HEBRIDES
INNER HEBRIDES
North Channel
St. George's Channel
Bristol Channel
Strait of Dover
Firth of Forth
Firth of Clyde
Moray Firth
Solway Firth
The Wash
Isle of Man
Isle of Wight
Ben Nevis 4,406
Snowdon 3,560
Scafell Pike 3,210
Slieve Donard 2,796
Carrantuohill 3,414
Longitude West of Greenwich
London
Edinburgh
Belfast
Dublin (Baile Átha Cliath)
Cardiff
Glasgow
Liverpool
Manchester
Birmingham
GREATER LONDON
0 2 4 6 8 10 MILES

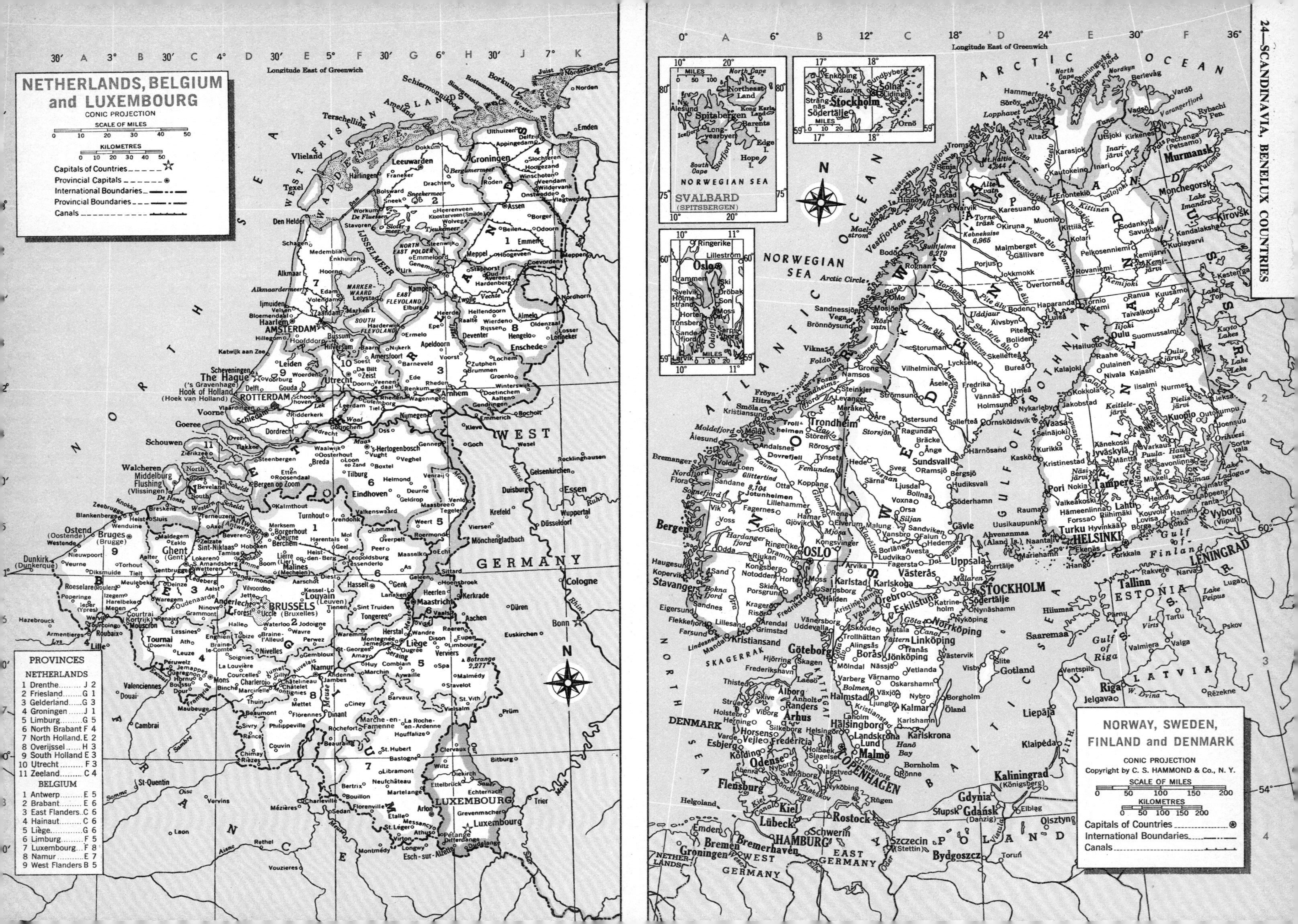
NETHERLANDS, BELGIUM and LUXEMBOURG
CONIC PROJECTION
SCALE OF MILES
0 10 20 30 40 50
KILOMETRES
0 10 20 30 40 50
Capitals of Countries
Provincial Capitals
International Boundaries
Provincial Boundaries
Canals
PROVINCES
NETHERLANDS
1 Drenthe J 2
2 Friesland G 1
3 Gelderland G 3
4 Groningen J 1
5 Limburg G 5
6 North Brabant F 4
7 North Holland E 2
8 Overijssel H 3
9 South Holland E 3
10 Utrecht F 3
11 Zeeland C 4
BELGIUM
1 Antwerp E 5
2 Brabant E 6
3 East Flanders C 6
4 Hainaut C 6
5 Liège G 6
6 Limburg F 5
7 Luxembourg F 8
8 Namur E 7
9 West Flanders B 5
NORWAY, SWEDEN, FINLAND and DENMARK
CONIC PROJECTION
Copyright by C. S. HAMMOND & Co., N. Y.
SCALE OF MILES
0 50 100 150 200
KILOMETRES
0 50 100 150 200
Capitals of Countries
International Boundaries
Canals
SVALBARD (SPITSBERGEN)

GERMANY
CONIC PROJECTION
SCALE OF MILES
SCALE OF KILOMETERS
Capitals of Countries
State and District Capitals
International Boundaries
State and District Boundaries
Canals
East Germany is divided into districts bearing the same name as their respective capitals.
Longitude East 10° of Greenwich
DENMARK
NORTH SEA
BALTIC SEA
NORTH FRISIAN ISLANDS
EAST FRISIAN ISLANDS
WEST FRISIAN ISLANDS
SCHLESWIG-HOLSTEIN
MECKLENBURG
LOWER SAXONY
BRANDENBURG
EAST GERMANY
NORTH RHINE-WESTPHALIA
HESSE
THURINGIA
SAXONY
RHINELAND PALATINATE
SAARLAND
BADEN-WÜRTTEMBERG
GERMANY
BAVARIA
NETHERLANDS
BELGIUM
LUXEMBOURG
FRANCE
SWITZERLAND
AUSTRIA
CZECHOSLOVAKIA
POLAND
Hamburg
Bremen
Hannover
Berlin
Potsdam
Magdeburg
Halle
Leipzig
Dresden
Karl-Marx-Stadt (Chemnitz)
Erfurt
Düsseldorf
Cologne (Köln)
Bonn
Frankfurt
Wiesbaden
Mainz
Stuttgart
Munich (München)
Nuremberg (Nürnberg)
Kiel
Rostock
Schwerin
Saarbrücken
Szczecin (Stettin)
BERLIN
WEST
EAST
© Copyright by C.S. HAMMOND & Co., Maplewood, N.J.

FRANCE
CONIC PROJECTION
SCALE OF MILES
0 20 40 60 80 100
SCALE OF KILOMETRES
0 20 40 60 80 100
Capitals of Countries
Capitals of Departments
International Boundaries
Department Boundaries
Canals
© C.S. HAMMOND & Co., N.Y.
PARIS and ENVIRONS
CORSICA
Same Scale as Main Map
MEDITERRANEAN SEA
Longitude 2° West of Greenwich 0° Longitude East of 2° Greenwich
UNITED KINGDOM
ENGLAND
LONDON
NORTH SEA
NETHERLANDS
Amsterdam
The Hague
Rotterdam
BELGIUM
Brussels
LUXEMBOURG
Luxembourg
GERMANY
SWITZERLAND
Bern
Geneva
ENGLISH CHANNEL (La Manche)
CHANNEL ISLANDS
BAY OF BISCAY
Gulf of Lions
SPAIN
ANDORRA
MEDITERRANEAN SEA
PARIS
SEINE-MARITIME
CALVADOS
MANCHE
ORNE
EURE
EURE-ET-LOIR
CÔTES-DU-NORD
FINISTÈRE
MORBIHAN
ILLE-ET-VILAINE
MAYENNE
SARTHE
LOIRE-ATLANTIQUE
MAINE-ET-LOIRE
INDRE-ET-LOIRE
LOIR-ET-CHER
LOIRET
VENDÉE
DEUX-SÈVRES
VIENNE
INDRE
CHER
NIÈVRE
YONNE
AUBE
MARNE
ARDENNES
AISNE
OISE
SOMME
PAS-DE-CALAIS
NORD
MEUSE
MOSELLE
MEURTHE-ET-MOSELLE
VOSGES
BAS-RHIN
HAUT-RHIN
HAUTE-MARNE
HAUTE-SAÔNE
CÔTE-D'OR
DOUBS
JURA
SAÔNE-ET-LOIRE
ALLIER
CREUSE
HAUTE-VIENNE
CHARENTE
CHARENTE-MARITIME
CORRÈZE
PUY-DE-DÔME
LOIRE
RHÔNE
AIN
HAUTE-SAVOIE
SAVOIE
ISÈRE
DRÔME
HAUTE-LOIRE
CANTAL
LOZÈRE
ARDÈCHE
GIRONDE
DORDOGNE
LOT
LOT-ET-GARONNE
LANDES
GERS
TARN-ET-GARONNE
TARN
AVEYRON
GARD
HÉRAULT
VAUCLUSE
BOUCHES-DU-RHÔNE
VAR
ALPES-MARITIMES
ALPES-DE-HAUTE-PROVENCE
HAUTES-ALPES
PYRÉNÉES-ATLANTIQUES
HAUTES-PYRÉNÉES
HAUTE-GARONNE
ARIÈGE
AUDE
PYRÉNÉES-ORIENTALES
SEINE-ET-MARNE
ESSONNE
YVELINES
VAL-D'OISE
VAL-DE-MARNE
SEINE-ST-DENIS
Bordeaux
Toulouse
Marseille
Lyon
Nantes
Rennes
Strasbourg
Nice
Montpellier
Limoges
Dijon
Orléans
Tours
Lille
Reims
Rouen
Le Havre
Brest
Grenoble
Clermont-Ferrand
Perpignan
Bayonne
Toulon
Ajaccio
Bastia
Massif Central
Mt. Blanc 15,781
Mt. Cinto 8,891
Mont Perdido 10,997
Pico de Aneto 11,168
Vignemale 10,820
Puy-de-Dôme 4,872
Plomb du Cantal 6,096
Monts Dore 6,188
Mt. Mézenc 5,754
Mt. Viso 12,601
Les Écrins 13,461
Mt. l'Incudine 7,007
Str. of Bonifacio

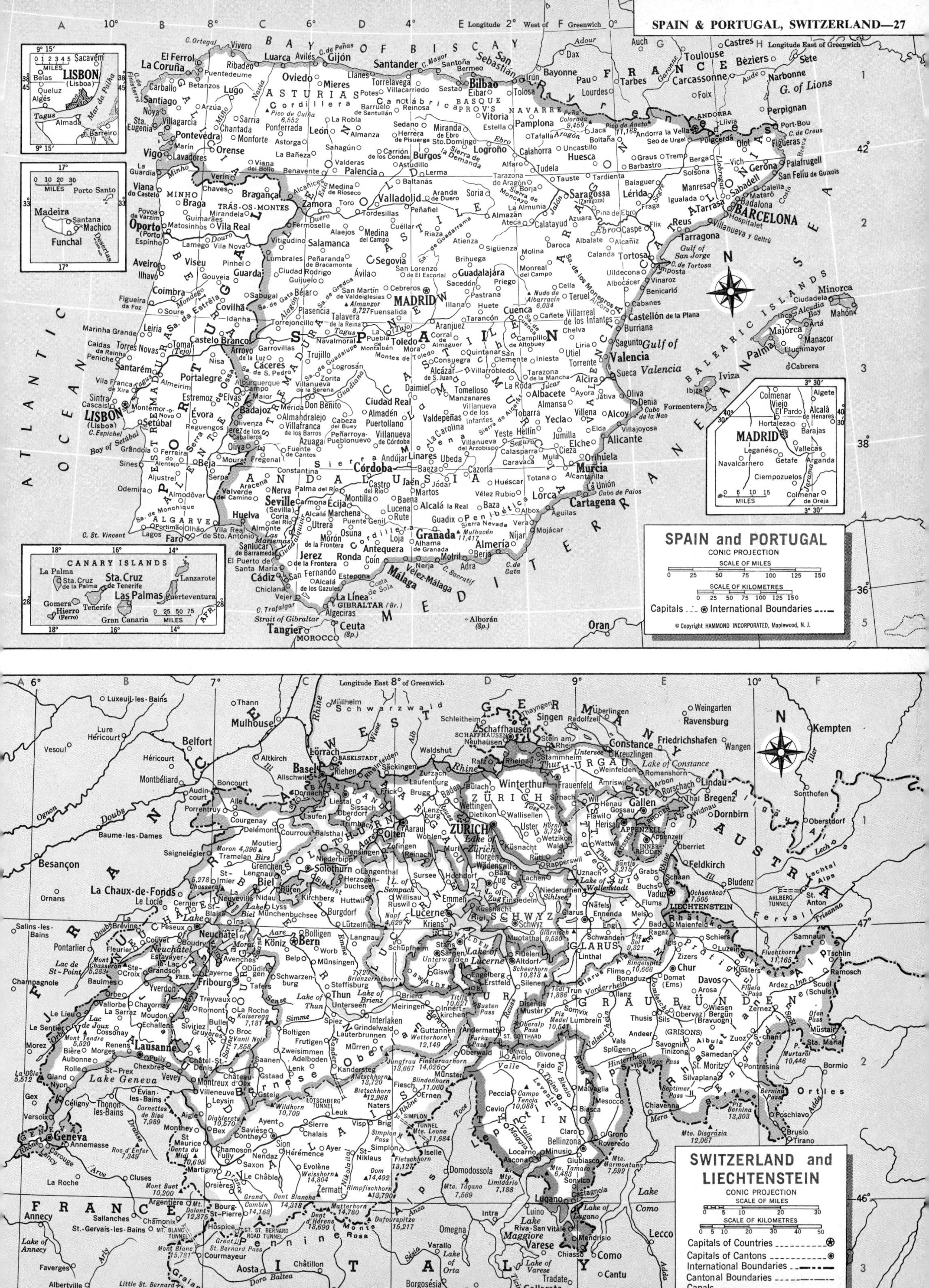
SPAIN and PORTUGAL
CONIC PROJECTION
SCALE OF MILES
0 25 50 75 100 125 150
SCALE OF KILOMETRES
0 25 50 75 100 125 150
Capitals ⊛ International Boundaries
© Copyright HAMMOND INCORPORATED, Maplewood, N. J.
BAY OF BISCAY
ATLANTIC OCEAN
MEDITERRANEAN SEA
CANARY ISLANDS
SWITZERLAND and LIECHTENSTEIN
CONIC PROJECTION
SCALE OF MILES
0 5 10 20 30
SCALE OF KILOMETRES
0 10 20 30 40 50
Capitals of Countries
Capitals of Cantons
International Boundaries
Cantonal Boundaries
Canals

ITALY
CONIC PROJECTION
SCALE OF MILES
0 20 40 60 80 100
SCALE OF KILOMETERS
0 20 40 60 80 100
Capitals of Countries
Regional Capitals
Provincial Capitals
International Boundaries
Regional Boundaries
The regions are subdivided into provinces bearin
the same names as their respective capitals, except
PROVINCE
MASSA-CARRARA
PESARO & URBINO
CAPITA
Massa
Pesar
Copyright by C.S. HAMMOND & Co., N.Y.
SWITZERLAND
HUNGARY
AUSTRIA
YUGOSLAVIA
LIECHTENSTEIN
FRANCE
CORSICA
SARDINIA
SICILY
TUNISIA
MALTA
SAN MARINO
VATICAN CITY
LIGURIAN SEA
TUSCAN ARCH.
TYRRHENIAN SEA
ADRIATIC SEA
IONIAN SEA
MEDITERRANEAN SEA
Gulf of Venice
Gulf of Taranto
Strait of Sicily
Malta Channel
Strait of Messina
G. of Manfredonia
Gulf of Gaeta
Gulf of Salerno
G. of Policastro
Gulf of Sant'Eufemia
Gulf of Squillace
Gulf of Hammamet
G. of Tunis
G. of Genoa
G. of Trieste
G. of Orosei
G. of Oristano
G. of Cagliari
G. of Asinara
G. of Ajaccio
Str. of Bonifacio
LIPARI ISLANDS
EGADI ISLANDS
PONTINE ISLANDS
PELAGIE ISLANDS
ROME
MILAN
Turin (Torino)
Genoa (Genova)
Venice (Venezia)
Florence (Firenze)
Naples
Palermo
Bari
Bologna
Trieste
Leghorn (Livorno)
Messina
Catania
Cagliari
Taranto
Reggio di Calabria
Syracuse (Siracusa)
Ancona
Pescara
Perugia
Trento
Bolzano
Aosta
Udine
Padua
Verona
Brescia
Bergamo
Parma
Modena
Ravenna
Rimini
Pisa
Siena
Arezzo
Grosseto
Viterbo
Terni
L'Aquila
Chieti
Foggia
Potenza
Cosenza
Catanzaro
Salerno
Benevento
Avellino
Campobasso
Sassari
Nuoro
Agrigento
Caltanissetta
Enna
Ragusa
Trapani
Marsala
Ajaccio
Bastia
Bern
Lucerne
Lausanne
Innsbruck
Graz
Ljubljana
Zagreb
Rijeka (Fiume)
Split
Tunis
Bizerte
Valletta
Nice
Monaco
Elba
Capri
Ischia
Stromboli
Ustica
Pantelleria
Lampedusa
Etna 10,741
Mt. Blanc 15,781
M. Corno 9,560
M. Cinto 8,891
VATICAN CITY
SCALE
0 300 600 900 Ft.
St. Peters
Piazza S. Pietro
ROME and ENVIRONS
L. Bracciano
Cerveteri
Ladispoli
Maccarese
Fregene
Fiumicino
Ostia Antica
Lido di Roma
TYRRHENIAN SEA
Monterotondo
Tivoli
Frascati
Ciampino
Castel Gandolfo
Albano Laziale
Velletri
Pomezia
Genzano
Nemi
Lanuvio
MILES
0 5 10 15 20

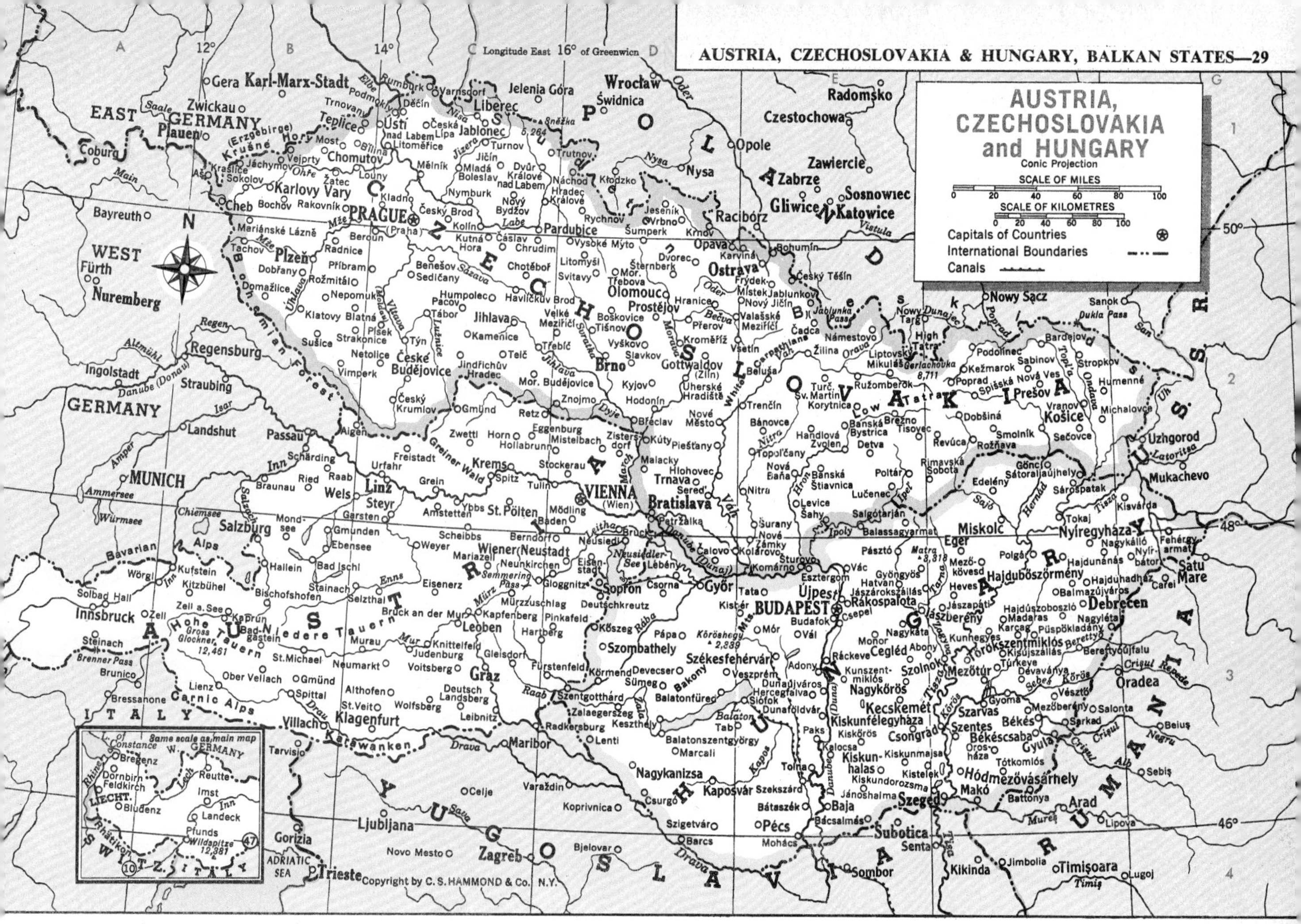

AUSTRIA, CZECHOSLOVAKIA and HUNGARY

Conic Projection

SCALE OF MILES

0 20 40 60 80 100

SCALE OF KILOMETRES

0 20 40 60 80 100

Capitals of Countries

International Boundaries

Canals

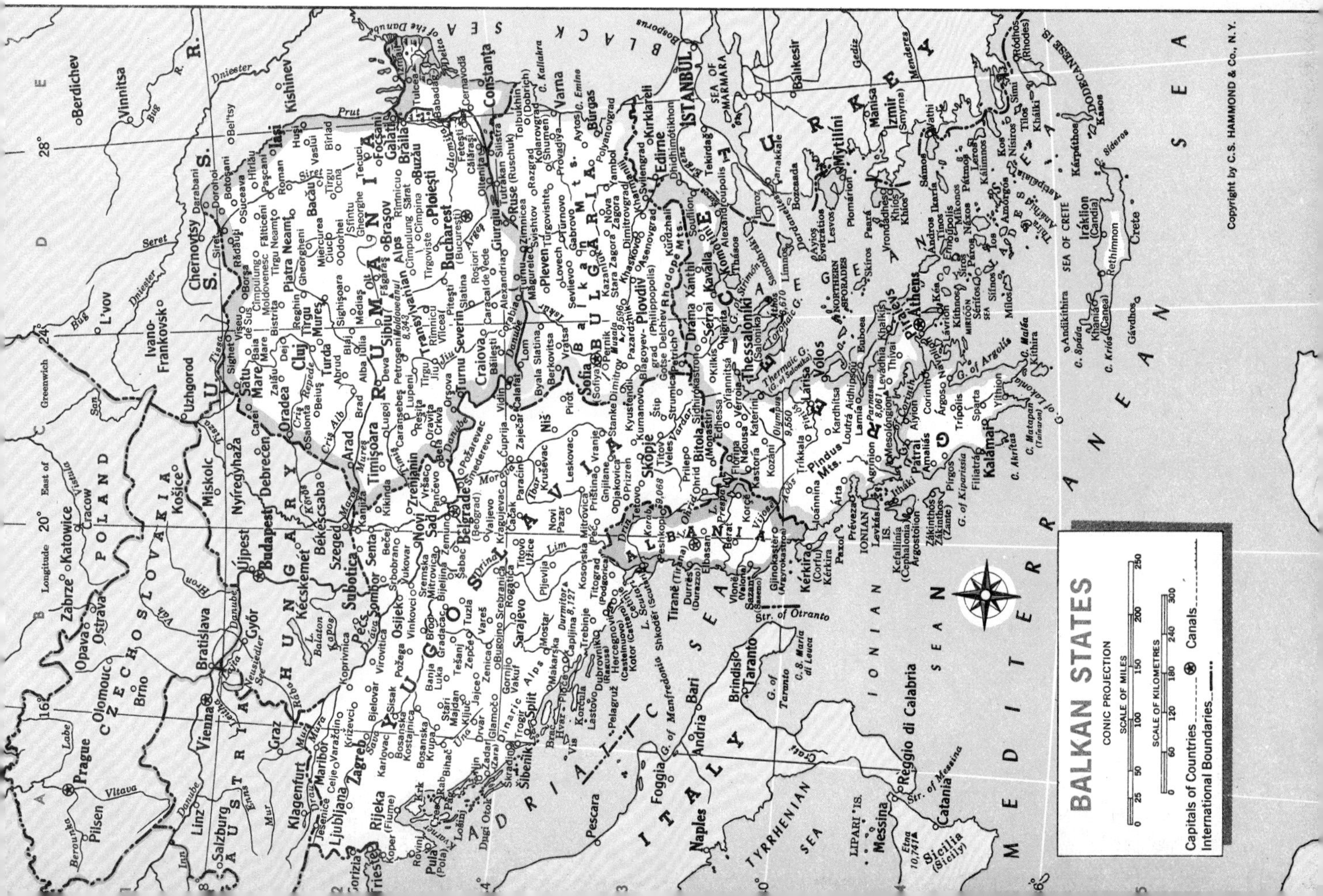

BALKAN STATES

CONIC PROJECTION

SCALE OF MILES

0 25 50 100 150 200 250

SCALE OF KILOMETRES

0 60 120 180 240 300

Capitals of Countries

International Boundaries

Canals

ADMINISTRATIVE DIVISIONS NOT NAMED ON MAP

Division	Ref.	Division	Ref.
1. Abkhaz A.S.S.R.	E5	13. Khakass Aut. Oblast	J4
2. Adygey Aut. Oblast	D5	14. Komi-Permyak Nat'l Okrug	F4
3. Adzhar A.S.S.R.	E5	15. Mari A.S.S.R.	E4
4. Aginsk Nat'l Okrug	M4	16. Mordvinian A.S.S.R.	E4
5. Chechen-Ingush A.S.S.R.	E5	17. Nagorno-Karabakh Aut. Oblast	E5
6. Chuvash A.S.S.R.	E4	18. Nakhichevan' A.S.S.R.	E6
7. Gorno-Altay Aut. Oblast	J4	19. North Ossetian A.S.S.R.	E5
8. Gorno-Badakhshan Aut. Oblast	H6	20. South Ossetian Aut. Oblast	E5
9. Jewish Aut. Oblast	O5	21. Tatar A.S.S.R.	F4
10. Kabardin-Balkar A.S.S.R.	E5	22. Tuvinian A.S.S.R.	K4
11. Karachay-Cherkess Aut. Oblast	E5	23. Udmurt A.S.S.R.	F4
12. Kara-Kalpak A.S.S.R.	G5	24. Ust'-Ordynskiy Nat'l Okrug	L4

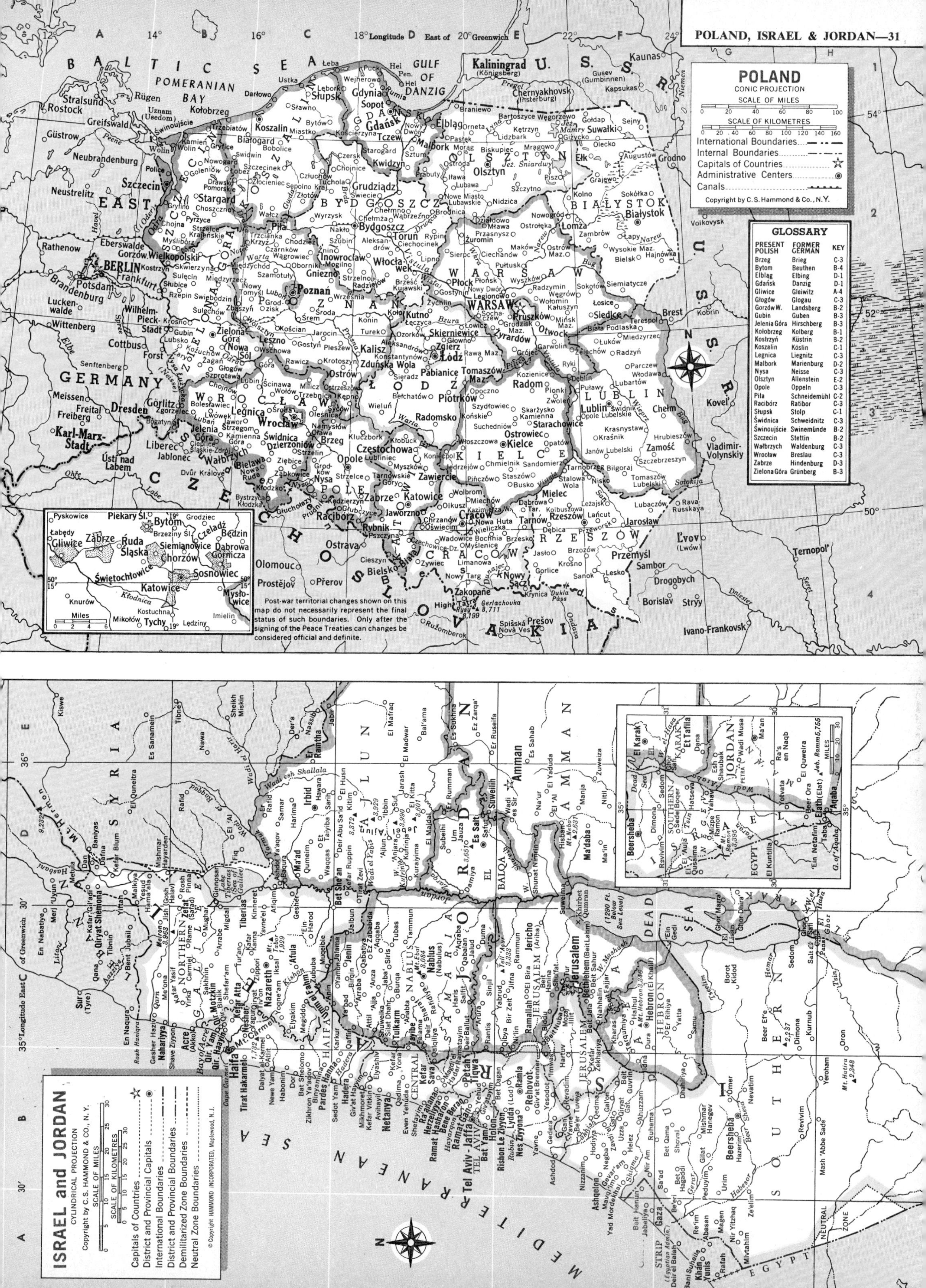
POLAND
CONIC PROJECTION
SCALE OF MILES
SCALE OF KILOMETRES
International Boundaries
Internal Boundaries
Capitals of Countries
Administrative Centers
Canals
Copyright by C. S. Hammond & Co., N.Y.
GLOSSARY
PRESENT POLISH | FORMER GERMAN | KEY
Brzeg | Brieg | C-3
Bytom | Beuthen | B-4
Elbląg | Elbing | D-1
Gdańsk | Danzig | D-1
Gliwice | Gleiwitz | A-4
Głogów | Glogau | C-3
Gorzów W. | Landsberg | B-2
Gubin | Guben | B-3
Jelenia Góra | Hirschberg | B-3
Kołobrzeg | Kolberg | B-1
Kostrzyń | Küstrin | B-2
Koszalin | Köslin | C-1
Legnica | Liegnitz | C-3
Malbork | Marienburg | D-2
Nysa | Neisse | C-3
Olsztyn | Allenstein | E-2
Opole | Oppeln | C-3
Piła | Schneidemühl | C-2
Racibórz | Ratibor | C-3
Słupsk | Stolp | C-1
Świdnica | Schweidnitz | C-3
Świnoujście | Swinemünde | B-2
Szczecin | Stettin | B-2
Wałbrzych | Waldenburg | C-3
Wrocław | Breslau | C-3
Zabrze | Hindenburg | D-3
Zielona Góra | Grünberg | B-3
Post-war territorial changes shown on this map do not necessarily represent the final status of such boundaries. Only after the signing of the Peace Treaties can changes be considered official and definite.
Longitude East of Greenwich
BALTIC SEA
POMERANIAN BAY
GULF OF DANZIG
GERMANY
EAST
U.S.S.R.
CZECHOSLOVAKIA
WARSAW
Poznań
Łódź
Kraków
Wrocław
Gdańsk
Szczecin
Białystok
Lublin
Kielce
Rzeszów
Olsztyn
Bydgoszcz
Katowice
Opole
Koszalin
ISRAEL and JORDAN
CYLINDRICAL PROJECTION
Copyright by C. S. HAMMOND & CO., N. Y.
SCALE OF MILES
SCALE OF KILOMETRES
Capitals of Countries
District and Provincial Capitals
International Boundaries
Demilitarized Zone Boundaries
Neutral Zone Boundaries
© Copyright HAMMOND INCORPORATED, Maplewood, N. J.
MEDITERRANEAN SEA
SYRIA
JORDAN
EGYPT
DEAD SEA
Jerusalem
Amman
Tel Aviv-Jaffa
Haifa
Beersheba
GAZA STRIP (Egyptian Admin.)
NEUTRAL ZONE

ASIA
LAMBERT AZIMUTHAL EQUAL-AREA PROJECTION
SCALE OF MILES
0 150 300 600 900 1200
SCALE OF KILOMETRES
0 300 600 900 1200
Capitals of Countries
Canals
International Boundaries
ATLANTIC OCEAN
GREENLAND
Iceland
North Pole
Longitude East of Greenwich
ARCTIC OCEAN
BARENTS SEA
KARA SEA
LAPTEV SEA
Novaya Zemlya
Severnaya Zemlya
New Siberian Is.
Franz Josef Ld.
Svalbard (Spitsbergen)
UNITED STATES (ALASKA)
Bering Str.
BERING SEA
Aleutian Is.
Wrangel I.
St. Lawrence I.
Nunivak I.
NORTH SEA
BALTIC SEA
BLACK SEA
CASPIAN SEA
MEDITERRANEAN SEA
ADRIATIC SEA
UNION OF SOVIET SOCIALIST REPUBLICS
RUSSIAN SOVIET FEDERATED SOCIALIST REPUBLIC
SIBERIA
KAZAKH S.S.R.
UZBEK S.S.R.
TURKMEN S.S.R.
KIRGIZ S.S.R.
Arctic Circle
SEA OF OKHOTSK
Sakhalin
KAMCHATKA PEN.
Kolyma Range
PACIFIC OCEAN
SEA OF JAPAN
JAPAN
TOKYO
Hokkaido
Honshu
Kyushu
Shikoku
MANCHURIA
MONGOLIA
Gobi
Ulan Bator
INNER MONGOLIA
SINKIANG
Tien Shan
Kun lun
TIBET
CHINA
PEKING
Yellow Sea
NANKING
SHANGHAI
EAST CHINA SEA
Taiwan (Formosa)
HONG KONG
MACAO
Tropic of Cancer
PHILIPPINES
Manila
SOUTH CHINA SEA
Hainan
VIETNAM
BURMA
THAILAND (SIAM)
Bangkok
Saigon
MALAYA
MALAYSIA
SINGAPORE
SARAWAK
SABAH
Borneo
KALIMANTAN
CELEBES SEA
Celebes (Sulawesi)
Sumatra
JAVA SEA
Djakarta (Batavia)
INDONESIA
Lesser Sunda Islands
Equator
AFGHANISTAN
PAKISTAN
INDIA
New Delhi
CALCUTTA
BOMBAY
Madras
BAY OF BENGAL
ARABIAN SEA
SRI LANKA (CEYLON)
Colombo
Andaman Is.
Nicobar Is.
Laccadive Is.
MALDIVES
IRAN (PERSIA)
Tehran
IRAQ
Baghdad
TURKEY
Ankara
Istanbul
SYRIA
Damascus
SAUDI ARABIA
Riyadh
Mecca
RED SEA
Rub' al Khali
YEMEN
Aden
Gulf of Aden
Gulf of Oman
Muscat
Persian Gulf
KUWAIT
QATAR
AFRICA
Djibouti
Mogadishu
Socotra
INDIAN OCEAN
Seychelles (Br.)
BRITISH INDIAN OCEAN TERR.
Chagos Archipelago
Diego Garcia
Madagascar
Tananarive
Comoro Is.
Réunion (Fr.)
MAURITIUS
Rodrigues (To Mauritius)
St. Brandon Group (To Mauritius)
Christmas I. (Australia)
Cocos (Keeling) Is. (Australia)
Tropic of Capricorn
AUSTRALIA
Perth
Fremantle
Port Hedland
Broome
Great Victoria Desert
Amsterdam I.

NEAR and MIDDLE EAST
CONIC PROJECTION
SCALE OF MILES
0 50 100 200 300 400
SCALE OF KILOMETRES
0 100 200 300 400
Capitals of Countries
International Boundaries
Copyright by C.S. Hammond & Co., N.Y.
BLACK SEA
CASPIAN SEA
MEDITERRANEAN SEA
ARABIAN SEA
GULF OF OMAN
RED SEA
TURKEY
SYRIA
IRAQ
IRAN
AFGHANISTAN
PAKISTAN
INDIA
SAUDI ARABIA
JORDAN
EGYPT
SUDAN
ETHIOPIA
YEMEN
OMAN
Rub' al Khali
Tehran
Baghdad
Kabul
Karachi
Riyadh
Mecca
Cairo
Damascus
Beirut
Ankara
Tashkent
Aden

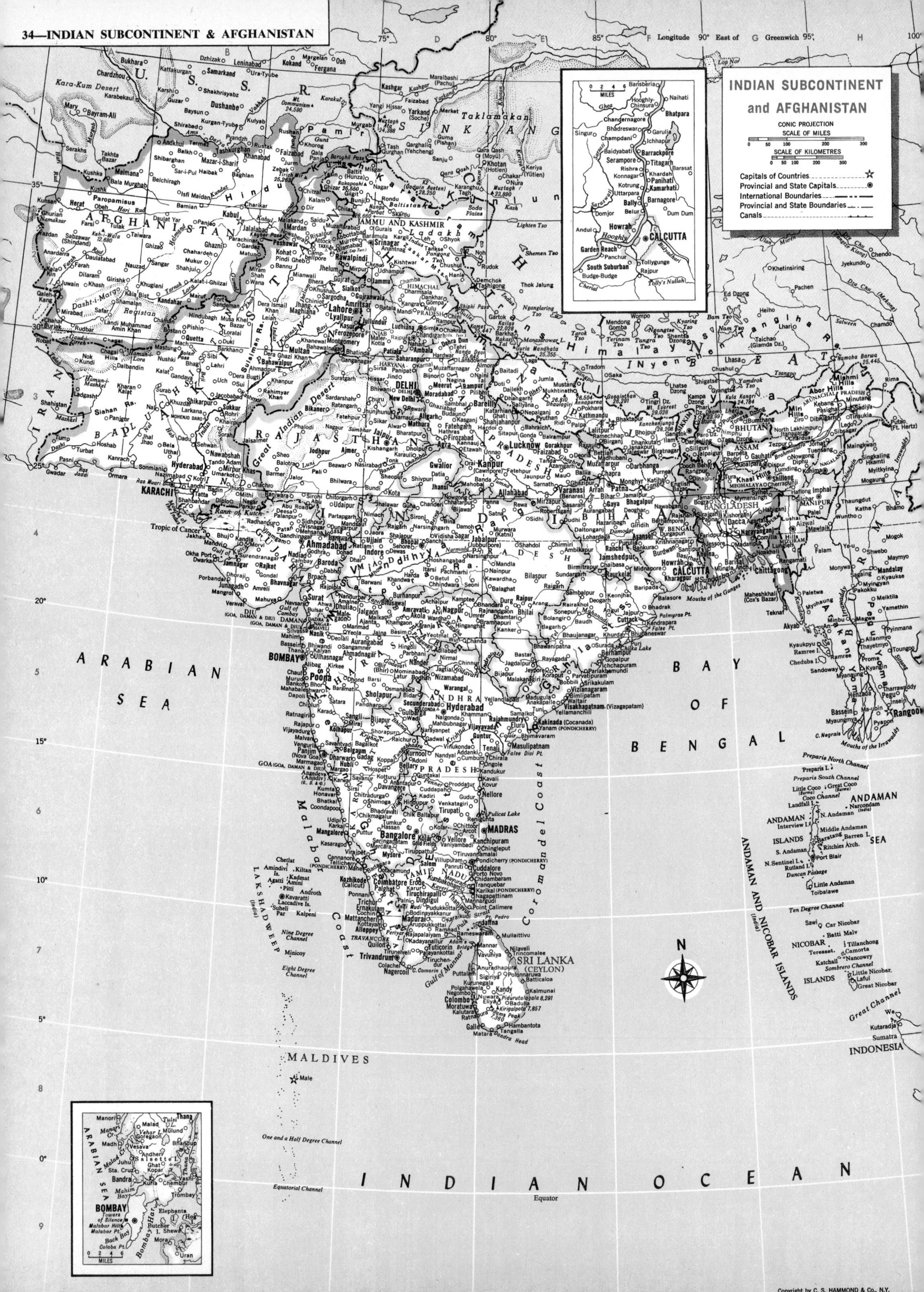
INDIAN SUBCONTINENT
and AFGHANISTAN
CONIC PROJECTION
SCALE OF MILES
0 50 100 200 300
SCALE OF KILOMETRES
0 50 100 200 300
Capitals of Countries
Provincial and State Capitals
International Boundaries
Provincial and State Boundaries
Canals
Longitude 90° East of G Greenwich 95°
MILES
CALCUTTA
Howrah
Hooghly
Garden Reach
South Suburban
Budge-Budge
Tollygunge
Barrackpore
Titagarh
Serampore
Chandernagore
Bhatpara
Naihati
AFGHANISTAN
Kabul
Kandahar
Herat
U. S. S. R.
SINKIANG
Taklamakan
Kara-Kum Desert
JAMMU AND KASHMIR
Ladakh
HIMACHAL PRADESH
PUNJAB
HARYANA
DELHI
New Delhi
RAJASTHAN
Great Indian Desert
UTTAR PRADESH
NEPAL
Kathmandu
BHUTAN
SIKKIM
ASSAM
MEGHALAYA
NAGALAND
MANIPUR
TRIPURA
MIZORAM
ARUNACHAL PRADESH
BANGLADESH
Dacca
BIHAR
W. BENGAL
CALCUTTA
GUJARAT
Ahmadabad
Tropic of Cancer
MADHYA PRADESH
ORISSA
MAHARASHTRA
BOMBAY
Poona
Nagpur
ANDHRA PRADESH
Hyderabad
Secunderabad
KARNATAKA
Bangalore
Mysore
TAMIL NADU
MADRAS
KERALA
Trivandrum
Malabar Coast
Coromandel Coast
LAKSHADWEEP
(India)
SRI LANKA
(CEYLON)
Colombo
Kandy
PAKISTAN
Karachi
Hyderabad
Lahore
Rawalpindi
Peshawar
Quetta
BALUCHISTAN
SIND
IRAN
TIBET
Himalaya
Lhasa
BURMA
Mandalay
Rangoon
Chittagong
ARABIAN SEA
BAY OF BENGAL
ANDAMAN SEA
ANDAMAN AND NICOBAR ISLANDS
(India)
ANDAMAN ISLANDS
Port Blair
NICOBAR ISLANDS
Ten Degree Channel
Nine Degree Channel
Eight Degree Channel
One and a Half Degree Channel
Equatorial Channel
MALDIVES
Male
INDIAN OCEAN
Equator
INDONESIA
Sumatra
Great Channel
Gulf of Mannar
Palk Strait
Mouths of the Ganges
Mouths of the Irrawaddy
BOMBAY
ARABIAN SEA
Thana
Salsette I.
Elephanta
Trombay
Colaba Pt.
Back Bay
Bombay Harbour
Malabar Hill
Towers of Silence
Uran
MILES

BURMA, THAILAND, INDOCHINA and MALAYA
CONIC PROJECTION
SCALE OF MILES
0 50 100 150 200
SCALE OF KILOMETRES
0 50 100 200 300
International Boundaries
Provincial and State Boundaries
Capitals of Countries
Provincial and State Capitals
INDIA
CHINA
BURMA
THAILAND (SIAM)
LAOS
CAMBODIA
NORTH VIETNAM
SOUTH VIETNAM
MALAYA
MALAYSIA
SUMATRA
INDONESIA
BANGLADESH
BAY OF BENGAL
ANDAMAN SEA
GULF OF SIAM
GULF OF TONKIN
SOUTH CHINA SEA
Strait of Malacca
HAINAN
ANDAMAN IS. (India)
NICOBAR IS. (India)
Tropic of Cancer
Longitude East of Greenwich
JOHORE
SINGAPORE
MILES 0 10 20
Copyright by C. S. HAMMOND & Co., N.Y.

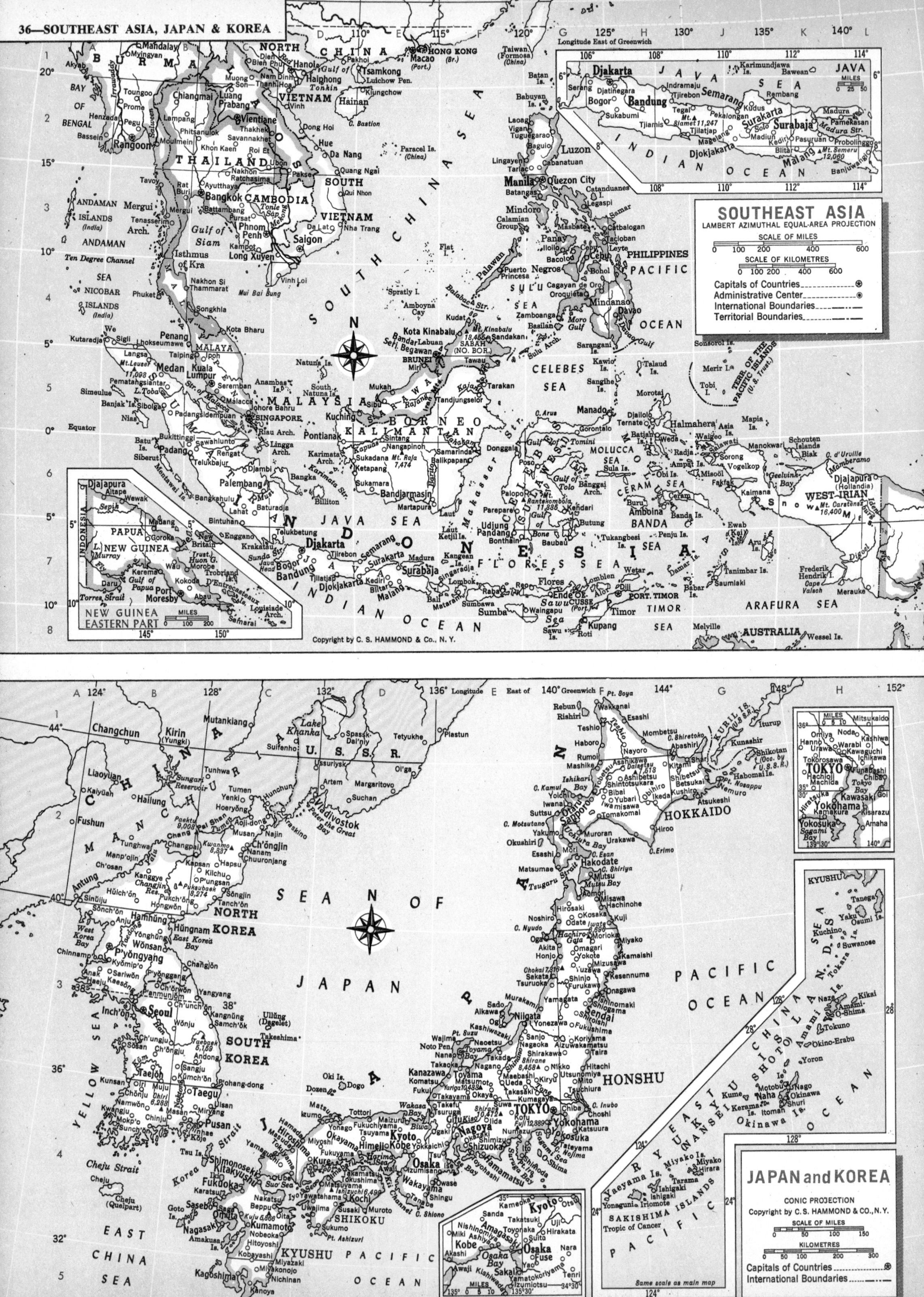
SOUTHEAST ASIA
LAMBERT AZIMUTHAL EQUAL-AREA PROJECTION
SCALE OF MILES
0 100 200 400 600
SCALE OF KILOMETRES
0 100 200 400 600
Capitals of Countries
Administrative Center
International Boundaries
Territorial Boundaries
Copyright by C. S. HAMMOND & Co., N. Y.
JAVA
NEW GUINEA EASTERN PART
BURMA
THAILAND
LAOS
CAMBODIA
NORTH VIETNAM
SOUTH VIETNAM
CHINA
MALAYA
MALAYSIA
SINGAPORE
BORNEO
KALIMANTAN
SARAWAK
SABAH (NO. BOR.)
BRUNEI
INDONESIA
SUMATRA
CELEBES
PHILIPPINES
WEST IRIAN
PORT. TIMOR
AUSTRALIA
SOUTH CHINA SEA
JAVA SEA
FLORES SEA
CELEBES SEA
SULU SEA
BANDA SEA
TIMOR SEA
ARAFURA SEA
ANDAMAN SEA
BAY OF BENGAL
INDIAN OCEAN
PACIFIC OCEAN
JAPAN and KOREA
CONIC PROJECTION
Copyright by C.S. HAMMOND & CO., N.Y.
SCALE OF MILES
0 50 100 150
KILOMETRES
0 50 100 200 300
Capitals of Countries
International Boundaries
Same scale as main map
TOKYO
KYUSHU
SAKISHIMA ISLANDS
RYUKYU (NANSEI SHOTO) ISLANDS
CHINA
MANCHURIA
U.S.S.R.
NORTH KOREA
SOUTH KOREA
JAPAN
HOKKAIDO
HONSHU
SHIKOKU
KYUSHU
SEA OF JAPAN
YELLOW SEA
EAST CHINA SEA
PACIFIC OCEAN

CHINA and MONGOLIA
CONIC PROJECTION
SCALE OF MILES
0 100 200 300 400 500
SCALE OF KILOMETRES
0 100 200 300 400 500
Capitals of Countries
International Boundaries
Provincial Capitals
Provincial Boundaries
Canals
Walls
© Copyright HAMMOND INCORPORATED, Maplewood, N.J.
Longitude East of Greenwich
SEA OF JAPAN
PACIFIC OCEAN
EAST CHINA SEA
YELLOW SEA
SOUTH CHINA SEA
BAY OF BENGAL
SEA OF OKHOTSK
INNER MONGOLIAN AUTONOMOUS REGION
SINKIANG-UIGHUR AUTONOMOUS REGION
TIBETAN AUTONOMOUS REGION
KWANGSI CHUANG AUTONOMOUS REGION
*Wuhan municipality consists of Hankow, Hanyang and Wuchang

AFRICA
LAMBERT AZIMUTHAL EQUAL-AREA PROJECTION
SCALE OF MILES
0 100 200 400 600
SCALE OF KILOMETRES
0 100 200 400 600
Capitals of Countries
Other Capitals
International Boundaries
Internal Boundaries
Canals
Wells
Copyright by C. S. Hammond & Co., N.Y.

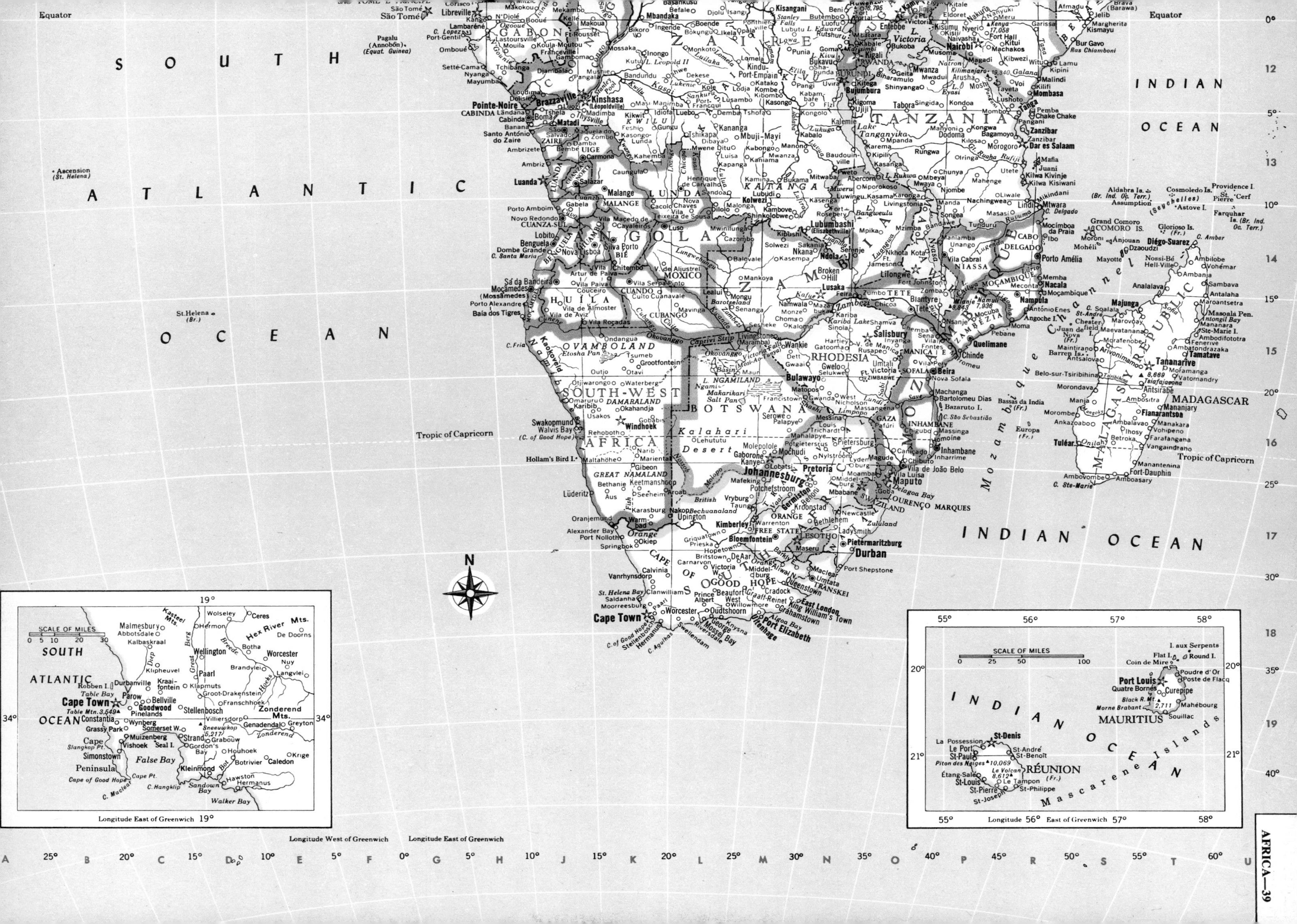

SOUTH ATLANTIC OCEAN
INDIAN OCEAN
Equator
Tropic of Capricorn
Mozambique Channel
MALAGASY REPUBLIC
MADAGASCAR
Tananarive
TANZANIA
Dar es Salaam
Zanzibar
Mombasa
Nairobi
ZAIRE
Kinshasa
Brazzaville
GABON
Libreville
ANGOLA
Luanda
ZAMBIA
Lusaka
RHODESIA
Salisbury
Bulawayo
BOTSWANA
Kalahari Desert
SOUTH-WEST AFRICA
Windhoek
Maputo
Beira
SWAZILAND
LESOTHO
ORANGE FREE STATE
CAPE OF GOOD HOPE
Johannesburg
Pretoria
Bloemfontein
Kimberley
Durban
Pietermaritzburg
East London
Port Elizabeth
Cape Town
Ascension (St. Helena)
St. Helena (Br.)
Mascarene Islands
MAURITIUS
Port Louis
RÉUNION
St-Denis
SCALE OF MILES
Longitude East of Greenwich
Longitude West of Greenwich
False Bay
Table Bay
Cape of Good Hope
Stellenbosch
Paarl
Worcester
Hex River Mts.
Zonderend Mts.

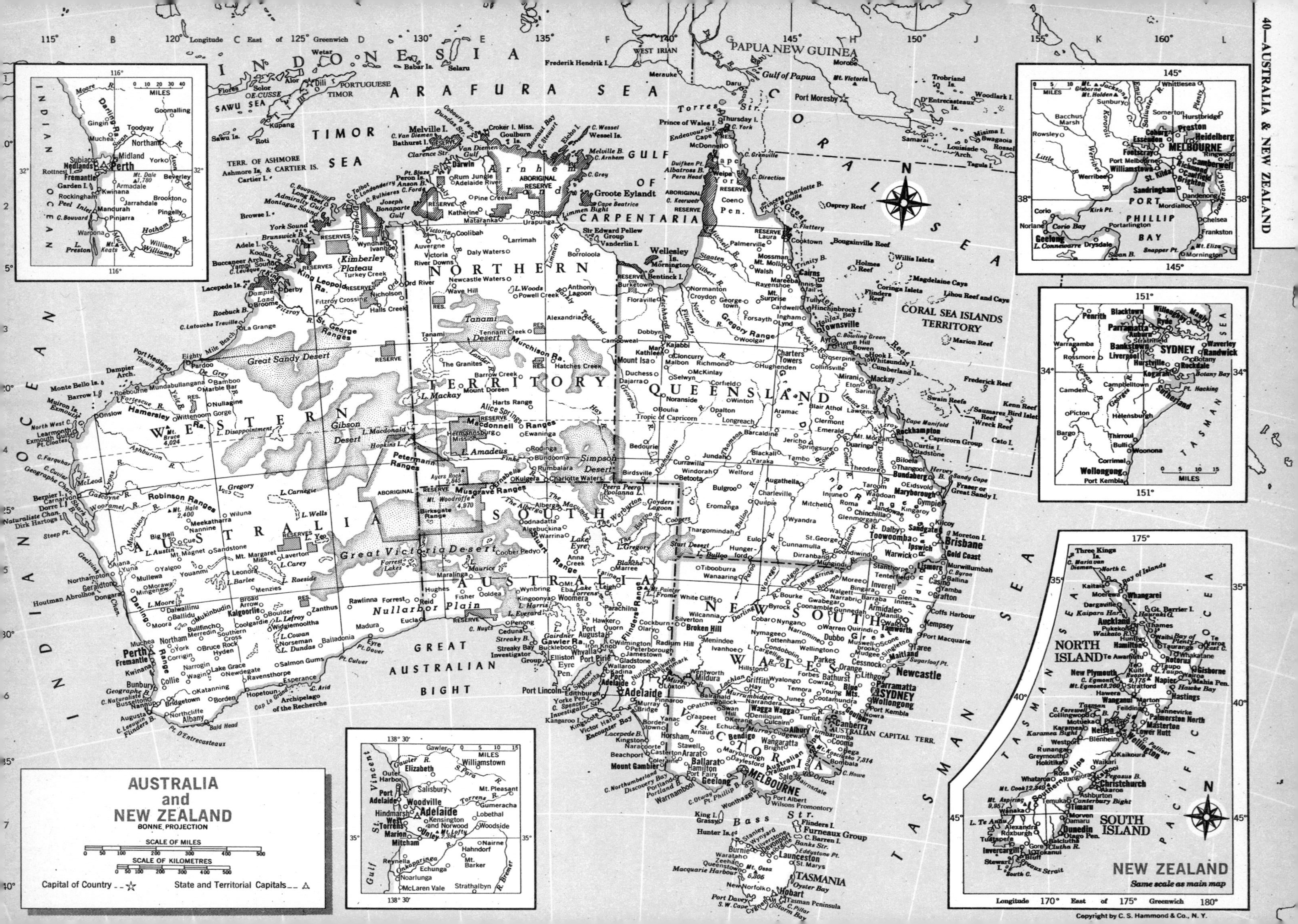
AUSTRALIA
and
NEW ZEALAND
BONNE PROJECTION
SCALE OF MILES
SCALE OF KILOMETRES
Capital of Country
State and Territorial Capitals
NEW ZEALAND
Same scale as main map
NORTH ISLAND
SOUTH ISLAND
INDONESIA
PAPUA NEW GUINEA
ARAFURA SEA
TIMOR SEA
CORAL SEA
TASMAN SEA
INDIAN OCEAN
GREAT AUSTRALIAN BIGHT
CORAL SEA ISLANDS TERRITORY
GULF OF CARPENTARIA
WESTERN AUSTRALIA
NORTHERN TERRITORY
SOUTH AUSTRALIA
QUEENSLAND
NEW SOUTH WALES
VICTORIA
TASMANIA
AUSTRALIAN CAPITAL TERR.
PORT PHILLIP BAY
Copyright by C. S. Hammond & Co., N. Y.

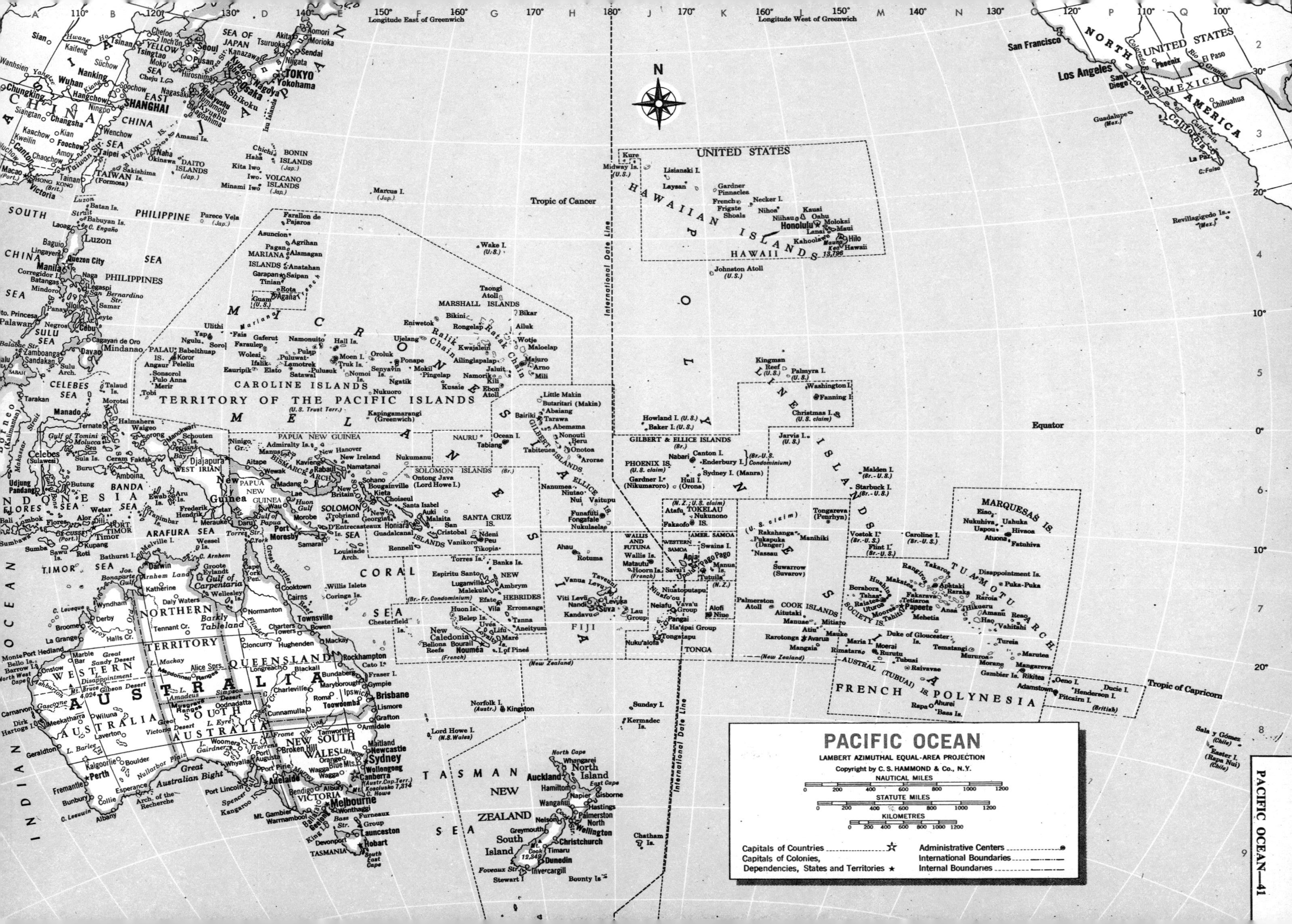
PACIFIC OCEAN
LAMBERT AZIMUTHAL EQUAL-AREA PROJECTION
Copyright by C. S. HAMMOND & Co., N.Y.
NAUTICAL MILES
STATUTE MILES
KILOMETRES
Capitals of Countries
Capitals of Colonies, Dependencies, States and Territories
Administrative Centers
International Boundaries
Internal Boundaries
Longitude East of Greenwich
Longitude West of Greenwich
Equator
Tropic of Cancer
Tropic of Capricorn
International Date Line
NORTH AMERICA
UNITED STATES
MEXICO
HAWAIIAN ISLANDS
HAWAII
LINE ISLANDS
POLYNESIA
MICRONESIA
MELANESIA
TERRITORY OF THE PACIFIC ISLANDS
CAROLINE ISLANDS
MARSHALL ISLANDS
MARIANA ISLANDS
GILBERT & ELLICE ISLANDS
PHOENIX IS.
SOLOMON ISLANDS
NEW HEBRIDES
FIJI
TONGA
COOK ISLANDS
SOCIETY IS.
MARQUESAS IS.
TUAMOTU ARCH.
FRENCH POLYNESIA
NEW ZEALAND
TASMAN SEA
CORAL SEA
ARAFURA SEA
AUSTRALIA
PAPUA NEW GUINEA
PHILIPPINES
PHILIPPINE SEA
SOUTH CHINA SEA
CHINA
JAPAN
INDIAN OCEAN

CARIBBEAN SEA
ATLANTIC OCEAN
PACIFIC
Longitude 55° West of Greenwich
NETH. ANTILLES
WEST INDIES
BARBADOS
TRINIDAD AND TOBAGO
GRENADA
VENEZUELA
COLOMBIA
ECUADOR
GUYANA
SURINAM
FRENCH GUIANA
AMAPÁ
RORAIMA
AMAZONAS
PARÁ
MARANHÃO
PIAUÍ
CEARÁ
RIO GRANDE DO NORTE
PARAÍBA
PERNAMBUCO
ALAGOAS
SERGIPE
BAHIA
GOIÁS
DISTRITO FEDERAL
MATO GROSSO
MINAS GERAIS
RONDÔNIA (GUAPORÉ)
ACRE
BOLIVIA
Equator
Caracas
Bogotá
Quito
Lima
La Paz
Sucre
Manaus
Belém
Brasília
Recife
Salvador (Bahia)
Fortaleza (Ceará)
Georgetown
Paramaribo
Cayenne
Panamá
GALÁPAGOS ISLANDS
(Archipiélago de Colón)
(To Ecuador)

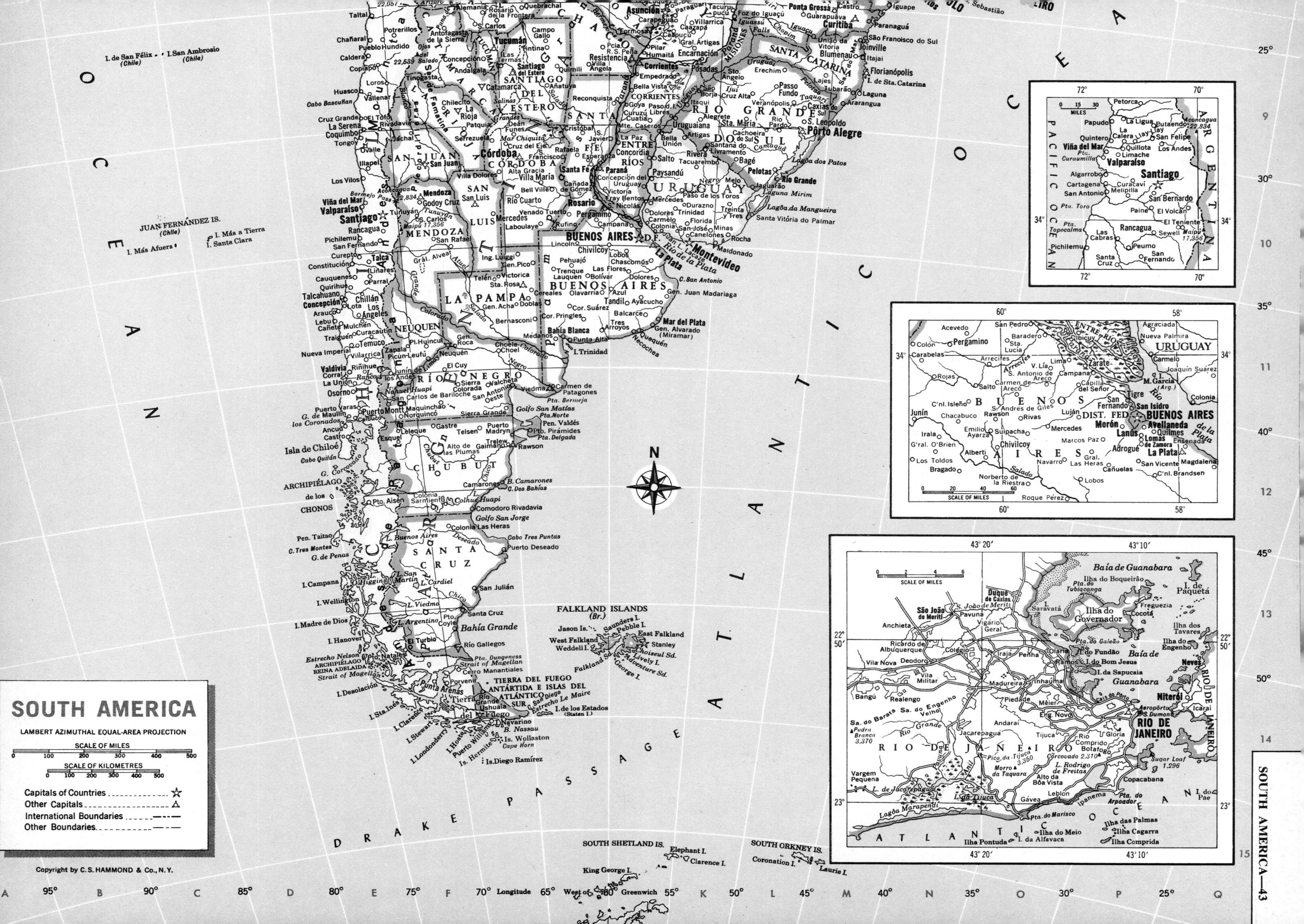
SOUTH AMERICA
LAMBERT AZIMUTHAL EQUAL-AREA PROJECTION
SCALE OF MILES
SCALE OF KILOMETRES
Capitals of Countries
Other Capitals
International Boundaries
Other Boundaries
Copyright by C.S. HAMMOND & Co., N.Y.
OCEAN
ATLANTIC OCEAN
DRAKE PASSAGE
I. de San Félix (Chile)
I. San Ambrosio (Chile)
JUAN FERNÁNDEZ IS. (Chile)
I. Más a Tierra
I. Santa Clara
I. Más Afuera
FALKLAND ISLANDS (Br.)
West Falkland
East Falkland
Stanley
TIERRA DEL FUEGO
ANTÁRTIDA E ISLAS DEL ATLÁNTICO SUR
Cape Horn
SOUTH SHETLAND IS.
SOUTH ORKNEY IS.
ARCHIPIÉLAGO de los CHONOS
Isla de Chiloé
Santiago
Valparaíso
Viña del Mar
Mendoza
Córdoba
Rosario
BUENOS AIRES
Montevideo
La Plata
Mar del Plata
Bahía Blanca
Asunción
Curitiba
Pôrto Alegre
URUGUAY
CHUBUT
SANTA CRUZ
RIO NEGRO
NEUQUEN
LA PAMPA
RIO GRANDE DO SUL
SANTA CATARINA
Longitude West of Greenwich
PACIFIC OCEAN
ARGENTINA
DIST. FED.
RIO DE JANEIRO
Baía de Guanabara
Niterói
Copacabana
Sugar Loaf 1,296
SCALE OF MILES

NORTH AMERICA
LAMBERT AZIMUTHAL EQUAL-AREA PROJECTION
SCALE OF MILES
0 100 200 400 600 800
SCALE OF KILOMETRES
0 200 400 600 800
Capitals of Countries
International Boundaries
Other Boundaries
Canals
© C.S. HAMMOND & Co., N.Y.
North Pole
ARCTIC OCEAN
Longitude West of Greenwich
GREENLAND SEA
BEAUFORT SEA
QUEEN ELIZABETH ISLANDS
GREENLAND (Den.)
ICELAND
UNITED KINGDOM
Denmark Str.
Davis Strait
Baffin Bay
Baffin I.
Hudson Strait
LABRADOR SEA
Hudson Bay
James Bay
Bering Strait
BERING SEA
ALASKA
UNITED STATES
YUKON TERR.
NORTHWEST TERRITORIES
BRITISH COLUMBIA
ALBERTA
SASKATCHEWAN
MANITOBA
ONTARIO
QUEBEC
NEWFOUNDLAND
CANADA
Great Bear Lake
Great Slave L.
Lake Superior
Gulf of St. Lawrence
PACIFIC OCEAN
ATLANTIC OCEAN
UNITED STATES
MONT.
N. DAK.
S. DAK.
MINN.
WIS.
MICH.
IDAHO
WYO.
NEBR.
IOWA
ILL.
IND.
OHIO
PA.
N.Y.
OREG.
WASH.
CALIF.
NEV.
UTAH
COLO.
KANS.
MO.
KY.
TENN.
ARIZ.
N. MEX.
OKLA.
ARK.
TEXAS
LA.
MISS.
ALA.
GA.
FLA.
S.C.
N.C.
VA.
W. VA.
MAINE
Chicago
New York
Philadelphia
Washington
Detroit
Los Angeles
San Francisco
New Orleans
Montréal
Québec
Toronto
Winnipeg
Vancouver
Tropic of Cancer
Gulf of Mexico
BAHAMAS
CUBA
Havana
JAMAICA
HAITI
DOMINICAN REP.
Hispaniola
WEST INDIES
GREATER ANTILLES
LESSER ANTILLES
CARIBBEAN SEA
MEXICO
Mexico City
LOWER CALIFORNIA
Gulf of California
YUCATAN PENINSULA
Bay of Campeche
BELIZE
GUATEMALA
HONDURAS
EL SALVADOR
NICARAGUA
COSTA RICA
PANAMA
Clipperton (Fr.)
Cocos I. (C.R.)
Malpelo I. (Col.)
GALÁPAGOS IS. (Ecuador)
Equator
VENEZUELA
COLOMBIA
Bogotá
ECUADOR
Quito
PERU
BRAZIL
SOUTH AMERICA
Amazon
Orinoco
Bermuda (Br.)

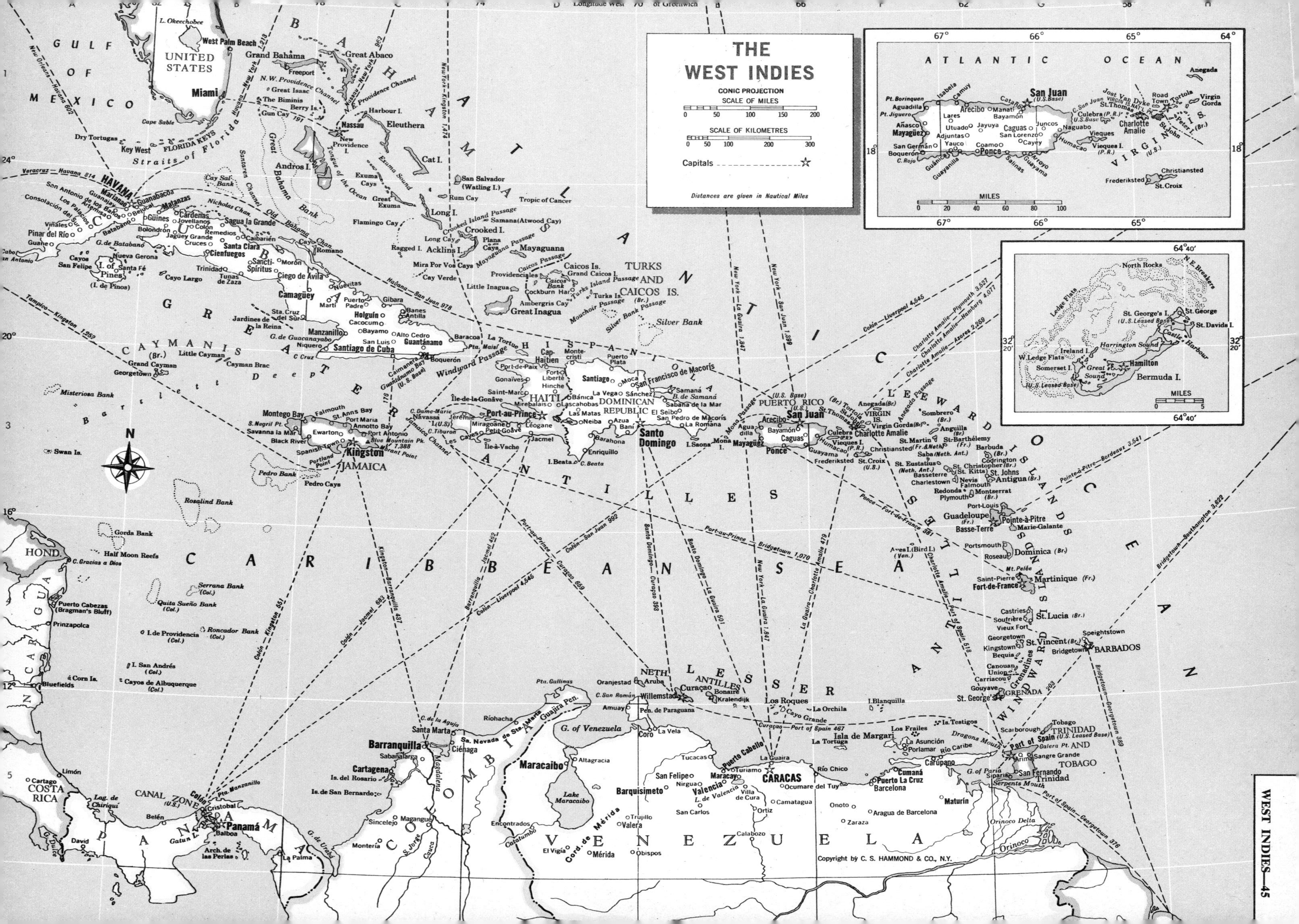
THE WEST INDIES
CONIC PROJECTION
SCALE OF MILES
SCALE OF KILOMETRES
Capitals
Distances are given in Nautical Miles
Copyright by C. S. HAMMOND & CO., N.Y.
Longitude West 70 of Greenwich
ATLANTIC OCEAN
GULF OF MEXICO
CARIBBEAN SEA
GREATER ANTILLES
LESSER ANTILLES
LEEWARD ISLANDS
WINDWARD ISLANDS
BAHAMA IS.
TURKS AND CAICOS IS.
HISPANIOLA
CAYMAN IS.
UNITED STATES
CUBA
HAITI
DOMINICAN REPUBLIC
PUERTO RICO
JAMAICA
VENEZUELA
COLOMBIA
PANAMA
COSTA RICA
HOND.
NICARAGUA
CANAL ZONE (U.S.)
HAVANA
Kingston
Port-au-Prince
Santo Domingo
San Juan
CARACAS
Bridgetown
Port of Spain
Fort-de-France
Basse-Terre
Charlotte Amalie
Nassau
Willemstad
Panamá
Miami
Key West
BARBADOS
TRINIDAD
TOBAGO
Tropic of Cancer
New York—San Juan 1,399
New York—La Guaira 1,847
New York—Kingston 1,474
Santo Domingo—Curaçao 393
Santo Domingo—La Guaira 501
Kingston—Barranquilla 437
Charlotte Amalie—Port of Spain 518
Bridgetown—Georgetown 389
Port of Spain—Georgetown 376
New Orleans—Havana 602
Veracruz—Havana 814
Tampico—Kingston 1,259
Habana—San Juan 978
Port-au-Prince—Bridgetown 1,070
Ponce—Fort-de-France 381
Bridgetown—Southampton 3,622
Pointe-à-Pitre—Bordeaux 3,541
Bermuda I.
Hamilton
St. George
MILES

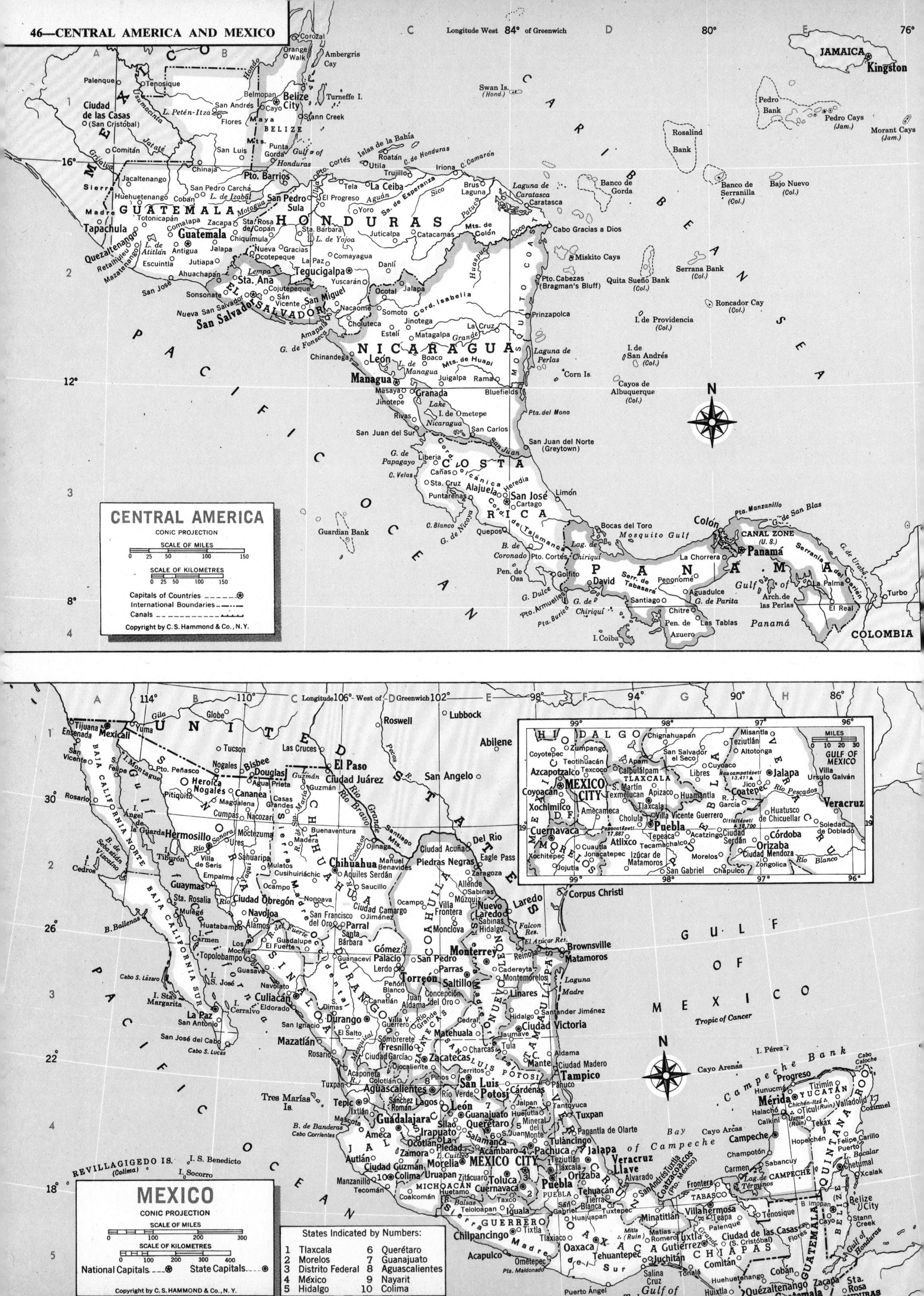
CENTRAL AMERICA
CONIC PROJECTION
SCALE OF MILES
0 25 50 100 150
SCALE OF KILOMETRES
0 25 50 100 150
Capitals of Countries
International Boundaries
Canals
Copyright by C.S. Hammond & Co., N.Y.
Longitude West 84° of Greenwich
80°
76°
16°
12°
8°
CARIBBEAN SEA
PACIFIC OCEAN
MEXICO
GUATEMALA
HONDURAS
EL SALVADOR
NICARAGUA
COSTA RICA
PANAMA
BELIZE
JAMAICA
Kingston
COLOMBIA
CANAL ZONE (U.S.)
Guatemala
Tegucigalpa
San Salvador
Managua
San José
Panamá
Belize City
Belmopan
Palenque
Tenosique
Ciudad de las Casas (San Cristóbal)
Comitán
Tapachula
Quezaltenango
Flores
San Andrés
Puerto Barrios
San Pedro Sula
La Ceiba
Tela
Trujillo
Juticalpa
Catacamas
Choluteca
León
Granada
Masaya
Jinotepe
Rivas
Bluefields
San Juan del Norte (Greytown)
San Juan del Sur
Liberia
Puntarenas
Alajuela
Heredia
Cartago
Limón
Bocas del Toro
Colón
David
Santiago
Chitré
Las Tablas
La Palma
Turbo
Swan Is. (Hond.)
Pedro Bank
Pedro Cays (Jam.)
Morant Cays (Jam.)
Rosalind Bank
Banco de Gorda
Banco de Serranilla (Col.)
Bajo Nuevo (Col.)
Cabo Gracias a Dios
Miskito Cays
Quita Sueño Bank (Col.)
Serrana Bank (Col.)
Roncador Cay (Col.)
I. de Providencia (Col.)
I. de San Andrés (Col.)
Cayos de Albuquerque (Col.)
Corn Is.
Gulf of Honduras
G. de Fonseca
Mosquito Gulf
Gulf of Panamá
G. de Chiriquí
Guardian Bank
I. Coiba
MEXICO
CONIC PROJECTION
SCALE OF MILES
0 100 200 300
SCALE OF KILOMETRES
0 100 200 300 400
National Capitals
State Capitals
Copyright by C.S. HAMMOND & Co., N.Y.
States Indicated by Numbers:
1 Tlaxcala
2 Morelos
3 Distrito Federal
4 México
5 Hidalgo
6 Querétaro
7 Guanajuato
8 Aguascalientes
9 Nayarit
10 Colima
Longitude 106° West of Greenwich 102°
114°
110°
98°
94°
90°
86°
30°
26°
22°
18°
UNITED STATES
GULF OF MEXICO
PACIFIC OCEAN
Tropic of Cancer
Bay of Campeche
Campeche Bank
MEXICO CITY
BAJA CALIFORNIA NORTE
BAJA CALIFORNIA SUR
SONORA
CHIHUAHUA
COAHUILA
NUEVO LEÓN
TAMAULIPAS
SINALOA
DURANGO
ZACATECAS
SAN LUIS POTOSÍ
JALISCO
MICHOACÁN
GUERRERO
OAXACA
VERACRUZ
PUEBLA
CHIAPAS
TABASCO
CAMPECHE
YUCATÁN
QUINTANA ROO
Tijuana
Mexicali
Ensenada
Hermosillo
Chihuahua
Ciudad Juárez
El Paso
Monterrey
Saltillo
Torreón
Durango
Culiacán
Mazatlán
La Paz
Zacatecas
Aguascalientes
San Luis Potosí
Guadalajara
León
Guanajuato
Querétaro
Morelia
Toluca
Cuernavaca
Puebla
Jalapa
Veracruz Llave
Oaxaca
Tuxtla Gutiérrez
Villahermosa
Campeche
Mérida
Chetumal
Tampico
Ciudad Victoria
Matamoros
Brownsville
Nuevo Laredo
Laredo
Acapulco
Chilpancingo
Tepic
Colima
REVILLAGIGEDO IS. (Colima)
Tres Marías Is.
HIDALGO
MEXICO CITY
TLAXCALA
MORELOS
PUEBLA
VERACRUZ
Cuernavaca
Puebla
Jalapa
Veracruz
Orizaba
Córdoba
GULF OF MEXICO
MILES 0 10 20 30

CANADA
CONIC PROJECTION
SCALE OF MILES
0 50 100 200 300
SCALE OF KILOMETRES
0 50 100 200 300 400 500
Capitals of Countries
Provincial Capitals
International Boundaries
Provincial Boundaries
Canals
Copyright by C.S. HAMMOND & Co., N.Y.
QUEEN ELIZABETH ISLANDS
Scale of Miles
ARCTIC
OCEAN
SVERDRUP ISLANDS
PARRY ISLANDS
ATLANTIC OCEAN
PACIFIC OCEAN
HUDSON BAY
BAFFIN BAY
DAVIS STRAIT
BEAUFORT SEA
GREENLAND
UNITED STATES
ALASKA
YUKON TERRITORY
BRITISH COLUMBIA
ALBERTA
SASKATCHEWAN
MANITOBA
ONTARIO
QUEBEC
NEW BRUNSWICK
NOVA SCOTIA
NEWFOUNDLAND
PRINCE EDWARD I.
NORTHWEST TERRITORIES
DISTRICT OF MACKENZIE
DISTRICT OF KEEWATIN
DISTRICT OF FRANKLIN
ROCKY MTS.
Ungava Peninsula
Hudson Str.
James Bay
Great Bear Lake
Great Slave Lake
Victoria Island
Banks Island
Baffin Island
Southampton I.
Gulf of St. Lawrence
Ottawa
Toronto
Montréal
Québec
Halifax
Winnipeg
Regina
Edmonton
Calgary
Vancouver
Victoria
Whitehorse
Yellowknife
St. John's
Boston
New York
Detroit
Seattle
Spokane
Cheyenne
Helena
MONTANA
WYOMING

POPULATION DISTRIBUTION

DENSITY PER SQ. MILE

- Over 260
- 130-260
- 25-130
- 3-25
- Under 3

- • Cities with over 1,000,000 inhabitants (including suburbs)
- ○ Cities with over 500,000 inhabitants (including suburbs)

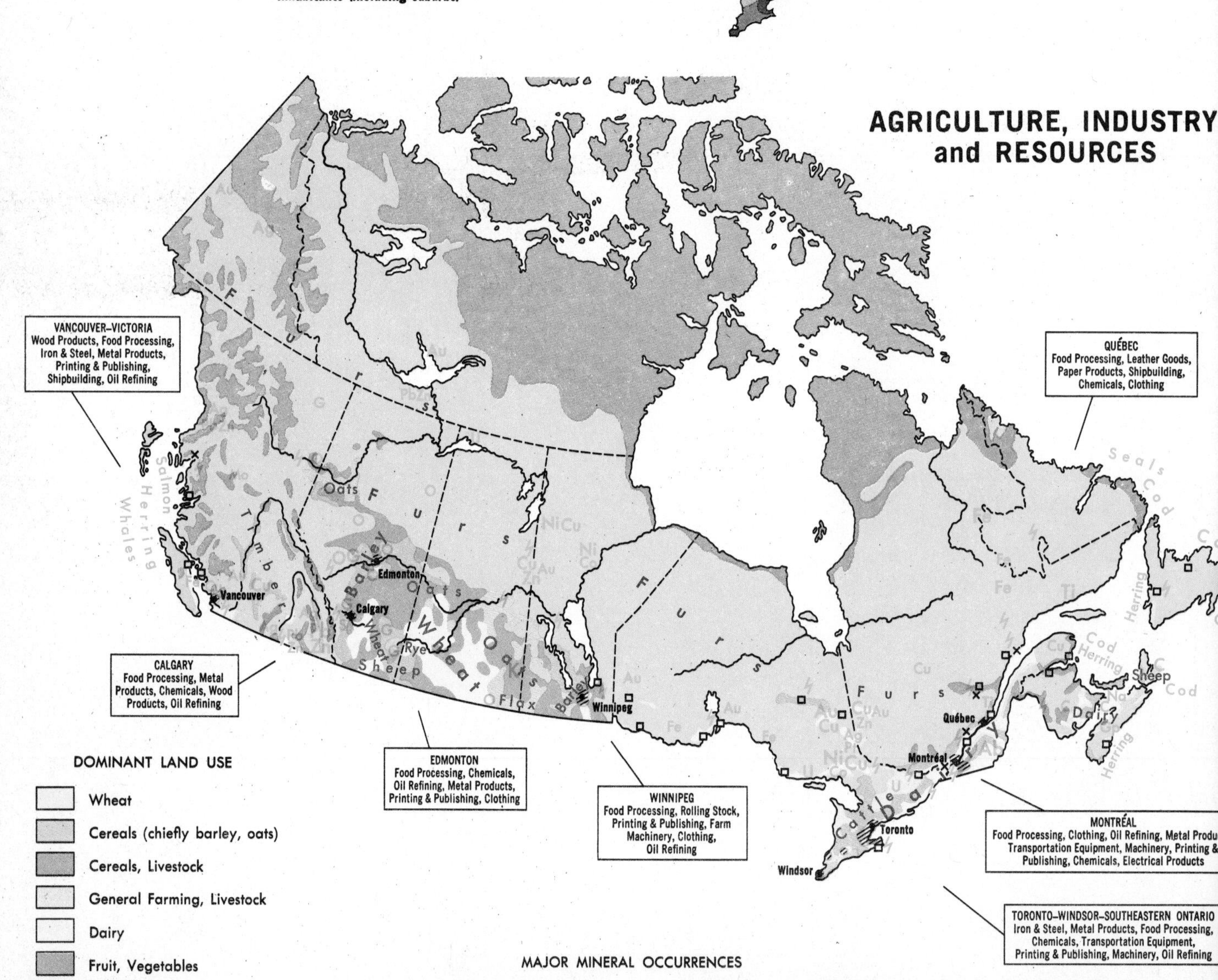

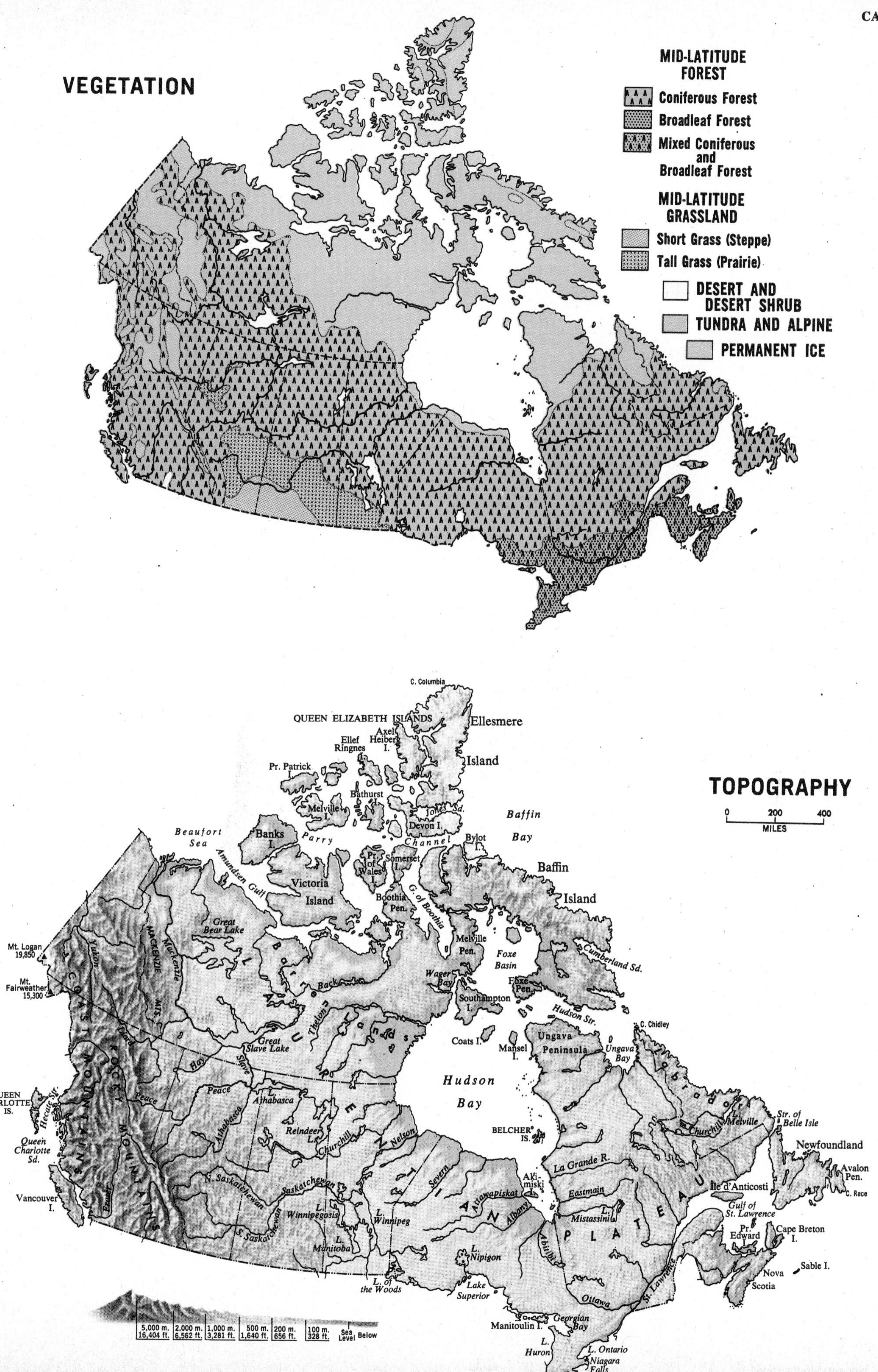
VEGETATION
MID-LATITUDE FOREST
Coniferous Forest
Broadleaf Forest
Mixed Coniferous and Broadleaf Forest
MID-LATITUDE GRASSLAND
Short Grass (Steppe)
Tall Grass (Prairie)
DESERT AND DESERT SHRUB
TUNDRA AND ALPINE
PERMANENT ICE
TOPOGRAPHY
0 200 400
MILES
C. Columbia
QUEEN ELIZABETH ISLANDS
Ellesmere Island
Axel Heiberg I.
Ellef Ringnes I.
Pr. Patrick I.
Bathurst I.
Melville I.
Jones Sd.
Devon I.
Baffin Bay
Bylot I.
Beaufort Sea
Banks I.
Parry Channel
Amundsen Gulf
Pr. of Wales I.
Somerset I.
Victoria Island
Boothia Pen.
G. of Boothia
Baffin Island
Great Bear Lake
Mt. Logan 19,850
Mt. Fairweather 15,300
Yukon
MACKENZIE MTS.
Mackenzie
Melville Pen.
Foxe Basin
Cumberland Sd.
Back
Wager Bay
Foxe Pen.
Southampton I.
Hudson Str.
Thelon
C. Chidley
Great Slave Lake
Coats I.
Mansel I.
Ungava Peninsula
Ungava Bay
Liard
Hay
Slave
LAURENTIAN UPLANDS
Hudson Bay
QUEEN CHARLOTTE IS.
Hecate Str.
Peace
Athabasca
Labrador
COAST MOUNTAINS
ROCKY MOUNTAINS
Reindeer L.
Churchill
BELCHER IS.
Melville
Str. of Belle Isle
Queen Charlotte Sd.
Nelson
Newfoundland
Akimiski I.
La Grande R.
Avalon Pen.
Vancouver I.
Fraser
N. Saskatchewan
Saskatchewan
Severn
Attawapiskat
Eastmain
Île d'Anticosti
C. Race
L. Winnipegosis
L. Winnipeg
Albany
L. Mistassini
Gulf of St. Lawrence
S. Saskatchewan
PLATEAU
Pr. Edward I.
Cape Breton I.
L. Manitoba
Abitibi
L. Nipigon
Sable I.
Nova Scotia
L. of the Woods
Lake Superior
Ottawa
St. Lawrence
Manitoulin I.
Georgian Bay
L. Huron
L. Ontario
Niagara Falls
5,000 m. 16,404 ft.
2,000 m. 6,562 ft.
1,000 m. 3,281 ft.
500 m. 1,640 ft.
200 m. 656 ft.
100 m. 328 ft.
Sea Level
Below

NEWFOUNDLAND
INCLUDING LABRADOR
SCALE
0 25 50 100 150 MI.
0 25 50 100 150 KM.
Capitals of Provinces
Provincial Boundaries
Provincial Boundary according to Imperial Privy Council decision, 1927
LABRADOR SEA
ATLANTIC OCEAN
Ungava Bay
QUÉBEC
LABRADOR
SAGUENAY PROVINCIAL PARK
Gulf of St. Lawrence
Honguedo Passage
Jacques Cartier (Mingan) Passage
Île d'Anticosti
St. Lawrence River
Gaspé Pen.
NEW BRUNSWICK
PRINCE EDWARD ISLAND
MAGDALEN ISLANDS (Quebec)
Cabot Strait
Str. of Belle Isle
Newfoundland
ST PIERRE & MIQUELON (Fr.)
Schefferville (Knob Lake)
Wabush
Labrador City
Churchill Falls
Goose Bay
Happy Valley
North West River
Smallwood Reservoir
Lake Melville
MEALY MTS.
Hamilton Inlet
Nain
Hopedale
Makkovik
Cartwright
Sept-Îles
Havre-St-Pierre
Natashquan
Gaspé
Campbellton
Bathurst
Chatham
Newcastle
Corner Brook
Stephenville
Deer Lake
Channel-Port aux Basques
Grand Falls
Gander
Lewisporte
Botwood
Windsor
Bishop's Falls
Springdale
Baie Verte
St. Anthony
Twillingate
Bonavista
Carbonear
Harbour Grace
Wabana
ST. JOHN'S
Placentia
Avalon Peninsula
Trinity Bay
Conception Bay
Placentia Bay
Bonavista Bay
Notre Dame Bay
White Bay
Fortune Bay
St. Mary's Bay
LONG RANGE MTS.
ANNIEOPSQUOTCH MTS.
GROS MORNE NAT'L PARK
TERRA NOVA NAT'L PARK
Grand Bank
St-Pierre
Miquelon
Longitude West of Greenwich
60° 55° 50°

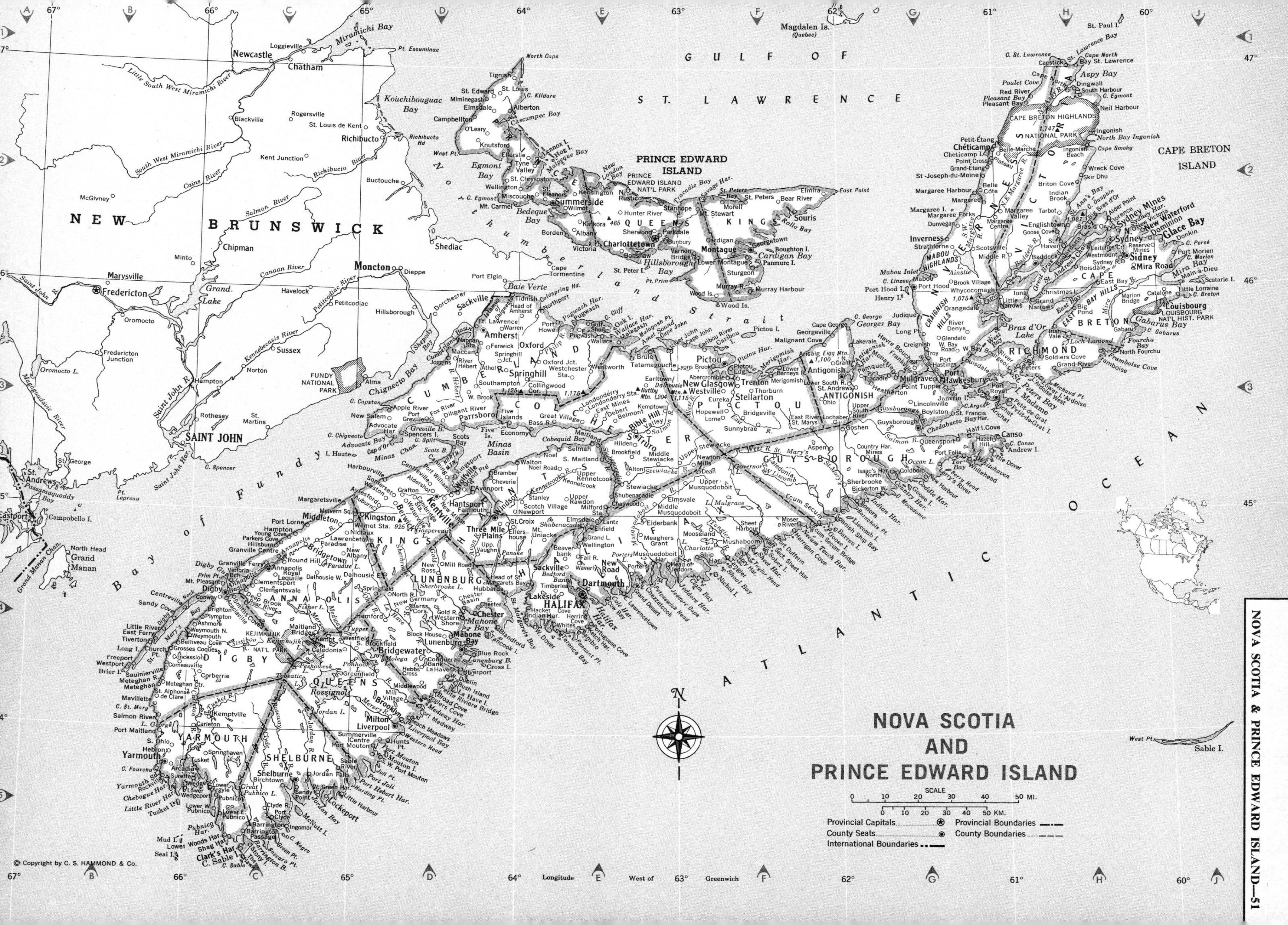
NOVA SCOTIA
AND
PRINCE EDWARD ISLAND
SCALE
0 10 20 30 40 50 MI.
0 10 20 30 40 50 KM.
Provincial Capitals
County Seats
International Boundaries
Provincial Boundaries
County Boundaries
GULF OF ST. LAWRENCE
ATLANTIC OCEAN
Bay of Fundy
Northumberland Strait
CAPE BRETON ISLAND
PRINCE EDWARD ISLAND
NEW BRUNSWICK
Magdalen Is. (Quebec)
Sable I.
Halifax
Dartmouth
Charlottetown
Summerside
Fredericton
Saint John
Moncton
Sydney
Truro
Yarmouth
Amherst
New Glasgow
Kentville
Lunenburg
Longitude West of Greenwich
© Copyright by C. S. HAMMOND & Co.

NEW BRUNSWICK
SCALE
0 5 10 20 30 40 MI.
0 5 10 20 30 40 KM.
Provincial Capitals
County Seats
International Boundaries
Provincial Boundaries
County Boundaries
GULF OF ST. LAWRENCE
CHALEUR BAY
PRINCE EDWARD ISLAND
Northumberland Strait
BAY OF FUNDY
Minas Basin
Minas Channel
NOVA SCOTIA
QUÉBEC
MAINE
RESTIGOUCHE
GLOUCESTER
NORTHUMBERLAND
VICTORIA
MADAWASKA
KENT
WESTMORLAND
ALBERT
YORK
CARLETON
SUNBURY
QUEENS
KINGS
ST. JOHN
CHARLOTTE
Fredericton
Saint John
Moncton
Campbellton
Dalhousie
Bathurst
Chatham
Newcastle
Edmundston
Woodstock
Charlottetown
Summerside
Halifax
Dartmouth
Truro
Amherst
Bangor
© Copyright by C. S. HAMMOND & Co.

QUEBEC
SOUTHERN PART
SCALE
0 5 10 20 30 40 MI.
0 5 10 20 30 40 KM.
National Capital
Provincial Capital
County Seats
International Boundaries
Provincial & State Boundaries
County Boundaries
GASPÉ PENINSULA
COUNTIES indicated by numbers:
1 Iberville D4
2 Napierville D4
3 Rouville E4
4 St-Hyacinthe D4
5 Île-de-Montréal D4
6 Deux-Montagnes D4
7 Soulanges C4
8 Beauharnois C4
9 Hull B4
10 Île-Jésus D4
11 Richelieu D4
12 Vaudreuil C4
Internal divisions represent Municipal Counties
Copyright by C.S. HAMMOND & Co., N.Y.
NEW BRUNSWICK
MAINE
NEW YORK
VERMONT
N.H.
Longitude 72° West of Greenwich

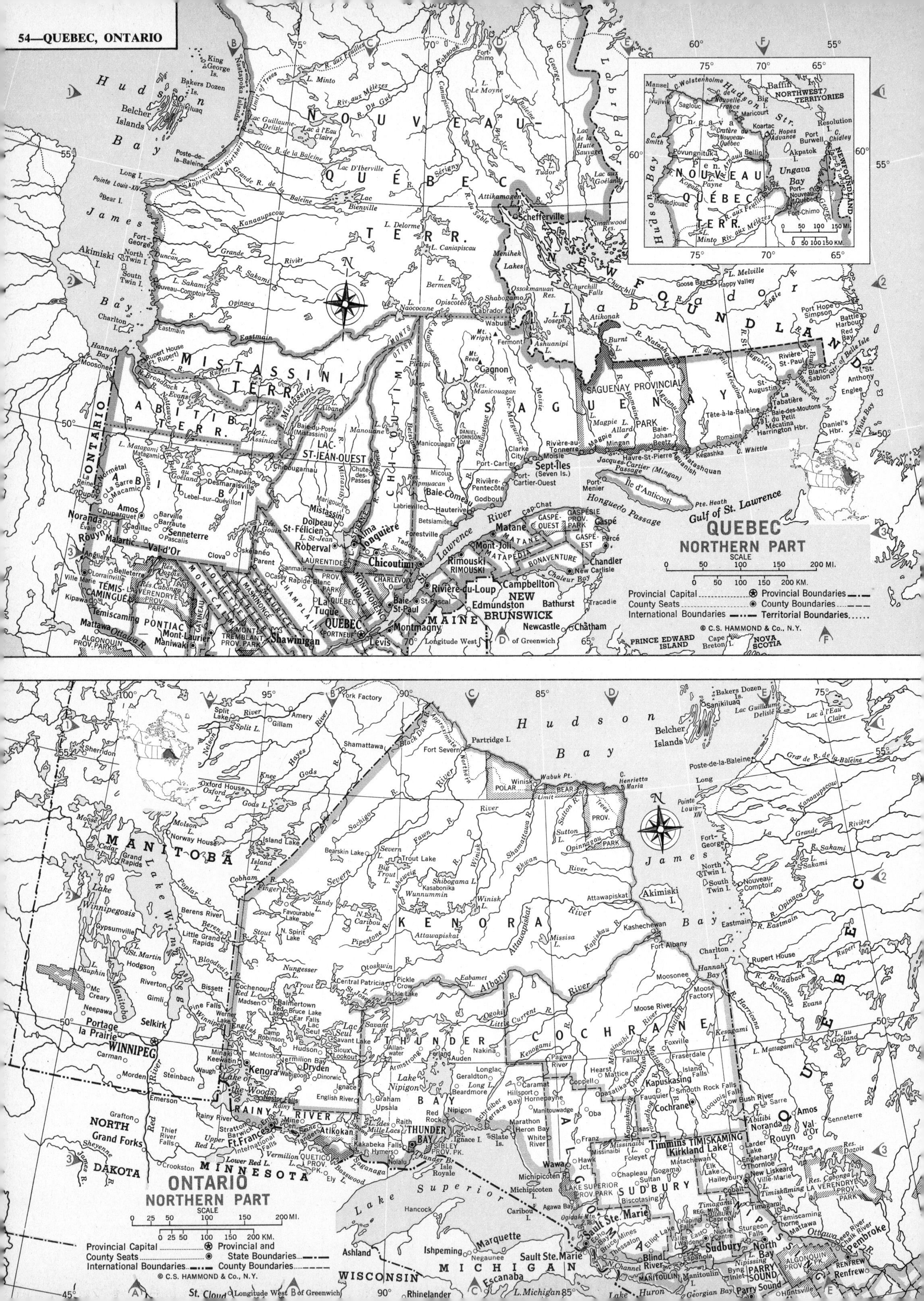
QUEBEC
NORTHERN PART
SCALE
0 50 100 150 200 MI.
0 50 100 150 200 KM.
Provincial Capital
Provincial Boundaries
County Seats
County Boundaries
International Boundaries
Territorial Boundaries
© C.S. HAMMOND & Co., N.Y.
Longitude West of Greenwich
Hudson Bay
James Bay
Gulf of St. Lawrence
NOUVEAU-QUÉBEC TERR.
MISTASSINI TERR.
ABITIBI TERR.
NEWFOUNDLAND
Labrador
SAGUENAY PROVINCIAL PARK
NEW BRUNSWICK
MAINE
PRINCE EDWARD ISLAND
NOVA SCOTIA
QUEBEC
Chicoutimi
Rimouski
Sept-Iles
Schefferville
Gaspé
ONTARIO
NORTHERN PART
SCALE
0 25 50 100 150 200 MI.
0 25 50 100 150 200 KM.
Provincial Capital
Provincial and State Boundaries
County Seats
International Boundaries
County Boundaries
© C.S. HAMMOND & Co., N.Y.
Longitude West of Greenwich
Hudson Bay
James Bay
Lake Superior
MANITOBA
WINNIPEG
KENORA
THUNDER BAY
COCHRANE
ALGOMA
SUDBURY
TIMISKAMING
NIPISSING
RAINY RIVER
MINNESOTA
NORTH DAKOTA
WISCONSIN
MICHIGAN
QUEBEC
Sault Ste. Marie
Timmins
Kapuskasing
Moosonee

ONTARIO
SOUTHERN PART
SCALE
0 10 20 30 40 50 MI.
0 10 20 30 40 50 KM.
National Capital
Provincial Capital
County Seats
International Boundaries
Provincial & State Boundaries
County Boundaries
Canals
ONTARIO
CENTRAL PART
0 25 50 75 100 125 MI.
0 25 50 75 100 125 KM.
TORONTO
LAKE ONTARIO
LAKE HURON
LAKE ONTARIO
LAKE ERIE
GEORGIAN BAY
LAKE SUPERIOR
QUÉBEC
NEW YORK
MICHIGAN
MINN.
WIS.
OTTAWA
TORONTO
HAMILTON
LONDON
WINDSOR
KINGSTON
SUDBURY
THUNDER BAY
ALGONQUIN PROVINCIAL PARK
Copyright by C. S. HAMMOND & CO., N. Y.

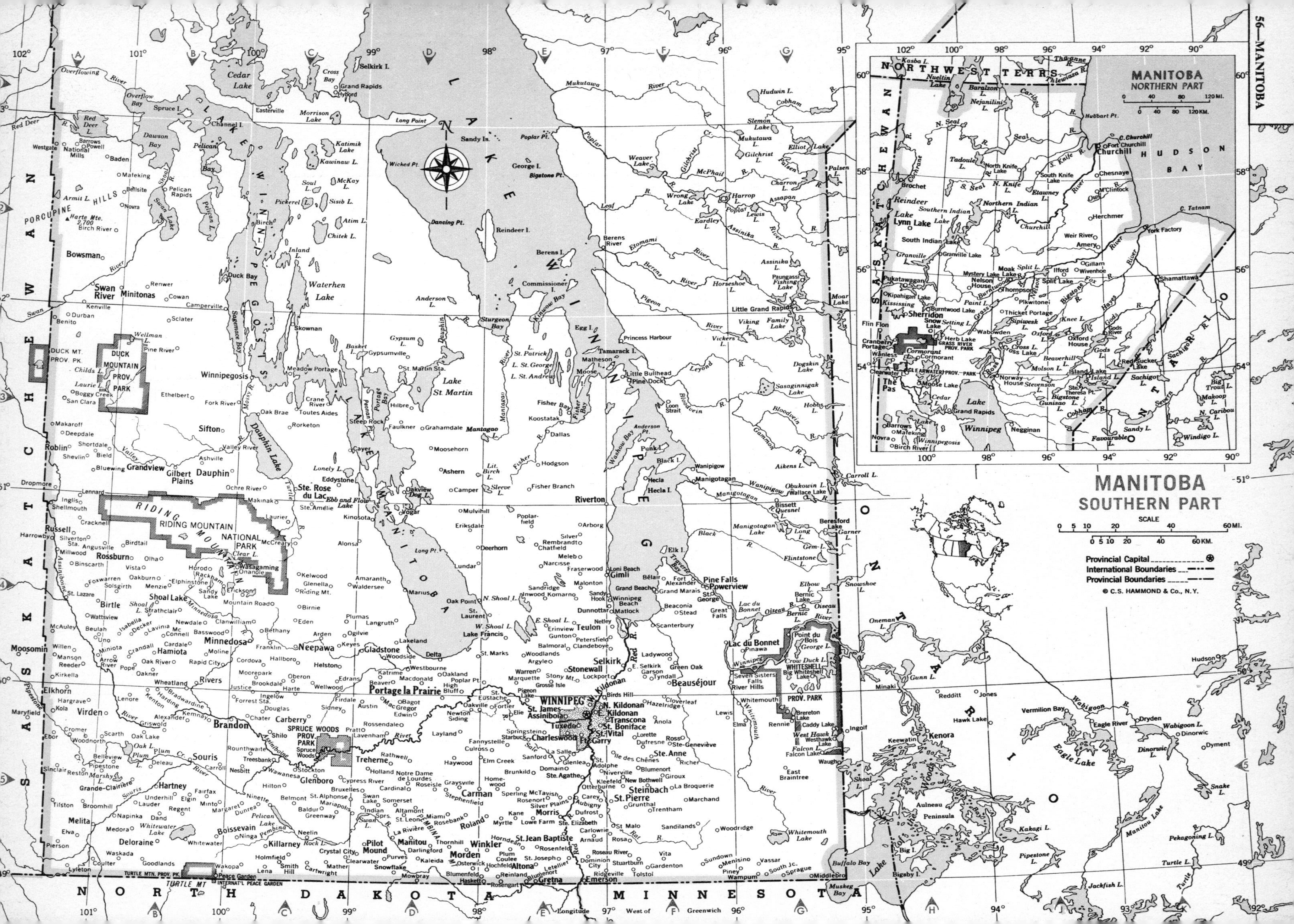
MANITOBA
SOUTHERN PART
SCALE
Provincial Capital
International Boundaries
Provincial Boundaries
© C.S. HAMMOND & Co., N.Y.
MANITOBA
NORTHERN PART
HUDSON BAY
LAKE WINNIPEG
LAKE WINNIPEGOSIS
LAKE MANITOBA
WINNIPEG
RIDING MOUNTAIN NATIONAL PARK
DUCK MOUNTAIN PROV. PARK
SPRUCE WOODS PROV. PARK
WHITESHELL PROV. PARK
NORTH DAKOTA
MINNESOTA
ONTARIO
SASKATCHEWAN

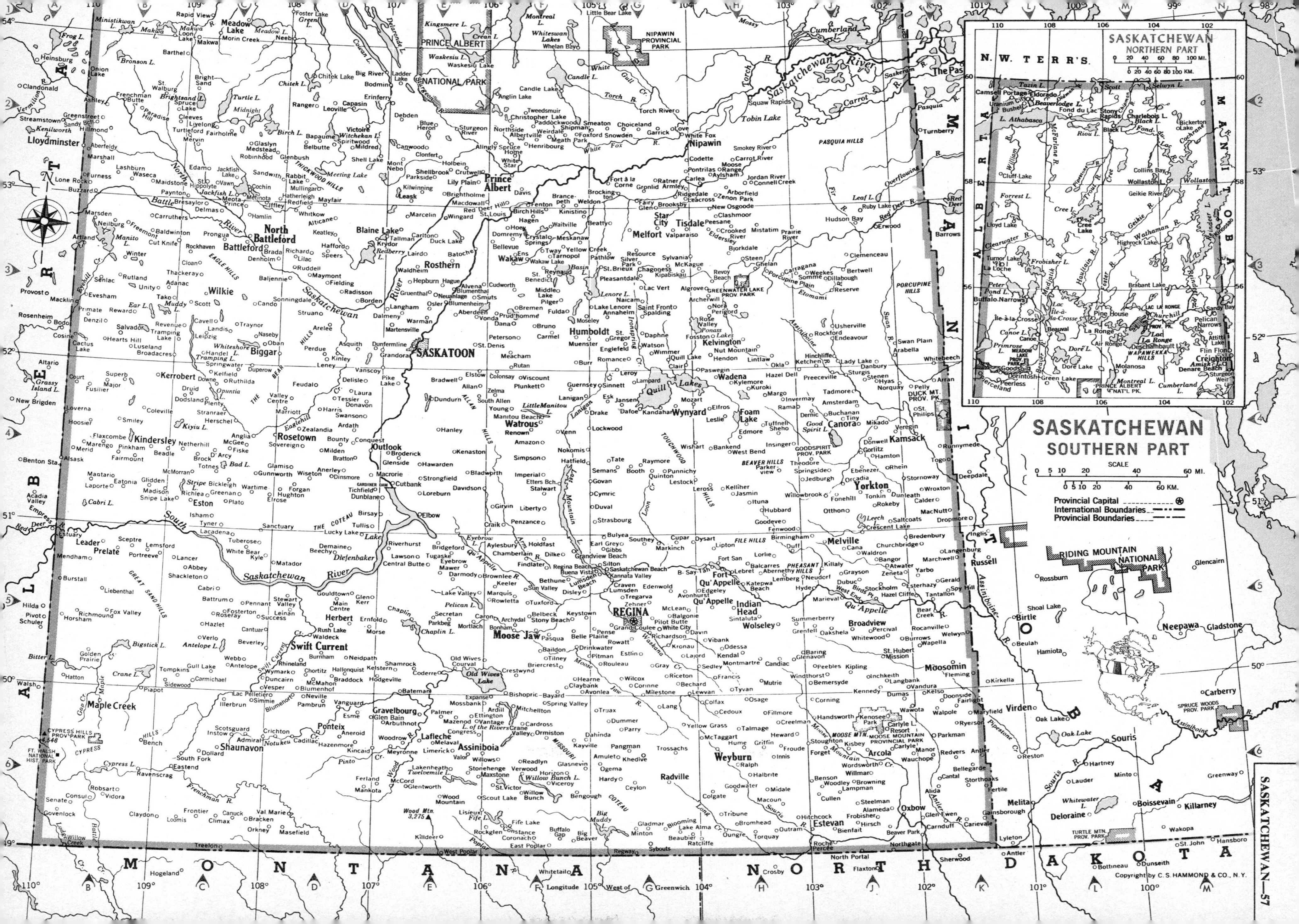
SASKATCHEWAN
SOUTHERN PART
SCALE
0 5 10 20 40 60 MI.
0 5 10 20 40 60 KM.
Provincial Capital
International Boundaries
Provincial Boundaries
SASKATCHEWAN
NORTHERN PART
0 20 40 60 80 100 MI.
0 20 40 60 80 100 KM.
N. W. TERR'S.
MANITOBA
ALBERTA
NORTH DAKOTA
MONTANA
REGINA
SASKATOON
Moose Jaw
Prince Albert
North Battleford
Swift Current
Yorkton
Weyburn
Estevan
Lloydminster
Copyright by C. S. HAMMOND & CO., N. Y.

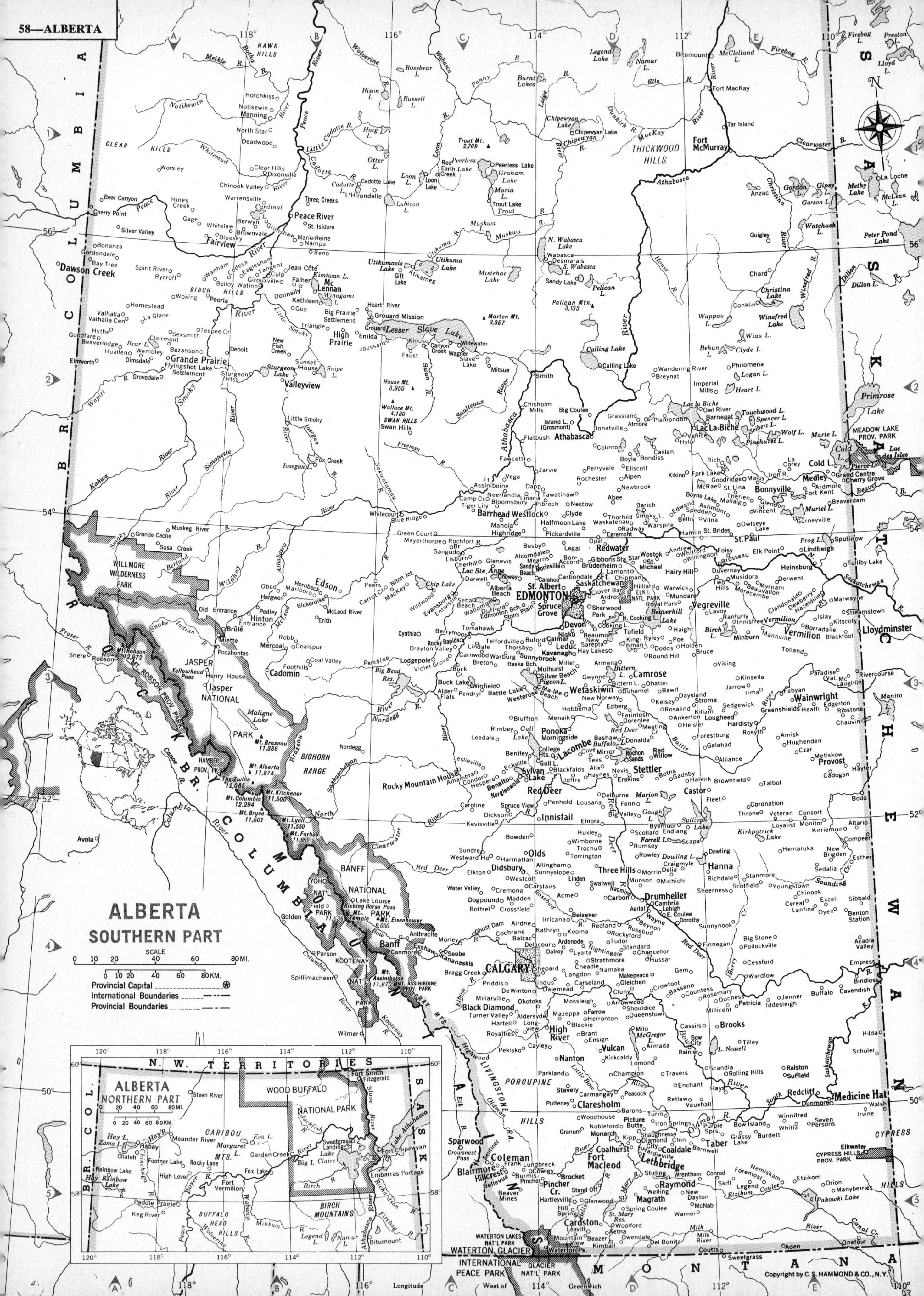
ALBERTA
SOUTHERN PART
SCALE
0 10 20 40 60 80 MI.
0 10 20 40 60 80 KM.
Provincial Capital
International Boundaries
Provincial Boundaries
BRITISH COLUMBIA
SASKATCHEWAN
MONTANA
ALBERTA
NORTHERN PART
0 20 40 60 80 MI.
0 20 40 60 80 KM.
N. W. TERRITORIES
BR. COL.
SASK.
WOOD BUFFALO
NATIONAL PARK
CARIBOU MTS.
BIRCH MOUNTAINS
BUFFALO HEAD HILLS
Steen River
Meander River
Hay L.
Zama L.
Habay
Chateh
Footner Lake
Rocky Lane
Rainbow Lake
High Level
Fort Vermilion
Paddle Prairie
Keg River
Garden Creek
Fox Lake
Fort Smith
Fitzgerald
Fort Chipewyan
Lake Athabasca
Embarras Portage
Bitumount
EDMONTON
CALGARY
Red Deer
Lethbridge
Medicine Hat
Grande Prairie
Peace River
Fort McMurray
Athabasca
Lac La Biche
Lesser Slave Lake
Jasper
JASPER NATIONAL PARK
BANFF NATIONAL PARK
Banff
WILLMORE WILDERNESS PARK
HAMBER PROV. PK.
MT. ROBSON PROV. PARK
YOHO NAT'L PARK
KOOTENAY NAT'L PARK
MT. ASSINIBOINE PROV. PARK
WATERTON LAKES NAT'L PARK
WATERTON GLACIER INTERNATIONAL PEACE PARK
GLACIER NAT'L PARK
CYPRESS HILLS PROV. PARK
MEADOW LAKE PROV. PARK
THICKWOOD HILLS
CLEAR HILLS
BIRCH HILLS
SWAN HILLS
BIGHORN RANGE
PORCUPINE HILLS
LIVINGSTONE RA.
ROCKY MTS.
Dawson Creek
Fairview
Grimshaw
Manning
High Prairie
Valleyview
Whitecourt
Barrhead
Westlock
St. Albert
Spruce Grove
Stony Plain
Leduc
Camrose
Wetaskiwin
Ponoka
Lacombe
Innisfail
Olds
Didsbury
Drumheller
Hanna
Stettler
Vegreville
Vermilion
Lloydminster
Wainwright
Provost
Coronation
Brooks
High River
Okotoks
Nanton
Claresholm
Fort Macleod
Pincher Cr.
Cardston
Magrath
Raymond
Taber
Vulcan
Coleman
Blairmore
Hillcrest
Canmore
Hinton
Edson
Cadomin
Bonnyville
Cold L.
St. Paul
Smoky Lake
Redwater
Fort Saskatchewan
Devon
Mt. Robson 12,972
Mt. Alberta 11,874
Mt. Columbia 12,294
Mt. Brazeau 11,386
Mt. Assiniboine 11,870
Trout Mt. 2,709
House Mt. 3,950
Wallace Mt. 4,130
Marten Mt. 3,357
Pelican Mtn. 3,135
Copyright by C. S. HAMMOND & CO., N.Y.
Longitude West of Greenwich

BRITISH COLUMBIA
SOUTHERN PART
SCALE
0 15 30 60 90 120 MI.
0 15 30 60 90 120 KM.
Provincial Capital
State Capital
International Boundaries
Provincial Boundaries
© C.S. HAMMOND & Co., N.Y.
BRITISH COLUMBIA
NORTHERN PART
YUKON
N.W.T.
PACIFIC OCEAN
ALBERTA
WASHINGTON
IDAHO
MONTANA
ALASKA
ROCKY MOUNTAINS
COAST MOUNTAINS
MONASHEE MTS.
SELKIRK MTS.
CARIBOO MTS.
SKEENA MOUNTAINS
HAZELTON MOUNTAINS
OMINECA MTS.
QUEEN CHARLOTTE SOUND
HECATE STRAIT
QUEEN CHARLOTTE ISLANDS
VANCOUVER ISLAND
Prince George
VANCOUVER
Victoria
Kamloops
Prince Rupert
Calgary

YUKON AND NORTHWEST TERRITORIES
SCALE
0 50 100 200 300 MI.
0 50 100 200 300 KM.
Territorial Capitals
International Boundaries
Provincial & Territorial Boundaries
District Boundaries
All islands in Hudson and James Bays lie within the District of Keewatin.
© Copyright by C. S. HAMMOND & Co.
Longitude West of Greenwich
ARCTIC OCEAN
BEAUFORT SEA
QUEEN ELIZABETH ISLANDS
SVERDRUP ISLANDS
PARRY ISLANDS
ELLESMERE ISLAND
GREENLAND (Denmark)
Baffin Bay
Davis Strait
Hudson Strait
Hudson Bay
Foxe Basin
Foxe Channel
Ungava Bay
Devon Island
Lancaster Sound
Jones Sound
Melville Island
Prince Patrick Island
Banks Island
Viscount Melville Sound
M'Clintock Chan.
Amundsen Gulf
Coronation Gulf
Queen Maud Gulf
Gulf of Boothia
Somerset Island
Prince of Wales Island
King William I.
Southampton I.
Melville Pen.
Boothia Pen.
DISTRICT OF FRANKLIN
VICTORIA ISLAND
NORTHWEST TERRITORIES
DISTRICT OF MACKENZIE
DISTRICT OF KEEWATIN
Great Bear Lake
Great Slave Lake
Yellowknife
Inuvik
Mackenzie River
YUKON TERRITORY
Whitehorse
Dawson
RICHARDSON MTS.
MACKENZIE MTS.
BRITISH MTS.
DAVIDSON MTS.
BROOKS RANGE
UNITED STATES
ALASKA
Fairbanks
BRITISH COLUMBIA
ALBERTA
SASKATCHEWAN
MANITOBA
QUÉBEC
Ungava Pen.

UNITED STATES
POLYCONIC PROJECTION
SCALE
0 50 100 200 300 400 MI.
0 50 100 200 300 400 KM.
Capitals of Countries
State Capitals
International Boundaries
State Boundaries
© C.S. HAMMOND & Co., N.Y.
ATLANTIC OCEAN
PACIFIC OCEAN
GULF OF MEXICO
CANADA
MEXICO
CUBA
BAHAMAS
HAWAII
ALASKA
Gulf of California
Lower California

POPULATION DISTRIBUTION

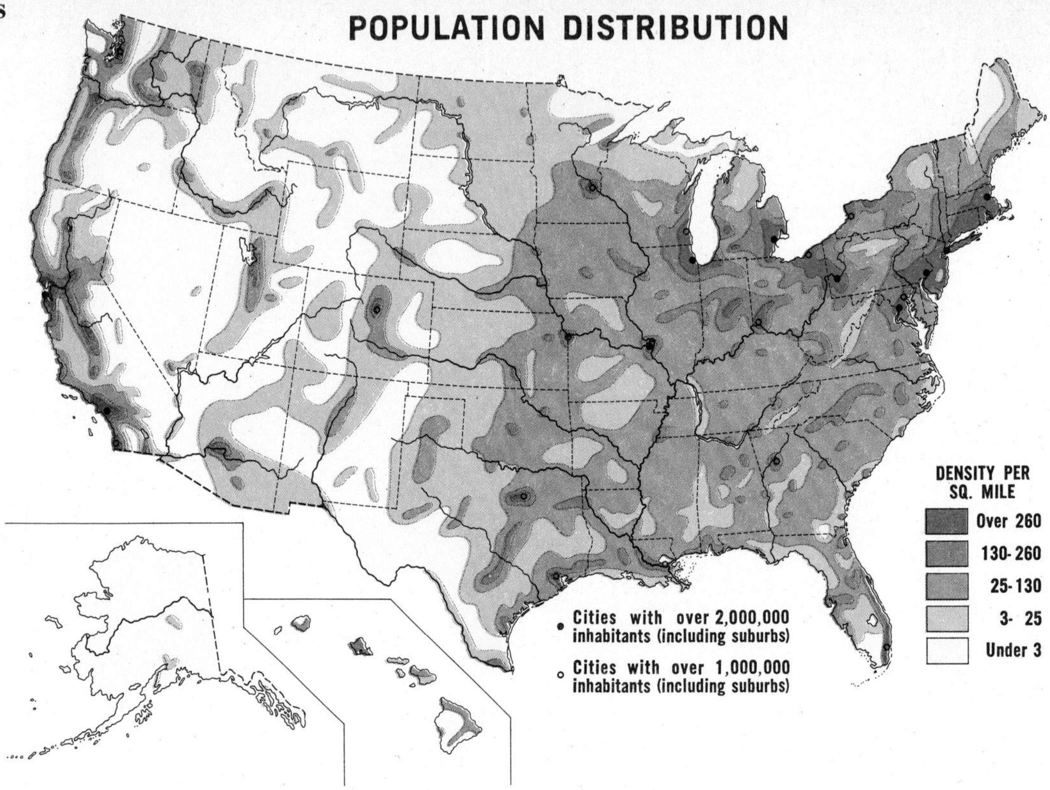

DENSITY PER SQ. MILE

- Over 260
- 130-260
- 25-130
- 3- 25
- Under 3

● Cities with over 2,000,000 inhabitants (including suburbs)

○ Cities with over 1,000,000 inhabitants (including suburbs)

AGRICULTURE, INDUSTRY and RESOURCES

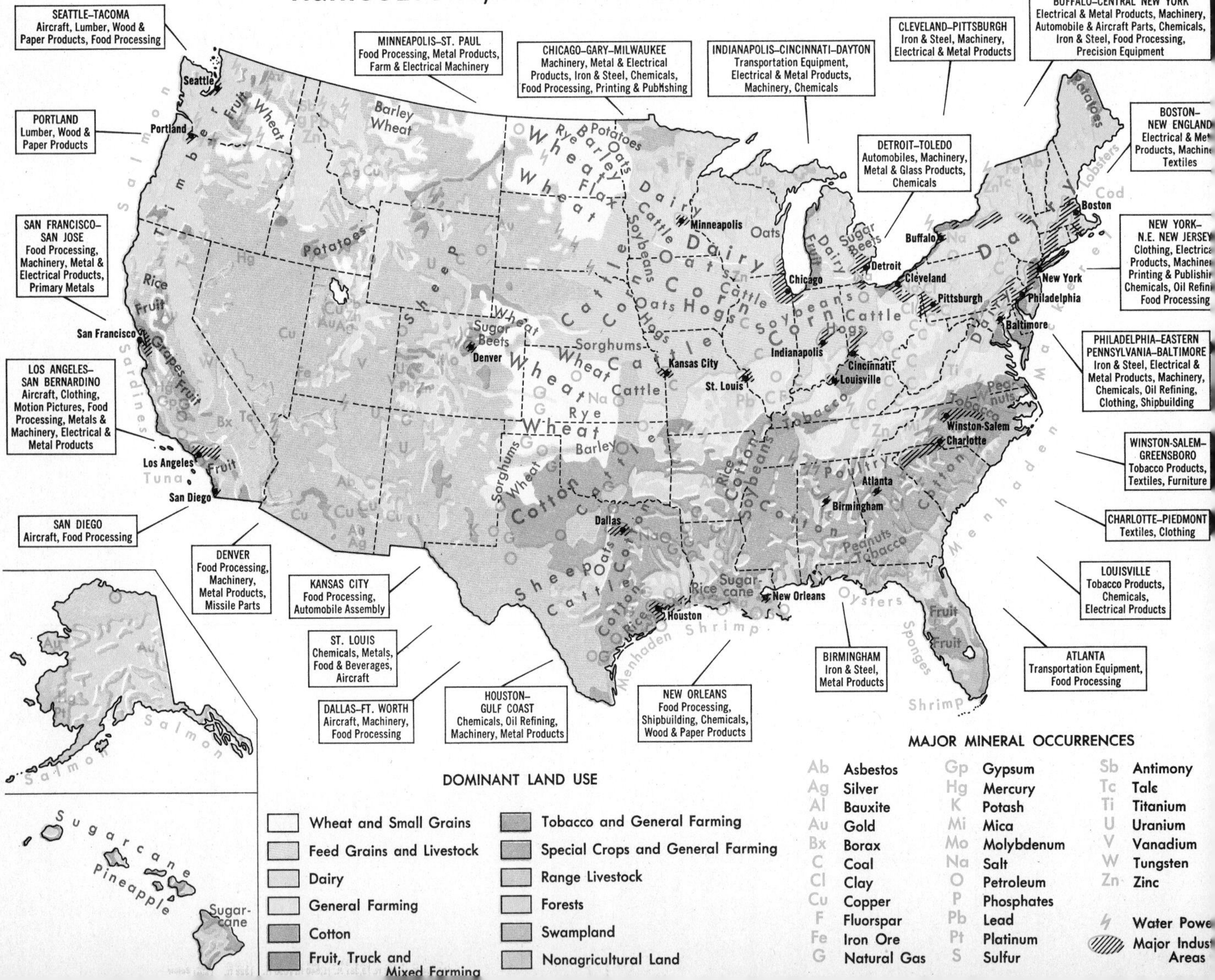

SEATTLE–TACOMA
Aircraft, Lumber, Wood & Paper Products, Food Processing

PORTLAND
Lumber, Wood & Paper Products

SAN FRANCISCO–SAN JOSE
Food Processing, Machinery, Metal & Electrical Products, Primary Metals

LOS ANGELES–SAN BERNARDINO
Aircraft, Clothing, Motion Pictures, Food Processing, Metals & Machinery, Electrical & Metal Products

SAN DIEGO
Aircraft, Food Processing

DENVER
Food Processing, Machinery, Metal Products, Missile Parts

KANSAS CITY
Food Processing, Automobile Assembly

ST. LOUIS
Chemicals, Metals, Food & Beverages, Aircraft

DALLAS–FT. WORTH
Aircraft, Machinery, Food Processing

HOUSTON–GULF COAST
Chemicals, Oil Refining, Machinery, Metal Products

NEW ORLEANS
Food Processing, Shipbuilding, Chemicals, Wood & Paper Products

BIRMINGHAM
Iron & Steel, Metal Products

MINNEAPOLIS–ST. PAUL
Food Processing, Metal Products, Farm & Electrical Machinery

CHICAGO–GARY–MILWAUKEE
Machinery, Metal & Electrical Products, Iron & Steel, Chemicals, Food Processing, Printing & Publishing

INDIANAPOLIS–CINCINNATI–DAYTON
Transportation Equipment, Electrical & Metal Products, Machinery, Chemicals

DETROIT–TOLEDO
Automobiles, Machinery, Metal & Glass Products, Chemicals

CLEVELAND–PITTSBURGH
Iron & Steel, Machinery, Electrical & Metal Products

BUFFALO–CENTRAL NEW YORK
Electrical & Metal Products, Machinery, Automobile & Aircraft Parts, Chemicals, Iron & Steel, Food Processing, Precision Equipment

BOSTON–NEW ENGLAND
Electrical & Me[tal] Products, Machine[ry], Textiles

NEW YORK–N.E. NEW JERSEY
Clothing, Electrica[l] Products, Machine[ry], Printing & Publishi[ng], Chemicals, Oil Refin[ing], Food Processing

PHILADELPHIA–EASTERN PENNSYLVANIA–BALTIMORE
Iron & Steel, Electrical & Metal Products, Machinery, Chemicals, Oil Refining, Clothing, Shipbuilding

WINSTON-SALEM–GREENSBORO
Tobacco Products, Textiles, Furniture

CHARLOTTE–PIEDMONT
Textiles, Clothing

LOUISVILLE
Tobacco Products, Chemicals, Electrical Products

ATLANTA
Transportation Equipment, Food Processing

DOMINANT LAND USE

Wheat and Small Grains	Tobacco and General Farming
Feed Grains and Livestock	Special Crops and General Farming
Dairy	Range Livestock
General Farming	Forests
Cotton	Swampland
Fruit, Truck and Mixed Farming	Nonagricultural Land

MAJOR MINERAL OCCURRENCES

Ab	Asbestos	Gp	Gypsum	Sb	Antimony		
Ag	Silver	Hg	Mercury	Tc	Talc		
Al	Bauxite	K	Potash	Ti	Titanium		
Au	Gold	Mi	Mica	U	Uranium		
Bx	Borax	Mo	Molybdenum	V	Vanadium		
C	Coal	Na	Salt	W	Tungsten		
Cl	Clay	O	Petroleum	Zn	Zinc		
Cu	Copper	P	Phosphates				
F	Fluorspar	Pb	Lead	ϟ	Water Pow[er]		
Fe	Iron Ore	Pt	Platinum	▨	Major Indus[trial] Areas		
G	Natural Gas	S	Sulfur				

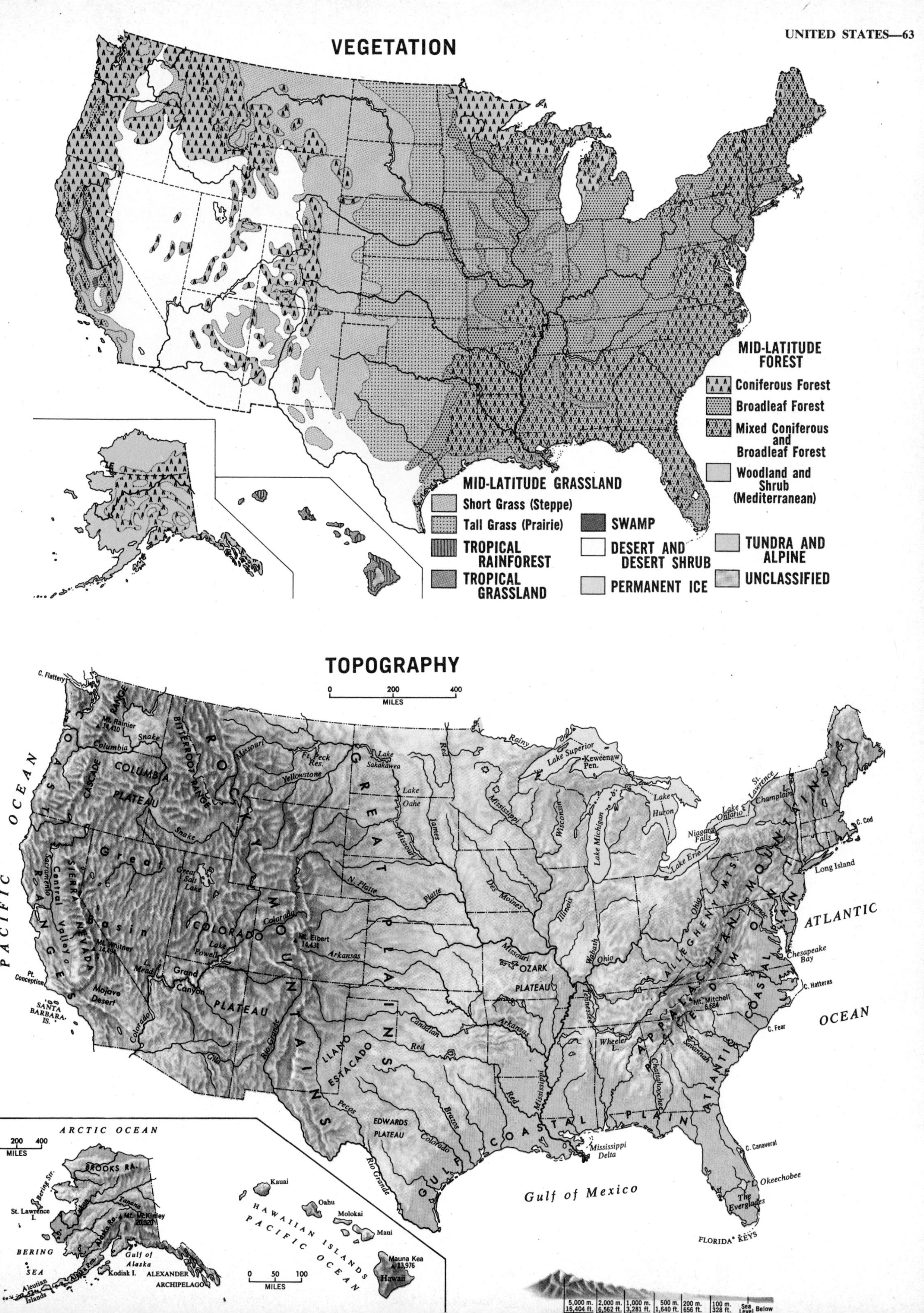
VEGETATION
MID-LATITUDE FOREST
Coniferous Forest
Broadleaf Forest
Mixed Coniferous and Broadleaf Forest
Woodland and Shrub (Mediterranean)
MID-LATITUDE GRASSLAND
Short Grass (Steppe)
Tall Grass (Prairie)
TROPICAL RAINFOREST
TROPICAL GRASSLAND
SWAMP
DESERT AND DESERT SHRUB
PERMANENT ICE
TUNDRA AND ALPINE
UNCLASSIFIED
TOPOGRAPHY
0 200 400 MILES
PACIFIC OCEAN
ATLANTIC OCEAN
Gulf of Mexico
C. Flattery
Mt. Rainier 14,410
CASCADE RANGE
COAST RANGES
COLUMBIA PLATEAU
BITTERROOT RANGE
ROCKY MOUNTAINS
GREAT PLAINS
Great Basin
SIERRA NEVADA
Central Valley
Mt. Whitney 14,494
Great Salt Lake
COLORADO PLATEAU
Mt. Elbert 14,431
Lake Powell
L. Mead
Grand Canyon
Mojave Desert
Pt. Conception
SANTA BARBARA IS.
LLANO ESTACADO
EDWARDS PLATEAU
OZARK PLATEAU
GULF COASTAL PLAIN
ATLANTIC COASTAL PLAIN
APPALACHIAN MOUNTAINS
ALLEGHENY MTS.
PIEDMONT
Mt. Mitchell 6,684
Lake Superior
Keweenaw Pen.
Lake Michigan
Lake Huron
Lake Erie
Lake Ontario
Niagara Falls
L. Champlain
St. Lawrence
C. Cod
Long Island
Chesapeake Bay
C. Hatteras
C. Fear
C. Canaveral
L. Okeechobee
The Everglades
FLORIDA KEYS
Mississippi Delta
Wheeler L.
Lake Sakakawea
Ft. Peck Res.
Lake Oahe
Columbia
Snake
Missouri
Yellowstone
Rainy
Red
James
Mississippi
Wisconsin
Des Moines
Illinois
Wabash
Ohio
Tennessee
Potomac
Savannah
Chattahoochee
N. Platte
Platte
Arkansas
Canadian
Red
Brazos
Colorado
Pecos
Rio Grande
Gila
Colorado
ARCTIC OCEAN
200 400 MILES
BROOKS RA.
Bering Str.
Yukon
Tanana
St. Lawrence I.
Alaska Ra.
Mt. McKinley 20,320
BERING SEA
Gulf of Alaska
Alaska Pen.
Kodiak I.
ALEXANDER ARCHIPELAGO
Aleutian Islands
HAWAIIAN ISLANDS
PACIFIC OCEAN
Kauai
Oahu
Molokai
Maui
Mauna Kea 13,976
Hawaii
0 50 100 MILES
5,000 m. 16,404 ft.
2,000 m. 6,562 ft.
1,000 m. 3,281 ft.
500 m. 1,640 ft.
200 m. 656 ft.
100 m. 328 ft.
Sea Level
Below

TEMPERATURE

AVERAGE JANUARY TEMPERATURE

Seattle 39°
Bismarck 9°
Minneapolis 12°
New York 30°
Chicago 25°
San Francisco 48°
Denver 30°
St. Louis 31°
Washington 34°
Los Angeles 55°
Phoenix 52°
Atlanta 43°
Dallas 46°
Chicago 25° Average January temperature at selected stations
New Orleans 55°
Fairbanks -11°
Honolulu 73°
Miami 69°
FAHRENHEIT
Over 68°
50° to 68°
32° to 50°
14° to 32°
-4° to 14°
Under -4°

AVERAGE JULY TEMPERATURE

Seattle 59°
Bismarck 70°
Minneapolis 73°
Chicago 75°
San Francisco 61°
Denver 72°
St. Louis 81°
Washington 77°
Los Angeles 72°
Phoenix 90°
Atlanta 79°
Dallas 85°
Chicago 75°
New Orleans 83°
Fairbanks 57°
Honolulu 79°
Miami 81°
FAHRENHEIT
Over 86°
68° to 86°
50° to 68°
Under 50°

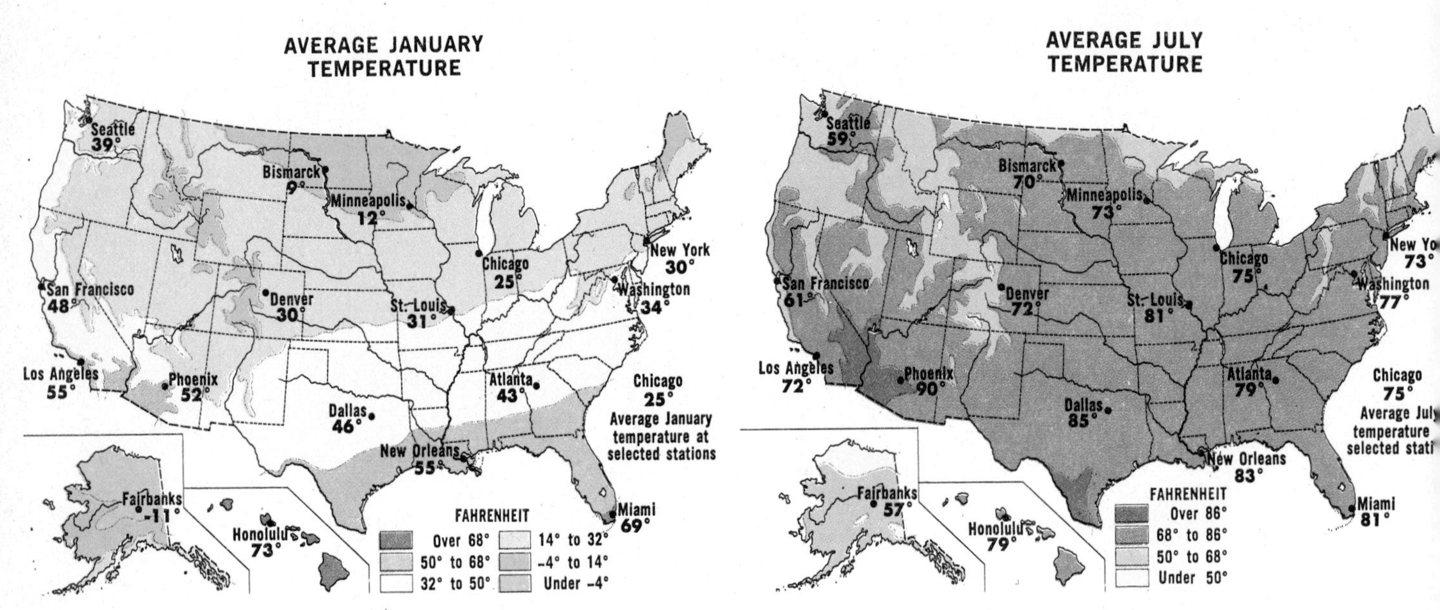

RAINFALL

Tatoosh 85
Portland 43
Helena 11
Bismarck 15
Presque Isle 37
Duluth 29
Boston 52
Salt Lake City 14
Chicago 34
New York 41
San Francisco 21
Denver 12
Washington, D.C. 42
St. Louis 32
Los Angeles 13
Albuquerque 7
Cape Hatteras 56
Yuma 2
Birmingham 49
Abilene 21
New Orleans 62
Nome 18
Mt. Waialeale 460
Honolulu 22
Juneau 72
Miami 60
AVERAGE ANNUAL RAINFALL
INCHES
Over 80
60-80
40-60
20-40
10-20
Under 10
Boston 52 Average annual rainfall at selected stations

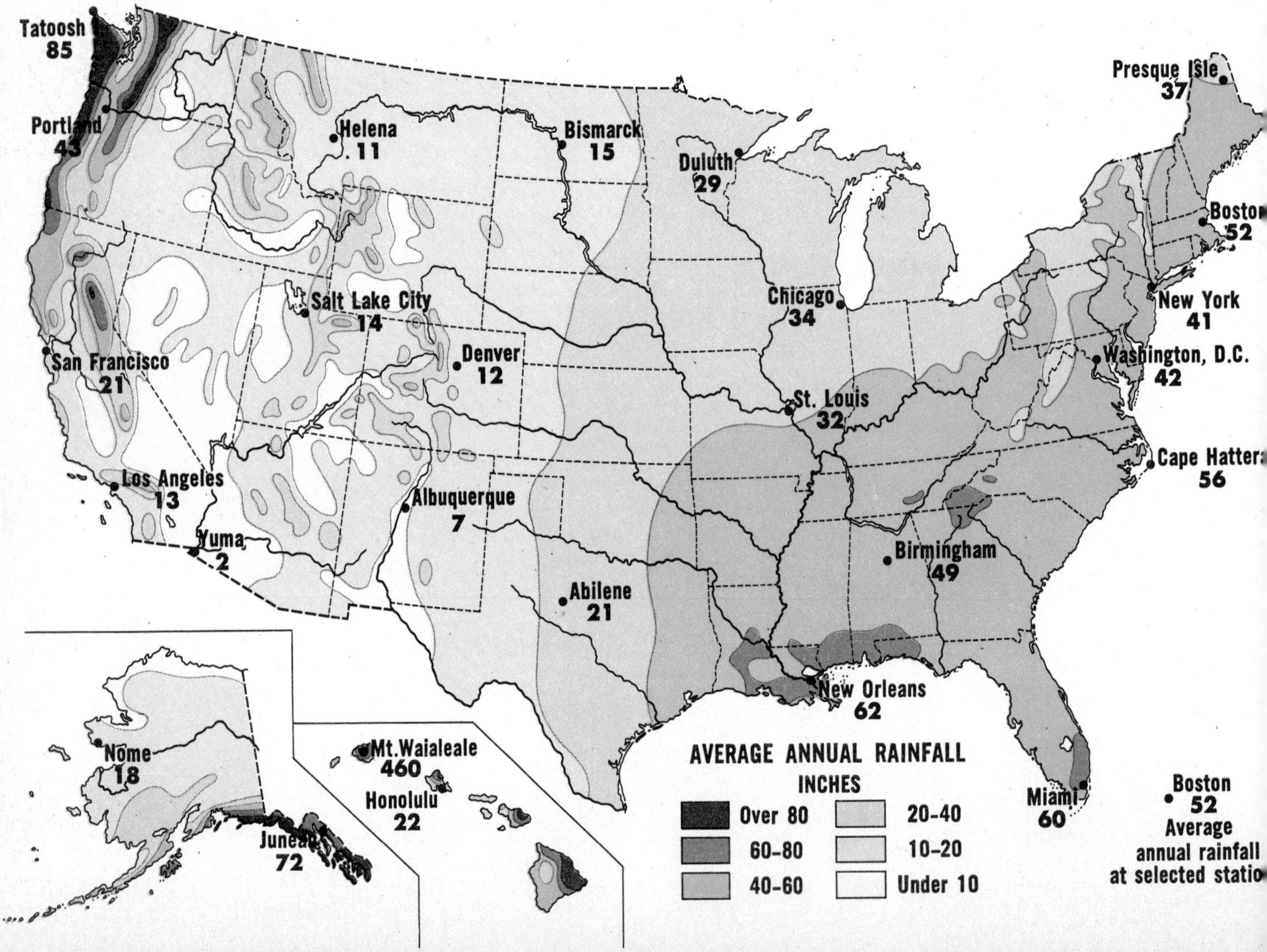

ALABAMA
SCALE
0 5 10 20 30 40 MI.
0 5 10 20 30 40 KM.
State Capitals
County Seats
Copyright by C. S. Hammond & Co., N. Y.
87° Longitude West of Greenwich
T E N N E S S E E
G E O R G I A
M I S S I S S I P P I
F L O R I D A
GULF OF MEXICO
LAUDERDALE
LIMESTONE
MADISON
JACKSON
COLBERT
LAWRENCE
MORGAN
MARSHALL
DE KALB
FRANKLIN
MARION
WINSTON
CULLMAN
BLOUNT
ETOWAH
CHEROKEE
LAMAR
FAYETTE
WALKER
JEFFERSON
ST. CLAIR
CALHOUN
CLEBURNE
PICKENS
TUSCALOOSA
SHELBY
TALLADEGA
CLAY
RANDOLPH
GREENE
HALE
BIBB
CHILTON
COOSA
TALLAPOOSA
CHAMBERS
SUMTER
PERRY
AUTAUGA
ELMORE
LEE
MARENGO
DALLAS
LOWNDES
MONTGOMERY
MACON
RUSSELL
BULLOCK
CHOCTAW
WILCOX
BUTLER
CRENSHAW
PIKE
BARBOUR
CLARKE
MONROE
CONECUH
COVINGTON
COFFEE
DALE
HENRY
WASHINGTON
ESCAMBIA
GENEVA
HOUSTON
MOBILE
BALDWIN
BIRMINGHAM
MONTGOMERY
MOBILE
HUNTSVILLE
TUSCALOOSA
ATLANTA
CHATTANOOGA
COLUMBUS
PENSACOLA

ALASKA
POLYCONIC PROJECTION
SCALE
State and Territorial Capitals
Court Houses
International Boundaries
Senatorial District Boundaries
ARCTIC OCEAN
BEAUFORT SEA
CHUKCHI SEA
BERING SEA
NORTON SOUND
BRISTOL BAY
GULF OF ALASKA
PACIFIC OCEAN
BROOKS RANGE
ALASKA RANGE
ALEXANDER ARCHIPELAGO
YUKON TERRITORY
BRITISH COLUMBIA
ALEUTIAN ISLANDS
Anchorage
Fairbanks
Juneau
Nome
Kodiak
Ketchikan
Sitka
Prince Rupert
Longitude West of Greenwich
©C. S. HAMMOND & Co., Maplewood, N. J.

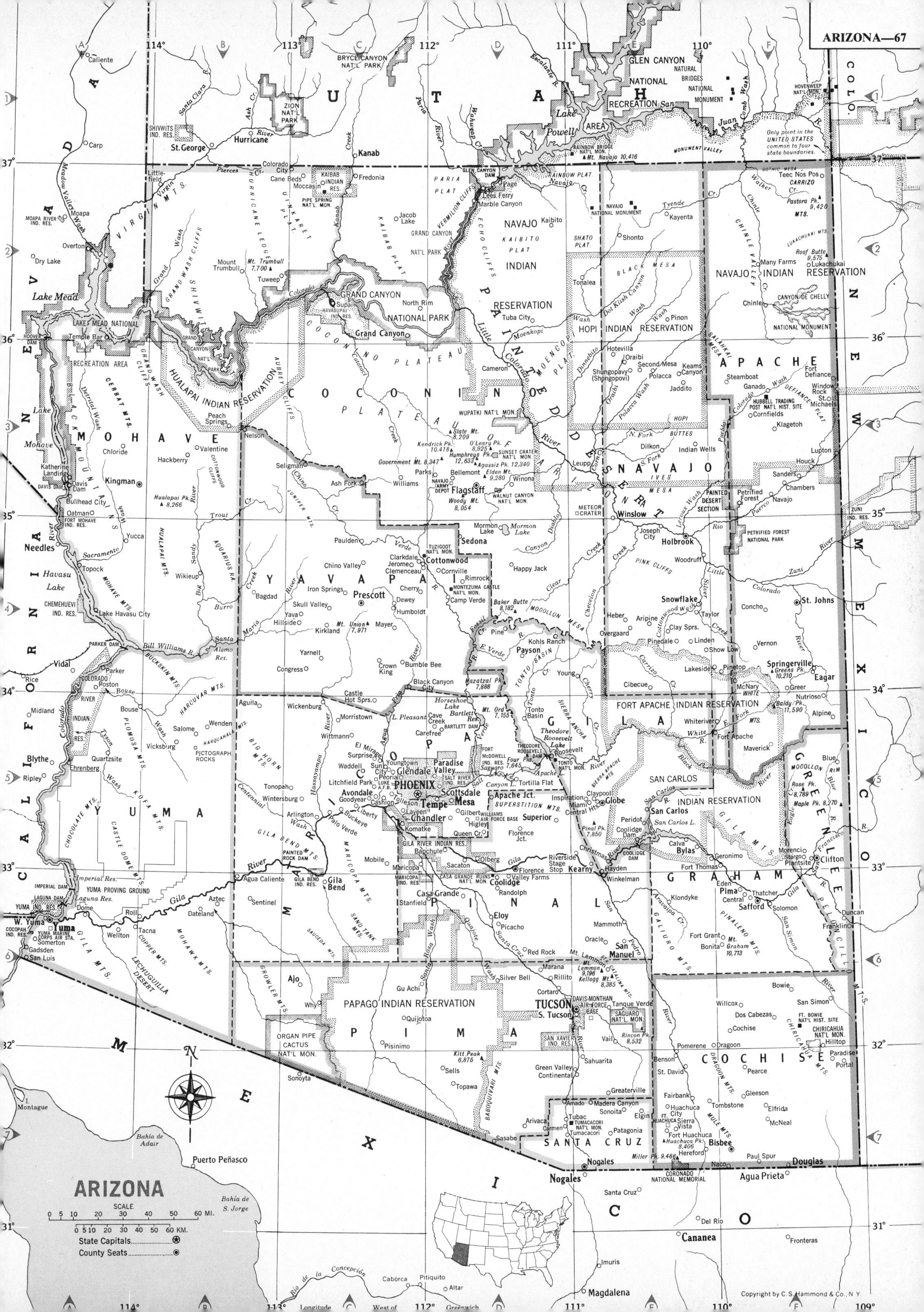
ARIZONA
State Capitals
County Seats
MOHAVE
COCONINO
NAVAJO
APACHE
YAVAPAI
MARICOPA
GILA
GREENLEE
GRAHAM
PINAL
PIMA
SANTA CRUZ
COCHISE
YUMA
PHOENIX
Tucson
Flagstaff
Prescott
Kingman
Yuma
Holbrook
St. Johns
Globe
Clifton
Safford
Florence
Nogales
Bisbee
Parker
GRAND CANYON NATIONAL PARK
NAVAJO INDIAN RESERVATION
HOPI INDIAN RESERVATION
FORT APACHE INDIAN RESERVATION
SAN CARLOS INDIAN RESERVATION
PAPAGO INDIAN RESERVATION
HUALAPAI INDIAN RESERVATION
GLEN CANYON NATIONAL RECREATION AREA
LAKE MEAD NATIONAL RECREATION AREA
PAINTED DESERT
UTAH
NEVADA
CALIFORNIA
NEW MEXICO
COLO.
MEXICO
Only point in the UNITED STATES common to four state boundaries.
Copyright by C.S. Hammond & Co., N.Y.

ARKANSAS
SCALE
0 5 10 20 30 40 MI.
0 5 10 20 30 40 KM.
State Capitals
County Seats
Copyright by C. S. HAMMOND & CO., N. Y.

CALIFORNIA
SCALE
0 10 20 40 60 80 MI.
0 10 20 40 60 80 KM.
State Capitals
County Seats
Canals
SAN FRANCISCO AND VICINITY
0 5 10 15 20MI.
0 5 10 15 20KM.
SACRAMENTO AND VICINITY
0 5 10 15 20MI.
0 5 10 15 20KM.
LOS ANGELES AND VICINITY
0 5 10 15 20MI.
0 5 10 15 20KM.
OREGON
NEVADA
ARIZONA
MEXICO
PACIFIC OCEAN
SANTA BARBARA IS.
Santa Barbara Channel
Gulf of Santa Catalina
Mojave Desert
LAKE MEAD NATIONAL RECREATION AREA
DEATH VALLEY NATIONAL MONUMENT
JOSHUA TREE NAT'L MON.
SEQUOIA NATIONAL PARK
YOSEMITE NATIONAL PARK
Lake Tahoe
Salton Sea
Sacramento
San Francisco
Los Angeles
San Diego
Fresno
Bakersfield
Longitude 119° West of Greenwich 118°
Copyright by C. S. Hammond & Co., N. Y.

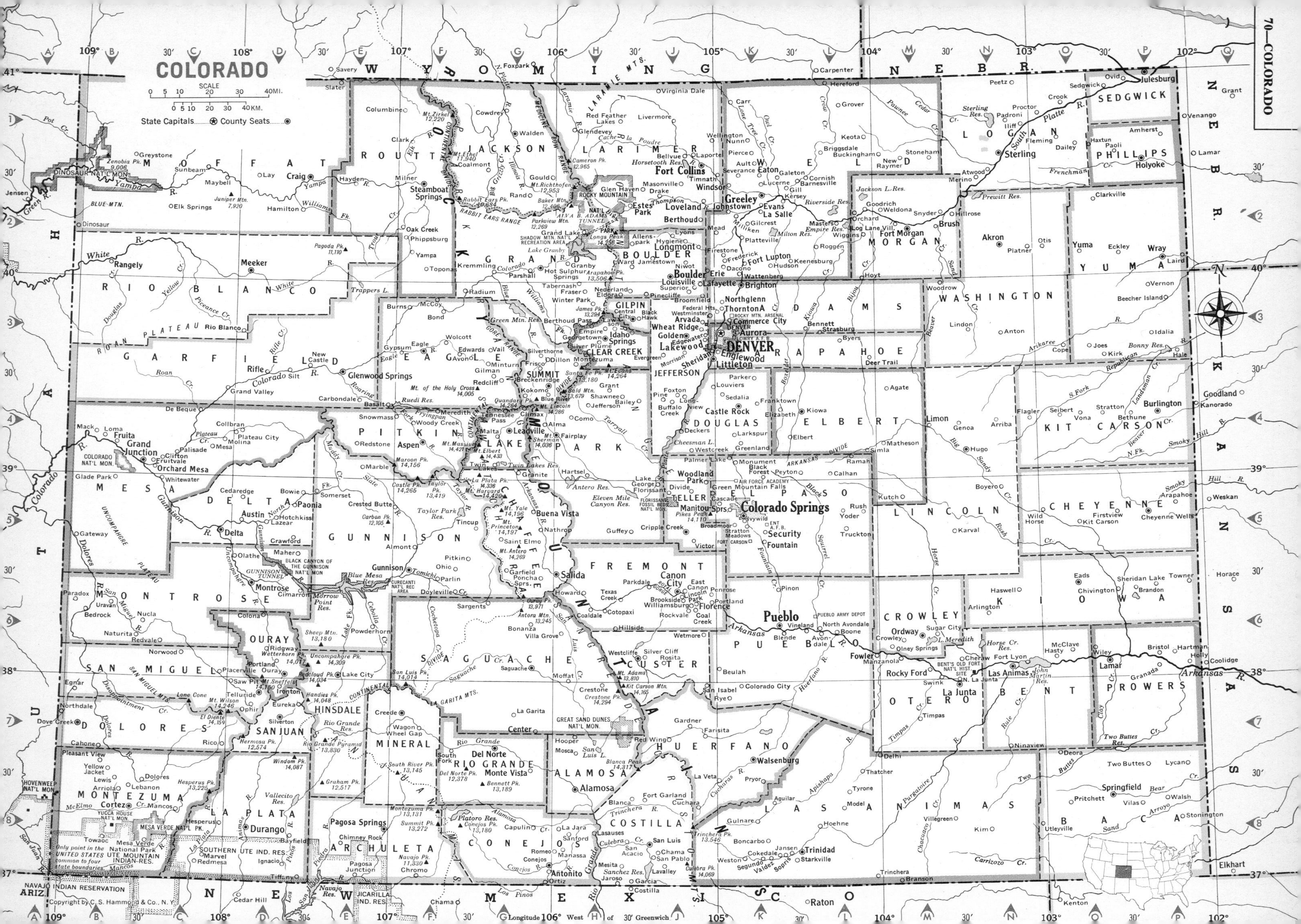
COLORADO
SCALE
0 5 10 20 30 40 MI.
0 5 10 20 30 40 KM.
State Capitals
County Seats
Copyright by C. S. Hammond & Co., N. Y.
WYOMING
NEBR.
NEBRASKA
KANSAS
NEW MEXICO
UTAH
ARIZ.
SEDGWICK
PHILLIPS
LOGAN
YUMA
WASHINGTON
MORGAN
KIT CARSON
CHEYENNE
KIOWA
PROWERS
BENT
BACA
OTERO
CROWLEY
LINCOLN
ELBERT
ARAPAHOE
ADAMS
WELD
LARIMER
BOULDER
JEFFERSON
DOUGLAS
EL PASO
PUEBLO
LAS ANIMAS
HUERFANO
CUSTER
FREMONT
TELLER
PARK
CLEAR CREEK
GILPIN
GRAND
JACKSON
ROUTT
MOFFAT
RIO BLANCO
GARFIELD
EAGLE
SUMMIT
LAKE
CHAFFEE
PITKIN
GUNNISON
DELTA
MESA
MONTROSE
OURAY
SAN MIGUEL
DOLORES
MONTEZUMA
LA PLATA
SAN JUAN
HINSDALE
MINERAL
RIO GRANDE
SAGUACHE
ALAMOSA
CONEJOS
COSTILLA
ARCHULETA
DENVER
Colorado Springs
Pueblo
Boulder
Fort Collins
Greeley
Grand Junction
Durango
Trinidad
Sterling
Julesburg
Lamar
La Junta
Gunnison
Leadville
Alamosa
Salida
Montrose
Craig
Meeker
Glenwood Springs
Pikes Peak 14,110
Mt. Elbert 14,433
ROCKY MOUNTAIN NAT'L PARK
GREAT SAND DUNES NAT'L MON.
MESA VERDE NAT'L PK.
DINOSAUR NAT'L MON.
COLORADO NAT'L MON.
BLACK CANYON OF THE GUNNISON NAT'L MON.
SOUTHERN UTE IND. RES.
UTE MOUNTAIN INDIAN RES.
NAVAJO INDIAN RESERVATION
Only point in the UNITED STATES common to four state boundaries
Longitude 106° West of 30' Greenwich

CONNECTICUT
SCALE
0 5 10 15 MI.
0 5 10 15 KM.
State Capitals
Longitude West of Greenwich
Copyright by C. S. Hammond & Co., N. Y.
LONG ISLAND SOUND
ATLANTIC OCEAN
GARDINERS BAY
THE RACE
LONG ISLAND
MASSACHUSETTS
RHODE ISLAND
NEW YORK
LITCHFIELD
HARTFORD
TOLLAND
WINDHAM
FAIRFIELD
NEW HAVEN
MIDDLESEX
NEW LONDON
HARTFORD
SPRINGFIELD
WATERBURY
NEW HAVEN
BRIDGEPORT
STAMFORD

FLORIDA
SCALE
0 5 10 20 30 40 50 MI.
0 5 10 20 30 40 50 KM.
State Capitals
County Seats
Canals
GEORGIA
ALA.
ATLANTIC OCEAN
GULF OF MEXICO
STRAITS OF FLORIDA
FLORIDA KEYS
Apalachee Bay
Okefenokee Swamp
Lake Okeechobee
Big Cypress Swamp
EVERGLADES NATIONAL PARK
Florida Bay
JACKSON
CALHOUN
GADSDEN
LEON
JEFFERSON
MADISON
HAMILTON
NASSAU
BAKER
DUVAL
COLUMBIA
SUWANNEE
TAYLOR
LAFAYETTE
UNION
BRADFORD
CLAY
ST. JOHNS
PUTNAM
ALACHUA
GILCHRIST
DIXIE
LEVY
MARION
FLAGLER
VOLUSIA
LAKE
SEMINOLE
CITRUS
SUMTER
HERNANDO
PASCO
ORANGE
BREVARD
OSCEOLA
POLK
HILLSBOROUGH
PINELLAS
MANATEE
HARDEE
HIGHLANDS
OKEECHOBEE
INDIAN RIVER
ST. LUCIE
MARTIN
SARASOTA
DE SOTO
CHARLOTTE
GLADES
LEE
HENDRY
PALM BEACH
COLLIER
BROWARD
DADE
MONROE
LIBERTY
WAKULLA
FRANKLIN
GULF
Tallahassee
Jacksonville
Tampa
St. Petersburg
Orlando
Miami
Miami Beach
Fort Lauderdale
Key West
Pensacola
WESTERN PART OF FLORIDA
Same scale as main map
ALABAMA
ESCAMBIA
SANTA ROSA
OKALOOSA
WALTON
HOLMES
WASHINGTON
BAY
Longitude West of Greenwich
Copyright by C. S. Hammond & Co., N. Y.

GEORGIA
SCALE
0 5 10 20 30 40 MI.
0 5 10 20 30 40 KM.
State Capitals
County Seats
© C.S. HAMMOND & Co., N.Y.
TENNESSEE
NORTH CAROLINA
SOUTH CAROLINA
ALABAMA
FLORIDA
ATLANTIC OCEAN
SEA ISLANDS
GULF OF MEXICO
APALACHEE BAY
OKEFENOKEE SWAMP
Longitude West of Greenwich
ATLANTA
Savannah
Augusta
Macon
Columbus
Tallahassee
JACKSONVILLE
CHATTANOOGA
COLUMBIA
CHARLOTTE

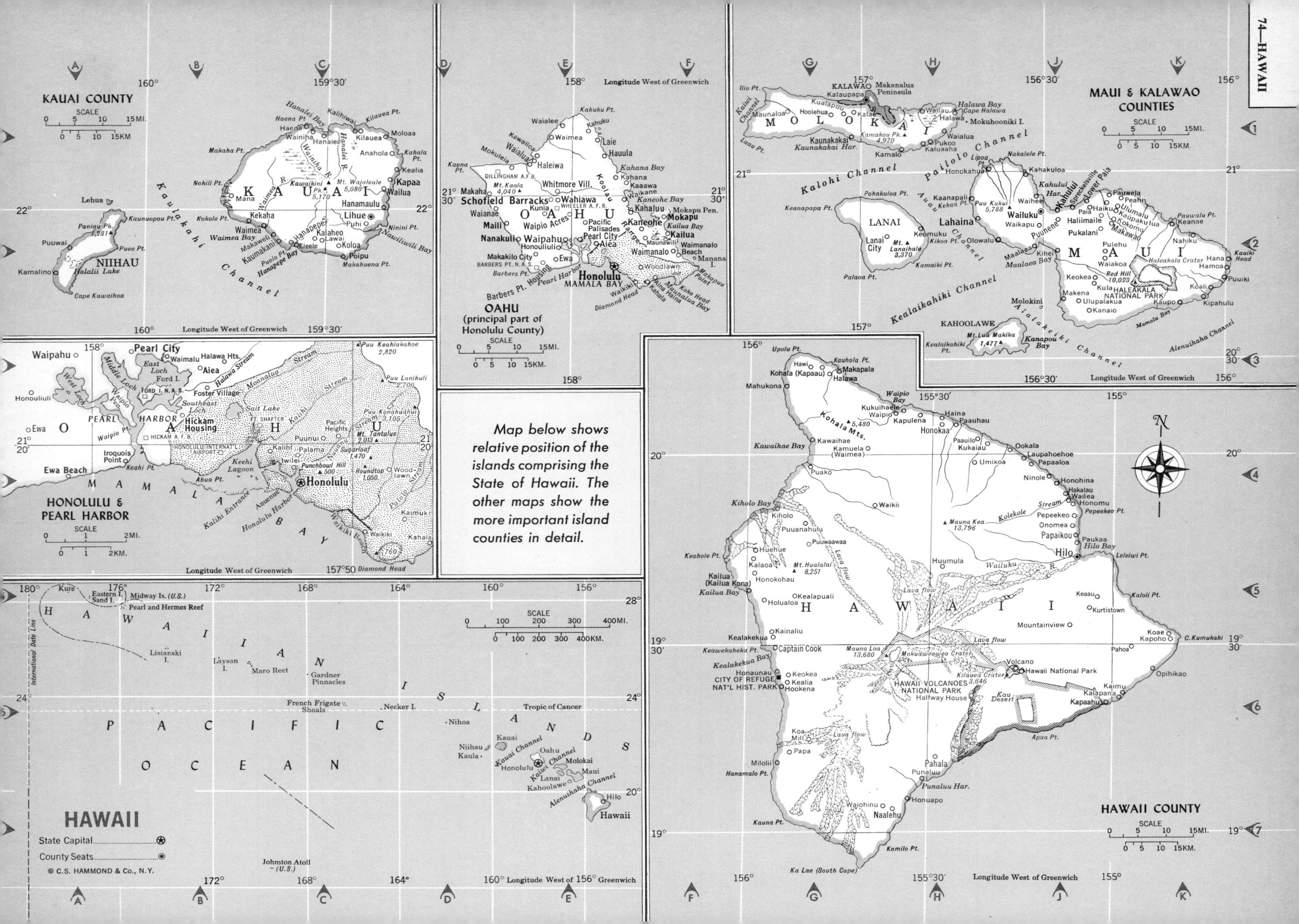
KAUAI COUNTY
SCALE
0 5 10 15MI.
0 5 10 15KM
KAUAI
NIIHAU
Kaulakahi Channel
Longitude West of Greenwich
OAHU
(principal part of Honolulu County)
SCALE
0 5 10 15MI.
0 5 10 15KM.
Schofield Barracks
Honolulu
MAMALA BAY
MAUI & KALAWAO COUNTIES
SCALE
0 5 10 15MI.
0 5 10 15KM.
MOLOKAI
LANAI
MAUI
KAHOOLAWE
Kalohi Channel
Pailolo Channel
Auau Channel
Kealaikahiki Channel
Alalakeiki Channel
Alenuihaha Channel
HALEAKALA NATIONAL PARK
HONOLULU & PEARL HARBOR
SCALE
0 1 2MI.
0 1 2KM.
Pearl City
Hickam Housing
Honolulu
Waikiki Beach
Diamond Head
Map below shows relative position of the islands comprising the State of Hawaii. The other maps show the more important island counties in detail.
HAWAII COUNTY
SCALE
0 5 10 15MI.
0 5 10 15KM.
HAWAII
Mauna Kea 13,796
Mauna Loa 13,680
Mt. Hualalai 8,251
Kohala Mts.
Hilo
Kailua (Kailua Kona)
HAWAII VOLCANOES NATIONAL PARK
CITY OF REFUGE NAT'L HIST. PARK
Ka Lae (South Cape)
HAWAII
State Capital
County Seats
HAWAIIAN ISLANDS
PACIFIC OCEAN
SCALE
0 100 200 300 400MI.
0 100 200 300 400KM.
Tropic of Cancer
International Date Line
Midway Is. (U.S.)
Pearl and Hermes Reef
Johnston Atoll (U.S.)
160° Longitude West of 156° Greenwich
© C.S. HAMMOND & Co., N.Y.

IDAHO
SCALE
0 5 10 20 30 40 50 60 MI.
0 5 10 20 30 40 50 60 KM.
State Capitals
County Seats
B. R. C O L U M B I A
A L T A.
W A S H I N G T O N
O R E G O N
M O N T A N A
N E V A D A
U T A H
W Y O M I N G
117°
116°
115°
114°
113°
112°
111°
49°
48°
47°
46°
45°
44°
43°
42°
BOUNDARY
BONNER
KOOTENAI
SHOSHONE
BENEWAH
LATAH
CLEARWATER
NEZ PERCE
LEWIS
IDAHO
ADAMS
VALLEY
WASHINGTON
PAYETTE
GEM
BOISE
CANYON
ADA
ELMORE
OWYHEE
CAMAS
BLAINE
CUSTER
LEMHI
CLARK
FREMONT
JEFFERSON
MADISON
TETON
BUTTE
BONNEVILLE
BINGHAM
POWER
BANNOCK
CARIBOU
BEAR LAKE
FRANKLIN
ONEIDA
CASSIA
TWIN FALLS
GOODING
LINCOLN
JEROME
MINIDOKA
Boise
Idaho Falls
Pocatello
Lewiston
Moscow
Coeur d'Alene
Sandpoint
Bonners Ferry
Wallace
Grangeville
Salmon
Challis
Ketchum
Hailey
Twin Falls
Burley
Rupert
Blackfoot
Rexburg
Driggs
Montpelier
Preston
Malad City
Mountain Home
Caldwell
Nampa
Weiser
Payette
Emmett
SPOKANE
Missoula
Helena
BUTTE
GREAT FALLS
Kalispell
Bozeman
Hamilton
Dillon
Anaconda
SALMON RIVER MTS.
BITTERROOT RANGE
CLEARWATER MTS.
SAWTOOTH NATIONAL RECREATION AREA
CRATERS OF THE MOON NATIONAL MON.
LOST RIVER RANGE
LEMHI RANGE
BEAVERHEAD MTS.
CENTENNIAL MTS.
CONTINENTAL DIVIDE
SEVEN DEVILS MTS.
IDAHO MOUNTAINS
GLACIER NATIONAL PARK
BLACKFEET INDIAN RESERVATION
YELLOWSTONE NATIONAL PARK
GRAND TETON NATIONAL PARK
FORT HALL INDIAN RES.
NAT'L REACTOR TESTING STA. U.S.A.E.C. RES.
Snake R.
Salmon R.
Clearwater R.
Borah Pk. 12,662
Copyright by C. S. Hammond & Co., N. Y.
Longitude West of Greenwich

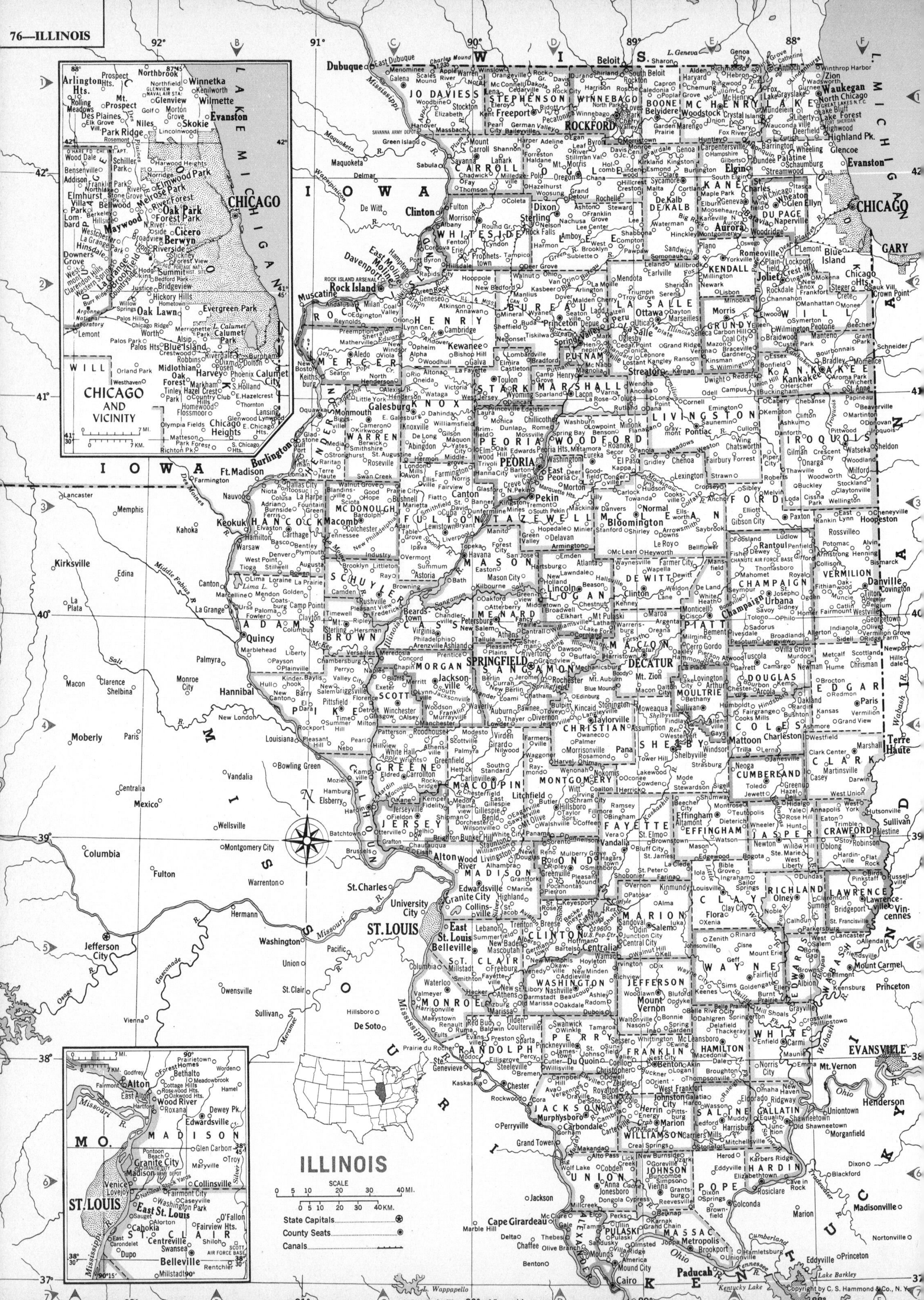
ILLINOIS
SCALE
0 5 10 20 30 40 MI.
0 5 10 20 30 40 KM.
State Capitals
County Seats
Canals
CHICAGO AND VICINITY
ST. LOUIS
MO.
MADISON
ST. CLAIR
IOWA
WISCONSIN
MISSOURI
KENTUCKY
INDIANA
LAKE MICHIGAN
JO DAVIESS
STEPHENSON
WINNEBAGO
BOONE
MC HENRY
LAKE
CARROLL
OGLE
DE KALB
KANE
DU PAGE
COOK
WHITESIDE
LEE
BUREAU
LA SALLE
KENDALL
GRUNDY
WILL
ROCK ISLAND
HENRY
MERCER
STARK
PUTNAM
MARSHALL
KANKAKEE
KNOX
WARREN
HENDERSON
PEORIA
WOODFORD
LIVINGSTON
IROQUOIS
MC DONOUGH
HANCOCK
FULTON
TAZEWELL
MC LEAN
FORD
SCHUYLER
MASON
DE WITT
CHAMPAIGN
VERMILION
ADAMS
BROWN
CASS
MENARD
LOGAN
PIATT
MORGAN
SANGAMON
MACON
DOUGLAS
EDGAR
PIKE
SCOTT
CHRISTIAN
MOULTRIE
COLES
GREENE
MACOUPIN
MONTGOMERY
SHELBY
CUMBERLAND
CLARK
JERSEY
CALHOUN
FAYETTE
EFFINGHAM
JASPER
CRAWFORD
MADISON
BOND
CLAY
RICHLAND
LAWRENCE
CLINTON
MARION
MONROE
WASHINGTON
JEFFERSON
WAYNE
EDWARDS
WABASH
RANDOLPH
PERRY
FRANKLIN
HAMILTON
WHITE
JACKSON
WILLIAMSON
SALINE
GALLATIN
UNION
JOHNSON
POPE
HARDIN
ALEXANDER
PULASKI
MASSAC
CHICAGO
ROCKFORD
PEORIA
SPRINGFIELD
DECATUR
ST. LOUIS
EVANSVILLE
Copyright by C. S. Hammond & Co., N.Y.

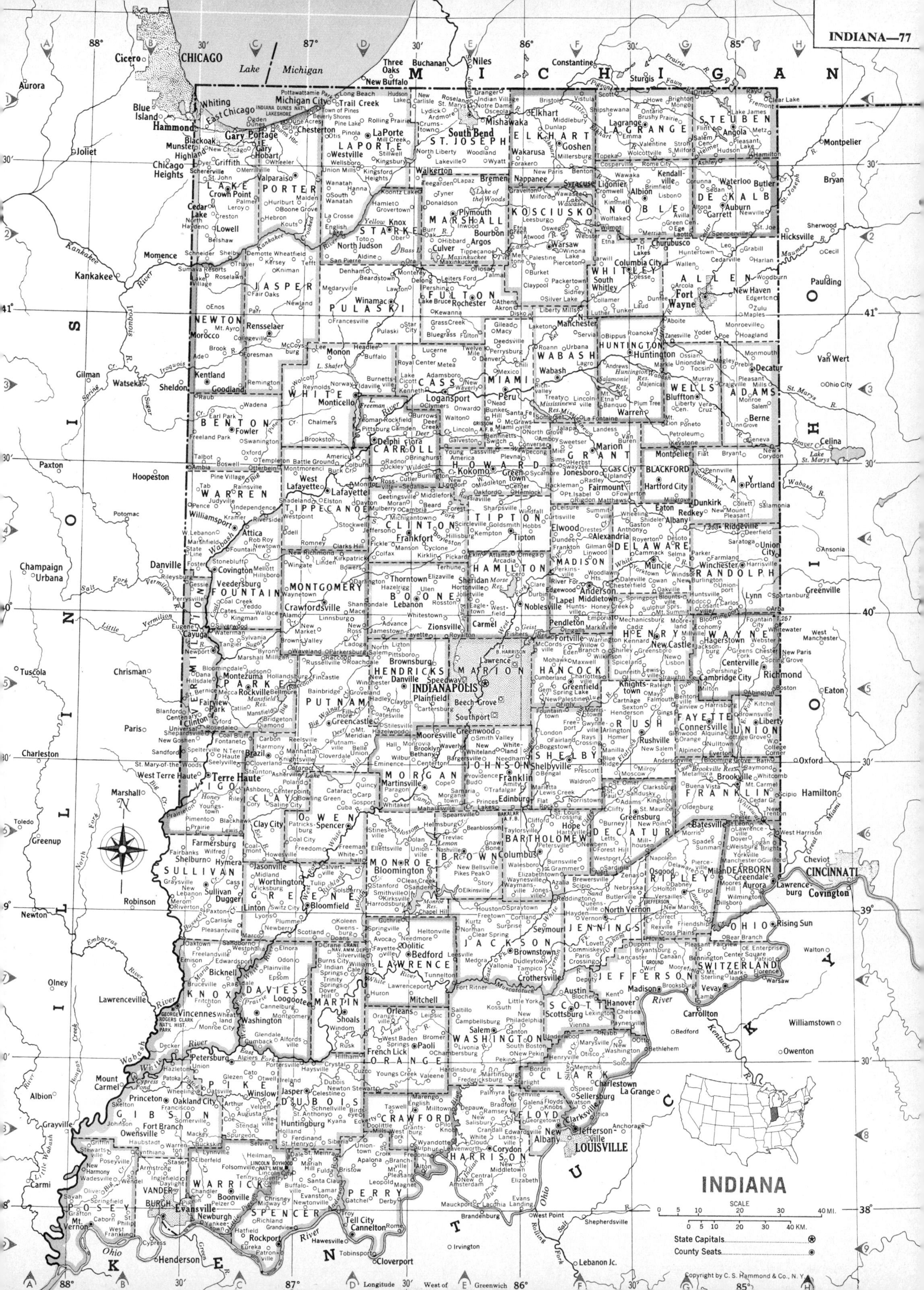
INDIANA
SCALE
0 5 10 20 30 40 MI.
0 5 10 20 30 40 KM.
State Capitals
County Seats
Copyright by C. S. Hammond & Co., N. Y.
Longitude West of Greenwich
MICHIGAN
ILLINOIS
OHIO
KENTUCKY
Lake Michigan
CHICAGO
CINCINNATI
LOUISVILLE
INDIANAPOLIS
South Bend
Fort Wayne
Gary
Hammond
Evansville
Terre Haute
Lafayette
Muncie
Kokomo
Anderson
Richmond
Bloomington
Columbus
New Albany
Jeffersonville
Vincennes
Logansport
Elkhart
Michigan City
Marion
LAKE
PORTER
LAPORTE
ST. JOSEPH
ELKHART
LAGRANGE
STEUBEN
NEWTON
JASPER
STARKE
MARSHALL
KOSCIUSKO
NOBLE
DE KALB
PULASKI
FULTON
WHITLEY
ALLEN
BENTON
WHITE
CASS
MIAMI
WABASH
HUNTINGTON
WELLS
ADAMS
WARREN
TIPPECANOE
CARROLL
HOWARD
GRANT
BLACKFORD
JAY
FOUNTAIN
MONTGOMERY
CLINTON
TIPTON
MADISON
DELAWARE
RANDOLPH
VERMILLION
PARKE
BOONE
HAMILTON
HENRY
WAYNE
PUTNAM
HENDRICKS
MARION
HANCOCK
VIGO
CLAY
OWEN
MORGAN
JOHNSON
SHELBY
RUSH
FAYETTE
UNION
FRANKLIN
SULLIVAN
GREENE
MONROE
BROWN
BARTHOLOMEW
DECATUR
RIPLEY
DEARBORN
KNOX
DAVIESS
MARTIN
LAWRENCE
JACKSON
JENNINGS
JEFFERSON
OHIO
SWITZERLAND
SCOTT
GIBSON
PIKE
DUBOIS
ORANGE
WASHINGTON
CLARK
POSEY
VANDERBURGH
WARRICK
SPENCER
PERRY
CRAWFORD
HARRISON
FLOYD
88°
87°
86°
85°
41°
40°
39°
38°

IOWA
SCALE
0 5 10 20 30 40 MI.
0 5 10 20 30 40 KM.
State Capitals
County Seats
Copyright by C. S. Hammond & Co., N. Y.
MINNESOTA
WISCONSIN
ILLINOIS
MISSOURI
NEBRASKA
S. DAK.
Mississippi River
Missouri River
Des Moines River
LYON
OSCEOLA
DICKINSON
EMMET
KOSSUTH
WINNEBAGO
WORTH
MITCHELL
HOWARD
WINNESHIEK
ALLAMAKEE
SIOUX
O'BRIEN
CLAY
PALO ALTO
HANCOCK
CERRO GORDO
FLOYD
CHICKASAW
FAYETTE
CLAYTON
PLYMOUTH
CHEROKEE
BUENA VISTA
POCAHONTAS
HUMBOLDT
WRIGHT
FRANKLIN
BUTLER
BREMER
BLACK HAWK
BUCHANAN
DELAWARE
DUBUQUE
WOODBURY
IDA
SAC
CALHOUN
WEBSTER
HAMILTON
HARDIN
GRUNDY
TAMA
BENTON
LINN
JONES
JACKSON
MONONA
CRAWFORD
CARROLL
GREENE
BOONE
STORY
MARSHALL
CLINTON
CEDAR
HARRISON
SHELBY
AUDUBON
GUTHRIE
DALLAS
POLK
JASPER
POWESHIEK
IOWA
JOHNSON
MUSCATINE
SCOTT
POTTAWATTAMIE
CASS
ADAIR
MADISON
WARREN
MARION
MAHASKA
KEOKUK
WASHINGTON
LOUISA
MILLS
MONTGOMERY
ADAMS
UNION
CLARKE
LUCAS
MONROE
WAPELLO
JEFFERSON
HENRY
DES MOINES
FREMONT
PAGE
TAYLOR
RINGGOLD
DECATUR
WAYNE
APPANOOSE
DAVIS
VAN BUREN
LEE
DES MOINES
DAVENPORT
CEDAR RAPIDS
SIOUX CITY
Council Bluffs
OMAHA
Dubuque
Waterloo
Rock Island

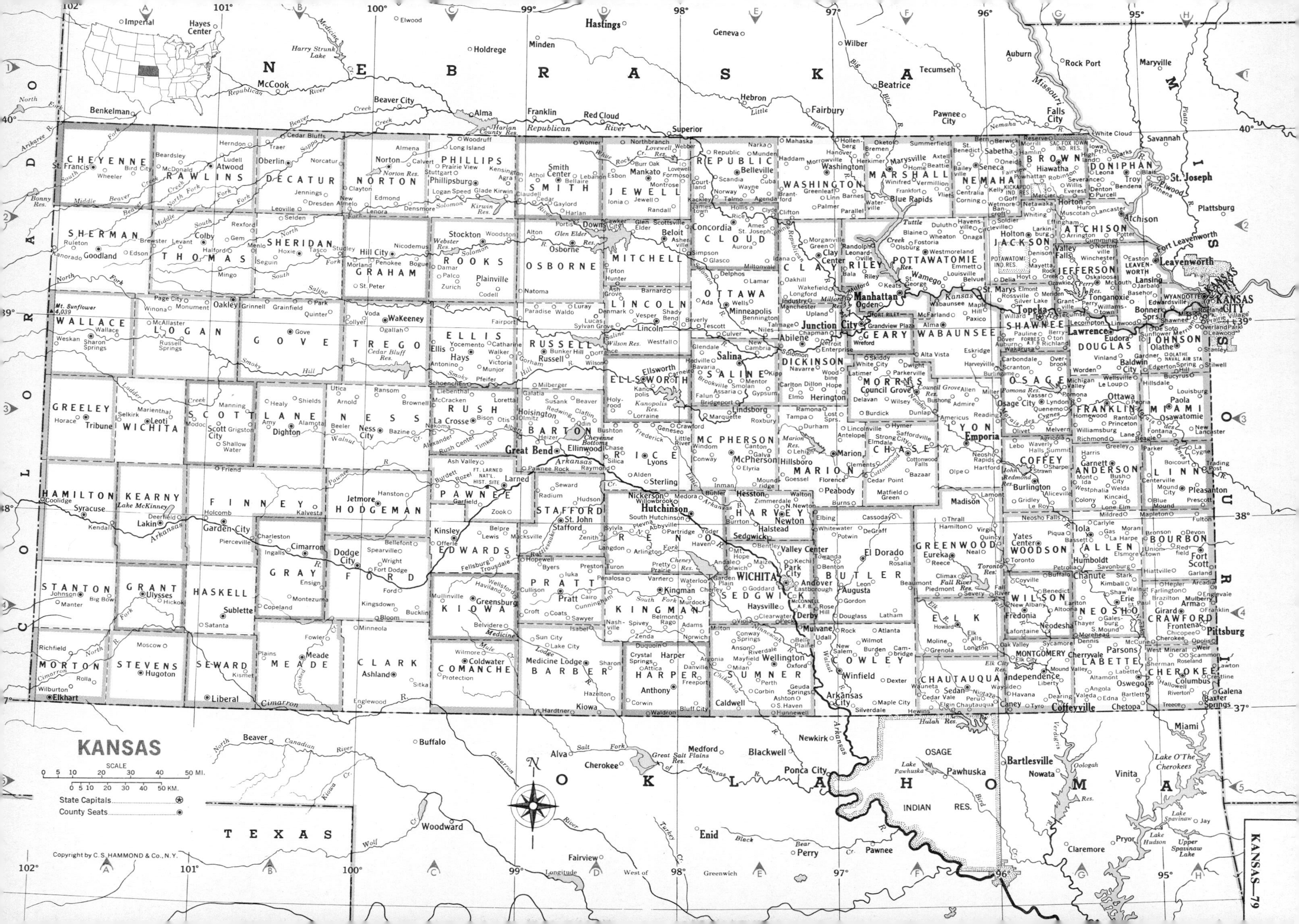
KANSAS
NEBRASKA
MISSOURI
OKLAHOMA
COLORADO
TEXAS
OSAGE INDIAN RES.
SCALE
0 5 10 20 30 40 50 MI.
0 5 10 20 30 40 50 KM.
State Capitals
County Seats
CHEYENNE
RAWLINS
DECATUR
NORTON
PHILLIPS
SMITH
JEWELL
REPUBLIC
WASHINGTON
MARSHALL
NEMAHA
BROWN
DONIPHAN
SHERMAN
THOMAS
SHERIDAN
GRAHAM
ROOKS
OSBORNE
MITCHELL
CLOUD
CLAY
RILEY
POTTAWATOMIE
JACKSON
ATCHISON
JEFFERSON
LEAVENWORTH
WYANDOTTE
WALLACE
LOGAN
GOVE
TREGO
ELLIS
RUSSELL
LINCOLN
OTTAWA
DICKINSON
GEARY
WABAUNSEE
SHAWNEE
DOUGLAS
JOHNSON
GREELEY
WICHITA
SCOTT
LANE
NESS
RUSH
BARTON
ELLSWORTH
SALINE
MORRIS
LYON
OSAGE
FRANKLIN
MIAMI
HAMILTON
KEARNY
FINNEY
HODGEMAN
PAWNEE
STAFFORD
RICE
McPHERSON
MARION
CHASE
COFFEY
ANDERSON
LINN
HARVEY
RENO
SEDGWICK
BUTLER
GREENWOOD
WOODSON
ALLEN
BOURBON
STANTON
GRANT
HASKELL
GRAY
FORD
EDWARDS
PRATT
KINGMAN
WILSON
NEOSHO
CRAWFORD
ELK
KIOWA
MORTON
STEVENS
SEWARD
MEADE
CLARK
COMANCHE
BARBER
HARPER
SUMNER
COWLEY
CHAUTAUQUA
MONTGOMERY
LABETTE
CHEROKEE
Topeka
Wichita
Kansas City
Hutchinson
Salina
Dodge City
Garden City
Emporia
Lawrence
Leavenworth
Manhattan
Junction City
Great Bend
Copyright by C. S. HAMMOND & Co., N. Y.

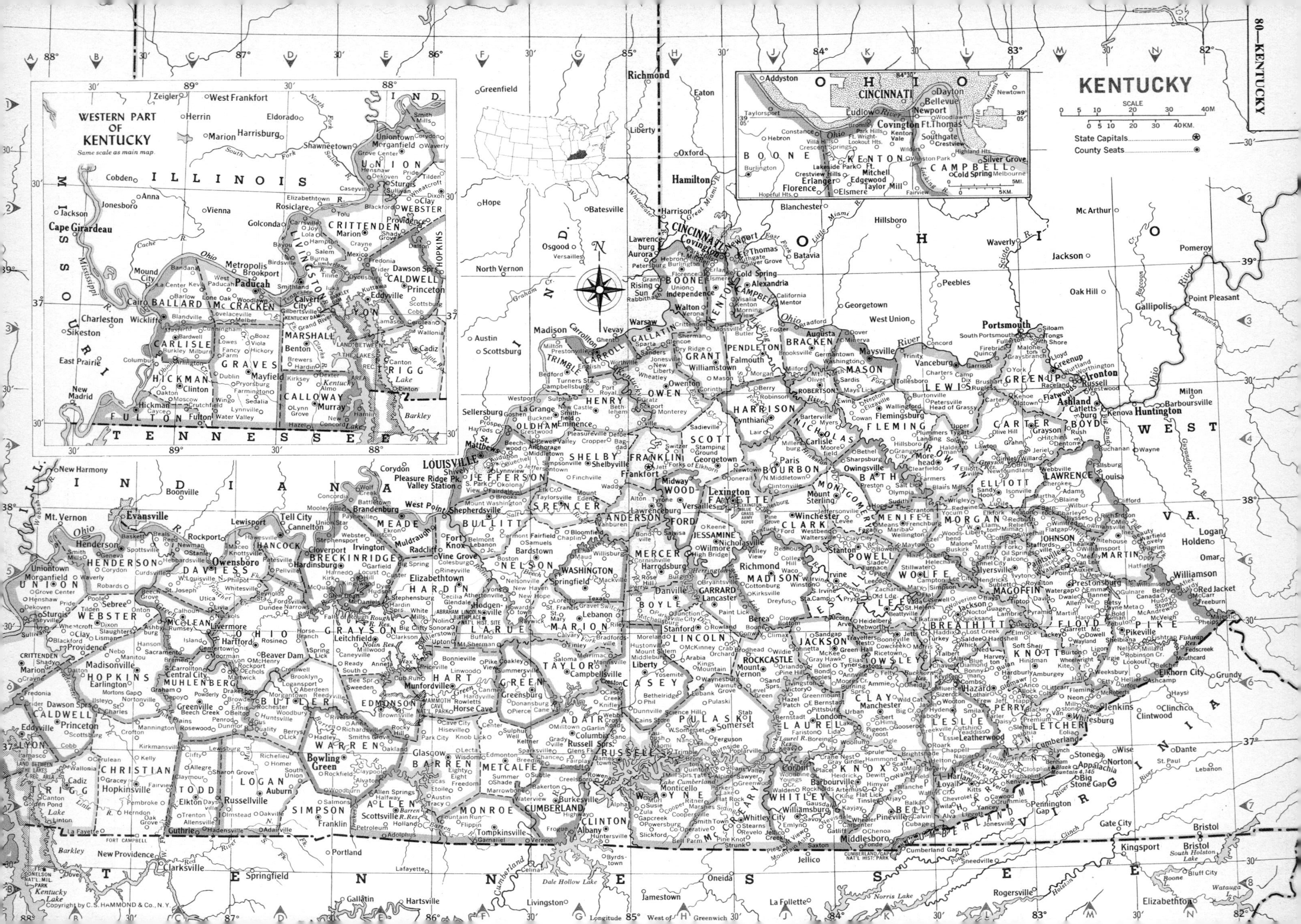

KENTUCKY
SCALE
State Capitals
County Seats
WESTERN PART OF KENTUCKY
Same scale as main map
ILLINOIS
INDIANA
OHIO
WEST VA.
VIRGINIA
TENNESSEE
MISSOURI
CINCINNATI
Covington
Newport
LOUISVILLE
Lexington
Frankfort
Paducah
Owensboro
Bowling Green
Ashland
Evansville
Huntington
Portsmouth
Copyright by C. S. HAMMOND & Co., N. Y.
Longitude 85° West of Greenwich

LOUISIANA
SCALE
0 5 10 20 30 40 MI.
0 5 10 20 30 40 KM.
State Capitals
Parish Seats
Canals
© C.S. HAMMOND & Co., N.Y.
NEW ORLEANS, BATON ROUGE AND VICINITY
0 5 10 15 20 MI.
0 5 10 15 20 KM.
LAKE PONTCHARTRAIN
LAKE MAUREPAS
NEW ORLEANS
BATON ROUGE
SHREVEPORT
Bossier City
MONROE
Alexandria
Lake Charles
Lafayette
Houma
GULF OF MEXICO
MISSISSIPPI SOUND
CHANDELEUR SOUND
BRETON SOUND
MOBILE BAY
ATCHAFALAYA BAY
SABINE LAKE
ARKANSAS
TEXAS
MISSISSIPPI
MISS.
ALA.
Longitude 91° West of Greenwich

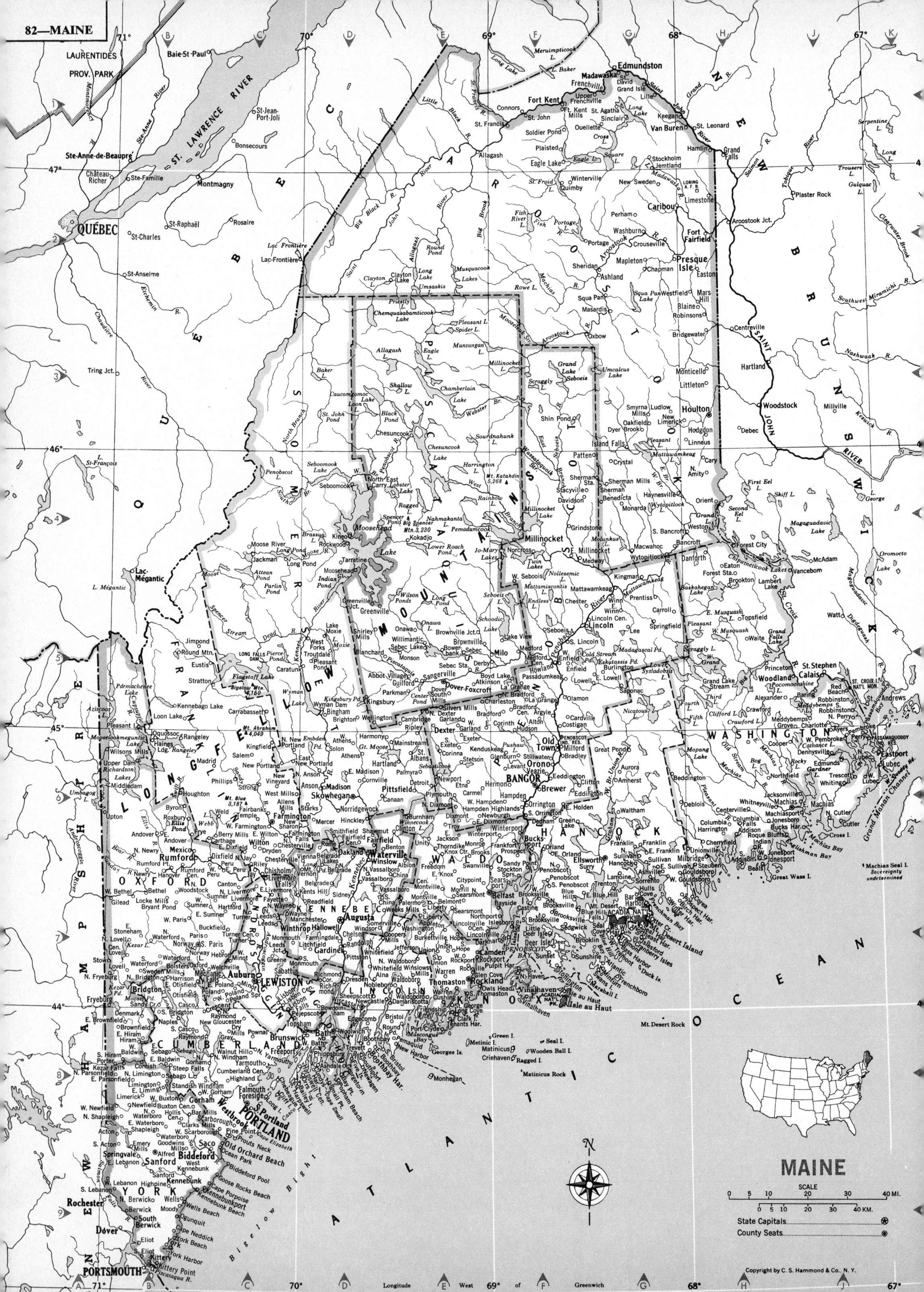
MAINE
SCALE
0 5 10 20 30 40 MI.
0 5 10 20 30 40 KM.
State Capitals
County Seats
ATLANTIC OCEAN
QUEBEC
NEW BRUNSWICK
NEW HAMPSHIRE
AROOSTOOK
PISCATAQUIS
SOMERSET
FRANKLIN
OXFORD
ANDROSCOGGIN
KENNEBEC
PENOBSCOT
WASHINGTON
HANCOCK
WALDO
KNOX
LINCOLN
SAGADAHOC
CUMBERLAND
YORK
LONGFELLOW MOUNTAINS
ST. LAWRENCE RIVER
SAINT JOHN RIVER
LAURENTIDES PROV. PARK
Québec
Edmundston
Fort Kent
Madawaska
Van Buren
Caribou
Presque Isle
Fort Fairfield
Houlton
Millinocket
Mt. Katahdin 5,268
Moosehead Lake
Greenville
Dover-Foxcroft
Old Town
Orono
BANGOR
Brewer
Ellsworth
Bucksport
Belfast
Camden
Rockland
Thomaston
Waterville
Skowhegan
Augusta
Gardiner
Hallowell
Farmington
Rumford
Auburn
LEWISTON
Brunswick
Bath
PORTLAND
South Portland
Westbrook
Saco
Biddeford
Sanford
Kennebunk
Kennebunkport
Old Orchard Beach
Calais
St. Stephen
Eastport
Lubec
Machias
Mt. Desert Island
ACADIA NAT'L PK.
Isle au Haut
Vinalhaven
Penobscot Bay
Monhegan
Matinicus Rock
Mt. Desert Rock
Bigelow Bight
Kittery
PORTSMOUTH
Dover
Rochester
Grand Manan Channel
Machias Seal I. Sovereignty undetermined
Longitude West 69° of Greenwich
Copyright by C. S. Hammond & Co., N. Y.

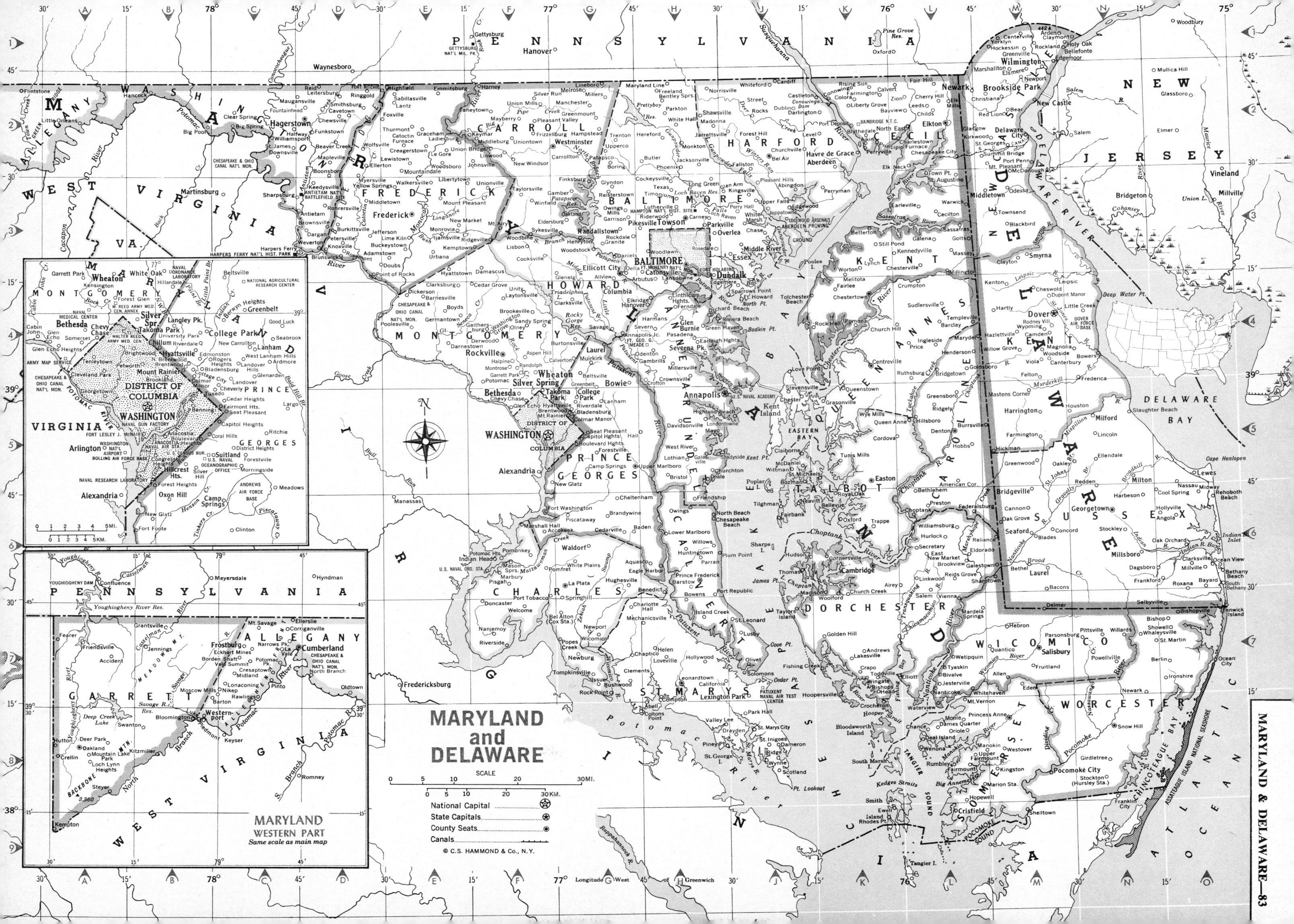
MARYLAND and DELAWARE
SCALE
0 5 10 20 30MI.
0 5 10 20 30KM.
National Capital
State Capitals
County Seats
Canals
© C.S. HAMMOND & Co., N.Y.
MARYLAND
WESTERN PART
Same scale as main map
DISTRICT OF COLUMBIA
WASHINGTON
BALTIMORE
Annapolis
Dover
Wilmington
ATLANTIC OCEAN
DELAWARE BAY
DELAWARE RIVER
NEW JERSEY
PENNSYLVANIA
WEST VIRGINIA
VIRGINIA
Longitude West of Greenwich

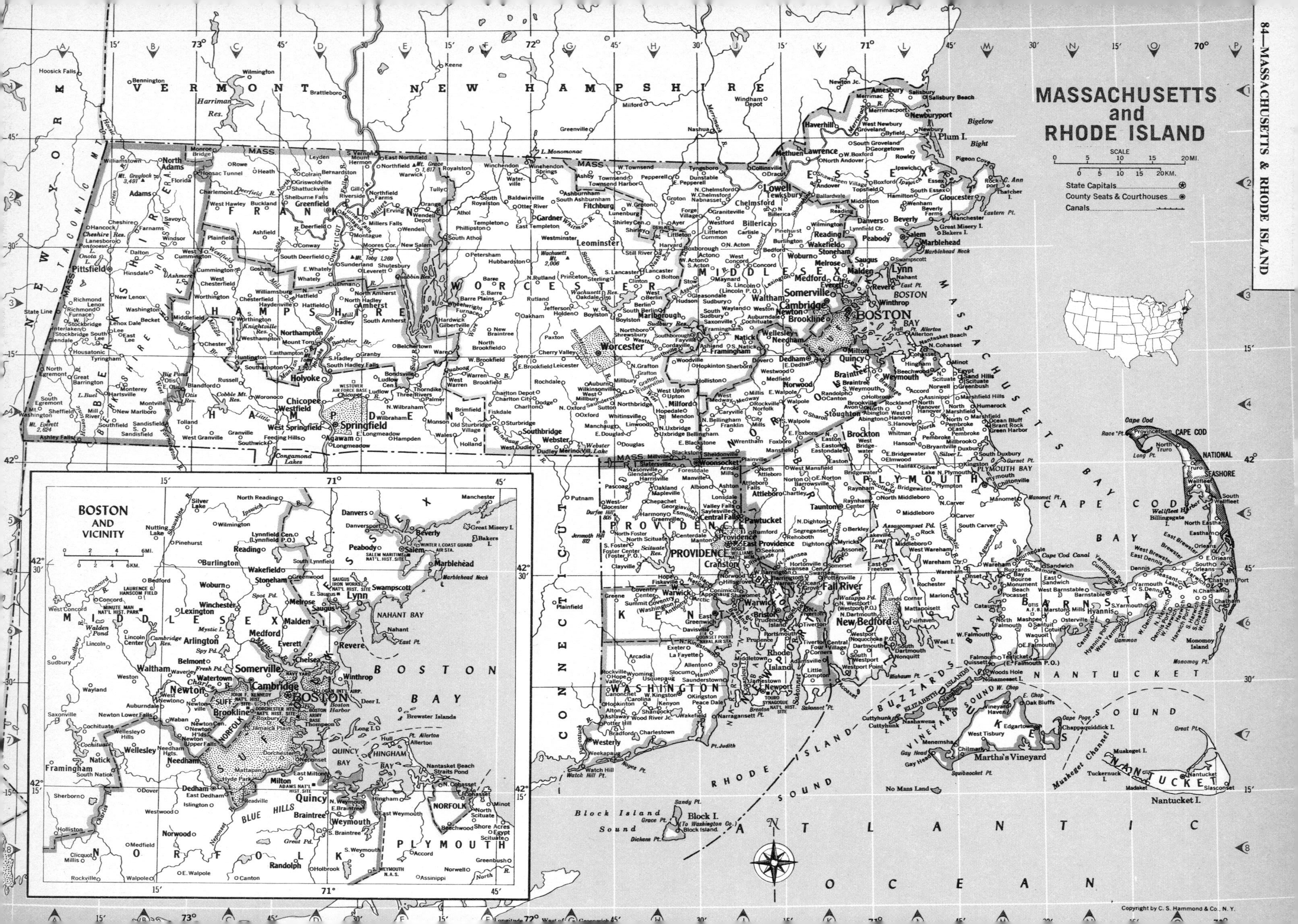

MASSACHUSETTS and RHODE ISLAND
SCALE
State Capitals
County Seats & Courthouses
Canals
BOSTON AND VICINITY
VERMONT
NEW HAMPSHIRE
NEW YORK
CONNECTICUT
MASSACHUSETTS BAY
CAPE COD BAY
BUZZARDS BAY
RHODE ISLAND SOUND
NANTUCKET SOUND
Block Island Sound
ATLANTIC OCEAN
BOSTON
PROVIDENCE
Worcester
Springfield
Martha's Vineyard
Nantucket I.
Copyright by C. S. Hammond & Co., N. Y.

MICHIGAN
SCALE
0 5 10 20 30 40 50 MI.
0 5 10 20 30 40 50 KM.
State Capitals
County Seats
Canals
ISLE ROYALE (NATIONAL PARK)
L. SUPERIOR
Same scale as main map
MICHIGAN WESTERN PART
Same scale as main map
LAKE SUPERIOR
LAKE MICHIGAN
LAKE HURON
LAKE ERIE
LAKE ST. CLAIR
ONTARIO
WISCONSIN
INDIANA
OHIO
KEWEENAW
HOUGHTON
ONTONAGON
GOGEBIC
BARAGA
IRON
MARQUETTE
DICKINSON
MENOMINEE
DELTA
ALGER
SCHOOLCRAFT
LUCE
CHIPPEWA
MACKINAC
EMMET
CHEBOYGAN
PRESQUE ISLE
CHARLEVOIX
ANTRIM
OTSEGO
MONTMORENCY
ALPENA
LEELANAU
GRAND TRAVERSE
KALKASKA
CRAWFORD
OSCODA
ALCONA
BENZIE
MANISTEE
WEXFORD
MISSAUKEE
ROSCOMMON
OGEMAW
IOSCO
MASON
LAKE
OSCEOLA
CLARE
GLADWIN
ARENAC
HURON
OCEANA
NEWAYGO
MECOSTA
ISABELLA
MIDLAND
BAY
TUSCOLA
SANILAC
MUSKEGON
MONTCALM
GRATIOT
SAGINAW
KENT
OTTAWA
IONIA
CLINTON
SHIAWASSEE
GENESEE
LAPEER
ST. CLAIR
ALLEGAN
BARRY
EATON
INGHAM
LIVINGSTON
OAKLAND
MACOMB
VAN BUREN
KALAMAZOO
CALHOUN
JACKSON
WASHTENAW
WAYNE
CASS
ST. JOSEPH
BRANCH
HILLSDALE
LENAWEE
MONROE
Lansing
DETROIT
GRAND RAPIDS
FLINT
MILWAUKEE
WINDSOR
TOLEDO
SOUTH BEND
ONT.
Copyright by C. S. Hammond & Co., N. Y.

MINNESOTA
SCALE
0 5 10 20 30 40 50 MI.
0 5 10 20 30 40 50 KM.
State Capitals
County Seats
MINNESOTA NORTHEASTERN PART
Same scale as main map
CANADA
MANITOBA
ONTARIO
NORTH DAKOTA
SOUTH DAKOTA
IOWA
WIS.
LAKE SUPERIOR
Lake of the Woods
KITTSON
ROSEAU
LAKE OF THE WOODS
MARSHALL
KOOCHICHING
PENNINGTON
BELTRAMI
RED LAKE
POLK
CLEARWATER
ITASCA
SAINT LOUIS
LAKE
COOK
NORMAN
MAHNOMEN
HUBBARD
CASS
CLAY
BECKER
WILKIN
OTTER TAIL
WADENA
CROW WING
AITKIN
CARLTON
PINE
TODD
MORRISON
MILLE LACS
KANABEC
GRANT
DOUGLAS
TRAVERSE
STEVENS
POPE
STEARNS
BENTON
SHERBURNE
ISANTI
CHISAGO
BIG STONE
SWIFT
KANDIYOHI
MEEKER
WRIGHT
ANOKA
WASHINGTON
HENNEPIN
RAMSEY
CHIPPEWA
LAC QUI PARLE
YELLOW MEDICINE
RENVILLE
MC LEOD
CARVER
SCOTT
DAKOTA
SIBLEY
LINCOLN
LYON
REDWOOD
NICOLLET
LE SUEUR
RICE
GOODHUE
WABASHA
BROWN
PIPESTONE
MURRAY
COTTONWOOD
WATONWAN
BLUE EARTH
WASECA
STEELE
DODGE
OLMSTED
WINONA
ROCK
NOBLES
JACKSON
MARTIN
FARIBAULT
FREEBORN
MOWER
FILLMORE
HOUSTON
DULUTH
MINNEAPOLIS
ST. PAUL

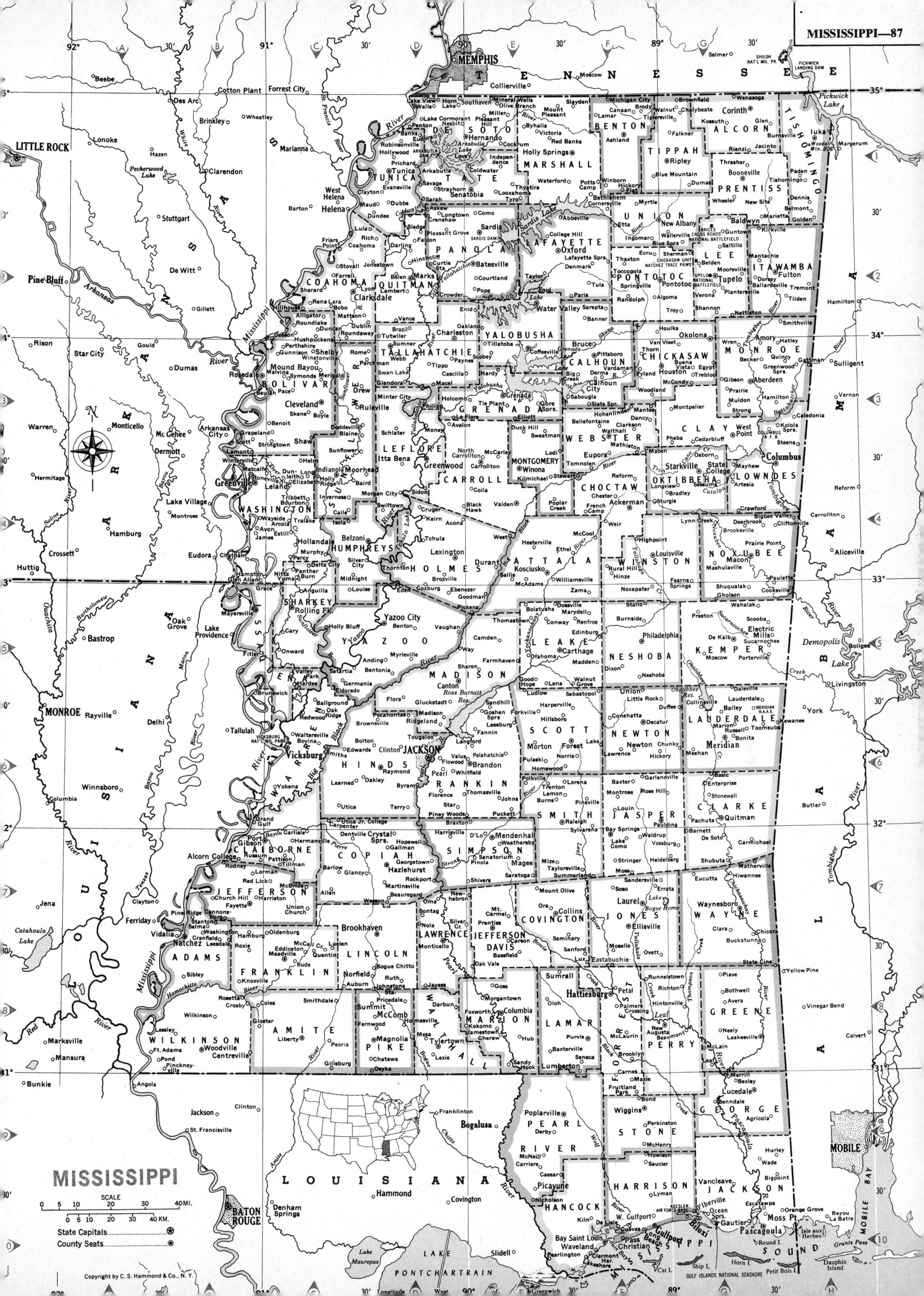
MISSISSIPPI
SCALE
0 5 10 20 30 40 MI.
0 5 10 20 30 40 KM.
State Capitals
County Seats
Copyright by C. S. Hammond & Co., N. Y.
TENNESSEE
ARKANSAS
LOUISIANA
ALABAMA
MEMPHIS
LITTLE ROCK
JACKSON
MOBILE
BATON ROUGE
MONROE
Mississippi River
Yazoo River
Big Black River
Pearl River
Pascagoula River
Tombigbee River
Sardis Lake
Grenada Lake
Enid Lake
Arkabutla Lake
Ross Barnett Res.
Pickwick Lake
Lake Pontchartrain
Mississippi Sound
Gulf Islands National Seashore
Ship I.
Horn I.
Cat I.
Petit Bois I.
Dauphin Island
Mobile Bay
DE SOTO
MARSHALL
BENTON
TIPPAH
ALCORN
TISHOMINGO
TUNICA
TATE
PRENTISS
UNION
LAFAYETTE
PANOLA
QUITMAN
COAHOMA
PONTOTOC
LEE
ITAWAMBA
YALOBUSHA
TALLAHATCHIE
CALHOUN
CHICKASAW
MONROE
BOLIVAR
SUNFLOWER
GRENADA
LEFLORE
CARROLL
MONTGOMERY
WEBSTER
CLAY
OKTIBBEHA
LOWNDES
CHOCTAW
WASHINGTON
HUMPHREYS
HOLMES
ATTALA
WINSTON
NOXUBEE
SHARKEY
YAZOO
LEAKE
NESHOBA
KEMPER
MADISON
ISSAQUENA
WARREN
HINDS
RANKIN
SCOTT
NEWTON
LAUDERDALE
CLAIBORNE
COPIAH
SIMPSON
SMITH
JASPER
CLARKE
JEFFERSON
LAWRENCE
JEFFERSON DAVIS
COVINGTON
JONES
WAYNE
ADAMS
FRANKLIN
LINCOLN
WILKINSON
AMITE
PIKE
WALTHALL
MARION
LAMAR
FORREST
PERRY
GREENE
PEARL RIVER
STONE
GEORGE
HANCOCK
HARRISON
JACKSON
Oxford
Tupelo
Columbus
Greenville
Greenwood
Vicksburg
Natchez
Meridian
Hattiesburg
Laurel
Gulfport
Biloxi
Pascagoula
Clarksdale
Cleveland
Starkville
Corinth
Brookhaven
McComb
Yazoo City
Canton
Grenada
Picayune
Bay Saint Louis

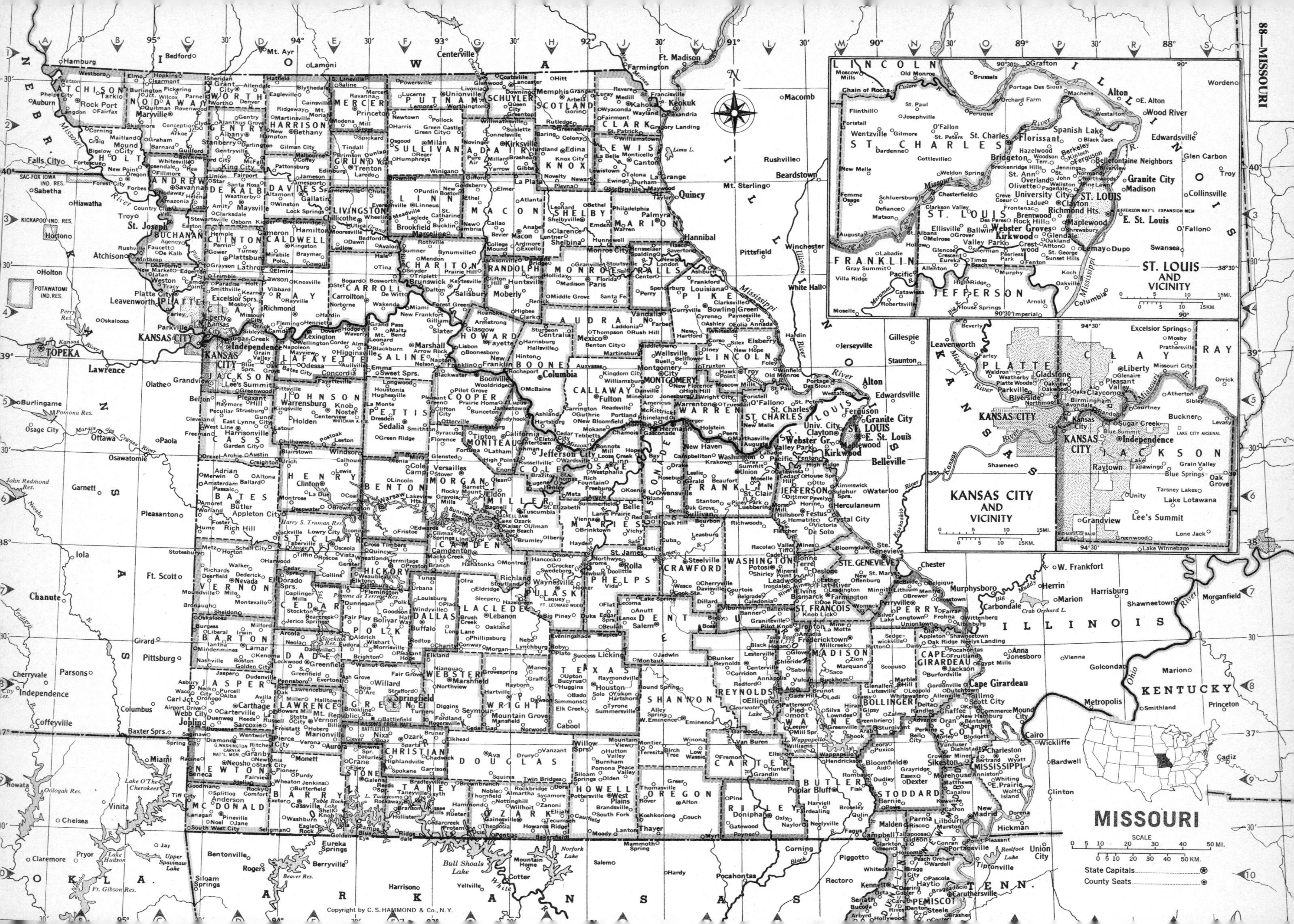

MISSOURI
SCALE
State Capitals
County Seats
ST. LOUIS AND VICINITY
KANSAS CITY AND VICINITY
IOWA
ILLINOIS
KENTUCKY
TENN.
ARKANSAS
OKLAHOMA
KANSAS
NEBRASKA
Copyright by C. S. HAMMOND & Co., N.Y.

MONTANA
SCALE
0 5 10 20 40 60 80 MI.
0 5 10 20 40 60 80 KM.
State Capitals
County Seats
© C.S. HAMMOND & Co., N.Y.
N. DAK.
S. DAK.
WYOMING
IDAHO
SASKATCHEWAN
ALBERTA
BRITISH COLUMBIA
CANADA
LINCOLN
FLATHEAD
GLACIER
TOOLE
LIBERTY
HILL
BLAINE
PHILLIPS
VALLEY
DANIELS
SHERIDAN
ROOSEVELT
RICHLAND
McCONE
DAWSON
WIBAUX
PRAIRIE
FALLON
CARTER
CUSTER
POWDER RIVER
ROSEBUD
TREASURE
BIG HORN
YELLOWSTONE
MUSSELSHELL
PETROLEUM
GARFIELD
FERGUS
JUDITH BASIN
GOLDEN VALLEY
WHEATLAND
STILLWATER
SWEET GRASS
CARBON
PARK
GALLATIN
MADISON
BEAVERHEAD
SILVER BOW
JEFFERSON
BROADWATER
MEAGHER
CASCADE
CHOUTEAU
TETON
PONDERA
LEWIS AND CLARK
POWELL
GRANITE
DEER LODGE
RAVALLI
MISSOULA
MINERAL
SANDERS
LAKE
YELLOWSTONE NATIONAL PARK
GLACIER NATIONAL PARK
BLACKFEET INDIAN RESERVATION
FORT BELKNAP INDIAN RES.
FLATHEAD INDIAN RESERVATION
CROW INDIAN RESERVATION
BITTERROOT RANGE
BIGHORN MTS.
Fort Peck Reservoir

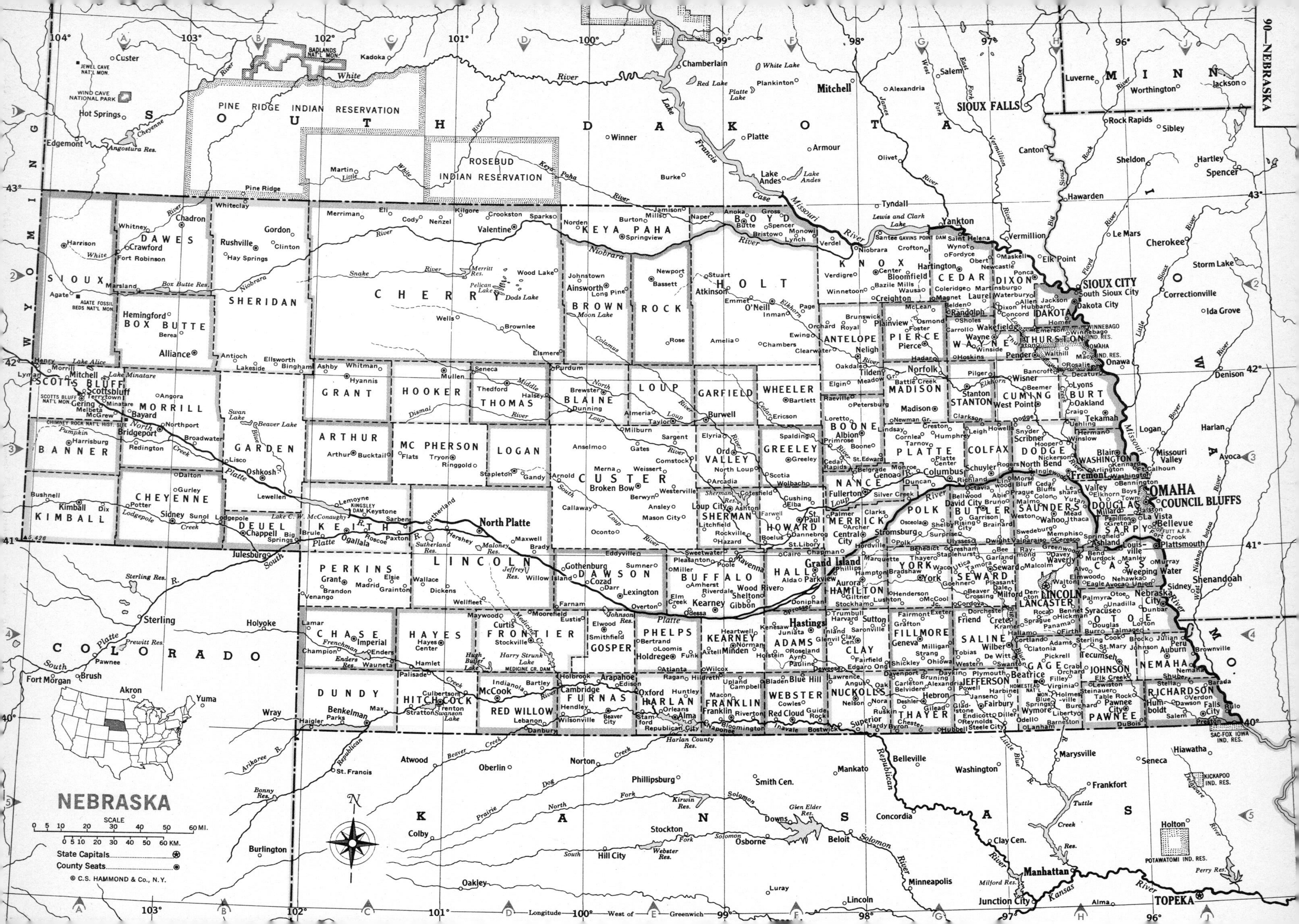
NEBRASKA
SCALE
0 5 10 20 30 40 50 60 MI.
0 5 10 20 30 40 50 60 KM.
State Capitals
County Seats
© C.S. HAMMOND & Co., N.Y.
SOUTH DAKOTA
IOWA
MINN.
MO.
KANSAS
COLORADO
WYOMING
PINE RIDGE INDIAN RESERVATION
ROSEBUD INDIAN RESERVATION
SIOUX
DAWES
BOX BUTTE
SHERIDAN
CHERRY
KEYA PAHA
BROWN
ROCK
HOLT
BOYD
KNOX
CEDAR
DIXON
DAKOTA
THURSTON
WAYNE
PIERCE
ANTELOPE
WHEELER
GARFIELD
LOUP
BLAINE
THOMAS
HOOKER
GRANT
ARTHUR
MC PHERSON
LOGAN
CUSTER
VALLEY
GREELEY
BOONE
MADISON
STANTON
CUMING
BURT
WASHINGTON
DODGE
COLFAX
PLATTE
NANCE
MERRICK
HOWARD
SHERMAN
BUFFALO
HALL
HAMILTON
POLK
BUTLER
SAUNDERS
DOUGLAS
SARPY
CASS
LANCASTER
SEWARD
YORK
FILLMORE
SALINE
GAGE
JOHNSON
NEMAHA
OTOE
PAWNEE
RICHARDSON
JEFFERSON
THAYER
NUCKOLLS
CLAY
ADAMS
WEBSTER
KEARNEY
FRANKLIN
PHELPS
HARLAN
GOSPER
FURNAS
DAWSON
FRONTIER
RED WILLOW
LINCOLN
HAYES
HITCHCOCK
CHASE
DUNDY
PERKINS
KEITH
DEUEL
GARDEN
MORRILL
CHEYENNE
KIMBALL
BANNER
SCOTTS BLUFF
LINCOLN
OMAHA
COUNCIL BLUFFS
SIOUX CITY
SIOUX FALLS
TOPEKA
North Platte
Grand Island
Hastings
Kearney
Missouri
Platte
Republican
Niobrara
Longitude West of Greenwich

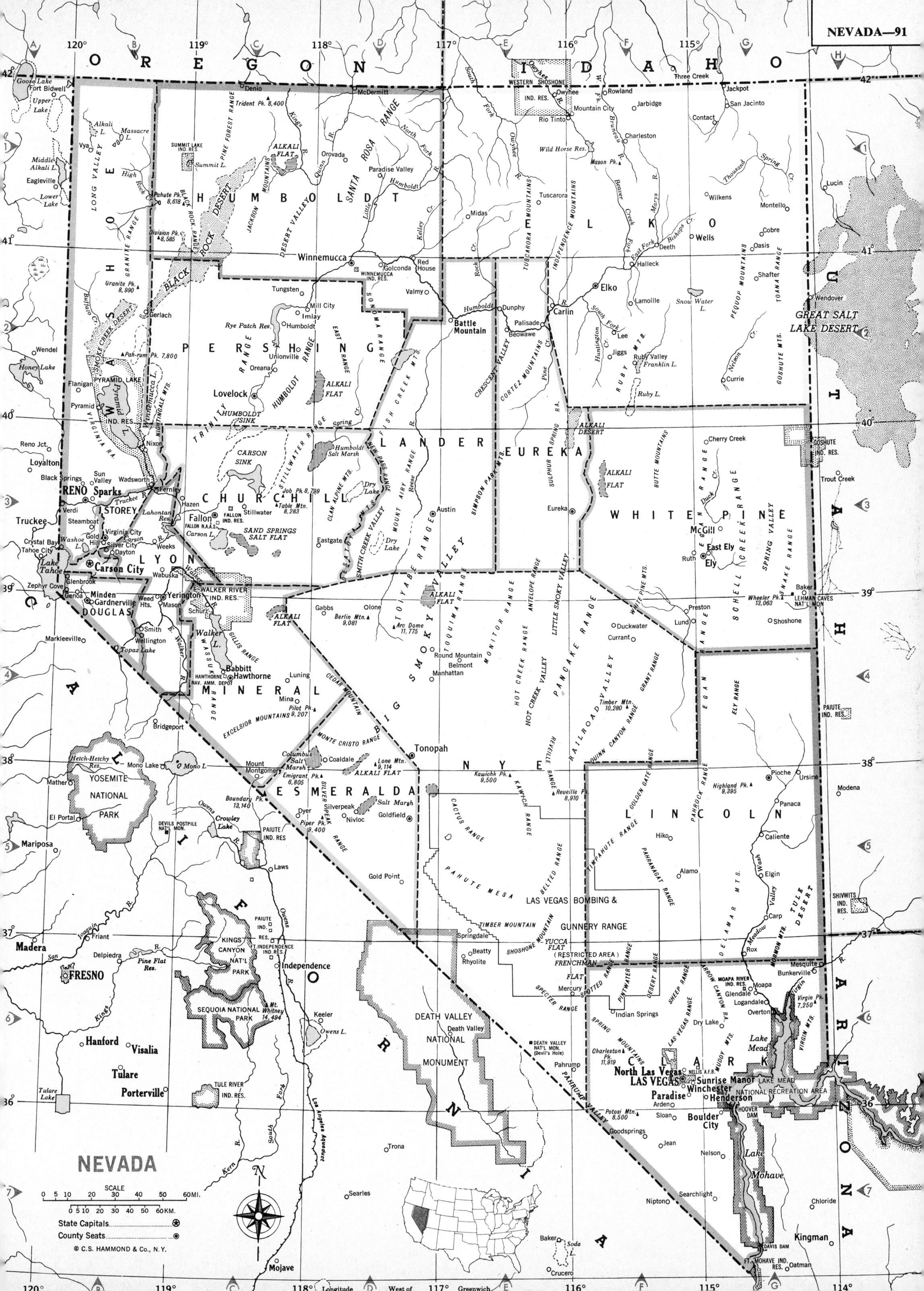
NEVADA
O R E G O N
I D A H O
U T A H
A R I Z O N A
C A L I F O R N I A
H U M B O L D T
E L K O
P E R S H I N G
W A S H O E
L A N D E R
E U R E K A
C H U R C H I L L
W H I T E P I N E
STOREY
L Y O N
DOUGLAS
M I N E R A L
N Y E
E S M E R A L D A
L I N C O L N
C L A R K
Carson City
RENO
Sparks
Winnemucca
Elko
Lovelock
Fallon
Austin
Eureka
Ely
East Ely
McGill
Tonopah
Goldfield
Hawthorne
Yerington
Minden
Gardnerville
Pioche
LAS VEGAS
North Las Vegas
Henderson
Boulder City
Battle Mountain
Wells
Carlin
Virginia City
Denio
McDermitt
Jackpot
Owyhee
Mountain City
Wendover
Caliente
Mesquite
Searchlight
Pahrump
Beatty
Rhyolite
Gerlach
Lake Tahoe
PYRAMID LAKE
Walker L.
Lake Mead
Lake Mohave
BLACK ROCK DESERT
SMOKE CREEK DESERT
GREAT SALT LAKE DESERT
CARSON SINK
HUMBOLDT SINK
SAND SPRINGS SALT FLAT
LAS VEGAS BOMBING & GUNNERY RANGE
(RESTRICTED AREA)
YUCCA FLAT
FRENCHMAN FLAT
DEATH VALLEY NATIONAL MONUMENT
YOSEMITE NATIONAL PARK
KINGS CANYON NAT'L PARK
SEQUOIA NATIONAL PARK
LAKE MEAD NATIONAL RECREATION AREA
HOOVER DAM
DAVIS DAM
LEHMAN CAVES NAT'L MON.
Wheeler Pk. 13,063
Boundary Pk. 13,140
Mt. Whitney 14,494
Charleston Pk. 11,919
Arc Dome 11,775
SANTA ROSA RANGE
RUBY MTS.
TOIYABE RANGE
TOQUIMA RANGE
MONITOR RANGE
SNAKE RANGE
SCHELL CREEK RANGE
EGAN RANGE
SPRING MOUNTAINS
SCALE
0 5 10 20 30 40 50 60 MI.
0 5 10 20 30 40 50 60 KM.
State Capitals
County Seats
120° 119° 118° 117° 116° 115° 114°
42° 41° 40° 39° 38° 37° 36°
Longitude West of Greenwich

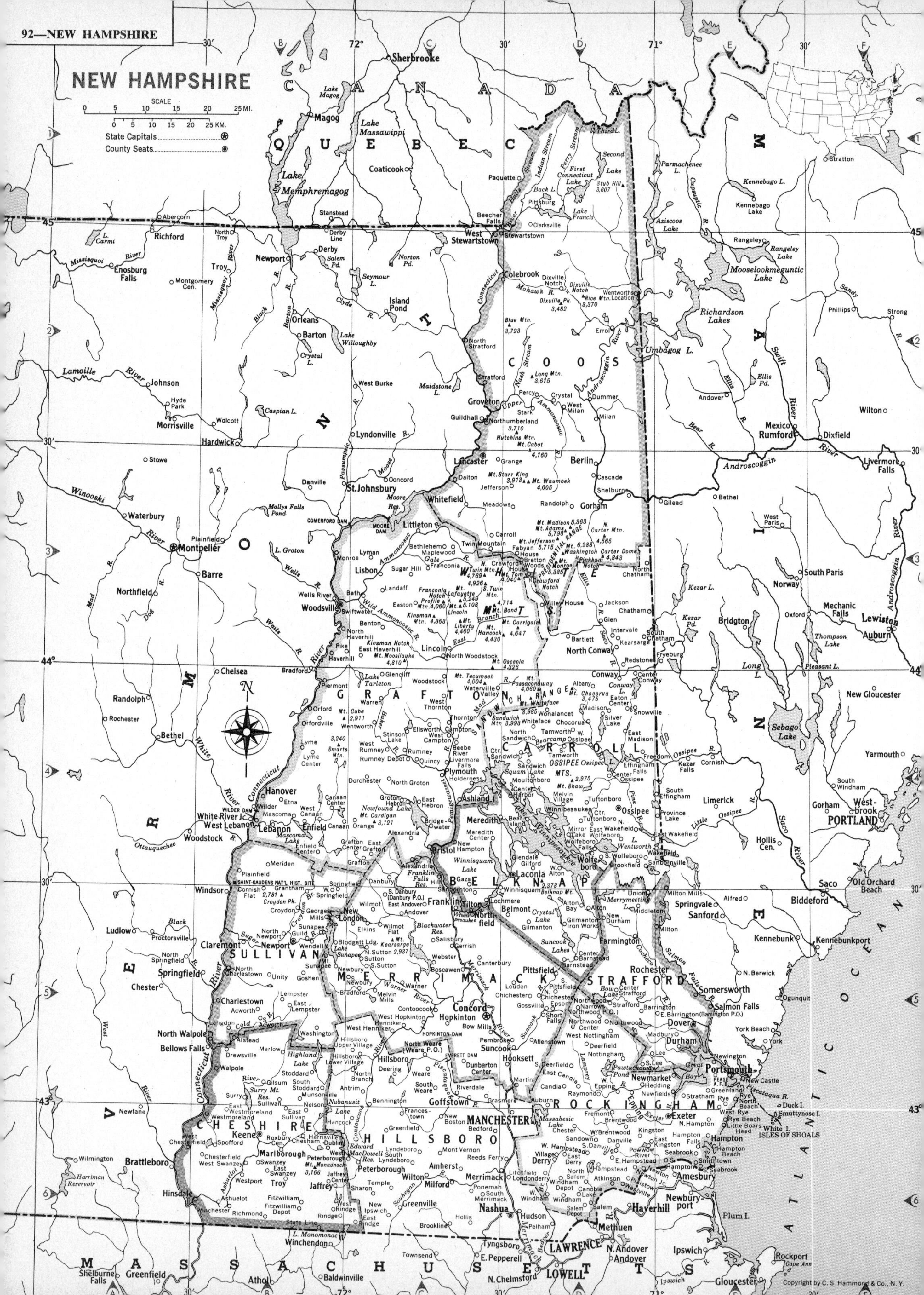
NEW HAMPSHIRE
SCALE
0 5 10 15 20 25 MI.
0 5 10 15 20 25 KM.
State Capitals
County Seats
CANADA
QUEBEC
VERMONT
MAINE
MASSACHUSETTS
ATLANTIC OCEAN
COOS
GRAFTON
CARROLL
BELKNAP
SULLIVAN
MERRIMACK
STRAFFORD
ROCKINGHAM
CHESHIRE
HILLSBORO
WHITE MTS.
PRESIDENTIAL RANGE
SANDWICH RANGE
OSSIPEE MTS.
Sherbrooke
Magog
Lake Magog
Lake Massawippi
Lake Memphremagog
Coaticook
Stanstead
Derby Line
Newport
Richford
Enosburg Falls
Troy
Barton
Orleans
Island Pond
St. Johnsbury
Lyndonville
Montpelier
Barre
Waterbury
Hardwick
Morrisville
Johnson
Stowe
Northfield
Randolph
Chelsea
Bradford
Woodstock
White River Jc.
West Lebanon
Windsor
Claremont
Springfield
Ludlow
Chester
Bellows Falls
North Walpole
Brattleboro
Hinsdale
Wilmington
Newfane
Pittsburg
First Connecticut Lake
Second Lake
Third L.
Lake Francis
West Stewartstown
Colebrook
Dixville Notch
Errol
Umbagog L.
North Stratford
Stratford
Groveton
Lancaster
Berlin
Gorham
Whitefield
Littleton
Twin Mountain
Bethlehem
Franconia
Lisbon
Woodsville
Haverhill
Lincoln
North Woodstock
North Conway
Conway
Jackson
Plymouth
Ashland
Meredith
Laconia
Bristol
Hanover
Lebanon
Enfield
Canaan
Franklin
Tilton
New London
Newport
Sunapee
Concord
Hopkinton
Henniker
Hillsboro
Pittsfield
Rochester
Farmington
Dover
Durham
Somersworth
Portsmouth
Exeter
Hampton
Newmarket
Manchester
Goffstown
Hooksett
Derry
Londonderry
Nashua
Hudson
Milford
Amherst
Merrimack
Keene
Marlborough
Jaffrey
Peterborough
Troy
Winchester
Walpole
Charlestown
Wolfeboro
Ossipee
Lake Winnipesaukee
Squam Lake
Newfound Lake
Mt. Washington 6,288
Mt. Adams 5,798
Mt. Jefferson 5,715
Mt. Madison 5,363
Mt. Monroe 5,385
Mt. Lafayette 5,249
Mt. Moosilauke 4,810
Mt. Chocorua 3,475
Mt. Kearsarge 2,937
Mt. Cardigan 3,121
Mt. Monadnock 3,166
Isles of Shoals
Haverhill
Lawrence
Lowell
Methuen
Newburyport
Amesbury
Winchendon
Greenfield
Gloucester
Portland
Lewiston
Auburn
Rumford
Biddeford
Saco
Sanford
Kennebunk
Sebago Lake
Mooselookmeguntic Lake
Rangeley Lake
Copyright by C. S. Hammond & Co., N. Y.

NEW JERSEY
SCALE
0 5 10 15 20 MI.
0 5 10 15 20 KM.
State Capitals
County Seats
Canals
Copyright by C. S. HAMMOND & CO., N. Y.
Longitude 75° West of Greenwich
PENNSYLVANIA
NEW YORK
DELAWARE
MARYLAND
ATLANTIC OCEAN
DELAWARE BAY
TRENTON
NEWARK
JERSEY CITY
PATERSON
ELIZABETH
CAMDEN
PHILADELPHIA
Atlantic City
Wilmington
SUSSEX
PASSAIC
BERGEN
MORRIS
ESSEX
HUDSON
UNION
WARREN
HUNTERDON
SOMERSET
MIDDLESEX
MERCER
MONMOUTH
OCEAN
BURLINGTON
CAMDEN
GLOUCESTER
SALEM
CUMBERLAND
ATLANTIC
CAPE MAY

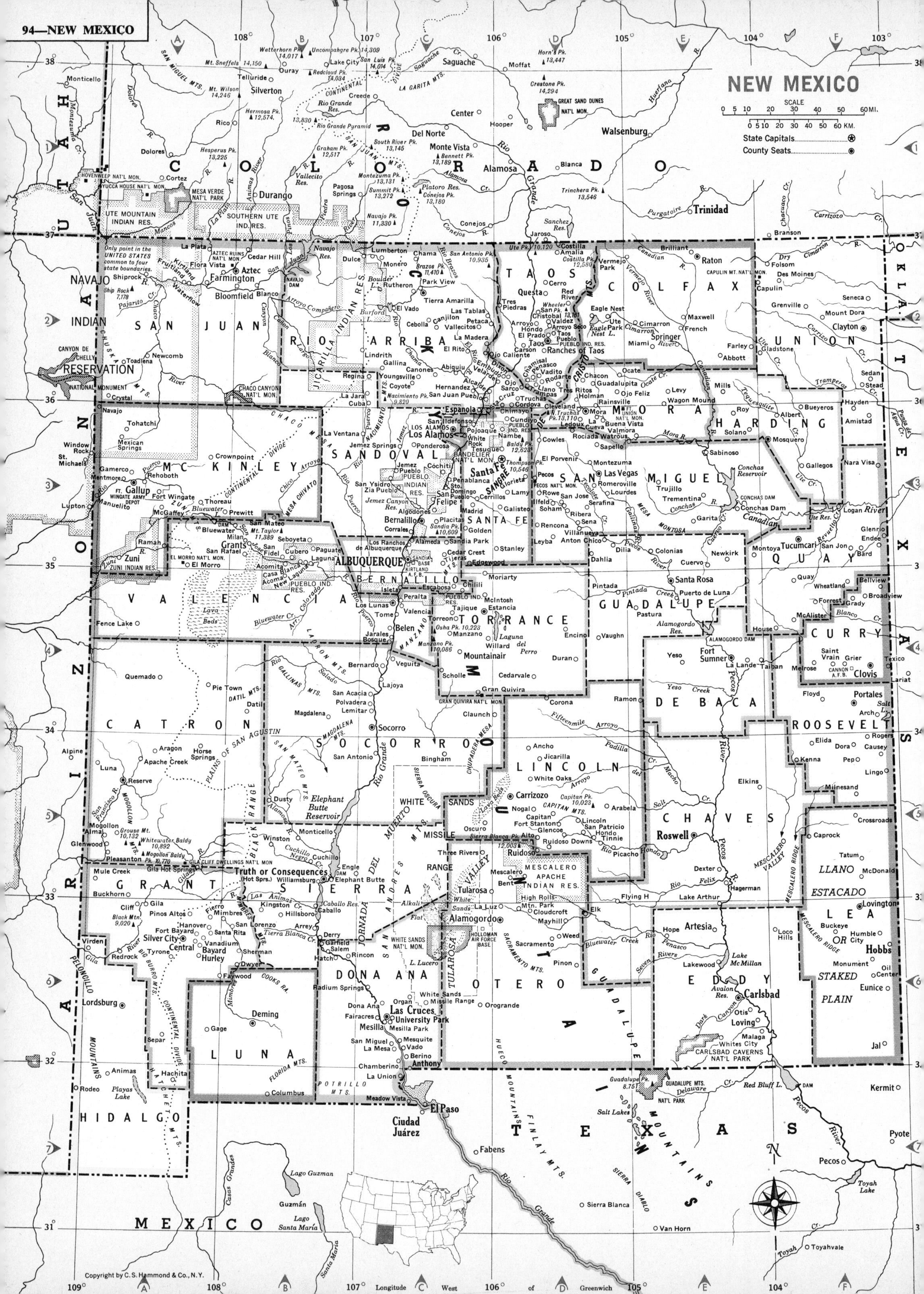
NEW MEXICO
SCALE
0 5 10 20 30 40 50 60 MI.
0 5 10 20 30 40 50 60 KM.
State Capitals
County Seats
COLORADO
UTAH
ARIZONA
OKLAHOMA
TEXAS
MEXICO
SAN JUAN
RIO ARRIBA
TAOS
COLFAX
UNION
MC KINLEY
SANDOVAL
LOS ALAMOS
SANTA FE
MORA
HARDING
SAN MIGUEL
QUAY
VALENCIA
BERNALILLO
TORRANCE
GUADALUPE
CURRY
DE BACA
ROOSEVELT
CATRON
SOCORRO
LINCOLN
CHAVES
GRANT
SIERRA
OTERO
LEA
EDDY
DONA ANA
LUNA
HIDALGO
Santa Fe
ALBUQUERQUE
Gallup
Farmington
Aztec
Raton
Clayton
Tucumcari
Clovis
Portales
Roswell
Carlsbad
Hobbs
Lovington
Alamogordo
Las Cruces
Deming
Lordsburg
Silver City
Socorro
Truth or Consequences
Los Alamos
Las Vegas
Taos
Espanola
Grants
Belen
Carrizozo
Artesia
Santa Rosa
Fort Sumner
Mosquero
Estancia
Reserve
Bernalillo
Tierra Amarilla
El Paso
Ciudad Juárez
Trinidad
Durango
Alamosa
Walsenburg
NAVAJO INDIAN RESERVATION
JICARILLA INDIAN RES.
MESCALERO APACHE INDIAN RES.
ZUNI INDIAN RES.
UTE MOUNTAIN INDIAN RES.
SOUTHERN UTE IND. RES.
CARLSBAD CAVERNS NAT'L PARK
WHITE SANDS NAT'L MON.
MESA VERDE NAT'L PARK
GREAT SAND DUNES NAT'L MON.
CHACO CANYON NAT'L MON.
CAPULIN MT. NAT'L MON.
GILA CLIFF DWELLINGS NAT'L MON.
EL MORRO NAT'L MON.
BANDELIER NAT'L MON.
LLANO ESTACADO
STAKED PLAIN
Elephant Butte Reservoir
Conchas Reservoir
Rio Grande
Pecos R.
Canadian River
Only point in the UNITED STATES common to four state boundaries.
Longitude West of Greenwich
109° 108° 107° 106° 105° 104° 103°
38° 37° 36° 35° 34° 33° 32° 31°

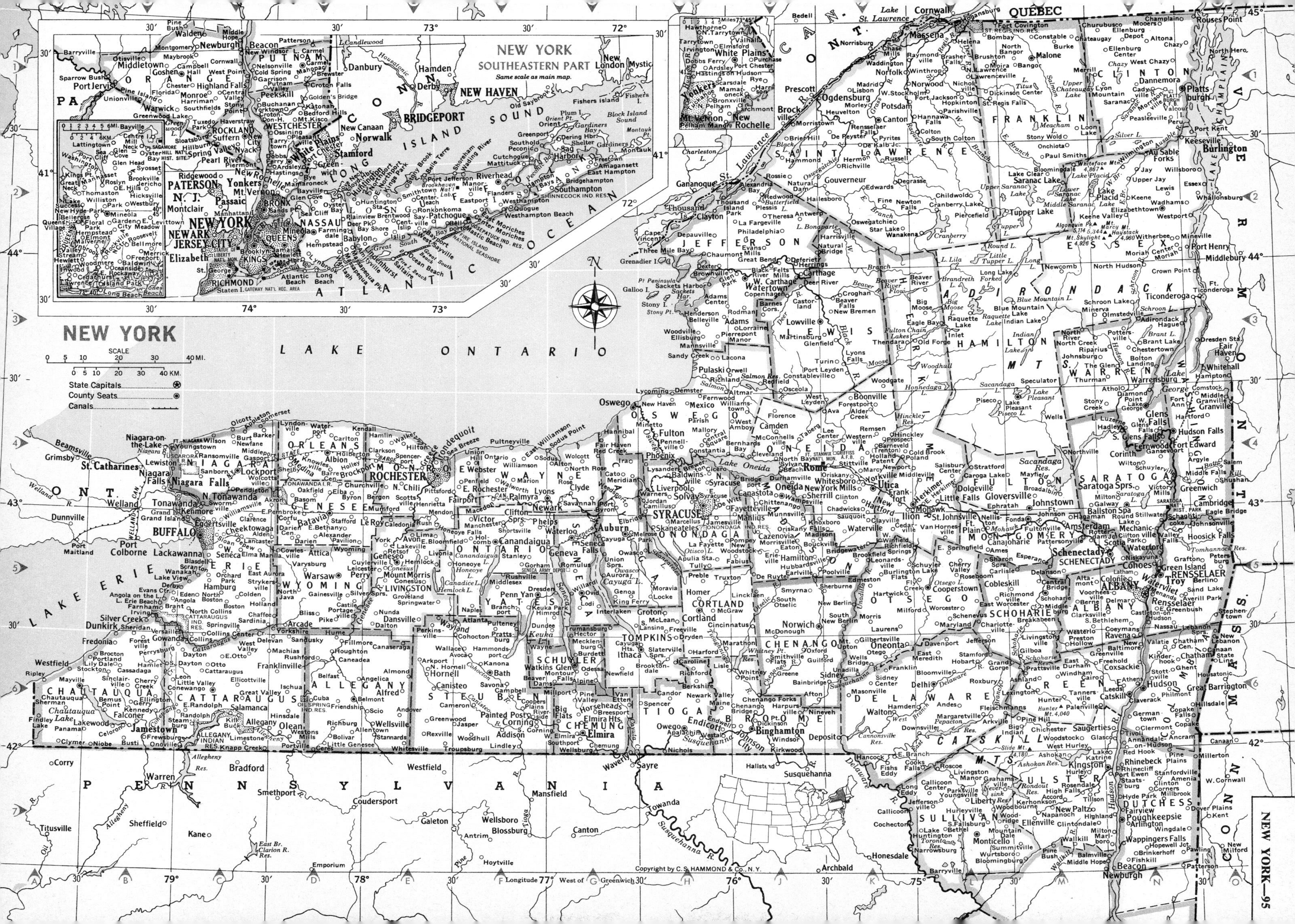
NEW YORK
SCALE
State Capitals
County Seats
Canals
LAKE ONTARIO
NEW YORK
SOUTHEASTERN PART
Same scale as main map.
LONG ISLAND SOUND
ATLANTIC OCEAN
QUEBEC
PENNSYLVANIA
ONT.
LAKE ERIE
ALBANY
BUFFALO
ROCHESTER
SYRACUSE
Copyright by C. S. HAMMOND & Co., N.Y.

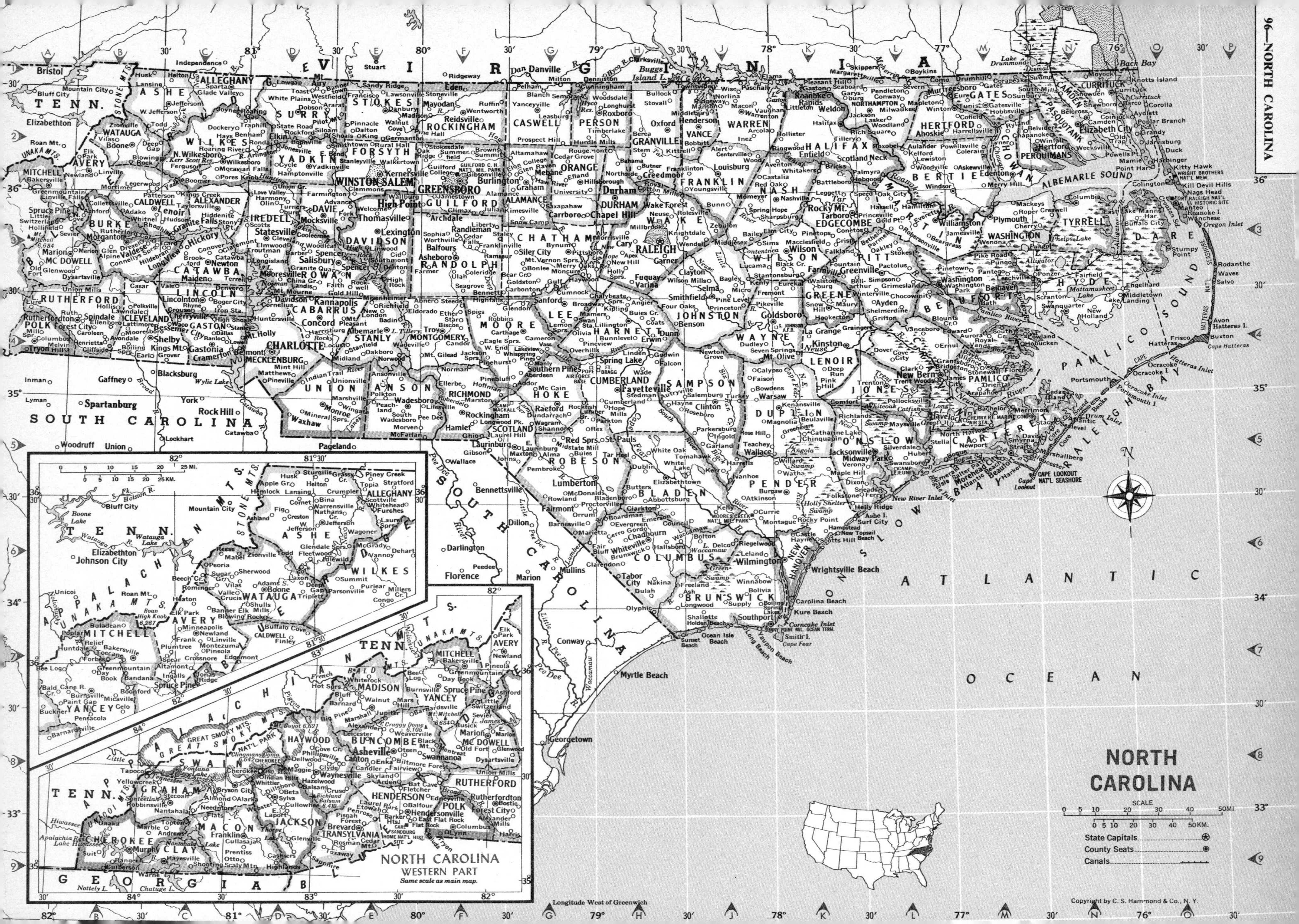
NORTH CAROLINA
SCALE
State Capitals
County Seats
Canals
Copyright by C. S. Hammond & Co., N. Y.
NORTH CAROLINA WESTERN PART
Same scale as main map.
ATLANTIC OCEAN
SOUTH CAROLINA
VIRGINIA
TENN.
GEORGIA
Longitude West of Greenwich

NORTH DAKOTA
SCALE
0 5 10 20 30 MI.
0 5 10 20 30 KM.
State Capitals
County Seats
Copyright by C. S. Hammond & Co., N. Y.
SASKATCHEWAN
MANITOBA
MINNESOTA
SOUTH DAKOTA
MONTANA
DIVIDE
BURKE
RENVILLE
BOTTINEAU
ROLETTE
TOWNER
CAVALIER
PEMBINA
WALSH
RAMSEY
BENSON
PIERCE
McHENRY
WARD
MOUNTRAIL
WILLIAMS
MC KENZIE
DUNN
MERCER
OLIVER
McLEAN
SHERIDAN
WELLS
EDDY
FOSTER
GRIGGS
STEELE
TRAILL
NELSON
GRAND FORKS
BARNES
CASS
STUTSMAN
KIDDER
BURLEIGH
MORTON
GRANT
EMMONS
LOGAN
MC INTOSH
LA MOURE
DICKEY
RANSOM
SARGENT
RICHLAND
STARK
BILLINGS
GOLDEN VALLEY
SLOPE
HETTINGER
ADAMS
BOWMAN
SIOUX
Lake Sakakawea
Lake Oahe
FORT BERTHOLD INDIAN RESERVATION
STANDING ROCK INDIAN RESERVATION
INTERNATIONAL PEACE GARDEN
Bismarck
Fargo
Grand Forks
Minot

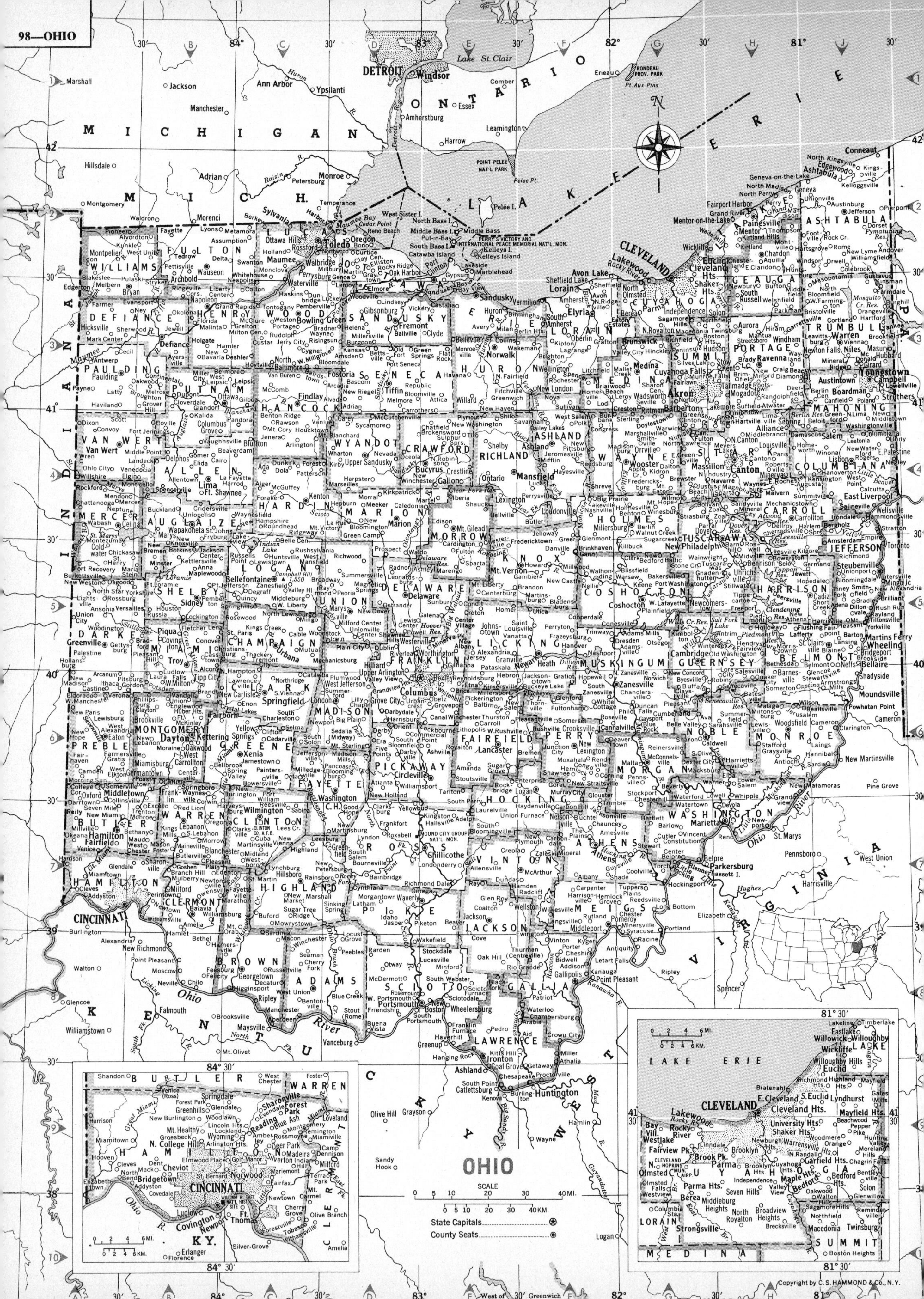
OHIO
MICHIGAN
INDIANA
ONTARIO
LAKE ERIE
KENTUCKY
WEST VIRGINIA
PENNSYLVANIA
WILLIAMS
FULTON
LUCAS
OTTAWA
DEFIANCE
HENRY
WOOD
SANDUSKY
ERIE
LORAIN
CUYAHOGA
LAKE
GEAUGA
ASHTABULA
TRUMBULL
PORTAGE
SUMMIT
MEDINA
HURON
SENECA
HANCOCK
PUTNAM
PAULDING
VAN WERT
ALLEN
HARDIN
WYANDOT
CRAWFORD
RICHLAND
ASHLAND
WAYNE
STARK
MAHONING
COLUMBIANA
MERCER
AUGLAIZE
MARION
MORROW
KNOX
HOLMES
TUSCARAWAS
CARROLL
JEFFERSON
SHELBY
LOGAN
UNION
DELAWARE
LICKING
COSHOCTON
HARRISON
DARKE
MIAMI
CHAMPAIGN
CLARK
FRANKLIN
MUSKINGUM
GUERNSEY
BELMONT
PREBLE
MONTGOMERY
GREENE
MADISON
FAIRFIELD
PERRY
NOBLE
MONROE
BUTLER
WARREN
CLINTON
FAYETTE
PICKAWAY
HOCKING
MORGAN
WASHINGTON
HAMILTON
CLERMONT
HIGHLAND
ROSS
VINTON
ATHENS
BROWN
ADAMS
PIKE
JACKSON
MEIGS
SCIOTO
GALLIA
LAWRENCE
Columbus
CLEVELAND
CINCINNATI
Toledo
Akron
Dayton
Youngstown
Canton
DETROIT
Windsor
Lake St. Clair
Pelee Pt.
Pelée I.
POINT PELEE NAT'L PARK
RONDEAU PROV. PARK
PERRY'S VICTORY AND INTERNATIONAL PEACE MEMORIAL NAT'L. MON.
MOUND CITY GROUP NAT'L. MON.
Campbell Hill 1,550
Ohio R.
84° 30' 83° 30' 82° 30' 81° 30'
42° 41° 40° 39° 38°
OHIO
SCALE
0 5 10 20 30 40 MI.
0 5 10 20 30 40 KM.
State Capitals
County Seats
West of Greenwich
Copyright by C. S. HAMMOND & Co., N.Y.

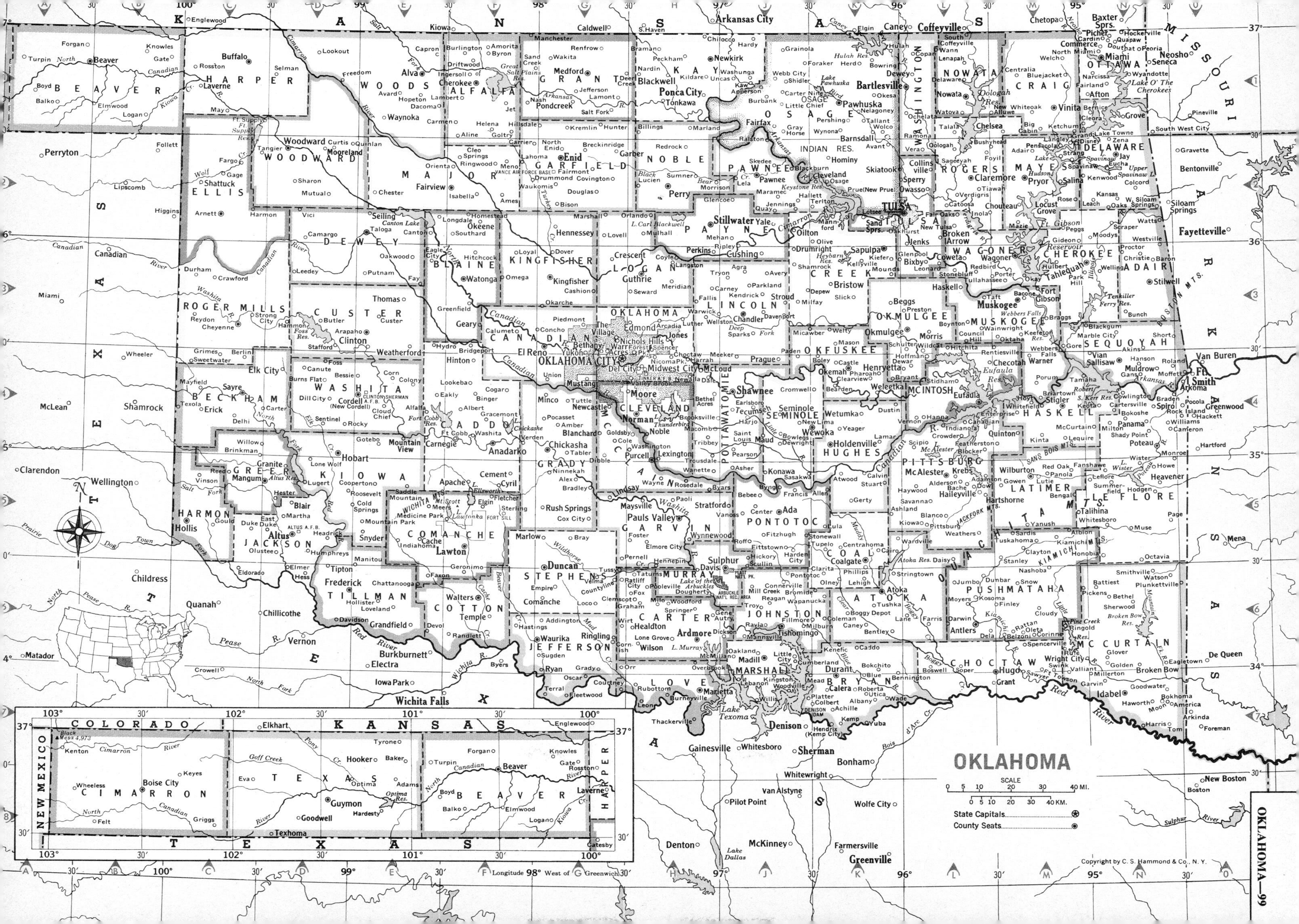
OKLAHOMA
SCALE
0 5 10 20 30 40 MI.
0 5 10 20 30 40 KM.
State Capitals
County Seats
Copyright by C. S. Hammond & Co., N. Y.
KANSAS
MISSOURI
ARKANSAS
TEXAS
COLORADO
NEW MEXICO
OKLAHOMA CITY
TULSA
Longitude 98° West of Greenwich

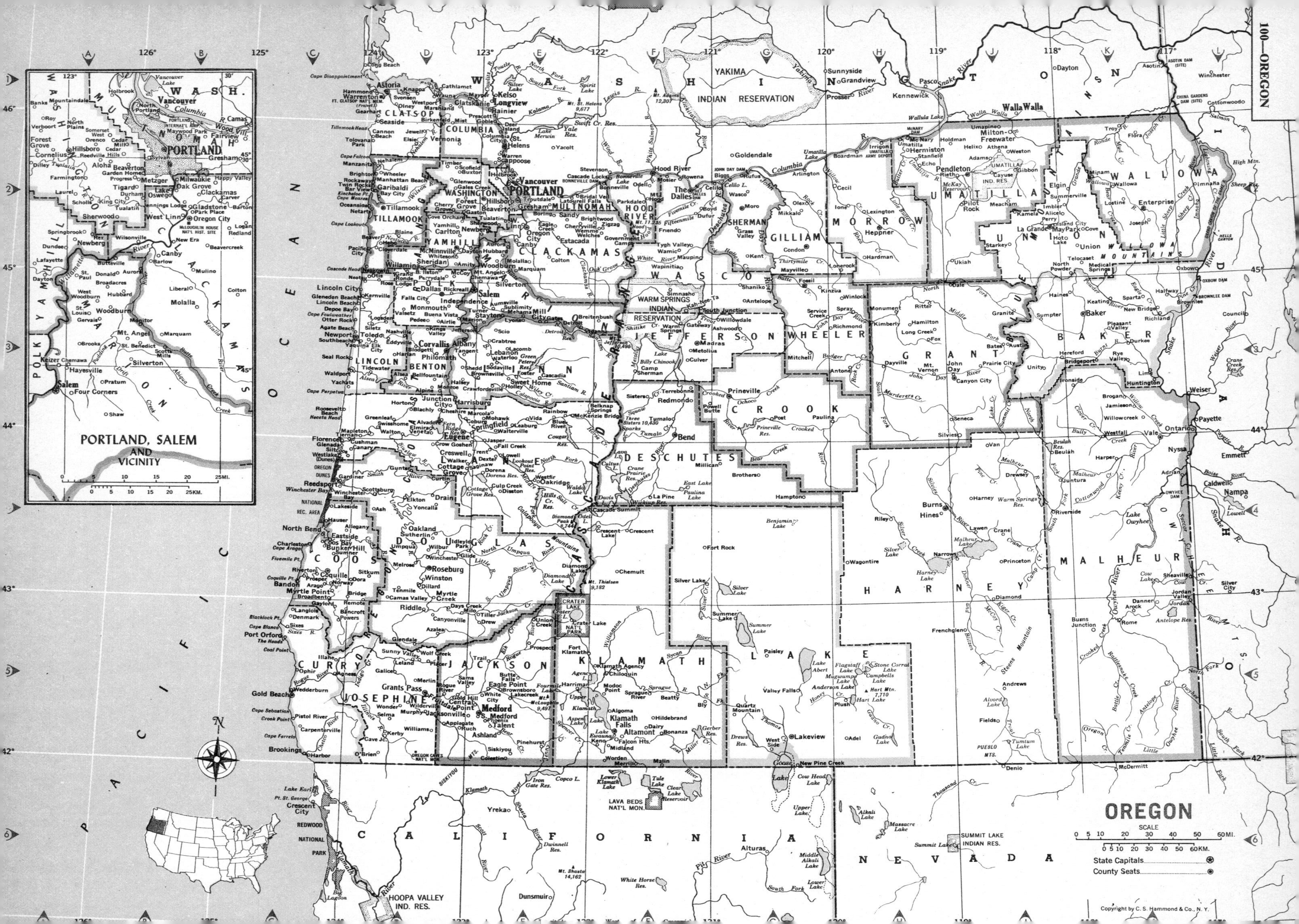
OREGON
SCALE
0 5 10 20 30 40 50 60 MI.
0 5 10 20 30 40 50 60 KM.
State Capitals
County Seats
Copyright by C. S. Hammond & Co., N. Y.
PORTLAND, SALEM AND VICINITY
0 5 10 15 20 25 MI.
0 5 10 15 20 25 KM.
W A S H I N G T O N
I D A H O
N E V A D A
C A L I F O R N I A
P A C I F I C O C E A N
YAKIMA INDIAN RESERVATION
WARM SPRINGS INDIAN RESERVATION
UMATILLA IND. RES.
CRATER LAKE NAT'L PARK
LAVA BEDS NAT'L MON.
HOOPA VALLEY IND. RES.
SUMMIT LAKE INDIAN RES.
CLATSOP
COLUMBIA
TILLAMOOK
WASHINGTON
MULTNOMAH
HOOD RIVER
WASCO
SHERMAN
GILLIAM
MORROW
UMATILLA
UNION
WALLOWA
BAKER
GRANT
WHEELER
JEFFERSON
CROOK
DESCHUTES
LAKE
HARNEY
MALHEUR
KLAMATH
JACKSON
JOSEPHINE
CURRY
COOS
DOUGLAS
LANE
LINCOLN
BENTON
LINN
MARION
POLK
YAMHILL
CLACKAMAS
PORTLAND
Salem
Eugene
Medford
Pendleton
Baker
Bend
Burns
Lakeview
Klamath Falls
Roseburg
Astoria
The Dalles
Walla Walla

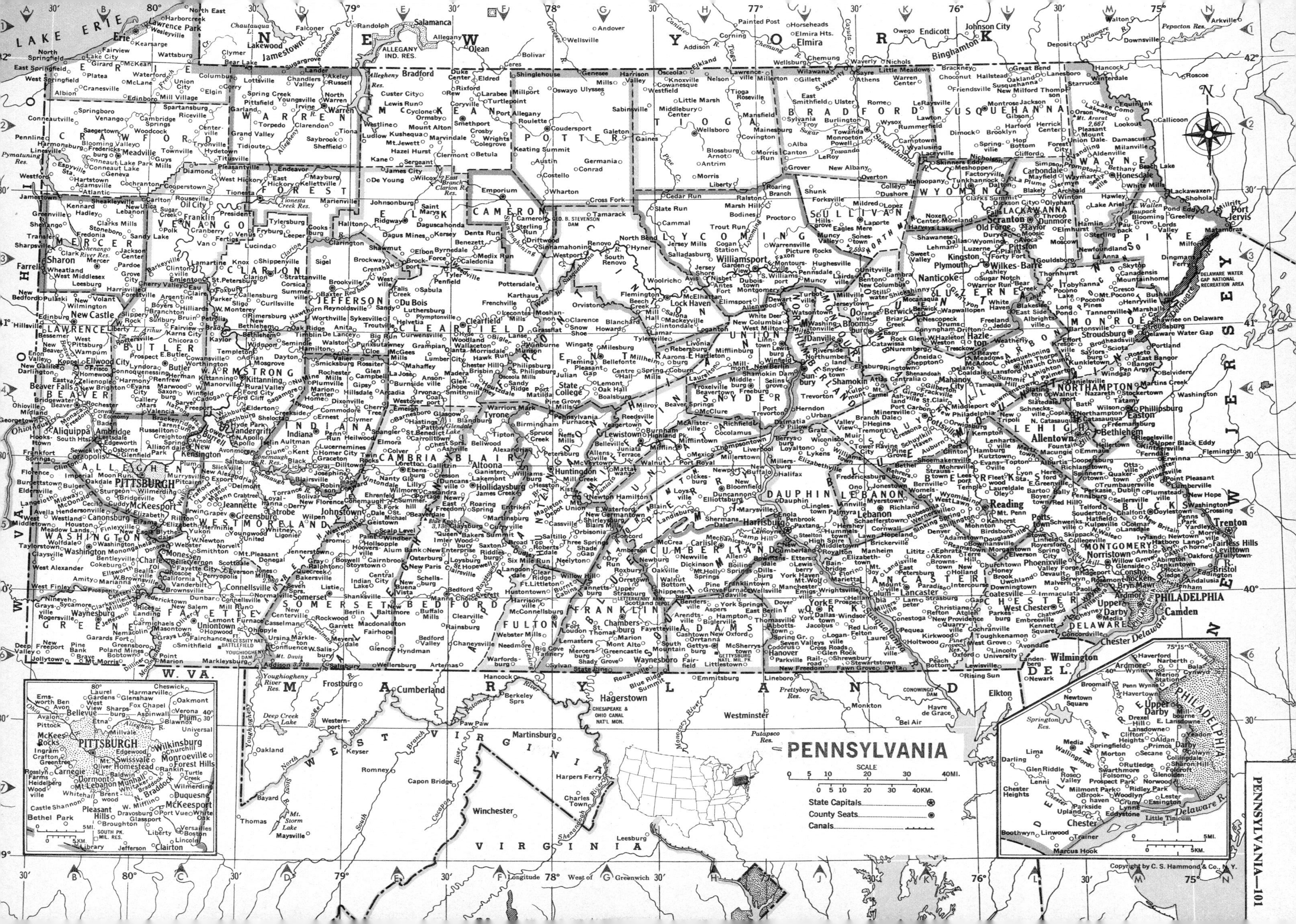
PENNSYLVANIA
SCALE
State Capitals
County Seats
Canals
PHILADELPHIA
PITTSBURGH
LAKE ERIE
NEW YORK
NEW JERSEY
MARYLAND
WEST VIRGINIA
VIRGINIA
DEL.
Copyright by C. S. Hammond & Co., N. Y.

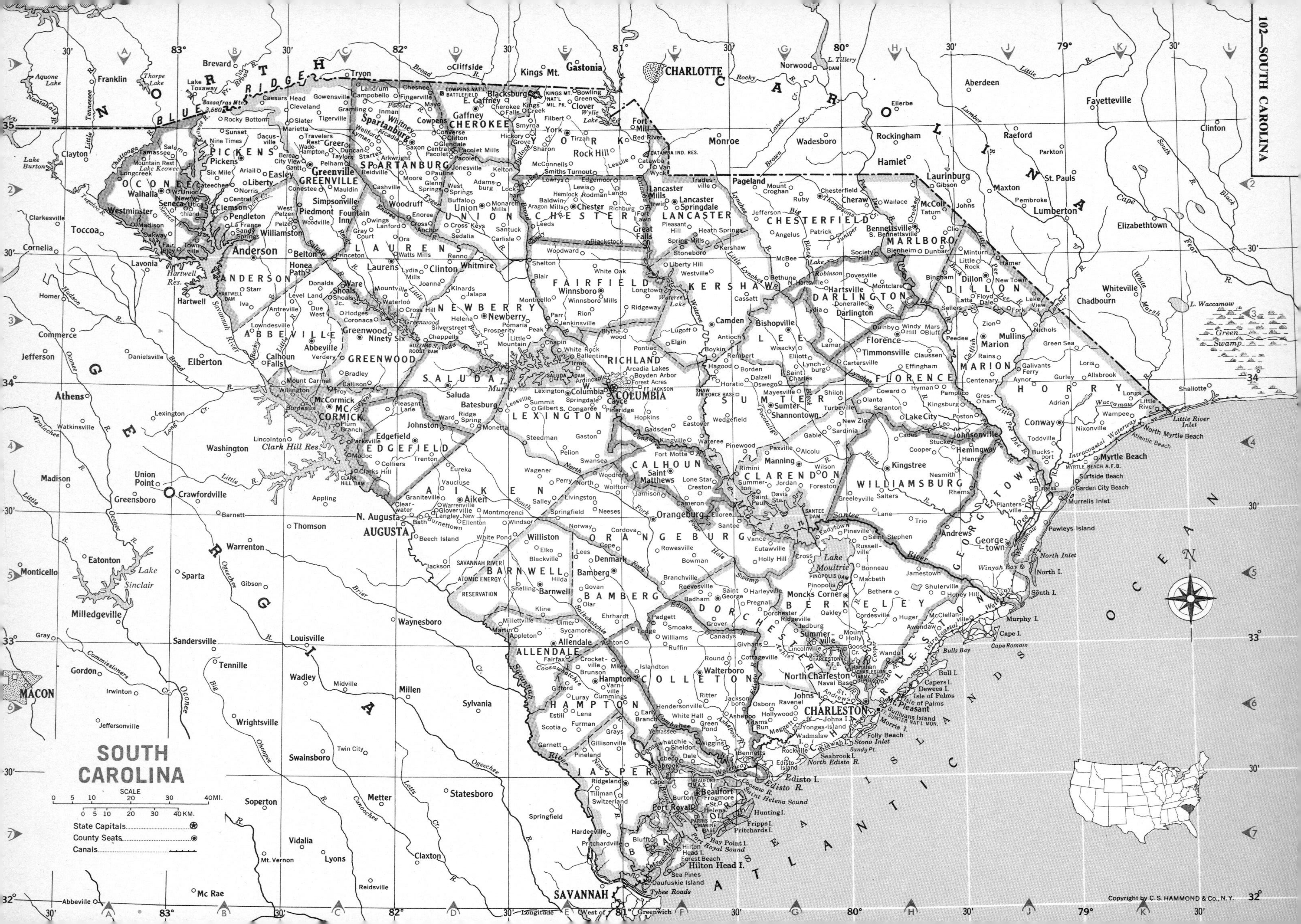
SOUTH CAROLINA
SCALE
0 5 10 20 30 40 MI.
0 5 10 20 30 40 KM.
State Capitals
County Seats
Canals
ATLANTIC OCEAN
NORTH CAROLINA
GEORGIA
BLUE RIDGE
COLUMBIA
CHARLESTON
GREENVILLE
SPARTANBURG
CHARLOTTE
AUGUSTA
SAVANNAH
OCONEE
PICKENS
ANDERSON
ABBEVILLE
GREENWOOD
McCORMICK
EDGEFIELD
AIKEN
BARNWELL
ALLENDALE
HAMPTON
JASPER
BEAUFORT
COLLETON
CHARLESTON
BERKELEY
DORCHESTER
ORANGEBURG
BAMBERG
CALHOUN
LEXINGTON
RICHLAND
SALUDA
NEWBERRY
LAURENS
UNION
CHEROKEE
YORK
CHESTER
FAIRFIELD
LANCASTER
KERSHAW
CHESTERFIELD
MARLBORO
DARLINGTON
LEE
SUMTER
CLARENDON
WILLIAMSBURG
FLORENCE
MARION
DILLON
HORRY
GEORGETOWN
SAVANNAH RIVER ATOMIC ENERGY RESERVATION
Copyright by C. S. HAMMOND & Co., N. Y.

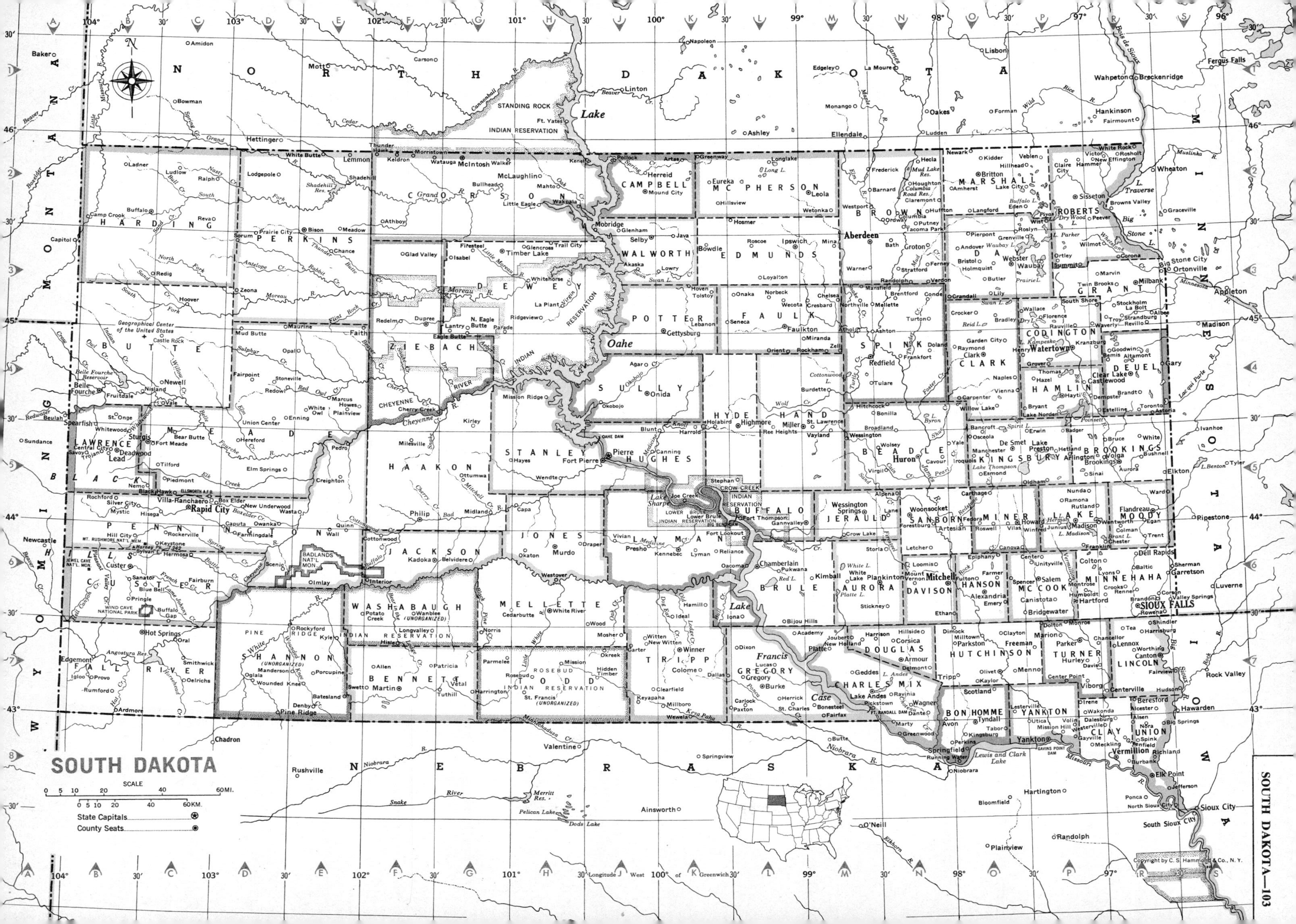
SOUTH DAKOTA
SCALE
0 5 10 20 40 60 MI.
0 5 10 20 40 60 KM.
State Capitals
County Seats
Copyright by C. S. Hammond & Co., N. Y.
NORTH DAKOTA
MINNESOTA
IOWA
NEBRASKA
WYOMING
MONTANA
Longitude West of Greenwich
STANDING ROCK INDIAN RESERVATION
ROSEBUD INDIAN RESERVATION
CROW CREEK INDIAN RESERVATION
LOWER BRULE INDIAN RESERVATION
BADLANDS NAT'L MON.
WIND CAVE NATIONAL PARK
Geographical Center of the United States
Lake Oahe
Lake Francis Case
Lewis and Clark Lake
Pierre
Sioux Falls
Rapid City
Aberdeen
Huron
Watertown
Mitchell
Yankton
HARDING
PERKINS
CORSON
BUTTE
ZIEBACH
DEWEY
MEADE
LAWRENCE
PENNINGTON
CUSTER
FALL RIVER
SHANNON
WASHABAUGH
JACKSON
HAAKON
STANLEY
JONES
MELLETTE
BENNETT
TODD
TRIPP
LYMAN
HUGHES
SULLY
POTTER
WALWORTH
CAMPBELL
MC PHERSON
EDMUNDS
FAULK
HYDE
HAND
BUFFALO
BRULE
GREGORY
CHARLES MIX
AURORA
JERAULD
BEADLE
SPINK
BROWN
MARSHALL
DAY
ROBERTS
GRANT
CODINGTON
CLARK
HAMLIN
DEUEL
KINGSBURY
BROOKINGS
SANBORN
MINER
LAKE
MOODY
DAVISON
HANSON
MC COOK
MINNEHAHA
DOUGLAS
HUTCHINSON
TURNER
LINCOLN
BON HOMME
YANKTON
CLAY
UNION

TENNESSEE
MISSOURI
KENTUCKY
ARK.
MISSISSIPPI
ALABAMA
VIRGINIA
NORTH CAROLINA
GEORGIA
S.C.
ALA.
NASHVILLE
MEMPHIS
KNOXVILLE
CHATTANOOGA
Longitude West of 88° Greenwich
Longitude West of 84° Greenwich
SCALE
0 5 10 20 30 40 MI.
0 5 10 20 30 40 KM.
State Capitals
County Seats
GREAT SMOKY MTS. NATIONAL PARK
APPALACHIAN MTS.
CUMBERLAND PLATEAU
Kentucky Lake
Pickwick Lake
Norris L.
Douglas L.
Cherokee L.

95111

TEXAS
0 20 40 60 80 100 MI.
0 20 40 60 80 100 KM.
State Capitals
County Seats
TEXAS
WESTERN PART
Same scale as main map
GULF OF MEXICO
MEXICO
NEW MEXICO
OKLAHOMA
ARK.
LA.
FORT WORTH
DALLAS
HOUSTON
Longitude 98° West of Greenwich 97°
Copyright by C. S. HAMMOND & Co., N.Y.

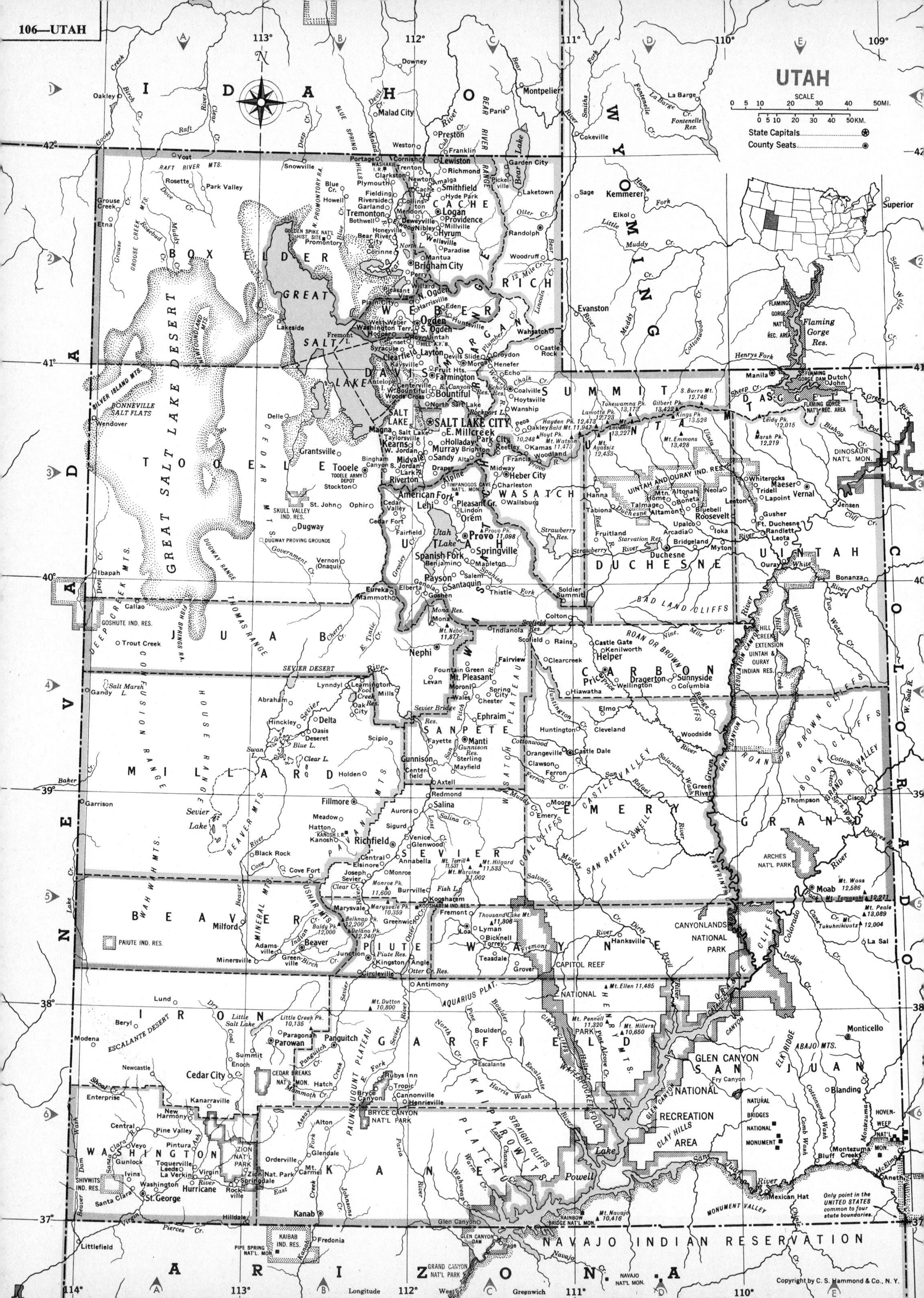

UTAH
SCALE
0 5 10 20 30 40 50MI.
0 5 10 20 30 40 50KM.
State Capitals
County Seats
IDAHO
WYOMING
NEVADA
COLORADO
ARIZONA
NAVAJO INDIAN RESERVATION
BOX ELDER
CACHE
RICH
WEBER
MORGAN
DAVIS
SALT LAKE
SUMMIT
DAGGETT
TOOELE
WASATCH
UTAH
DUCHESNE
UINTAH
JUAB
CARBON
SANPETE
MILLARD
EMERY
GRAND
SEVIER
BEAVER
PIUTE
WAYNE
IRON
GARFIELD
SAN JUAN
WASHINGTON
KANE
SALT LAKE CITY
Ogden
Logan
Provo
Brigham City
Tooele
Heber City
Nephi
Manti
Price
Castle Dale
Fillmore
Richfield
Beaver
Junction
Loa
Parowan
Panguitch
St. George
Kanab
Moab
Monticello
Vernal
Duchesne
Coalville
Randolph
Morgan
Farmington
Manila
GREAT SALT LAKE
GREAT SALT LAKE DESERT
BONNEVILLE SALT FLATS
SEVIER DESERT
ESCALANTE DESERT
Utah Lake
Sevier Lake
Bear Lake
Flaming Gorge Res.
Lake Powell
UINTA MTS.
WASATCH RANGE
HOUSE RANGE
DUGWAY PROVING GROUNDS
GOLDEN SPIKE NAT'L HIST. SITE
TIMPANOGOS CAVE NAT'L MON.
DINOSAUR NAT'L MON.
ARCHES NAT'L PARK
CANYONLANDS NATIONAL PARK
CAPITOL REEF NATIONAL PARK
BRYCE CANYON NAT'L PARK
ZION NAT'L PARK
CEDAR BREAKS NAT'L MON.
NATURAL BRIDGES NATIONAL MONUMENT
GLEN CANYON NATIONAL RECREATION AREA
RAINBOW BRIDGE NAT'L MON.
HOVENWEEP NAT'L MON.
PIPE SPRING NAT'L MON.
GRAND CANYON NAT'L PARK
NAVAJO NAT'L MON.
UINTAH AND OURAY IND. RES.
GOSHUTE IND. RES.
SKULL VALLEY IND. RES.
PAIUTE IND. RES.
SHIVWITS IND. RES.
KAIBAB IND. RES.
MONUMENT VALLEY
Kings Pk. 13,528
Mt. Nebo 11,877
Mt. Peale 13,089
Provo Pk. 11,098
Only point in the UNITED STATES common to four state boundaries.
Longitude 112° West of Greenwich
Copyright by C. S. Hammond & Co., N. Y.

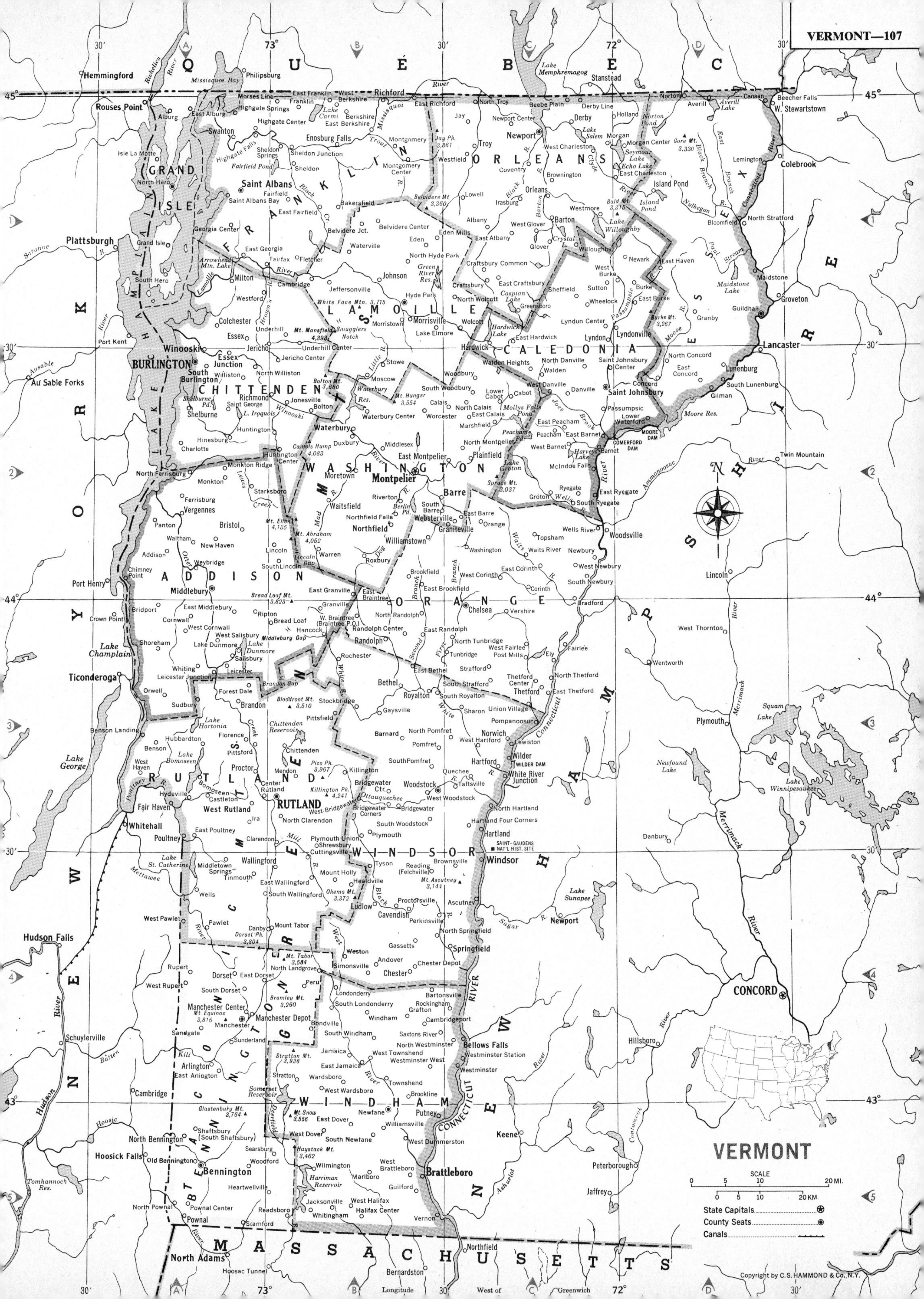

VERMONT
QUÉBEC
NEW YORK
NEW HAMPSHIRE
MASSACHUSETTS
GRAND ISLE
FRANKLIN
ORLEANS
ESSEX
LAMOILLE
CALEDONIA
CHITTENDEN
WASHINGTON
ADDISON
ORANGE
RUTLAND
WINDSOR
BENNINGTON
WINDHAM
73°
72°
30′
45°
44°
43°
Hemmingford
Philipsburg
Missisquoi Bay
Richelieu River
Lake Memphremagog
Stanstead
Morses Line
East Franklin
West Berkshire
Richford
East Richford
North Troy
Beebe Plain
Derby Line
Holland
Norton
Averill
Averill Lake
Canaan
Beecher Falls
W. Stewartstown
Rouses Point
Alburg
East Alburg
Highgate Springs
Franklin
Lake Carmi
Berkshire
East Berkshire
Jay
Newport Center
Derby
Norton Pond
Swanton
Highgate Center
Enosburg Falls
Montgomery
Jay Pk. 3,861
Troy
Newport
Lake Salem
Morgan
Morgan Center
Gore Mt. 3,330
Isle La Motte
Highgate Falls
Sheldon Springs
Sheldon Junction
Fairfield Pond
Sheldon
Montgomery Center
Westfield
West Charleston
Seymour Lake
Echo Lake
East Charleston
Lemington
Colebrook
North Hero
Saint Albans
Fairfield
Saint Albans Bay
Bakersfield
Belvidere Mt. 3,360
Lowell
Coventry
Brownington
Orleans
Irasburg
Island Pond
Bald Mt. 3,315
East Fairfield
Belvidere Center
Albany
Barton
Westmore
Lake Willoughby
Bloomfield
North Stratford
Plattsburgh
Georgia Center
Belvidere Jct.
Eden
Eden Mills
East Albany
West Glover
Crystal Lake
Glover
Willoughby
Grand Isle
East Georgia
Waterville
North Hyde Park
Newark
East Haven
Arrowhead Mtn. Lake
Fairfax
Fletcher
Green River Res.
Craftsbury Common
West Burke
Milton
Cambridge
Jeffersonville
Johnson
Craftsbury
East Craftsbury
Caspian Lake
Sheffield
Sutton
Burke
Maidstone
Maidstone Lake
South Hero
Westford
White Face Mtn. 3,715
Hyde Park
North Wolcott
Wheelock
East Burke
Greensboro
Groveton
Guildhall
Colchester
Underhill
Mt. Mansfield 4,393
Smugglers Notch
Morristown
Morrisville
Wolcott
Hardwick Lake
East Hardwick
Lyndon Center
Burke Mt. 3,267
Granby
Essex
Lake Elmore
Lyndon
Lyndonville
Port Kent
Winooski
Jericho
Underhill Center
Hardwick
Lancaster
BURLINGTON
Essex Junction
Jericho Center
Stowe
Walden Heights
North Danville
Saint Johnsbury Center
North Concord
Au Sable Forks
South Burlington
Williston
North Williston
Moscow
Walden
East Concord
Lunenburg
Bolton Mt. 3,680
Waterbury Res.
Woodbury
South Woodbury
Lower Cabot
Cabot
West Danville
Danville
Concord
South Lunenburg
Richmond
Mt. Hunger 3,554
Calais
North Calais
Mollys Falls Pond
Saint Johnsbury
Gilman
Shelburne Pd.
Saint George
Jonesville
Bolton
East Calais
Worcester
Passumpsic
Moore Res.
Shelburne
L. Iroquois
Waterbury Center
Marshfield
East Peacham
Lower Waterford
Moore Dam
Huntington
Waterbury
Peacham
East Barnet
Comerford Dam
Hinesburg
Duxbury
Middlesex
Peacham Pd.
North Montpelier
Barnet
Charlotte
Camels Hump 4,083
West Barnet
Harveys Lake
Twin Mountain
Huntington Center
East Montpelier
Plainfield
Lake Groton
North Ferrisburg
Monkton Ridge
Moretown
Montpelier
McIndoe Falls
Monkton
Starksboro
Spruce Mt. 3,037
Ryegate
Barre
Riverton
Berlin Pd.
Groton
South Ryegate
East Ryegate
Ferrisburg
Vergennes
Waitsfield
South Barre
Websterville
Panton
Bristol
Northfield Falls
Northfield
East Barre
Graniteville
Orange
Wells River
Woodsville
Mt. Ellen 4,135
Mt. Abraham 4,052
Williamstown
Topsham
Waltham
New Haven
Warren
Waits River
Newbury
Addison
Lincoln
Lincoln Gap
Washington
Weybridge
South Lincoln
Roxbury
West Newbury
Chimney Point
Brookfield
West Corinth
East Corinth
Port Henry
Middlebury
East Granville
East Brookfield
Corinth
South Newbury
Lincoln
Bread Loaf Mt. 3,823
East Braintree
Bradford
Bridport
East Middlebury
Granville
Chelsea
Vershire
Crown Point
Cornwall
Ripton
Bread Loaf
W. Braintree (Braintree P.O.)
North Randolph
West Cornwall
Hancock
Randolph Center
East Randolph
West Thornton
West Salisbury
Middlebury Gap
Randolph
North Tunbridge
Fairlee
Shoreham
Lake Dunmore
Salisbury
Tunbridge
West Fairlee
Post Mills
Ely
Lake Champlain
Rochester
Wentworth
Whiting
Leicester Junction
Leicester
Brandon Gap
Strafford
Ticonderoga
East Bethel
Thetford Center
North Thetford
Bethel
South Strafford
Thetford
East Thetford
Orwell
Forest Dale
Bloodroot Mt. 3,510
Stockbridge
Royalton
South Royalton
Sudbury
Brandon
Gaysville
Sharon
Union Village
Squam Lake
Lake Hortonia
Chittenden Reservoir
Pittsfield
Pompanoosuc
Plymouth
Benson Landing
Hubbardton
Florence
Barnard
North Pomfret
Norwich
Benson
Pittsford
Chittenden
Pomfret
West Hartford
Lewiston
Lake Bomoseen
Lake George
West Haven
Proctor
Pico Pk. 3,967
Killington
South Pomfret
Hartford
Wilder
Wilder Dam
Newfound Lake
Mendon
Quechee
White River Junction
Center Rutland
Killington Pk. 4,241
Bridgewater Ctr.
Woodstock
Taftsville
Lake Winnipesaukee
Hydeville
Castleton
Fair Haven
West Rutland
RUTLAND
West Bridgewater
Ottauquechee
Bridgewater Corners
West Woodstock
Bridgewater
North Hartland
Whitehall
Ira
North Clarendon
South Woodstock
Hartland Four Corners
Poultney
East Poultney
Clarendon
Plymouth Union
Plymouth
Hartland
Saint-Gaudens Nat'l Hist. Site
Danbury
Shrewsbury
Cuttingsville
Lake St. Catherine
Wallingford
Windsor
Brownsville
Mettawee
Middletown Springs
Tinmouth
Tyson
Reading (Felchville)
Mount Holly
Mt. Ascutney 3,144
Healdville
East Wallingford
South Wallingford
Okemo Mt. 3,372
Lake Sunapee
Wells
Ludlow
Proctorsville
Ascutney
West Pawlet
Cavendish
Perkinsville
Newport
Pawlet
Danby
Mount Tabor
North Springfield
Dorset Pk. 3,804
Hudson Falls
Weston
Gassetts
Springfield
Mt. Tabor 3,584
Andover
Chester Depot
Rupert
Simonsville
Chester
Dorset
East Dorset
North Landgrove
West Rupert
Peru
South Dorset
Bromley Mt. 3,260
Londonderry
Bartonsville
South Londonderry
Rockingham
Grafton
CONCORD
Manchester Center
Mt. Equinox 3,816
Manchester Depot
Manchester
Windham
Cambridgeport
Bondville
Sandgate
Sunderland
South Windham
Saxtons River
Schuylerville
North Westminster
Bellows Falls
Hillsboro
Batten Kill
Jamaica
West Townshend
Westminster West
Westminster Station
Stratton Mt. 3,936
Arlington
East Arlington
East Jamaica
Stratton
Wardsboro
Townshend
Westminster
Somerset Reservoir
West Wardsboro
Brookline
Cambridge
Glastenbury Mt. 3,764
Mt. Snow 3,556
Newfane
Putney
East Dover
Williamsville
Hoosic
Shaftsbury (South Shaftsbury)
North Bennington
West Dover
South Newfane
Keene
West Dummerston
Searsburg
Haystack Mt. 3,462
Hoosick Falls
Old Bennington
Woodford
Bennington
Wilmington
West Brattleboro
Peterborough
Harriman Reservoir
Marlboro
Brattleboro
Tomhannock Res.
Heartwellville
Guilford
Jaffrey
North Pownal
Pownal Center
Readsboro
Jacksonville
West Halifax
Halifax Center
Pownal
Whitingham
Vernon
Stamford
North Adams
Northfield
Hoosac Tunnel
Bernardston
Longitude
West of
Greenwich
Connecticut River
Hudson River
Merrimack River
Contoocook
Ashuelot
Sugar R.
Black R.
White River
Winooski
Lamoille River
Missisquoi
Passumpsic
Ammonoosuc
Nulhegan
Paul Stream
Saranac R.
Ausable
Otter Cr.
Lewis Creek
Dog R.
Mad R.
Deerfield
West R.
Mill R.
Waits R.
Wells R.
Joes Brook
Barton R.
Clyde R.
Moose R.
Black Branch
East Branch
Poultney R.
Castleton
Trout R.
Browns R.
Little R.
Second Br.
First Br.
SCALE
0 5 10 20 MI.
0 5 10 20 KM.
State Capitals
County Seats
Canals
Copyright by C. S. HAMMOND & Co., N.Y.

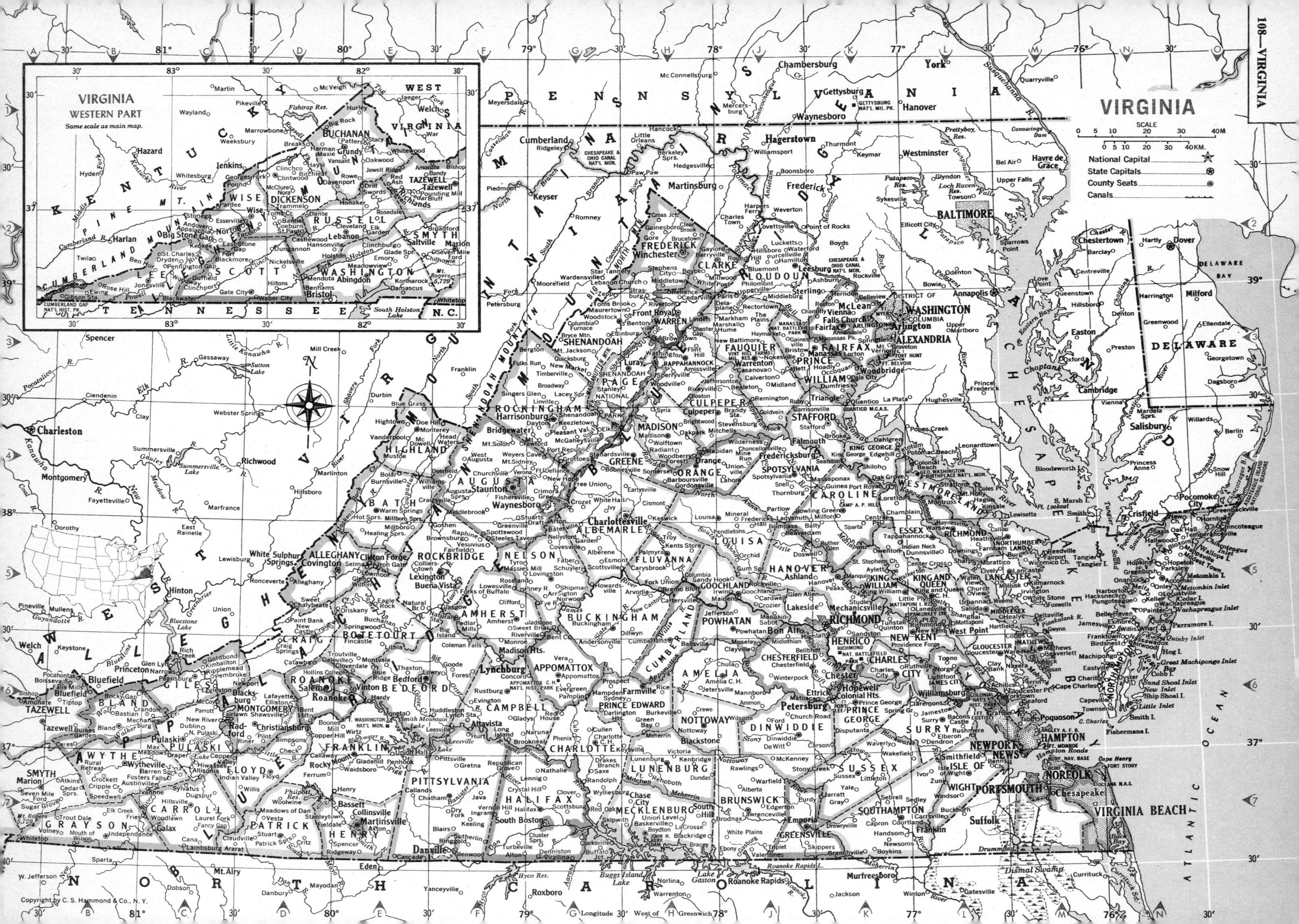
VIRGINIA
SCALE
0 5 10 20 30 40M
0 5 10 20 30 40KM.
National Capital
State Capitals
County Seats
Canals
VIRGINIA
WESTERN PART
Same scale as main map.
ATLANTIC
OCEAN
CHESAPEAKE
BAY
PENNSYLVANIA
MARYLAND
DELAWARE
WEST VIRGINIA
KENTUCKY
TENNESSEE
NORTH CAROLINA
WASHINGTON
DISTRICT OF COLUMBIA
BALTIMORE
RICHMOND
NORFOLK
PORTSMOUTH
VIRGINIA BEACH
Copyright by C. S. Hammond & Co., N. Y.

WASHINGTON
SCALE
0 5 10 20 30 40 MI.
0 5 10 20 30 40 KM.
State Capitals
County Seats
Copyright by C. S. HAMMOND & Co., N.Y.
Longitude 121° West of Greenwich
PACIFIC OCEAN
BRITISH COLUMBIA
IDAHO
OREGON
SEATTLE
Spokane
Olympia
Tacoma
Yakima
Walla Walla
PORTLAND
VANCOUVER
Victoria

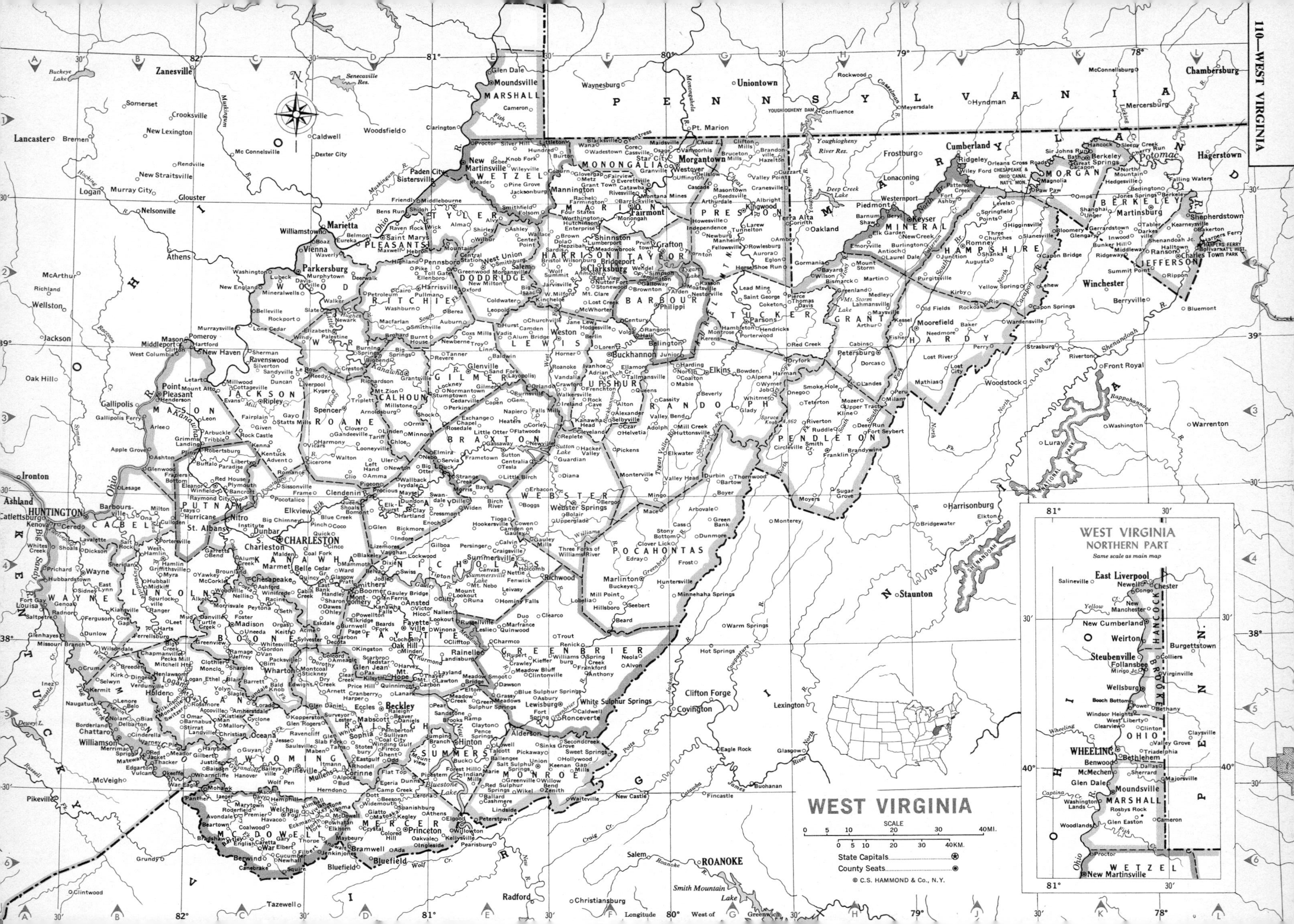
WEST VIRGINIA
SCALE
0 5 10 20 30 40 MI.
0 5 10 20 30 40 KM.
State Capitals
County Seats
© C.S. HAMMOND & Co., N.Y.
WEST VIRGINIA
NORTHERN PART
Same scale as main map
CHARLESTON
P E N N S Y L V A N I A
M A R Y L A N D
V I R G I N I A
K E N T U C K Y
O H I O

WISCONSIN

SCALE

0 5 10 20 30 40 MI.

0 5 10 20 30 40 KM.

State Capitals ⊛

County Seats ◉

Canals

LAKE SUPERIOR

MICHIGAN

MINNESOTA

IOWA

ILLINOIS

LAKE MICHIGAN

GREEN BAY

APOSTLE ISLANDS

MILWAUKEE

CHICAGO

Longitude West of Greenwich

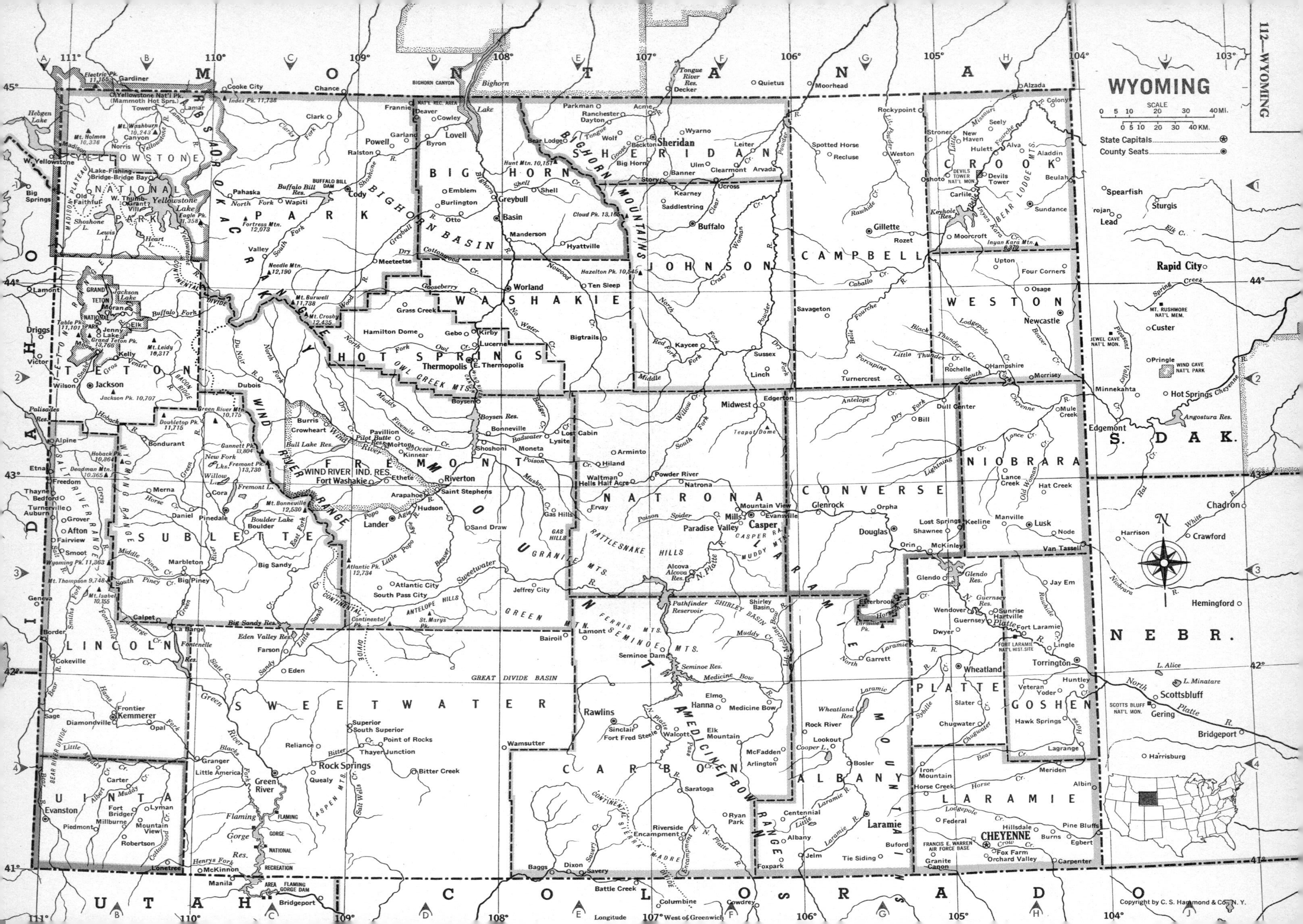
WYOMING
SCALE
0 5 10 20 30 40 MI.
0 5 10 20 30 40 KM.
State Capitals
County Seats
MONTANA
S. DAK.
NEBR.
COLORADO
UTAH
IDAHO
CROOK
WESTON
NIOBRARA
GOSHEN
LARAMIE
PLATTE
CONVERSE
CAMPBELL
SHERIDAN
JOHNSON
NATRONA
ALBANY
CARBON
SWEETWATER
FREMONT
WASHAKIE
HOT SPRINGS
BIG HORN
PARK
TETON
SUBLETTE
LINCOLN
UINTA
YELLOWSTONE NATIONAL PARK
CHEYENNE
Casper
Laramie
Rock Springs
Sheridan
Gillette
Rawlins
Riverton
Lander
Cody
Jackson
Evanston
Green River
Torrington
Douglas
Buffalo
Worland
Thermopolis
Kemmerer
Pinedale
Newcastle
Lusk
Sundance
Wheatland
Basin
BIGHORN MOUNTAINS
BIGHORN BASIN
ABSAROKA RANGE
WIND RIVER RANGE
GREAT DIVIDE BASIN
MEDICINE BOW MTS.
LARAMIE MOUNTAINS
WYOMING RANGE
SALT RIVER RANGE
GRANITE MTS.
RATTLESNAKE HILLS
CONTINENTAL DIVIDE
WIND RIVER IND. RES.
FLAMING GORGE NATIONAL RECREATION AREA
Rapid City
Scottsbluff
Longitude 107° West of Greenwich
Copyright by C. S. Hammond & Co., N. Y.

INDEX OF THE WORLD

(See Glossary of Abbreviations on Page 145)

A

B

C

D

E

F

G

J

K

L

M

N

O

P

S

T

U

V

GLOSSARY OF ABBREVIATIONS

A

Acad. — Academy
A.F.B. — Air Force Base
Afgh. — Afghanistan
Afr. — Africa
A. & I. — Territory of the Afars & Issas
Ala. — Alabama
Alb. — Albania
Alg. — Algeria
Alta. — Alberta
Amer. — American
Amer. Samoa — American Samoa
Ant. — Antarctica
Ar. — Arabia
arch. — archipelago
Arg. — Argentina
Ariz. — Arizona
Ark. — Arkansas
A. S. S. R. — Autonomous Soviet Socialist Republic
Aus. — Austria
Aust. — Australia
aut. — autonomous
Aut. Obl. — Autonomous Oblast
aut. prov. — autonomous province
Aut. Reg. — Autonomous Region

B

Bah. — Bahamas
Bang. — Bangladesh
Barb. — Barbados
B.C. — British Columbia
Bch. — Beach
Belg. — Belgium
Berm. — Bermuda
Bol. — Bolivia
Braz. — Brazil
B.I.O.T. — British Indian Ocean Territory
Bulg. — Bulgaria
B.V.I. — British Virgin Islands

C

. — cape
alif. — California
.A. — Central America
amb. — Cambodia
an. — Canada
ap. — capital
.A.R. — Central African Republic
. H. — Court House
han. — channel
han. Is. — Channel Islands
o. — county
ol. — Colombia
olo. — Colorado
onn. — Connecticut
.R. — Costa Rica
tr. — Center
Verde — Cape Verde
. Z. — Canal Zone
zech. — Czechoslovakia

D

el. — Delaware
en. — Denmark
epr. — depression
ept. — department
es. — desert
st. — district
om. Rep. — Dominican Republic

E

— East
cua. — Ecuador
Ger. — East Germany
Sal. — El Salvador
ng. — England
. Guin. — Equatorial Guinea
est. — estuary
Eth. — Ethiopia

F

Falk. Is. — Falkland Islands
Fin. — Finland
Fla. — Florida
for. — forest
Fr. — French
Fr. Gui. — French Guiana
Fr. Poly. — French Polynesia
Ft. — Fort

G

Ga. — Georgia
G. & E. Is. — Gilbert & Ellice Islands
Ger. — Germany
Greenl. — Greenland
Gt. — Great
Guad. — Guadeloupe
Guat. — Guatemala
Guin.-Biss. — Guinea-Bissau

H

hbr. — harbor
Hond. — Honduras
Hts. — Heights
Hung. — Hungary

I

i., isl., — island, isle
I.C. — Ivory Coast
Ice. — Iceland
Ill. — Illinois
Ind. — Indiana
Indon. — Indonesia
Int'l — International
Ire. — Ireland
is., isls. — islands
Isr. — Israel
isth. — isthmus

J

Jam. — Jamaica
Jct. — Junction

K

Kans. — Kansas
Ky. — Kentucky

L

La. — Louisiana
Lab. — Laboratory
Lak. — Lakeshore
Leb. — Lebanon
Lib. — Liberia
Liecht. — Liechtenstein
Lux. — Luxembourg

M

Mal. Rep. — Malagasy Republic
Mart. — Martinique
Mass. — Massachusetts
M.C.A.S. — Marine Corps Air Station
Md. — Maryland
Mem. — Memorial
Mex. — Mexico
Mich. — Michigan
Minn. — Minnesota
Miss. — Mississippi
Mo. — Missouri
Mong. — Mongolia
Mont. — Montana
Mor. — Morocco
Moz. — Mozambique
mt., mtn. — mount, mountain
mts. — mountains

N

N. — North
N.A. — North America
N.B. — National Battlefield
N.B.P. — National Battlefield Park
N.Br. — New Brunswick
N.B.S. — National Battlefield Site
N. C. — North Carolina
N. Dak. — North Dakota
Nebr. — Nebraska
Neth. — Netherlands
Neth. Ant. — Netherlands Antilles
Nev. — Nevada
New Cal. — New Caledonia
Newf. — Newfoundland
New Hebr. — New Hebrides
N. H. — New Hampshire
N.H.P. — National Historical Park
N.H.S. — National Historic Site
Nic. — Nicaragua
Nig. — Nigeria
N. Ire. — Northern Ireland
N. J. — New Jersey
N. Korea — North Korea
N. Lab. — National Laboratory
N. Lak. — National Lakeshore
N. M. — National Monument
N. M. C. — Naval Missile Center
N. Mem. — National Memorial
N. Mem. Pk. — National Memorial Park
N. Mex. — New Mexico
N. M. P. — National Military Park
No. — Northern
Nor. — Norway
N. P. — National Park
N. R. A. — National Recreation Area
N. S. — Nova Scotia
N. Sea — National Seashore
N. Viet. — North Vietnam
N. W. T. — Northwest Territories (Canada)
N. Y. — New York
N. Z. — New Zealand

O

Obl. — Oblast
Okla. — Oklahoma
Ont. — Ontario
Oreg. — Oregon

P

Pa. — Pennsylvania
Pak. — Pakistan
Pan. — Panama
Par. — Paraguay
P.D.R.Y. — Peoples Democratic Republic of Yemen
P.E.I. — Prince Edward Island
pen. — peninsula
Phil. — Philippines
Pk. — Park
plat. — plateau
P.N.G. — Papua New Guinea
Pol. — Poland
Port. — Portuguese
P. R. — Puerto Rico
prom. — promontory
Prot. — Protectorate
prov. — province, provincial
Prov. Pk. — Provincial Park
Pt., Pte. — Point, Pointe

Q

Que. — Quebec

R

reg. — region
Rep. — Republic
res. — reservoir
Rhod. — Rhodesia
R. I. — Rhode Island
riv. — river
Rum. — Rumania

S

S. — South
S. A. — South America
S. Afr. — South Africa
São T. & P. — São Tomé & Príncipe
Sask. — Saskatchewan
Saudi Ar. — Saudi Arabia
S. C. — South Carolina
Scot. — Scotland
S. Dak. — South Dakota
Sea. — Seashore
Sen. — Senegal
Seych. — Seychelles
S.F.S.R. — Soviet Federated Socialist Republic
Sing. — Singapore
S. Korea — South Korea
S. Leone — Sierra Leone
Sol. Is. — Solomon Islands
Sp. — Spanish
Spr., Sprs. — Spring, Springs
Sp. Sahara — Spanish Sahara
S. S. R. — Soviet Socialist Republic
St., Ste. — Saint, Sainte
Sta. — Santa
St. C.-N.-A. — Saint Christopher-Nevis-Anguilla
Sto. — Santo
str. — strait
Sur. — Surinam
S. Viet. — South Vietnam
S. W. Afr. — South-West Africa
Swaz. — Swaziland
Switz. — Switzerland

T

Tanz. — Tanzania
T. & C. Is. — Turks & Caicos Islands
Tenn. — Tennessee
terr. — territory
Tex. — Texas
Thai. — Thailand
T. & T. — Trinidad & Tobago
T. T. P. I. — Trust Territory of the Pacific Islands
Tun. — Tunisia

U

U. A. E. — United Arab Emirates
U. K. — United Kingdom
Urug. — Uruguay
U. S. — United States
U. S. S. R. — Union of Soviet Socialist Repubilcs

V

Va. —Virginia
Ven. — Venezuela
V. I. — Virgin Islands (U.S.)
Viet. — Vietnam
Vill. — Village
vol. — volcano
Vt. — Vermont

W

W. — West
Wash. — Washington
W. Ger. — West Germany
W. I. — West Indies
Wis. — Wisconsin
W. Samoa — Western Samoa
W. Va. — West Virginia
Wyo. — Wyoming

Y

Y.A.R. — Yemen Arab Republic
Yugo. — Yugoslavia

POLITICAL & ECONOMIC TABLES OF THE WORLD

POLITICAL DIVISION	GOVERNMENT	MAJOR PRODUCTS
AFARS & ISSAS, TERR. OF THE	French overseas territory with a high commissioner, council of government and territorial assembly.	Salt; hides & skins; livestock; boats.
AFGHANISTAN	Republic, at present under military rule, with a president, appointed cabinet and a ruling central committee.	Wheat, barley, corn, rice, sugar beets, nuts & seeds, fruits, cotton, tobacco; livestock; timber; natural gas, salt, copper, lead, talc, coal, lapis lazuli; hides & skins (karakul), wool, textiles, leather, carpets, cement.
ALBANIA	Soviet-type republic with a head of state, cabinet and unicameral legislature; controlled by the Communist party.	Corn, tobacco, wheat, potatoes, cotton, sugar beets, fruits; livestock; fish; timber; petroleum, bitumen, lignite, nickel, copper, iron ore, chromite; textiles, wool, tobacco products, chemicals.
ALGERIA	Centralized republic under a president, council of ministers, and a revolutionary council.	Wheat, barley, oats, corn, grapes, olives, dates, figs, citrus fruits, vegetables, tobacco; fish; livestock; timber; iron ore, petroleum, phosphates, zinc, natural gas, mercury, coal, lead; hides & skins, wine, olive oil, cork, food & tobacco products, leather goods, textiles, carpets, wool, plastics, chemicals, machinery, iron & steel, refined petroleum.
AMERICAN SAMOA	U.S. territory with a governor and an elected bicameral legislature.	Taro, breadfruit, yams, bananas, arrowroot, pineapples, coconuts, oranges; fish; livestock; canned fish, copra, mats.
ANDORRA	Co-principality of the president of France and the Spanish bishop of Seo de Urgel, with an elected executive and a council general.	Tobacco, potatoes, oats, barley; livestock; timber; iron ore, lead; dairy, tobacco, wood & wool products.
ANGOLA	Former Portuguese possession, now under an interim military government, pending independence.	Coffee, corn, sugarcane, peanuts, tobacco, rice, palm products, cotton, sisal; iron ore, petroleum, diamonds; fish; livestock; timber; refined petroleum, cement, paper, tires, refined sugar, food products, chemicals.
ANTIGUA	Associated British state, with governor, prime minister, cabinet and bicameral legislature.	Sugar, cotton, rice, molasses, fruits, vegetables; fish; processed sugar and cotton, rum.
ARGENTINA	A republic with a president, appointive cabinet, elective senate and chamber of deputies.	Wheat, corn, millet, cotton, sugarcane, tobacco, fruits; livestock; timber; petroleum, natural gas, zinc, silver, lead, coal, iron ore, tungsten; wine, vegetable oils, dairy products, meat & meat products, wool, hides, textiles, wood and metal products, iron & steel, machinery, autos, chemicals, leather, petroleum products, cement.
AUSTRALIA	Independent British Commonwealth member with a governor-general, prime minister, cabinet, and a bicameral parliament, composed of a senate and a house of representatives.	Wheat, oats, barley, fruits, vegetables; livestock; gold, coal, petroleum, copper, iron, lead, silver, bauxite, zinc; timber, iron & steel, wool, electrical and radio equipment, appliances, chemicals, petroleum products, optical & agricultural implements, machinery, textiles, leather, airplanes, engines, ships, processed meat, sugar, dairy products, building materials, autos, tires.
AUSTRIA	A federal republic with a president, chancellor, cabinet, and a bicameral elective assembly.	Rye, wheat, corn, oats, barley, potatoes, sugar beets, hops, flax, tobacco, grapes; livestock; timber; iron ore, copper, lead, graphite, coal, petroleum, salt, magnesite; wine, processed foods, dairy products, iron & steel, aluminum, machinery, tools, chemicals, paper, textiles, cement.
BAHAMAS	Independent British Commonwealth member, with a governor-general, prime minister, cabinet and bicameral legislature.	Tomatoes, pineapples, sugarcane, vegetables, sponges, citrus fruits, bananas; fish, crawfish, shells; timber; salt; handcraft products, cement, pulpwood, processed fish, rum, refined petroleum, drugs.
BAHRAIN	Constitutional emirate with a sheikh, prime minister and cabinet.	Vegetables, fruits, dates; fish, shellfish; petroleum; refined petroleum, processed aluminum, electrical goods, cement, flour.
BANGLADESH	Independent republic in the British Commonwealth, with a president, prime minister, cabinet, and a unicameral legislature.	Rice, sugarcane, jute, cotton, oilseeds, tobacco, tea, chilies, fruit; timber; cattle, fish; natural gas, coal; textiles, hides & skins, flour, refined petroleum, steel, chemicals, refined sugar, handicrafts, paper, leather goods, jute products.

POLITICAL DIVISION	GOVERNMENT	MAJOR PRODUCTS
BARBADOS	Independent British Commonwealth member, with a governor-general, prime minister, cabinet and a bicameral legislature.	Sugarcane, vegetables, cotton; fish; manjak (asphalt); sugar, molasses, rum, edible oils, margarine.
BELGIUM	Constitutional, hereditary monarchy, with a king, prime minister, cabinet, and a bicameral legislature.	Wheat, rye, oats, barley, potatoes, sugar beets, tobacco, vegetables, fruit, hops; livestock, poultry; fish; coal, iron, zinc, lead, dolomite; coke, iron & steel, machinery, metal products, textiles, lace, glass, chemicals, petroleum & uranium refining, sugar, beer, paper, wine, wool, cut diamonds, dairy products, aircraft, cement, autos.
BELIZE	Internally self-governing British colony with governor, prime minister, cabinet and bicameral legislature.	Rice, corn, bananas, vegetables, citrus fruits, cocoa, sugarcane; cattle; hard and softwoods; fish, shellfish; rum, meat, fruit & fish products.
BERMUDA	Partly self-governing British colony with a governor, prime minister, cabinet and a bicameral legislature.	Lily bulbs, onions, bananas, citrus fruits, vegetables, potatoes; coral; poultry, fish; limestone; perfume, pharmaceuticals, concrete.
BHUTAN	Monarchy with a king, cabinet, and an elected national assembly.	Rice, wheat, barley, millet, corn, fruits; timber; cattle, yaks; handicrafts, dairy products.
BOLIVIA	Centralized constitutional republic, with a president, cabinet and bicameral legislature, at present under military rule.	Potatoes, corn, wheat, barley, rice, cassava, sugarcane, cotton, coffee, fruits; timber; livestock; tin, zinc, lead, silver, antimony, copper, natural gas, petroleum, tungsten, gold, sulphur; hides & skins, textiles, chemicals, cement, beer, tobacco products.
BOTSWANA	Republic within the British Commonwealth, with a president, cabinet unicameral national assembly and advisory house of chiefs.	Kaffir cotton, sorghum, millet, corn, wheat, beans, fruits & nuts; livestock; diamonds, nickel, copper, coal, salt, talc, manganese ore; hides & skins, meat & dairy products, leather goods, brewing.
BRAZIL	Federal republic with a president, vice-president, appointive cabinet and a bicameral national congress.	Coffee, corn, rice, wheat, cotton, cocoa, sugarcane, soybeans, cassava, rubber, fibers, carnauba wax, medicinal plants, fruits & nuts, tobacco; livestock; timber; iron & manganese ore, diamonds, lead & zinc, bauxite, gold & silver, mica, asbestos, chromite, tungsten, petroleum, quartz, beryllium, copper, coal; meat products, hides, textiles, chemicals, petrochemicals, drugs, paper, lumber, machinery, autos, metal products, iron & steel, sugar, aluminum, tires, cement.
BRUNEI	Internally self-governing British protected sultanate, with a chief minister, legislative council and council of ministers.	Rice, sago, rubber, jelutong, cutch, tapioca, bananas; timber; livestock; petroleum, natural gas; boat building, cloth, brass and silverware, refined petroleum.
BULGARIA	Soviet-type republic with chief of state, cabinet, state council and unicameral assembly; controlled by the Communist party.	Wheat, corn, barley, cotton, tobacco, sugar beets, potatoes, seeds, fruits, vegetables; timber; livestock; fish; iron ore, copper, lead, coal, manganese, petroleum, zinc; food, leather & tobacco products, sugar, refined minerals & petroleum, textiles, wine, iron & steel, machinery, cement.
BURMA	One-party socialist republic with a president, state council, prime minister, cabinet and a unicameral assembly.	Rice, corn, cotton, pulses, sugarcane, tobacco, fruits & nuts, jute, rubber, sesame; livestock; timber (teak); petroleum, lead, zinc, tungsten, nickel, silver, copper, precious stones; sugar, food, tobacco & wood products, drugs, chemicals, textiles, cement, refined petroleum, steel.
BURUNDI	One-party republic with a president, cabinet, and an executive political bureau.	Coffee, tea, cotton, corn, beans, fruits & nuts, sweet potatoes, sorghum; cattle; fish; timber; nickel; hides & skins, textiles, cement, beer, soap, shoes, food products.
CAMBODIA	Nominal republic, at present under Communist military rule.	Rice, tobacco, corn, beans, sugarcane, rubber, cotton; cattle; fish; timber; phosphates, gold, precious stones; food products, textiles, sugar, glass, drugs.
CAMEROON	One-party republic, with a president, cabinet, and a unicameral national assembly.	Cocoa, coffee, rubber, nuts, tea, rice, tobacco, palm products, cotton; livestock; fish; timber; bauxite, gold, petroleum; hides & skins, wood, rubber & tobacco products, textiles, beer, food products, palm oil.

POLITICAL DIVISION	GOVERNMENT	MAJOR PRODUCTS
CANADA	Independent confederation of the British Commonwealth, with a governor-general, prime minister, cabinet and a bicameral parliament, composed of an elected senate and house of commons.	Wheat, oats, barley, corn, potatoes, vegetables, sugar beets, tobacco, fruits, oilseeds; livestock, poultry; fish, shellfish; timber; furs; gold, copper, nickel, zinc, lead, silver, potash, molybdenum, platinum, iron ore, titanium, cobalt, radium, uranium, petroleum, natural gas, coal, asbestos, salt, gypsum, sulphur; hydroelectric power; foods, apparel, meat & dairy products, transportation equipment, iron & steel, aluminum, metal products, lumber, pulp, paper & wood products, textiles, electric goods, chemicals, autos, cement, processed minerals, refined petroleum, machinery.
CAPE VERDE ISLANDS	Former Portuguese possession, now an independent republic.	Coffee, bananas, nuts, oilseeds, corn; livestock; salt, lime; hides & skins, preserved fish, sugar, cement.
CENTRAL AFRICAN REPUBLIC	One-party republic of the French Community, with a president (for life) and a revolutionary council.	Coffee, cotton, peanuts, tobacco, corn, rice, sorghum; timber; livestock; gold, diamonds, uranium; wood & palm products, textiles, flour, soap, beer.
CHAD	One-party republic of the French Community, under a prime minister, cabinet, & military council.	Millet, sorghum, rice, cotton, vegetables, dates, cassava, peanuts, gum arabic, ivory, ostrich feathers; livestock; fish; natron (salt); hides, cloth, meat products.
CHILE	Constitutional republic, at present ruled by a president and a military junta.	Cereal grains, seeds, sugar beets, potatoes, vegetables, fruits, tobacco; livestock; fish; timber; copper, nitrates, iron ore, manganese, silver, gold, molybdenum, zinc, coal, petroleum; chemicals, petrochemicals, wood & metal products, textiles, paper, pulp, drugs, wine, iron & steel, food & leather products, cement.
CHINA (PEOPLE'S REPUBLIC)	Nominal republic, ruled by a prime minister & cabinet (state council); controlled by Communist party's politburo, headed by the standing committee and its chairman.	Rice & cereal grains, soybeans, fruits, vegetables, nuts, oilseeds, tea, silk, cotton, sugarcane, tobacco; livestock, poultry; fish; timber; iron ore, petroleum, coal, tungsten, tin, antimony, magnetite, manganese, molybdenum, natural gas, mercury, bauxite, lead, zinc; meat & food products, textiles, apparel, ceramics, cement, iron & steel, machinery, metal products, aluminum, chemicals, vehicles, armaments.
CHINA (REPUBLIC OF): TAIWAN	Republic with a president, prime minister, cabinet, a legislative yuan and a national assembly, the latter electing the president.	Rice, sugarcane, tea, sweet potatoes, bananas, pineapples, mushrooms, soybeans, tobacco; livestock; fish; timber; coal, natural gas; food & wood products, cement, glass, chemicals, petrochemicals, steel, bicycles, sugar, electric & electronic goods, machinery, metal products, textiles, apparel.
COLOMBIA	A centralized federal republic with a president, appointed cabinet, and elected bicameral legislature.	Coffee, rice, cotton, sugarcane, bananas, cacao, wheat, corn, tobacco, rubber, fibers; livestock; fish; timber; petroleum, gold, platinum, emeralds, silver, salt; sugar, food & tobacco products, beer, textiles, cement, iron & steel, machinery, metal & leather products, chemicals, meat.
COMORO ISLANDS	Former French territory, now an independent republic with a president & assembly.	Sugarcane, vanilla, rice, root vegetables, copra, sisal, coffee, essential oils (ylang, citronella), cloves, cacao, perfume plants; timber; rum distilling.
CONGO	One-party republic of the French Community, with a president, prime minister, cabinet, and national revolutionary council.	Palm products, coffee, cocoa, bananas, tobacco, sugarcane, rice, corn, peanuts, fruits; livestock; timber; petroleum, potash, lead, zinc, gold; hardwoods & wood products, textiles, beer, cement, sugar, food products.
COOK ISLANDS	Internally self-governing state associated with New Zealand with a commissioner, prime minister, cabinet and legislative assembly.	Citrus fruits, coconuts, copra, oilseeds, tomatoes, arrowroot, pineapples, breadfruit, taro, kumaras, plantains, yams; mother-of-pearl, textiles, processed fruits.
COSTA RICA	Constitutional republic with president, appointed cabinet and unicameral legislature.	Coffee, bananas, cocoa, corn, sugarcane, rice, potatoes, tobacco; cattle; tuna; timber; gold, salt, bauxite; dairy, tobacco & food products; electrical goods, beef, sugar, textiles, furniture, cement, apparel.

POLITICAL DIVISION	GOVERNMENT	MAJOR PRODUCTS
CUBA	Soviet-type republic with a president, actually ruled by decree by the prime minister, who is head of the cabinet.	Sugarcane, tobacco, coffee, rice, fruits; cattle; timber; fish; nickel, iron ore, chromite, manganese, copper; sugar, tobacco, meat & food products, textiles, cement, chemicals, steel, refined petroleum & metals, electrical goods, rum.
CYPRUS	British Commonwealth republic, with a president (Greek), vice-president (Turkish), cabinet, Greek & Turkish communal chambers, & a unicameral legislature. At present politically unsettled.	Wheat, barley, grapes, raisins, olives, potatoes, carobs, nuts, citrus fruits, tobacco, vegetables; fish; livestock; copper & concentrates, iron pyrites, asbestos, chromite, gypsum, marble; tobacco, leather & food products, cement, wine, textiles, refined petroleum.
CZECHOSLOVAKIA	Soviet-type republic with a president, cabinet, bicameral legislature, and Czech and Slovak National Councils, with actual power residing in the Communist party presidium.	Wheat, rye, oats, barley, corn, sugar beets, potatoes; livestock; timber; coal, iron ore, magnesite, uranium, lead, salt; munitions, machinery, metal, rubber, leather & wood products, cement, iron & steel, textiles, shoes, porcelain, paper, chemicals, aircraft, autos, glass & glassware, beer, apparel, sugar, food products.
DAHOMEY	Republic, at present under a head of state and national revolutionary council.	Palm products, rice, peanuts, cotton, corn, beans, coffee, millet; livestock; fish; iron ore; oilseed milling, textiles, kenaf, cement, beer.
DENMARK	Constitutional, hereditary monarchy with a queen, prime minister, cabinet, and a unicameral legislature.	Barley, oats, rye, wheat, potatoes, sugar beets, vegetables; poultry, livestock; stone, clay, iron ore; meat & meat products, dairy products, canned foods, beverages, machinery, transportation equipment, metal & rubber products, chemicals, apparel, shoes, furniture, glassware, earthenware, electrical goods, ships, cement, paper, tobacco products.
DOMINICA	Associated British state, with governor, prime minister, cabinet and unicameral legislature.	Bananas, citrus fruits, coconuts, cocoa, vanilla, sugarcane, corn, rice, mangoes, avocados; livestock; fish; pumice; fruit & tobacco products, edible & essential oils, soap, copra, rum.
DOMINICAN REPUBLIC	Republic with a president, vice-president, appointed cabinet, and bicameral legislature.	Sugarcane, cacao, coffee, tobacco, bananas, rice, fruits, corn; cattle; lumber; nickel, bauxite; nickel & petroleum refining, chocolate, sugar, meat, cigars, textiles, cement, beer, flour, peanut oil, leather goods, rum.
ECUADOR	Constitutional republic at present under the rule of a president, cabinet & military junta.	Rice, cocoa, coffee, sugarcane, corn, bananas, cotton, cinchona; livestock; fish & shellfish; timber; petroleum, gold, silver; food, rubber, leather & wood products, textiles, toquilla (panama) hats, sugar, beer, cement, chemicals & petrochemicals, drugs, glass.
EGYPT	One-party Arab republic with a president (with supreme powers), cabinet, and a partly elected unicameral assembly.	Cotton, cereal grains, sugarcane, fruits, vegetables; livestock; fish; petroleum, phosphates, salt, iron ore, manganese, limestone; cotton ginning, iron & steel, refined petroleum, food processing, textiles, chemicals, cement, petrochemicals, sugar.
EL SALVADOR	Republic with a president, cabinet, and unicameral legislature.	Coffee, cotton, cereal grains, cacao, tobacco, henequén, sugarcane; fish, shellfish; livestock; timber; silver; sugar, textiles, food products, drugs, chemicals, electric goods.
ENGLAND AND WALES	Integral part of the United Kingdom, with executive power nominally residing in the Crown, but actually exercised by the prime minister, cabinet and bicameral parliament, composed of a house of lords and a house of commons.	Potatoes, vegetables, cereal grains, hay, beans, vetches, hops, fruits; livestock, poultry; fish; coal, natural gas, iron ore, copper, lead, nickel, tin; dairy products, wool, cotton & linen textiles, electrical goods, vehicles, steel, scientific instruments, cutlery, foods & beverages, leather & tobacco products, apparel, chemicals, petrochemicals, pottery, china, machinery, locomotives, knitwear, drugs.
EQUATORIAL GUINEA	One-party centralized republic, with a president, appointed cabinet and a unicameral legislature.	Cocoa, coffee, bananas, sugarcane, palm oil & kernels; timber, cabinet woods; fish; copra, beverages, soap.
ETHIOPIA	One-party centralized state, with an appointed cabinet and military government.	Coffee, wheat, corn, barley, durra, teff, pulses, oilseeds, chat, civet, fruits, vegetables, sugarcane, spices; poultry, livestock; gold, platinum; hides & skins, meat & food products, textiles, cement, sugar, refined petroleum, drugs.
FALKLAND ISLANDS	British colony with a governor, executive & legislative councils.	Oats, vegetables, hay; sheep; wool, hides & skins, tallow, animal & vegetable oil.

POLITICAL DIVISION	GOVERNMENT	MAJOR PRODUCTS
FIJI	Independent British Commonwealth member, with a governor-general, prime minister, cabinet, and a bicameral legislature.	Sugarcane, coconuts, rice, fruits, cotton, rubber, ginger, oilseeds, vegetables, bananas, cocoa, corn, tobacco; livestock; timber; fish; gold, silver, manganese; sugar, copra, coconut oil, molasses, candlenut oil, cement, beer, meat products, flour, shipbuilding.
FINLAND	Constitutional republic with a president, cabinet, and a unicameral legislature.	Hay, potatoes, cereal grains; livestock, poultry, reindeer; timber; fish; copper, iron ore, titanium, zinc, nickel; lumber, plywood, furniture, pulp, paper, wood products, textiles, food & dairy products, meat, chemicals, china, glass, machinery, ships, transportation equipment, electrical & metal products, vehicles, apparel, iron & steel.
FRANCE	A constitutional republic with a president, a bicameral elected legislature and appointive council of ministers.	Sugar beets, potatoes, cereal grains, turnips, fruits, nuts, grapes, buckwheat; livestock; fish; coal, iron ore, bauxite, pyrites, potash, salt, sulphur, natural gas; iron & steel, chemicals, machinery, metal & leather goods, autos, aircraft, ships, aluminum, porcelain, food & dairy products, apparel, cosmetics, perfumes, sugar, wines & spirits, electric & electronic goods, lace, silk, cotton, rayon, wool & linen textiles.
FRENCH GUIANA	Overseas department of France governed by a prefect with an elective general council.	Rice, bananas, sugarcane, corn, manioc; timber; livestock; shrimp; bauxite, gold; hides, shoes, rum, fish glue.
FRENCH POLYNESIA	Overseas territory of France, with a governor, government council, and an elected territorial assembly.	Coconuts, bananas, pineapples, oranges, vanilla, sugarcane, coffee, bamboo; fish; mother-of-pearl, sugar, rum, copra.
GABON	One-party republic of the French Community with a president, vice-president, cabinet & a unicameral legislature.	Coffee, cocoa, rubber, corn, rice, bananas, cassava; timber; fish; manganese, uranium, petroleum, iron ore, gold, natural gas, lead, zinc, copper, diamonds, phosphates; refined petroleum, processed metals, textiles, plywood.
GAMBIA	Republic of the British Commonwealth, with a president, vice-president, cabinet and unicameral legislature.	Peanuts, rice, millet, sorghum, fruits, palm kernels; livestock; fish; textiles, peanut oil refining, fish processing, palm products, beverages.
GERMANY	Divided country with two governments. The western democratic Federal Republic has a president, chancellor, cabinet & bicameral parliament. The eastern Democratic Republic is ruled by the chairman of the state council, a prime minister & cabinet, & a unicameral legislature; actual power resides in the head of the Communist party.	Cereal grains, potatoes, sugar beets, fruits, hops; livestock; fish; timber; coal, lignite, iron ore, potash, salt, uranium, lead, zinc, natural gas, fluorspar; iron & steel, autos, bicycles, machinery, aluminum, cement, electrical & transportation equipment, ships, metal & electronic products, cotton & woolen textiles & yarn, rayon fiber, precision & optical instruments, shoes, apparel, food products, sugar, beer, wine, chemicals, sulphuric acid, soda, ammonia, synthetic rubber, drugs, petrochemicals.
GHANA	Republic of the British Commonwealth, with a military council and appointed cabinet.	Cocoa, palm products, coconuts, kola nuts, fruits, tobacco, coffee, peanuts, rubber; livestock; fish; timber; gold, diamonds, manganese, bauxite; aluminum, refined petroleum, textiles.
GIBRALTAR	Partly self-governing British colony, with a governor, cabinet, house of assembly & local council.	Fish; ship repairing, beer, local food processing.
GILBERT AND ELLICE ISLS.	Self-governing British colony, with a governor and local councils.	Coconuts, breadfruit; phosphate of lime; pearl shell, fish; pigs, poultry; copra, palm products.
GREAT BRITAIN	See: England and Wales, Northern Ireland, Scotland.	
GREECE	Constitutional republic, with a president, prime minister, cabinet & an elected unicameral parliament.	Cereal grains, tobacco, sugar beets, cotton, fruits, olives; livestock; sponges, fish; iron ore, emery, manganese, magnesite, marble, silver, nickel, bauxite, salt, chromite; textiles, olive oil, processed meat, fruit & vegetables, dairy, wood & leather products, steel, machinery, refined aluminum & petroleum, chemicals, wine, olive oil, cement, drugs.
GREENLAND	Integral part of the Danish kingdom, with representation in Parliament, and an elected council.	Grass for fodder; cod and other fish; sheep, furs; cryolite, lead, zinc; processed fish, skins.
GRENADA	Independent British Commonwealth member, with a governor, premier, cabinet, and bicameral legislature.	Cocoa, nutmeg, coffee, mace, limes, bananas, sugarcane, coconuts, vegetables, cotton; fish; livestock; timber; sugar, cotton ginning, copra, lime oil, rum, beer, cigarettes.

POLITICAL DIVISION	GOVERNMENT	MAJOR PRODUCTS
GUADELOUPE	Overseas department of France with a prefect and elected general council.	Sugarcane, bananas, pineapples, mangoes, avocados, coffee, cotton, sisal, cocoa, vanilla, cassava; fish; rum, sugar.
GUAM	Unincorporated U.S. territory, with an elected governor, advisory staff, and a unicameral legislature.	Coconuts, corn, bananas, citrus fruits, mangoes, papayas, breadfruit, sweet potatoes, cassava, vegetables, sugarcane, pineapples; livestock, poultry; fish; dairy & coconut products.
GUATEMALA	Republic with a president, cabinet, council of state, and a unicameral legislature.	Coffee, bananas, sugarcane, tobacco, rubber, cotton, chicle, abacá; fish; cattle; mahogany; nickel, zinc, lead; textiles, chemicals, essential oils, wood, metal & electric goods, processed meat & foods, sugar, hides & skins, apparel.
GUINEA	One-party centralized republic, with a president, cabinet, and national assembly.	Rice, millet, coffee, kola nuts, peanuts, palm oil & kernels, quinine, pineapples, cassava, bananas; livestock; bauxite, iron ore, diamonds, gold; timber; hides & skins, textiles, wood & food products, cigarettes, aluminum.
GUINEA-BISSAU	Former Portuguese possession, now a republic with a president, council & an elected assembly.	Rice, millet, coconuts, peanuts, palm kernels & oil, oilseeds, wax; livestock; timber; hides & skins, copra.
GUYANA	"Co-operative" republic within the British Commonwealth, with president, prime minister, cabinet, and unicameral legislature.	Sugarcane, corn, rice, coconuts, coffee, citrus & tropical fruits, cacao, balata, rubber; timber; livestock; shrimp; bauxite, diamonds, manganese, gemstones, gold; textiles, milled rice, beer, rum, lime oil, sugar, wood & pulp, molasses, aluminum.
HAITI	Centralized republic, with a president, appointed cabinet, and a unicameral legislature.	Coffee, sugarcane, sisal, cotton, fruits, rice, corn, cocoa; livestock; shellfish; bauxite; fiber, cement, essential oils, handicrafts, molasses, textiles, cement, sugar, soap, rum.
HONDURAS	Republic at present under a head of state, appointed cabinet, and a military council.	Bananas, coffee, coconuts, tobacco, corn, beans, sugarcane, cotton, rice, henequén; mahogany; cattle; lead, zinc, gold, silver; meat & food products, sugar, lumber, vegetable oils.
HONG KONG	British colony ruled by a governor assisted by executive and legislative councils.	Rice, sugarcane, vegetables; fish; poultry, pigs; iron ore, wolfram, graphite; iron & steel, ships, enamel ware, apparel, textiles, cotton & plastic goods, toys, cameras, radios, electric & electronic goods.
HUNGARY	Soviet-type republic, with a presidential council, cabinet and a unicameral assembly. Actual power is in the hands of the politburo of the Communist party.	Cereal grains, sugar beets, tobacco, grapes, fruits, potatoes; livestock, poultry; fish; timber; coal, petroleum, natural gas, iron ore, bauxite; flour, sugar, iron & steel, wines, textiles, chemicals, cotton & woolen goods, dairy, food, wood & paper products, machinery, tools & metal products, transportation equipment, drugs, aluminum, bicycles, cement.
ICELAND	A republic with a president, prime minister, appointed cabinet and an elected bicameral legislature.	Hay, potatoes, turnips, fruits, vegetables; livestock; fish; diatomite; dairy products, processed fish & fish products, meat, hides & skins, textiles, apparel, chemicals, cement, motors, vegetable oils.
INDIA	An independent republic within the British Commonwealth with a president, vice-president, prime minister, cabinet and a bicameral parliament.	Cereal grains, peanuts, seeds, tea, tobacco, opium, jute, cotton, rubber, coffee, sugarcane; fish; livestock; timber; coal, manganese, iron ore, petroleum, salt, mica, chromite, ilmenite, clay, copper, bauxite, gypsum; textiles, silk, cotton & jute fabrics, carpets, wood & metalwork, leather, cement, ships, refined petroleum, sugar, iron & steel, machinery, typewriters, aluminum, autos, transportation equipment, aircraft, chemicals.
INDONESIA	Centralized republic headed by a president, appointed cabinet, a parliament and a consultative assembly.	Rice, sugarcane, corn, coconuts, cassava, sweet potatoes, spices, tea, coffee, fruits, rubber, tobacco, cotton, kapok; livestock; fish; timber; tin, petroleum, iron ore, natural gas, salt, bauxite, nickel, copper; refined petroleum & products, sugar, cement, copra, textiles, paper, ships, chemicals, palm oil, food products, glass, rubber goods, autos.
IRAN	Constitutional monarchy governed by a shah, an appointed prime minister & cabinet, and a partly elected bicameral legislature.	Cereal grains, cotton, dates, raisins, fruits, opium, sugar beets, nuts, tea, tobacco; livestock; fish; timber; petroleum, natural gas, copper, lead, coal, iron ore, salt; hides, wool, textiles, carpets, leather & tobacco products, caviar, sugar, glass, tools, vehicles, iron & steel, cement, aluminum, refined petroleum, metal products, chemicals & petrochemicals, vehicles, flour, processed foods.

POLITICAL DIVISION	GOVERNMENT	MAJOR PRODUCTS
IRAQ	Nominal republic headed by a revolutionary council and an appointed cabinet.	Dates, fruits, barley, wheat, rice, tobacco, cotton, vegetables, sorghum; livestock; petroleum, sulphur, salt; refined petroleum, cement, chemicals, drugs, hides & skins, wool, glass, textiles, processed foods, electrical equipment.
IRELAND	Republic with a president, prime minister, cabinet, and a partly-elected bicameral parliament.	Hay, potatoes, turnips, sugar beets, cereal grains; fish; livestock; lead, zinc, silver; tobacco, textiles, apparel, wood, clay, paper & metal products, machinery, dairy products, meat, processed foods, beer, malt, chemicals, vehicles.
ISRAEL	Republic with a president, prime minister, cabinet and elected unicameral parliament.	Wheat, cotton, tobacco, vegetables, fruits; livestock, poultry; fish; potash, salt, petroleum; textiles, apparel, processed foods, dairy products, glass, drugs, instruments, paper, metal, wood, rubber & leather products, polished diamonds, electric & electronic products, chemicals, wine, vehicles, refined petroleum, transportation equipment.
ITALY	Constitutional republic with a president, an appointed cabinet & an elected bicameral parliament.	Cereal grains, sugar beets, potatoes, tomatoes, olives, grapes, citrus fruits, tobacco; timber; fish; livestock; natural gas, sulphur iron ore, coal, zinc, bauxite, mercury, marble; textiles, chemicals, wine, autos, machinery, electrical goods, sugar, olive oil, apparel, processed foods, petrochemicals, typewriters, iron & steel, aluminum, shoes, transportation equipment.
IVORY COAST	One-party republic, with a president, cabinet, and a unicameral national assembly.	Coffee, cocoa, sugarcane, bananas, pineapples, nuts, rubber, cotton; tropical woods; livestock; fish; diamonds, iron ore; textiles, processed foods, lumber & wood products, refined petroleum, metal products, palm oil.
JAMAICA	Independent member of the British Commonwealth, with a governor-general, prime minister, cabinet, and bicameral parliament.	Sugarcane, bananas, tobacco, coconuts, coffee, citrus fruits, pimento, spices; fish; timber; bauxite, gypsum; rum, molasses, textiles, aluminum, copra, apparel, chemicals, processed foods, sugar, cement, metal, paper & rubber products.
JAPAN	Constitutional monarchy, with a prime minister, cabinet, and a bicameral diet. The duties of the emperor are merely ceremonial.	Rice, wheat, barley, potatoes, fruits, vegetables, sugarcane, hemp, tobacco, soybeans, tea; livestock; fish; timber; petroleum, iron ore, manganese, gold, silver, copper, coal, natural gas; textiles, silk, iron & steel, machinery, autos, ships, instruments, electric & electronic goods, paper, pulp, porcelain & earthenware, toys, sugar, chemicals, apparel, aluminum, fish products, metal products.
JORDAN	Constitutional monarchy, with king, prime minister, cabinet and a bicameral national assembly.	Wheat, barley, grapes, vegetables, fruits, olives; livestock; phosphates, potash, marble; wool, tobacco & leather products, cement, soap, olive oil, beverages, refined petroleum.
KENYA	One-party republic of the British Commonwealth, with a president, vice-president, cabinet, and unicameral national assembly.	Sisal, wheat, tea, coffee, pyrethrum, cotton, sugarcane, corn, peanuts, coconuts, wattle bark; livestock; timber; gold, silver, fluorspar, salt; sisal, meat & dairy products, sugar, cement, soda ash, hides & skins, petroleum products.
KOREA	Divided country with two governments. South Korea is a centralized republic with a president, prime minister, cabinet & unicameral assembly. North Korea is ruled by the politburo of the Communist party, and has a prime minister & unicameral assembly.	Rice, barley, wheat, soybeans, tobacco, corn, cotton, fruits; timber; livestock; fish; tungsten, gold, silver, iron ore, copper, coal, petroleum, lead, graphite, kaolin; textiles, silk, apparel, electric & electronic goods, metal, rubber, paper, wood & petroleum products, chemicals, cement, machinery, iron & steel.
KUWAIT	Constitutional state with a sheikh, prime minister, cabinet, and an elected unicameral assembly.	Fruits, vegetables; pearls; fish; petroleum, natural gas; refined petroleum & petroleum products, ammonia, chemicals, fertilizer, cement, fish products, wool.
LAOS	Constitutional monarchy with a king, prime minister, cabinet and a bicameral legislature.	Rice, coffee, tea, citrus fruits, corn, cinchona, opium, potatoes, tobacco, cardamon, stick-lac; livestock; timber; tin; textiles, cigarettes, beverages, lumber, milled rice.
LEBANON	Republic with a president, an appointed prime minister and cabinet, and an elected unicameral parliament.	Wheat, barley, corn, potatoes, fruits, onions, vegetables, olives, tobacco; livestock; iron ore; textiles, metal & tobacco products, refined petroleum, chemicals, processed foods, cement, olive oil.

POLITICAL DIVISION	GOVERNMENT	MAJOR PRODUCTS
LESOTHO	Nominal monarchy presently ruled by a prime minister, cabinet, and an appointed national assembly.	Cereal grains, beans, peas; livestock; diamonds; wool, mohair, hides & skins, carpets, textiles, shoes, candles, chemicals, jewelry, processed foods.
LIBERIA	One-party republic, with a president, cabinet, and a bicameral legislature.	Rubber, rice, coffee, sugarcane, cocoa, palm oil & kernels, piassava; timber; fish, shrimp; iron ore, diamonds; petroleum products, cement, processed foods & rubber, lumber.
LIBYA	Arab republic ruled by a revolutionary council and an appointed prime minister and cabinet.	Barley, wheat, olives, grapes, dates, vegetables, figs, peanuts, citrus fruits, almonds, esparto; livestock, sponge & tuna fishing; hides & skins; petroleum, natural gas; textiles, crude petroleum, processed foods, leather, olive oil.
LIECHTENSTEIN	Constitutional monarchy with a prince, cabinet and unicameral diet.	Corn, wheat, potatoes, grapes; livestock; textiles, wine, leather, dairy products, ceramics, precision instruments, drugs, canned foods, postage stamps.
LUXEMBOURG	Constitutional monarchy with a grand duke, prime minister, cabinet, and a bicameral parliament.	Oats, potatoes, wheat, rye, grapes; livestock; timber; iron ore, slate, salt, gypsum; iron & steel, metal products, chemicals, tobacco, leather, wine, dairy products, rubber products, fertilizers, plastic goods.
MACAO	Portuguese overseas province with a governor and advisory councils.	Rice, vegetables; fish; cement, metal work, lumber, processed tobacco, matches, wine, textiles, fireworks.
MALAGASY REPUBLIC	Republic of the French Community, at present under a head of state and a military directorate.	Cassava, rice, corn, sweet potatoes, vanilla, cloves, sugarcane, coffee, bananas, beans, manioc, sisal, tobacco, raffia; timber; livestock; fish; graphite, mica, chromite; textiles, processed meat & foods, refined petroleum & petroleum products, cement, paper, sugar, beer, leather.
MALAWI	One-party republic of the British Commonwealth, with president (for life), cabinet, and unicameral legislature.	Tobacco, tea, cotton, sugarcane, tung nuts, pulses, sisal, corn, fruits, sorghum, rice, millet, peanuts, rubber; timber; livestock; bauxite, stone, gold; hides & skins, tung oil, meat, transportation equipment, machinery, ghee, sugar.
MALAYSIA	Constitutional monarchy of the British Commonwealth, with a paramount ruler, cabinet and bicameral parliament.	Rubber, rice, coconuts, sugarcane, coffee, cocoa, pineapples, pepper, tea, tobacco, vegetables; livestock; fish; timber; tin, petroleum, copper, gold, antimony, bauxite, iron ore, manganese; rubber & wood products, steel, autos, refined petroleum, textiles, electric goods, sugar, fibers.
MALDIVES	Republic with a president, prime minister, cabinet and unicameral legislature.	Coconuts, corn, millet, pumpkins, sweet potatoes, fruits, nuts; fish, cowries; mats, boats, dried fish & fish products, handicrafts, copra, coir, ambergris, lace.
MALI	One-party republic at present under a military committee and a consultative cabinet. The president rules by decree.	Millet, rice, sorghum, peanuts, corn, cotton, tobacco, nuts, sisal; livestock; fish; salt, gold, bauxite, iron ore, uranium; hides & skins, ceramics, jewelry, leather, rice mills, soap, processed fish & foods, textiles, sugar, cement, meat, fibers.
MALTA	Independent republic of the British Commonwealth, with a president, prime minister, cabinet and unicameral parliament.	Wheat, barley, potatoes, onions, grapes, vegetables, fruits, cumin seed, cotton; livestock; fish; lace, wine, beer, cigarettes, buttons, pipes, gloves, textiles & yarn, flowers, ceramics, rubber & electronic goods, apparel.
MARTINIQUE	Overseas department of France, with a prefect and an elected general council.	Sugarcane, cocoa, mangoes, avocados, pineapples, bananas, coffee; fish; rum, sugar.
MAURITANIA	One-party, Islamic republic, with a president, appointed cabinet, and a unicameral assembly.	Cereal grains, beans, peanuts, melons, dates, gum arabic, henna, sweet potatoes; livestock; lobsters, fish; manganese, gypsum, iron ore, copper, salt; hides & skins, fish products.
MAURITIUS	Independent member of the British Commonwealth, with a governor, prime minister, cabinet, and unicameral assembly.	Sugarcane, aloe fiber, corn, coffee, vanilla beans, hemp, potatoes, sisal, peanuts, tea, yams, manioc, pineapples, tobacco, coconuts; molasses, rum, copra, sugar, dairy, tea & tobacco products, processed foods, textiles, fibers.
MEXICO	Constitutional federative republic with a president, council of ministers and a bicameral congress.	Cereal grains, coffee, cotton, sugarcane, bananas, chicle, beans, oranges, henequén; timber; fish; shrimp; livestock; silver, gold, lead, zinc, petroleum, coal, sulphur, manganese, natural gas, iron ore, copper; sugar, hides, textiles, fibers, chemicals, aluminum, machinery, autos, refined petroleum, petrochemicals, cement, paper, drugs, metal products.

POLITICAL DIVISION	GOVERNMENT	MAJOR PRODUCTS
MONACO	Constitutional hereditary principality, with a chief minister, cabinet, & a unicameral council.	Principal revenue from gambling casino and tourism. Postage stamps, perfume, liqueurs, olive oil, oranges, chemicals, instruments, glass, processed foods, ceramics.
MONGOLIA	Soviet-type republic, with a president (chairman of Communist party politburo) & unicameral legislature.	Grains; livestock; coal, petroleum, lead, gold; dairy products, wool, hides & skins, processed foods, machinery, furs, meat & dairy products, textiles, leather, cement.
MOROCCO	Constitutional monarchy, with a king, appointed prime minister, cabinet, and unicameral parliament.	Wheat, barley, legumes, olives, nuts, citrus fruits, sugar beets, grapes, vegetables; cork, timber; livestock; fish; phosphates, iron ore, fluorite, coal, lead, zinc, manganese, petroleum, cobalt; textiles, carpets, pulp, wine, essential oils, olive oil, food & fish products, perfumes, wool.
MOZAMBIQUE	Former Portuguese possession, now an independent "people's" republic.	Sugarcane, cereal grains, coconuts, cotton, cashew nuts, peanuts, sisal, beans, tea, tobacco; timber; livestock; fish, shellfish; gold, coal, iron ore, bauxite; sugar, textiles, milled rice, cement, vegetable oils, processed foods & fish, copra.
NAURU	Republic with a president, cabinet, and unicameral assembly.	Phosphates.
NEPAL	Constitutional monarchy, with king, prime minister, cabinet, and a unicameral legislature.	Rice, wheat, corn, millet, jute, sugarcane, potatoes, tea, oilseeds, medicinal herbs; timber, livestock; iron ore, copper; processed rice, tobacco, leather & wood products, textiles, sugar, chemicals, ghee, hides & skins.
NETHERLANDS	A constitutional, hereditary monarchy governed by the queen, a prime minister, cabinet, and bicameral partly elected parliament (states general).	Potatoes, sugar beets, cereal grains, flax, legumes, flower bulbs, seeds, vegetables, fruits; livestock; fish; coal, petroleum, natural gas, salt; metal products, textiles, paper, chemicals, processed foods, apparel, ships, ceramics, cement, dairy, wood & tobacco products, petroleum products, machinery, electric & electronic products, transportation equipment, flowers, glass, processed diamonds.
NETHERLANDS ANTILLES	Self-governing part of Netherlands Union with governor, minister-president, cabinet & unicameral legislature (staten).	Fish; salt, phosphates; refined petroleum, petrochemicals, electronic equipment, textiles, beer.
NEW CALEDONIA	French overseas territory with a governor, government council & an elected territorial assembly.	Coconuts, coffee, cotton, corn, tobacco, bananas, pineapples, vegetables, rice; timber; livestock; nickel, chrome, manganese, iron ore, cobalt, copper, lead, silver, gold; canned meat, nickel & coffee processing, copra.
NEW GUINEA, TERR. OF	U.N. trusteeship, governed by Australia. (For other details, see under PAPUA.)	
NEW HEBRIDES	British and French condominium under high commissioners, & a partly-elected advisory council.	Coconuts, cocoa, coffee, bananas, yams, taro, manioc, fruits; timber; cattle; fish, trochus shell; manganese; meat and fish products, copra, lumber.
NEW ZEALAND	An independent member of the British Commonwealth under a governor-general, prime minister, cabinet and a unicameral parliament.	Cereal grains; livestock; timber; fish; gold, coal, mineral sands, limestone, petroleum, natural gas; meat, wool, hides & skins, apparel, timber & wood products, dairy products, food & tobacco products, autos, chemicals, fertilizers, beer, bricks, cement, electrical goods, machinery, paper, rubber & petroleum products.
NICARAGUA	Republic under a president, cabinet & bicameral legislature.	Coffee, sugarcane, sesame, corn, bananas, rice, cocoa, tobacco, cotton, beans; cattle; fish; hardwoods; gold, copper, silver; sugar, wood products, meat products, textiles, cottonseed, chemicals, petroleum products, paper, food products.
NIGER	Nominal republic, now under a head of state, appointed cabinet & a military council.	Millet, rice, manioc, peanuts, cotton, gum arabic, beans, sorghum; livestock; uranium, cassiterite, limesetone, salt, natron; hides & skins, meat, food & leather products, textiles, cement, peanut oil.
NIGERIA	Federal republic of the British Commonwealth, now under a supreme military council and a federal executive council.	Palm oil and kernels, cocoa, spices, tobacco, peanuts, cotton, rubber, soybeans, corn, rice, millet, coffee; livestock; fish, shrimp; timber; tin, coal, limestone, natural gas, petroleum, marble; metal products, cement, timber & wood products, textiles, beer, refined petroleum, hides & skins, processed foods & oils.

POLITICAL DIVISION	GOVERNMENT	MAJOR PRODUCTS
NIUE	Internally self-governing state associated with New Zealand, with a commissioner, prime minister, cabinet & assembly.	Limes, kumaras, passion fruit, bananas; copra, woven handicrafts.
NORTHERN IRELAND	Integral part of the United Kingdom, with local government presently being reorganized.	Potatoes, oats, fruits, vegetables, barley, hay; poultry, livestock; limestone, basalt & igneous rocks, sand & gravel; linen, apparel, wool textiles, dairy products, meat & meat products, aircraft, machinery, tobacco, whiskey, electronic & transportation equipment, ships.
NORWAY	A constitutional hereditary monarchy with a king, prime minister, cabinet, and unicamerally elected but bicamerally operated legislature.	Hay, oats, barley, wheat, rye, potatoes, fruits; livestock; fish; timber; iron ore, petroleum, nickel, zinc, natural gas, coal; pulp, paper, cellulose, ships, aluminum, machinery, chemicals, metal & electro-chemical products, transportation equipment, iron & steel, processed & canned fish & foods, textiles, wool, dairy products, leather, furs.
OMAN	Independent Arab sultanate and an absolute monarchy.	Wheat, alfalfa, dates, limes, frankincense, coconuts, tobacco; livestock; fish; petroleum; dried fish & limes, ghee.
PACIFIC ISLANDS, TRUST TERR.	United States U. N. trusteeship, with a high commissioner and a bicameral Congress of Micronesia.	Vegetables, tropical fruits, coconuts; fish, trochus shell; poultry, livestock; copra, meat, handicrafts.
PAKISTAN	Federal centralized Islamic republic with a president, prime minister, cabinet and a bicameral legislature.	Cereal grains, cotton, sugarcane, citrus fruits, dates, tobacco; livestock; fish; petroleum, salt, chromite, natural gas, gypsum, limestone; textiles, rugs, apparel, leather, wool, hides & skins, handicrafts, surgical instruments, sporting goods, sugar, chemicals, cement, iron & steel, refined petroleum, electric goods, tires.
PANAMA	Centralized republic with a president, vice-president, cabinet & unicameral assembly, now ruled by decree by a military junta.	Bananas, cocoa, abacá, coconuts, rice, sugarcane, coffee, fruits; fish, shrimp; livestock; timber; beer, sugar, wood & leather products, textiles, refined petroleum, processed foods, cement, apparel, drugs, fishmeal.
PAPUA	Australian territory, self-governed jointly with New Guinea by an administrator, chief minister, council & unicameral assembly.	Coconuts, coffee, cocoa, rubber, rice, sago, tea, pyrethrum; cattle; fish, prawns; timber; gold, silver, copper; boats, tobacco products, lumber & wood products, copra, palm oil, beer, dairy products.
PARAGUAY	Centralized republic with a president, an appointed cabinet and a bicameral congress.	Cotton, tobacco, sugarcane, cereal grains, yerba maté, soybeans, coffee, citrus fruits; livestock; timber, quebracho; beef, meat products, flour, refined petroleum products, oilcake & essential oils, hides, textiles, cement.
PERU	Nominal republic with a president, prime minister & cabinet, presently ruled by decree under a military junta.	Cotton, sugarcane, potatoes, cereal grains, beans, potatoes, vegetables, fruits, coffee, guano; fish; livestock; petroleum, lead, zinc, copper, silver, gold, salt, iron ore; textiles, foodstuffs, fishmeal, sugar, cement, apparel, wool, paper, drugs, chemicals, refined metals & metal products, fibers, iron & steel, tires, hides & skins.
PHILIPPINES	Republic governed by a president, prime minister, cabinet and unicameral assembly.	Rice, sugarcane, abacá, corn, tobacco, cocoa, coffee, nuts, kapok, peanuts, vegetables, maguey, rubber, fruits; livestock; fish; timber, gum resins; gold, iron ore, copper, chromite, silver, manganese, salt, coal, petroleum; sugar, textiles, rubber & tobacco products; lumber & wood products, autos, handicrafts, milled coconut oil & rice, fruit canning, copra, steel, cement, glass, chemicals, paper.
PITCAIRN ISLANDS	British colony, with a governor, an island magistrate & council.	Fruits, vegetables; goats, poultry; handicrafts, postage stamps.
POLAND	Soviet-type republic with a president, cabinet, chief of (council of) state, & unicameral parliament; actual power lies with the politburo of the Communist party.	Potatoes, cereal grains, sugar beets; livestock; fish; timber; coal, lead, zinc, sulphur, iron ore, petroleum, copper, natural gas; iron & steel, chemicals & petrochemicals, coke, electric & electronic equipment, autos, ships, aluminum, metal, food & dairy products, sugar, glass, transportation equipment, cement, machinery, paper.
PORTUGAL	Nominal constitutional republic, at present ruled by a military junta.	Cereal grains, potatoes, tomatoes, citrus fruits, grapes, olives; livestock; fish; timber; coal, wolfram, iron ore, sulphur, tungsten; wine, olive oil, cork, canned fish, food products, pulp, refined petroleum, ships, autos, textiles, electronic equipment, machinery, cement, steel.
PORTUGUESE TIMOR	Portuguese overseas territory under a governor and a legislative assembly.	Coffee, coconuts, rubber, cocoa; sandalwood; livestock; hides, shells, wax, copra.

POLITICAL DIVISION	GOVERNMENT	MAJOR PRODUCTS
PUERTO RICO	Self-governing "free state" associated with the United States, with a governor, advisory council, and a bicameral congress.	Sugarcane, tobacco, fruits, coconuts, coffee, cotton, vegetables; livestock; stone, sand & gravel; rum, molasses, sugar, canned fish & fruit, tobacco products, cement, leather, textiles, apparel, petrochemicals, metal & electronic products.
QATAR	Arab state with an emir (with all authority), prime minister, cabinet & advisory council.	Dates, fruit, vegetables; shrimp, fish; livestock; natural gas, limestone, petroleum; fish products, cement, refined petroleum, petrochemicals.
RÉUNION	French overseas department, with a prefect and general council.	Sugarcane, tea, tobacco, vanilla, corn, manioc; livestock; essential oils, fruit & vegetable products, rum, sugar, molasses.
RHODESIA	Constitutional republic, with a president, cabinet, and bicameral parliament.	Corn, tobacco, peanuts, wheat, cotton, tea, sugarcane, citrus fruits; livestock; fish; copper, gold, asbestos, chromite, coal; textiles, apparel, cigarettes, wood, food, dairy & rubber products, meat & meat products, sugar, iron & steel, vehicles, electrical goods, metal products, chemicals, hides.
RUMANIA	A Soviet-type republic with a president, a state council, a cabinet, and a unicameral assembly; actual power resides in Communist party politburo.	Wheat, barley, corn, potatoes, sugar beets, tobacco, fruits; livestock; timber; petroleum, natural gas, coal, lignite, salt, iron ore, copper, bauxite, manganese, uranium; iron & steel, machinery, chemicals, lumber, wood & paper products, electric goods, refined petroleum, ships, cement, sugar, food products, textiles, metal products.
RWANDA	Nominal republic with president, cabinet & unicameral assembly, presently under military rule.	Coffee, cotton, rice, tea, corn, peanuts, pyrethrum, vegetables; livestock; cassiterite, tungsten, tantalite, beryl, wolfram; textiles, handicrafts, processed foods, beer, hides.
ST. CHRISTOPHER-NEVIS-ANGUILLA	Associated British state with a governor, prime minister, cabinet & unicameral assembly.	Sugarcane, cotton, rice, vegetables, tropical fruits, corn, yams, coconuts, livestock; fish, shellfish; salt; molasses.
ST. HELENA	British colony with a governor, legislative and executive councils.	Fruit, vegetables, lily bulbs, flax, sweet potatoes, potatoes; livestock, poultry; cordage, fibers, lace.
ST. LUCIA	Associated British state with a governor, prime minister, cabinet & unicameral assembly.	Bananas, coconuts, cocoa, tropical & citrus fruits, nutmeg, mace; fish; rum, copra, coconut oil, soap, cigarettes.
ST. PIERRE AND MIQUELON	French overseas territory with a governor, privy council and elective general council.	Codfish; cattle; sienna earth, yellow ocher; fish products, furs.
ST. VINCENT	Associated British state with a governor, prime minister, cabinet & bicameral assembly.	Bananas, arrowroot, coconuts, rice, tropical fruits, cotton, corn, spices, peanuts, cocoa; fish; livestock; copra, rum, processed foods, cigarettes.
SAN MARINO	Republic with two regents, cabinet, & a unicameral council.	Wheat, fruits, grapes, vegetables; stone; livestock; textiles, postage stamps, wine, pottery, hides, cement, paper, leather.
SÃO TOMÉ AND PRÍNCIPE	Former Portuguese possession, now an independent "democratic" republic.	Cacao, coffee, coconuts, cinchona, bananas; livestock; palm oil, copra.
SAUDI ARABIA	Absolute monarchy, with king (with all authority) & cabinet, with legislation by decree.	Dates, corn, wheat, coffee, fruits, henna, vegetables; fish; livestock; petroleum, gold, silver, gypsum, lead, copper; refined petroleum, petrochemicals, fertilizers, iron & steel, cement, meat & dairy products, hides, wool.
SCOTLAND	Integral part of United Kingdom, with secretary of state for Scotland in the U.K. cabinet, controlling local agriculture & fisheries, home & health, education, development, & economic planning.	Potatoes, sugar beets, wheat, barley, vegetables, fruits; livestock; fish, shellfish; petroleum, coal, iron ore, lead, stone; iron & steel, machinery, metal, dairy, tobacco & food products, textiles & yarn, watches, transportation equipment, electric & electronic goods, autos, ships, paper, whiskey, refined petroleum, aluminum, chemicals.
SENEGAL	One-party republic of the French Community, with a president, a prime minister, cabinet and unicameral assembly.	Millet, sorghum, rice, corn, peanuts, cotton, fruits, vegetables, sweet potatoes; livestock; fish; phosphates, titanium, limestone; textiles, processed fish & foods, cement, peanut oil & cakes, refined petroleum, chemicals.
SEYCHELLES	British colony with governor, chief minister, cabinet & assembly.	Coconuts, cinnamon, patchouli, vanilla, tea; fish, tortoise shell, guano; copra, coconut oil, dried fish, coir, essential oils.
SIERRA LEONE	One-party republic of the British Commonwealth, with a president, prime minister, cabinet & unicameral parliament.	Palm oil & kernels, rice, coffee, kola nuts, ginger, vegetables, cassava, piassava, peanuts, cocoa; livestock; fish, shrimp; diamonds, iron ore, bauxite, rutile; palm products, rice & oil milling.

POLITICAL DIVISION	GOVERNMENT	MAJOR PRODUCTS
SINGAPORE	Republic of the British Commonwealth, with a president & advisory council, prime minister, cabinet & unicameral parliament.	Rubber, coconuts, fruits, vegetables, rice, coffee, tapioca, tobacco; livestock; fish; tin, rubber & petroleum processing, rice & coconut milling, steel, chemicals, cement, lumber & wood products, textiles, bricks, palm & food products, paper, refined petroleum, drugs, ships, electric goods.
SOLOMON ISLANDS PROT.	British protectorate, with high commissioner and partly elected governing council.	Coconuts, rice, sorghum, cocoa; livestock, poultry; fish, trochus & turtle shell, bêche-de-mer; timber; bauxite, gold; copra, palm oil, tobacco products.
SOMALIA	Republic with a president, three vice-presidents, cabinet & a ruling military council.	Sugarcane, cotton, cereal grains, peanuts, sesame, tobacco, bananas, beans; livestock; fish, shellfish; salt; fish, food & meat products, sugar, textiles, hides & skins.
SOUTH AFRICA	Constitutional republic, with a state president, prime minister, cabinet & bicameral parliament.	Cereal grains, tobacco, sugarcane; fruits, peanuts; livestock; fish, lobsters; gold, coal, diamonds, copper, asbestos, manganese, limestone, platinum, chromite, iron ore, vanadium, tin, antimony, uranium; timber; chemicals, wool, iron & steel, machinery, apparel, textiles, fish & food products, sugar, aluminum, metal products, hides, autos, cement, transportation equipment, dairy products.
SOUTH-WEST AFRICA	South African controlled territory with an administrator & legislative assembly, & representation in the South African legislature.	Livestock; fish, shellfish; diamonds, copper, lead, zinc, salt, tin, manganese, vanadium, iron ore, cadmium, silver, fluorspar, tantalite, phosphate, sulfur, germanium; karakul wool & hides, fish processing, dairy products.
SPAIN	Nominal monarchy governed by a chief of state and cabinet, prime minister, and unicameral legislature. A king is to be sworn in as chief of state upon death or retirement of the chief of state.	Cereal grains, potatoes, legumes, citrus fruits, vegetables, olives, grapes, sugar beets, esparto, flax, hemp, pulses, nuts, sugarcane; livestock, poultry; fish; timber; coal, lignite, iron ore & pyrites, lead, zinc, mercury, copper, uranium, gypsum; textiles, paper, cement, hides, wine, olive oil, processed foods, cork, machinery, chemicals, leather, autos, refined petroleum, apparel, silk, shoes, processed foods & fruit, iron & steel.
SPANISH SAHARA	Overseas Spanish province, with governor general & assembly.	Barley, corn, dates, fruits, vegetables; livestock; fish; cork; phosphates, iron ore; skins, fish products, oilcake.
SRI LANKA (CEYLON)	Independent republic of the British Commonwealth, with a president, a prime minister, a cabinet and a unicameral assembly.	Tea, coconuts, rubber, rice, cotton, spices, cocoa, nuts, sugarcane, fruits; fish; livestock; graphite, mineral sands, ilmenite, gem stones, limestone, salt, pearls; copra, plywood, leather, shoes, glass, steel, acetic acid, ceramics, quinine, strychnine, chemicals, drugs, textiles, cement, beer, refined petroleum, coconut & tobacco products, paper, apparel.
SUDAN	Centralized one-party Arab republic with a president, cabinet & ruling military council, aided by an assembly.	Cotton, cereal grains, gum arabic, oilseeds, senna, castor beans, resins, peanuts, sesame, dom & shea nuts, dates; livestock; ivory, trochus shell, mother-of-pearl; iron ore, manganese, chromite, salt, gold; textiles, cement, hides & skins, cottonseed, oilcake, sugar, leather, paint, soap.
SURINAM	Self-governing part of the Netherlands Union, with governor, minister-president, cabinet and unicameral legislature (staten).	Rice, citrus fruits, coconuts, coffee, bananas, sugarcane, cacao, balata, corn, tobacco; livestock; shrimp; timber, balata; gold, bauxite; sugar, rum, lumber & plywood, molasses, aluminum, food & dairy products.
SWAZILAND	Monarchy within the British Commonwealth, with a prime minister, cabinet and bicameral parliament, at present under rule by decree.	Tobacco, corn, peanuts, sugarcane, sorghum, cotton, rice, pineapples, citrus fruits; livestock; timber; asbestos, iron ore, coal; meat & dairy products, sugar, pulp, canned fruits, textiles, hides & skins, wood & tobacco products.
SWEDEN	A constitutional hereditary monarchy with a titular king, prime minister, cabinet and a unicameral parliament.	Hay, sugar beets, potatoes, oilseeds, oats, wheat, rye, barley; timber; livestock; fish; iron ore, zinc, copper, lead; lumber, paper & wood products, machinery, textiles, iron & steel, metal & electric goods, chemicals, dairy, food & tobacco products, porcelain, glass, ships, furs, transportation equipment, matches, autos, munitions, liquor, instruments.
SWITZERLAND	Federal republic with a president, vice-president & executive federal council, & a bicameral elected federal assembly.	Cereal grains, sugar beets, potatoes, vegetables, fruits, tobacco; livestock; timber; salt, iron ore, manganese; dairy & tobacco products, watches & clocks, electric & glass products, instruments, jewelry, machinery, metal products, chocolate, wine, drugs, textiles & yarn, chemicals, aluminum, iron & steel, cement, sugar, meat, apparel, dyes, foods.

POLITICAL DIVISION	GOVERNMENT	MAJOR PRODUCTS
SYRIA	Arab republic with a president (who rules by decree), prime minister, and legislative people's council.	Cereal grains, cotton, vegetables, olives, grapes, sugar beets, tobacco; livestock; petroleum, natural gas, phosphates, gypsum; leather, textiles, cement, refined petroleum, wool, hides & skins, sugar, processed foods & oils, apparel, glass, tobacco goods.
TANZANIA	One-party united republic of the British Commonwealth, with a president, two vice-presidents, cabinet, and unicameral assembly.	Sisal, fruits, cocoa, coconuts, cotton, cloves, pyrethrum, spices, coffee, tobacco, nuts, tea, oilseeds, sugarcane; livestock; hides & skins; diamonds, gold, phosphates, mica, salt, tin, gem stones; processed foods, cement, textiles, refined petroleum, copra, hides & skins, sugar, dairy & wood products, cordage, rolled iron & aluminum.
THAILAND (SIAM)	Centralized constitutional monarchy with a king, prime minister, cabinet, & partly elected bicameral assembly.	Rice, coconuts, sugarcane, rubber, peanuts, tobacco, tapioca, jute, kenaf, cotton, corn; teak & other timber; livestock; fish; tin, wolfram, lead; lac, sugar, cement, textiles, tobacco & petroleum products, paper.
TOGO	One-party republic ruled by decree by a president & an appointed cabinet.	Palm oil & kernels, manioc, kapok, cocoa, coconuts, yams, cereal grains, coffee, cotton, peanuts, nuts, cassava; livestock; timber; phosphates, limestone; textiles, copra, cement.
TOKELAU ISLANDS	An island territory of New Zealand governed by an administrator.	Coconuts, fiber, taro; pigs, chickens; fish; hats, mats, copra.
TONGA	Constitutional monarchy of the British Commonwealth, with king, prime minister & partly elected unicameral assembly.	Coconuts, bananas, yams, breadfruit, taro, cassava, papayas, pineapples, melons, tobacco, corn, peanuts, candlenuts; fish; livestock, poultry; copra, processed fruits.
TRINIDAD AND TOBAGO	Independent British Commonwealth member, with a governor-general, prime minister, cabinet, & a bicameral parliament.	Coffee, cocoa, coconuts, sugarcane, citrus fruits; cattle; timber; petroleum, natural gas, asphalt, coal, clay; rum, textiles, sugar, chemicals, plastic, glass, clay, wood & food products, cement, electric goods, refined petroleum.
TUNISIA	A republic with a president (for life), an appointed cabinet, a prime minister, and an elected unicameral assembly.	Cereal grains, grapes, esparto, olives, vegetables, nuts, fruits, dates; cork, timber; livestock; fish; phosphates, petroleum, iron ore, lead, zinc; flour, wine, olive oil, sugar, wool, pottery, leather, textiles, food processing, chemicals, iron & steel, paper, refined petroleum, metal & electric goods.
TURKEY	Constitutional republic with a president, an appointed prime minister, a cabinet, and a bicameral parliament.	Tobacco, cereal grains, cotton, fruits, opium, seeds, olives, nuts, sugar beets; livestock; fish; timber; chromite, iron ore, petroleum, copper, coal, lignite; textiles, iron & steel, chemicals, refined petroleum, rugs, paper, olive oil, wool, furs, sugar, mohair, silk, cement, skins.
UGANDA	Centralized republic of the British Commonwealth, under a president (who rules by decree), a military council & cabinet.	Cotton, coffee, tea, plaintains, sisal, peanuts, millet, corn, tobacco, sugarcane; livestock; salt, copper, gold, phosphates, tin; cement, beverages, sugar, chemicals, smelted copper, processed foods, textiles, hides & skins, steel.
U.S.S.R.	Federation of 15 union republics with a bicameral Supreme Soviet, which elects the presidium & council of ministers. Real power is largely exercised by the politburo & secretariat (under its general secretary) of the central committee of the Communist party.	Cereal grains, sugar beets, cotton, flax, potatoes, seeds, vegetables, tobacco; livestock; fish; timber; petroleum, natural gas, bauxite, uranium, platinum, iron ore, lead, zinc, copper, phosphates, mercury, gold, manganese, nickel, chromite, asbestos, potash; iron & steel, machinery, chemicals, refined petroleum, petrochemicals, ships, autos, aircraft, lumber & wood products, meat & dairy products, textiles, wool, sugar, tools & metal products, aluminum, furs, cement, paper, electric goods, instruments, transportation equipment, foods & beverages.
UNITED ARAB EMIRATES	Constitutional Arab federation of seven sheikhdoms, with president, vice-president, prime minister & cabinet & government councils.	Dates, cereal grains, vegetables; livestock; fish, pearl fishing; petroleum; cement, refined petroleum, petrochemicals, postage stamps, dried fish.
UNITED KINGDOM	See: England and Wales, Northern Ireland, Scotland.	
UNITED STATES	Federal republic with a president, vice-president, an appointed cabinet, and a bicameral congress (senate and house of representatives). It consists of 50 states, each with a governor and a state legislature (all except Nebraska being bicameral).	Cereal grains, hay, soybeans, potatoes, peanuts, sugar beets, sugarcane, vegetables, nuts, fruits, cotton, tobacco, flax; livestock, poultry; fish, shellfish; timber; petroleum, natural gas, coal, iron ore, copper, lead, zinc, gold, silver, molybdenum, bauxite, gypsum, phosphates, sulphur, stone, sand & gravel; iron & steel, machinery, transportation equipment, metal products, electric & electronic goods, autos, ships, aircraft, munitions, chemicals, tobacco, leather, rubber & plastic products, glass, wool, textiles, cement, food & dairy products, lumber & wood products, paper, refined petroleum, petrochemicals.

POLITICAL DIVISION	GOVERNMENT	MAJOR PRODUCTS
UPPER VOLTA	Centralized republic with a president (who rules by decree) and a military cabinet.	Cereal grains, sweet potatoes, peanuts, cassava, karite (shea nuts), vegetables, cotton, sisal, sesame, tea; livestock; gold, manganese, copper; hides & skins, meat products, sugar, flour, textiles, processed foods & oils, soap, cigarettes.
URUGUAY	A republic governed by a president, cabinet and a legislative council of state.	Cereal grains, seeds, peanuts, fruits, hops, sugar beets, grapes, tobacco; livestock, meat & meat products, hides, wool, textiles, leather, wines, chemicals, refined petroleum, aluminum, steel, cement, sugar, metal products.
VATICAN CITY	The Pope exercises absolute legislative, executive & judicial power.	Postage stamps, religious articles.
VENEZUELA	Constitutional federal republic with a president, appointive cabinet, and an elected bicameral congress.	Coffee, cotton, cocoa, sugarcane, cereal grains, tobacco, beans, sisal, balata, rubber, bananas; livestock; fish, shrimp; petroleum, natural gas, iron ore, gold, coal, phosphates, nickel, salt, diamonds; leather, rubber, metal & wood products, sugar, food, dairy & meat products, vehicles, chemicals, refined petroleum, petrochemicals, paper, steel, transportation equipment, apparel.
VIETNAM	At present divided into two Communist-controlled republics in the north and south.	Rice, corn, sugarcane, coffee, fruits, nuts, vegetables, tea, manioc, peanuts, sweet potatoes, tobacco, cotton, rubber, silk; livestock, poultry; fish, shellfish; timber; coal, iron ore, chromite, uranium, phosphates, gold, tin; paper, textiles, chemicals, machinery, tobacco, lumber & wood products, sugar, processed foods, glass, beer, handicrafts, steel.
VIRGIN ISLANDS (BR.)	British colony with an administrator, chief minister and councils.	Bananas, tropical fruits, coconuts, vegetables; livestock, poultry; fish, shellfish, turtles; handicrafts, rum.
VIRGIN ISLANDS (U.S.)	Unincorporated U.S. territory with an elected governor & unicameral legislature.	Vegetables, sugarcane, citrus fruits, coconuts; cattle; fish; rum, bay rum & oil, molasses, handicrafts, sugar, lime juice, hides, bitters.
WALLIS & FUTUNA	French overseas territory with an administrator, & a local council and assembly.	Coconuts, bananas, taro, yams, cassava, arrowroot, vegetables; livestock, poultry; fish, trochus shell; copra, handicrafts.
WESTERN SAMOA	Independent member of the British Commonwealth, with head of state, prime minister, cabinet & assembly.	Breadfruit, coconuts, coffee, fruits, seeds, yams, pawpaws, cocoa, bananas, taro; fish; timber; livestock; copra, handicrafts, hides, lumber, processed foods, apparel, beverages, soap.
YEMEN ARAB REP.	Arab republic under a seven-man military council & head of state.	Coffee, cereal grains, cotton, grapes, fruits, qat, sesame; cattle; fish; rock salt; textiles, hides, leather, handicrafts.
YEMEN, PEOPLES DEM. REP. OF	One-party Arab socialist republic, ruled by a three-man presidential council, cabinet & council.	Dates, cereal grains; coffee, qat, gums, tobacco, cotton, fruit, sesame; livestock; fish; salt; ship bunkering, refined petroleum, hides & skins, textiles, fish products.
YUGOSLAVIA	Federal republic with a president, prime minister, cabinet & bicameral assembly; actually under control of the Communist party.	Cereal grains, sugar beets, tobacco, potatoes, seeds, hemp, nuts, fruits; livestock; fish; timber; coal, gold, iron ore, manganese, petroleum, bauxite, chromite, mercury, antimony, copper, lead, zinc, salt; textiles, lumber & wood products, cement, sugar, food & metal products, machinery, chemicals, iron & steel, ships, wine.
ZAIRE	Centralized one-party republic with a president (who rules by decree), prime minister, cabinet & legislative council.	Palm oil & kernels, cotton, coffee, tea, cocoa, rice, sugarcane, rubber; livestock; ivory, timber; copper, diamonds, gold, cobalt, tantalite, petroleum, zinc, manganese, bauxite, cassiterite; textiles, processed foods, sugar, rubber products.
ZAMBIA	One-party republic of the British Commonwealth, with a president, vice-president, cabinet, and a unicameral assembly.	Cereal grains, tobacco, peanuts, cassava, sugarcane, fruits, cotton; timber; fish; livestock; copper, lead, coal, manganese, zinc, cobalt; iron & steel, metal & tobacco products, textiles, chemicals, refined petroleum & copper, processed foods & beverages, sugar, drugs, tires.

SELF-SUFFICIENCY IN RAW MATERIALS

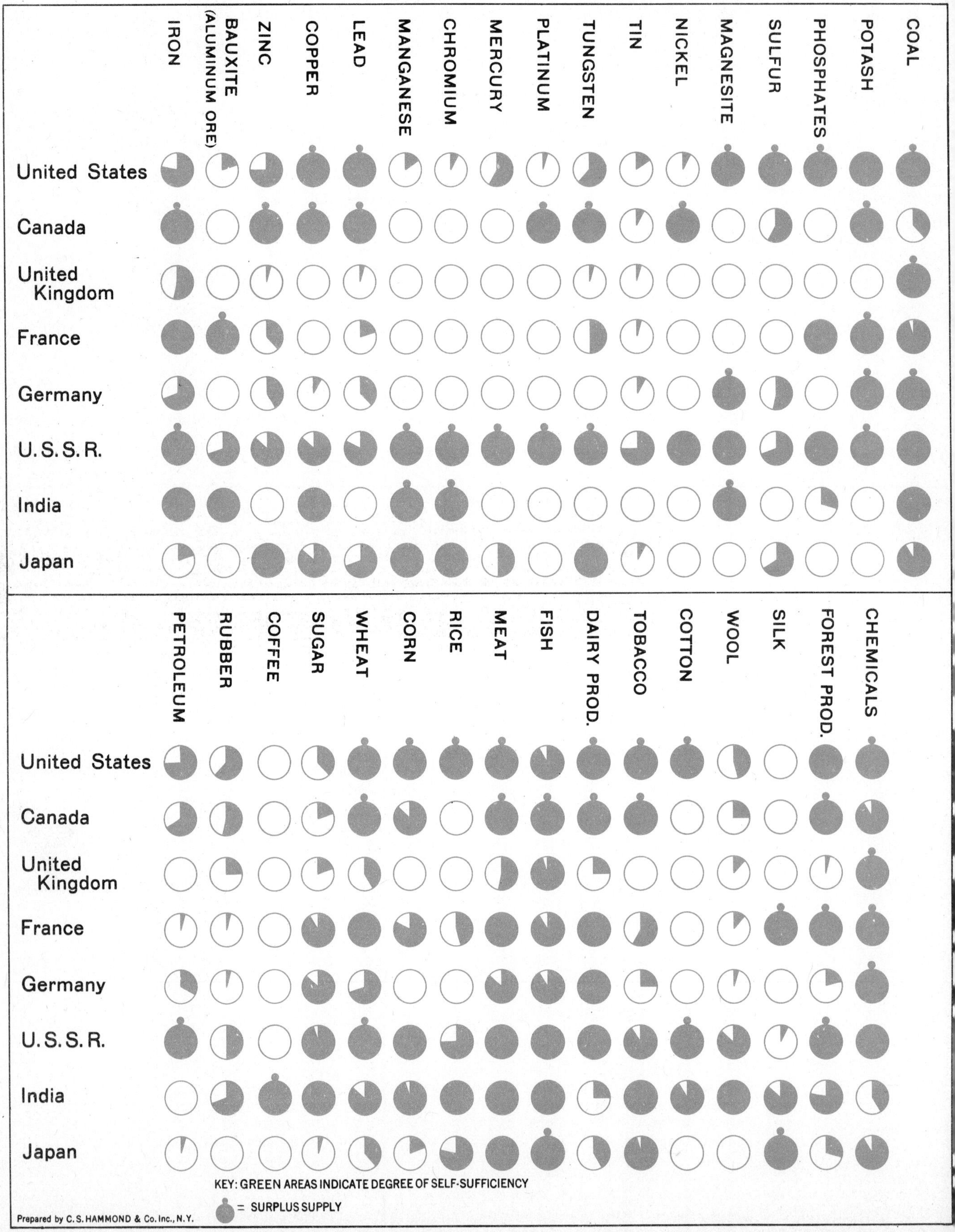

IRON
BAUXITE (ALUMINUM ORE)
ZINC
COPPER
LEAD
MANGANESE
CHROMIUM
MERCURY
PLATINUM
TUNGSTEN
TIN
NICKEL
MAGNESITE
SULFUR
PHOSPHATES
POTASH
COAL

United States
Canada
United Kingdom
France
Germany
U.S.S.R.
India
Japan

PETROLEUM
RUBBER
COFFEE
SUGAR
WHEAT
CORN
RICE
MEAT
FISH
DAIRY PROD.
TOBACCO
COTTON
WOOL
SILK
FOREST PROD.
CHEMICALS

United States
Canada
United Kingdom
France
Germany
U.S.S.R.
India
Japan

KEY: GREEN AREAS INDICATE DEGREE OF SELF-SUFFICIENCY

= SURPLUS SUPPLY

Prepared by C. S. HAMMOND & Co. Inc., N.Y.

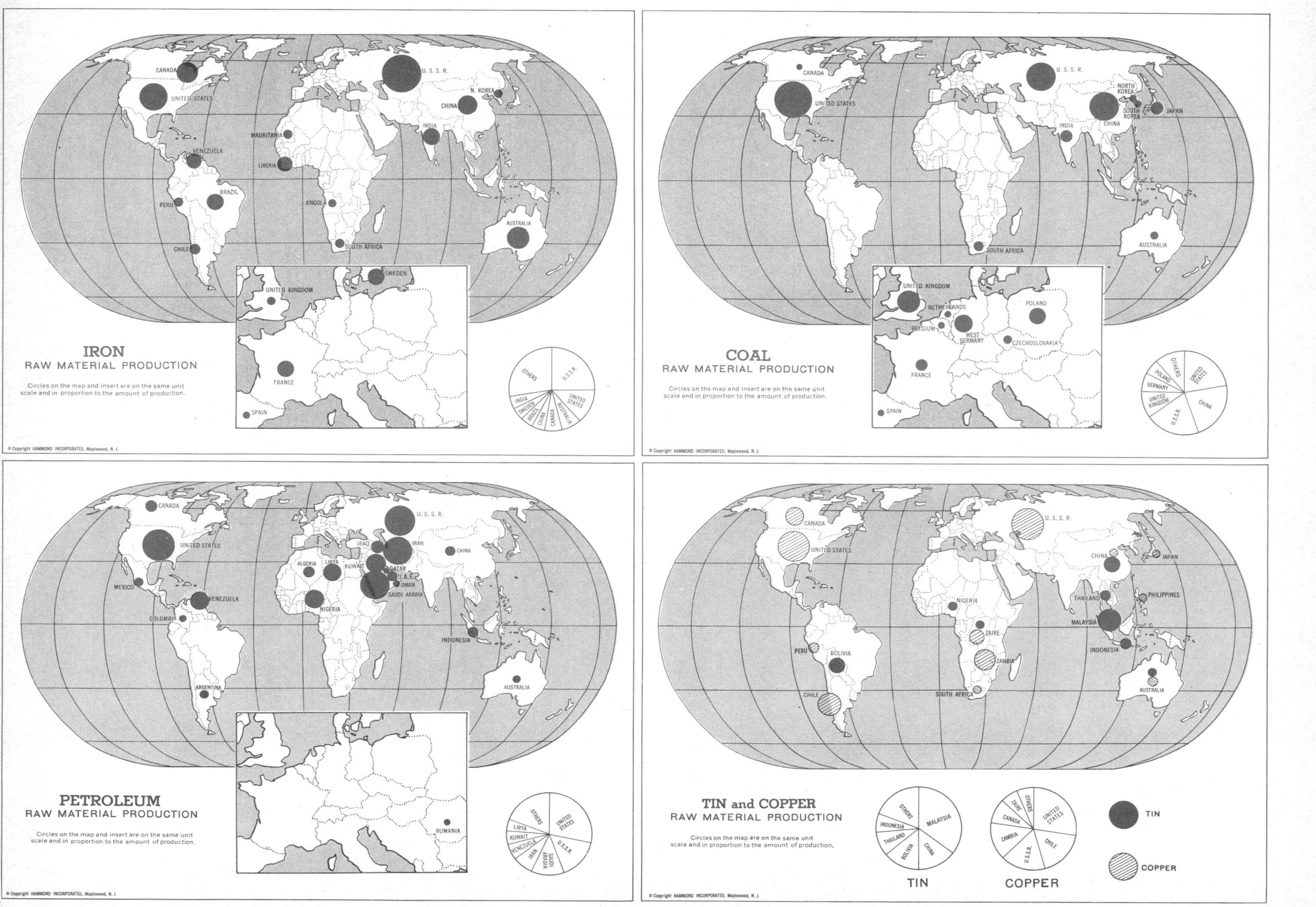
IRON
RAW MATERIAL PRODUCTION
Circles on the map and insert are on the same unit scale and in proportion to the amount of production.
CANADA
UNITED STATES
VENEZUELA
BRAZIL
PERU
CHILE
MAURITANIA
LIBERIA
ANGOLA
SOUTH AFRICA
U. S. S. R.
N. KOREA
CHINA
INDIA
AUSTRALIA
SWEDEN
UNITED KINGDOM
FRANCE
SPAIN
OTHERS
U.S.S.R.
UNITED STATES
AUSTRALIA
CANADA
CHINA
BRAZIL
SWEDEN
INDIA
© Copyright HAMMOND INCORPORATED, Maplewood, N. J.
COAL
RAW MATERIAL PRODUCTION
Circles on the map and insert are on the same unit scale and in proportion to the amount of production.
CANADA
UNITED STATES
U. S. S. R.
NORTH KOREA
SOUTH KOREA
JAPAN
CHINA
INDIA
SOUTH AFRICA
AUSTRALIA
UNITED KINGDOM
NETHERLANDS
BELGIUM
WEST GERMANY
POLAND
CZECHOSLOVAKIA
FRANCE
SPAIN
OTHERS
UNITED STATES
CHINA
U.S.S.R.
UNITED KINGDOM
GERMANY
POLAND
© Copyright HAMMOND INCORPORATED, Maplewood, N. J.
PETROLEUM
RAW MATERIAL PRODUCTION
Circles on the map and insert are on the same unit scale and in proportion to the amount of production.
CANADA
UNITED STATES
MEXICO
VENEZUELA
COLOMBIA
ARGENTINA
U. S. S. R.
IRAQ
IRAN
CHINA
ALGERIA
LIBYA
KUWAIT
QATAR
U.A.E.
OMAN
SAUDI ARABIA
NIGERIA
INDONESIA
AUSTRALIA
RUMANIA
OTHERS
UNITED STATES
U.S.S.R.
SAUDI ARABIA
IRAN
VENEZUELA
KUWAIT
LIBYA
© Copyright HAMMOND INCORPORATED, Maplewood, N. J.
TIN and COPPER
RAW MATERIAL PRODUCTION
Circles on the map are on the same unit scale and in proportion to the amount of production.
CANADA
UNITED STATES
PERU
BOLIVIA
CHILE
U. S. S. R.
CHINA
JAPAN
PHILIPPINES
THAILAND
MALAYSIA
INDONESIA
NIGERIA
ZAIRE
ZAMBIA
SOUTH AFRICA
AUSTRALIA
OTHERS
MALAYSIA
INDONESIA
THAILAND
BOLIVIA
CHINA
TIN
OTHERS
ZAIRE
CANADA
UNITED STATES
ZAMBIA
U.S.S.R.
CHILE
COPPER
TIN
COPPER
© Copyright HAMMOND INCORPORATED, Maplewood, N. J.

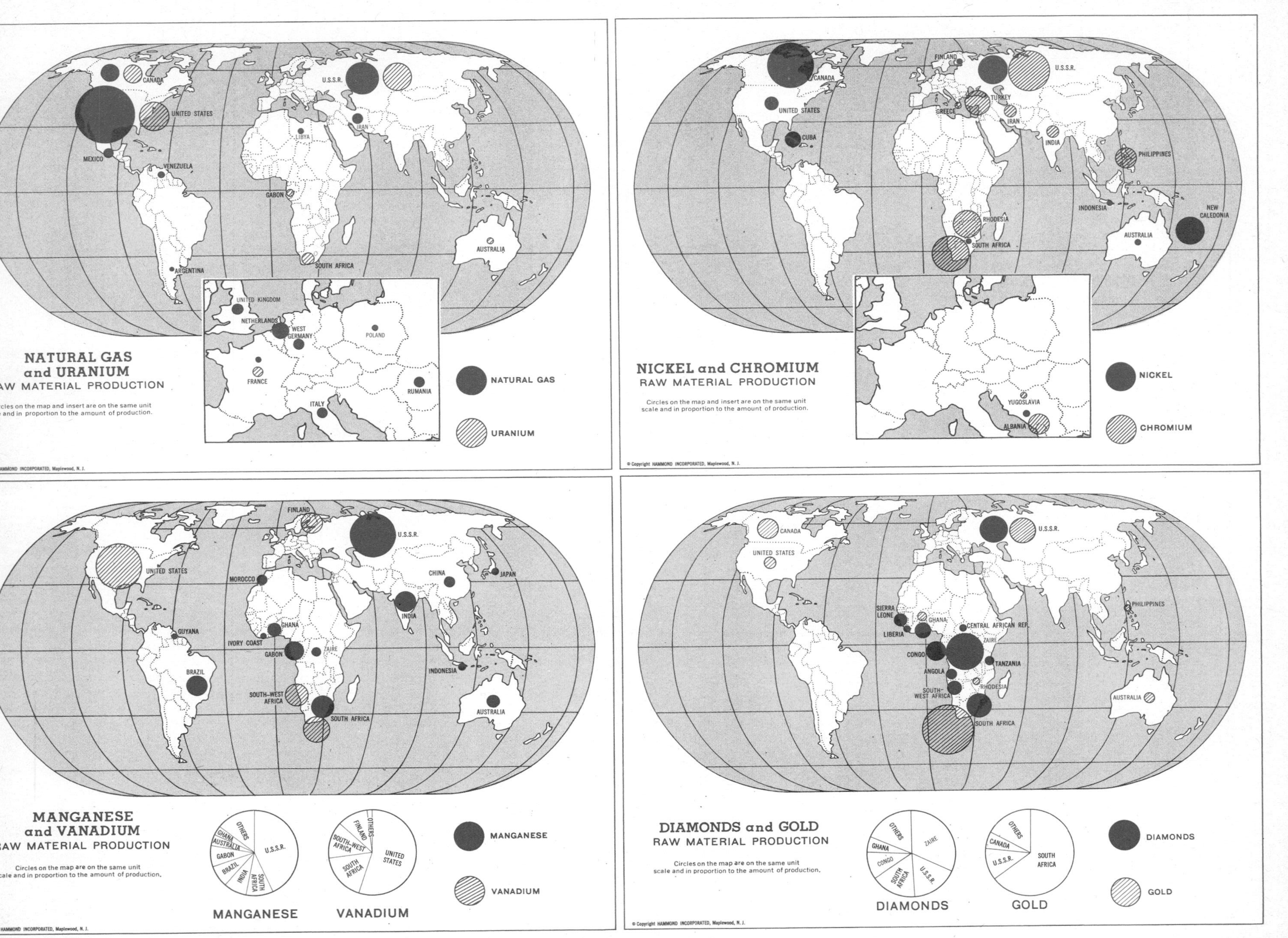
CANADA
UNITED STATES
MEXICO
VENEZUELA
ARGENTINA
U.S.S.R.
IRAN
LIBYA
GABON
SOUTH AFRICA
AUSTRALIA
UNITED KINGDOM
NETHERLANDS
WEST GERMANY
POLAND
FRANCE
RUMANIA
ITALY
NATURAL GAS and URANIUM
RAW MATERIAL PRODUCTION
Circles on the map and insert are on the same unit scale and in proportion to the amount of production.
NATURAL GAS
URANIUM
© Copyright HAMMOND INCORPORATED, Maplewood, N.J.
FINLAND
CANADA
UNITED STATES
CUBA
GREECE
TURKEY
IRAN
U.S.S.R.
INDIA
PHILIPPINES
INDONESIA
NEW CALEDONIA
AUSTRALIA
RHODESIA
SOUTH AFRICA
YUGOSLAVIA
ALBANIA
NICKEL and CHROMIUM
RAW MATERIAL PRODUCTION
Circles on the map and insert are on the same unit scale and in proportion to the amount of production.
NICKEL
CHROMIUM
© Copyright HAMMOND INCORPORATED, Maplewood, N.J.
FINLAND
U.S.S.R.
UNITED STATES
MOROCCO
CHINA
JAPAN
INDIA
GUYANA
GHANA
IVORY COAST
GABON
ZAIRE
INDONESIA
BRAZIL
SOUTH-WEST AFRICA
SOUTH AFRICA
AUSTRALIA
MANGANESE and VANADIUM
RAW MATERIAL PRODUCTION
Circles on the map are on the same unit scale and in proportion to the amount of production.
OTHERS
GHANA
AUSTRALIA
GABON
BRAZIL
INDIA
SOUTH AFRICA
U.S.S.R.
MANGANESE
OTHERS
FINLAND
SOUTH-WEST AFRICA
SOUTH AFRICA
UNITED STATES
VANADIUM
MANGANESE
VANADIUM
© Copyright HAMMOND INCORPORATED, Maplewood, N.J.
CANADA
UNITED STATES
U.S.S.R.
PHILIPPINES
SIERRA LEONE
GHANA
CENTRAL AFRICAN REP.
LIBERIA
ZAIRE
CONGO
TANZANIA
ANGOLA
RHODESIA
SOUTH-WEST AFRICA
SOUTH AFRICA
AUSTRALIA
DIAMONDS and GOLD
RAW MATERIAL PRODUCTION
Circles on the map are on the same unit scale and in proportion to the amount of production.
OTHERS
GHANA
CONGO
SOUTH AFRICA
U.S.S.R.
ZAIRE
DIAMONDS
OTHERS
CANADA
U.S.S.R.
SOUTH AFRICA
GOLD
DIAMONDS
GOLD
© Copyright HAMMOND INCORPORATED, Maplewood, N.J.

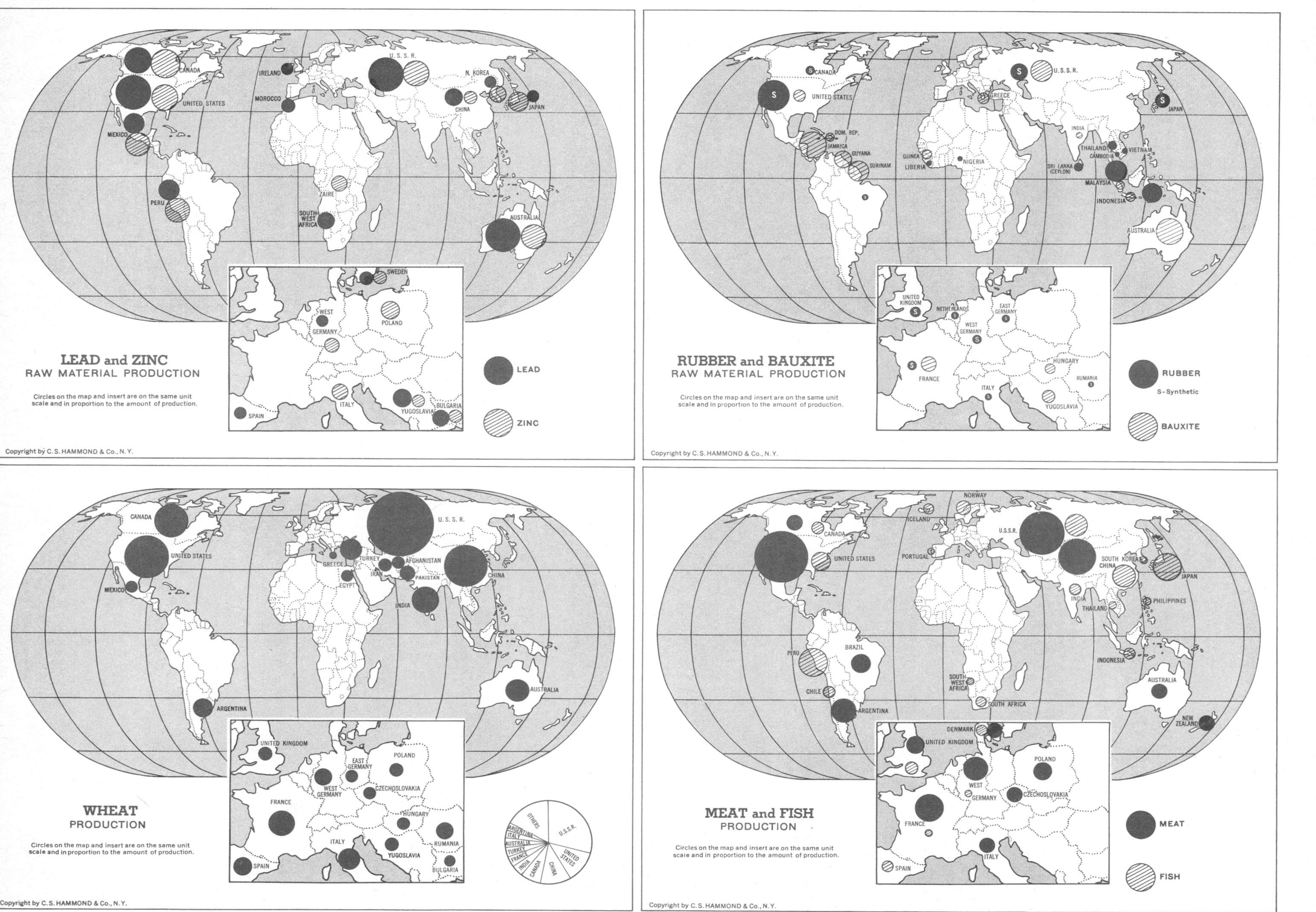
LEAD and ZINC
RAW MATERIAL PRODUCTION
Circles on the map and insert are on the same unit scale and in proportion to the amount of production.
LEAD
ZINC
CANADA
UNITED STATES
MEXICO
PERU
IRELAND
MOROCCO
ZAIRE
SOUTH WEST AFRICA
U.S.S.R.
N. KOREA
CHINA
JAPAN
AUSTRALIA
SWEDEN
WEST GERMANY
POLAND
ITALY
YUGOSLAVIA
BULGARIA
SPAIN
Copyright by C. S. HAMMOND & Co., N. Y.
RUBBER and BAUXITE
RAW MATERIAL PRODUCTION
Circles on the map and insert are on the same unit scale and in proportion to the amount of production.
RUBBER
S-Synthetic
BAUXITE
CANADA
UNITED STATES
DOM. REP.
JAMAICA
GUYANA
SURINAM
GUINEA
LIBERIA
NIGERIA
GREECE
U.S.S.R.
INDIA
THAILAND
CAMBODIA
VIETNAM
SRI LANKA (CEYLON)
MALAYSIA
INDONESIA
JAPAN
AUSTRALIA
UNITED KINGDOM
NETHERLANDS
EAST GERMANY
WEST GERMANY
FRANCE
HUNGARY
RUMANIA
ITALY
YUGOSLAVIA
Copyright by C. S. HAMMOND & Co., N. Y.
WHEAT
PRODUCTION
Circles on the map and insert are on the same unit scale and in proportion to the amount of production.
CANADA
UNITED STATES
MEXICO
ARGENTINA
U.S.S.R.
GREECE
TURKEY
IRAN
EGYPT
AFGHANISTAN
PAKISTAN
INDIA
CHINA
AUSTRALIA
UNITED KINGDOM
EAST GERMANY
POLAND
WEST GERMANY
CZECHOSLOVAKIA
FRANCE
HUNGARY
ITALY
RUMANIA
YUGOSLAVIA
BULGARIA
SPAIN
OTHERS
ARGENTINA
ITALY
AUSTRALIA
TURKEY
FRANCE
INDIA
CANADA
CHINA
UNITED STATES
U.S.S.R.
Copyright by C. S. HAMMOND & Co., N. Y.
MEAT and FISH
PRODUCTION
Circles on the map and insert are on the same unit scale and in proportion to the amount of production.
MEAT
FISH
CANADA
UNITED STATES
PERU
BRAZIL
CHILE
ARGENTINA
ICELAND
NORWAY
PORTUGAL
SOUTH WEST AFRICA
SOUTH AFRICA
U.S.S.R.
SOUTH KOREA
CHINA
JAPAN
INDIA
THAILAND
PHILIPPINES
INDONESIA
AUSTRALIA
NEW ZEALAND
DENMARK
UNITED KINGDOM
WEST GERMANY
POLAND
CZECHOSLOVAKIA
FRANCE
ITALY
SPAIN
Copyright by C. S. HAMMOND & Co., N. Y.

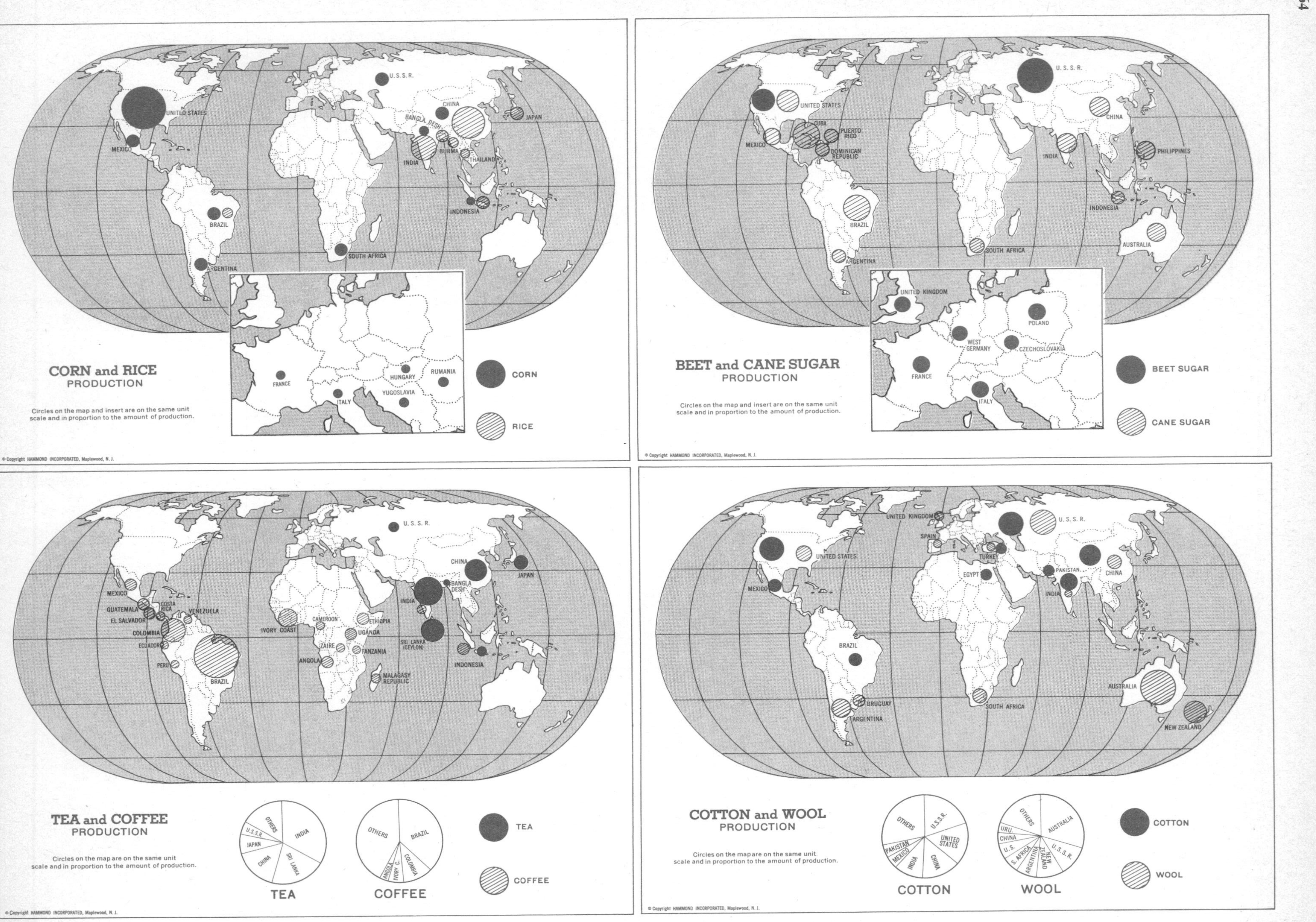

CORN and RICE
PRODUCTION
Circles on the map and insert are on the same unit scale and in proportion to the amount of production.
UNITED STATES
MEXICO
BRAZIL
ARGENTINA
U.S.S.R.
CHINA
BANGLA DESH
INDIA
BURMA
THAILAND
JAPAN
INDONESIA
SOUTH AFRICA
FRANCE
ITALY
HUNGARY
RUMANIA
YUGOSLAVIA
CORN
RICE
© Copyright HAMMOND INCORPORATED, Maplewood, N. J.
BEET and CANE SUGAR
PRODUCTION
Circles on the map and insert are on the same unit scale and in proportion to the amount of production.
UNITED STATES
MEXICO
CUBA
PUERTO RICO
DOMINICAN REPUBLIC
BRAZIL
ARGENTINA
U.S.S.R.
CHINA
INDIA
PHILIPPINES
INDONESIA
AUSTRALIA
SOUTH AFRICA
UNITED KINGDOM
POLAND
WEST GERMANY
CZECHOSLOVAKIA
FRANCE
ITALY
BEET SUGAR
CANE SUGAR
© Copyright HAMMOND INCORPORATED, Maplewood, N. J.
TEA and COFFEE
PRODUCTION
Circles on the map are on the same unit scale and in proportion to the amount of production.
U.S.S.R.
CHINA
JAPAN
BANGLA DESH
INDIA
SRI LANKA (CEYLON)
INDONESIA
MEXICO
GUATEMALA
COSTA RICA
EL SALVADOR
VENEZUELA
COLOMBIA
ECUADOR
PERU
BRAZIL
IVORY COAST
CAMEROON
ETHIOPIA
UGANDA
ZAIRE
TANZANIA
ANGOLA
MALAGASY REPUBLIC
OTHERS
U.S.S.R.
JAPAN
CHINA
INDIA
SRI LANKA
TEA
OTHERS
BRAZIL
ANGOLA
IVORY C.
COLOMBIA
COFFEE
TEA
COFFEE
© Copyright HAMMOND INCORPORATED, Maplewood, N. J.
COTTON and WOOL
PRODUCTION
Circles on the map are on the same unit. scale and in proportion to the amount of production.
UNITED KINGDOM
SPAIN
U.S.S.R.
UNITED STATES
MEXICO
TURKEY
EGYPT
PAKISTAN
INDIA
CHINA
BRAZIL
URUGUAY
ARGENTINA
SOUTH AFRICA
AUSTRALIA
NEW ZEALAND
OTHERS
U.S.S.R.
UNITED STATES
CHINA
INDIA
MEXICO
PAKISTAN
COTTON
OTHERS
AUSTRALIA
U.S.S.R.
NEW ZEALAND
ARGENTINA
S. AFRICA
U.S.
CHINA
URU.
WOOL
COTTON
WOOL
© Copyright HAMMOND INCORPORATED, Maplewood, N. J.

THE SOLAR SYSTEM

The *solar system* consists of the sun, nine planets and their 32 satellites, thousands of asteroids, millions of meteors and many comets. All these bodies travel around the sun in nearly circular paths called *orbits*. The planets are held in their orbits by the sun's gravity.

The nine planets surrounding the sun are commonly divided into two groups called the *inner planets* and the *outer planets*. The inner planets, those that are closest to the sun, include Mercury, Venus, Earth and Mars. Mercury is nearest the sun and, in this group, Mars is farthest from the sun. In the outer planets, or those farther from the sun, we find Jupiter, Saturn, Uranus, Neptune and Pluto.

The two planet groups are separated from one another by the *asteroid belt* which lies between Mars and Jupiter, forming the outer boundary of the inner group and the inner boundary of the outer planets.

Asteroids are small planets, most of which are only a few miles or less in diameter. The largest is Ceres, with a diameter of 480 miles, about 1/300 the size of the smallest planet, Mercury. Thousands of these small bodies go into making up the asteroid belt and it is worth noting that some scientists believe they once may have been one planet that was broken up.

In thinking of distances we tend to focus our attention on one dimension — the farther away something is the smaller it appears to be. Of course, with the solar system this is untrue. The largest of the planets, Jupiter, is in the outer planet group. The smallest planet, Mercury, is closest of all to the sun. To put these sizes in another perspective we should first look at the dimension of the sun.

In comparison with the Earth and the eight other planets in our solar system the sun is a gigantic sphere. In diameter it is approximately 864,000 miles, which is 100 times longer than Earth and 10 times longer than Jupiter, the biggest planet. In terms of volume, over 1½ million earth-size planets could fit into a sphere the size of the sun. But, although the sun is the largest body in our solar system, it is a relatively small *star* when viewed as part of our galaxy which contains more than 100 billion stars.

RELATIVE DIAMETERS OF THE PLANETS AND SUN

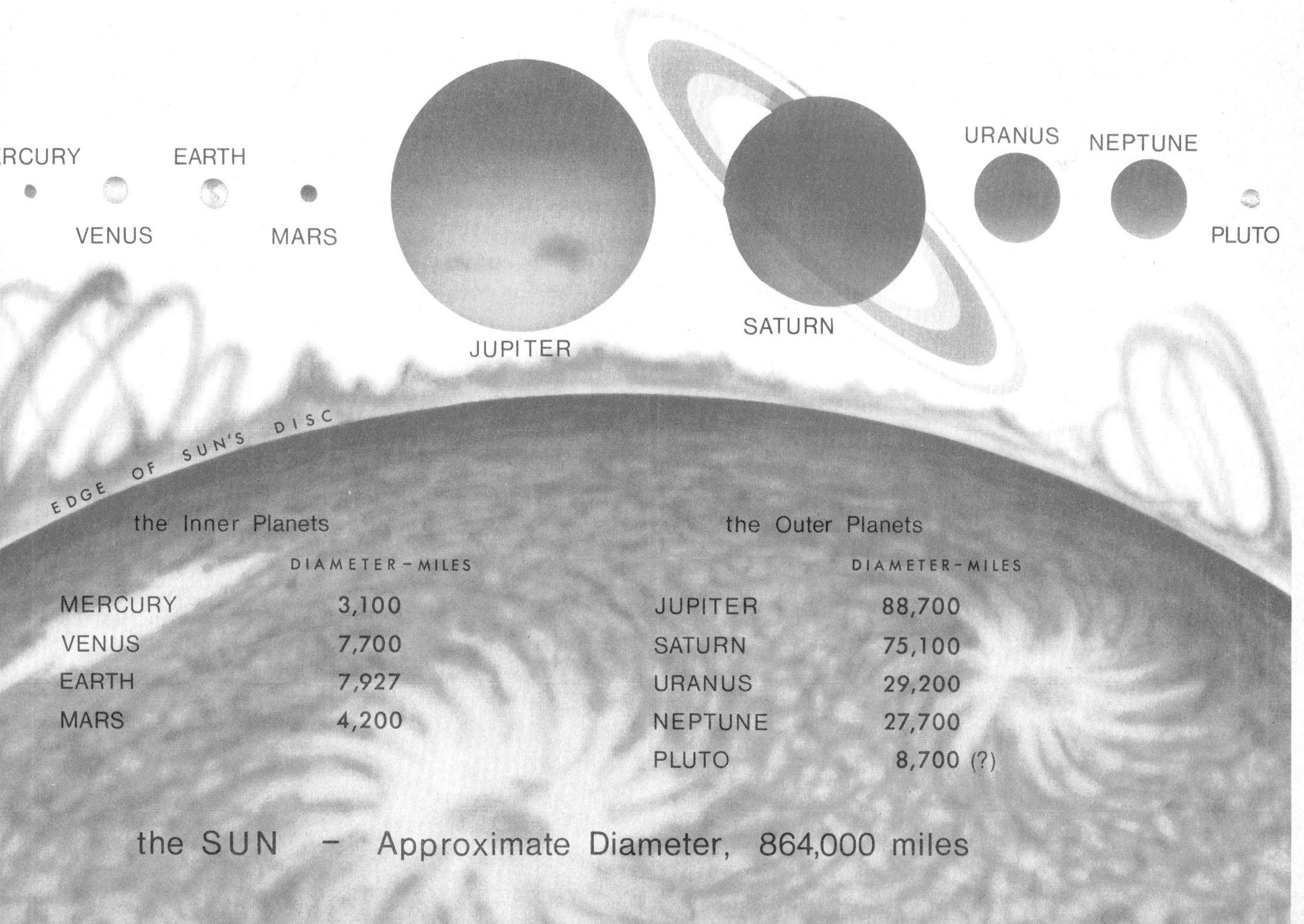

the Inner Planets

	DIAMETER – MILES
MERCURY	3,100
VENUS	7,700
EARTH	7,927
MARS	4,200

the Outer Planets

	DIAMETER – MILES
JUPITER	88,700
SATURN	75,100
URANUS	29,200
NEPTUNE	27,700
PLUTO	8,700 (?)

the SUN – Approximate Diameter, 864,000 miles

THE SOLAR SYSTEM
(continued)

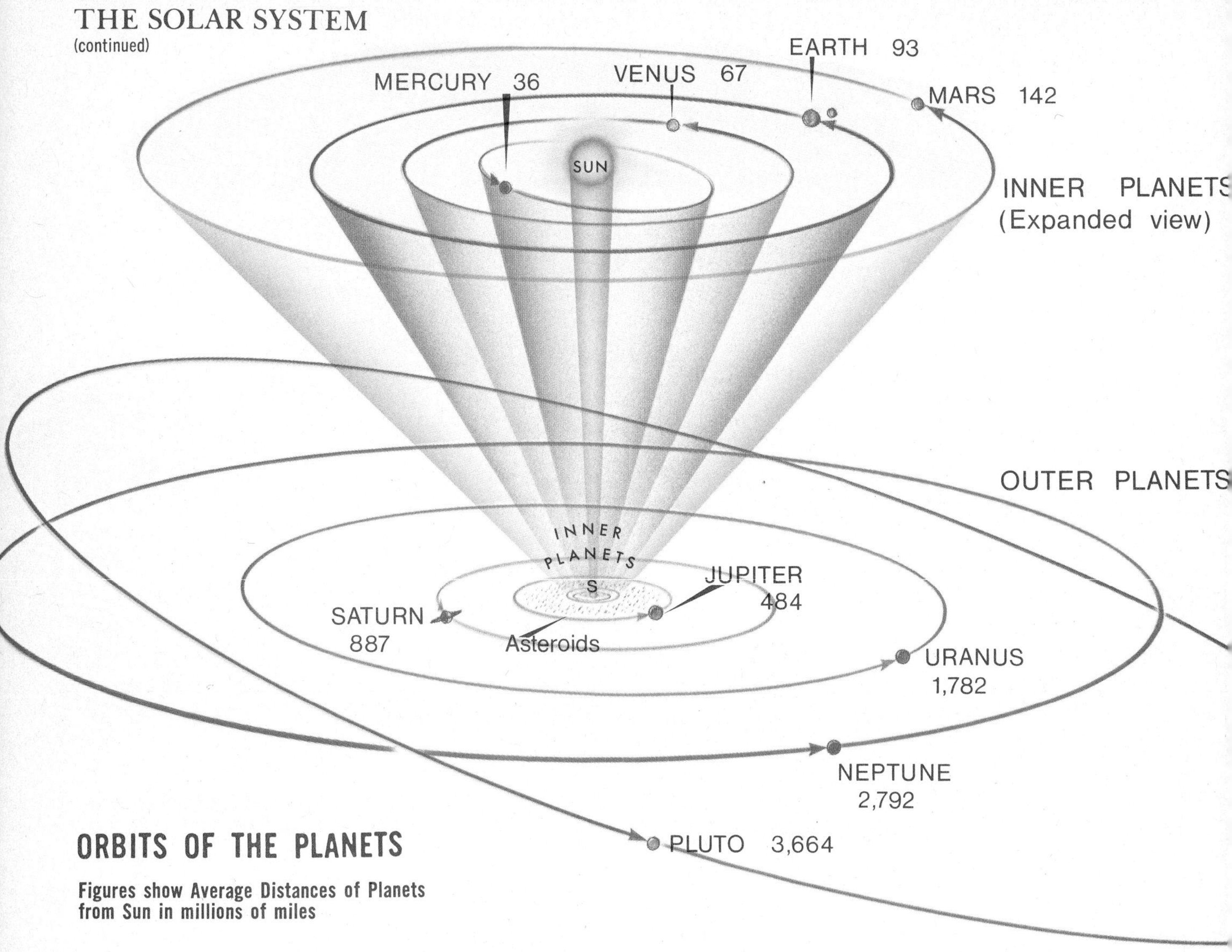

ORBITS OF THE PLANETS

Figures show Average Distances of Planets from Sun in millions of miles

All the planets within our solar system move in the same direction around the sun and their orbits lie in nearly the same plane (within 3½ percent of the plane of the Earth's orbit). The orbits of Mercury and Pluto are exceptions to this. Mercury's orbit is inclined 7°; Pluto's orbit, inclined by over 17°, is highly eccentric. During part of its orbit Pluto lies within the orbit of Neptune. However the two planets do not collide because of the inclination of Pluto's orbit. Rotation and revolution are other factors of interest in studying planet characteristics. How much time does it take for each planet to rotate on its axis and to revolve around the sun? Mercury, for example, is closest to the sun and takes 88 days to make one revolution around the sun (the Earth takes 365¼ days or one earth-year). Pluto, on the other hand, is farthest from the sun and takes 248 earth-years to make one revolution. Pluto's axial rotation speed is also slow as compared with the 23 hours and 56 minutes it takes Earth to rotate once. It takes Pluto over six earth-days to make one rotation.

Temperature, weight (or gravity) and atmospheric density are other areas we study to understand our planet neighbors.

Mercury, for example, has no atmosphere. Its density indicates that its composition is probably similar to that of Earth, yet its temperatures are a study in extremes. On the sunny side of Mercury temperatures may soar as high as, 770°F., while on the shadowed side the temperature approaches absolute zero (-459.6°F.). The gravitational pull on Mercury differs from Earth too. A man weighing 150 pounds on Earth would weigh 45 on Mercury.

Venus, closest to Earth, has a dense atmosphere composed mainly of carbon dioxide. Surface temperatures are considered to be quite hot.

Mars has an atmosphere considerably less than that of Earth so its surface is visible. Seasonal variations on Mars are indicated by the polar caps, believed to be ice and snow, which disappear in summer. This would indicate that Mars' atmosphere contains some water vapor.

Jupiter, Saturn, Uranus and Neptune are much larger than the other planets and differ from the others in several ways. Their bulk compositions include considerably more gaseous substance and less rock material. This is reflected in their densities, which are much less than that of Earth. Also, they have extremely low surface temperatures. Relatively little is known about *Pluto* because it is so distant from Earth.

A MAN'S WEIGHT AND JUMP ON EACH PLANET

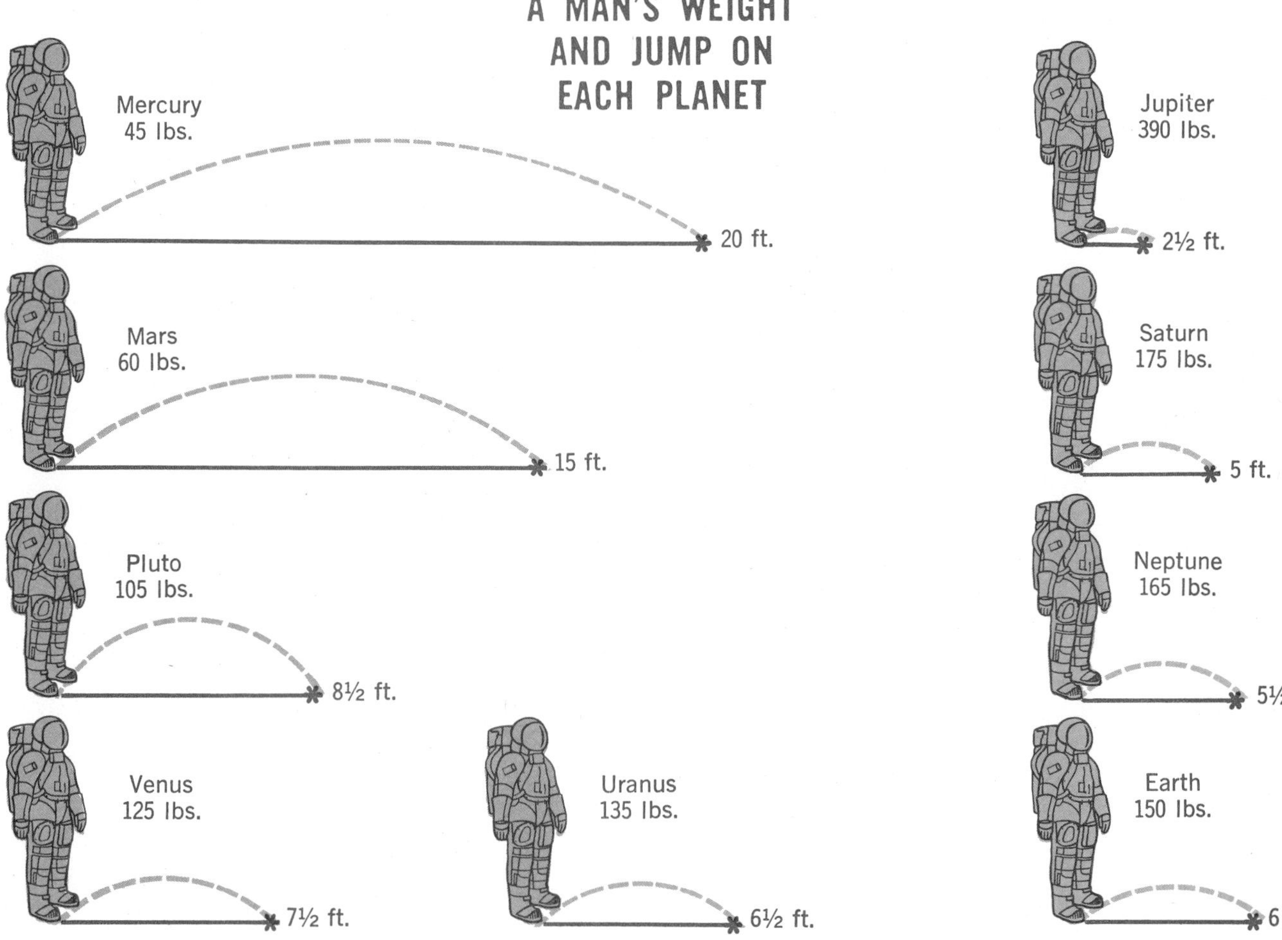

FACTS ABOUT THE PLANETS

	MERCURY	VENUS	EARTH	MARS	JUPITER	SATURN	URANUS	NEPTUNE	PLUTO
Period of Revolution Around the Sun	87.97 days	224.7 days	365.26 da.	687 days	11.86 years	29.46 years	84.02 years	164.79 yrs.	247.7 years
Period of Rotation on Axis	59 days	250 days	23 hours 56 min.	24 hours 37 min.	9 hours 50 min.	10 hours 14 min.	10 hours 45 min.	15 hours 48 min.	6 days 9 hours ?
Inclination of Axis	?	?	23.5°	24°	3.1°	26.8°	98°	29°	?
Minimum Distance from Earth (millions of miles)	49	26	—	34	362	773	1,594	2,654	2,605
Maximum Distance from Earth (millions of miles)	137	161	—	247	597	1,023	1,946	2,891	4,506
Escape Velocity (miles per hour)	7,920	22,700	25,200	11,200	133,200	79,200	46,800	55,400	?
Mass or Weight (compared to Earth)	.05	.81	1.0	.11	318	95	14.6	17.2	?
Volume (compared to Earth)	.06	.92	1.0	.15	1,318	736	64	60	.10
Density (water = 1.0)	5.3	4.9	5.5	4.0	1.3	0.7	1.3	1.6	?
Number of Moons	0	0	1	2	12	10	5	2	0

THE MOON: EARTH'S NATURAL SATELLITE

The moon, man's first stepping stone into the silent seas of space, actually is a gigantic stone in the sky . . . an airless, waterless sphere of towering mountain ranges, broad craters, great plains and powdery, gray-brown dust. It rotates around the earth keeping its far side always hidden from our sight. One-quarter the diameter of the earth and having one-sixth its gravity, this uninviting neighbor only 238,000 miles away was formed, we speculate, when

NEAR SIDE

(photo mosaic)

NORTH
PHILOLAUS
METON
PYTHAGORAS
BIRMINGHAM
W. BOND
STRABO
J. HERSCHEL
MARE HUMBOLDTIANUM (Humboldt's Sea)
MARE FRIGORIS (Sea of Cold)
DE LA RUE
SINUS RORIS (Bay of Dew)
REPSOLD
PLATO
ALPS
ENDYMION
ARISTOTELES
JURA MOUNTAINS
ALPINE VALLEY
HERCULES
ATLAS
SHARP
SINUS IRIDUM (Bay of Rainbows)
LAPLACE PROM.
MT. PICO
EUDOXUS
BURG
MAIRAN
MESSALA
HERACLIDES PROM.
MT. PITON
CASSINI
CAUCASUS MOUNTAINS
LACUS SOMNIORUM (Lake of Dreams)
FRANKLIN
ARISTILLUS
MARE IMBRIUM (Sea of Rains)
GEMINUS
POSIDONIUS
DELISLE
AUTOLYCUS
CHACORNAC
ARCHIMEDES
MARE SERENITATIS (Sea of Serenity)
TIMOCHARIS
TAURUS MOUNTAINS
PALUS PUTREDINIS (Marsh of Decay)
LAMBERT
CLEOMEDES
O. STRUVE
ARISTARCHUS
EULER
SELEUCUS
HERODOTUS
MACROBIUS
APENNINES
OCEANUS PROCELLARUM (Ocean of Storms)
HAEMUS MOUNTAINS
MENELAUS
PLINIUS
MARE CRISIUM (Sea of Crises)
CARPATHIANS
MARE VAPORUM (Sea of Vapors)
MANILIUS
PALUS SOMNII (Marsh of Sleep)
KRAFFT
ERATOSTHENES
SINUS AESTUUM (Seething Bay)
COPERNICUS
JULIUS CAESAR
MARE TRANQUILLITATIS (Sea of Tranquility)
CONDORCET
KEPLER
HYGINUS CLEFT
ARIADAEUS CLEFT
REINER
CAVALERIUS
ENCKE
PALLAS
TRIESNECKER
TARUNTIUS
HEVELIUS
REINHOLD
AGRIPPA
APOLLONIUS
SINUS MEDII (Central Bay)
GODIN
MASKELYNE
+APOLLO 11 LANDING JULY 20, 1969
MARE SPUMANS (Foaming Sea)
LANSBERG
MÖSTING
DELAMBRE
MARE FECUNDITATIS (Sea of Fertility)
FRA MAURO
HERSCHEL
HIPPARCHUS
GRIMALDI
GUTENBERG
RIPHAEUS MTS.
PARRY
PTOLEMAEUS
THEOPHILUS
LANGRENUS
ALBATEGNIUS
HANSTEEN
LETRONNE
GUERICKE
CYRILLUS
BILLY
ALPHONSUS
ABULFEDA
MARE NECTARIS (Sea of Nectar)
PYRENEES
VENDELINUS
COLOMBO
CRÜGER
ALPETRAGIUS
GASSENDI
CATHARINA
BULLIALDUS
MARE NUBIUM (Sea of Clouds)
STRAIGHT WALL
ARZACHEL
ALTAI MOUNTAINS
MERSENIUS
MARE HUMORUM (Sea of Moisture)
FRACASTORIUS
SANTBECH
HIPPALUS
PURBACH
PETAVIUS
SACROBOSCO
WERNER
VIETA
MERCATOR
REGIOMONTANUS
SNELLIUS
DOPPELMAYER
VITELLO
PITATUS
WILKINS
ZAGUT
PICCOLOMINI
WALTER
ALIACENSIS
STEVINUS
CAPUANUS
LEXELL
WURZELBAUER
RABBI LEVI
RHEITA
STÖFLER
FURNERIUS
HAINZEL
ORONTIUS
METIUS
WILHELM
TYCHO
MAUROLYCUS
FABRICIUS
SCHICKARD
SAUSSURE
BAROCIUS
MAGINUS
MARE AUSTRALE (Southern Sea)
PITISCUS
SCHILLER
CUVIER
LONGOMONTANUS
PHOCYLIDES
VLACQ
CLAVIUS
SCHEINER
MUTUS
BLANCANUS
CURTIUS
MORETUS
MANZINUS
SOUTH

a swirling cloud of cosmic gas and particles separated into eddies which contracted to become the sun, the planets and their satellites. Unshielded by protective air, temperatures on its surface range from over 200°F. by day to –200°F. after dark. Yet some day we shall launch space vehicles from there, virtually without gravitational drag, and, because it has no atmosphere, clearly observe the furthest heavens on ever-cloudless nights.

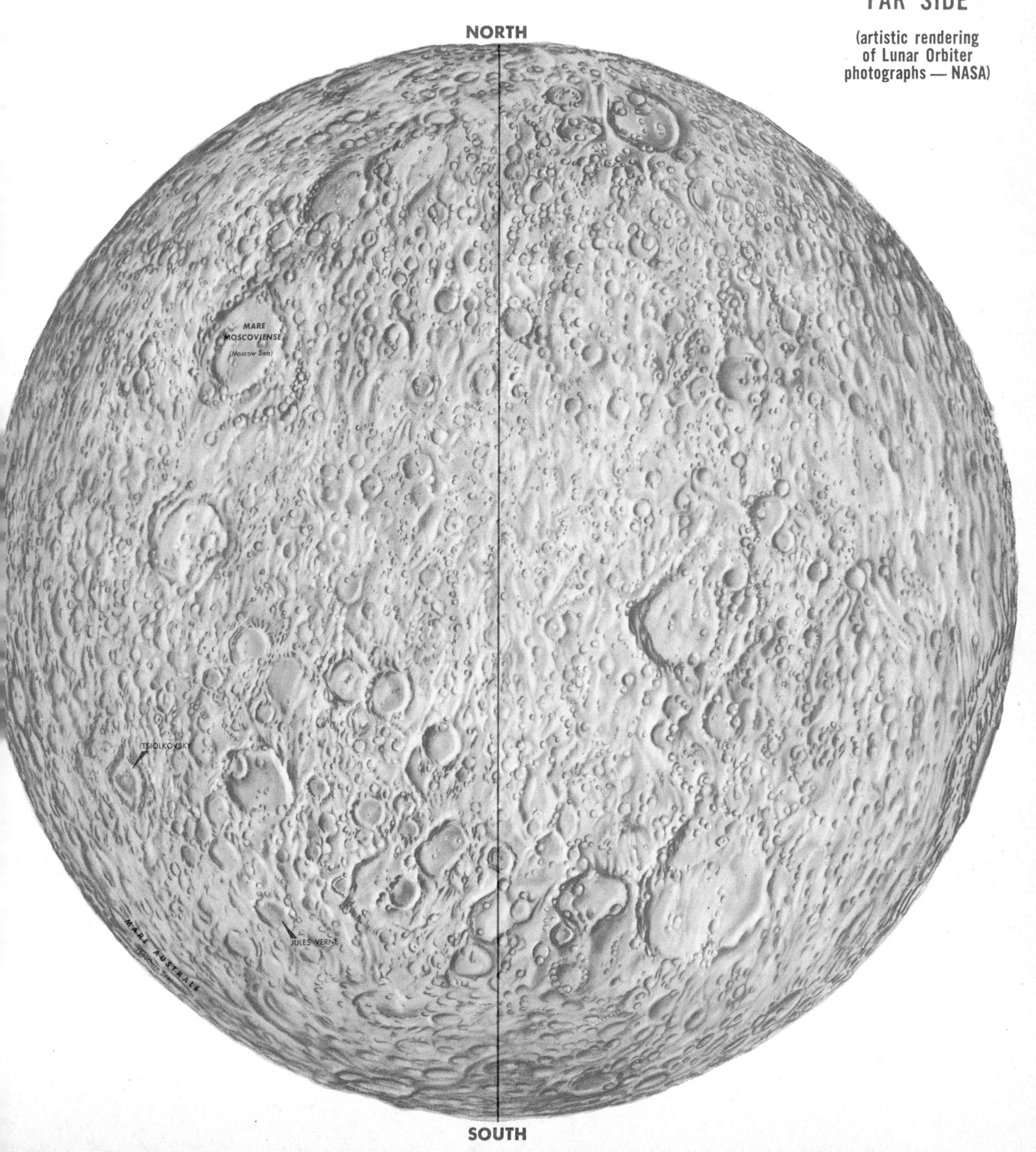

FAR SIDE

(artistic rendering of Lunar Orbiter photographs — NASA)

DEVELOPMENT OF CONTINENTS AND OCEANS

If we can envision the continents of the world as seated firmly on massive rafts of rock and moving across the surface of the earth at a rate of about 6 feet every 60 years we have a basic notion of what is meant by continental drift and the manner in which land and sea masses have been formed.

The original concept of continental drift was proposed in the 1920s, but only during the past three years or so have geologists and geophysicists accepted as fact the seemingly preposterous notion that the surface of the earth is constantly in motion.

The making of the continents began more than 200 million years ago during the Permian period with the splitting of a gigantic landmass known as Pangaea. Two continents, Laurasia to the north and Gondwana to the south, were formed by the initial division. Over a period of many millions of years these landmasses subdivided into smaller parts approximately the shapes of Africa, Eurasia, North and South America, Australia, and Antarctica as we know them today.

CONTINENTAL DRIFT

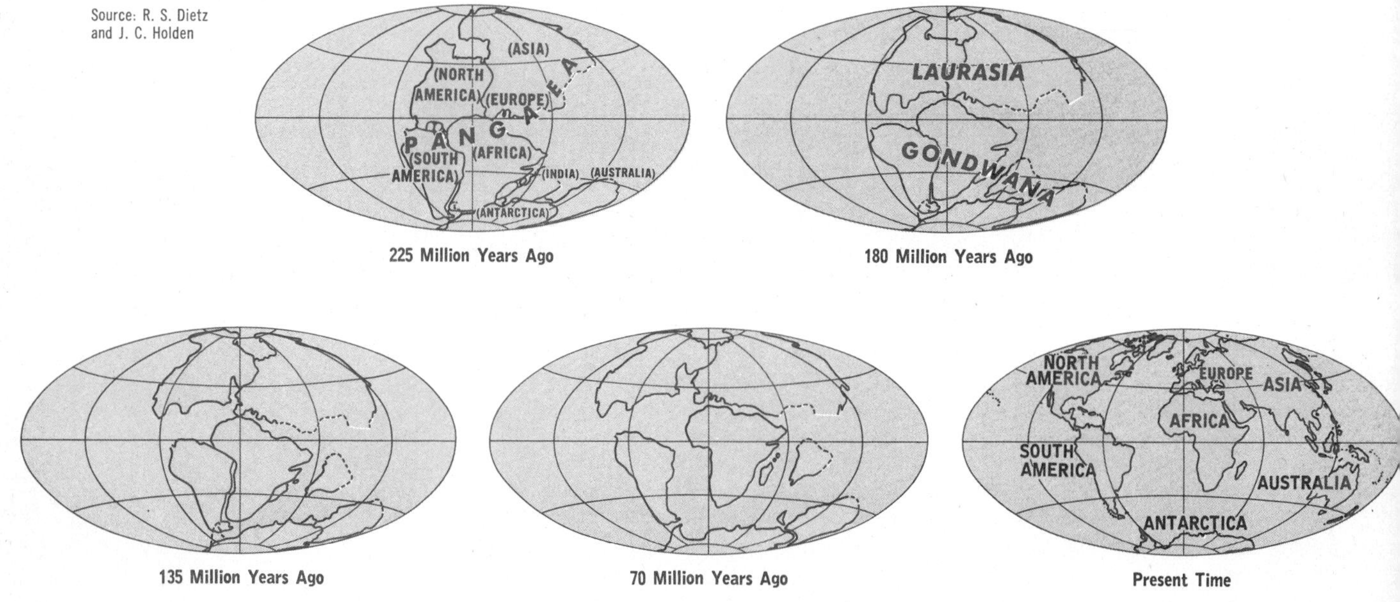

CRUSTAL MOVEMENT

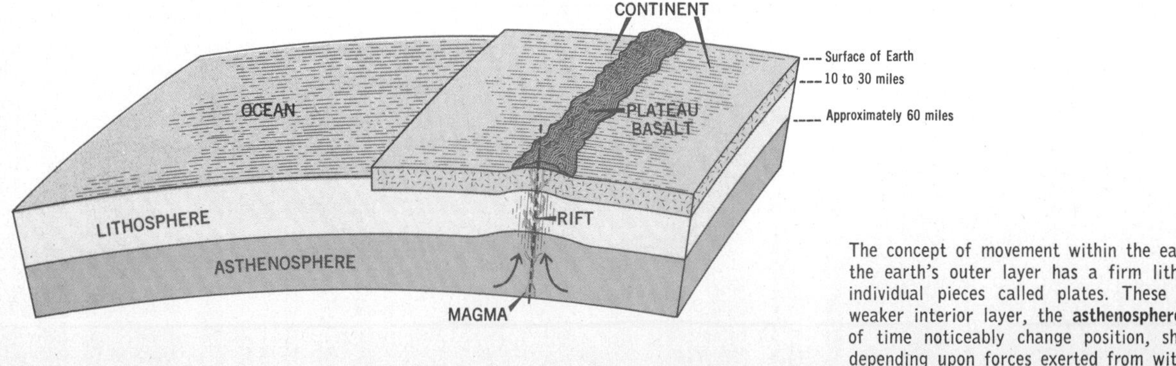

The concept of movement within the earth's crust assumes that the earth's outer layer has a firm lithosphere divided up into individual pieces called plates. These plates "float" above a weaker interior layer, the **asthenosphere**, and over vast periods of time noticeably change position, shape, size and direction depending upon forces exerted from within the earth.

THE ICE AGES

Far from being an isolated instance, the movement of glaciers over the face of the earth has been a natural phenomenon for many thousands of years. Stimulated by changes in climate and resulting changes in sea level—perhaps induced by shifts in the earth's axis—glaciers have followed a rather unpredictable course of advance and retreat continuing into the 20th century.

At some point in unrecorded history during the greatest ice age, or the Pleistocene epoch, as much as 27 percent of the earth's surface was covered by glacial ice to a depth of up to 10,000 feet. The icy masses moved across the earth as far south as New York City and the Missouri River in North America, burying much of Europe and blanketing vast areas in northern Asia.

Many of the great ice sheets retreated as the climate became warmer, leaving deposits of soil and rock picked up as they traveled southward in the Northern Hemisphere. The landscape changed as the glaciers left behind their typical U-shaped valleys, amphitheater-like hollows and jagged mountain ridges, altering to a large extent the former ecological zones which changed again and again as the ice reformed and melted.

Although not enough is known about glaciers to predict accurately their future behavior, we do know that they react to climatic changes. Glaciers were advancing in Alpine regions during the 19th century until a global warm up in the beginning of this century caused their retreat. Recently the trend has been toward cooler and moister climate and, on a limited scale, glaciers are beginning to advance once more.

EXTENT OF GLACIATION IN THE NORTHERN HEMISPHERE DURING THE ICE AGES

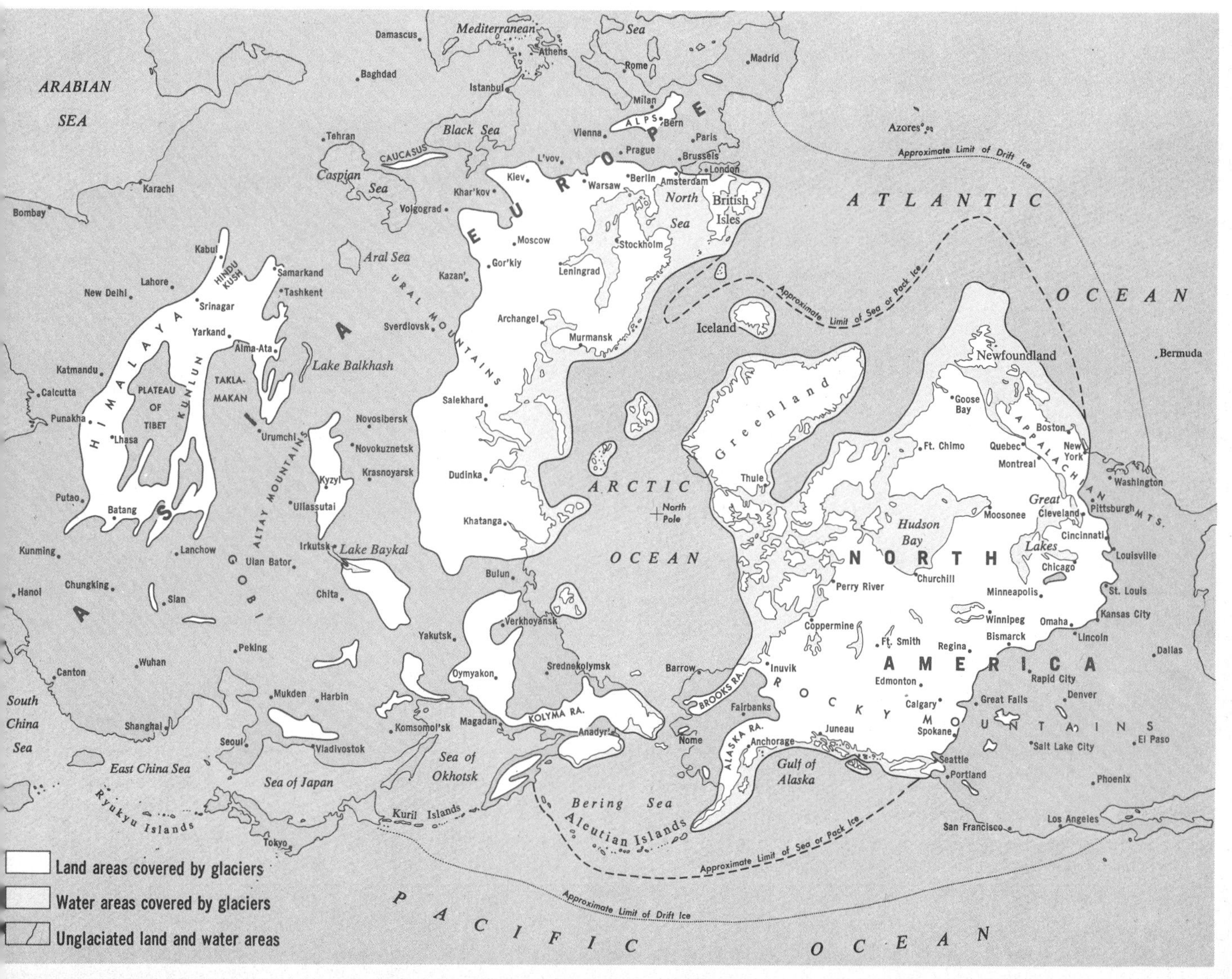

THE GEOLOGIC RECORD

GEOLOGIC TIME

Era	Period	Time Division	Years Ago	Major Geologic Developments
CENOZOIC ERA	QUATERNARY PERIOD	RECENT		
			10,000	GREAT LAKES, NORWEGIAN FJORDS
		PLEISTOCENE		ICE AGES
			1-2 million	BLACK SEA
	TERTIARY PERIOD	PLIOCENE		CASPIAN SEA
			11 million	
		MIOCENE		HIMALAYAS
			25 million	
		OLIGOCENE		ALPS
			40 million	
		EOCENE		
			60 million	
		PALEOCENE		ANDES MOUNTAINS
			70 million	ROCKY MOUNTAINS
MESOZOIC ERA		CRETACEOUS PERIOD		CHALK DEPOSITS
			135 million	COAST RANGES, SIERRA NEVADA, JURA MOUNTAINS
		JURASSIC PERIOD		
			180 million	NEW JERSEY PALISADES
		TRIASSIC PERIOD		CAUCASUS
			225 million	URAL MOUNTAINS, APPALACHIAN MOUNTAINS
PALEOZOIC ERA		PERMIAN PERIOD		POTASH DEPOSITS
			270 million	
		PENNSYLVANIAN PERIOD		COAL DEPOSITS
			300 million	
		MISSISSIPPIAN PERIOD		
			350 million	ACADIAN MOUNTAINS
		DEVONIAN PERIOD		
			400 million	
		SILURIAN PERIOD		NIAGARA FALLS CAPROCK
			440 million	TACONIC MOUNTAINS
		ORDOVICIAN PERIOD		LIMESTONE DEPOSITS
			500 million	VERMONT MOUNTAINS
		CAMBRIAN PERIOD		
			600 million	ARIZONA MOUNTAINS
		PRE-CAMBRIAN		METALLIC ORE DEPOSITS, LAURENTIAN MOUNTAINS, ADIRONDACK MOUNTAINS

Like a giant Rosetta stone the secrets of the earth's creation lie spread in strata beneath our feet, revealing their hieroglyphic message to a few of the initiated.

For billions of years layers of rock — the sedimentary deposits of ages — have piled up on the earth's surface, entrapping the characteristics of time. Time when a lifeless nature prepared for the first microscopic living organisms; time when these organisms were destroyed or became extinct, time when, through endless subtle mutations, they evolved into new forms of life.

The Paleozoic, ancient era; Mesozoic, middle era; and

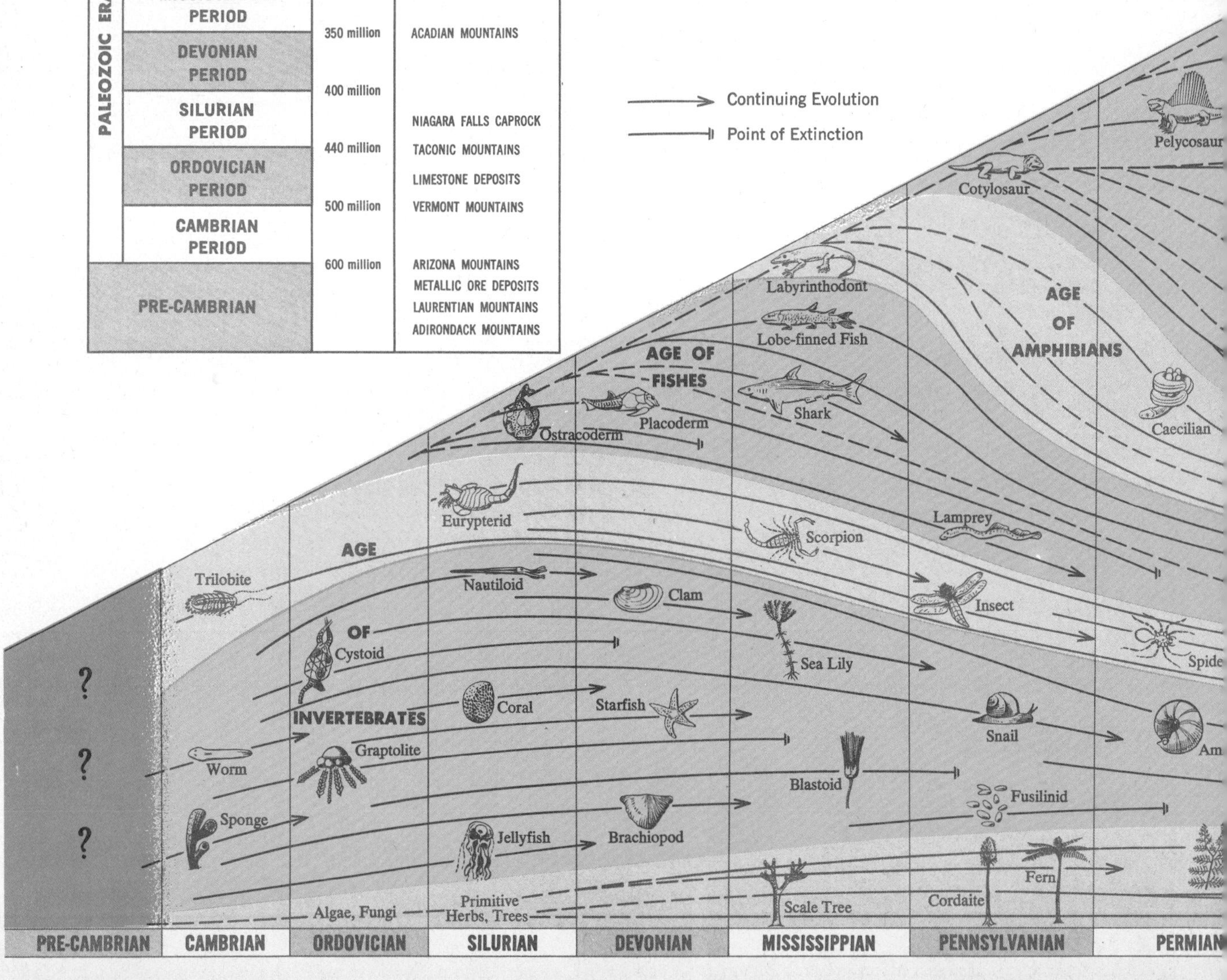

Continuing Evolution
Point of Extinction

Pelycosaur
Cotylosaur
Labyrinthodont
AGE OF AMPHIBIANS
Lobe-finned Fish
AGE OF FISHES
Shark
Caecilian
Ostracoderm
Placoderm
Eurypterid
Lamprey
Scorpion
AGE OF INVERTEBRATES
Trilobite
Nautiloid
Clam
Insect
Cystoid
Sea Lily
Spide
Coral
Starfish
Snail
Graptolite
Am
Worm
Blastoid
Fusilinid
Sponge
Jellyfish
Brachiopod
Fern
Algae, Fungi
Primitive Herbs, Trees
Scale Tree
Cordaite
?
?
?

PRE-CAMBRIAN | CAMBRIAN | ORDOVICIAN | SILURIAN | DEVONIAN | MISSISSIPPIAN | PENNSYLVANIAN | PERMIAN

Cenozoic, recent era, are the designations used for the broad periods of time during which life evolved. Locked within strata of rock, vestiges of life are found in the fossilized remains of creatures over a billion years old. In succeeding layers geologists and anthropologists find other clues to the mystery of time and life: the appearance of the lowest forms of animal life; the evolution of fish, amphibians, reptiles, birds and mammals. Late in the schedule of creation traces of a strange and wonderful animal appear, for it was only one million years ago that man left his first imprint on the geologic record.

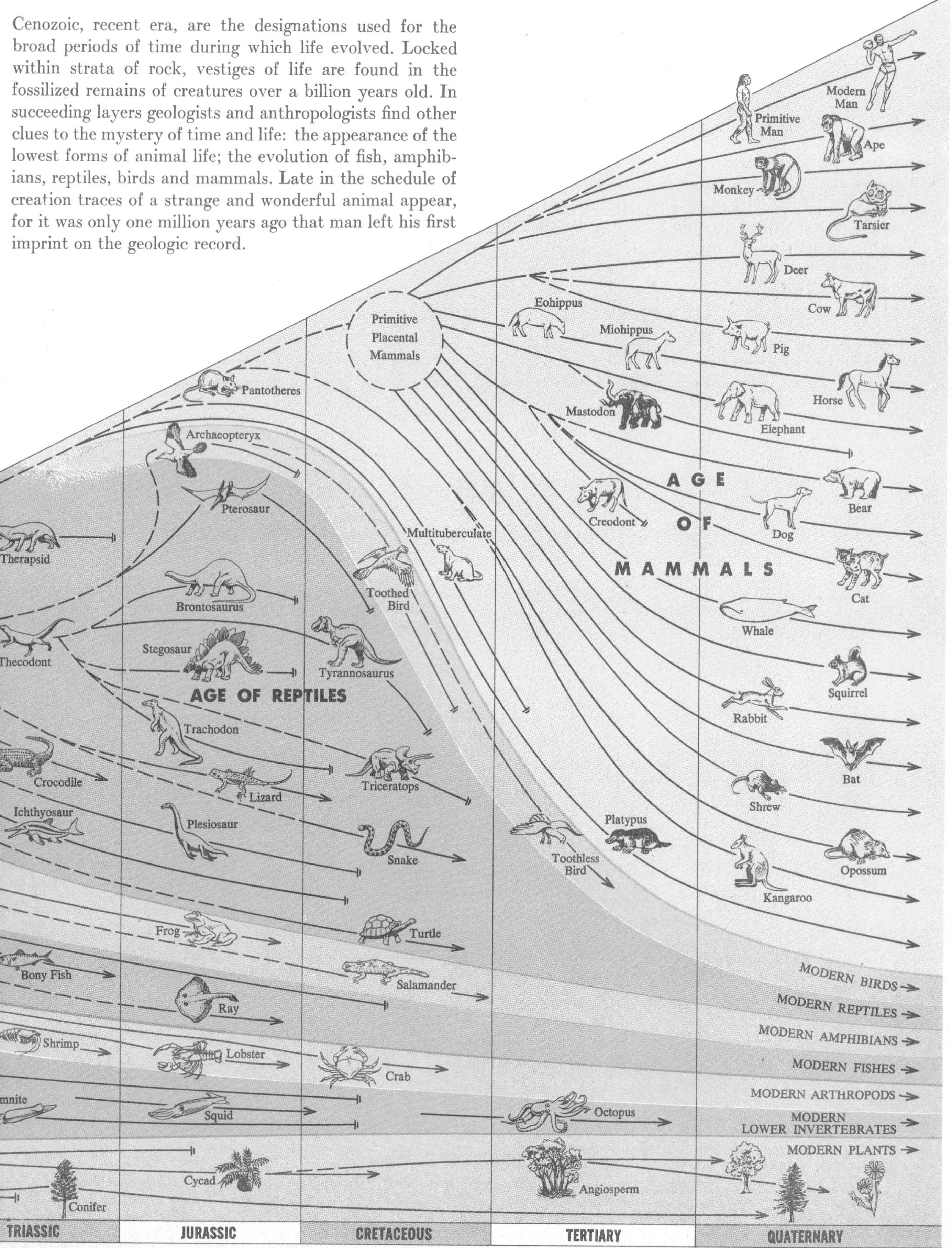

LIFE SUPPORT CYCLES

With an intuition clearly beyond their scientific knowledge, the ancients of India developed a theory of reincarnation which, in some philosophic ways, parallels what science has learned of the workings of the biosphere. In the remarkable thrift of nature nothing is lost — in tremendous complex cycles atoms from the first life on earth still move through the biosphere.

The miracle of energy is constantly performed in the cycles of the "life-giving" elements. Carbon, hydrogen, oxygen, nitrogen, sulfur and phosphorus act together to produce all living matter. While many other elements such as calcium, iodine and iron are also found in living things, they are not absolute essentials in all cases. Carbon, hydrogen and oxygen are vital for photosynthesis and are the components of the basic food substances — carbohydrates and fats. Carbon, in its common gaseous form, carbon dioxide, is absorbed by green plants and triggers the production of carbohydrate compounds by reacting with molecules of water.

Some "energy" is stored within the plant in the form of new tissue; other "energy," in the form of oxygen is released into the air to be used by other organisms. The seemingly inexhaustible supply of carbon dioxide available for use is replenished in the atmosphere through the respiration of all living things, and in the soil as bacteria and fungi break down plant and animal cells,

Nitrogen, sulfur and phosphorus are essential to animals and plants for the production and maintenance of protein. Nitrogen, with carbon, hydrogen and oxygen, is used for the growth and repair of tissue. Sulfur acts as a "stiffening" agent in all protein. To perform their functions proteins must be folded and shaped in a particular way, and their structure is maintained by bonds between sulfur atoms. While phosphorus is not a constituent of protein,

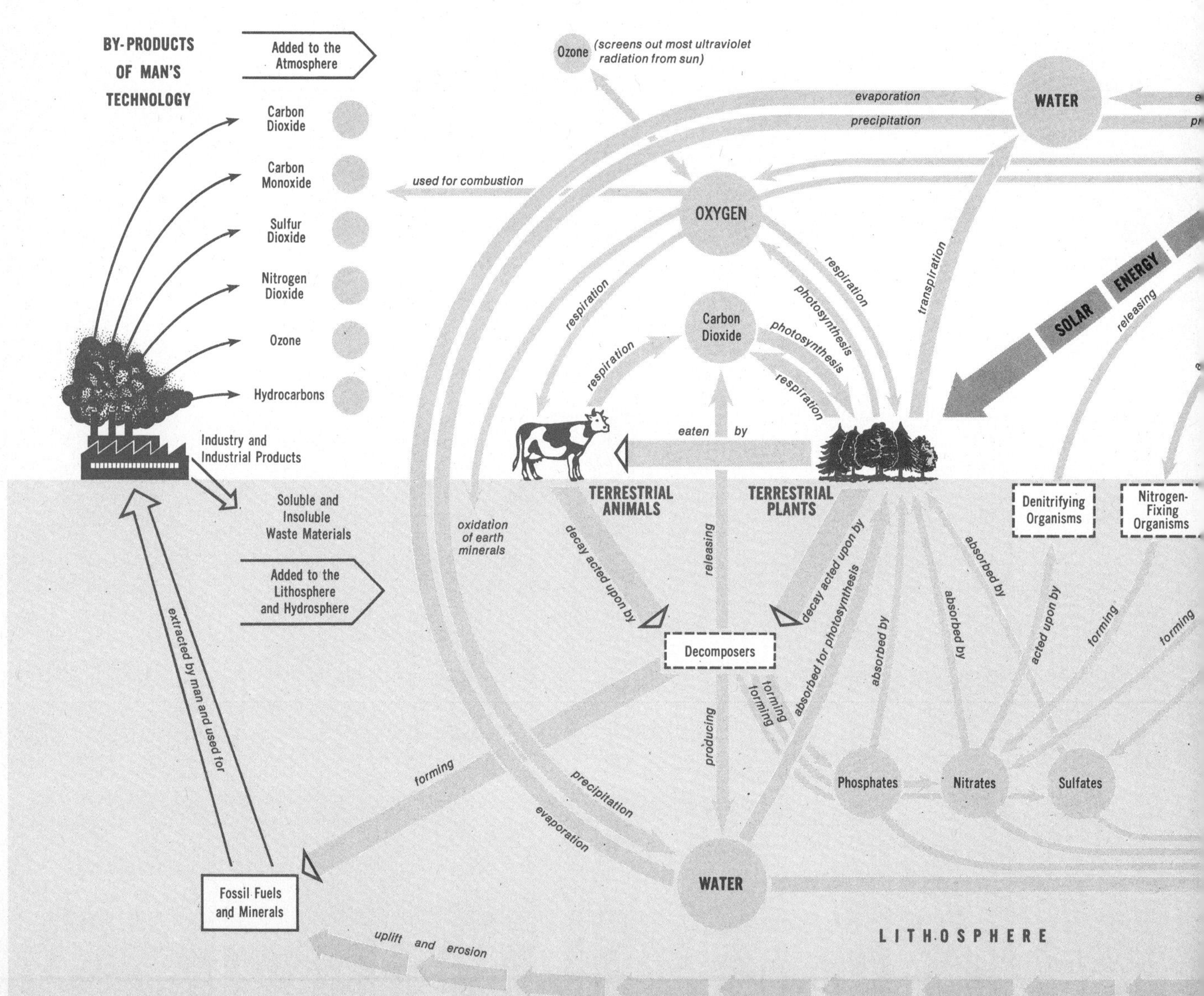

no protein can be made without it. Special phosphate compounds are the "fuel" for all biochemical work within the cell.

Although about four-fifths of the atmosphere is nitrogen, higher forms of life cannot make use of it in its "free" state and must absorb it at one or more points in its biospheric cycle. The decomposers — bacteria and fungi — act on waste matter, breaking down complex compounds into simpler usable forms including nitrogen. Some nitrogen-fixing bacteria are able to utilize atmospheric nitrogen in their own metabolism, while others convert it to those nitrogen-enriched substances necessary for all plant growth.

In nature, no part is greater than the whole and almost every element is dependent on another for some essential part of its cycle. Water, which is incorporated into every organism, is essential in the formation of free oxygen which in turn sustains the life of that organism. Water is also the principal "carrier" in the cycling of all elements. When it evaporates, water returns certain elements to the atmosphere; when it seeps through the soil on its return to the sea, water distributes nutrients to plant roots.

Carbon monoxide, sulfur and nitrogen oxides, hydrocarbons — by-products of man's industry — are being injected into the biosphere in ever-increasing amounts. There, as the "new compounds," they must in some way co-exist with the life-support cycles established throughout millions of years of evolution. Their compatability with these cycles and the organisms they nurture will determine the future of life on our planet.

Already man has learned one thing. Although the question of reincarnation or any form of life after death remains unanswered for many, science has proved that there is no natural end to the raw materials of nature or to the "new compounds" man has made from them.

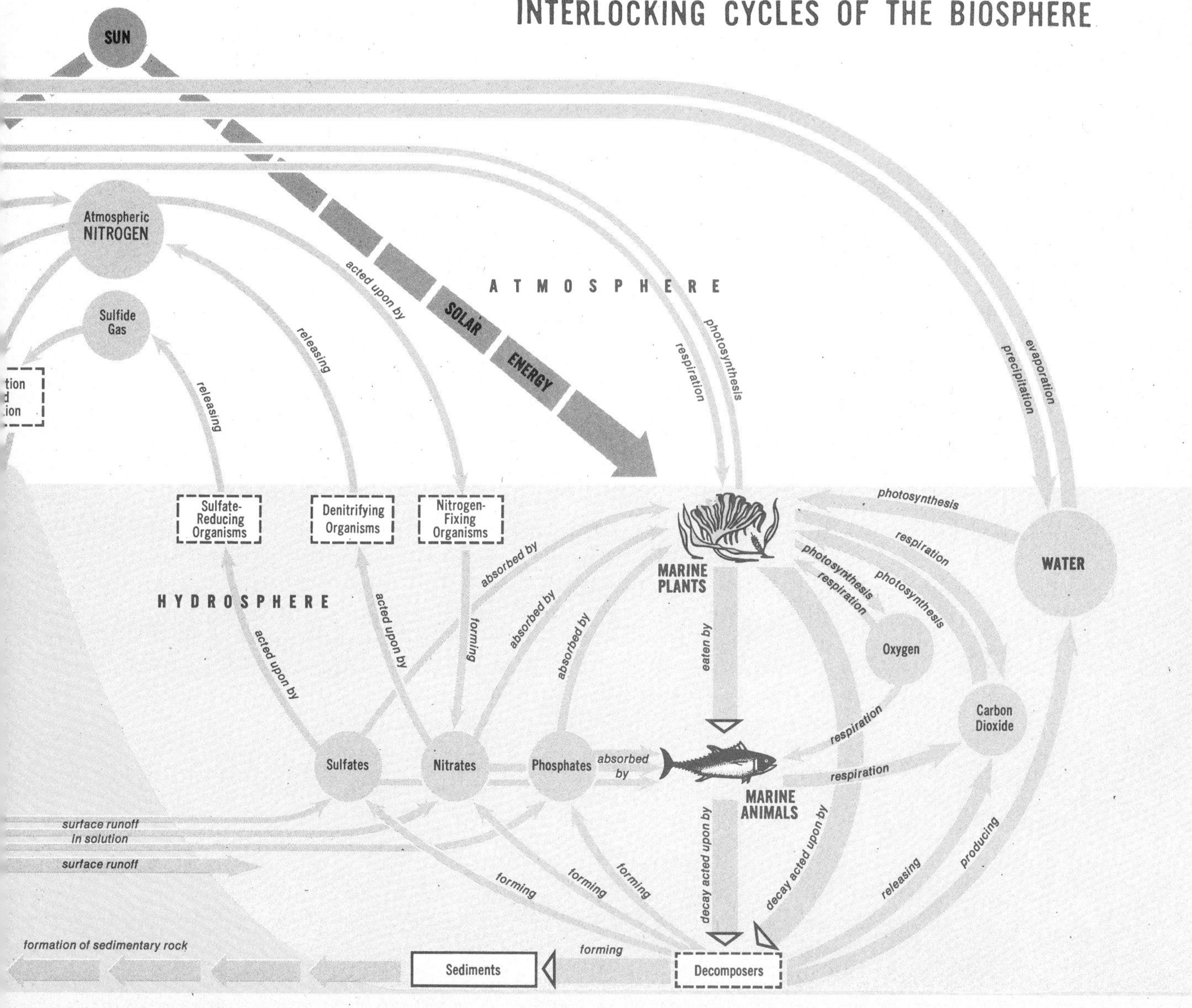

MAN'S IMPACT UPON NATURE

Since he could think man has been at war with death. He has fought his battles against destruction with science and technology as his weapons, virtually eliminating his own annihilation by predatory animals and from diseases such as leprosy, tuberculosis and diphtheria. He has walked into many valleys of death to fight malaria and yellow fever, and he has resolved that each year more of his own kind will live to finish out their threescore years and ten.

However, the victory over nature, which had balanced population with food supply and space, is bitter, for the population has "exploded" leaving man with the seemingly insolvable problem of providing more food and space for himself or reducing his numbers by starvation or by war.

Man outsmarted himself in many ways as he worked toward creating a more perfect world for himself without understanding that natural laws go beyond human manipulation. He has destroyed forests and meadows, polluted the water and air, eliminated organisms that tried to share his bread. However, he has yet to learn to recreate the wood and brush or the interdependent communities of bacteria, insects and animals that he learned — too late — enrich the air, the soil and the water and without which he cannot function.

Modern man knows how to manufacture "miraculous" materials to work for his pleasure or his seemingly insatiable needs, but the sophistications of technology have yet to control effectively the by-products. These new materials, still subject to the order of nature's cycles penetrate the biosphere and eventually come to roost in his own vulnerable body.

New battles are being fought throughout the world and new standards bearing the slogans of ecology float in the "unsafe" air. It is somehow ironic to find that many people now believe that man has been fighting the wrong fight in his gigantic struggle with nature. That, after all, nature never was his enemy.

Man cannot turn back to his beginnings when he lived with, and not against, the natural world. But a compromise between technology and nature must take place for our "plundered planet" cries out for the day of reckoning.

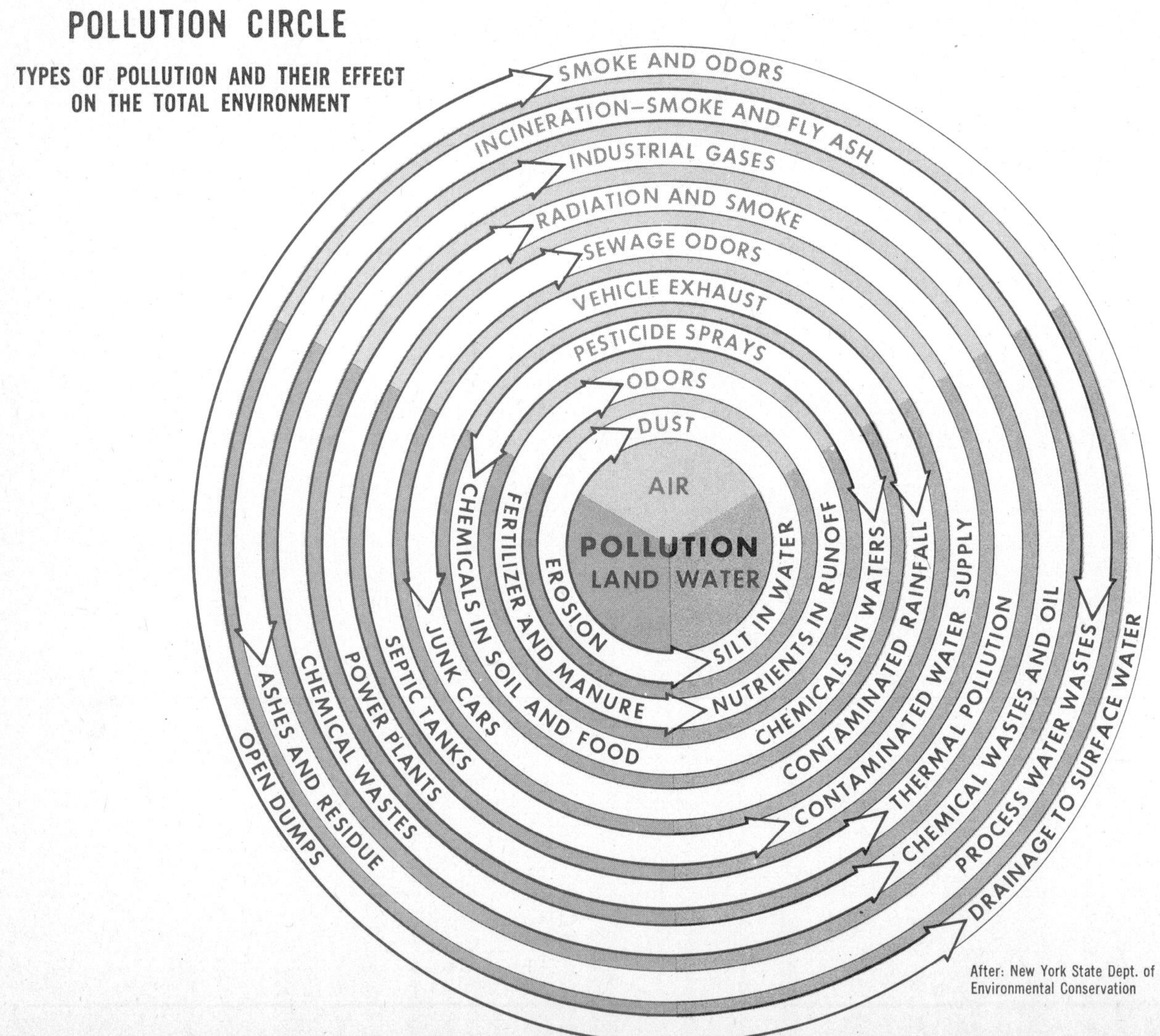

WORLD HISTORY SECTION

CONTENTS

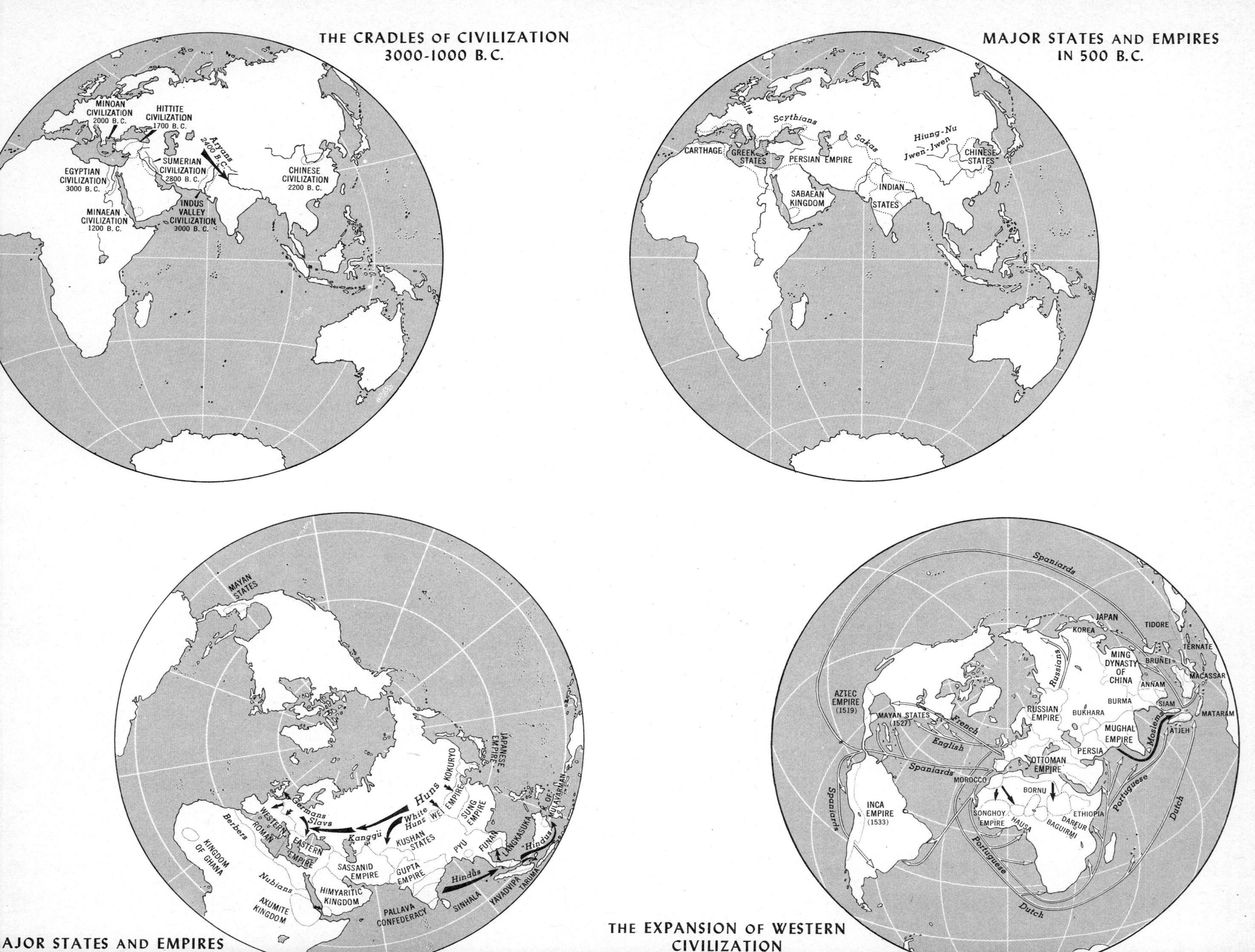
THE CRADLES OF CIVILIZATION
3000-1000 B.C.
MINOAN CIVILIZATION 2000 B.C.
HITTITE CIVILIZATION 1700 B.C.
Aryans 2400 B.C.
EGYPTIAN CIVILIZATION 3000 B.C.
SUMERIAN CIVILIZATION 2800 B.C.
CHINESE CIVILIZATION 2200 B.C.
MINAEAN CIVILIZATION 1200 B.C.
INDUS VALLEY CIVILIZATION 3000 B.C.
MAJOR STATES AND EMPIRES
IN 500 B.C.
Celts
Scythians
Sakas
Hiung-Nu
Jwen-Jwen
CARTHAGE
GREEK STATES
PERSIAN EMPIRE
CHINESE STATES
SABAEAN KINGDOM
INDIAN STATES
MAJOR STATES AND EMPIRES
MAYAN STATES
Huns
KOKURYO
JAPANESE EMPIRE
Germans
Slavs
WESTERN ROMAN EMPIRE
EASTERN EMPIRE
White Huns
WEI EMPIRE
SUNG EMPIRE
Berbers
Kanggü
KUSHAN STATES
PYU
FUNAN
LANGKASUKA
K. OF MULAVARMAN
Hindus
KINGDOM OF GHANA
Nubians
SASSANID EMPIRE
GUPTA EMPIRE
HIMYARITIC KINGDOM
AXUMITE KINGDOM
PALLAVA CONFEDERACY
SINHALA
YAVADVIPA
TARUMA
THE EXPANSION OF WESTERN
CIVILIZATION
Spaniards
JAPAN
KOREA
TIDORE
TERNATE
Russians
MING DYNASTY OF CHINA
BRUNEI
MACASSAR
ANNAM
AZTEC EMPIRE (1519)
BURMA
SIAM
MATARAM
MAYAN STATES (1527)
RUSSIAN EMPIRE
BUKHARA
French
MUGHAL EMPIRE
Moslems
ATJEH
English
PERSIA
OTTOMAN EMPIRE
Spaniards
MOROCCO
BORNU
Portuguese
INCA EMPIRE (1533)
SONGHOY EMPIRE
HAUSA
ETHIOPIA
DARFUR
BAGUIRMI
Dutch
Portuguese
Dutch

ANCIENT SEMITIC WORLD
Copyright by C. S. HAMMOND & Co., N. Y.
Scale of Miles
0 100 200 300 400
Black Sea
Caspian Sea
ASIA MINOR
Mt. Ararat
Hittite Kingdom
Lycia
Cilicia
Carchemish
Mitanni
Haran
Nineveh
Assyria
Asshur
Media
Hatti
Kittim (Cyprus)
Arvad
Amurru
Hamath
ARAM (Syria)
Naharina
Mediterranean Sea
Phoenicia
Sidon
Damascus
Tyre
Canaan
Euphrates R.
Akkad
Tigris R.
Elam
Susa
Babylon
BABYLONIA
Sumer
Ammon
Jerusalem
Moab
Ur
Chaldea
Persian Gulf
Memphis
Mizraim
Nile R.
Mt. Sinai
ARABIA
EGYPT
Pathros (Upper Egypt)
Arabian Desert
Thebes
Red Sea
Cush
Ethiopia

CANAAN BEFORE THE CONQUEST
Copyright by C. S. HAMMOND & Co., N. Y.
Scale of Miles
0 10 20 30 40
Capitals
HITTITE EMPIRE
Damascus
Sidon
Sidonians (Phoenicians)
MOUNT LEBANON
Leontes R.
MT. HERMON
Tyre
Laish (Dan)
BASHAN (KINGDOM OF OG)
Kedesh
Hazor
Merom
Accho
Sea of Chinnereth
Ashtaroth
Mt. Tabor
Yarmuk R.
Edrei
Kishon R.
MT. CARMEL
Canaanites
Dor
Megiddo
Beth-shan
Dothan
Mahanaim
Plain of Sharon
The Great Sea (Mediterranean Sea)
Shechem
Mt. Ebal
Mt. Gerizim
Jordan
Succoth
Penuel
Jabbok R.
Joppa
Hivites
Bethel
Ai
Jericho
River
Gilgal
Rabbath-ammon
Amorites
KINGDOM OF SIHON
Heshbon
Mt. Nebo
Medeba
Ekron
Jebusites
Jerusalem (Jebus)
Bethlehem
Ashdod
Ashkelon
CANAAN
Lachish
Hebron
Hittites
Salt Sea (Dead Sea)
Dibon
AMMON
Gaza
Eglon
Debir
Gerar
Arnon R.
Raphia
Besor
Beer-sheba
Arad
Kenites
Kir-moab
MOAB
Amalekites
Rehoboth
Zoar
Zered R.
River of Egypt
Wilderness of Zin
Arabah
EDOM
MT. SEIR
Bozrah
Kadesh-barnea

CANAAN AS DIVIDED AMONG THE TWELVE TRIBES
c. 1200-1020 B.C.
Copyright by C. S. HAMMOND & Co., N. Y.
Scale of Miles
0 10 20 30 40
Sidon
Sidonians (Phoenicians)
MOUNT LEBANON
Leontes R.
Damascus
Zarephath
MT. HERMON
Tyre
Kanah
DAN
Laish (Dan)
ASHER
NAPHTALI
Kedesh
Bashan
Hazor
MANASSEH
Accho
Cabul
Sea of Chinnereth
Ashtaroth
ZEBULUN
Kishon R.
MT. CARMEL
Hammath
Aphek
Mt. Tabor
Yarmuk R.
Edrei
Dor
Megiddo
Shunem
ISSACHAR
Ramoth-gilead
Taanach
Jezreel
Beth-shan
The Great Sea (Mediterranean Sea)
Plain of Sharon
MANASSEH
Mahanaim
GAD
Mt. Ebal
Shechem
Mt. Gerizim
Jordan
Succoth
Jabbok R.
Penuel
AMMON
Kanah
Shiloh
GILEAD
Joppa (Japho)
Ajalon
EPHRAIM
River
Jazer
Rabbath-ammon
Beth-horon
Bethel
DAN
Jabneel
Gibeon
Jericho
Gezer
BENJAMIN
Gilgal
Heshbon
Mt. Nebo
Ashdod
Jerusalem (Jebus)
Medeba
Philistines
Libnah
Beth-shemesh
Bethlehem
Ashkelon
JUDAH
REUBEN
Gaza
Lachish
Hebron
Salt Sea (Dead Sea)
Aroer
Caleb
En-gedi
Arnon R.
Gerar
Ziklag
Raphia
Cherethites
Beer-sheba
Kenites
MOAB
Hormah
SIMEON
Rehoboth
Zered R.
River of Egypt
Wilderness of Zin
EDOM

THE KINGDOMS OF ISRAEL AND JUDAH
c. 925-842 B.C.
Copyright by C. S. HAMMOND & Co., N. Y.
Scale of Miles
0 10 20 30 40
Capitals
Sidon
MOUNT LEBANON
Leontes R.
Damascus
Zarephath
MT. HERMON
PHOENICIA
ARAM
Syrians
Tyre
Ijon
Dan
Kedesh
Hazor
Accho
Chinnereth
GESHUR
Cabul
Sea of Chinnereth
Kishon R.
MT. CARMEL
Hammath
Aphek
Bashan
Mt. Tabor
Yarmuk R.
Edrei
Dor
Megiddo
Shunem
Jezreel
Ramoth-gilead
Taanach
Beth-shan
ISRAEL
The Great Sea (Mediterranean Sea)
Plain of Sharon
Jordan
GILEAD
Samaria
Mt. Ebal
Mt. Gerizim
Shechem
Penuel
Jabbok R.
AMMON
Shiloh
Joppa
River
Beth-horon
Bethel
Jericho
Rabbath-ammon
Jabneel
Gezer
Gilgal
PHILISTIA
Ekron
Jerusalem
Heshbon
Mt. Nebo
Ashdod
Bethlehem
Medeba
Ashkelon
JUDAH
Lachish
Hebron
Wilderness of Judah
Salt Sea (Dead Sea)
Aroer
MOAB
Gaza
Arnon R.
Gerar
Raphia
Beer-sheba
Kir-moab
Valley of Salt
Zered R.
River of Egypt
EDOM

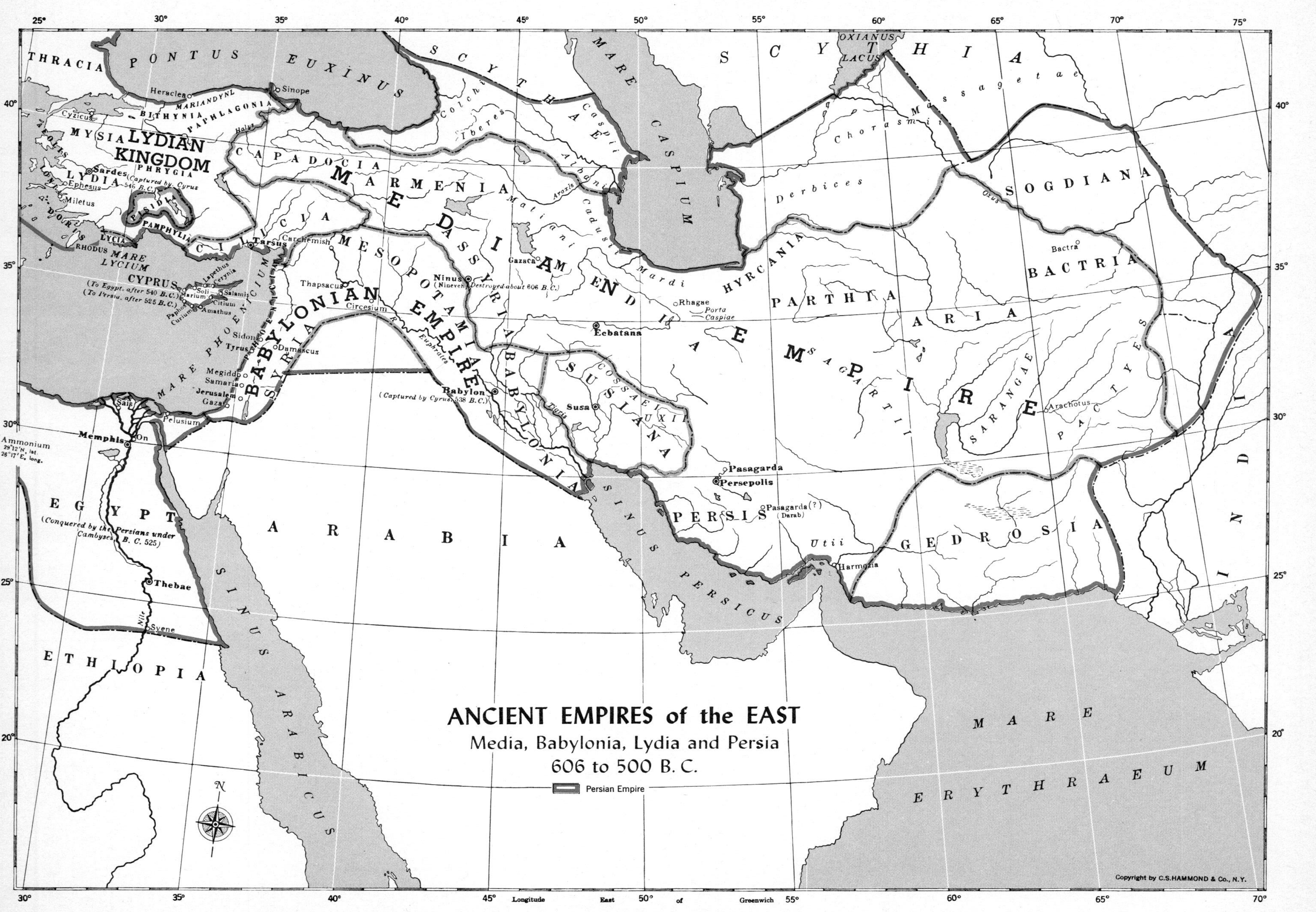
ANCIENT EMPIRES of the EAST
Media, Babylonia, Lydia and Persia
606 to 500 B.C.
Persian Empire
THRACIA
PONTUS EUXINUS
LYDIAN KINGDOM
MYSIA
LYDIA
PHRYGIA
BITHYNIA
PAPHLAGONIA
MARIANDYNI
Heraclea
Sinope
Cyzicus
Sardes (Captured by Cyrus 546 B.C.)
Ephesus
Miletus
PAMPHYLIA
LYCIA
RHODUS
MARE LYCIUM
CYPRUS
(To Egypt, after 540 B.C.)
(To Persia, after 525 B.C.)
Salamis
Citium
Amathus
CAPADOCIA
CILICIA
Tarsus
Carchemish
ARMENIA
MEDIAN EMPIRE
ASSYRIA
MESOPOTAMIA
BABYLONIAN EMPIRE
BABYLONIA
SYRIA
PHOENICIA
Thapsacus
Circesium
Ninus (Nineveh) Destroyed about 606 B.C.
Babylon (Captured by Cyrus, 538 B.C.)
Euphrates
Tigris
Damascus
Sidon
Tyrus
Megiddo
Samaria
Jerusalem
Gaza
Pelusium
Sais
Memphis
On
Ammonium 29°12' N. lat. 26°17' E. long.
EGYPT (Conquered by the Persians under Cambyses, B.C. 525)
Thebae
Syene
Nile
ETHIOPIA
ARABIA
SINUS ARABICUS
MARE PHOENICIUM
SCYTHAE
SCYTHIA
Colchi
Iberes
Caspii
Albani
Cadusii
Matiani
Araxis
MARE CASPIUM
Gazaca
Ecbatana
Mardi
Rhagae
Porta Caspiae
HYRCANIA
PARTHIA
ARIA
Derbices
Chorasmii
Massagetae
OXIANUS LACUS
SOGDIANA
BACTRIA
Bactra
Oxus
PERSIAN EMPIRE
SAGARTII
SARANGAE
PACTYES
Arachotus
SUSIANA
COSSAEI
UXII
Susa
Pasagarda
Persepolis
Pasagarda (?) (Darab)
PERSIS
Utii
Harmozia
GEDROSIA
INDI
SINUS PERSICUS
MARE ERYTHRAEUM
Longitude East of Greenwich

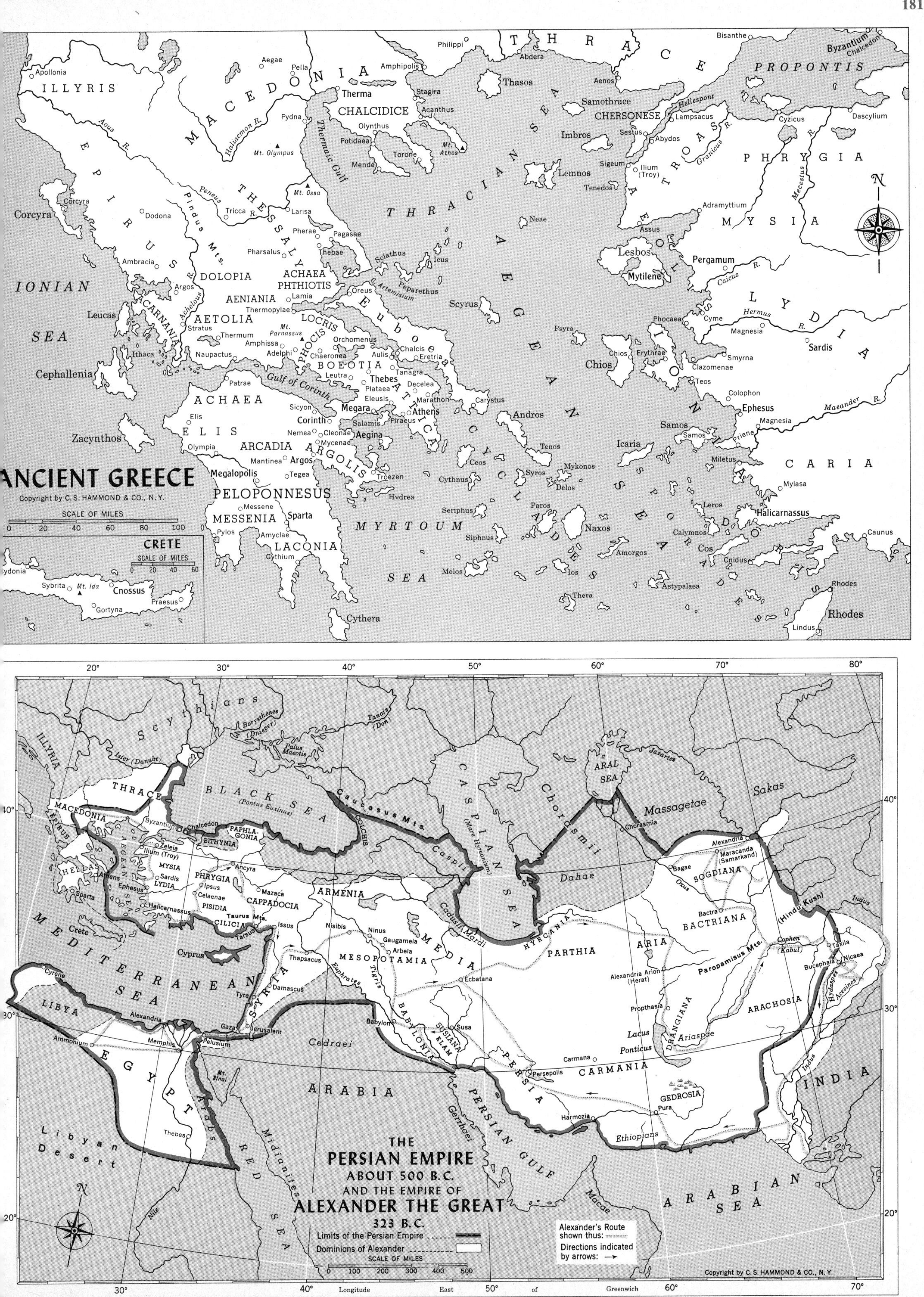
ANCIENT GREECE
Copyright by C. S. HAMMOND & CO., N. Y.
SCALE OF MILES
0 20 40 60 80 100
CRETE
SCALE OF MILES
0 20 40 60
Sybrita
Mt. Ida
Cnossus
Praesus
Gortyna
ILLYRIS
Apollonia
MACEDONIA
Aegae
Pella
Amphipolis
Philippi
THRACE
Abdera
Bisanthe
Byzantium
Chalcedon
PROPONTIS
Thasos
Aenos
Samothrace
CHERSONESE
Hellespont
Lampsacus
Cyzicus
Dascylium
Therma
Stagira
Acanthus
CHALCIDICE
Olynthus
Potidaea
Torone
Mende
Mt. Athos
Thermaic Gulf
Pydna
Haliacmon R.
Mt. Olympus
Aous R.
EPIRUS
Corcyra
Dodona
Ambracia
THESSALY
Peneus
Tricca
Larisa
Mt. Ossa
Pindus Mts.
Pherae
Pagasae
Pharsalus
Thebae
Sciathus
Icus
Peparethus
Artemisium
DOLOPIA
ACHAEA PHTHIOTIS
Lamia
Oreus
AENIANIA
Thermopylae
Argos
Achelous
ACARNANIA
AETOLIA
Stratus
Thermum
LOCRIS
PHOCIS
Mt. Parnassus
Amphissa
Delphi
Orchomenus
Chaeronea
BOEOTIA
Aulis
Chalcis
Eretria
Euboea
Leuctra
Thebes
Tanagra
Decelea
Plataea
Eleusis
Marathon
Carystus
ATTICA
Athens
Piraeus
Megara
Salamis
Aegina
IONIAN SEA
Leucas
Ithaca
Cephallenia
Zacynthos
Naupactus
Patrae
Gulf of Corinth
ACHAEA
ELIS
Elis
Olympia
Sicyon
Corinth
Nemea
Cleonae
Mycenae
ARCADIA
ARGOLIS
Mantinea
Argos
Tegea
Troezen
Hydrea
Megalopolis
PELOPONNESUS
Messene
MESSENIA
Sparta
Pylos
Amyclae
LACONIA
Gythium
Cythera
MYRTOUM SEA
THRACIAN SEA
AEGEAN SEA
Imbros
Lemnos
Sestus
Abydos
Sigeum
Ilium (Troy)
Tenedos
TROAS
Granicus R.
Neae
Scyrus
PHRYGIA
Macestus R.
Adramyttium
MYSIA
Assus
Lesbos
Mytilene
AEOLIS
Pergamum
Caicus R.
LYDIA
Hermus R.
Phocaea
Cyme
Magnesia
Sardis
Psyra
Chios
Erythrae
Smyrna
Clazomenae
Teos
Colophon
Ephesus
IONIA
Maeander R.
Magnesia
Samos
Priene
Andros
Icaria
Tenos
Ceos
Mykonos
Syros
Delos
Cythnus
CYCLADES
Miletus
CARIA
Mylasa
Seriphus
Paros
Naxos
Siphnus
Melos
Ios
Amorgos
Thera
Astypalaea
SPORADES
Leros
Calymnos
Halicarnassus
Cos
DORIS
Cnidus
Caunus
Rhodes
Lindus
THE PERSIAN EMPIRE ABOUT 500 B.C. AND THE EMPIRE OF ALEXANDER THE GREAT 323 B.C.
Limits of the Persian Empire
Dominions of Alexander
SCALE OF MILES
0 100 200 300 400 500
Alexander's Route shown thus:
Directions indicated by arrows:
Copyright by C. S. HAMMOND & CO., N. Y.
Longitude East of Greenwich
20° 30° 40° 50° 60° 70° 80°
Scythians
Borysthenes (Dnieper)
Tanais (Don)
Palus Maeotis
Ister (Danube)
ILLYRIA
THRACE
MACEDONIA
EPIRUS
BLACK SEA (Pontus Euxinus)
Caucasus Mts.
COLCHIS
CASPIAN SEA (Mare Hyrcanium)
Caspii
ARAL SEA
Jaxartes
Chorasmii
Massagetae
Sakas
Chorasmia
Byzantium
Chalcedon
PAPHLAGONIA
BITHYNIA
Zeleia
Ilium (Troy)
MYSIA
Sardis
LYDIA
HELLAS
Athens
Sparta
Ephesus
AEGEAN SEA
Ancyra
PHRYGIA
Ipsus
Celaenae
PISIDIA
Mazaca
CAPPADOCIA
ARMENIA
Halicarnassus
Taurus Mts.
CILICIA
Tarsus
Issus
Crete
MEDITERRANEAN SEA
Cyprus
Cyrene
LIBYA
Alexandria
Ammonium
Memphis
Pelusium
EGYPT
Mt. Sinai
Thebes
Arabs
Nile
Libyan Desert
RED SEA
Midianites
Tyre
Damascus
Gaza
Jerusalem
SYRIA
Thapsacus
Nisibis
Ninus
Gaugamela
Arbela
MESOPOTAMIA
Euphrates
Tigris
Babylon
BABYLONIA
SUSIANA
ELAM
Susa
MEDIA
Ecbatana
Cadusii
Mardi
HYRCANIA
Dahae
PARTHIA
Cedraei
ARABIA
Gerrhaei
PERSIAN GULF
Macae
PERSIA
Persepolis
CARMANIA
Carmana
Harmozia
GEDROSIA
Pura
Ethiopians
Lacus Ponticus
DRANGIANA
Ariaspae
Propthasia
Alexandria Arion (Herat)
ARIA
Bagae
Oxus
SOGDIANA
Alexandria
Maracanda (Samarkand)
Bactra
BACTRIANA
Paropamisus Mts.
Cophen (Kabul)
(Hindu Kush)
Taxila
Bucephala
Nicaea
Hydaspes
Acesines
Indus
ARACHOSIA
INDIA
ARABIAN SEA

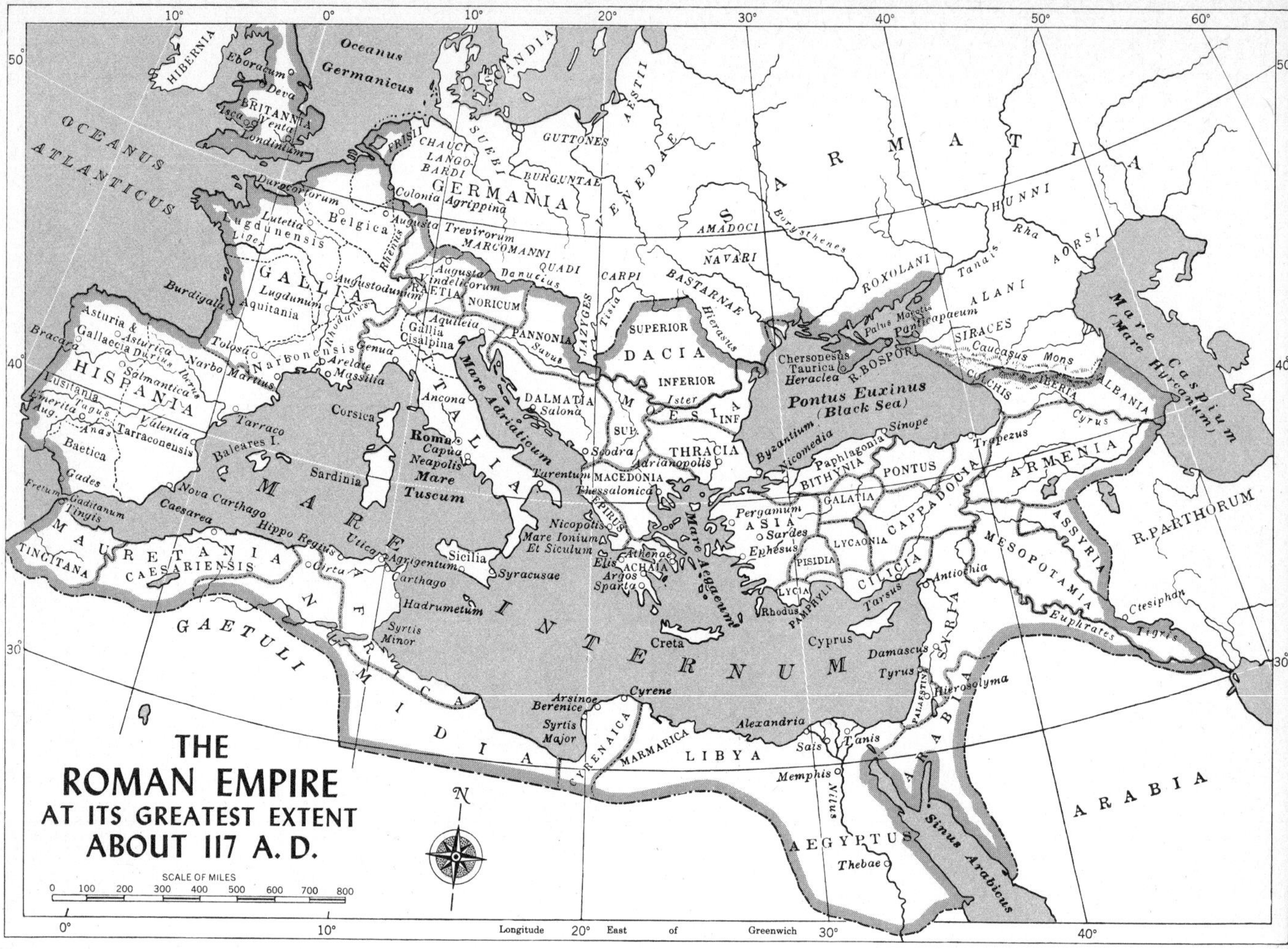

THE
ROMAN EMPIRE
AT ITS GREATEST EXTENT
ABOUT 117 A. D.
SCALE OF MILES
0 100 200 300 400 500 600 700 800
Longitude East of Greenwich
Oceanus Germanicus
OCEANUS ATLANTICUS
HIBERNIA
Eboracum
Deva
BRITANNIA
Venta
Londinium
Durocortorum
Lutetia
Lugdunensis
Liger
Belgica
Augusta Trevirorum
Colonia Agrippina
GERMANIA
FRISII
CHAUCI
LANGOBARDI
SUEBI
GUTTONES
BURGUNTAE
VENEDAE
AESTII
MARCOMANNI
QUADI
GALLIA
Lugdunum
Augustodunum
Aquitania
Burdigala
Narbonensis
Narbo Martius
Tolosa
Arelate
Massilia
Genua
Gallia Cisalpina
Aquileia
RAETIA
NORICUM
PANNONIA
Danuvius
Asturia
Gallaecia
Bracara
HISPANIA
Lusitania
Emerita Aug.
Tagus
Anas
Salmantica
Valentia
Tarraco
Tarraconensis
Baetica
Gades
Baleares I.
Corsica
Sardinia
ITALIA
Roma
Capua
Neapolis
Ancona
Mare Tuscum
Mare Adriaticum
DALMATIA
Salona
Tarentum
Sicilia
Syracusae
MARE INTERNUM
Nova Carthago
Caesarea
Hippo Regius
Utica
Carthago
Cirta
Agrigentum
Hadrumetum
Syrtis Minor
MAURETANIA
TINGITANA
CAESARIENSIS
Tingis
GAETULI
AFRICA
NUMIDIA
Mare Ionium Et Siculum
Nicopolis
EPIRUS
MACEDONIA
Thessalonica
Scodra
THRACIA
Adrianopolis
MOESIA
SUP.
INF.
Ister
DACIA
SUPERIOR
INFERIOR
JAZYGES
CARPI
BASTARNAE
AMADOCI
NAVARI
ROXOLANI
SARMATIA
Borysthenes
HUNNI
Rha
AORSI
ALANI
Tanais
Palus Maeotis
Panticapaeum
SIRACES
Caucasus Mons
Chersonesus Taurica
Heraclea
R. BOSPORI
Pontus Euxinus (Black Sea)
Byzantium
Nicomedia
Sinope
Trapezus
Paphlagonia
BITHYNIA
PONTUS
GALATIA
CAPPADOCIA
ARMENIA
COLCHIS
IBERIA
ALBANIA
Cyrus
Mare Caspium (Mare Hyrcanium)
ASIA
Pergamum
Sardes
Ephesus
LYCAONIA
PISIDIA
LYCIA
PAMPHYLIA
CILICIA
Tarsus
Rhodus
Antiochia
SYRIA
MESOPOTAMIA
ASSYRIA
Euphrates
Tigris
Ctesiphon
R. PARTHORUM
Mare Aegaeum
Athenae
ACHAIA
Elis
Argos
Sparta
Creta
Cyprus
Damascus
Tyrus
Hierosolyma
PALAESTINA
Arsinoe
Berenice
Cyrene
Syrtis Major
CYRENAICA
MARMARICA
LIBYA
Alexandria
Sais
Tanis
Memphis
Nilus
AEGYPTUS
Thebae
Sinus Arabicus
ARABIA

EUROPE
BARBARIC MIGRATIONS
IN THE FOURTH AND
FIFTH CENTURIES
Copyright by C. S. HAMMOND & CO., N. Y.
SCALE OF MILES
0 100 200 300 400 500
Goths
Huns
Alans, Suevi, Vandals
Angles, Saxons, Jutes
ATLANTIC OCEAN
NORTH SEA
BALTIC SEA
BLACK SEA
PICTS
SCOTS
BRITONS
BRITAIN
JUTES
ANGLES
SAXONS
5th Cent.
FRANKS
Rhine R.
Turnacum
Remi
BURGUNDIANS
WESTERN
GAUL
ROMAN
Tolosa
Pyrenees
Massilia
Barcino
EMPIRE
SPAIN
VANDALS
SUEVI
ALANS
Carthago Nova
MAURETANIA
NUMIDIA
AFRICA
Carthage
Rome
ITALY
ILLYRICUM
Danube R.
GOTHS
After 150
BURGUNDIANS
VANDALS
SUEVI
HUNS
EAST GOTHS
WEST GOTHS
Attila's Capital?
ALANS
EASTERN
ROMAN
EMPIRE
Constantinople
Athens
Sparta
Crete
Cyprus
MEDITERRANEAN SEA
EGYPT
ORIENS

EUROPE
IN 600
Copyright by C. S. HAMMOND & CO., N. Y.
SCALE OF MILES
0 100 200 300 400 500
ATLANTIC OCEAN
NORTH SEA
BALTIC SEA
BLACK SEA
PICTS
ANGLES
SAXONS
NORSEMEN
SWEDES
DANES
FRISIANS
SAXONS
THURINGIANS
BAVARIANS
AUSTRASIA
NEUSTRIA
FRANKISH
KINGDOMS
Paris
Soissons
Metz
Orleans
Chalon
BRITTANY
AQUITAINE
Toulouse
BURGUNDY
BASQUES
SUEVI
WEST GOTHIC
KINGDOM
Toledo
LOMBARD
KDM.
Pavia
Ravenna
Rome
ADRIATIC SEA
Carthage
AFRICA
EASTERN
ROMAN
EMPIRE
MEDITERRANEAN SEA
BERBERS
GARAMANTES
WESTERN SLAVS
LITHUANIAN PEOPLES
EASTERN SLAVS
FINNISH PEOPLES
Volga R.
ALANS
AVAR KINGDOM
Danube
Viminacium
BULGARS
SOUTHERN SLAVS
Constantinople
ASIA MINOR
KHAZARS
MAGYARS
KDM. OF THE VOLGA BULGARS
SASSANID EMPIRE
LAKHMID KDM.
GHASSANID KDM.
Petra
ARABS

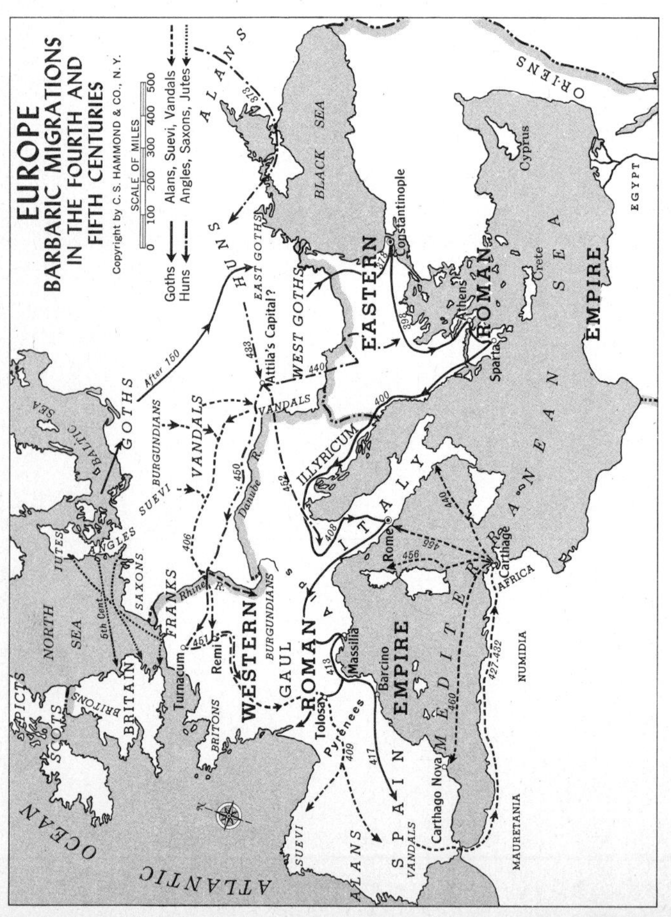

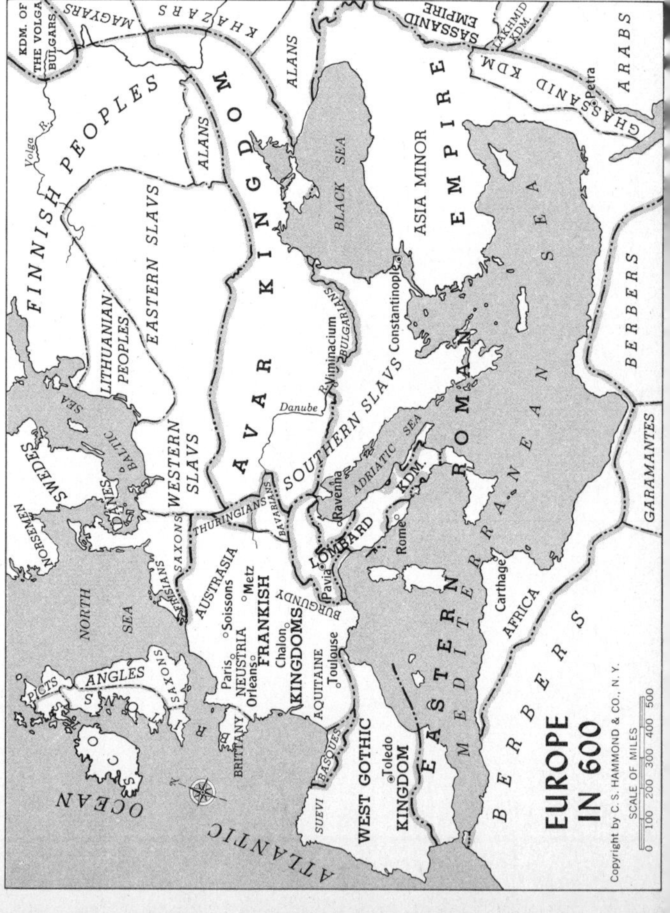

BRITANNIA
about 350 A. D
Showing the
CELTIC TRIBES
and approximately
The 4 Divisions of DIOCLETIAN
SCALE OF MILES
0 20 40 60 80 100
CALEDONIA
Boderiae (Bodotriae) Aestuarium (Firth of Forth)
ANTONINE WALL
DAMNONII
Trimontium
OTADINI
Blatum Bulgium
NOVANTAE
SELGOVAE
HADRIAN'S WALL
Segedunum
Corstopitum
Luguvallium
Uxellodunum
Brocavum
Ituna Aestuarium
Monapia (Mona)
Cataractonium
BRIGANTES
PARISI
Isurium
Bremetennacum
MAXIMA
CAESARIENSIS
Eburacum (York)
SETANTII
Legiolium
Abus (R. Humber)
Mancunium (Manchester)
Danum (Doncaster)
Segelocum
Lindum (Lincoln)
Mona
DRUIDS
Deva (Chester)
CORNAVII
Segontium (Caernarvon)
Causennae
CORITANI
Metaris Aest. The Wash
Branodunum
ORDOVICES
Viroconium (Wroxeter)
BRITANNIA
Ratae (Leicester)
Venonae
Durobrivae
Venta Icenorum (Caistor)
ICENI
PRIMA
CATUVELLAUNI
CASSII
Bravonium (Leintwardine)
BRITANNIA
SECUNDA
DEMETAE
Maridunum
SILURES
Isca
Nidum
DOBUNI
Glevum (Gloucester)
Verulamium
FLAVIA
TRINOBANTES
Chesterford
Camulodunum (Colchester)
Venta Silurum
Corinium
CAESARIENSIS
Londinium
Tanatis
Rutupiae
Sabrinae Aest.
ATREBATII
Calleva
Tamesis
Aquae Solis (Bath)
BELGAE
Venta Belgarum (Winchester)
REGNI
CANTII
Durovernum (Canterbury)
Dubris (Dover)
Sorbiodunum (Salisbury)
Clausentum
Lemanis (Lympne)
Fretum Gallicum
OCEANUS
VERGIONIUS
Isca Dumnoniorum (Exeter)
DUMNONII
DUROTRIGES
Durnovaria (Dorchester)
Regnum (Chichester)
Magnus Portus
Vectis I.
OCEANUS HIBERNICUS
OCEANUS GERMANICUS
OCEANUS BRITANNICUS
HIBERNIA
GALLIA
N
Longitude West of Greenwich

ENGLISH CONQUEST
From 450 to the End of the 6th Century
Showing the Settlements of the Jutes,
Saxons and Angles. Also the Sections
of the Country which were retained by
the Britons (Celtic Tribes).
SCALE OF MILES
0 20 40 60 80 100
Iona
SCOTS
PICTS
Forth
Alcluyd
Tweed
Melrose
Lindisfarne (Holy I.)
Bamborough (Bebbanburh)
BERNICIA
STRATHCLYDE
Solway
Caerleol
ANGLES
OCEANUS GERMANICUS
(German Ocean)
CUMBRIA
DEIRA
Usa
York (Eoforwic)
OCEANUS HIBERNICUS (Irish Sea)
SOUTH-UMBRIANS
Humbra (Humber)
LINDISWARAS
Lindum (Lincoln)
MERCIANS
Treonta
The Wash
Chester
Branodunum (Brancaster)
Northfolc
Uriconium (Wroxeter)
MIDDLE ANGLES
Venta Icenorum (Caistor)
EAST ANGLES
CAMBRIA
NORTH WEALAS
Suthfolc
Stour
Menevia (St. David)
Gleawanceaster (Gloucester)
Cirenceaster
SAXONS
Camulodunum (Colchester)
Deorham
London
EAST SAXONS
Richborough
Thanet I.
Bathanceaster (Bath)
Taemese
Aegelesford
Sabrina or Suefern
WEST SAXONS
Andredsweald
JUTES
Cantwarabyrig (Canterbury)
SOUTH SAXONS
Lynne
Wintanceaster (Winchester)
Cissanceaster (Chichester)
Cerdicesford (Charford)
Anderida (Pevensey)
WESTWEALAS
BRITONS
DAMNONIA
Wihtgara Burh (Wight)
OCEANUS BRITANNICUS
(English Channel)
GAUL
© C. S. HAMMOND & Co., N.Y.
Longitude West of Greenwich

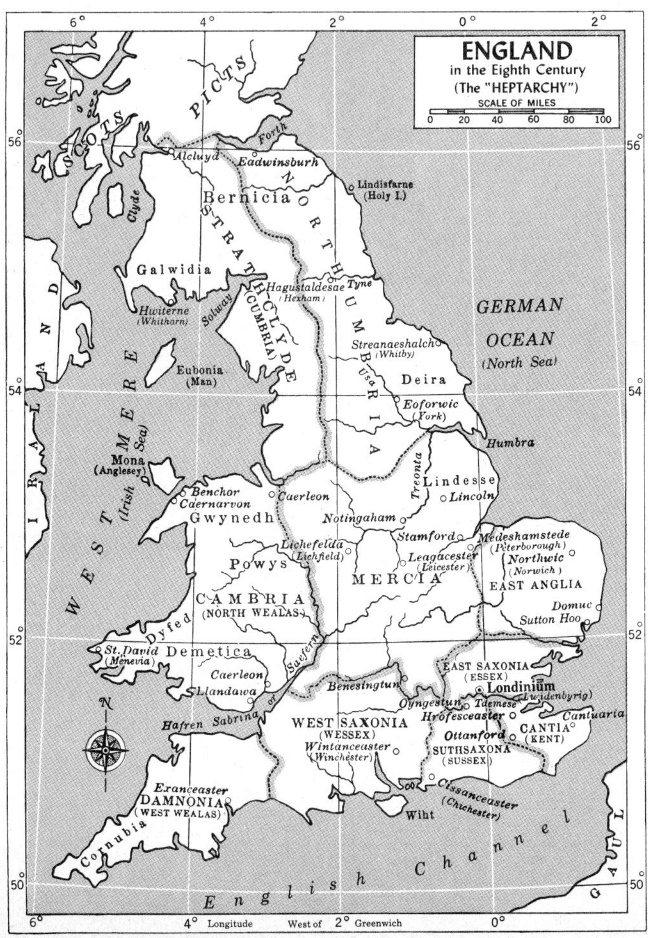
ENGLAND
in the Eighth Century
(The "HEPTARCHY")
SCALE OF MILES
0 20 40 60 80 100
SCOTS
PICTS
Forth
Alcluyd
Eadwinsburh
Lindisfarne (Holy I.)
Clyde
Bernicia
NORTHUMBRIA
STRATCLYDE (CUMBRIA)
Galwidia
Hwiterne (Whithorn)
Solway
Hagustaldesae (Hexham)
Tyne
GERMAN OCEAN
(North Sea)
Streanaeshalch (Whitby)
Eubonia (Man)
Usa
Deira
Eoforwic (York)
WESTERE MERE (Irish Sea)
IRALAND
Humbra
Mona (Anglesey)
Treonta
Lindesse
Lincoln
Benchor
Caernarvon
Gwynedh
Caerleon
Notingaham
Stamford
Medeshamstede (Peterborough)
Lichefelda (Lichfield)
Leagacester (Leicester)
Northwic (Norwich)
Powys
MERCIA
EAST ANGLIA
CAMBRIA
(NORTH WEALAS)
Domuc
Sutton Hoo
Dyfed
St. David (Menevia)
Demetica
Caerleon
Llandawa
Saefern
EAST SAXONIA (ESSEX)
Benesingtun
Londinium (Lundenbyrig)
Oyngestun
Taemese
Hrofesceaster
Cantuaria
Hafren
Sabrina
WEST SAXONIA (WESSEX)
Wintanceaster (Winchester)
Ottanford
CANTIA (KENT)
SUTHSAXONA (SUSSEX)
Cissanceaster (Chichester)
Exanceaster
DAMNONIA
(WEST WEALAS)
Cornubia
Wiht
English Channel
GAUL
Longitude West of Greenwich

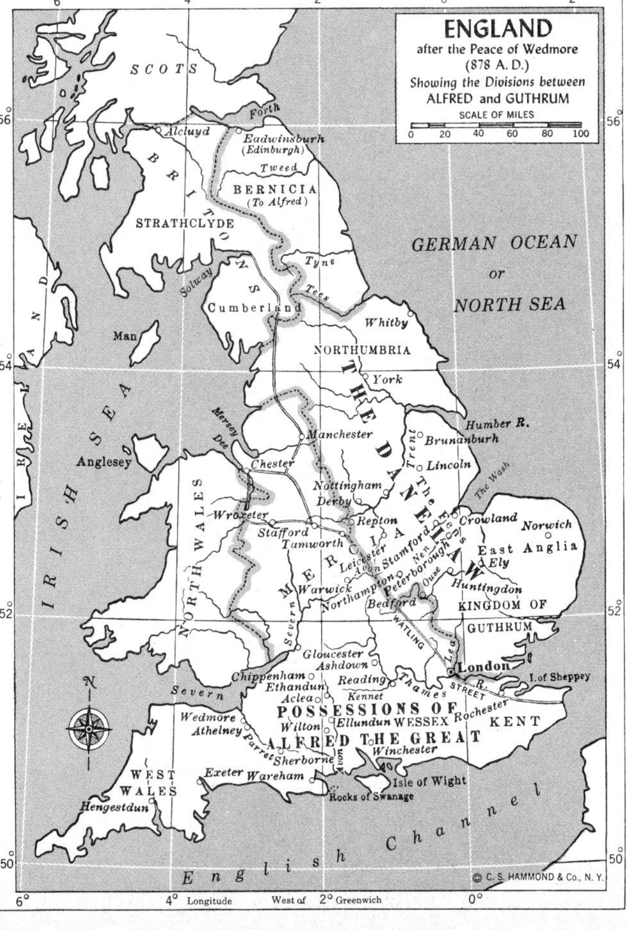
ENGLAND
after the Peace of Wedmore
(878 A.D.)
Showing the Divisions between
ALFRED and GUTHRUM
SCALE OF MILES
0 20 40 60 80 100
SCOTS
Forth
Alcluyd
Eadwinsburh (Edinburgh)
Tweed
BRITONS
BERNICIA
(To Alfred)
STRATHCLYDE
Tyne
GERMAN OCEAN
or
NORTH SEA
Solway
Tees
Cumberland
Whitby
Man
NORTHUMBRIA
THE DANELAW
York
IRELAND
IRISH SEA
Mersey
Dee
Manchester
Humber R.
Brunanburh
Anglesey
Chester
Lincoln
Trent
The Wash
Nottingham
Derby
NORTH WALES
Wroxeter
Repton
Crowland
Norwich
Stafford
Tamworth
MERCIA
Leicester
Stamford
Peterborough
East Anglia
Ely
Warwick
Northampton
Ouse
Huntingdon
Severn
Bedford
KINGDOM OF
GUTHRUM
WATLING
Gloucester
Ashdown
London
STREET
I. of Sheppey
Chippenham
Ethandun
Reading
Thames
Rochester
Severn
Aclea
Kennet
KENT
Wedmore
Athelney
POSSESSIONS OF
ALFRED THE GREAT
Wilton
Ellundun WESSEX
Parret
Sherborne
Winchester
Exeter
Wareham
Isle of Wight
WEST WALES
Rocks of Swanage
Hengestdun
English Channel
© C. S. HAMMOND & Co., N. Y.
Longitude West of Greenwich

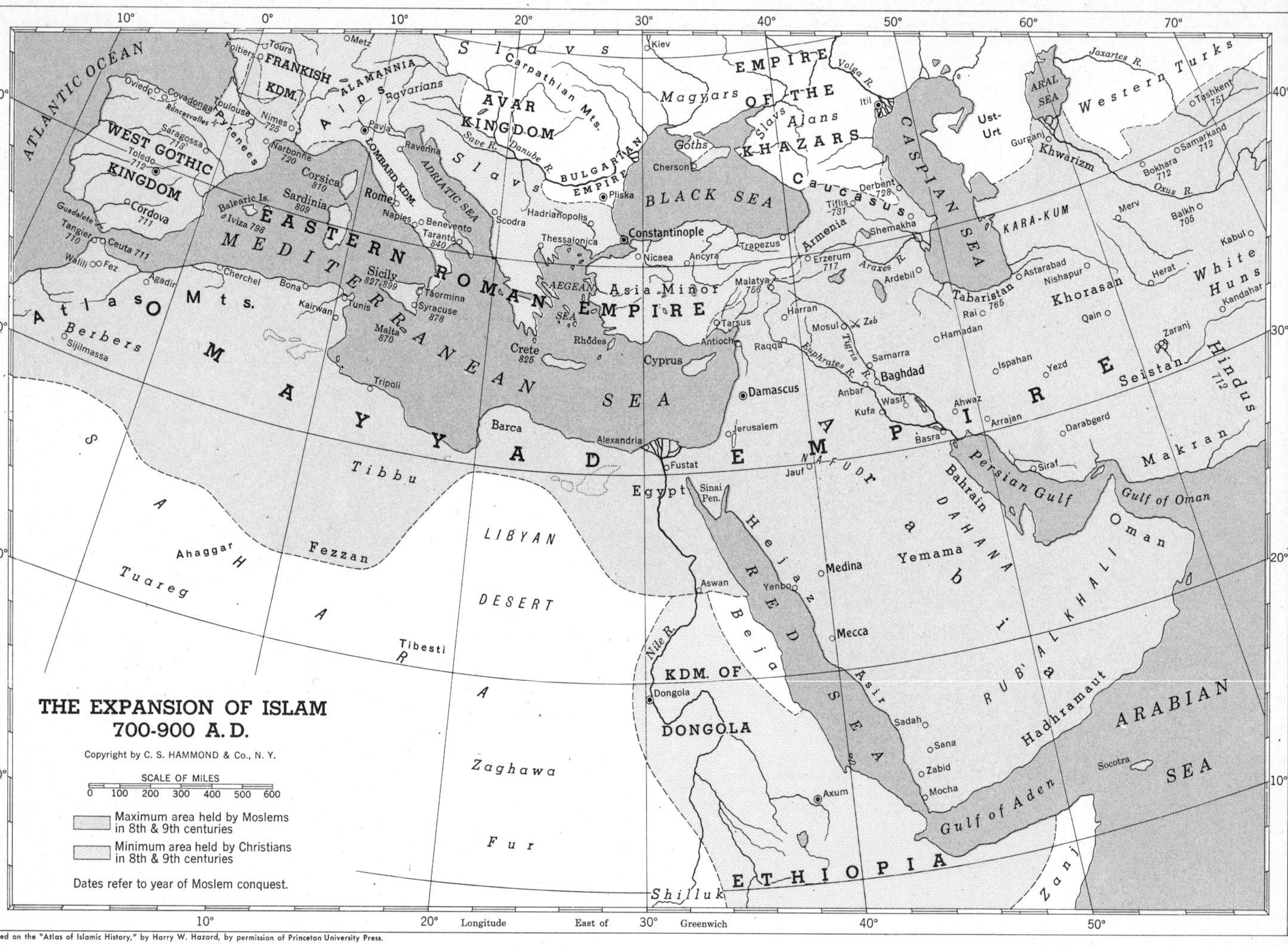

THE EXPANSION OF ISLAM 700-900 A.D.

SCALE OF MILES
0 100 200 300 400 500 600

Maximum area held by Moslems in 8th & 9th centuries

Minimum area held by Christians in 8th & 9th centuries

Dates refer to year of Moslem conquest.

Based on the "Atlas of Islamic History," by Harry W. Hazard, by permission of Princeton University Press.

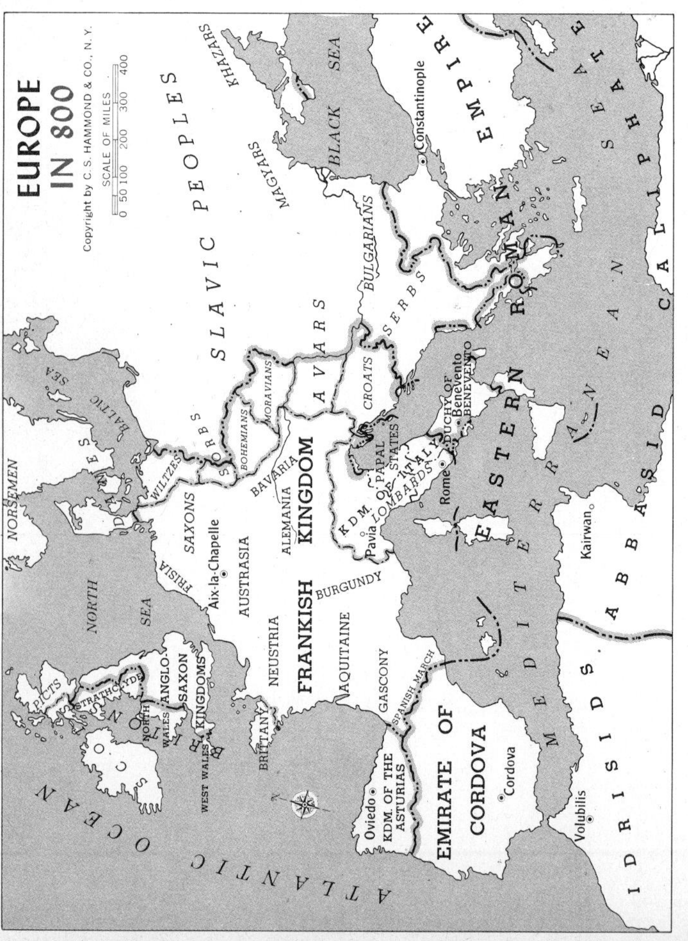

ENGLISH POSSESSIONS IN FRANCE
Possessions of William the Conqueror:
Possessions of Henry II, about 1180:
Possessions of Henry III, 1272:
French Crown Lands, 1180:
Boundary of France in the 12th Century:
SCALE OF MILES
0 50 100 150
ENGLAND
WALES
Bedford
Gloucester
London
Thames
Canterbury
Dover
Southampton
Portsmouth
Hastings
Exeter
Plymouth
English Channel
PONTHIEU
FLANDERS
Calais
Bruges
Antwerp
Brussels
Liège
Cambrai
Scheldt
Meuse
Utrecht
Rhine
Moselle
Amiens
Noyon
Laon
Reims
Verdun
Seine
Rouen
Bayeux
Caen
Bec
NORMANDY
Mortain
Beaumont
Marne
Châlons
Paris
ISLE OF FRANCE
CHAMPAGNE
St.-Pol-de-Léon
BRITTANY
Alencon
Chartres
Rennes
MAINE
Sens
Troyes
Vannes
Le Mans
Orléans
Langres
Angers
ANJOU
Tours
Blois
Sancerre
BURGUNDY
Dijon
Doubs
Loire
TOURAINE
Cher
Nantes
Autun
BERRY
BOURGES
Nevers
Saône
FRANCE
Châlon
Poitiers
POITOU
Chateauroux
L. Geneva
LA MARCHE
Bourbon
BOURBON
Geneva
Vienne
Clermont
Allier
Lyon
ATLANTIC OCEAN
Angoulême
AUVERGNE
FOREZ
Vienne
AQUITAINE
(GUYENNE)
Dordogne
VELAY
Bordeaux
Valence
Rhône
La Teste-de-Buch
Lot
QUERCY
Mende
VIVARAIS
Viviers
Cahors
Albret
Agen
Rodez
Uzes
Avignon
GASCONY
Adour
Bayonne
Albi
Nimes
Arles
PROVENCE
Toulouse
Montpellier
TOULOUSE
NAVARRE
BÉARN
Béziers
BIGORRE
Narbonne
Carcassonne
COMMINGES
MEDITERRANEAN SEA
ARAGON
THE EMPIRE

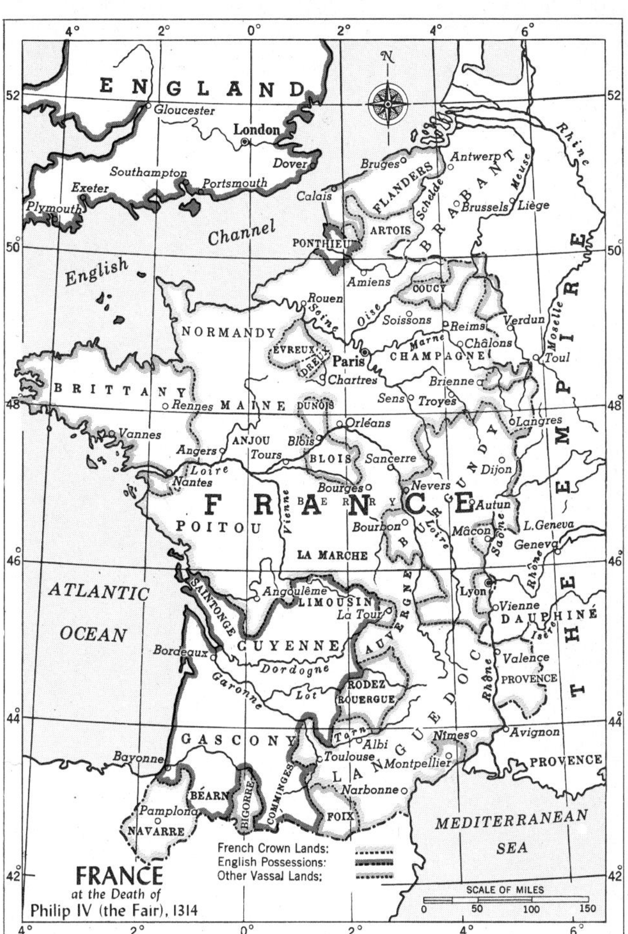
FRANCE
at the Death of
Philip IV (the Fair), 1314
French Crown Lands:
English Possessions:
Other Vassal Lands:
SCALE OF MILES
0 50 100 150
ENGLAND
Gloucester
London
Dover
Southampton
Portsmouth
Exeter
Plymouth
English Channel
Calais
Bruges
FLANDERS
Antwerp
BRABANT
Scheldt
Brussels
Liège
Meuse
Rhine
Moselle
PONTHIEU
ARTOIS
Amiens
COUCY
Rouen
Seine
Oise
Soissons
Reims
Verdun
NORMANDY
ÉVREUX
DREUX
Paris
Marne
CHAMPAGNE
Châlons
Toul
Chartres
Brienne
BRITTANY
Rennes
MAINE
DUNOIS
Sens
Troyes
Langres
Vannes
Orléans
Angers
ANJOU
Tours
Blois
BLOIS
Sancerre
BURGUNDY
Dijon
Loire
Nantes
Bourges
Nevers
FRANCE
Autun
BERRY
POITOU
Vienne
Bourbon
Mâcon
Saône
L. Geneva
Geneva
LA MARCHE
Lyon
ATLANTIC OCEAN
SAINTONGE
Angoulême
LIMOUSIN
La Tour
AUVERGNE
Vienne
DAUPHINÉ
Isère
Bordeaux
GUYENNE
Valence
Dordogne
PROVENCE
Rhône
Garonne
Lot
RODEZ
ROUERGUE
GASCONY
Tarn
Nimes
Avignon
Bayonne
Albi
Toulouse
Montpellier
LANGUEDOC
PROVENCE
BÉARN
Narbonne
Pamplona
NAVARRE
BIGORRE
COMMINGES
FOIX
MEDITERRANEAN SEA
THE EMPIRE

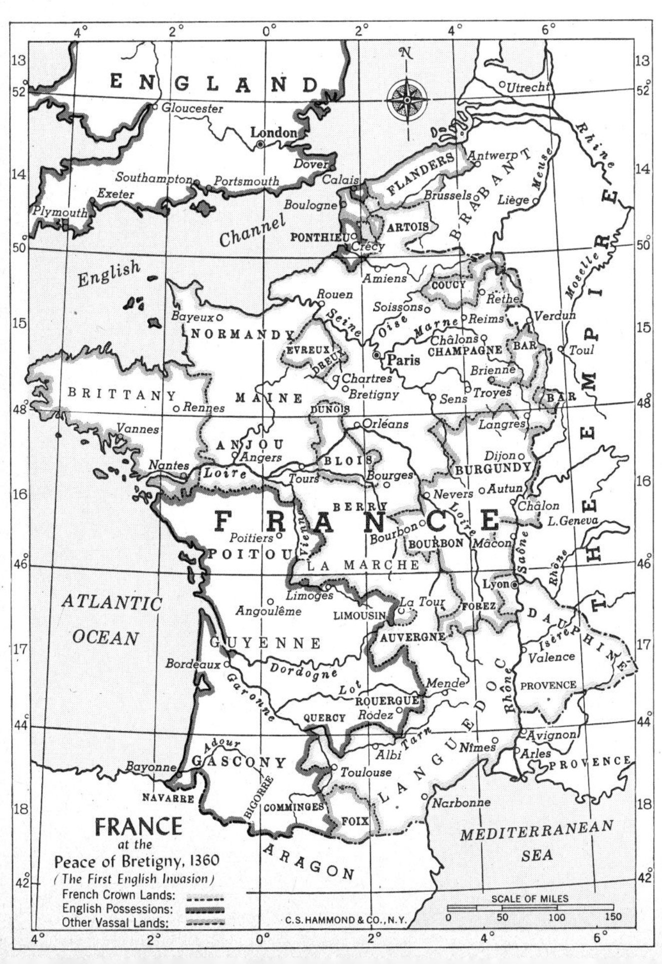
FRANCE
at the
Peace of Bretigny, 1360
(The First English Invasion)
French Crown Lands:
English Possessions:
Other Vassal Lands:
C.S. HAMMOND & CO., N.Y.
SCALE OF MILES
0 50 100 150
ENGLAND
Gloucester
London
Dover
Southampton
Portsmouth
Exeter
Plymouth
Calais
Boulogne
English Channel
PONTHIEU
Crécy
FLANDERS
Antwerp
BRABANT
Brussels
Liège
Meuse
Utrecht
Rhine
Moselle
ARTOIS
Amiens
COUCY
Rethel
Bayeux
Rouen
Seine
Oise
Soissons
Reims
Verdun
NORMANDY
ÉVREUX
DREUX
Paris
Marne
Châlons
CHAMPAGNE
BAR
Toul
Chartres
Bretigny
Brienne
BRITTANY
Rennes
MAINE
DUNOIS
Sens
Troyes
BAR
Vannes
Orléans
Langres
ANJOU
Angers
BLOIS
Dijon
BURGUNDY
Nantes
Loire
Tours
Bourges
Nevers
Autun
Châlon
BERRY
FRANCE
L. Geneva
Poitiers
POITOU
Vienne
Bourbon
BOURBON
Mâcon
Saône
LA MARCHE
Lyon
Rhône
Limoges
ATLANTIC OCEAN
Angoulême
LIMOUSIN
La Tour
FOREZ
DAUPHINÉ
Isère
GUYENNE
AUVERGNE
Bordeaux
Valence
Dordogne
Mende
PROVENCE
Lot
Garonne
ROUERGUE
QUERCY
Rodez
Adour
Albi
Tarn
Avignon
Bayonne
GASCONY
Nimes
Arles
PROVENCE
Toulouse
LANGUEDOC
NAVARRE
BIGORRE
COMMINGES
FOIX
Narbonne
MEDITERRANEAN SEA
ARAGON
THE EMPIRE

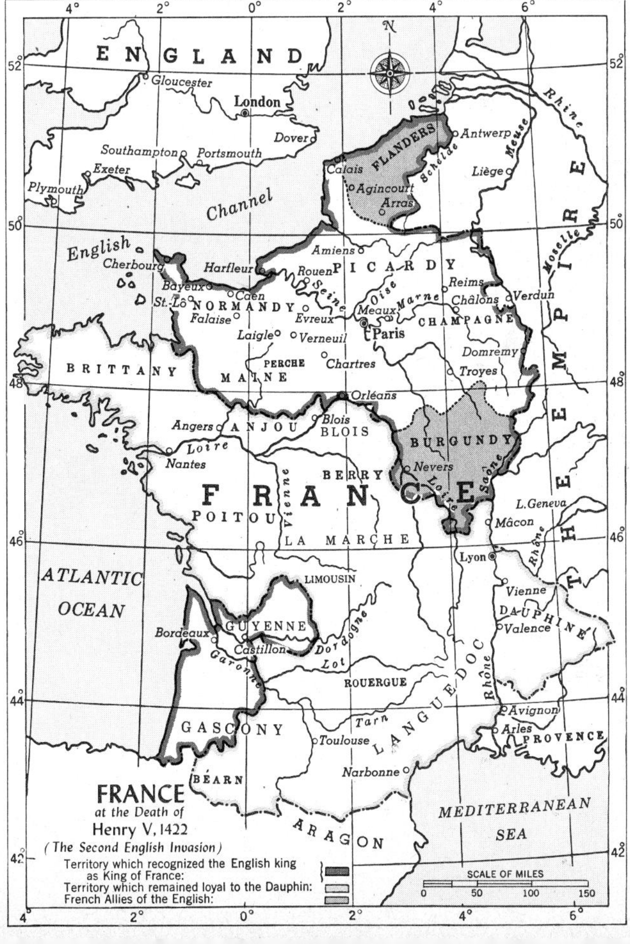
FRANCE
at the Death of
Henry V, 1422
(The Second English Invasion)
Territory which recognized the English king as King of France:
Territory which remained loyal to the Dauphin:
French Allies of the English:
SCALE OF MILES
0 50 100 150
ENGLAND
Gloucester
London
Dover
Southampton
Portsmouth
Exeter
Plymouth
English Channel
FLANDERS
Antwerp
Scheldt
Calais
Agincourt
Arras
Liège
Meuse
Rhine
Moselle
Cherbourg
Harfleur
Amiens
Rouen
PICARDY
Bayeux
Caen
St.-Lô
NORMANDY
Falaise
Seine
Oise
Meaux
Marne
Reims
Châlons
Verdun
Evreux
Paris
CHAMPAGNE
Laigle
Verneuil
Domremy
PERCHE
Chartres
BRITTANY
MAINE
Troyes
Orléans
Angers
ANJOU
Blois
BLOIS
BURGUNDY
Loire
Nantes
Nevers
BERRY
Saône
FRANCE
L. Geneva
POITOU
Vienne
Mâcon
LA MARCHE
Lyon
Rhône
ATLANTIC OCEAN
LIMOUSIN
Vienne
DAUPHINÉ
GUYENNE
Valence
Bordeaux
Castillon
Dordogne
Lot
Garonne
ROUERGUE
LANGUEDOC
GASCONY
Tarn
Avignon
Arles
PROVENCE
Toulouse
Narbonne
BÉARN
ARAGON
MEDITERRANEAN SEA
THE EMPIRE

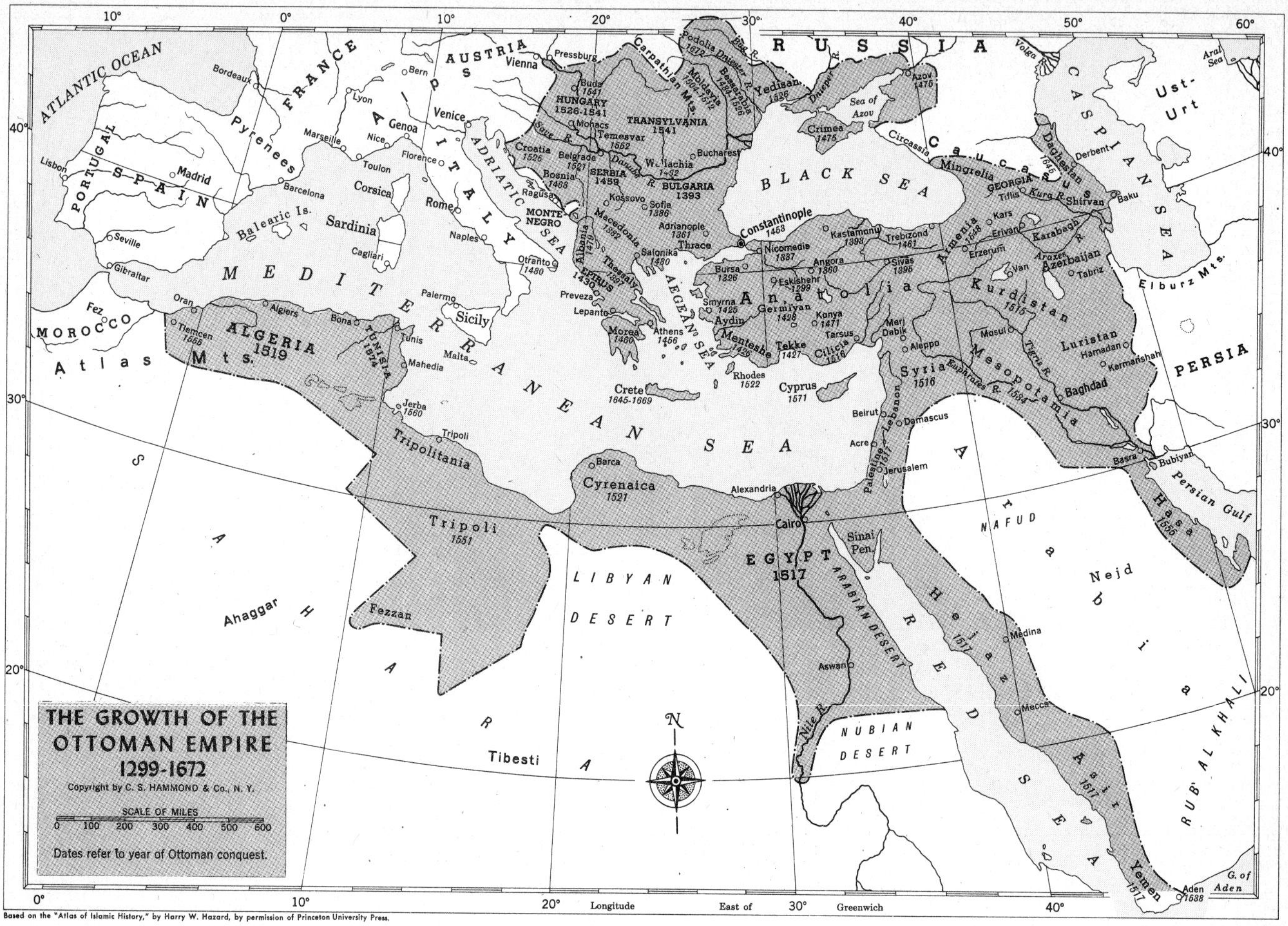

THE GROWTH OF THE OTTOMAN EMPIRE 1299-1672

SCALE OF MILES

0 100 200 300 400 500 600

Dates refer to year of Ottoman conquest.

Longitude East of Greenwich

Based on the "Atlas of Islamic History," by Harry W. Hazard, by permission of Princeton University Press.

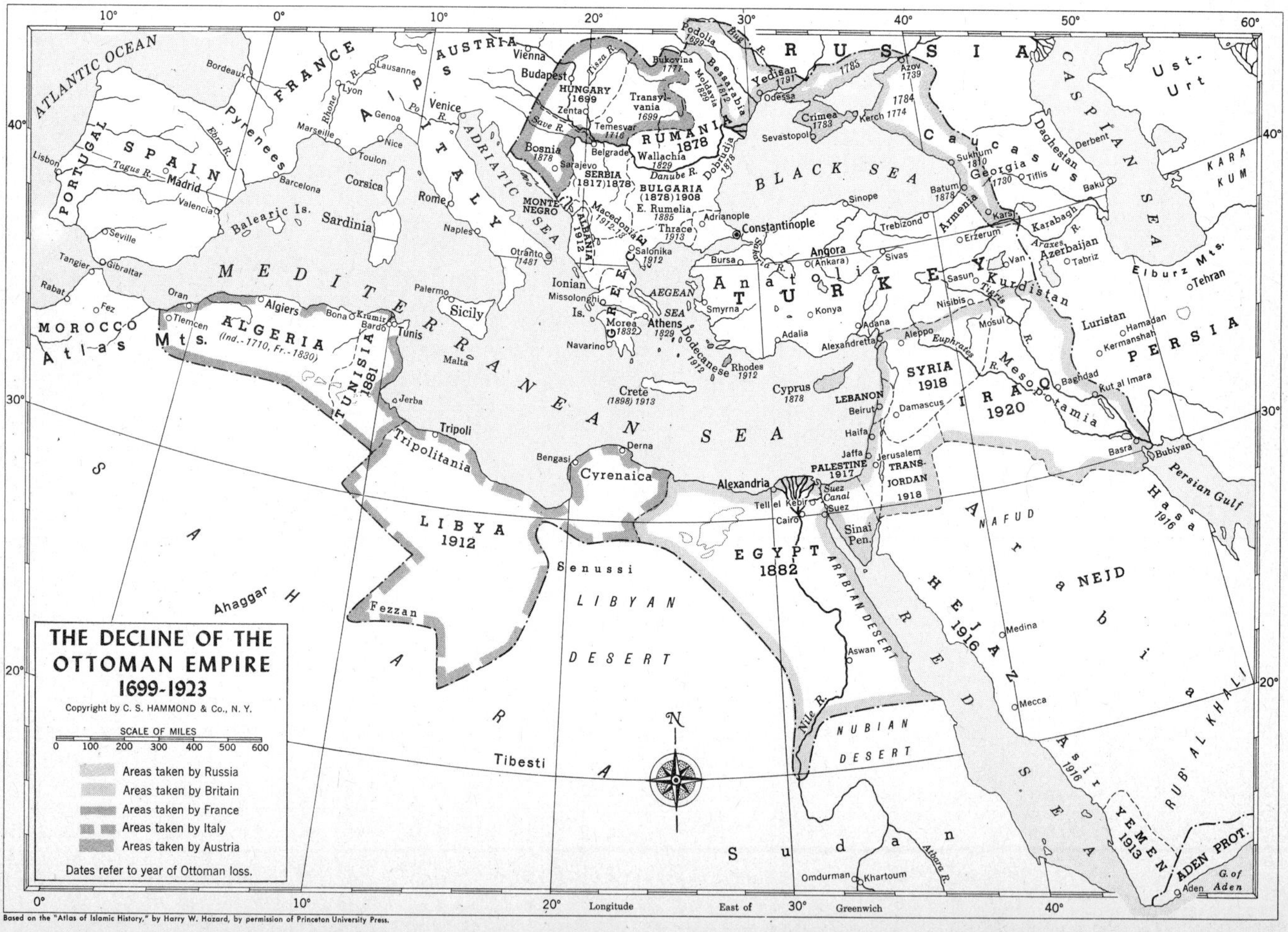

THE DECLINE OF THE OTTOMAN EMPIRE 1699-1923

SCALE OF MILES

0 100 200 300 400 500 600

- Areas taken by Russia
- Areas taken by Britain
- Areas taken by France
- Areas taken by Italy
- Areas taken by Austria

Dates refer to year of Ottoman loss.

Longitude East of Greenwich

Based on the "Atlas of Islamic History," by Harry W. Hazard, by permission of Princeton University Press.

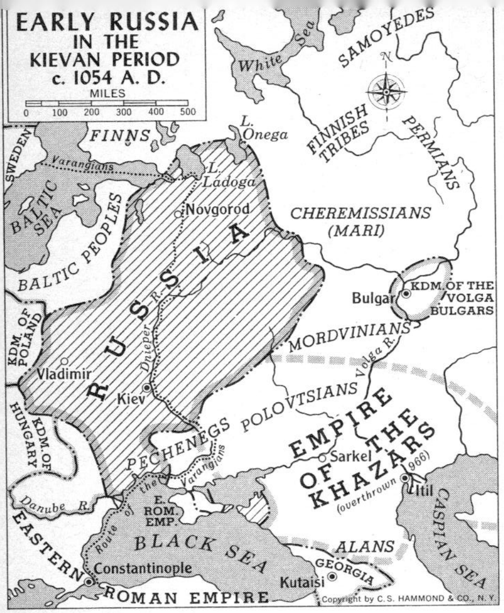
EARLY RUSSIA
IN THE
KIEVAN PERIOD
c. 1054 A. D.
MILES
0 100 200 300 400 500
RUSSIA
SAMOYEDES
FINNISH TRIBES
PERMIANS
CHEREMISSIANS (MARI)
FINNS
Varangians
BALTIC SEA
BALTIC PEOPLES
L. Onega
L. Ladoga
Novgorod
Bulgar
KDM. OF THE VOLGA BULGARS
MORDVINIANS
KDM. OF POLAND
Vladimir
Kiev
POLOVTSIANS
PECHENEGS
EMPIRE OF THE KHAZARS
Sarkel
(overthrown 966)
Itil
KDM. OF HUNGARY
E. ROM. EMP.
BLACK SEA
ALANS
GEORGIA
Kutaisi
CASPIAN SEA
Constantinople
EASTERN ROMAN EMPIRE
Copyright by C. S. HAMMOND & CO., N. Y.

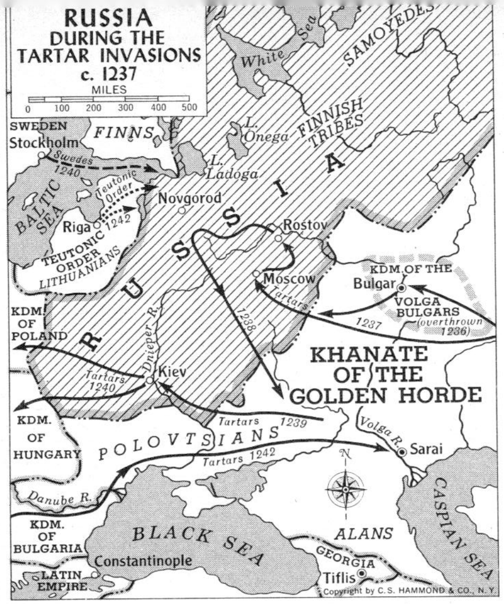
RUSSIA
DURING THE
TARTAR INVASIONS
c. 1237
MILES
0 100 200 300 400 500
SWEDEN
Stockholm
FINNS
Swedes 1240
Teutonic Order
Riga 1242
TEUTONIC ORDER
LITHUANIANS
Novgorod
L. Ladoga
L. Onega
FINNISH TRIBES
SAMOYEDES
RUSSIA
Rostov
Moscow
Tartars
1238
KDM. OF THE VOLGA BULGARS
Bulgar
(overthrown 1236)
1237
KHANATE OF THE GOLDEN HORDE
KDM. OF POLAND
Kiev
Tartars 1240
KDM. OF HUNGARY
POLOVTSIANS
Tartars 1239
Tartars 1242
Sarai
KDM. OF BULGARIA
BLACK SEA
Constantinople
LATIN EMPIRE
ALANS
GEORGIA
Tiflis
CASPIAN SEA
Copyright by C. S. HAMMOND & CO., N. Y.

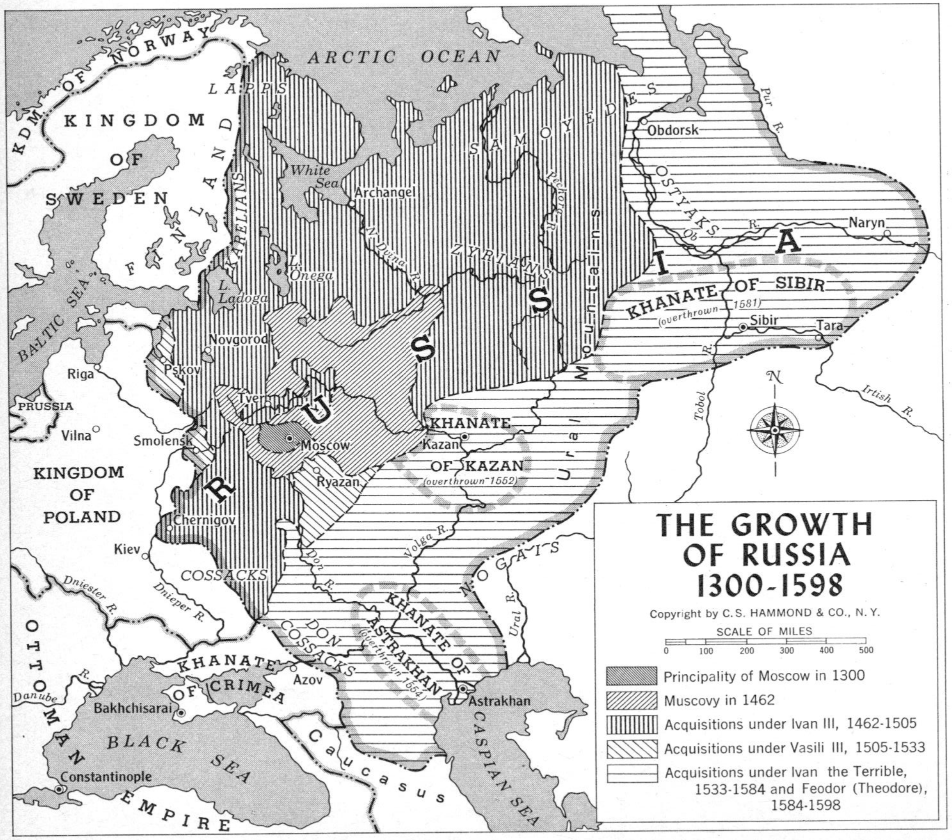
THE GROWTH
OF RUSSIA
1300-1598
Copyright by C. S. HAMMOND & CO., N. Y.
SCALE OF MILES
0 100 200 300 400 500
Principality of Moscow in 1300
Muscovy in 1462
Acquisitions under Ivan III, 1462-1505
Acquisitions under Vasili III, 1505-1533
Acquisitions under Ivan the Terrible, 1533-1584 and Feodor (Theodore), 1584-1598
ARCTIC OCEAN
KDM. OF NORWAY
KINGDOM OF SWEDEN
LAPPS
KARELIANS
FINLAND
White Sea
Archangel
SAMOYEDES
ZYRIANS
OSTYAKS
Obdorsk
Naryn
KHANATE OF SIBIR (overthrown 1581)
Sibir
Tara
Ural Mountains
RUSSIA
L. Onega
L. Ladoga
Novgorod
Pskov
Tver
Moscow
Ryazan
KHANATE OF KAZAN (overthrown 1552)
Kazan
BALTIC SEA
Riga
PRUSSIA
Vilna
Smolensk
KINGDOM OF POLAND
Chernigov
Kiev
COSSACKS
DON COSSACKS
NOGAIS
KHANATE OF ASTRAKHAN (overthrown 1554)
Astrakhan
KHANATE OF CRIMEA
Bakhchisarai
Azov
BLACK SEA
Caucasus
CASPIAN SEA
Constantinople
OTTOMAN EMPIRE

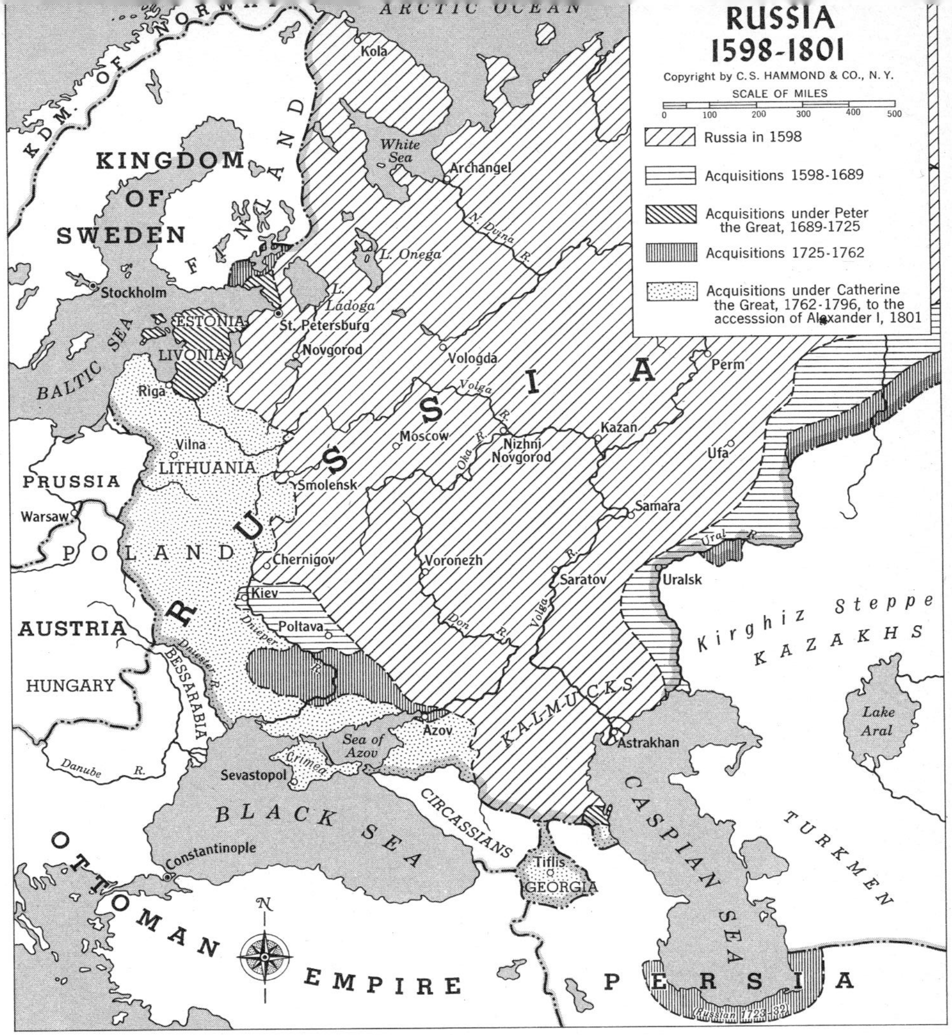
RUSSIA
1598-1801
Copyright by C. S. HAMMOND & CO., N. Y.
SCALE OF MILES
0 100 200 300 400 500
Russia in 1598
Acquisitions 1598-1689
Acquisitions under Peter the Great, 1689-1725
Acquisitions 1725-1762
Acquisitions under Catherine the Great, 1762-1796, to the accesssion of Alexander I, 1801
ARCTIC OCEAN
KDM. OF NORWAY
KINGDOM OF SWEDEN
FINLAND
Stockholm
Kola
White Sea
Archangel
L. Onega
L. Ladoga
St. Petersburg
Novgorod
ESTONIA
LIVONIA
Riga
BALTIC SEA
Vologda
Perm
Kazan
Ufa
Moscow
Nizhni Novgorod
Smolensk
Vilna
LITHUANIA
PRUSSIA
Warsaw
POLAND
Chernigov
Kiev
Poltava
Voronezh
Samara
Saratov
Uralsk
RUSSIA
AUSTRIA
HUNGARY
BESSARABIA
Kirghiz Steppe
KAZAKHS
Lake Aral
KALMUCKS
Azov
Sea of Azov
Crimea
Sevastopol
Astrakhan
BLACK SEA
CIRCASSIANS
Tiflis
GEORGIA
CASPIAN SEA
TURKMEN
Constantinople
OTTOMAN EMPIRE
PERSIA
(Russian 1723-32)

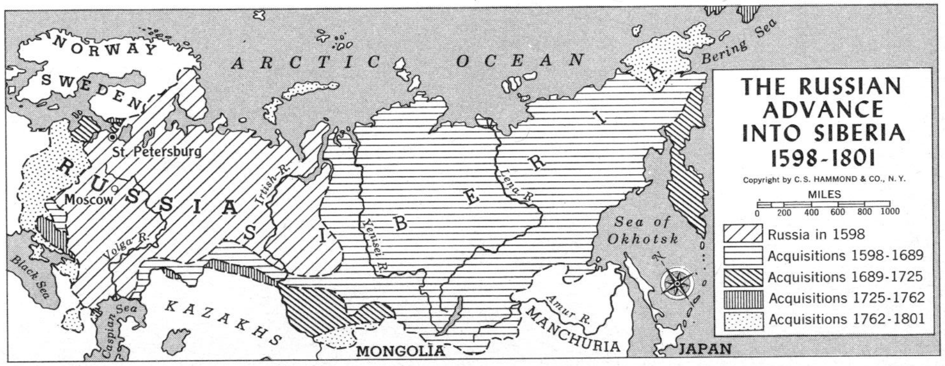
THE RUSSIAN
ADVANCE
INTO SIBERIA
1598-1801
Copyright by C. S. HAMMOND & CO., N. Y.
MILES
0 200 400 600 800 1000
Russia in 1598
Acquisitions 1598-1689
Acquisitions 1689-1725
Acquisitions 1725-1762
Acquisitions 1762-1801
ARCTIC OCEAN
NORWAY
SWEDEN
St. Petersburg
Moscow
RUSSIA
SIBERIA
Bering Sea
Sea of Okhotsk
KAZAKHS
MONGOLIA
MANCHURIA
JAPAN
Black Sea
Caspian Sea

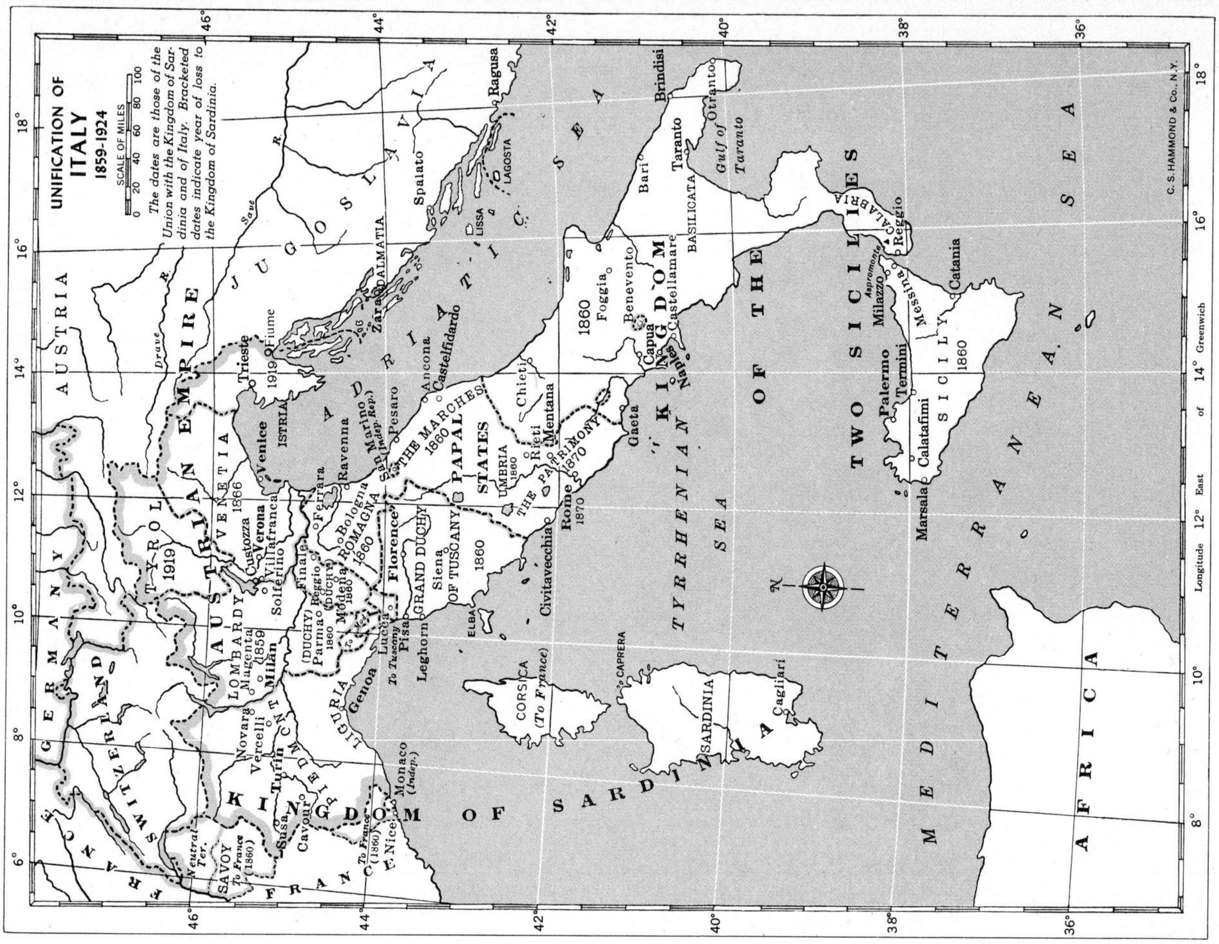

UNIFICATION OF ITALY 1859-1924

SCALE OF MILES 0 20 40 60 80 100

The dates are those of the Union with the Kingdom of Sardinia and of Italy. Bracketed dates indicate year of loss to the Kingdom of Sardinia.

Longitude 12° East of 14° Greenwich

C.S. HAMMOND & Co., N.Y.

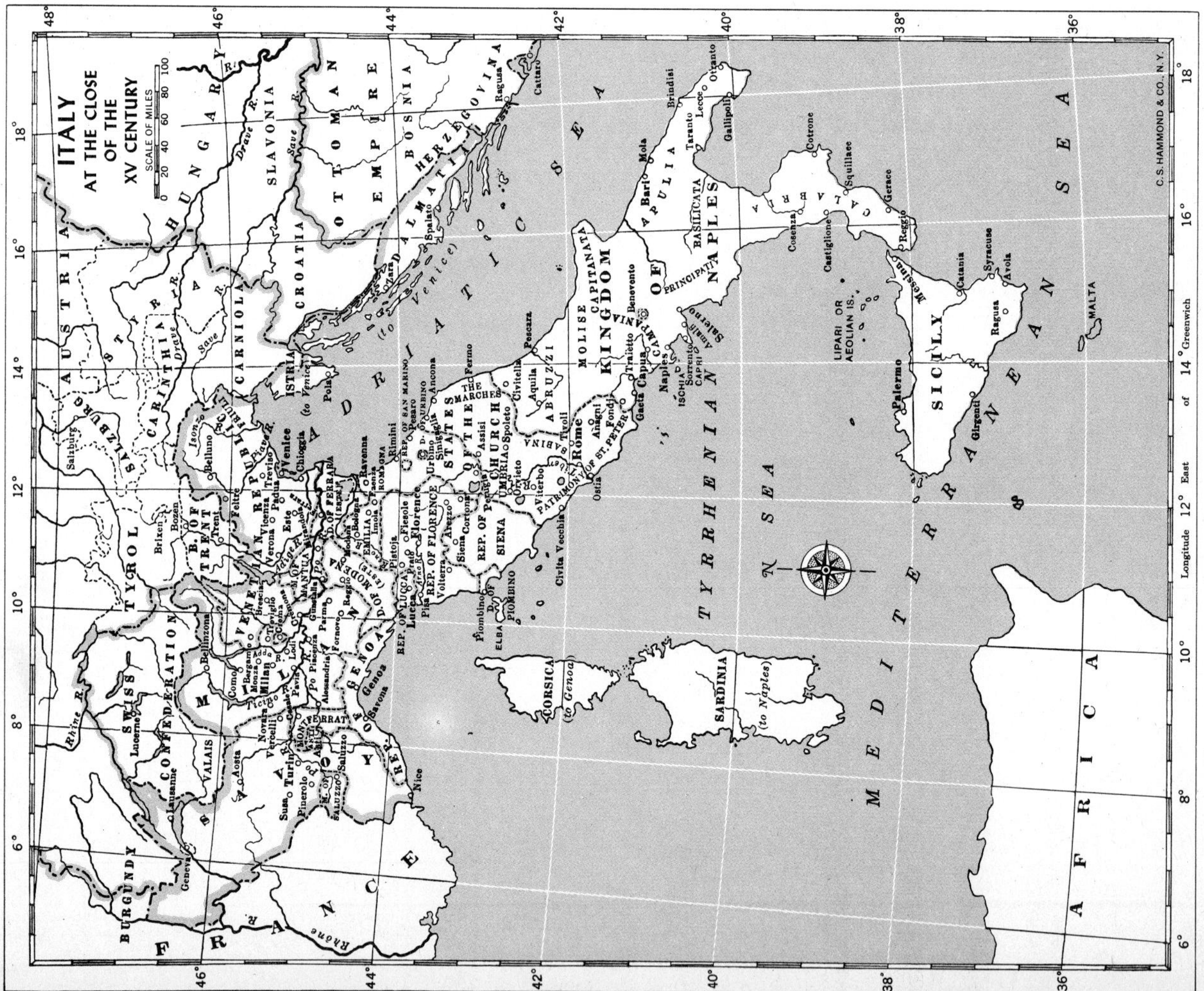

ITALY AT THE CLOSE OF THE XV CENTURY

SCALE OF MILES 0 20 40 60 80 100

Longitude 12° East of 14° Greenwich

C.S. HAMMOND & CO., N.Y.

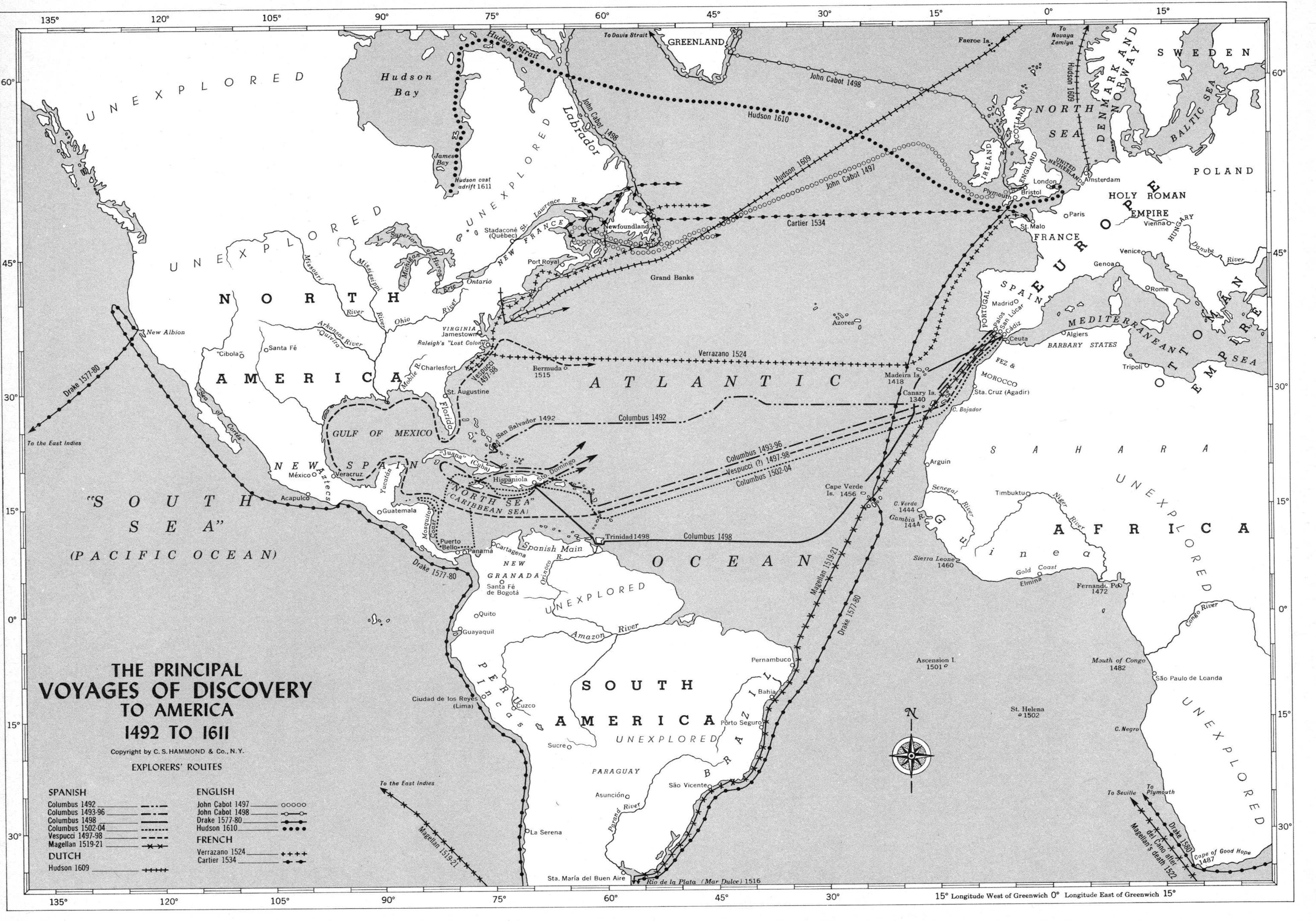
THE PRINCIPAL
VOYAGES OF DISCOVERY
TO AMERICA
1492 TO 1611
Copyright by C. S. HAMMOND & Co., N.Y.
EXPLORERS' ROUTES
SPANISH
Columbus 1492
Columbus 1493-96
Columbus 1498
Columbus 1502-04
Vespucci 1497-98
Magellan 1519-21
DUTCH
Hudson 1609
ENGLISH
John Cabot 1497
John Cabot 1498
Drake 1577-80
Hudson 1610
FRENCH
Verrazano 1524
Cartier 1534
UNEXPLORED
Hudson Bay
James Bay
Hudson cast adrift 1611
Hudson Strait
To Davis Strait
GREENLAND
Labrador
NORTH AMERICA
NEW FRANCE
Stadaconé (Québec)
Newfoundland
Port Royal
Grand Banks
VIRGINIA
Jamestown
Raleigh's "Lost Colony"
Charlesfort
St. Augustine
Florida
Bermuda 1515
GULF OF MEXICO
NEW SPAIN
México
Veracruz
Aztecs
Yucatan
Guatemala
Acapulco
"Cibola"
Santa Fé
"Quivira"
New Albion
To the East Indies
"SOUTH SEA"
(PACIFIC OCEAN)
San Salvador 1492
"Juana" (Cuba)
Hispaniola
Sto. Domingo
"NORTH SEA" (CARIBBEAN SEA)
Mosquito Coast
Puerto Bello
Panama
Cartagena
Spanish Main
NEW GRANADA
Santa Fé de Bogotá
Trinidad 1498
Quito
Guayaquil
PERU
Incas
Cuzco
Ciudad de los Reyes (Lima)
SOUTH AMERICA
Amazon River
Orinoco R.
Pernambuco
Bahia
Porto Seguro
BRAZIL
PARAGUAY
Asunción
Paraná River
São Vicente
Sucre
La Serena
Sta. María del Buen Aire
Rio de la Plata (Mar Dulce) 1516
ATLANTIC OCEAN
Azores
Madeira Is. 1418
Canary Is. 1340
Cape Verde Is. 1456
C. Bojador
Arguin
C. Verde 1444
Gambia R. 1444
Sierra Leone 1460
Ascension I. 1501
St. Helena 1502
SAHARA
AFRICA
Guinea
Gold Coast
Elmina
Timbuktu
Niger River
Senegal River
Fernando Po 1472
Congo River
Mouth of Congo 1482
São Paulo de Loanda
C. Negro
Cape of Good Hope 1487
To Seville
To Plymouth
Drake 1580
del Cano after Magellan's death 1522
EUROPE
PORTUGAL
SPAIN
Madrid
Palos
San Lúcar
Cádiz
Ceuta
FEZ & MOROCCO
Sta. Cruz (Agadir)
Algiers
BARBARY STATES
MEDITERRANEAN SEA
Tripoli
OTTOMAN EMPIRE
FRANCE
St. Malo
Paris
ENGLAND
IRELAND
SCOTLAND
Plymouth
Bristol
London
UNITED NETHERLANDS
Amsterdam
NORTH SEA
DENMARK AND NORWAY
SWEDEN
BALTIC SEA
POLAND
HOLY ROMAN EMPIRE
Vienna
HUNGARY
Danube River
Venice
Genoa
Rome
Faeroe Is.
To Novaya Zemlya
15° Longitude West of Greenwich 0° Longitude East of Greenwich 15°

UNITED STATES

INDIAN TRIBES AND LINGUISTIC FAMILIES

after Powell and Kroeber

The various Indian tribes are shown where they were located during the period of their greatest significance in American history.

LINGUISTIC FAMILIES

No.	Family	No.	Family	No.	Family
1	ALGONQUIAN	12	KITUNAHAN	21	TONKAWAN
2	ARAWAKAN	13	MUSKOGEAN	22	TUNICAN
3	ATHAPASCAN	14	PIMAN	23	UCHEAN
4	ATTACAPAN	15	SALISHAN	24	WAIILATPUAN
5	CADDOAN	16	SHAHAPTIAN	25	WAKASHAN
6	CHITIMACHAN	17	SHOSHONEAN	26	YUMAN
7	COAHUILTECAN	18	SIOUAN	27	ZUÑIAN
8	IROQUOIAN	19	TANOAN	28	Miscellaneous Pacific Coast Linguistic Families.
9	KARANKAWAN	20	TIMUCUAN	29	Linguistic affinity uncertain.
10	KERESAN				
11	KIOWAN				

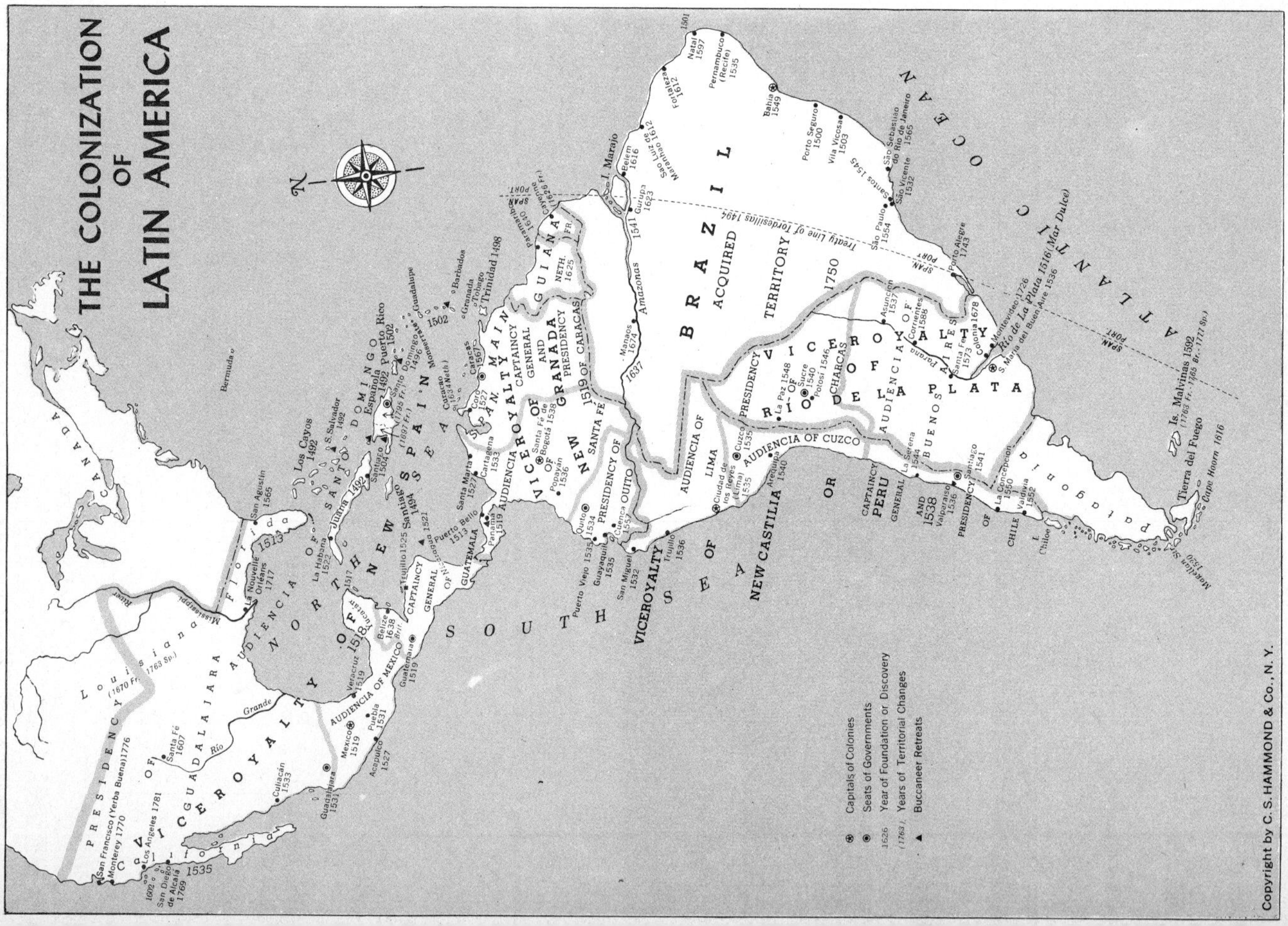

THE COLONIZATION OF LATIN AMERICA

- ⊛ Capitals of Colonies
- ◉ Seats of Governments
- 1626 Year of Foundation or Discovery
- (1763) Years of Territorial Changes
- ▲ Buccaneer Retreats

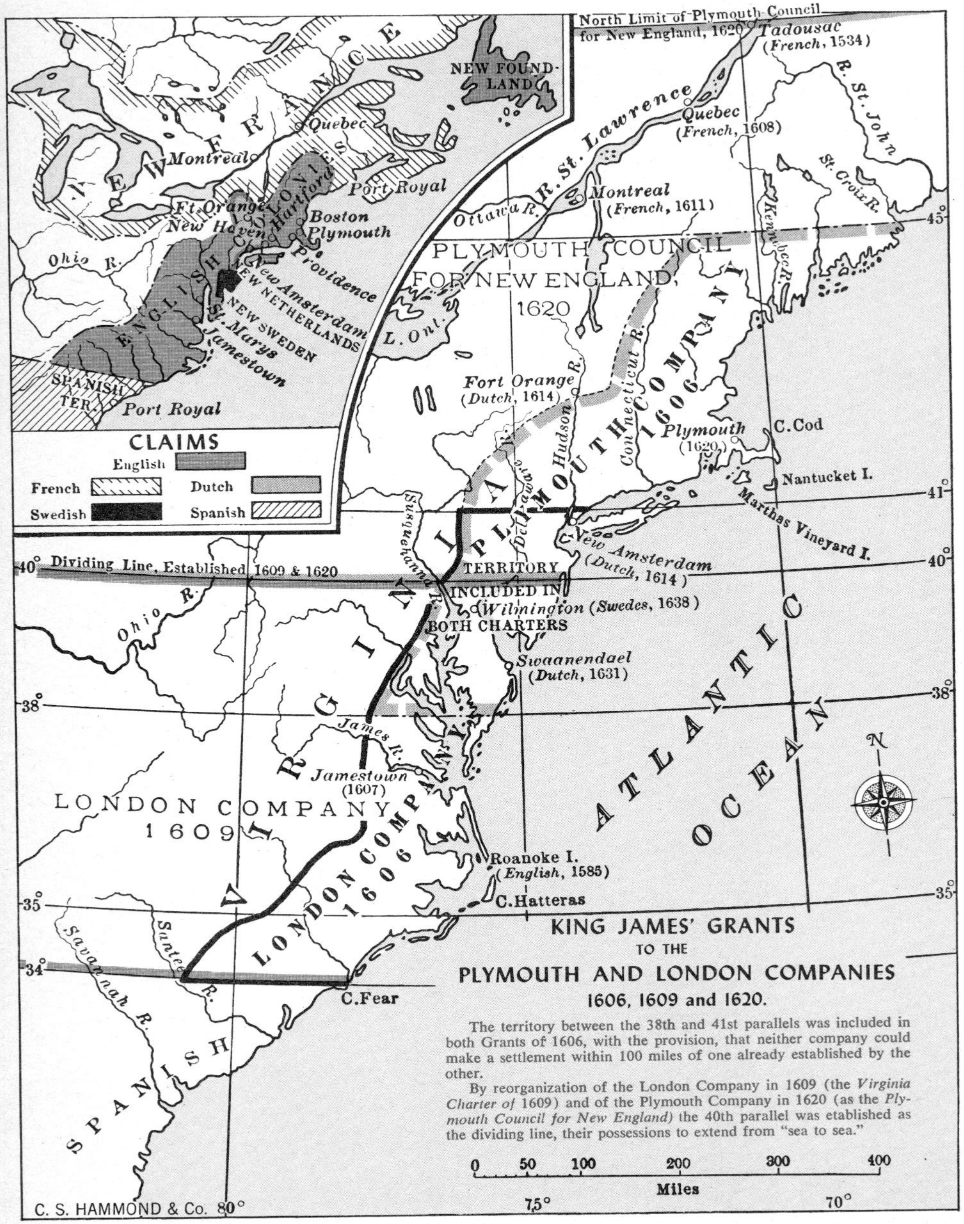

KING JAMES' GRANTS
TO THE
PLYMOUTH AND LONDON COMPANIES
1606, 1609 and 1620.

The territory between the 38th and 41st parallels was included in both Grants of 1606, with the provision, that neither company could make a settlement within 100 miles of one already established by the other.

By reorganization of the London Company in 1609 (the *Virginia Charter of 1609*) and of the Plymouth Company in 1620 (as the *Plymouth Council for New England)* the 40th parallel was established as the dividing line, their possessions to extend from "sea to sea."

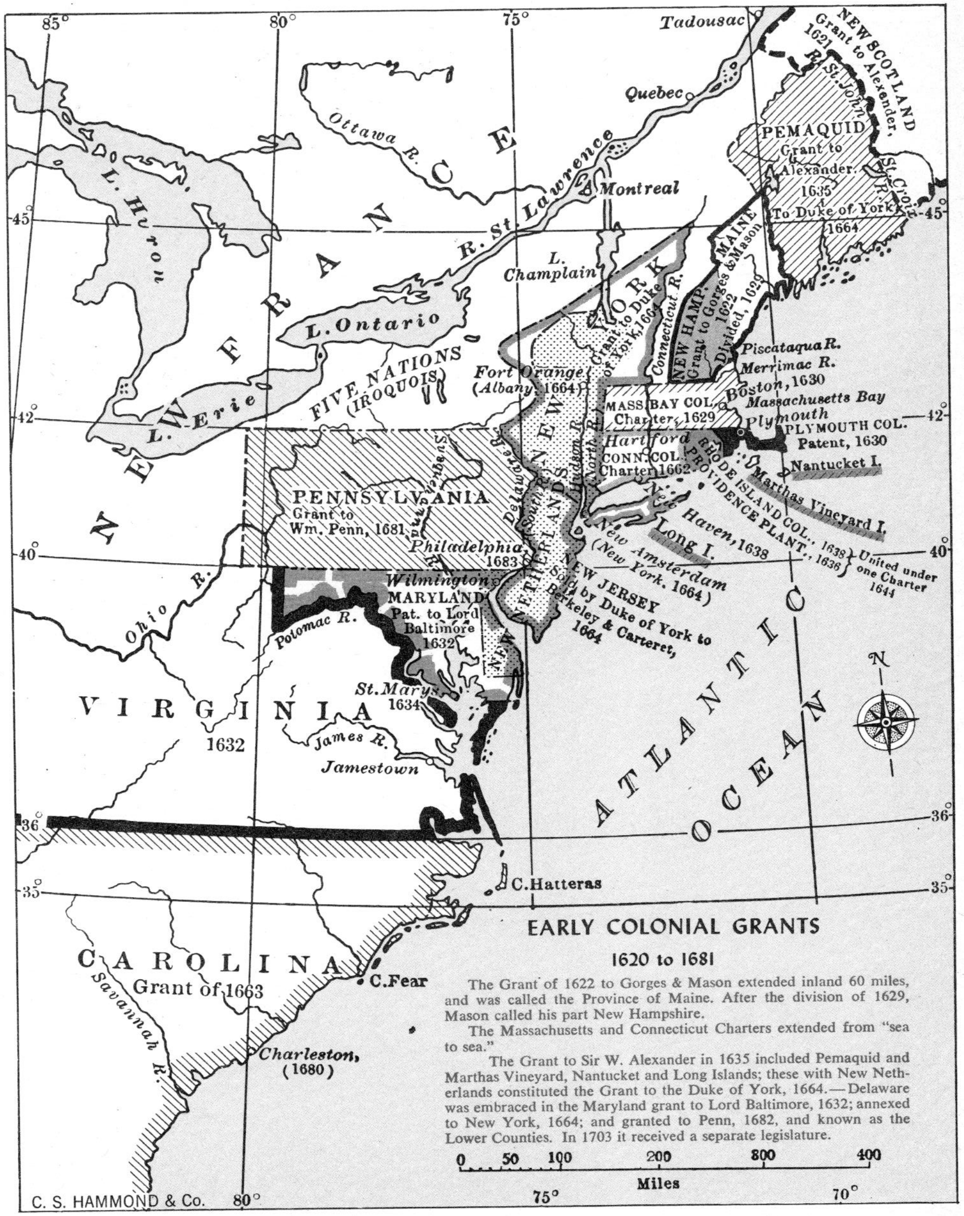

C. S. HAMMOND & Co.

EARLY COLONIAL GRANTS
1620 to 1681

The Grant of 1622 to Gorges & Mason extended inland 60 miles, and was called the Province of Maine. After the division of 1629, Mason called his part New Hampshire.

The Massachusetts and Connecticut Charters extended from "sea to sea."

The Grant to Sir W. Alexander in 1635 included Pemaquid and Marthas Vineyard, Nantucket and Long Islands; these with New Netherlands constituted the Grant to the Duke of York, 1664.—Delaware was embraced in the Maryland grant to Lord Baltimore, 1632; annexed to New York, 1664; and granted to Penn, 1682, and known as the Lower Counties. In 1703 it received a separate legislature.

C. S. HAMMOND & Co.

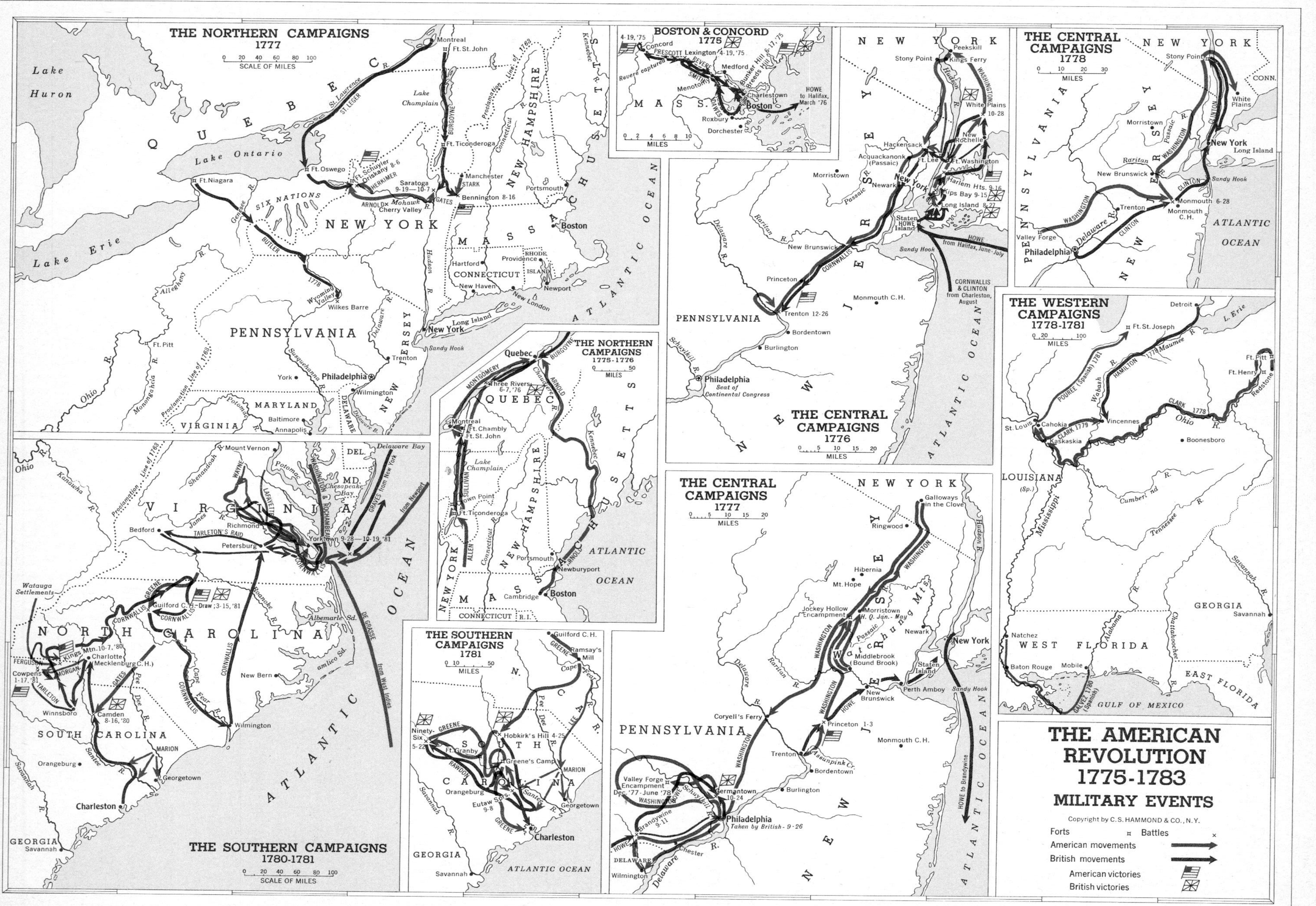
THE AMERICAN REVOLUTION 1775-1783
MILITARY EVENTS
Copyright by C.S. HAMMOND & CO., N.Y.
Forts
Battles
American movements
British movements
American victories
British victories
THE NORTHERN CAMPAIGNS 1777
SCALE OF MILES
BOSTON & CONCORD 1775
MILES
THE CENTRAL CAMPAIGNS 1776
MILES
THE CENTRAL CAMPAIGNS 1778
MILES
THE WESTERN CAMPAIGNS 1778-1781
MILES
THE NORTHERN CAMPAIGNS 1775-1776
MILES
THE CENTRAL CAMPAIGNS 1777
MILES
THE SOUTHERN CAMPAIGNS 1781
MILES
THE SOUTHERN CAMPAIGNS 1780-1781
SCALE OF MILES
ATLANTIC OCEAN
GULF OF MEXICO
9488

POLAND
TO 1667
Boundary of Poland previous to 1629
Lands ceded to Sweden in 1629 (confirmed 1660)
Lands ceded to Russia at the Peace of Andrussof, 1667
SCALE OF MILES
0 50 100 200 300
Longitude 25° East of Greenwich
FINLAND
SWEDEN
BALTIC SEA
Gulf of Finland
Stockholm
ESTHONIA
LIVONIA
Riga
COURLAND
SAMOGITIA
LITHUANIA
PRUSSIA
BRANDENBURG
POLAND
BLACK RUSSIA
WHITE RUSSIA
GREAT POLAND
Warsaw
PODLESIA
LITTLE POLAND
VOLHYNIA
LITTLE RUSSIA
UKRAINE
PODOLIA
GALICIA
SILESIA
AUSTRIA
HUNGARY
MOLDAVIA
TURKISH EMPIRE
KHANATE OF CRIMEA
BLACK SEA
RUSSIA

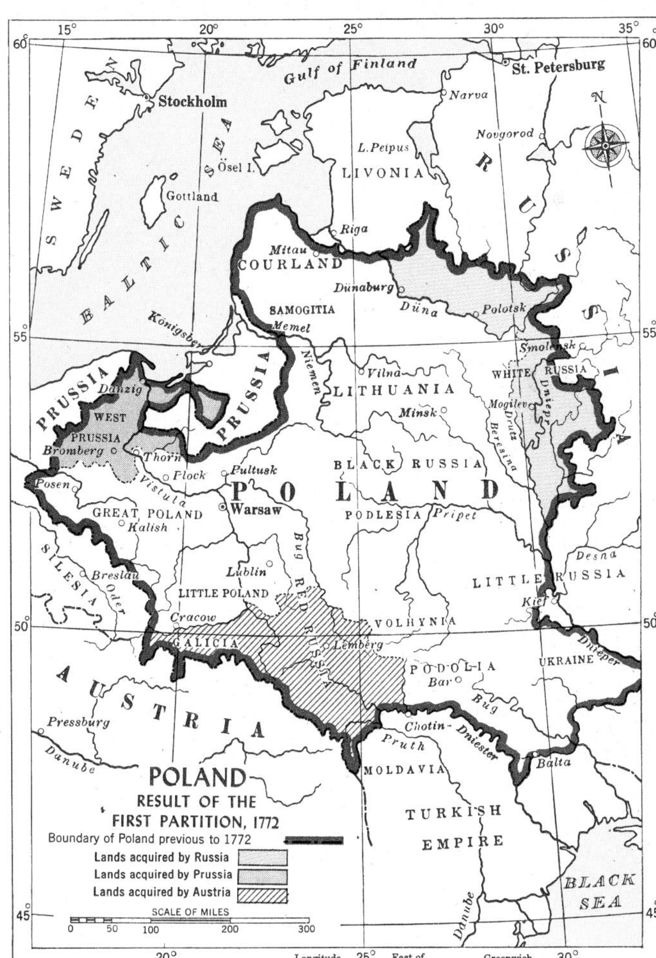
POLAND
RESULT OF THE
FIRST PARTITION, 1772
Boundary of Poland previous to 1772
Lands acquired by Russia
Lands acquired by Prussia
Lands acquired by Austria
SCALE OF MILES
0 50 100 200 300
Longitude 25° East of Greenwich
Gulf of Finland
St. Petersburg
Stockholm
SWEDEN
BALTIC SEA
LIVONIA
COURLAND
SAMOGITIA
PRUSSIA
WEST PRUSSIA
LITHUANIA
WHITE RUSSIA
BLACK RUSSIA
POLAND
GREAT POLAND
Warsaw
PODLESIA
LITTLE POLAND
VOLHYNIA
LITTLE RUSSIA
GALICIA
PODOLIA
UKRAINE
AUSTRIA
MOLDAVIA
TURKISH EMPIRE
BLACK SEA
RUSSIA

POLAND
RESULT OF THE
SECOND PARTITION, 1793
Boundary of Poland from 1772 to 1793
Lands acquired by Russia
Lands acquired by Prussia
Austria took no part in this partition.
SCALE OF MILES
0 50 100 200 300
Longitude 25° East of Greenwich
Gulf of Finland
St. Petersburg
Stockholm
SWEDEN
BALTIC SEA
LIVONIA
COURLAND
SAMOGITIA
PRUSSIA
BLACK RUSSIA
GREAT POLAND
Warsaw
POLAND
PODLESIA
VOLHYNIA
LITTLE RUSSIA
PODOLIA
GALICIA
SILESIA
AUSTRIA
MOLDAVIA
TURKISH EMPIRE
BLACK SEA
RUSSIA

POLAND
RESULT OF THE
THIRD PARTITION, 1795
Boundary of Poland from 1793 to 1795
Lands acquired by Russia
Lands acquired by Prussia
Lands acquired by Austria
SCALE OF MILES
0 50 100 200 300
Longitude 25° East of Greenwich
Gulf of Finland
St. Petersburg
Stockholm
SWEDEN
BALTIC SEA
LIVONIA
COURLAND
SAMOGITIA
LITHUANIA
PRUSSIA
POLAND
Warsaw
VOLHYNIA
AUSTRIA
TURKISH EMPIRE
BLACK SEA
RUSSIA

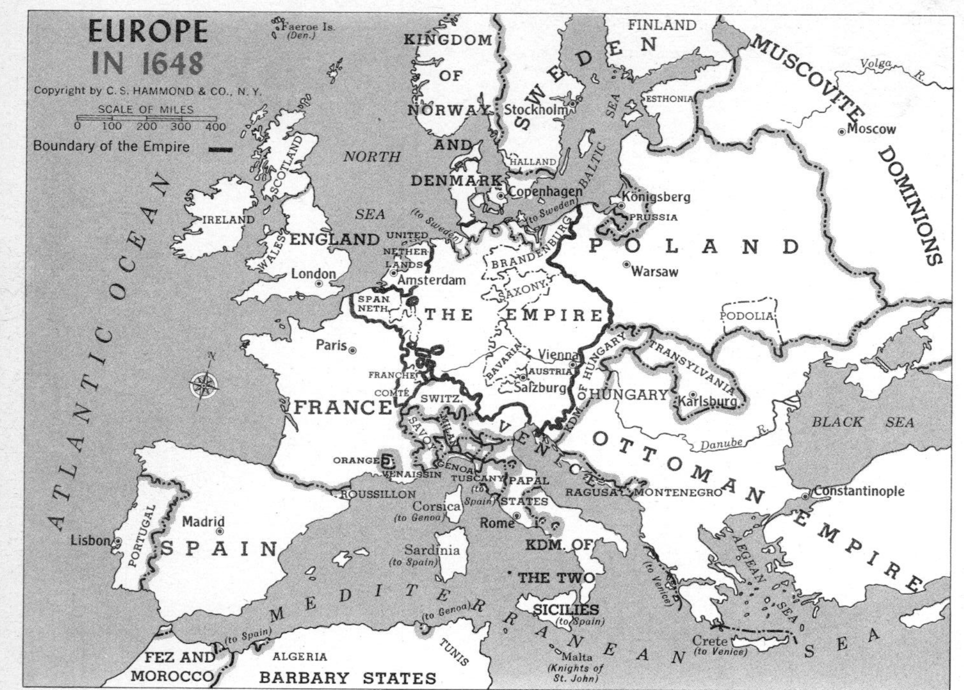
EUROPE
IN 1648
Copyright by C. S. HAMMOND & CO., N. Y.
SCALE OF MILES
0 100 200 300 400
Boundary of the Empire
MUSCOVITE DOMINIONS
POLAND
PRUSSIA
THE EMPIRE
HUNGARY
TRANSYLVANIA
OTTOMAN EMPIRE
KINGDOM OF NORWAY AND DENMARK
SWEDEN
ENGLAND
SCOTLAND
WALES
IRELAND
UNITED NETHERLANDS
SPAN. NETH.
FRANCE
SPAIN
PORTUGAL
PAPAL STATES
KDM. OF THE TWO SICILIES
ALGERIA
TUNIS
BARBARY STATES
FEZ AND MOROCCO
ATLANTIC OCEAN
MEDITERRANEAN SEA
BLACK SEA
AEGEAN SEA
NORTH SEA
BALTIC SEA
Moscow
Warsaw
Königsberg
Stockholm
Copenhagen
Amsterdam
London
Paris
Vienna
Salzburg
Karlsburg
Constantinople
Madrid
Lisbon
Rome

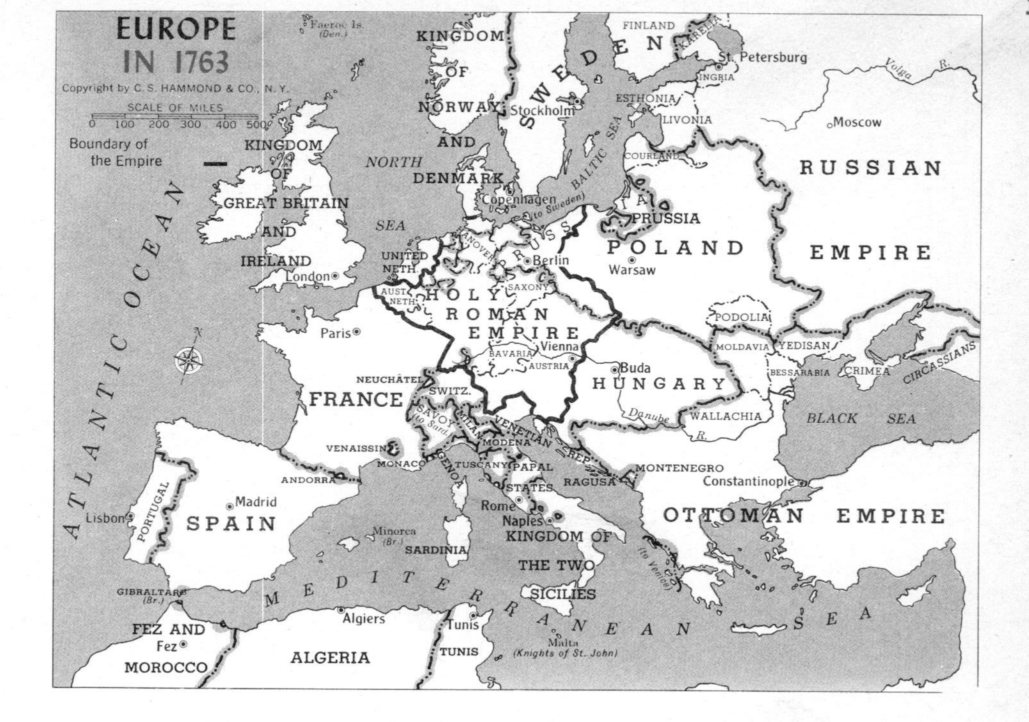
EUROPE
IN 1763
Copyright by C. S. HAMMOND & CO., N. Y.
SCALE OF MILES
0 100 200 300 400 500
Boundary of the Empire
RUSSIAN EMPIRE
POLAND
PRUSSIA
HOLY ROMAN EMPIRE
HUNGARY
OTTOMAN EMPIRE
KINGDOM OF NORWAY AND DENMARK
SWEDEN
KINGDOM OF GREAT BRITAIN AND IRELAND
FRANCE
SPAIN
PORTUGAL
KINGDOM OF THE TWO SICILIES
SARDINIA
ALGERIA
TUNIS
FEZ AND MOROCCO
ATLANTIC OCEAN
MEDITERRANEAN SEA
BLACK SEA
NORTH SEA
BALTIC SEA
St. Petersburg
Moscow
Warsaw
Berlin
Vienna
Buda
Constantinople
Stockholm
Copenhagen
London
Paris
Madrid
Lisbon
Rome
Naples
Algiers
Tunis
Fez

EUROPE
IN 1812
Copyright by C. S. HAMMOND & CO., N. Y.
SCALE OF MILES
0 100 200 300 400 500
Boundary of the Confederation of the Rhine
RUSSIAN EMPIRE
GRAND DUCHY OF WARSAW
PRUSSIA
EMPIRE OF AUSTRIA
KDM. OF HUNGARY
CONF. OF THE RHINE
OTTOMAN EMPIRE
KINGDOM OF NORWAY AND DENMARK
SWEDEN
UNITED KINGDOM
EMPIRE OF THE FRENCH
ITALY
NAPLES
SPAIN
PORTUGAL
SARDINIA
SICILY
ALGERIA
TUNIS
MOROCCO
ATLANTIC OCEAN
MEDITERRANEAN SEA
ADRIATIC SEA
BLACK SEA
NORTH SEA
St. Petersburg
Moscow
Helsingfors
Stockholm
Copenhagen
Berlin
Warsaw
Erfurt
Kassel
Vienna
Laibach
Constantinople
London
Paris
Milan
Rome
Naples
Palermo
Cagliari
Madrid
Lisbon
Algiers

EUROPE
1815-1839
Copyright by C. S. HAMMOND & CO., N. Y.
SCALE OF MILES
0 50 100 200 300 400
Boundary of the Germanic Confederation
Boundaries as of 1839
RUSSIAN EMPIRE
POLAND
CRACOW
PRUSSIA
GERMANIC CONFEDERATION
AUSTRIAN EMPIRE
HUNGARY
OTTOMAN EMPIRE
GREECE
SWEDEN
NORWAY
DENMARK
UNITED KINGDOM
NETHERLANDS
BELGIUM
FRANCE
SPAIN
PORTUGAL
SARDINIA
STATES OF THE CHURCH
KINGDOM OF THE TWO SICILIES
ALGERIA
TUNIS
MOROCCO
ATLANTIC OCEAN
MEDITERRANEAN SEA
BLACK SEA
NORTH SEA
St. Petersburg
Moscow
Stockholm
Christiania
Copenhagen
Frankfurt
Vienna
Belgrade
Constantinople
Athens
Corfu
London
Paris
Turin
Rome
Naples
Madrid
Lisbon
Algiers

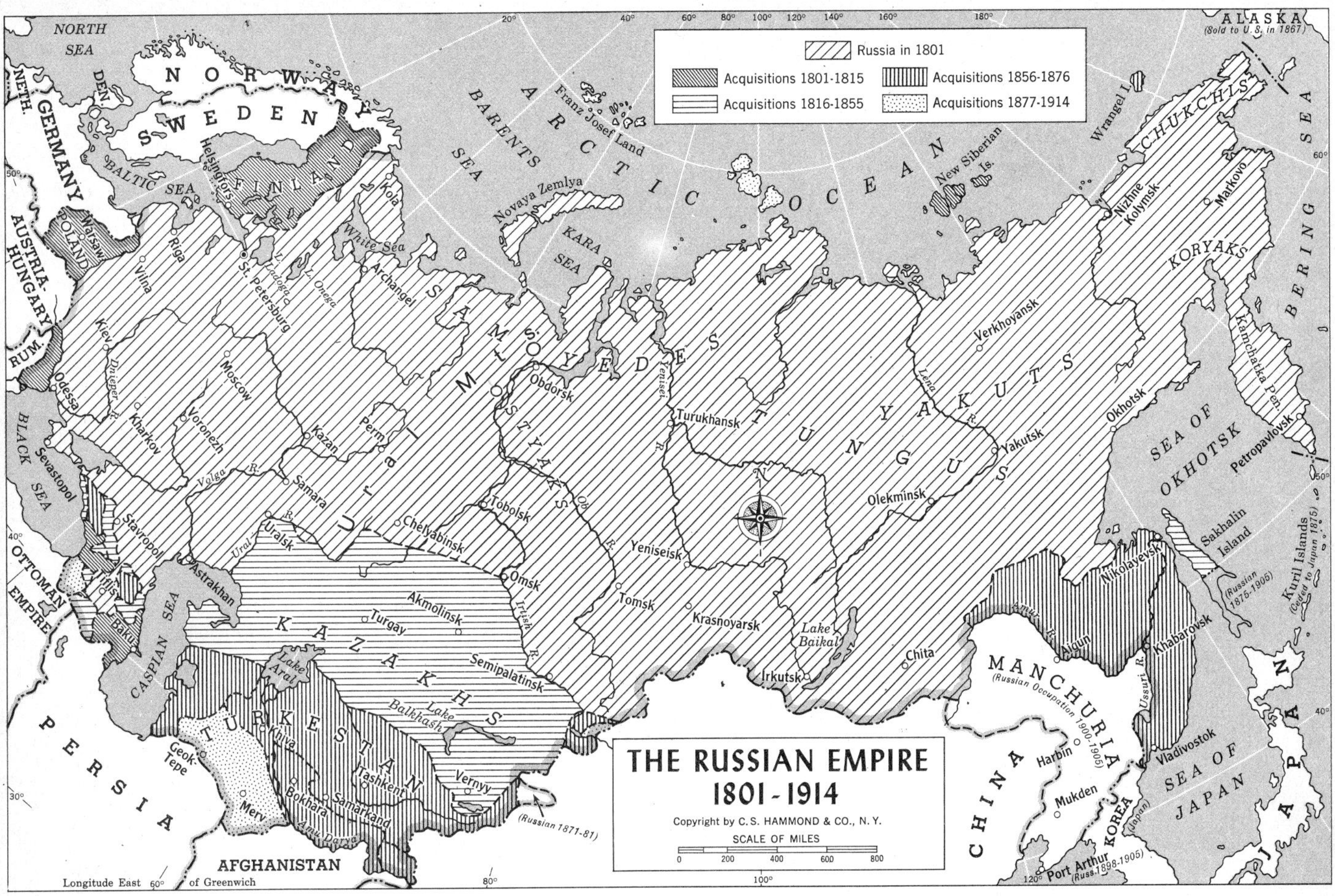
THE RUSSIAN EMPIRE
1801-1914
Copyright by C.S. HAMMOND & CO., N.Y.
SCALE OF MILES
0 200 400 600 800
Russia in 1801
Acquisitions 1801-1815
Acquisitions 1816-1855
Acquisitions 1856-1876
Acquisitions 1877-1914
NORTH SEA
NORWAY
SWEDEN
FINLAND
DEN.
NETH.
GERMANY
AUSTRIA-HUNGARY
RUM.
BALTIC SEA
Helsingfors
Warsaw
POLAND
Riga
Vilna
Kiev
Odessa
BLACK SEA
Sevastopol
Kharkov
Voronezh
Moscow
St. Petersburg
L. Ladoga
L. Onega
White Sea
Archangel
Kola
BARENTS SEA
ARCTIC OCEAN
Franz Josef Land
Novaya Zemlya
KARA SEA
New Siberian Is.
Wrangel I.
CHUKCHIS
ALASKA
(Sold to U.S. in 1867)
BERING SEA
Nizhne Kolymsk
Markovo
KORYAKS
Kamchatka Pen.
Petropavlovsk
SEA OF OKHOTSK
Okhotsk
Verkhoyansk
YAKUTS
TUNGUS
Yakutsk
Olekminsk
SAMOYEDES
OSTYAKS
Obdorsk
Turukhansk
Yeniseisk
Tomsk
Krasnoyarsk
Irkutsk
Lake Baikal
Chita
Kazan
Perm
Samara
Ural Mts.
Volga R.
Stavropol
Astrakhan
Tiflis
Baku
CASPIAN SEA
Uralsk
Chelyabinsk
Tobolsk
Omsk
Akmolinsk
Turgay
Semipalatinsk
KAZAKHS
Lake Aral
Lake Balkhash
Vernyy
(Russian 1871-81)
TURKESTAN
Khiva
Tashkent
Samarkand
Bokhara
Merv
Geok-Tepe
Amu Darya
PERSIA
AFGHANISTAN
OTTOMAN EMPIRE
MANCHURIA
(Russian Occupation 1900-1905)
Aigun
Khabarovsk
Nikolayevsk
Sakhalin Island
(Russian 1875-1905)
Kuril Islands
(Ceded to Japan 1875)
Harbin
Mukden
Vladivostok
Port Arthur
(Russ.1898-1905)
KOREA
(Japan)
SEA OF JAPAN
JAPAN
CHINA
Longitude East of Greenwich

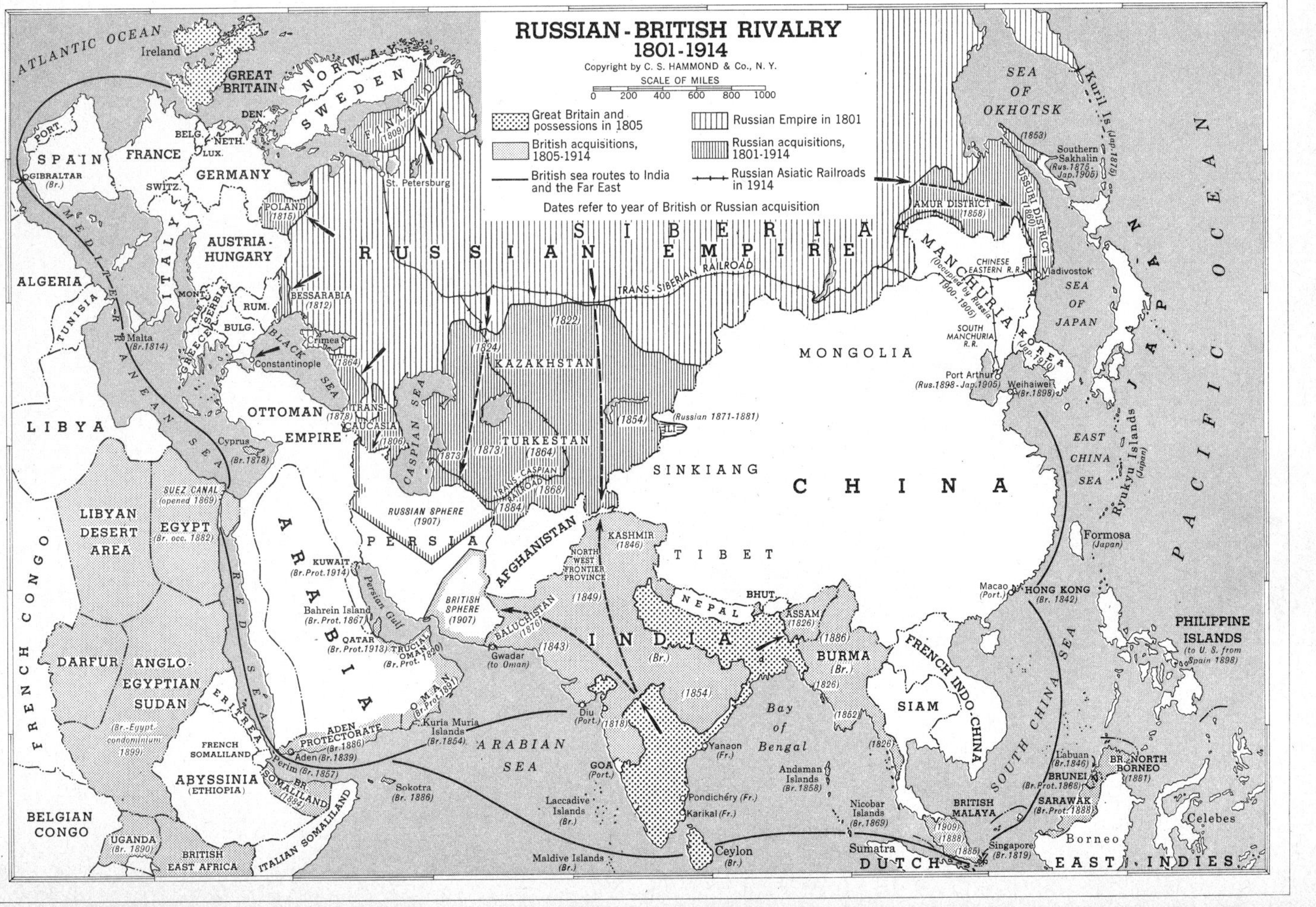
RUSSIAN-BRITISH RIVALRY
1801-1914
Copyright by C. S. HAMMOND & Co., N. Y.
SCALE OF MILES
0 200 400 600 800 1000
Great Britain and possessions in 1805
British acquisitions, 1805-1914
British sea routes to India and the Far East
Russian Empire in 1801
Russian acquisitions, 1801-1914
Russian Asiatic Railroads in 1914
Dates refer to year of British or Russian acquisition
ATLANTIC OCEAN
Ireland
GREAT BRITAIN
NORWAY
SWEDEN
FINLAND
(1809)
DEN.
BELG.
NETH.
LUX.
PORT.
SPAIN
GIBRALTAR
(Br.)
FRANCE
SWITZ.
GERMANY
POLAND
(1815)
St. Petersburg
AUSTRIA-HUNGARY
ITALY
ALGERIA
TUNISIA
Malta
(Br.1814)
MONT.
SERBIA
RUM.
BULG.
GREECE
BESSARABIA
(1812)
Crimea
Constantinople
BLACK SEA
(1864)
MEDITERRANEAN SEA
LIBYA
OTTOMAN EMPIRE
Cyprus
(Br.1878)
TRANS-CAUCASIA
(1878)
(1806)
SIBERIA
RUSSIAN EMPIRE
TRANS-SIBERIAN RAILROAD
(1822)
(1824)
KAZAKHSTAN
CASPIAN SEA
(1873)
TURKESTAN
(1864)
TRANS-CASPIAN RAILROAD
(1884)
(1868)
(1854)
(Russian 1871-1881)
RUSSIAN SPHERE
(1907)
PERSIA
SUEZ CANAL
(opened 1869)
LIBYAN DESERT AREA
EGYPT
(Br. occ. 1882)
ARABIA
KUWAIT
(Br.Prot.1914)
Persian Gulf
Bahrein Island
(Br. Prot. 1867)
QATAR
(Br. Prot.1913)
TRUCIAL OMAN
(Br. Prot. 1820)
OMAN
(Br. Prot. 1891)
BRITISH SPHERE
(1907)
AFGHANISTAN
BALUCHISTAN
(1876)
Gwadar
(to Oman)
KASHMIR
(1846)
NORTH WEST FRONTIER PROVINCE
(1849)
(1843)
INDIA
(Br.)
(1854)
Diu
(Port.)
(1818)
GOA
(Port.)
Laccadive Islands
(Br.)
Maldive Islands
(Br.)
Ceylon
(Br.)
Pondichéry (Fr.)
Karikal (Fr.)
Yanaon
(Fr.)
Bay of Bengal
Andaman Islands
(Br. 1858)
Nicobar Islands
(Br. 1869)
NEPAL
BHUT.
ASSAM
(1826)
(1886)
BURMA
(Br.)
(1826)
(1852)
TIBET
SINKIANG
MONGOLIA
CHINA
RED SEA
DARFUR
ANGLO-EGYPTIAN SUDAN
(Br.-Egypt. condominium 1899)
ERITREA
FRENCH SOMALILAND
ADEN PROTECTORATE
(Br. 1886)
Aden (Br. 1839)
Perim (Br. 1857)
BR. SOMALILAND
(1884)
Kuria Muria Islands
(Br. 1854)
ARABIAN SEA
Sokotra
(Br. 1886)
ABYSSINIA
(ETHIOPIA)
FRENCH CONGO
BELGIAN CONGO
UGANDA
(Br. 1890)
BRITISH EAST AFRICA
ITALIAN SOMALILAND
SIAM
FRENCH INDO-CHINA
BRITISH MALAYA
(1909)
(1888)
(1885)
Singapore
(Br. 1819)
Sumatra
DUTCH EAST INDIES
Borneo
Celebes
Labuan
(Br. 1846)
BRUNEI
(Br. Prot. 1888)
SARAWAK
(Br. Prot. 1888)
BR. NORTH BORNEO
(1881)
SOUTH CHINA SEA
PHILIPPINE ISLANDS
(to U. S. from Spain 1898)
Macao
(Port.)
HONG KONG
(Br. 1842)
Formosa
(Japan)
EAST CHINA SEA
Ryukyu Islands
(Japan)
Weihaiwei
(Br. 1898)
Port Arthur
(Rus.1898 - Jap.1905)
KOREA
(Jap. 1910)
SOUTH MANCHURIA R.R.
MANCHURIA
(Occupied by Russia 1900-1905)
CHINESE EASTERN R.R.
Vladivostok
SEA OF JAPAN
JAPAN
AMUR DISTRICT
(1858)
USSURI DISTRICT
(1860)
SEA OF OKHOTSK
(1853)
Southern Sakhalin
(Rus.1875 - Jap.1905)
Kuril Is.
(Jap. 1875)
PACIFIC OCEAN

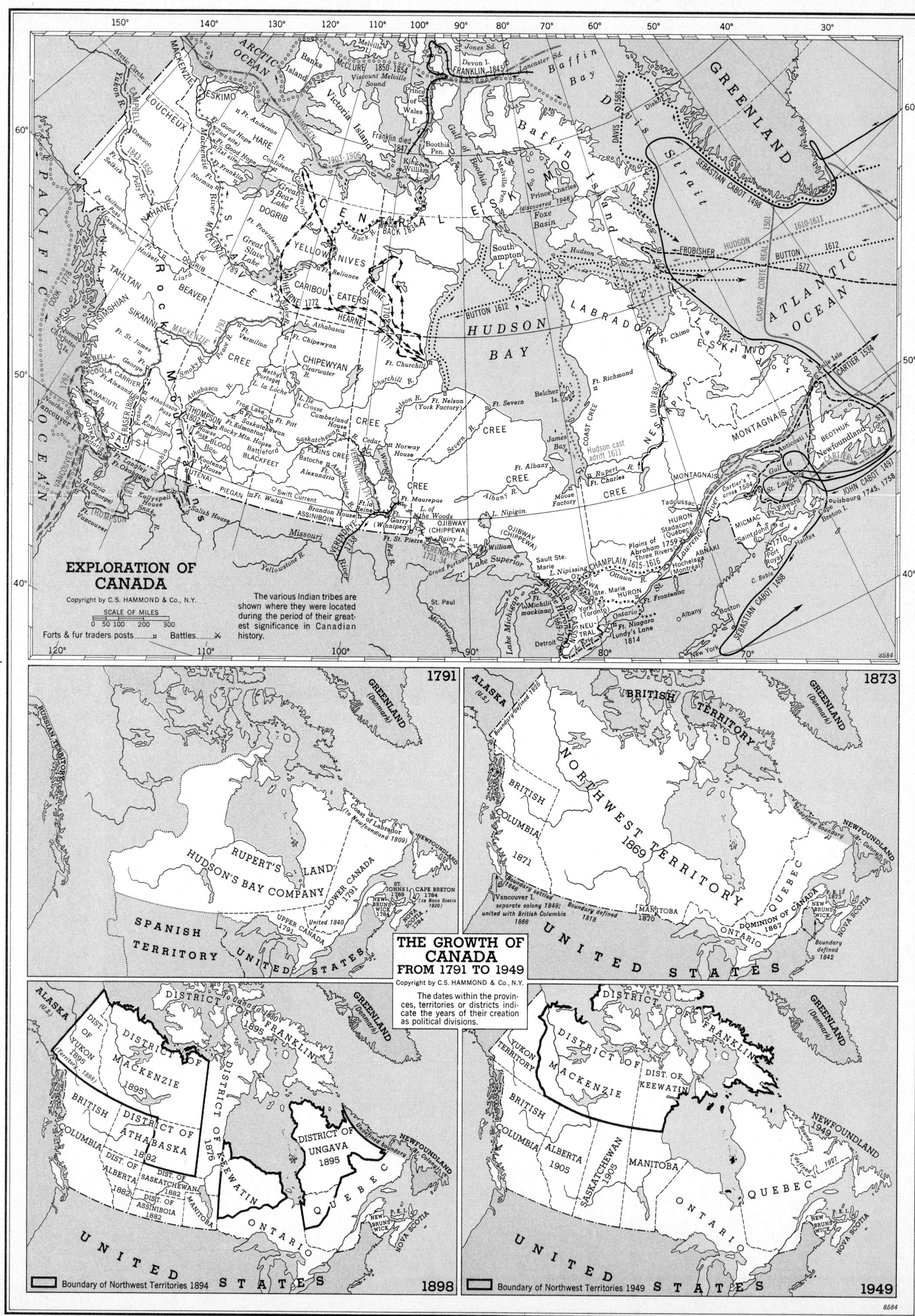
EXPLORATION OF CANADA
Copyright by C.S. HAMMOND & Co., N.Y.
SCALE OF MILES
0 50 100 200 300
Forts & fur traders posts
Battles
The various Indian tribes are shown where they were located during the period of their greatest significance in Canadian history.
1791
1873
1898
1949
THE GROWTH OF CANADA FROM 1791 TO 1949
Copyright by C.S. HAMMOND & Co., N.Y.
The dates within the provinces, territories or districts indicate the years of their creation as political divisions.
Boundary of Northwest Territories 1894
Boundary of Northwest Territories 1949
8584

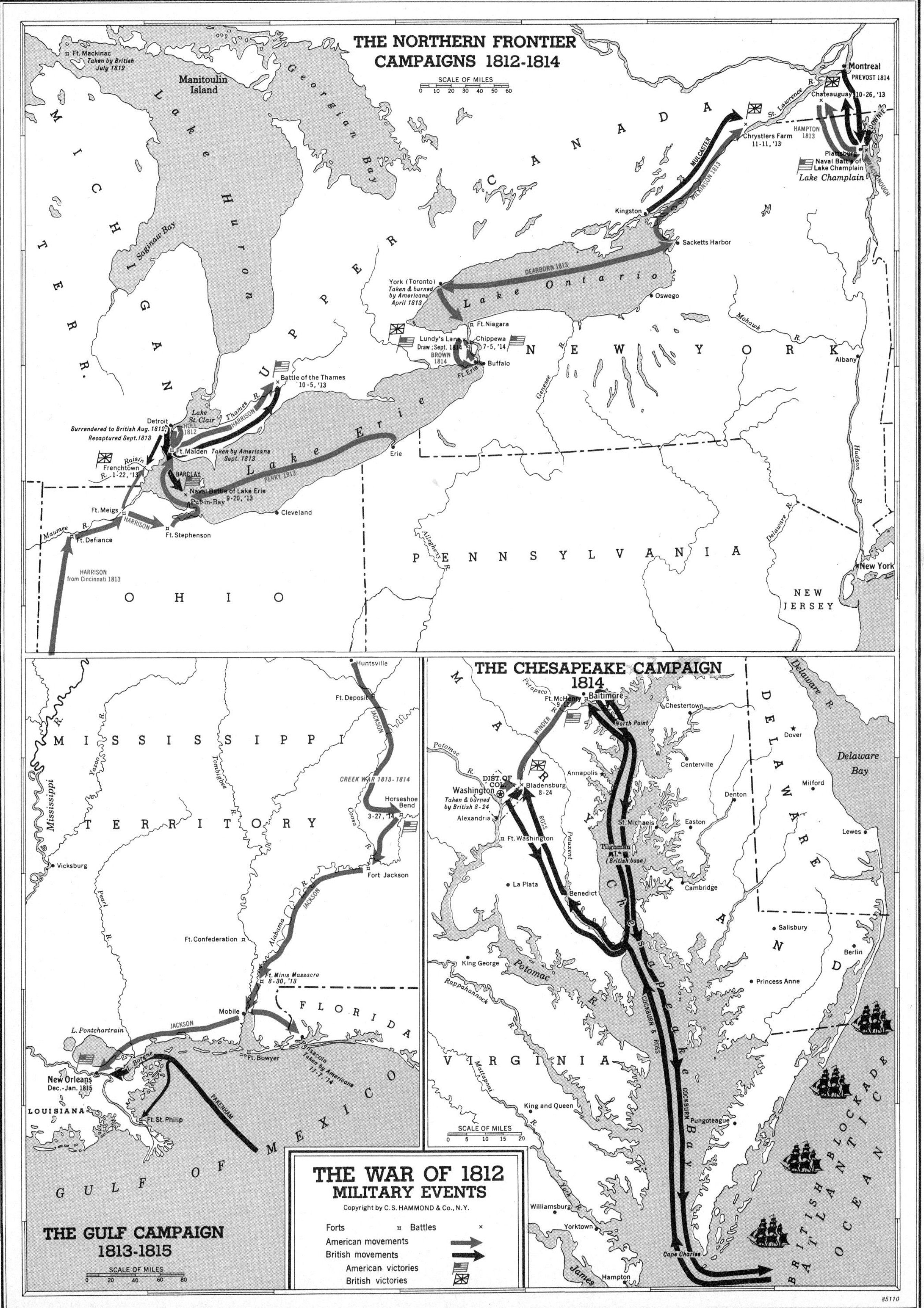
THE NORTHERN FRONTIER CAMPAIGNS 1812-1814
SCALE OF MILES
0 10 20 30 40 50 60
Ft. Mackinac
Taken by British July 1812
Manitoulin Island
Lake Huron
Georgian Bay
Saginaw Bay
MICHIGAN TERR.
UPPER CANADA
Montreal
PREVOST 1814
Chateauguay 10-26, '13
HAMPTON 1813
St. Lawrence R.
Chryslers Farm 11-11, '13
MULCASTER
WILKINSON 1813
Plattsburg
Naval Battle of Lake Champlain
Lake Champlain
MACDONOUGH
Kingston
Sacketts Harbor
DEARBORN 1813
Lake Ontario
York (Toronto)
Taken & burned by Americans April 1813
Oswego
Ft. Niagara
Lundy's Lane
Draw; Sept. 1814
Chippewa 7-5, '14
BROWN 1814
Ft. Erie
Buffalo
Mohawk R.
Genesee R.
NEW YORK
Albany
Battle of the Thames 10-5, '13
Thames R.
HARRISON
Lake St. Clair
Detroit
Surrendered to British Aug. 1812
Recaptured Sept. 1813
HULL 1812
Ft. Malden
Taken by Americans Sept. 1813
Raisin R.
Frenchtown 1-22, '13
BARCLAY
PERRY 1813
Naval Battle of Lake Erie 9-20, '13
Put-in-Bay
Lake Erie
Erie
Cleveland
Ft. Meigs
Ft. Stephenson
Maumee R.
Ft. Defiance
HARRISON from Cincinnati 1813
OHIO
PENNSYLVANIA
Allegheny R.
Delaware R.
Hudson R.
New York
NEW JERSEY
THE GULF CAMPAIGN 1813-1815
SCALE OF MILES
0 20 40 60 80
Huntsville
Ft. Deposit
JACKSON
CREEK WAR 1813-1814
MISSISSIPPI TERRITORY
Mississippi
Yazoo R.
Tombigbee R.
Coosa R.
Horseshoe Bend 3-27, '14
Fort Jackson
Vicksburg
Pearl R.
Alabama R.
Ft. Confederation
Ft. Mims Massacre 8-30, '13
Mobile
FLORIDA
L. Pontchartrain
Ft. Bowyer
Pensacola
Taken by Americans 11-7, '14
L. Borgne
New Orleans
Dec.-Jan. 1815
LOUISIANA
Ft. St. Philip
PAKENHAM
GULF OF MEXICO
THE CHESAPEAKE CAMPAIGN 1814
Patapsco
Ft. McHenry 9-12
Baltimore
North Point
Chestertown
WINDER
Potomac R.
DIST. OF COL.
Washington
Taken & burned by British 8-24
Bladensburg 8-24
Annapolis
Alexandria
ROSS
Ft. Washington
Patuxent
St. Michaels
Easton
Tilghman I.
(British base)
La Plata
Benedict
Cambridge
MARYLAND
DELAWARE
Dover
Centerville
Delaware R.
Delaware Bay
Milford
Denton
Lewes
Salisbury
Berlin
King George
Rappahannock
Princess Anne
Chesapeake Bay
COCKBURN & ROSS
COCKBURN
VIRGINIA
Mattaponi
King and Queen
Pungoteague
SCALE OF MILES
0 5 10 15 20
York R.
Williamsburg
Yorktown
James
Hampton
Cape Charles
BRITISH BLOCKADE
ATLANTIC OCEAN
THE WAR OF 1812
MILITARY EVENTS
Copyright by C.S. HAMMOND & Co., N.Y.
Forts
Battles
American movements
British movements
American victories
British victories
85110

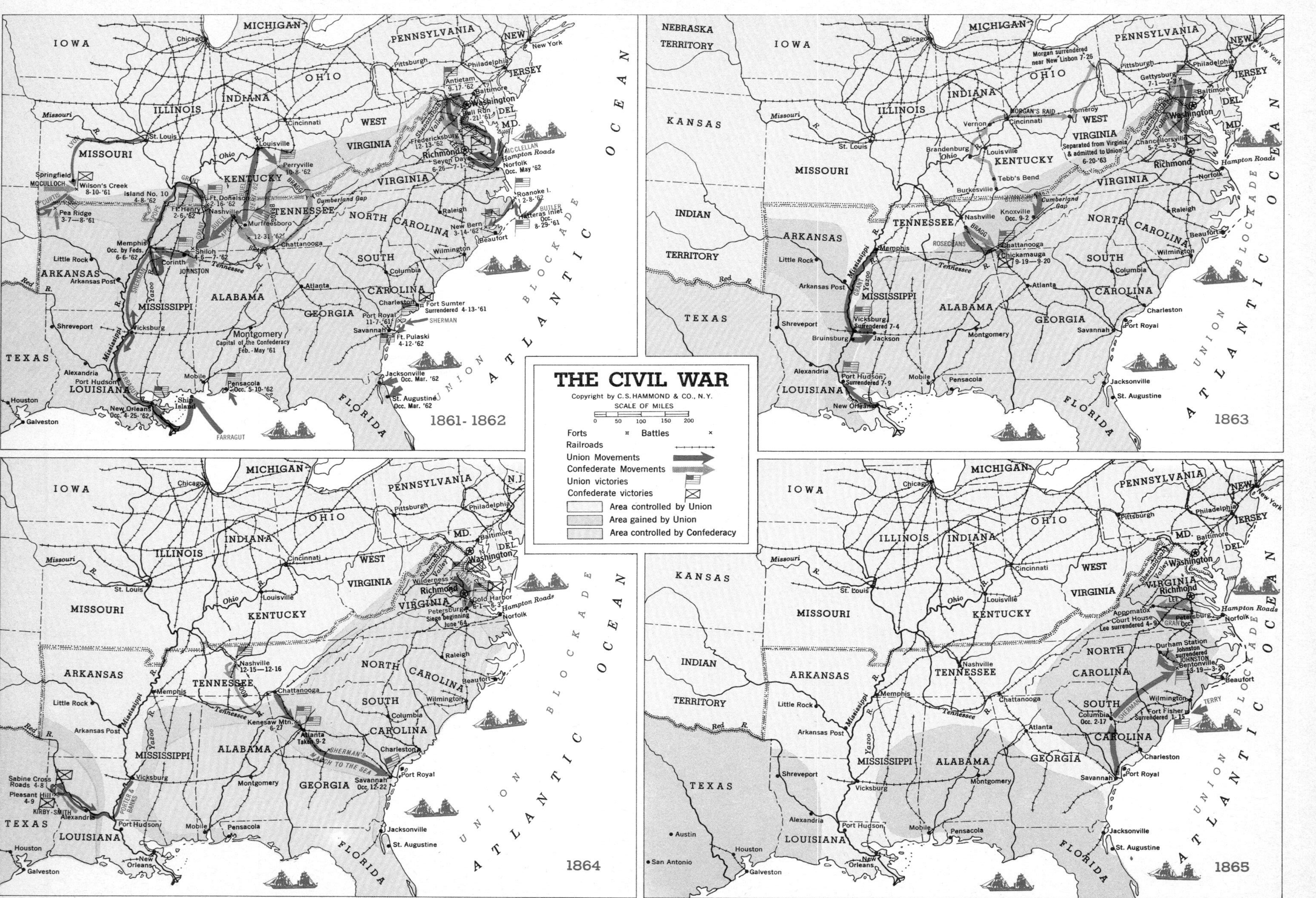
THE CIVIL WAR
Copyright by C. S. HAMMOND & CO., N.Y.
SCALE OF MILES
0 50 100 150 200
Forts
Battles
Railroads
Union Movements
Confederate Movements
Union victories
Confederate victories
Area controlled by Union
Area gained by Union
Area controlled by Confederacy
1861-1862
1863
1864
1865
ATLANTIC OCEAN
UNION BLOCKADE

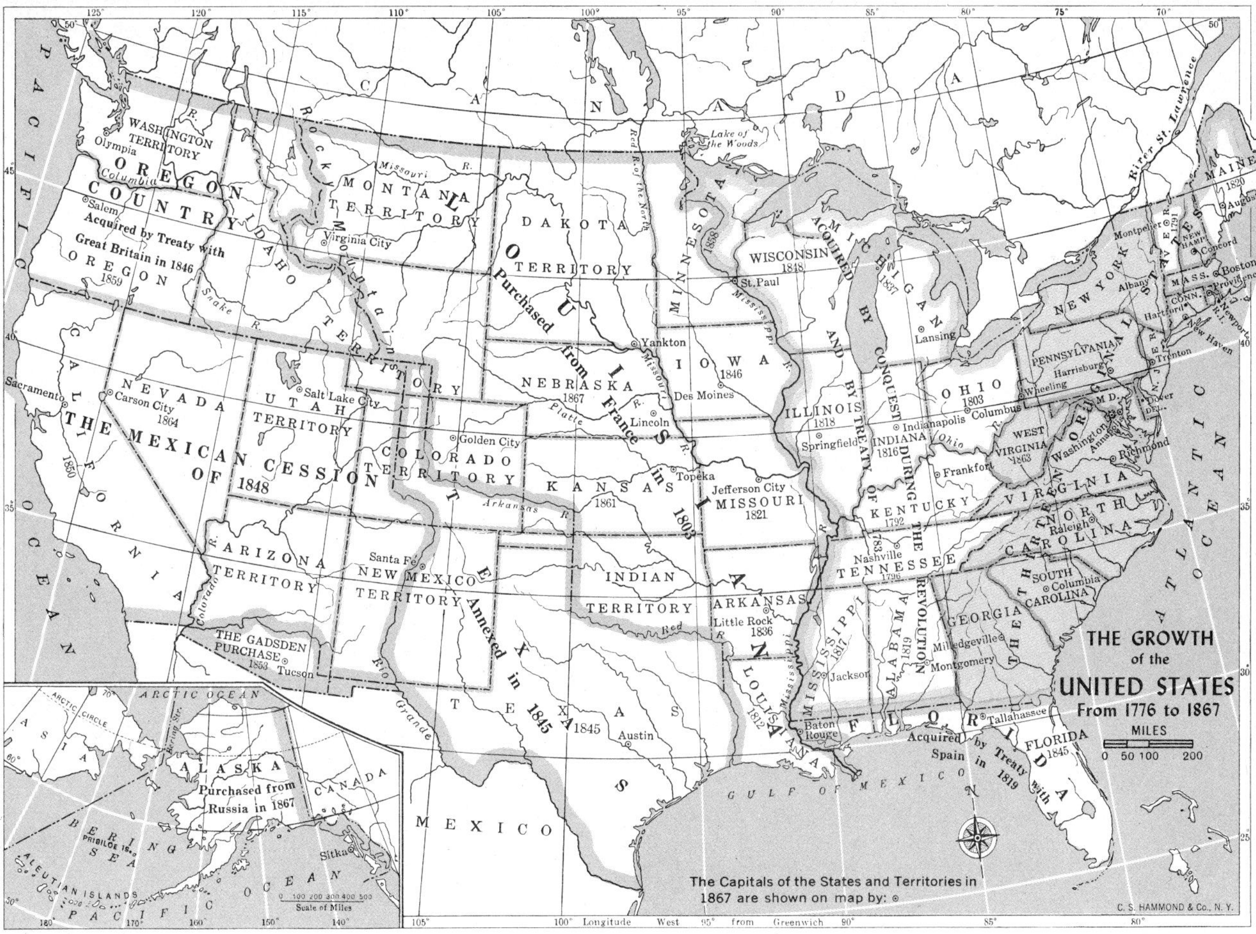

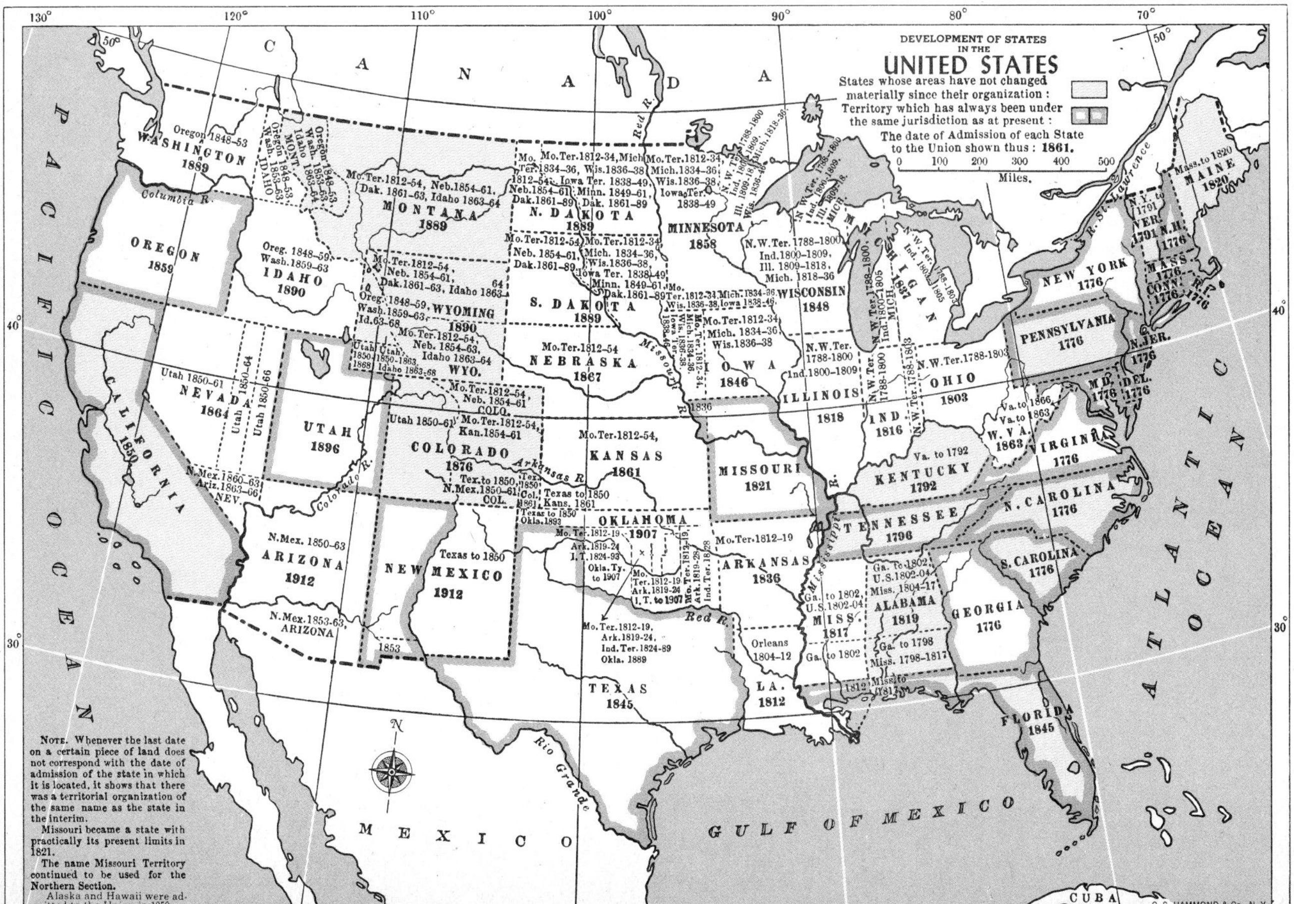

THE GROWTH of the UNITED STATES From 1776 to 1867

MILES
0 50 100 200

The Capitals of the States and Territories in 1867 are shown on map by: ⊙

C. S. HAMMOND & Co., N. Y.

DEVELOPMENT OF STATES IN THE UNITED STATES

States whose areas have not changed materially since their organization :

Territory which has always been under the same jurisdiction as at present :

The date of Admission of each State to the Union shown thus : **1861.**

0 100 200 300 400 500
Miles.

NOTE. Whenever the last date on a certain piece of land does not correspond with the date of admission of the state in which it is located, it shows that there was a territorial organization of the same name as the state in the interim.

Missouri became a state with practically its present limits in 1821.

The name Missouri Territory continued to be used for the Northern Section.

Alaska and Hawaii were admitted to the Union in 1959.

C. S. HAMMOND & Co., N. Y.

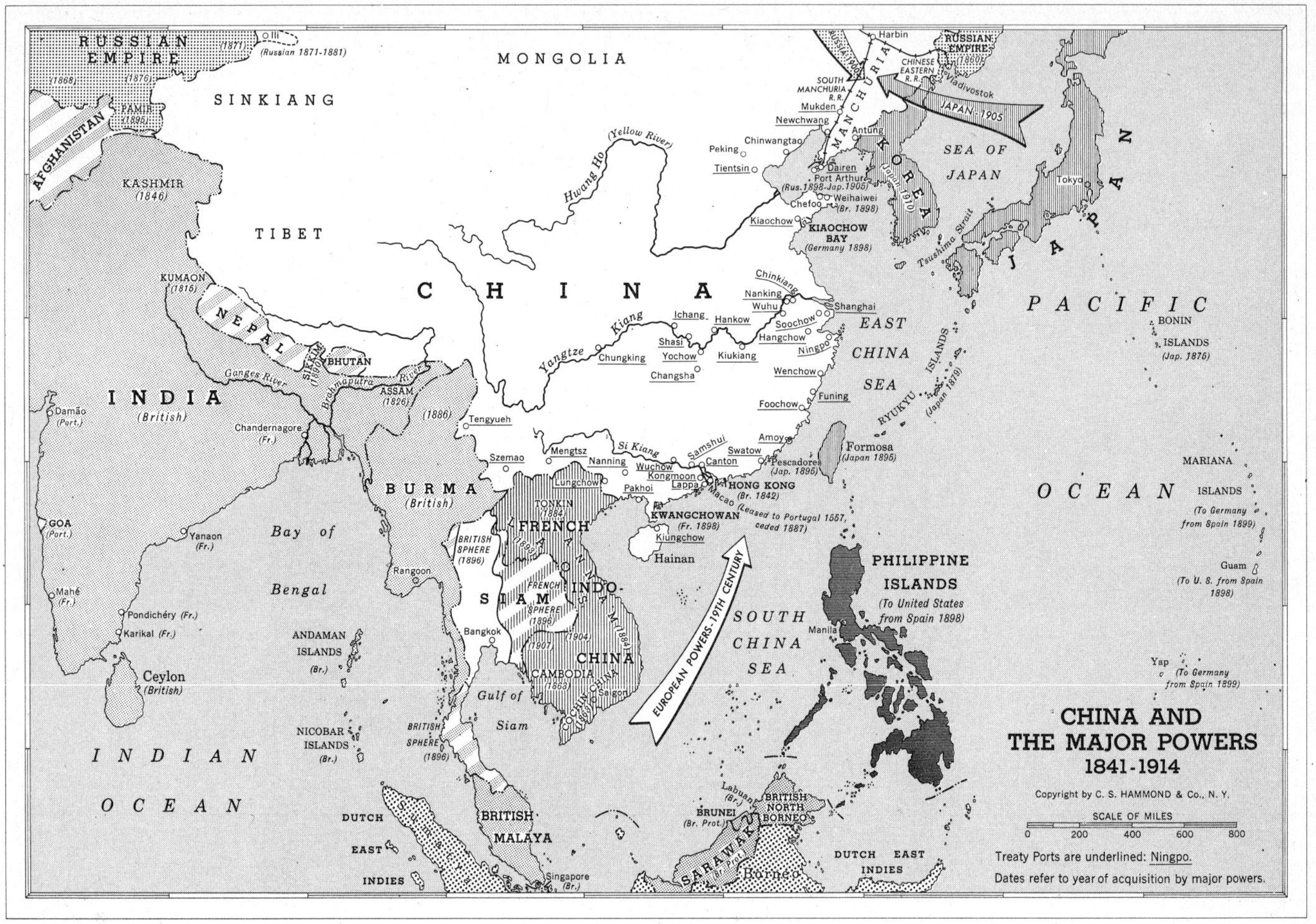

CHINA AND THE MAJOR POWERS 1841-1914

SCALE OF MILES
0 200 400 600 800

Treaty Ports are underlined: Ningpo.

Dates refer to year of acquisition by major powers.

RUSSIAN EMPIRE
MONGOLIA
SINKIANG
AFGHANISTAN
PAMIR (1895)
KASHMIR (1846)
TIBET
CHINA
KUMAON (1816)
NEPAL
SIKKIM (1890)
BHUTAN
ASSAM (1826)
INDIA (British)
BURMA (British)
Ceylon (British)
ANDAMAN ISLANDS (Br.)
NICOBAR ISLANDS (Br.)
Bay of Bengal
INDIAN OCEAN
MANCHURIA
KOREA
JAPAN
SEA OF JAPAN
JAPAN-1905
EAST CHINA SEA
RYUKYU ISLANDS (Japan 1879)
PACIFIC OCEAN
BONIN ISLANDS (Jap. 1876)
MARIANA ISLANDS (To Germany from Spain 1899)
Guam (To U. S. from Spain 1898)
Yap (To Germany from Spain 1899)
Formosa (Japan 1895)
Pescadores (Jap. 1895)
HONG KONG (Br. 1842)
Macao (Leased to Portugal 1557, ceded 1887)
KWANGCHOWAN (Fr. 1898)
KIAOCHOW BAY (Germany 1898)
Weihaiwei (Br. 1898)
Port Arthur (Rus. 1898-Jap. 1905)
PHILIPPINE ISLANDS (To United States from Spain 1898)
SOUTH CHINA SEA
EUROPEAN POWERS-19TH CENTURY
FRENCH INDO-CHINA
TONKIN (1884)
ANNAM (1884)
CAMBODIA (1863)
COCHIN CHINA
SIAM
BRITISH SPHERE (1896)
FRENCH SPHERE (1896)
Gulf of Siam
BRITISH MALAYA
Singapore (Br.)
DUTCH EAST INDIES
BRUNEI (Br. Prot.)
BRITISH NORTH BORNEO
SARAWAK (Br. Prot.)
Borneo
Hainan

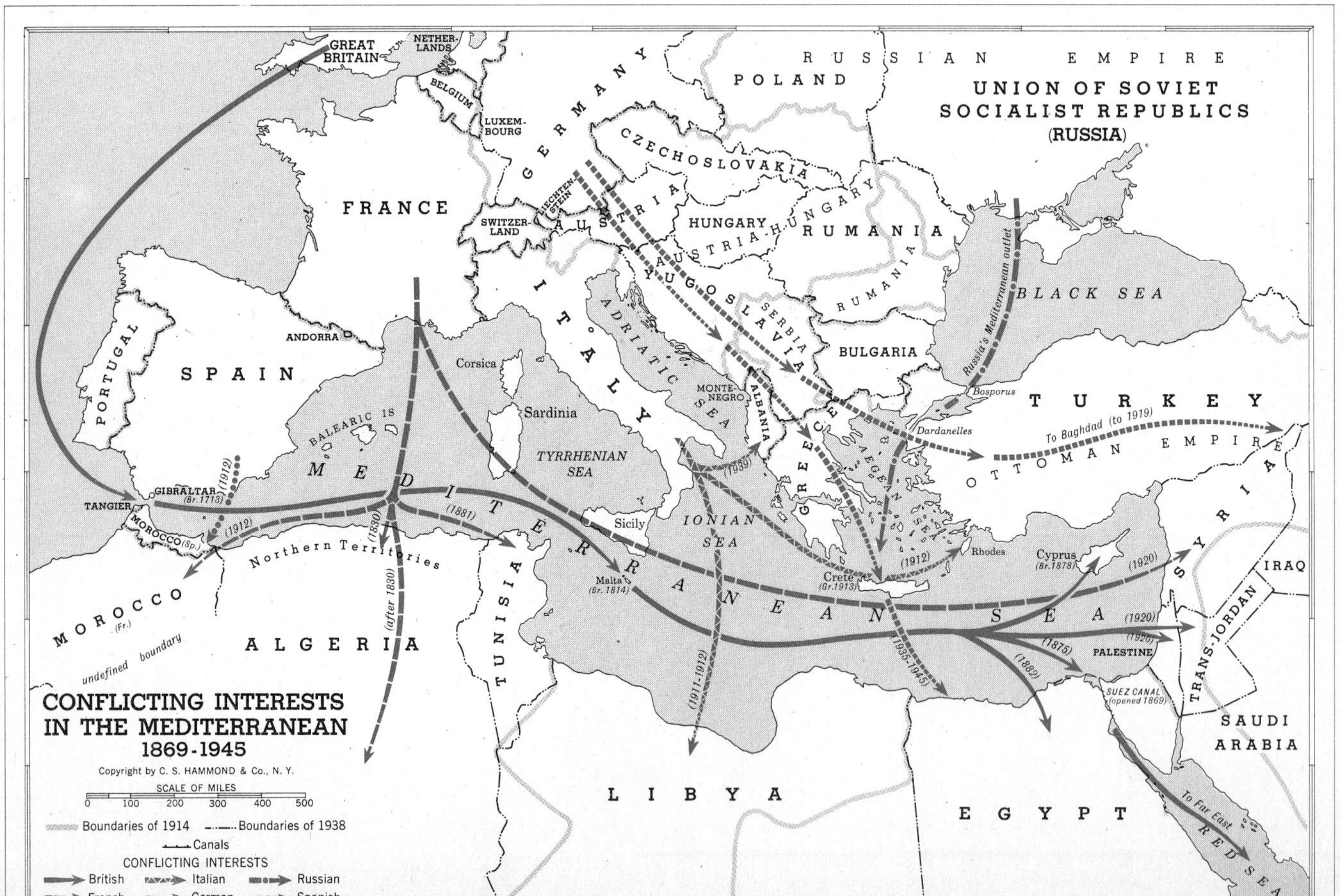

CONFLICTING INTERESTS IN THE MEDITERRANEAN 1869-1945

SCALE OF MILES
0 100 200 300 400 500

Boundaries of 1914 —— Boundaries of 1938 —— Canals

CONFLICTING INTERESTS
British — Italian — Russian
French — German — Spanish

GREAT BRITAIN
NETHERLANDS
BELGIUM
LUXEMBOURG
GERMANY
POLAND
RUSSIAN EMPIRE
UNION OF SOVIET SOCIALIST REPUBLICS (RUSSIA)
CZECHOSLOVAKIA
FRANCE
SWITZERLAND
LIECHTENSTEIN
AUSTRIA
HUNGARY
AUSTRIA-HUNGARY
RUMANIA
YUGOSLAVIA
SERBIA
BULGARIA
BLACK SEA
Russia's Mediterranean outlet
Bosporus
Dardanelles
TURKEY
OTTOMAN EMPIRE
To Baghdad (to 1919)
PORTUGAL
SPAIN
ANDORRA
ITALY
Corsica
Sardinia
ADRIATIC SEA
MONTENEGRO
ALBANIA
GREECE
AEGEAN SEA
TYRRHENIAN SEA
IONIAN SEA
Sicily
MEDITERRANEAN SEA
BALEARIC IS.
GIBRALTAR (Br. 1713)
TANGIER
MOROCCO (Sp.)
MOROCCO (Fr.)
Northern Territories
undefined boundary
ALGERIA
TUNISIA
Malta (Br. 1814)
Crete (Gr. 1913)
Rhodes
Cyprus (Br. 1878)
SYRIA
IRAQ
TRANS-JORDAN
PALESTINE
SUEZ CANAL (opened 1869)
SAUDI ARABIA
LIBYA
EGYPT
To Far East
RED SEA

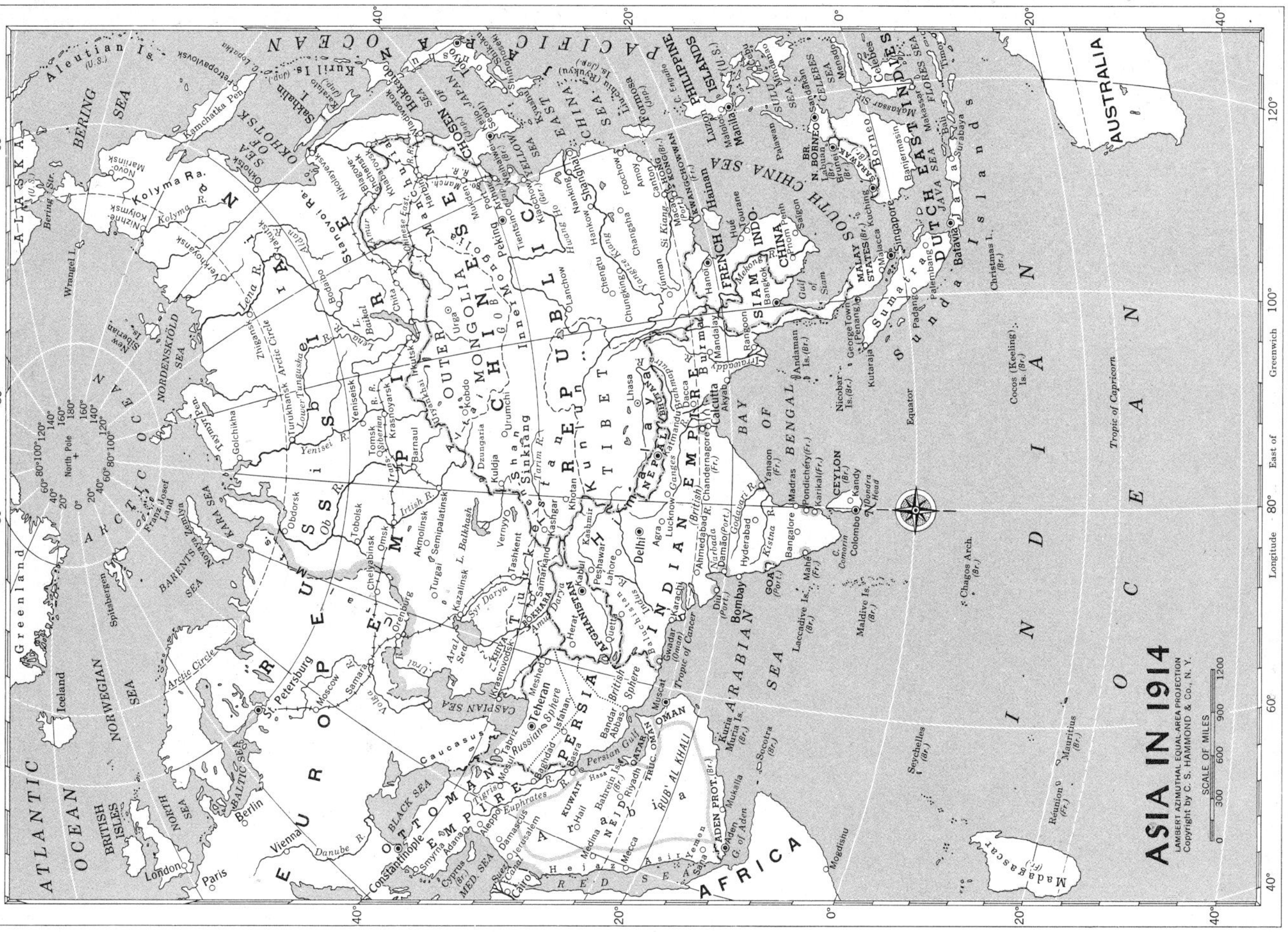
ASIA IN 1914
LAMBERT AZIMUTHAL EQUAL AREA PROJECTION
Copyright by C. S. HAMMOND & Co., N. Y.
SCALE OF MILES
0 300 600 900 1200

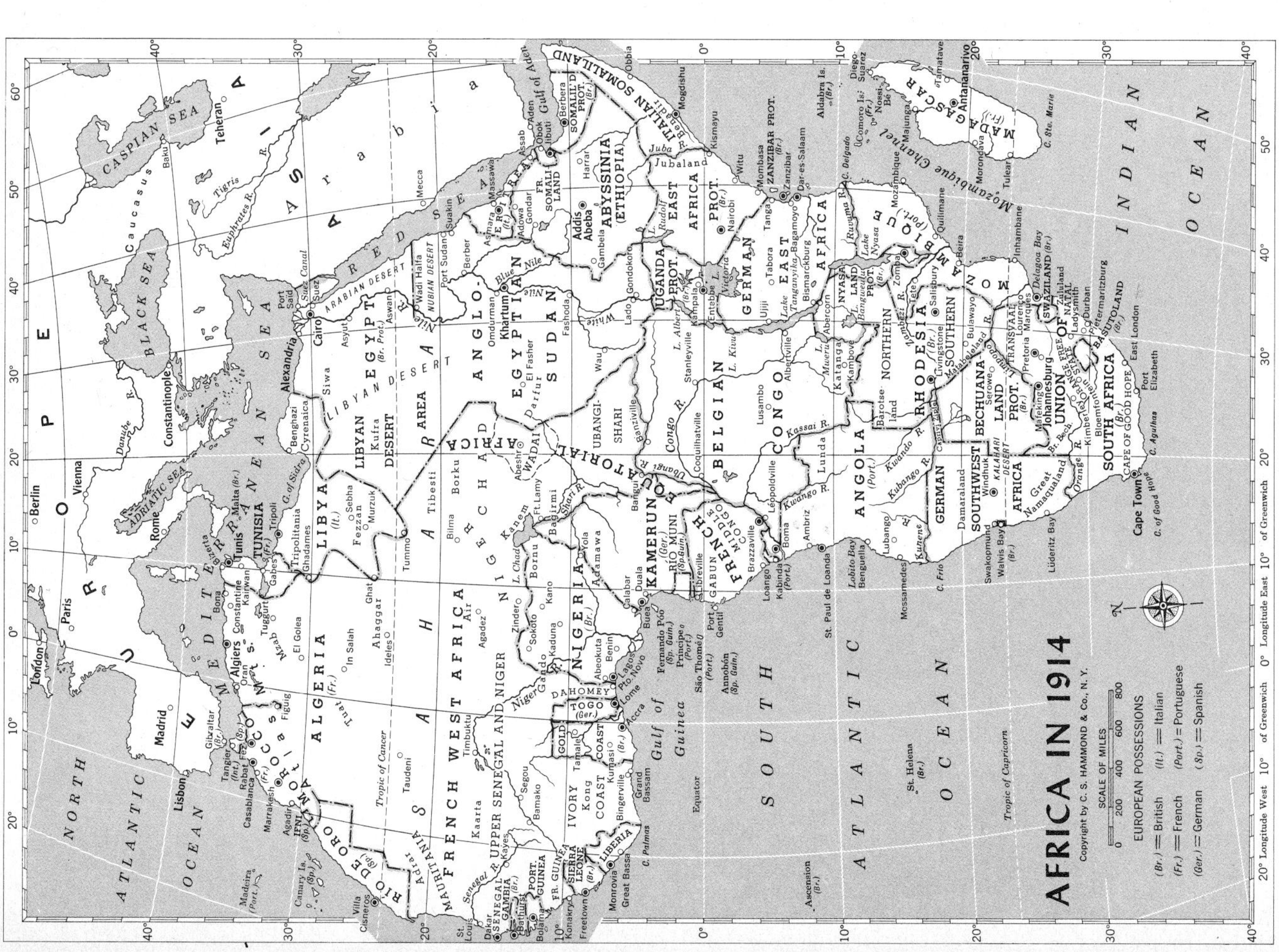
AFRICA IN 1914
Copyright by C. S. HAMMOND & Co., N. Y.
SCALE OF MILES
0 200 400 600 800
EUROPEAN POSSESSIONS
(Br.) = British (It.) = Italian
(Fr.) = French (Port.) = Portuguese
(Ger.) = German (Sp.) = Spanish

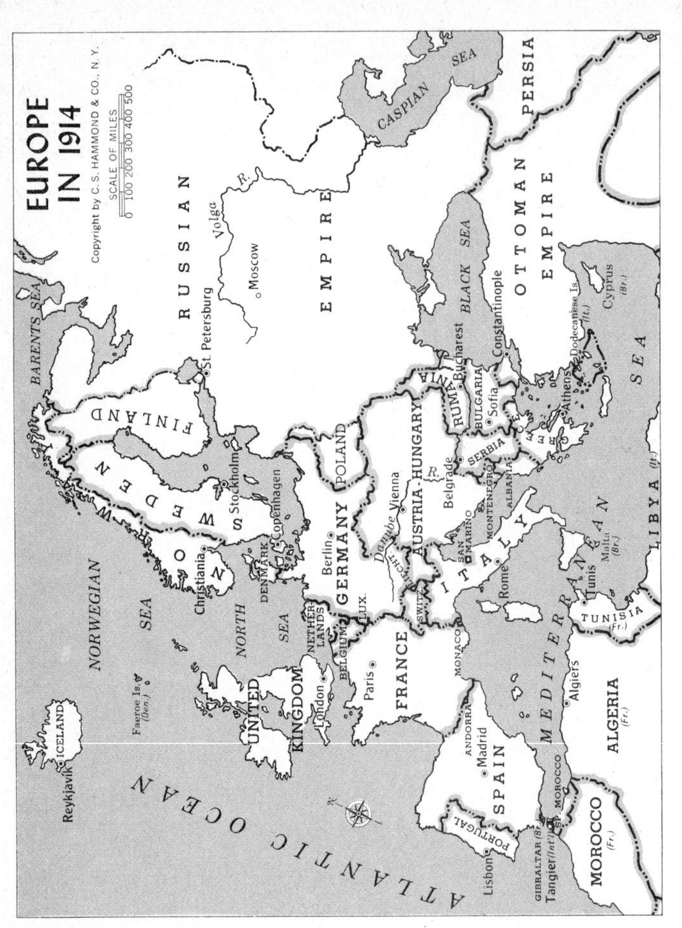

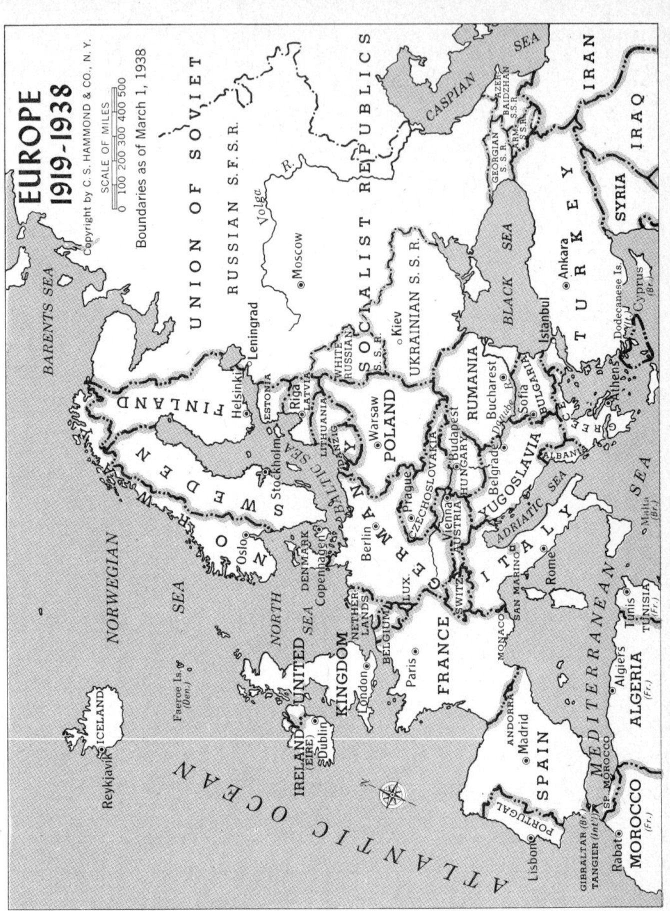

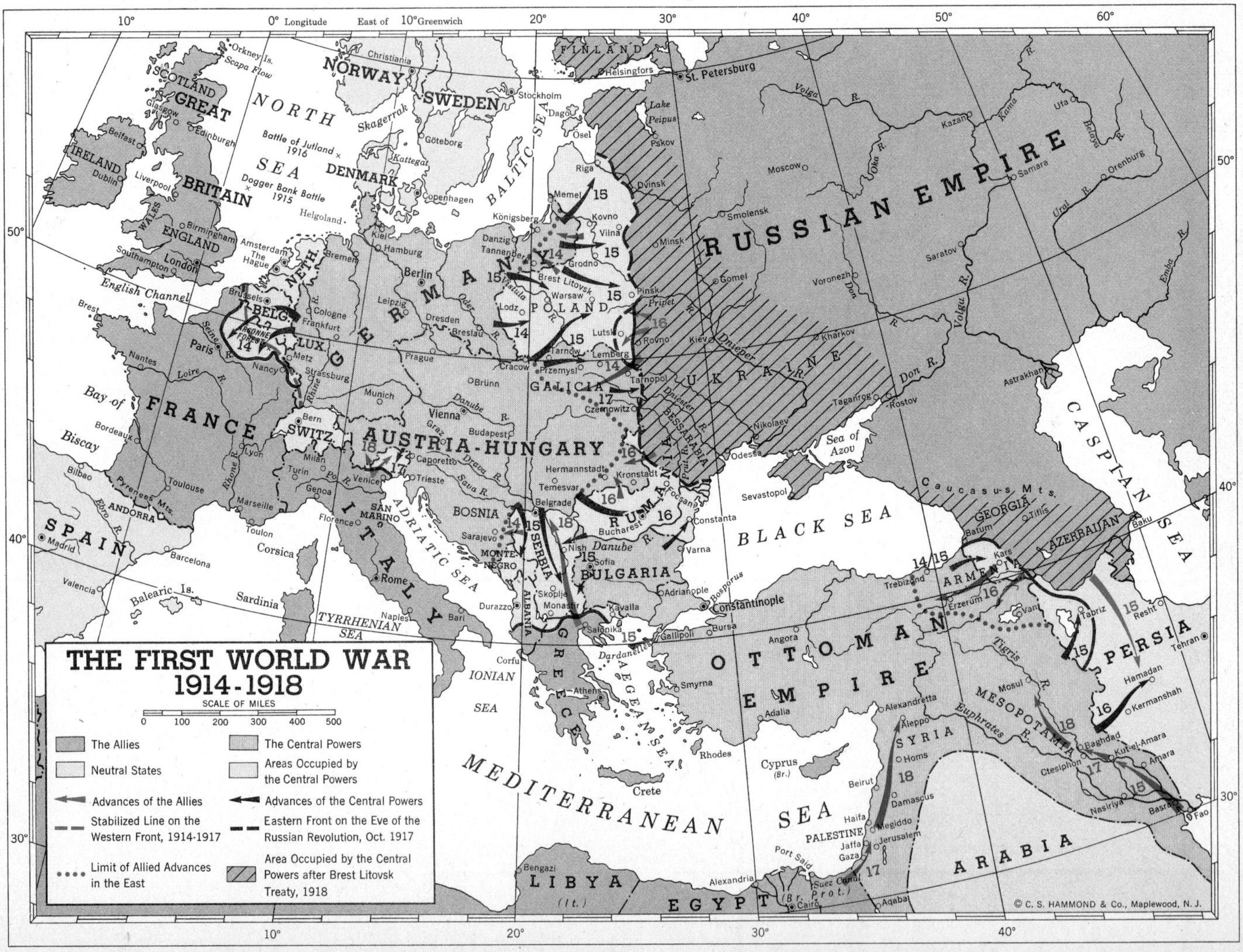

THE FIRST WORLD WAR 1914-1918

SCALE OF MILES

0 100 200 300 400 500

- The Allies
- The Central Powers
- Neutral States
- Areas Occupied by the Central Powers
- Advances of the Allies
- Advances of the Central Powers
- Stabilized Line on the Western Front, 1914-1917
- Eastern Front on the Eve of the Russian Revolution, Oct. 1917
- Limit of Allied Advances in the East
- Area Occupied by the Central Powers after Brest Litovsk Treaty, 1918

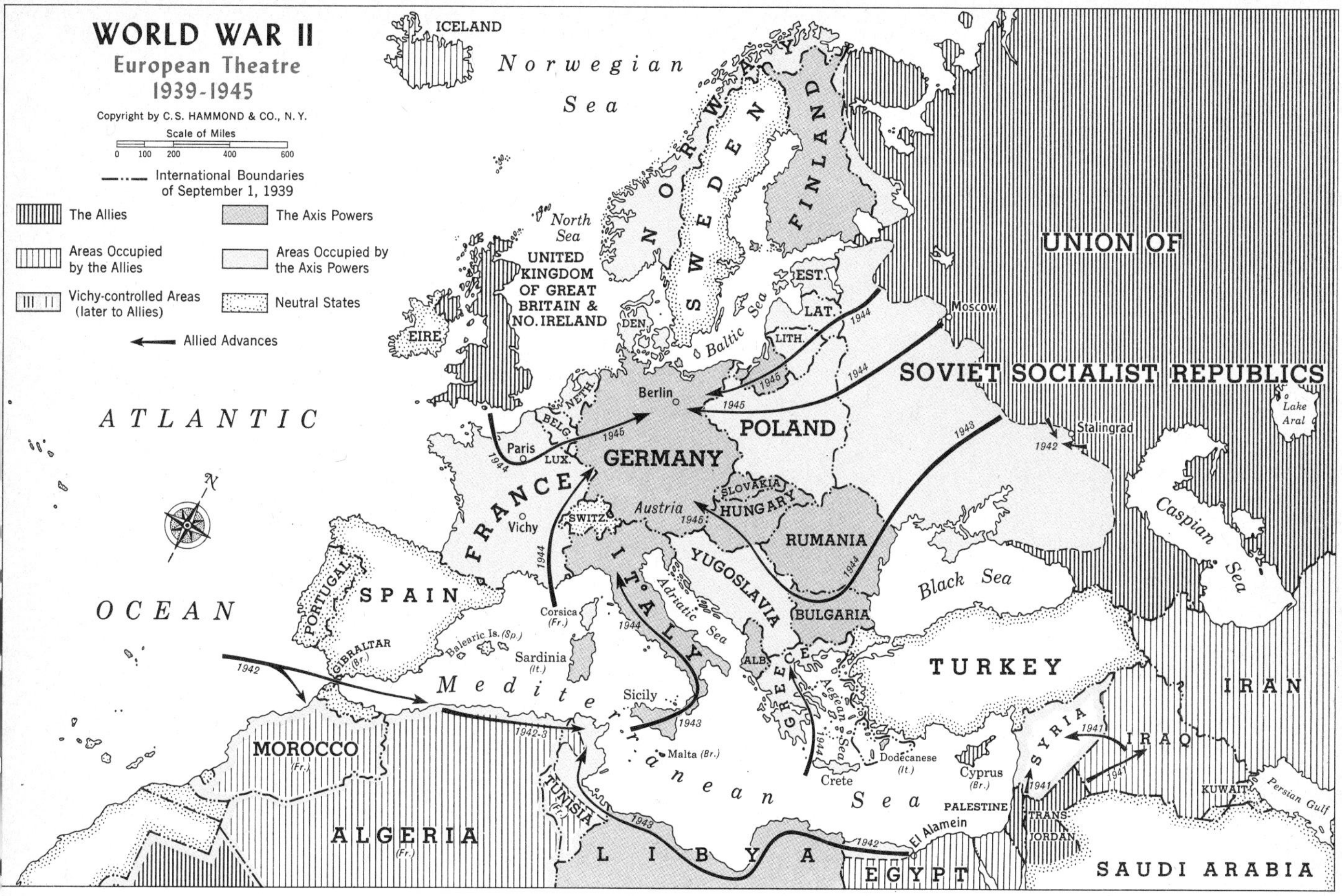
WORLD WAR II
European Theatre
1939-1945
Copyright by C.S. HAMMOND & CO., N.Y.
Scale of Miles
0 100 200 400 600
International Boundaries of September 1, 1939
The Allies
The Axis Powers
Areas Occupied by the Allies
Areas Occupied by the Axis Powers
Vichy-controlled Areas (later to Allies)
Neutral States
Allied Advances
ICELAND
Norwegian Sea
NORWAY
SWEDEN
FINLAND
North Sea
UNITED KINGDOM OF GREAT BRITAIN & NO. IRELAND
EIRE
DEN.
Baltic Sea
EST.
LAT.
LITH.
Moscow
UNION OF SOVIET SOCIALIST REPUBLICS
Lake Aral
Stalingrad
Berlin
NETH.
BELG.
LUX.
Paris
GERMANY
POLAND
FRANCE
Vichy
SWITZ.
Austria
SLOVAKIA
HUNGARY
RUMANIA
Caspian Sea
ATLANTIC OCEAN
PORTUGAL
SPAIN
GIBRALTAR (Br.)
Balearic Is. (Sp.)
Corsica (Fr.)
Sardinia (It.)
ITALY
Adriatic Sea
YUGOSLAVIA
BULGARIA
Black Sea
ALB.
GREECE
Aegean Sea
TURKEY
IRAN
Sicily
Malta (Br.)
Mediterranean Sea
Dodecanese (It.)
Crete
Cyprus (Br.)
SYRIA
IRAQ
KUWAIT
Persian Gulf
MOROCCO (Fr.)
ALGERIA (Fr.)
TUNISIA
LIBYA
PALESTINE
TRANS JORDAN
El Alamein
EGYPT
SAUDI ARABIA
1942
1942-3
1943
1944
1945
1941

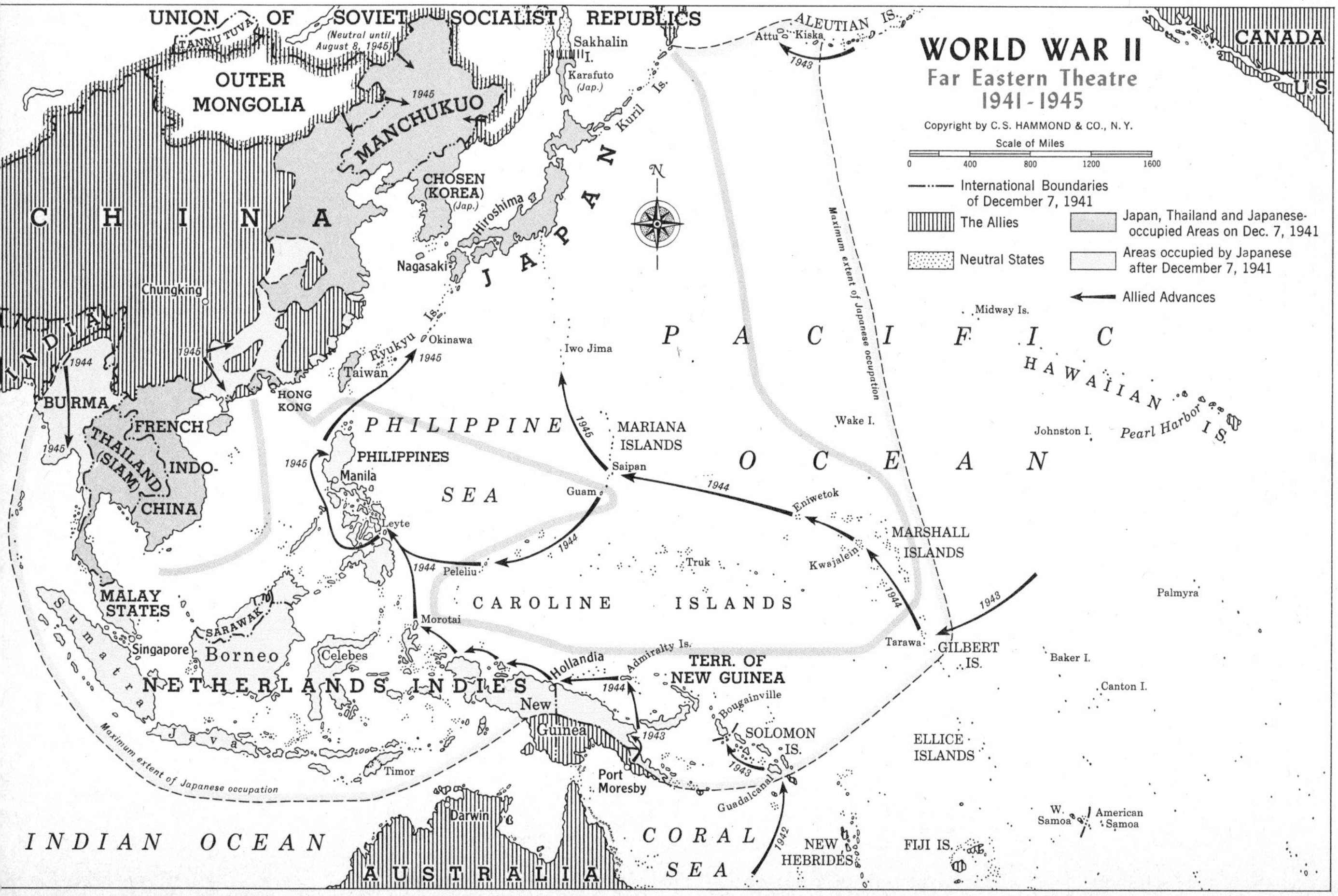
WORLD WAR II
Far Eastern Theatre
1941-1945
Copyright by C.S. HAMMOND & CO., N.Y.
Scale of Miles
0 400 800 1200 1600
International Boundaries of December 7, 1941
The Allies
Japan, Thailand and Japanese-occupied Areas on Dec. 7, 1941
Neutral States
Areas occupied by Japanese after December 7, 1941
Allied Advances
UNION OF SOVIET SOCIALIST REPUBLICS
TANNU TUVA
(Neutral until August 8, 1945)
Sakhalin I.
Karafuto (Jap.)
ALEUTIAN IS.
Attu
Kiska
CANADA
U.S.
OUTER MONGOLIA
MANCHUKUO
CHOSEN (KOREA) (Jap.)
Kuril Is.
JAPAN
Hiroshima
Nagasaki
CHINA
Chungking
INDIA
BURMA
FRENCH INDO-CHINA
THAILAND (SIAM)
HONG KONG
Taiwan
Ryukyu Is.
Okinawa
Iwo Jima
Maximum extent of Japanese occupation
Midway Is.
PACIFIC OCEAN
HAWAIIAN IS.
Pearl Harbor
Johnston I.
Wake I.
PHILIPPINE SEA
PHILIPPINES
Manila
Leyte
MARIANA ISLANDS
Saipan
Guam
Eniwetok
MARSHALL ISLANDS
Kwajalein
Truk
Peleliu
CAROLINE ISLANDS
MALAY STATES
Sumatra
Singapore
SARAWAK
Borneo
Celebes
Morotai
NETHERLANDS INDIES
Java
Timor
Hollandia
Admiralty Is.
TERR. OF NEW GUINEA
New Guinea
Port Moresby
Bougainville
SOLOMON IS.
Guadalcanal
Tarawa
GILBERT IS.
Palmyra
Baker I.
Canton I.
ELLICE ISLANDS
W. Samoa
American Samoa
FIJI IS.
NEW HEBRIDES
CORAL SEA
Darwin
AUSTRALIA
INDIAN OCEAN
1942
1943
1944
1945

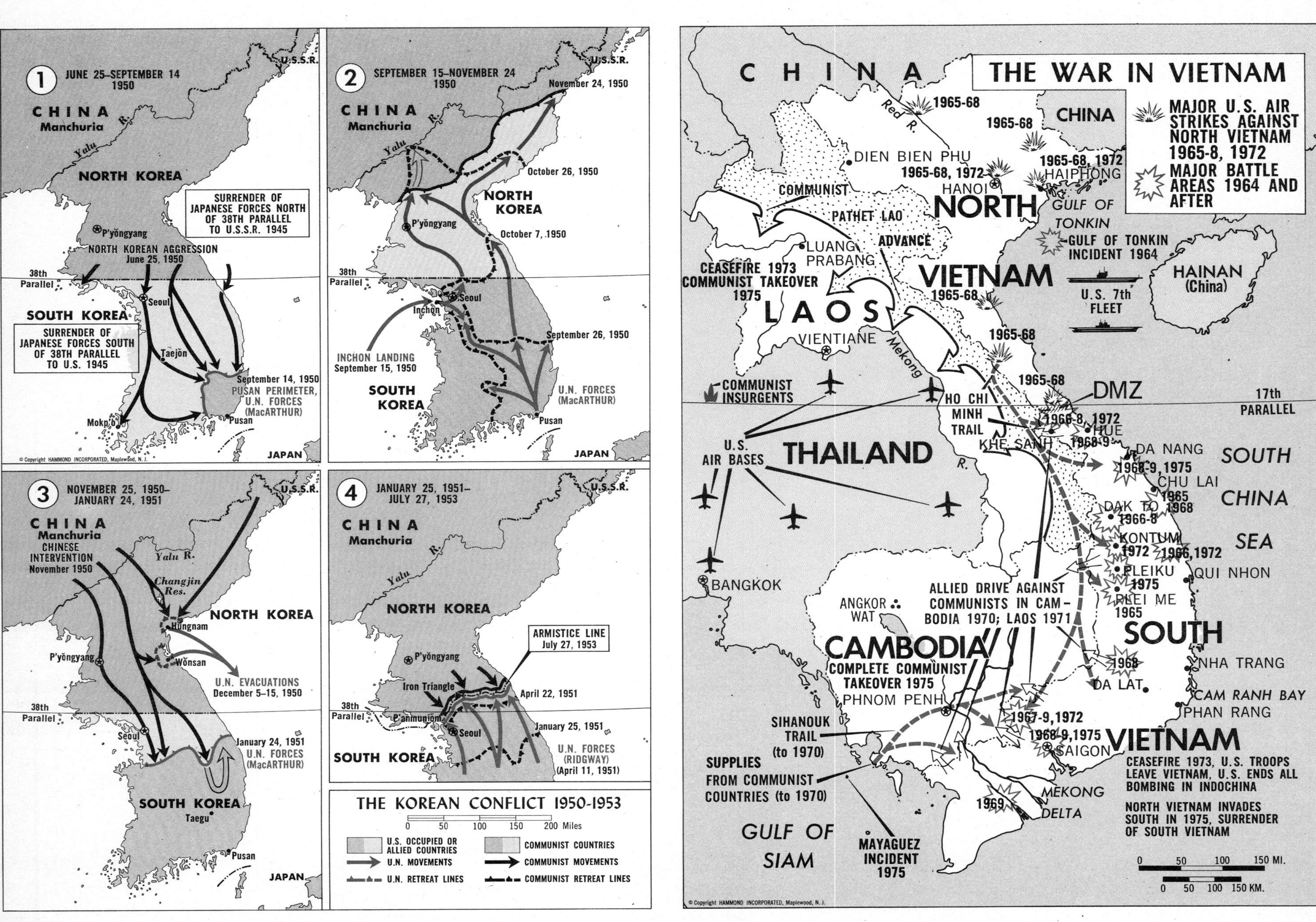
THE KOREAN CONFLICT 1950-1953
U.S. OCCUPIED OR ALLIED COUNTRIES
COMMUNIST COUNTRIES
U.N. MOVEMENTS
COMMUNIST MOVEMENTS
U.N. RETREAT LINES
COMMUNIST RETREAT LINES
0 50 100 150 200 Miles
1 JUNE 25–SEPTEMBER 14 1950
CHINA Manchuria
NORTH KOREA
SURRENDER OF JAPANESE FORCES NORTH OF 38TH PARALLEL TO U.S.S.R. 1945
NORTH KOREAN AGGRESSION June 25, 1950
SOUTH KOREA
SURRENDER OF JAPANESE FORCES SOUTH OF 38TH PARALLEL TO U.S. 1945
September 14, 1950 PUSAN PERIMETER, U.N. FORCES (MacARTHUR)
2 SEPTEMBER 15–NOVEMBER 24 1950
November 24, 1950
October 26, 1950
October 7, 1950
INCHON LANDING September 15, 1950
September 26, 1950
U.N. FORCES (MacARTHUR)
3 NOVEMBER 25, 1950– JANUARY 24, 1951
CHINESE INTERVENTION November 1950
U.N. EVACUATIONS December 5–15, 1950
January 24, 1951 U.N. FORCES (MacARTHUR)
4 JANUARY 25, 1951– JULY 27, 1953
ARMISTICE LINE July 27, 1953
Iron Triangle
April 22, 1951
January 25, 1951
U.N. FORCES (RIDGWAY) (April 11, 1951)
THE WAR IN VIETNAM
MAJOR U.S. AIR STRIKES AGAINST NORTH VIETNAM 1965-8, 1972
MAJOR BATTLE AREAS 1964 AND AFTER
CEASEFIRE 1973 COMMUNIST TAKEOVER 1975
COMMUNIST PATHET LAO ADVANCE
GULF OF TONKIN INCIDENT 1964
U.S. 7th FLEET
COMMUNIST INSURGENTS
U.S. AIR BASES
HO CHI MINH TRAIL
ALLIED DRIVE AGAINST COMMUNISTS IN CAMBODIA 1970; LAOS 1971
CAMBODIA
COMPLETE COMMUNIST TAKEOVER 1975
SIHANOUK TRAIL (to 1970)
SUPPLIES FROM COMMUNIST COUNTRIES (to 1970)
MAYAGUEZ INCIDENT 1975
CEASEFIRE 1973, U.S. TROOPS LEAVE VIETNAM, U.S. ENDS ALL BOMBING IN INDOCHINA
NORTH VIETNAM INVADES SOUTH IN 1975, SURRENDER OF SOUTH VIETNAM
0 50 100 150 MI.
0 50 100 150 KM.

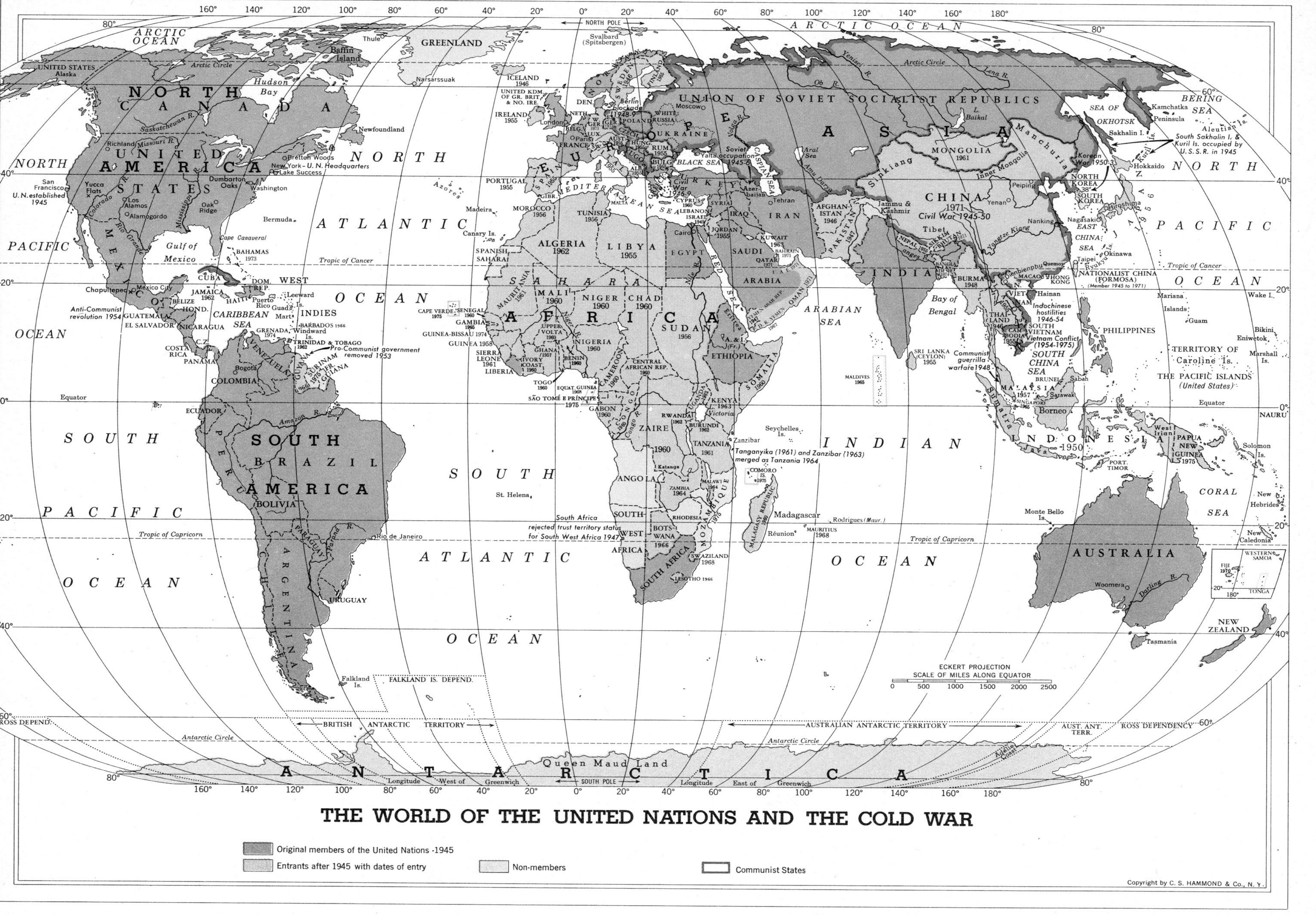
THE WORLD OF THE UNITED NATIONS AND THE COLD WAR
Original members of the United Nations -1945
Entrants after 1945 with dates of entry
Non-members
Communist States
ECKERT PROJECTION
SCALE OF MILES ALONG EQUATOR
0 500 1000 1500 2000 2500
Copyright by C. S. HAMMOND & Co., N. Y.
NORTH AMERICA
CANADA
UNITED STATES
MEXICO
SOUTH AMERICA
BRAZIL
ARGENTINA
EUROPE
AFRICA
ASIA
UNION OF SOVIET SOCIALIST REPUBLICS
CHINA 1971 Civil War 1945-50
INDIA
AUSTRALIA
ANTARCTICA
ARCTIC OCEAN
NORTH PACIFIC OCEAN
SOUTH PACIFIC OCEAN
NORTH ATLANTIC OCEAN
SOUTH ATLANTIC OCEAN
INDIAN OCEAN
San Francisco U.N. established 1945
New York - U. N. Headquarters
Lake Success
Berlin blockade 1948-9
Soviet occupation 1945-6
Korean War 1950-3
South Sakhalin I. & Kuril Is. occupied by U.S.S.R. in 1945
Indochinese hostilities 1946-54
Vietnam Conflict (1954-1975)
Communist guerrilla warfare 1948
Anti-Communist revolution 1954
Pro-Communist government removed 1953
Tanganyika (1961) and Zanzibar (1963) merged as Tanzania 1964
South Africa rejected trust territory status for South West Africa 1947
NATIONALIST CHINA (FORMOSA) (Member 1945 to 1971)
TERRITORY OF THE PACIFIC ISLANDS (United States)
BRITISH ANTARCTIC TERRITORY
AUSTRALIAN ANTARCTIC TERRITORY
ROSS DEPENDENCY
FALKLAND IS. DEPEND.
Tropic of Cancer
Equator
Tropic of Capricorn
Arctic Circle
Antarctic Circle

THE WORLD TODAY

Western Hemisphere

THE UNITED NATIONS

Afghanistan
Albania
Algeria
Argentina
Australia
Austria
Bahamas
Bahrain
Bangladesh
Barbados
Belgium
Benin
Bhutan
Bolivia
Botswana
Brazil
Bulgaria
Burma
Burundi
Cambodia
Cameroon
Canada
Cape Verde
Central African Republic
Chad
Chile
China
Colombia
Comoro Islands
Congo, Rep. of (Brazzaville)
Costa Rica
Cuba
Cyprus
Czechoslovakia
Denmark
Dominican Republic
Ecuador
Egypt
El Salvador
Equatorial Guinea
Ethiopia
Fiji
Finland
France
Gabon
Gambia
Germany, East
Germany, West
Ghana
Greece
Grenada
Guatemala
Guinea
Guinea-Bissau
Guyana
Haiti
Honduras
Hungary
Iceland
India
Indonesia
Iran
Iraq
Ireland
Israel
Italy
Ivory Coast
Jamaica
Japan
Jordan
Kenya
Kuwait
Laos
Lebanon
Lesotho
Liberia
Libya
Luxembourg
Malagasy Rep.
Malawi
Malaysia
Maldives
Mali
Malta
Mauritania
Mauritius
Mexico
Mongolia
Morocco
Mozambique
Nepal
Netherlands
New Zealand
Nicaragua
Niger
Nigeria
Norway
Oman
Pakistan
Panama
Papua New Guinea
Paraguay
Peru
Philippines
Poland
Portugal
Qatar
Rumania
Rwanda
São Tomé e Príncipe
Saudi Arabia
Senegal
Sierra Leone
Singapore
Somalia
South Africa
Soviet Union
Byelorussian S.S.R.
Ukrainian S.S.R.
Spain
Sri Lanka
Sudan
Surinam
Swaziland
Sweden
Syria
Tanzania
Thailand
Togo
Trinidad and Tobago
Tunisia
Turkey
Uganda
United Arab Emirates
United Kingdom
United States
Upper Volta
Uruguay
Venezuela
Yemen, P.D.R. of
Yemen Arab Rep.
Yugoslavia
Zaire
Zambia

NORTH ATLANTIC TREATY ORGANIZATION (NATO)

elgium
anada
enmark
rance
erman Federal Rep. (West Ger.)
reece
celand
Italy
Luxembourg
Netherlands
Norway
Portugal
Turkey
United Kingdom
United States

ORGANIZATION OF AMERICAN STATES (OAS-Rio Pact)

Argentina
Barbados
Bolivia
Brazil
Chile
Colombia
Costa Rica
Dominican Republic
Ecuador
El Salvador
Guatemala
Haiti
Honduras
Jamaica
Mexico
Nicaragua
Panama
Paraguay
Peru
Trinidad & Tobago
United States
Uruguay
Venezuela
Cuba*

* Expelled from activities of O.A.S.

SOUTH-EAST ASIA TREATY ORGANIZATION (SEATO)

Australia
France
New Zealand
Pakistan
Philippines
Thailand
United Kingdom
United States

CENTRAL TREATY ORGANIZATION* (CENTO)

Iran
Pakistan
Turkey
United Kingdom

* Formerly Baghdad Pact

WARSAW PACT COUNTRIES ("SOVIET BLOC")

Soviet Union
Bulgaria
Czechoslovakia
German Democratic Rep. (East Ger.)
Hungary
Poland
Rumania

VOYAGES OF DISCOVERY & EXPLORATION

Year	Explorer and Nationality	Discovery — Exploration — Journey
B. C.		
500	Himilco (Carthage)	Explores Atlantic Coast of Europe.
470	Hanno (Carthage)	Leads a colonizing expedition to West Africa, as far as Cape Palmas.
330	Pytheas of Massilia (Greek)	Explores coast of Spain, Gaul and Great Britain.
332-326	Alexander the Great (Macedonia)	Enters India in 326.
325	Nearcnus (Macedonia)	Sails from the Indus to the Euphrates River.
120	Eudoxus of Cnidus (Greek)	Attempts circumnavigation of Africa.
A. D.		
84	Gnaeus Julius Agricola (Roman)	Circumnavigates Great Britain.
861	Norsemen	Explore Faeroe Islands and Iceland; round north cape of Europe.
876	Gunnbjörn (Norse)	Sights Greenland Coast.
982	Eric the Red (Norse)	Discovers and names Greenland.
1000	Leif Ericson (Norse)	Discovers Newfoundland (Helluland), and Coast of New England (Vinland).
1160	Benjamin of Tudela (Navarre)	Travels in Turkey, Egypt, Assyria and Persia, penetrating to the frontiers of China.
1200	Arabs	Trading merchants discover Siberia.
1253	Jan van Ruysbroek (Dutch)	Reaches Karakorum, the ancient seat of the Mongol Empire.
1271-1295	Marco Polo (Venetian)	Travels in Central Asia, India, Persia. First to travel in China.
1325-1352	Ibn Batuta (Arabian)	Travels through North Africa, East Africa, South Russia, Arabia, India and China.
1487	Bartholomew Dias (Portuguese)	Rounds Cape of Good Hope to a point beyond Algoa Bay.
1492-1494	Christopher Columbus (Genoan)	Discovers the West Indies on Oct. 12, 1492; Dominica, Puerto Rico and several of the Windward Islands on Nov. 3, 1493 during his second voyage; Jamaica on May 3, 1494.
1497	Amerigo Vespucci (Florentine)	Discovers Venezuela and the continent of South America.
1497	John Cabot (Anglo-Venetian)	Sails along the northeast coast of America, discovering Cape Breton Islands and Nova Scotia.
1498	Vasco da Gama (Portuguese)	Takes route to India via Cape of Good Hope.
1498	Sebastian Cabot (English)	Explores American Coast from Gulf of Saint Lawrence to Chesapeake Bay.
1499	Christopher Columbus (Genoan)	Discovers Trinidad on July 31st; enters mouth of Orinoco River on August 1st.
1499	Alonso de Ojeda (Italian)	Discovers Gulf of Venezuela and New Granada.
1500	Vicente Pinzon (Spanish)	Discovers mouth of the Amazon.
1501	Pedro Alvarez Cabral (Portuguese)	Explores Coast of Brazil which he names Santa Cruz.
1502	Amerigo Vespucci (Florentine)	Discovers Bay of Rio de Janeiro.
1502	Christopher Columbus (Genoan)	Visits Central America on his fourth voyage; discovers Martinique.
1513	Ponce de Leon (Spanish)	Discovers Florida and sails up the west coast of the Peninsula.
1513	Vasco Nunez de Balboa (Spanish)	Crosses Isthmus of Panama and discovers the Pacific Ocean.
1518	Juan de Grijalva (Spanish)	Discovers east coast of Mexico.
1519-1521	Hernando Cortez (Spanish)	Conquers Mexico.
1519-1521	Ferdinand Magellan (Spanish), del Cano (after Magellan's death)	First to circumnavigate the globe. Passes thru the Strait of Magellan, crosses the Pacific and discovers the Philippines.
1524	Giovanni Verrazano (Italian)	Explores coast of North Carolina, Maryland, New Jersey and New York.
1524-1535	Jacques Cartier (French)	Explores Gulf of St. Lawrence and ascends river to Montreal.
1534	Francisco Pizarro (Spanish)	Completes the conquest of Peru.
1540-1541	Francisco de Orellana (Spanish)	Crosses Andes east of Quito and descends Amazon River to mouth.
1541	Fernando de Soto (Spanish)	Discovers the Mississippi River.
1576	Sir Martin Frobisher (English)	Explores Labrador and Baffin Bay; discovers Frobisher Bay.
1577-1580	Sir Francis Drake (English)	Second circumnavigation of the globe; explores west coast of North America as far as Oregon.
1592	John Davis (English)	Discovers the Falkland Islands.
1595	Sir Walter Raleigh (English)	Explores Guiana and ascends the Orinoco 4 miles.
1596	William Barents (Dutch)	Discovers Spitzbergen, Nova Zemlya a Barents Sea.
1606	Pedro Fernandez de Queiros (Spanish)	Discovers the New Hebrides.
1608	Samuel de Champlain (French)	Discovers Lake Ontario.
1608	John Smith (English)	Explores Chesapeake Bay and its tributaries.
1609-1610	Henry Hudson (English)	Explores Hudson River and Hudson Bay.
1616	William Baffin (English)	Enters Baffin Bay in quest of Northwe Passage.
1642	Abel Tasman (Dutch)	Discovers Van Dieman's Land (Tasmania) a New Zealand.
1673	Jacques Marquette and Louis Joliet (French)	Explore the Mississippi River from the nor
1681	Renè R. C. La Salle (French)	Explores Lower Mississippi and takes possessi for Louis XIV.
1701	Father Kino	Explores California.
1728	Vitus Bering (Dane)	Discovers Bering Strait and proves that As and America are not connected.
1768-1775	Capt. James Cook (English)	Circumnavigates the globe and makes hydr graphic surveys of the Society Islands, San wich Islands, east coast of Australia, Co Strait in New Zealand.
1789-1793	Alex. Mackenzie (Scotch)	Explores Mackenzie River; first to make ove land trip to Pacific Coast.
1792	George Vancouver (English)	Circumnavigates Vancouver Island, explor Gulf of Georgia.
1803-1806	Capt. Meriwether Lewis and Capt. Wm. Clark (U.S.)	Explore northwestern part of U. S. ascendi Missouri River, crossing headwaters of Colur bia River and following this river to the Pacif
1819	Sir Wm. E. Parry (English)	Discovers Parry Archipelago.
1821	Fabian von Bellinghausen (Russian)	Explores Antarctic and discovers Peter Isla and Alexander Island.
1830	Chas. Sturt (English)	Discovers the Murray River and Lake Alexa drina, Australia.
1841	Sir James C. Ross (English)	Commands expedition to Victoria Land a Volcanoes Erebus and Terror.
1849-1873	David Livingstone (Scotch)	Discovers Lakes Ngami, Shirwa, Nyasa a Victoria Falls.
1850	Sir R. M'Clure (Irish)	Discovers Northwest Passage.
1876	H. M. Stanley (Welsh)	Discovers Lakes Albert and Edward.
1881-1884	Lieut. A. W. Greely (U.S.)	Explores Grinnell Land and N.E. coast of Gree land. Expedition reaches 83° 24½' N. 1882.
1909	Robert E. Peary (U.S.)	Reaches North Pole with Henson and fo Eskimos on April 6.
1909	Sir Ernest H. Shackleton (English)	Reaches lat. 88° 23' S.; ascends Mt. Ereb organizes party which determines the locati of the South Magnetic Pole.
1911	Capt. Roald Amundsen (Norwegian)	Discovers the South Pole on December 18.
1911-1914	Sir Douglas Mawson (British)	Explores Antarctic and discovers King Geor V Land.
1914	Col. Theodore Roosevelt (U.S.)	Discovers Roosevelt River, S. America.
1927	C. H. Karius (Australian)	Crosses central New Guinea for first time.
1929	Comm. R. E. Byrd (U.S.)	Makes 1600 mile airplane flight to the So Pole and back, from base at "Little Americ
1933-1935	Rear Adm. R. E. Byrd (U.S.)	Discovers Roosevelt Island on Second Antarc Expedition.
1939-1941	Rear Adm. R. E. Byrd (U.S.)	Explores coast of Palmer Peninsula and ad cent islands.
1946-1948	Comm. Finn Ronne (U.S.)	Explores area south of Weddell Sea, provi existence of undivided Antarctic continent.
1948	R.C.A.F. fliers (Canadian)	Discover 85 mile long Prince Charles Island Canadian Arctic.
1951	Maj. Franz Risquez (Venezuela)	Discovers source of Orinoco River.
1953	Col. John Hunt (leader) (British)	Commands expedition making first success ascent of Mt. Everest; summit reached Edmond Hillary and Tensing Norkay.
1958	Cmdr. William R. Anderson (U.S.)	First underwater traverse of the Arctic atomic submarine; reaches North Pole un polar ice pack.
1960	Jacques Piccard (director) (French)	Exploration in bathyscaph reaches record oc depth in Mariana Trench.
1961	Yuri A. Gagarin (U.S.S.R.)	First manned space flight.
1969	Neil A. Armstrong, Edwin E. Aldrin, Michael Collins (U.S.)	First landing of man on the moon.
1973	Charles Conrad, Joseph P. Kerwin, Paul J. Weitz (U.S.)	First manned flight to a space station.